Zulu Beer Vessels

IN THE TWENTIETH CENTURY

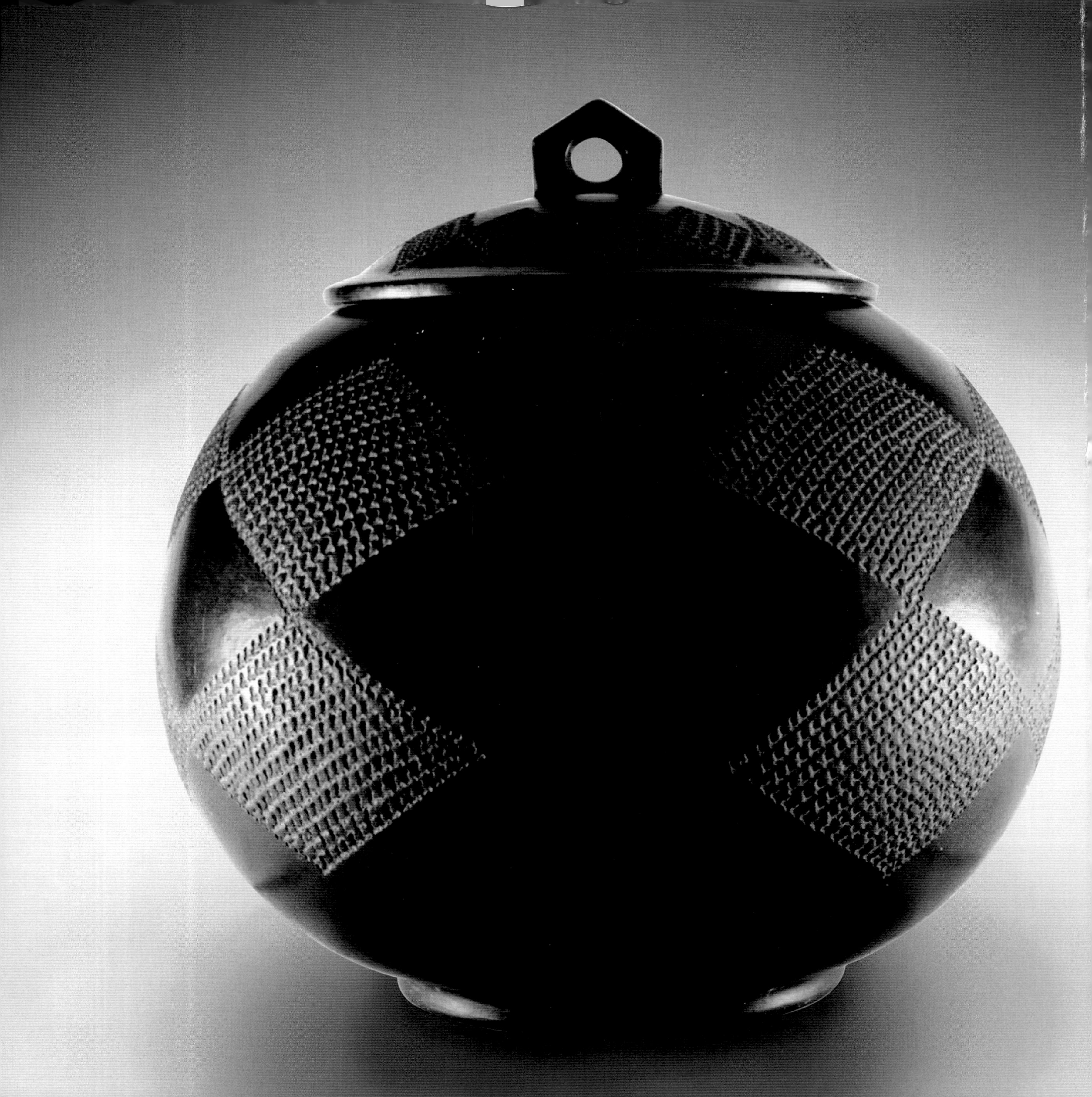

Zulu Beer Vessels

IN THE TWENTIETH CENTURY

Their History, Classification and Geographical Distribution

Frank Jolles

ARNOLDSCHE
Art Publishers

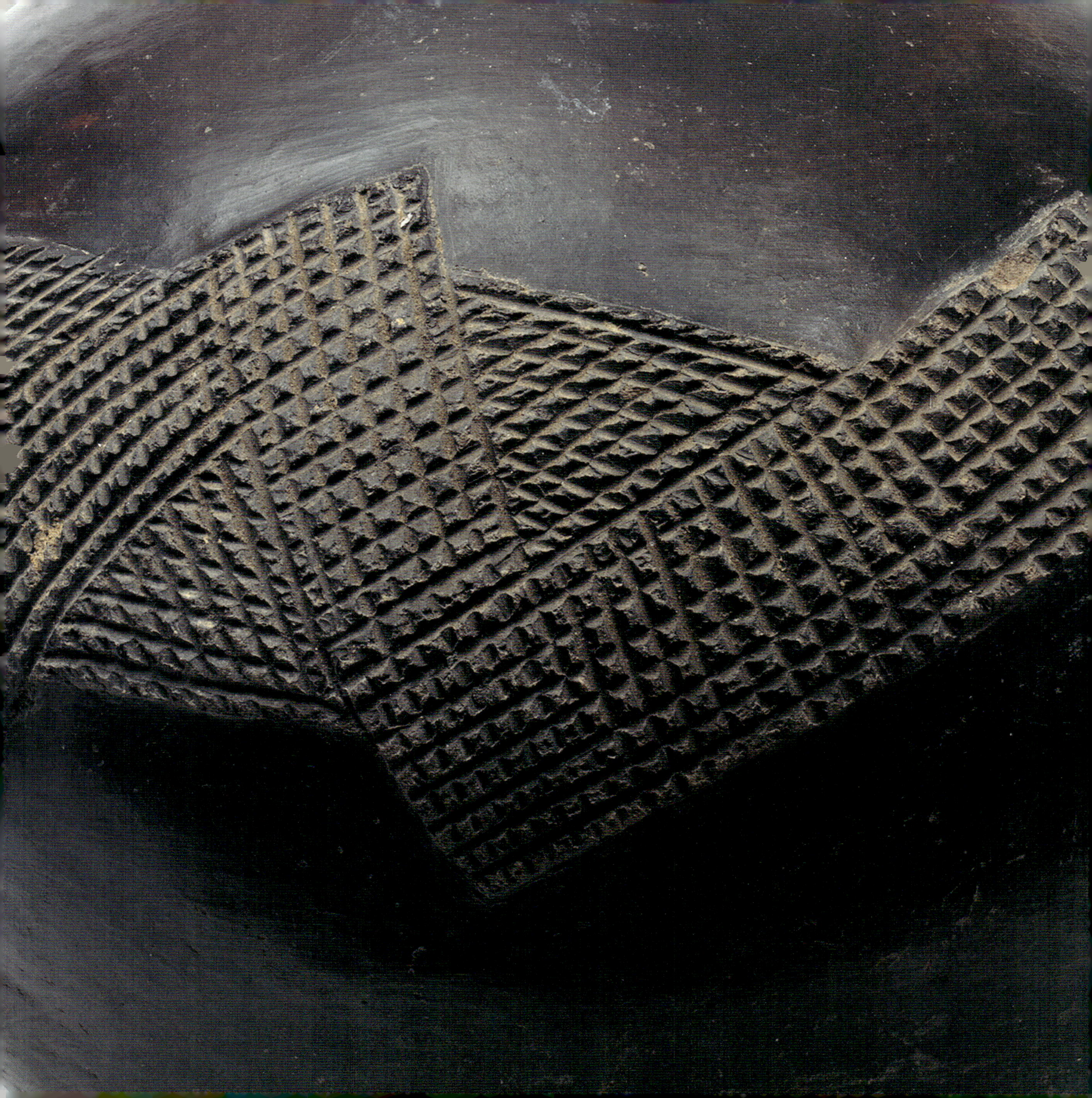

To the author, our beloved and extraordinary father.
Sadly, he did not live to see this, his final work, published.
He dedicated the last 20 years of his life to documenting
Zulu culture in transition, to the benefit of future generations.

PHILIP, ANNA AND STEPHEN JOLLES

Dedicated by the author to the memory of Juliet Armstrong
(1950–2012), exquisite ceramicist, scholar, teacher and friend.

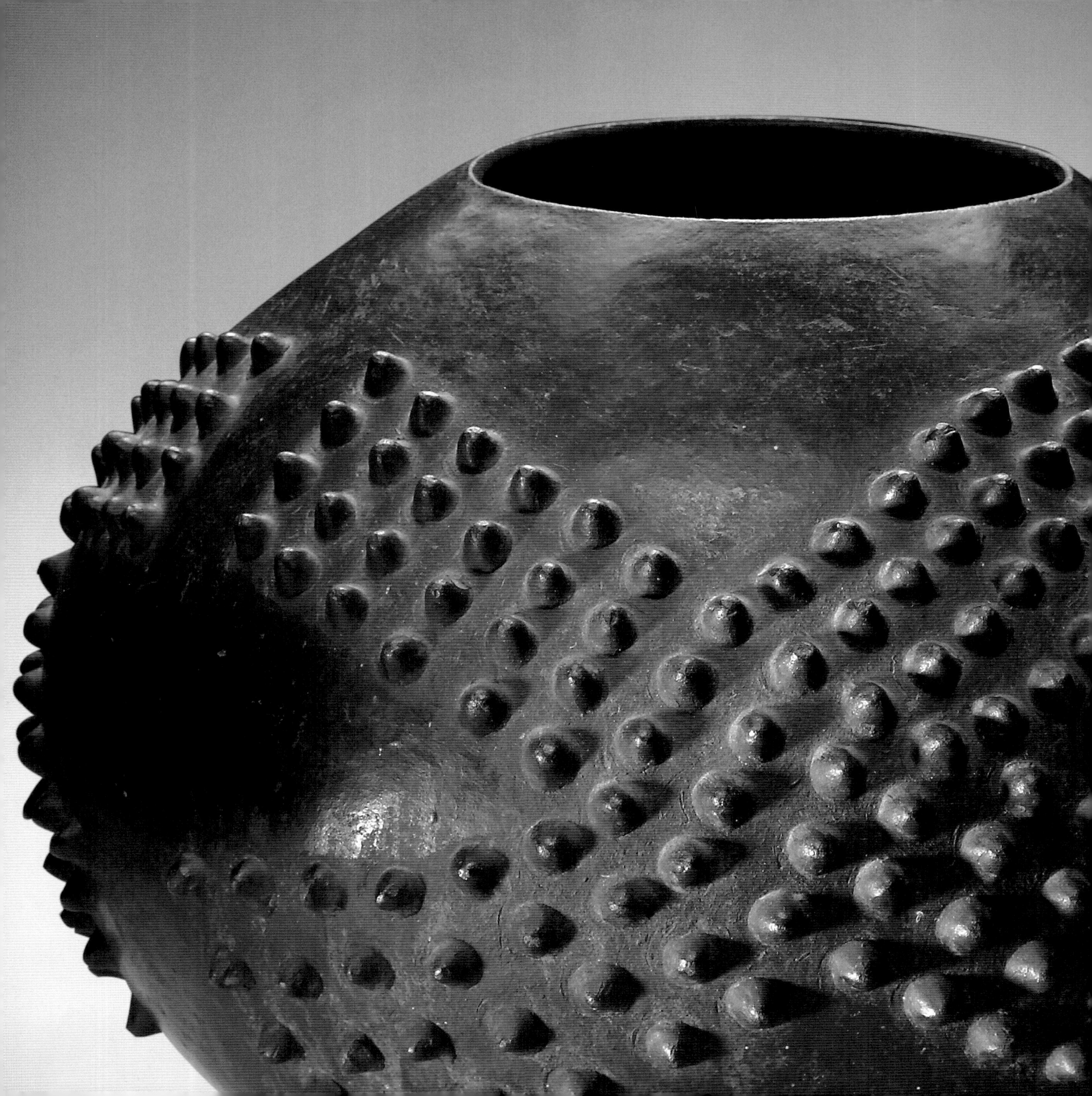

Contents

PAGE ii
King Dinizulu's Pot *c.*1960?
H: 220 mm with lid D: *c.*230 mm G: 720 mm

PAGE iv
POT NUMBER 407 Ukhamba H: 310 mm

LEFT
POT NUMBER 229 Ukhamba H: 305 mm, W: 394 mm

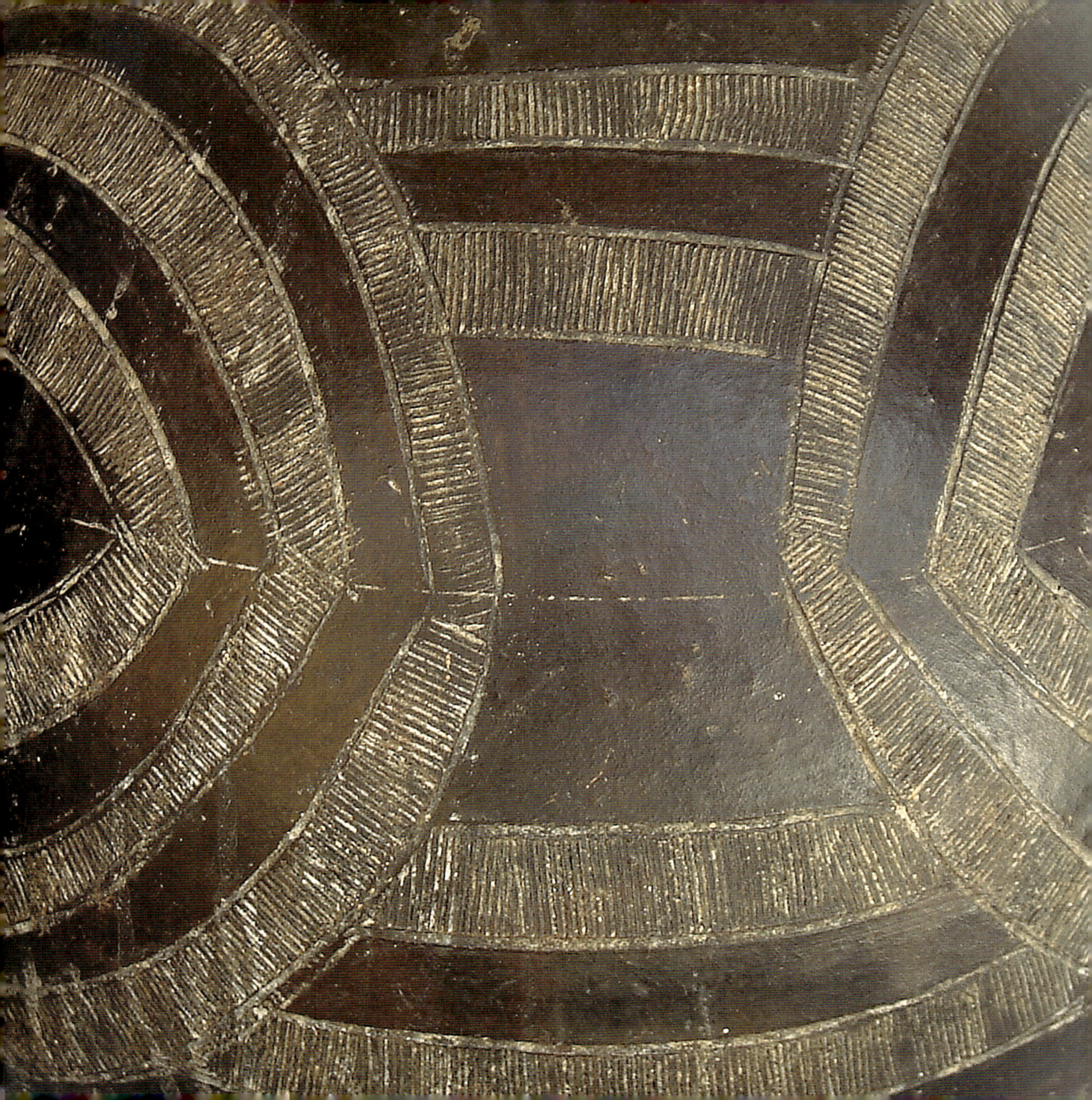

Karel Nel

Foreword

I have always been struck by the stark simplicity and spare embellishment of great Zulu[1] vessels. Their controlled and rhythmic use of pattern plays out in mathematical sequences of double curves, or in syncopated cadences, a series of sophisticated visual counterpoints that are mirrored and inverted across the pot surfaces. These surfaces are also often decorated with geometric zigzags that flow – or break – into stark staccato series, punctuating the sheer spherical volume of the vessel. These calculated embellishments are scored at times into the surface or applied in relief patterns in the form of small raised pellets or slabs into which chamfered, pyramidal elements are incised.

The vessels themselves, generally pure in form, are a testament to Zulu women potters' enormous skill and acumen: the double curved surfaces are systematically built coil by coil, their cambered surfaces embodying a taut internalised strength which is refined by external burnishing before being fired.

Most casual viewers are unaware of the importance of these vessels in Zulu culture. The pots are fashioned by women to be used for the brewing and fermentation both of sorghum and of the precious milk, central to Nguni[2] culture. They are containers of nourishment for the living, sustaining the family and, by extension, the group. At the same time the pots and their use pay deference to and honour the ancestors, bringing together the worlds of the living and the ancestral.

Frank Jolles and I have shared a great appreciation and passion for Zulu ceramic

1 See Hamilton, C and Leibhammer, N. Forthcoming 'Introduction: Tribing and Untribing the Archive' in *Tribing and Untribing the Archive: an investigation into the constituting of the material record pertinent to the late independent and colonial periods of Southern KwaZulu-Natal and its contemporary theorisation.*

2 For a complex reading of the making of identity in south-eastern Southern Africa see Wright, J, 'Making identities in the Thukela-Mzimvubu region, c. 1770 – c. 1940' in Hamilton, C and Leibhammer, N. Forthcoming *Tribing and Untribing the Archive: an investigation into the constituting of the material record pertinent to the late independent and colonial periods of southern KwaZulu-Natal and its contemporary theorisation*, and Mahoney, M. 2012. *The Other Zulus: The Spread of Zulu Ethnicity in Colonial South Africa.* Durham, NC: Duke University Press.

POT NUMBER 231 Ukhamba H: 360 W: 370 mm.

vessels. Over the years we spent many hours cataloguing, looking, and he helping me to identify the possible regional origins of vessels in my collection, made since boyhood. I spent time at his hilltop home in Hilton, KwaZulu-Natal, working through his archive of Zulu pots, learning from his very specific knowledge of each vessel. We would both be engrossed in the sheer inventiveness and beauty, attempting to understand the nuance of each object which he had carefully collected, documented and located regionally.

We shared a passion for the idea that an object can be deciphered, that it acts as a complex barometer of many factors, that, when decoded, reveals an inordinate amount about the nature of the society within which it was created and used, revealing clues as to the identity of the maker and the larger social and historical context. Through shifts in the shape and decoration of the pots, one is able to trace either the sedentary nature of the society from which they came, or the disruptive impacts of migration, conflict or conquest.

Jolles, a trained linguist, came late to the study of African art, but made a significant contribution through his disciplined and meticulous approach to the study of material culture of the Southern African region. He first set his sights on the study of Zulu beadwork, circumscribing his focus to the Msinga region. This led to an in-depth visual analysis of the material using systematic, analytic techniques from his linguistic training. He perspicaciously was able to perceive the body of beadwork in terms of its syntax, looking at its grammar, finding its patterns, colour sequences and anomalies. His work highlighted how the beadwork of one region abutted against that of another, some characteristics spilling over and being shared while others remained distinctive, creating, as it were, beadwork dialects.

Then, using a similar approach, he set about carefully studying the genesis of the Zulu earplug tradition and its evolution from the first plain wooden examples to those engraved and coloured with enamel paint, followed by the flourishing fashion for earplugs decorated with the first plastics. These earplugs consisted of light wooden disks, embellished with precisely inlaid and pinned geometric patterns in brilliant blues, reds, greens, cream, black and white.

More recently, he had focused on the emergence of a contemporary Zulu doll-making industry, producing a book on this quirky and inventive phenomenon, a blend of an old impulse and a new market.

Now, in this publication dealing with the Zulu beer vessels of the twentieth century, the focus is on both a particular time period and the specific regions of pot making that he personally visited, and where he had had access to the local makers and opportunities to engage meaningfully with the complexities of each context.

Jolles' research involved meticulous fieldwork, interviewing owners of the pots in the various localities, tracking down the living potters, returning for successive discussions, casually chatting with women, following their arguments and disagreements, finding ways of questioning without pre-empting answers, thereby avoiding a mechanical and statistical approach, and embracing a live garnering of knowledge.

Jolles recounted how oral history lives on amongst many of the old women, some still remembering the 'flu epidemic of 1918–1924 and other significant events, and recalled how the pots and their makers intermeshed with these long-lived experiences.

During his fieldwork Jolles not only systematically collected vessels but also the *isimbenge* or grass basket lids that covered the pots. He recorded the history of each in order to attempt to map out stylistic epicentres and soft outer peripheries – developing an understanding of how styles moved and morphed. He

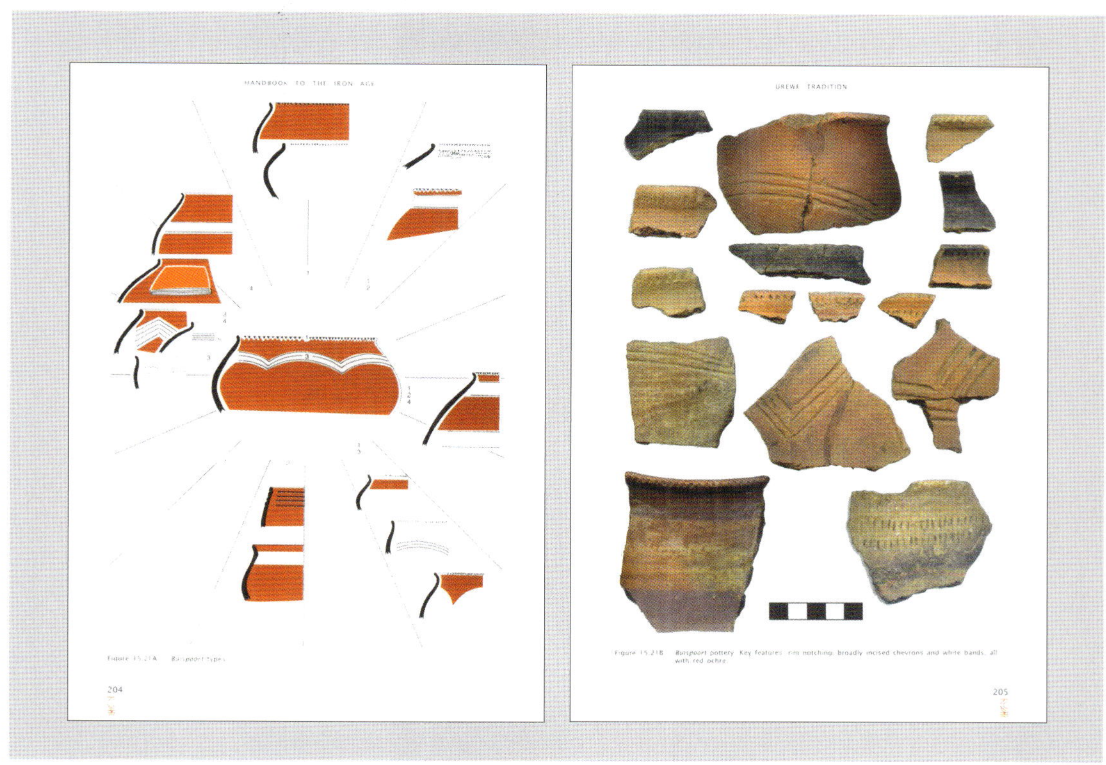

T. N. Huffman *Handbook to the Iron Age, The Archaeology of Pre-Colonial Farming Societies in Southern Africa*, pp 204–205.

worked at comprehending the reasons for such stylistic shifts, sketching the historical and political forces at play and also alluding to the economic imperatives for which these vessels were made.

It is to be understood that no two pots are exactly alike, each fashioned by individuals who, on the one hand, are part of a continuum of a longstanding 'language' of traditional vessels, but whose personal inflection is nevertheless evident. Evident too is the subliminal influence of the end users of the vessel: the pot is tenderly created for personal or family use, more generally made for local village use and even more generically crafted and scaled down to be carried to some distant external market.

Jolles' study of twentieth century Zulu ceramics drew substantially on living memory and worked within a relatively narrow focus. This is in contrast to, for example, the work of archaeologist Thomas Huffman whose study of the Iron Age looks at regional distribution of ceramic styles in pre-colonial farming societies over a large time span, considering shards from archaeological sites dating as far back as 1800 years before the present. He studies ceramics within the broader Southern African region, focusing on the 'big picture' and the relatively slower rate of change in comparison to Jolles' period of the twentieth century, which was characterised by rapid changes brought about by colonial rule, migration, political disruptions and cultural dismemberment.

Huffman traces ceramic sequences using vessel fragments to reconstruct their profile, shape and decoration. Their distinctive applied pattern and overall

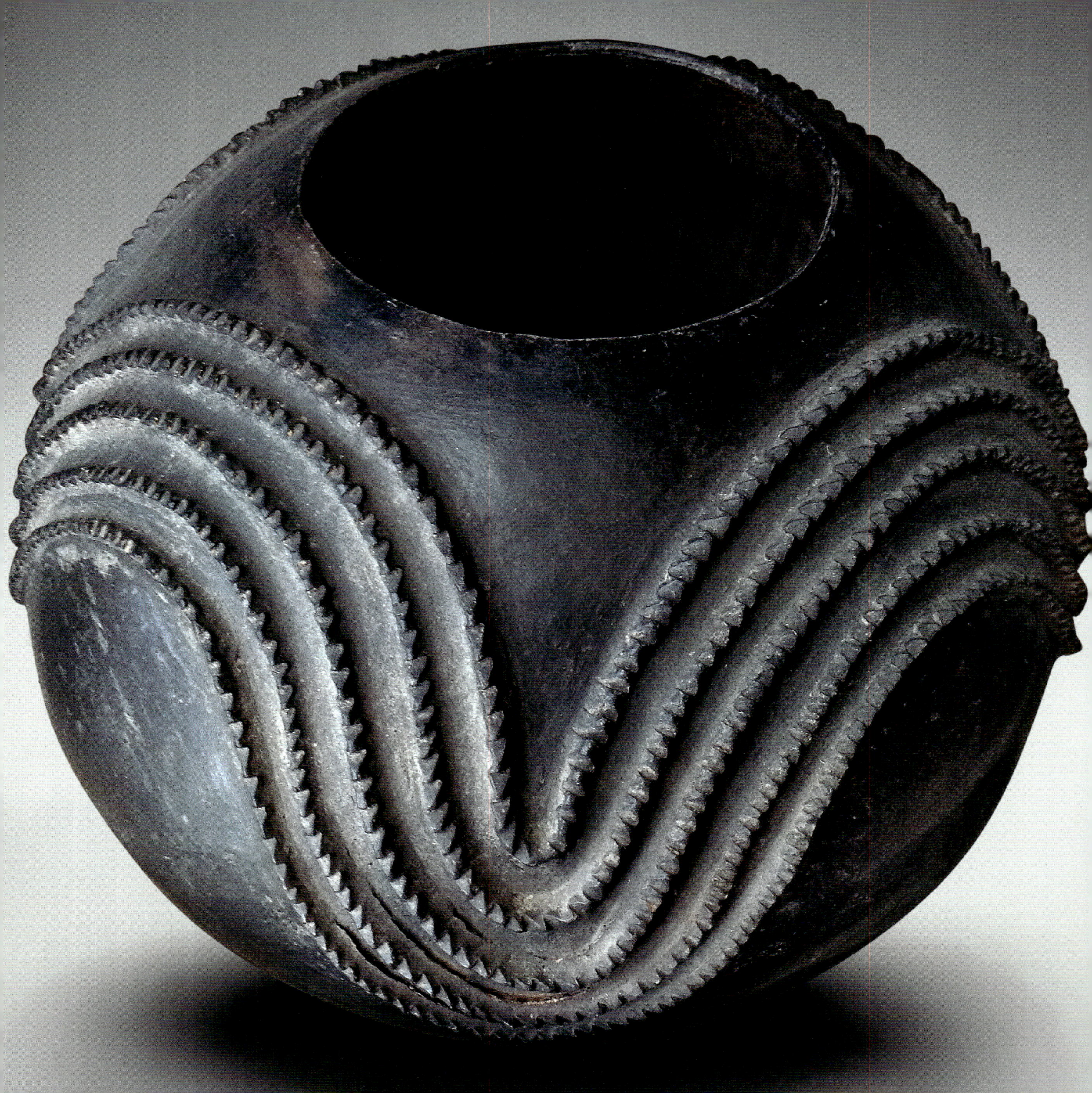

characteristics are used to designate stylistic regions, facilitating a theory on migratory trends and filial associations. Huffman is fortunate in that his shards are found *in situ* within the stratigraphies of his designated archaeological site, enabling him to make considered deductions about regional stylistic epicentres and broad regions of shared style.

Jolles, on the other hand, found his pots whole, above the ground, but described how some regions left him frustrated – finding only new or meagre examples due to the pots having been collected by 'runners', removed from their context, and sold to dealers. These valuable examples end up in the market without any information recorded about the owners of the vessels, who the makers were, how they were used, or the village from where they were sourced.

Historically, this total loss of contextual information has been one of our greatest challenges as scholars of the material culture of the Southern African region. Early pieces were plucked from their context by missionaries, travellers and soldiers returning from British–Zulu wars at the time of the first inroads into the area and then taken back to England and Europe as curiosities, mostly erasing any detailed field information. In the past three decades, as historic collections have slowly returned to South African museums, contemporary scholars are slowly and painstakingly attempting to locate each item regionally through stylistic affinities. This can now only be done through the fragmentary information gleaned from cursory labels, historic writings or tracing the movements of particular individuals on their colonial journeys.

So, Jolles' real contribution is his single-minded research in response to this past. Even at this late stage, he attempted to put in place a few fixed co-ordinates through the collecting and careful documentation of material, and by recording any additional traces that remained within his geographic area of research. Jolles interacted with the last exponents of an etiolated tradition of pot making. Using the detailed stylistic data gathered, he created precise maps of six major regional styles of Zulu beer vessels. His seminal work thus allows for the retrospective repositioning of objects displaced by indiscriminate collecting in the past. The quality of Jolles' work is evidence of his deep respect for the originating people and culture within which these vessels were created.

In this volume, he describes the techniques used in the making and decorating of the vessels, the source of the clay, the firing materials, and how these seemingly limited resources contribute to the austere beauty of the pots. He extrapolates on the place of the pots within society, their use, their aesthetic qualities and their link with the ancestral realm. He traces the movement of skills of pot making and decoration as it was related to marriage – as the woman left her own family and was faced with having to fit into her husband's familial context and its style of pot making. Having to negotiate this highly charged new context, the woman learned to adapt her skills to the new domain, seeking a fine balance of being respectful yet needing to establish her own self-worth and so, in time, changing both her own as well as the style of pot making into which she had been relocated.

This phenomenon is also corroborated in the archaeological record of the eighteenth century as homestead styles crossed 'borders' in much the same way. This fusion and alteration of styles is reminiscent of how vocabularies are shared and languages evolve by contact. Alternatively, differences may reflect the desire to distinguish oneself as different.

Studying the sequences of pots is a powerful way to understand a form of female genealogy, a covert history in genre, shape and pattern in this powerfully desig-

POT NUMBER **232**
Ukhamba, H: 350 W: 390 mm

nated female domain. I first became aware of this many years ago on a study trip to Swaziland. After acquiring a fine vessel in a small market in Manzini, I duly paid for the pot and the maker offered to carry it to my vehicle. I declined, thinking I was saving her the effort and sparing her the necessity of having to leave her wares unattended. She looked somewhat disbelieving of me, but I picked up the vessel and started to walk through the market. A commotion ensued. She ran, caught up with me, gracefully relieved me of the pot, and walked us both to the vehicle. I learned that day that in Southern African traditional societies men do *not* carry pots! These are specifically located within the female domain, and I had unwittingly transgressed.

Wooden objects, such as milk pails and meat platters, are, on the other hand, a counterpoint: exclusively carved by men, used by men and associated with the male domain. As with pot making, carving is handed down through generations within a family, and levels of skill vary.

Jolles spoke at times of his contact with the Nala family, the great pot makers whose vessels created a demand on both the local and international art market. Here, exceptional skills were handed from mother to daughter as they worked together, one style flowing into another, creating continuity and individuality, emerging in equal measure, the same but different. Their vessels moved from being purely functional to being artefacts entering another realm and market altogether.

Unfortunately Jolles' study cuts off at the end of the twentieth century, thereby excluding consideration of the Nala phenomenon which gained impetus after 2000.

Jolles' archived vessels should find their way into safekeeping within a public museum as a historical resource. Substantive documented museum collections of pots, as Jolles pointed out, are few and far between: the Shaw and Lawton collection, put together in the 1960s, housed at the Iziko/National Museum in Cape Town; Nicholas Penny's collection of Zulu pots, collected in the 1980s, at the KwaZulu Cultural Museum in Ulundi; and the collection of pots also made in the 1980s by Tom Huffman for the Wits Art Museum in Gauteng are the most significant.

Nineteenth-century ceramic material is rare, while much beadwork and wooden objects survive from this period. Readily collected, they were easily transportable and survived the long journeys at sea back to Europe and Britain. Pots, on the other hand, due to their fragility and bulkiness, were seldom collected, or if collected, rarely survived the journey intact. Vessels *in situ* generally were 'used up', and were, for the most part, not collected by South Africans, who have paid scant attention to this extraordinary tradition right in front of them. There are, however, important scholars and archaeologists who have paid due attention to the archaeological and historical aspects of this tradition.

Apart from the two exhibitions of Zulu beer vessels curated by Jolles at the Heath Gallery of the University of KwaZulu-Natal, very few exhibitions of Southern African traditional ceramics have ever been curated. The exception is *Emhlabeni: From the Earth*, a broad survey of Southern African ceramics, curated by Fiona Rankin-Smith and shown at the Standard Bank Gallery, Johannesburg (10 June – 24 July 1993). The exhibition was drawn from the Wits Art Museum holdings, which includes the large sample collected by Huffman.

Token vessels of great beauty have been included in important museum exhibitions locally in South Africa, such as in *Democracy X*, curated at the Castle in Cape Town to celebrate 10 years of democracy, and more frequently abroad in major exhibitions such as *Africa: The Art of a Continent*, shown in London in 1995 and New York in 1996; *Ubuntu: Arts et cultures d'Afrique du Sud,* exhibited in Paris in 2002;

and *The Art of Daily Life* shown in 2011 at the Cleveland Museum of Art in the United States of America. In 2009, the Barbier-Müller Museum in Geneva undertook a major Pan-African exhibition of ceramics, *Terres Cuites Africaines*, leading the way in more recent years. Jolles was a contributing author to the exhibition publication, performing a review of the Barbier-Müller collection.

It surely is time that a major specialist exhibition of this extraordinary Southern African female ceramic tradition be undertaken either in South Africa or internationally. Perhaps Jolles' timeous publication will prove a catalyst for such an exhibition.

Finally, it must be said that Frank Jolles and I differed somewhat in our evaluation of the Zulu vessels. I am taken by the sheer beauty and control of the form of the vessel, and the consummate precision required in calculating the pattern sequences. Jolles, on the other hand, also saw value in vessels which to my eye seem to lack conviction and the expertise in execution, yet he was able to see the explanatory value in a particular sequence of patterns – both in the ceramics and the beadwork – or an echo of a bygone form that has a resonance with the developmental syntax of a particular region, which he had resolutely sleuthed and made sense of.

While I would like to see a publication of the finest Zulu vessels ever made, Frank, on the other hand, determinedly – and to my utmost admiration – focused his sights only on the parameters where he could make accurate deductions about their context, history and stylistic sequence. His work stands testimony to the fact that he was a truly precise surveyor, interpreter and cartographer of twentieth-century Zulu ceramics.

References

Hamilton, C and Leibhammer, N. Forthcoming 'Introduction: Tribing and Untribing the Archive' in *Tribing and Untribing the Archive: an investigation into the constituting of the material record pertinent to the late independent and colonial periods of Southern KwaZulu-Natal and its contemporary theorisation*.

Huffman, Thomas H. 2007. *Handbook to the Iron Age: The Archaeology of Pre-Colonial Framing Societies in Southern Africa*. University of KwaZulu-Natal Press: Scottsville.

Mahoney, M. 2012. *The Other Zulus: The Spread of Zulu Ethnicity in Colonial South Africa*. Durham, NC: Duke University Press.

Wright, J. Forthcoming 'Making identities in the Thukela-Mzimvubu region, c. 1770 – c. 1940' in Hamilton, C and Leibhammer, N, *Tribing and Untribing the Archive: an investigation into the constituting of the material record pertinent to the late independent and colonial periods of Southern KwaZulu-Natal and its contemporary theorisation*.

Acknowledgements

With particular thanks to Elizabeth Burroughs for her meticulous editing and to both Nessa Leibhammer and Philip Jolles for their thoughtful contributions. Finally, to Kevin Shenton for the continued pleasure at working together in designing the book.

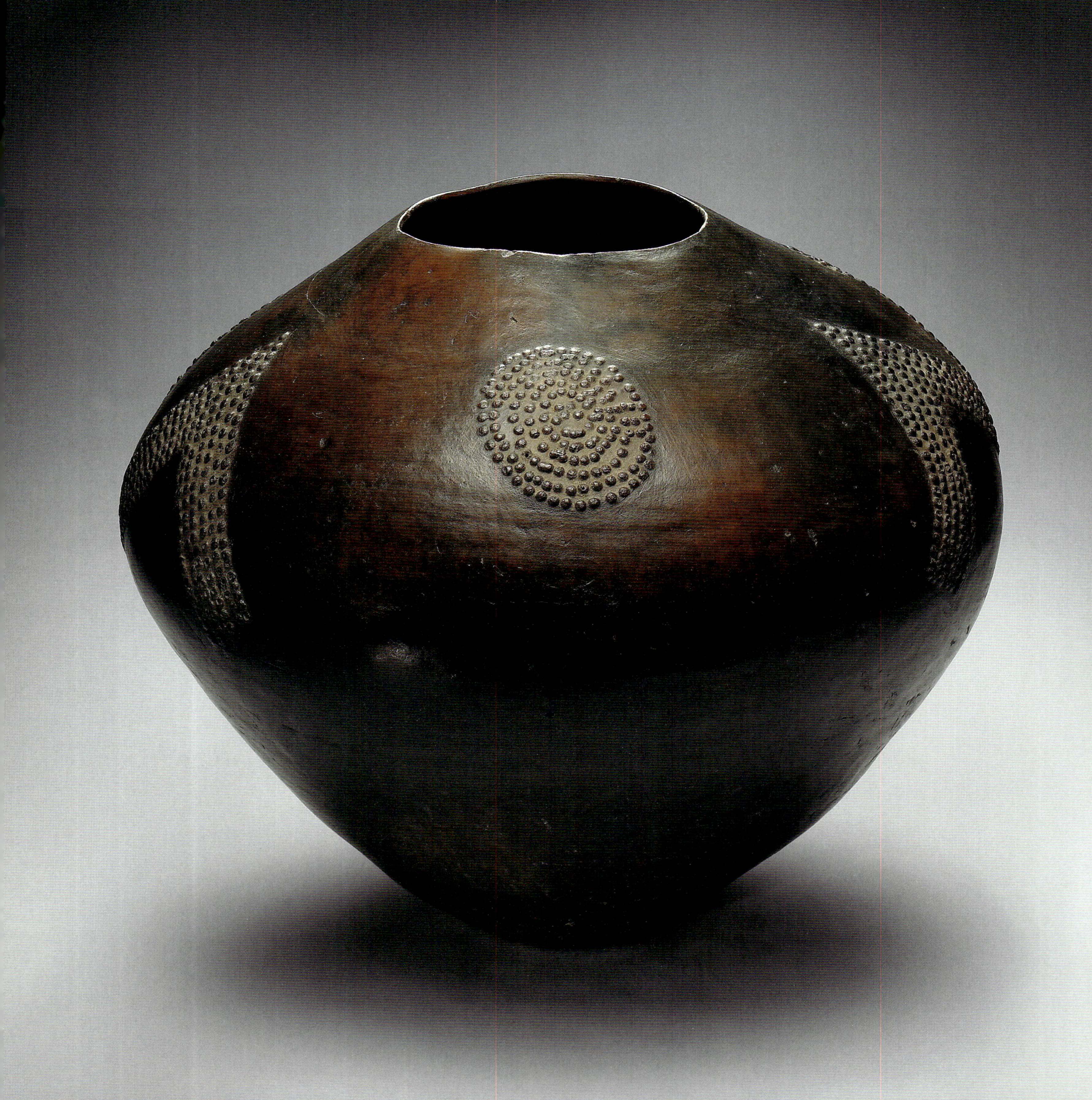

Introduction

Large Hlabisa beer vessel *c.*1960?
H: 220 mm D: 440 mm
COLLECTION: WB SIMMONS, NEW YORK

Twenty years of collecting Zulu beer vessels, interviewing the makers and cataloguing information have taught me that a survey such as the one presented here can never hope to be comprehensive. Each vessel is unique, combining features derived from local stylistic conventions with others specific to its maker. In an environment in which objects of daily use are dominated by industrial designs which can be replicated at will, it is good to keep this, obvious as it may seem, in mind.

Any survey of indigenous ceramics should be regarded as open-ended. It is impossible to trace every vessel to its place of origin and its maker. Potters may marry out of their districts, whole families tend to move in troubled times, vessels get broken and entire districts may even be 'collected out' by dealers selling their wares worldwide without keeping any record of their sources. Individually made vessels are often replete with information lacking in their industrial counterparts: regional styles preserve data about the migration of clans, whilst innovations often reflect social changes in the lives of the potters. Such information is lost when pots are collected indiscriminately.

Production processes, the so-called *chaînes opératives,* from the mixing of clays to the final firing, determine the nature of ceramics. In pre-colonial southern Africa the potters' wheel was unknown. Clay vessels were made by coiling: gradually building up a pot by adding coils of soft clay from a base upwards until the required height and shape are reached. A vessel turned on a wheel is by nature symmetrical.[1] If it has

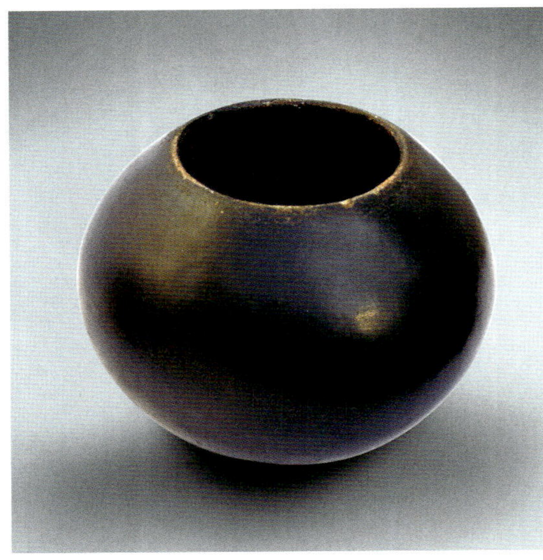

a flat base, however narrow, it will stand securely. This is not necessarily the case with a coiled pot, which depends on the eye and the hand of the potter to ensure that balance is maintained. Such pots may be off-centre, yet a small departure from perfect symmetry can serve to highlight the ideal and their proximity to it. This is an aesthetic outcome that distinguishes them from run-of-the-mill turned vessels. Add the urge to create vessels that are a pleasure to handle, functional and pleasing to the eye, and you have the foundations of an aesthetic of the potters' craft – both tactile and visual: an aesthetic that embraces technical refinement and individual creativity in the context of a local historical tradition.

Mastering the technical challenges is part of the process in realising this aesthetic. In fact it is a prerequisite. In pottery it might include features such as the harmony of symmetry and surface in the simplest of shapes as in Siphiwe Nala's *umancishana* above, or the form of the *imbiza* from Msinga bellowing out from a base less than a third of its diameter (see No. 704, p. 192), or the near-horizontal upper surface of the tra-

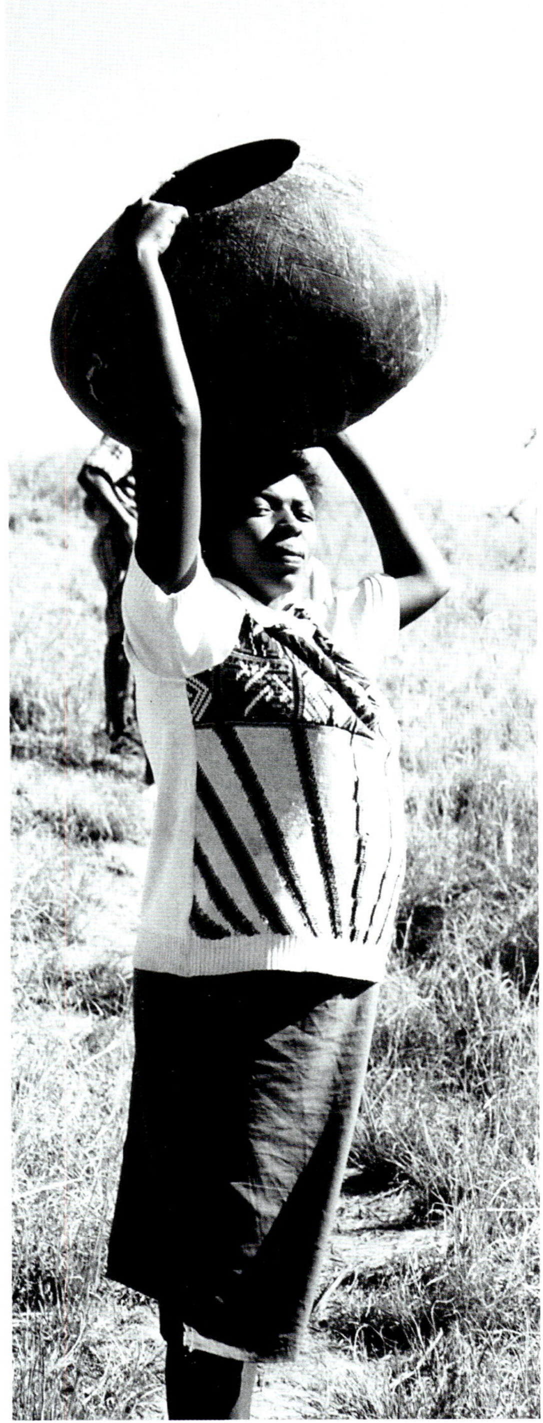

TOP LEFT: Siphiwe Nala. *Umancishana, c.*1960.
PHOTO: Frank Jolles

LEFT: Field photo (*c.*1990) of girl carrying the Simmons pot near the collection site in Hlabisa.

RIGHT: Large Hlabisa beer vessel *c.*1960?
H: 381 mm D: 622 mm
COLLECTION: FRANK JOLLES, HLABISA

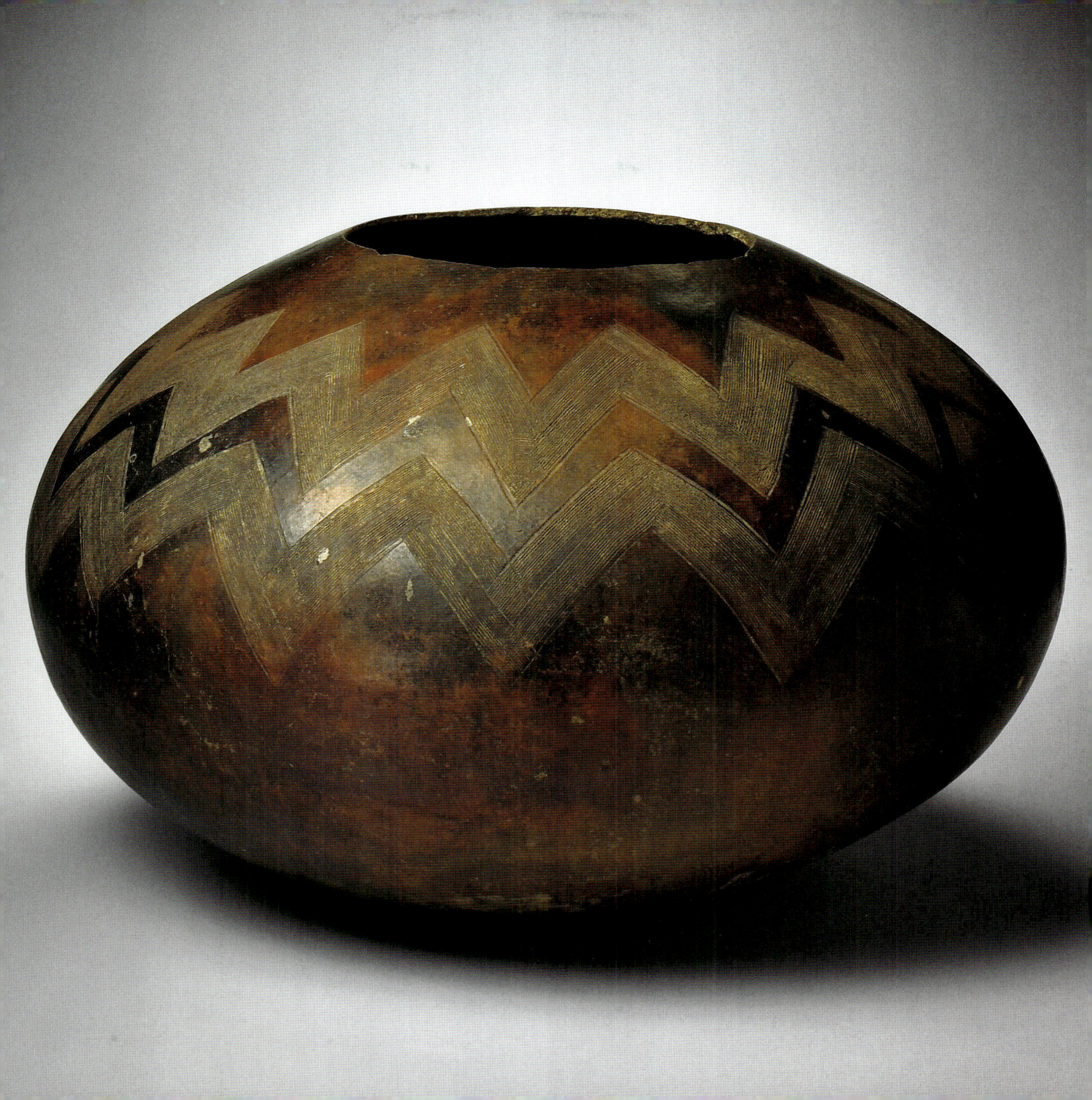

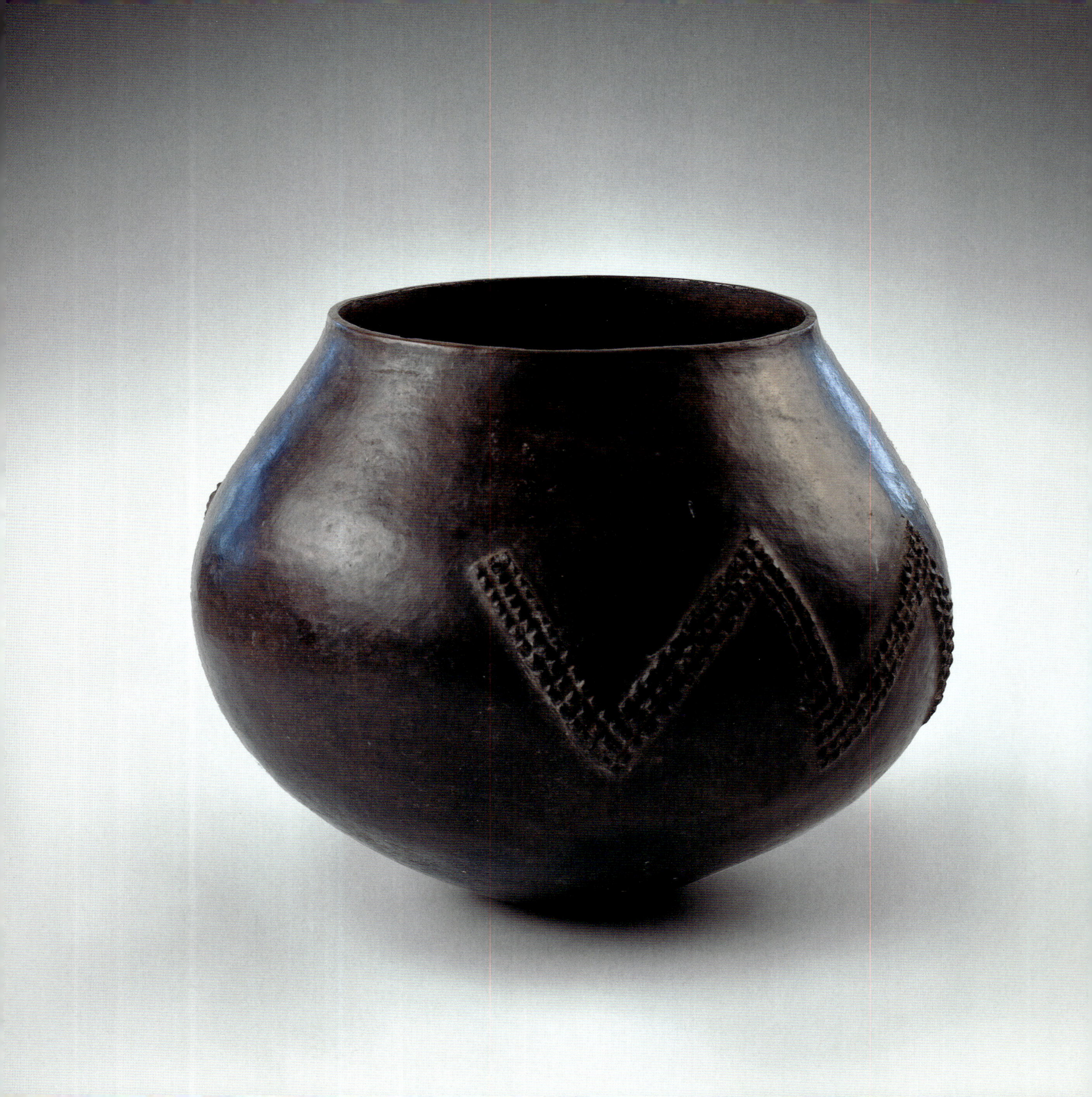

ditional Hlabisa *ukhamba* here in a magnificent example from the Simmons Collection in New York (page 3).

The ideal of a stable pot with as narrow a base as possible is encountered over a wide range of places and periods as exemplified by this early 1930s pot from Phongolo. It has a ratio of base to diameter of 1:4.2.

Such features are often embedded in the regional styles, in other words, they are typical of the vessels from those areas, yet the realisation of the ideal rests with the personal skill and motivation of the individual. To give an example: Thangithile MaNgobese Mhlongo (born 1946) is an outstanding potter from Hlabisa. I interviewed her at her brother's house at Umgangatho in March 2000. She told me that when she started she was unable to make pots in the traditional Hlabisa style because they were 'very difficult to make. You have to build it up little by little, leaving it to harden and then continuing.' So she made 'bag-shaped' pots that were just as functional as their more sophisticated decorated counterparts (see p. 109). Although she could provide for her livelihood in that way, her abiding ambition was to achieve perfection in the traditional forms: whatever the commercial benefit, her main motivation was an aesthetic one.[2]

It is surprising that clay beer vessels should have survived the onslaught of the industrial age at all: the introduction of iron cooking pots, aluminium containers, enamel ware, imported cheap ceramics and glass and finally plastics. All these found their way into Zulu rural culture. Many might be considered more suitable for brewing and serving beer than the traditional clay vessels: they are lighter, less fragile and completely waterproof. In fact, plastic containers are occasionally used for brewing and there was a time in the 1960s and 1970s when medium-sized black plastic *izinkamba* were manufactured in Dur-

ban. Yet the traditional clay vessels not only survived but flourished both in quality of workmanship and sophistication of design so that the twentieth century may be regarded as a golden age of Zulu ceramics. It is only in those areas ceded to white settlement in 1904[3] that the ancient craft of pottery has declined to the point of extinction.

Historical background

The century opened on a particularly inauspicious note. A series of natural disasters swept over Zululand, causing widespread malnutrition and starvation, and disrupting the traditional way of life based on agriculture and animal husbandry. Between 1895 and 1907 there were six years of serious drought. In 1895–96 and again in 1898, 1903–04 and 1906 swarms of red locusts devastated the crops. In 1897 an epidemic of rinderpest wiped out an estimated 85% of the cattle, and before the herds had time to regenerate they were struck down by East Coast Fever in 1904–05.[4] The effects of these natural disasters were aggravated by the degradation of the environment, which had taken place in the last decades of the nineteenth century. The wholesale slaughter of wild life through indiscriminate hunting for its own sake and for the trade in ivory and skins, the destruction of the forests, soil erosion caused by overgrazing in the pre-rinderpest years and the introduction of ploughing profoundly altered the entire physical environment and deprived the African population of their traditional safety-net of natural resources in times of drought. The situation was exacerbated by a rapid rise in the population, which increased by about a third between 1891 and 1904.[5]

REGION: Phongolo, Skosana Family, Shoba, 1930s.
PROVENANCE: African Art Centre, Durban.
COLLECTOR: Nomusa Dube.
H: 157 mm. D: 210 mm. B: 50 mm.

The impact of colonialism was hardly less disastrous. As early as 1872 taxes, duties and fines imposed on Africans in the colony of Natal accounted for approximately 75% of total revenue, whilst less than 4% of total expenditure was devoted to 'Native Purposes' – a spectacular transfer of wealth. As Etherington (1989: 175) puts it: '… while Africans suffered taxation without representation, white settlers enjoyed representation virtually without taxation'. Many of the levies, such as the hut tax and the surprisingly high fee of £5 for the registration of African marriages, had to be paid in cash. This in turn forced Africans onto the labour market – be it in the cities or on settler-owned farms – thereby undermining the homestead economy and its social order.

With the introduction of 'Responsible Government' in May 1893 the Africans were deprived of what little protection they had enjoyed under the previous dispensation enshrined in the Natal Constitution. The Imperial Government was aware of the pressures to which the African population were likely to be subjected. It attempted to forestall some of them in the Natal Constitution Amendment Law of 1875, which, in the words of Sir Garnet Wolseley, Special Commissioner to Natal, was intended to 'enable Her Majesty's Ministers through the Governor here to direct the future policy of Natal and to prevent hasty and dangerous local legislation'.[6] Such legislation was not slow in coming once 'Responsible Government' had been instituted. Between 1893 and the end of the first decade of the twentieth century a cascade of new acts and measures were introduced, the general effect of which was to 'deprive Africans of access to land, to destroy their independence and to make it difficult for them to work outside the Colony'. This process reached its final conclusion in the Land Act of 1913, after Natal had become a part of the Union of South Africa (1910). It 'prevented Africans from purchasing land or remaining as squatters on the property of white land-owners'.[7]

The crisis came in 1906 when the Government decided to impose an additional tax on the already indebted and impoverished population – a poll tax of £1 on every adult male excepting those liable for hut tax.[8] Sporadic resistance to the tax over a wide area was met with 'much criticized measures of defence and reprisal' by the obviously insecure administration.[9] These included the declaration of martial law, public executions, floggings and extensive burning of dwellings and crops. The situation escalated into what has become known as the 'Bambatha rebellion', in which a minor chief of the Umvoti area and his followers resorted to force in resisting payment of the tax and then fled into the Nkandla forest. The 'rebellion' was broken in an encounter on 10 June 1906 when Bambatha was taken by surprise in the nearby Mome Gorge. Bambatha and nearly 600 of his followers were massacred, with no opportunity given for surrender. In the aftermath over 5 000 'rebels' faced court martial, and Dinuzulu, the Zulu King, was sentenced to four years' imprisonment.

The Bambatha uprising marks the end of an epoch in more than one sense. Although the break-up of the kingdom dated from the settlement at the end of the Anglo-Zulu War in 1879, widespread loyalty to the institution of the monarchy and the person of the King survived the political demise of the kingdom, despite his banishment after the annexation of Zululand in 1887, to St Helena for ten years. Even after his return from St Helena, and in spite of his installation as salaried 'Government Induna', most Zulus still regarded Dinuzulu as the head of their nation. His imprisonment after the uprising[10] and subsequent death in 'exile' in 1913 on a farm in the

Transvaal spelled the end of the spiritual authority of the monarchy (at least until its revival two generations later in the guise of a new nationalism). This was reflected in much of the material culture of the period by the loss of normative styles and the disintegration of Zululand into distinct stylistic regions. Furthermore, the Zulu royal family had come to be feared 'as a focus of national resistance to the ambitions of white settlers to obtain Zulu land and labour'.[11] Whether or not such fears were justified, large-scale settler penetration into the interior of Zululand, with all its consequences for the indigenous population, first took place in the post-Bambatha period.

The emergence of the main stylistic regions of the twentieth century and their origins in nineteenth-century land allocations

Very few Zulu ceramics from the nineteenth century have survived. Beer pots, unlike weapons, beadwork and carvings, were not collectors' items and did not make it into European or North American collections. Whilst they occasionally figure in early paintings and photographs, they are outnumbered by baskets for storing and transporting water and beer. So it is difficult to trace twentieth-century Zulu pottery styles

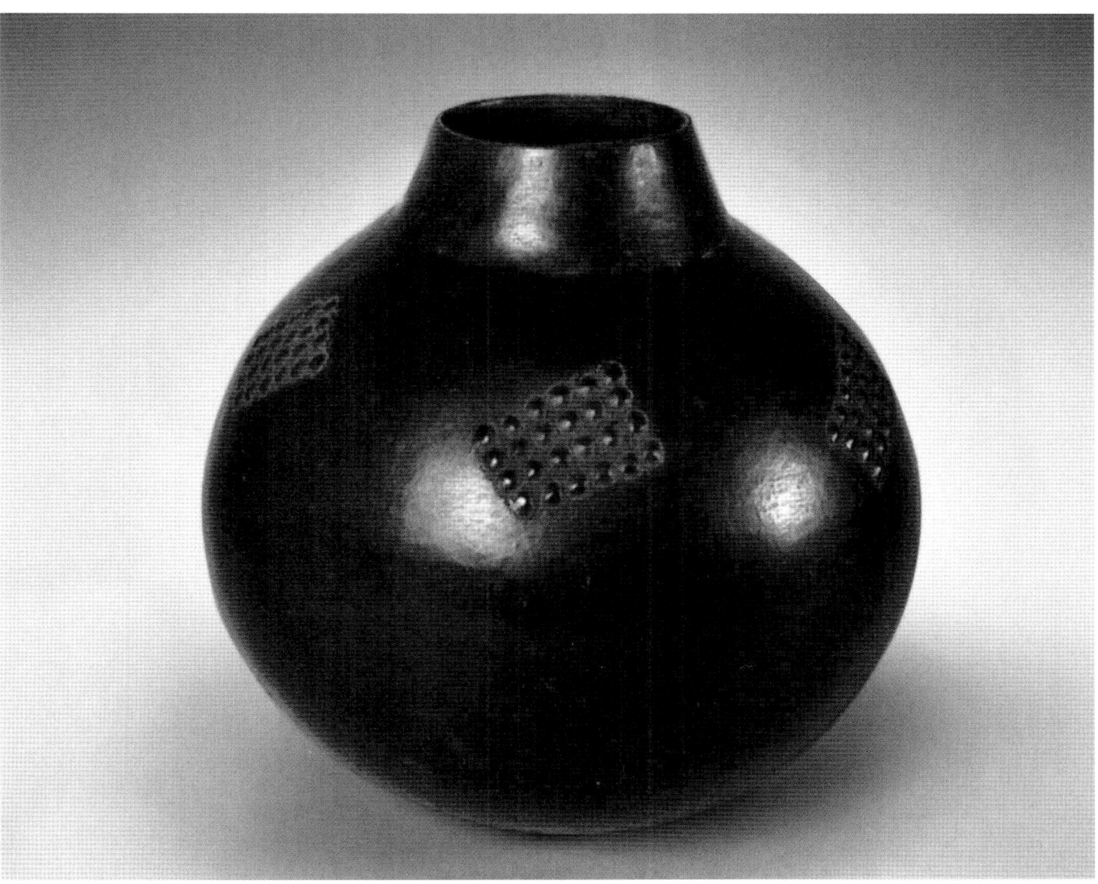

Uphiso from Zululand before 1904,
NATAL MUSEUM

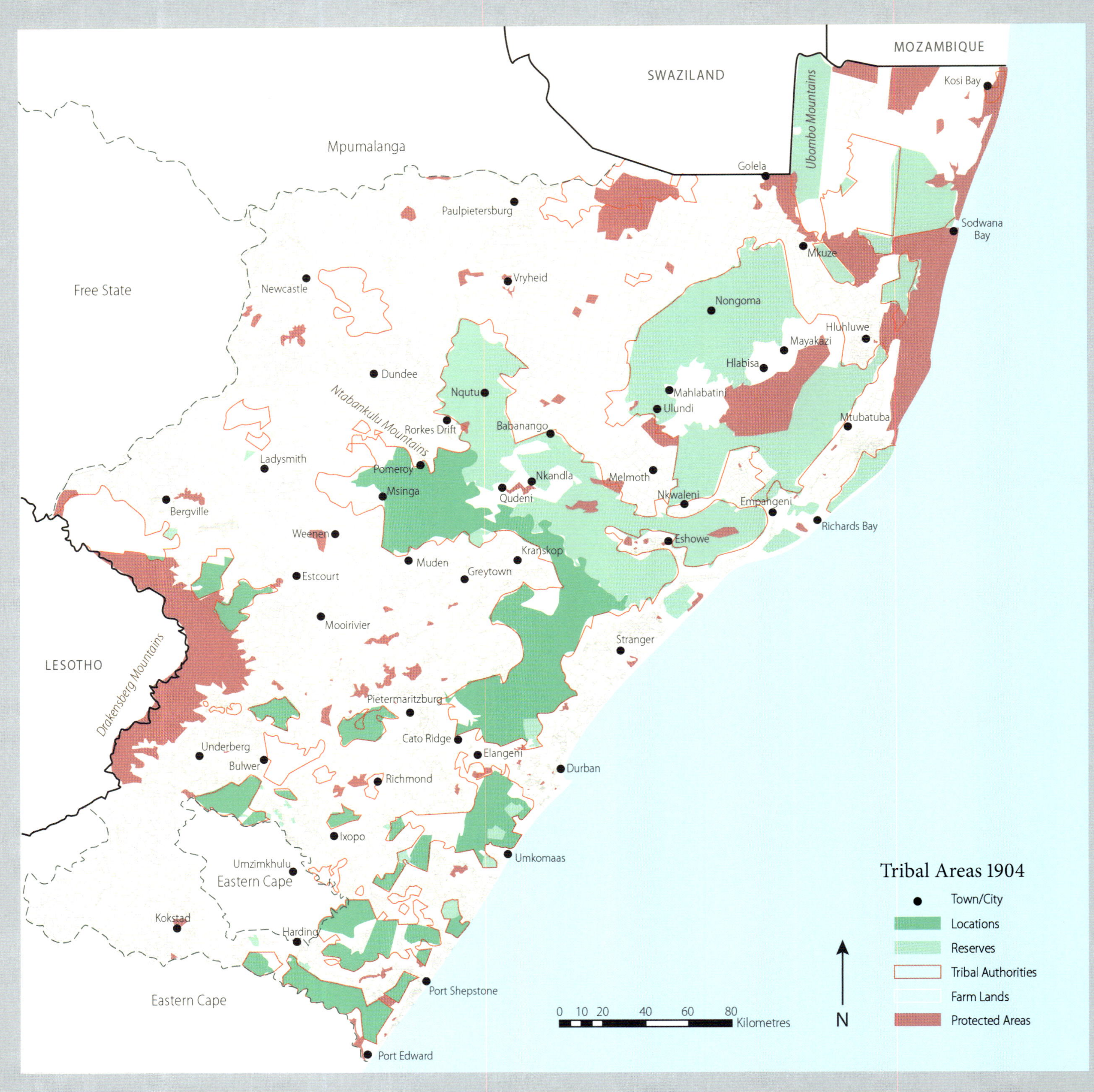

MOZAMBIQUE
SWAZILAND
Mpumalanga
Free State
LESOTHO
Eastern Cape
Eastern Cape
Ubombo Mountains
Ntabankulu Mountains
Drakensberg Mountains
Kosi Bay
Golela
Sodwana Bay
Mkuze
Paulpietersburg
Vryheid
Nongoma
Hluhluwe
Mayakazi
Hlabisa
Newcastle
Mahlabatini
Ulundi
Mtubatuba
Dundee
Nqutu
Rorkes Drift
Babanango
Ladysmith
Pomeroy
Nkandla
Melmoth
Msinga
Qudeni
Nkwaleni
Bergville
Empangeni
Eshowe
Richards Bay
Weenen
Kranskop
Estcourt
Muden
Greytown
Mooirivier
Stranger
Pietermaritzburg
Cato Ridge
Underberg
Elangeni
Bulwer
Durban
Richmond
Ixopo
Umkomaas
Umzimkhulu
Kokstad
Harding
Port Shepstone
Port Edward

Tribal Areas 1904
Town/City
Locations
Reserves
Tribal Authorities
Farm Lands
Protected Areas

0 10 20   40   60   80
Kilometres
N

back into the nineteenth century. On the other hand many twentieth-century regional stylistic features can be shown to follow late nineteenth-century political and administrative boundaries. This is quite evident in the case of beadwork;[12] to a lesser extent it also holds good for woodcarving.[13] In order to determine whether twentieth-century ceramics fit into the same pattern as the other forms of Zulu material culture, it is necessary to sketch the historical subdivisions of to-day's KwaZulu-Natal as they developed in the course of the nineteenth century.

The first major partition of the region in the post-Shakan period was the annexation of Natal as an autonomous district of the Cape Colony on 31 May 1844. The appointment of Theophilus Shepstone as Diplomatic Agent to the Native Tribes in 1846 saw the creation of subdivisions within Natal as 'locations'[14] (reserves) for the indigenous population. In 1846 and 1847 Shepstone 'supervised the movement of nearly 80 000 Natal Africans … into locations he had demarcated for their occupation, the rest of the area being cut up into farms for white ownership'.[15] With relatively minor alterations Shepstone's dispensation remained the basis of land allocation in Natal until the end of white rule in 1994. In the meanwhile the borders of the Kingdom of Zululand suffered a series of revisions under the encroachments of the Boers and the British until it was finally annexed in 1887. By that time the British policy of weakening the influence of the royal house by playing off the various factions of the Zulus against each other, coupled with the establishment of the Boer New Republic in the north, had effectively redrawn most of the internal tribal territorial divisions of Zululand.

Finally, on 29 December 1897, Zululand was incorporated into Natal. A land commission set up in 1902 submitted its report in 1904. The former Kingdom was divided into regions for white settlement (1 057 467 hectares or 40.2%) and black reserves (1 573 047 hectares, 59.8%). Laband comments as follows:[16]

In going about their task, the commissioners … were consciously 'actuated by a desire to exclude from the Reserves, which were to be inalienable, as much land as [they] conscientiously could'. Put in another way, this meant that they identified as reserves regions undesirable in terms of their potential for commercial agriculture and white settlement.

First in Natal and subsequently in Zululand, people of diverse tribal backgrounds were resettled in reservations with well-defined permanent borders. Such reservations often lay outside the main routes linking different parts of the country. Large tracts of white farmlands separated many of them from one another. As a result, people tended to travel between their homes in the reservations and their places of work in the cities rather than between one reservation and the next. This pattern was supported and formalised by Act 49 of 1901, 'To Facilitate the Identification of Native Servants', which decreed that all Africans other than labour tenants had to possess an identification pass by means of which their movements could be controlled.[17] The relative paucity of local transport in the reservations during the first half of the twentieth century meant that many people spent their lives within a radius of a few miles of their homesteads. In the course of time the reservations developed identities of their own, which redefined the previous tribal allegiances that had been imported into the communities when they were formed.[18]

This is the basis of the so-called fourth-world entities, pseudo-polities without representation or self-determination, dependent for their survival on the shedding of population to the outside world, in this case to the cities. In Natal and Zululand they languished on throughout most of the twentieth century with little change in the rhythm of daily life. The self-contained nature of the reservations preserved them from many of the incursions of the outside world and enabled the creation of a relatively stable social environment for those who stayed behind.[19] This lasted into the 1970s when the effects of overcrowding and soil erosion began to make themselves felt. As a mitigating factor the reservations benefited from the general growth of the economy with its concomitant transfer payments. That may account for what seems to have been a widely held impression that disposable income and the quality of life were slowly but surely improving. This was reflected in a renaissance of the crafts for local use, including pottery, carving, grass weaving and beadwork, during the second and third quarters of the twentieth century. Based on the study of beadwork three main periods emerge: up to the 1940s, when the old rural order was still largely the norm, from the 1950s to about 1980, the migrant labour epoch, and the last two decades of the twentieth century, which witnessed the general decline of traditional beadwork (except the religious beadwork of the Shembe sect) and the emergence of a commercial tourist craft industry.

Sources and current distribution of twentieth-century ceramic beer vessels

Most twentieth-century ceramic vessels were made in the locations and reserves. There seems to have been no continuous tradition of pottery on white-owned farms. Within the locations there were certain regions in which the making of beer vessels, cooking pots and large storage containers flourished, reaching a high degree of technical perfection and developing distinctive styles. In other regions only small to medium-sized rather basic sparsely decorated forms could be found in the field. In some others, particularly those in which communities of Christianised blacks (*amakholwa*) settled and purchased land in the nineteenth century, ceramic pots have not been in use for a long time.[20]

From the late 1980s onwards, partly as a result of publications and partly dealer-driven, a collectors' market for 'antique' Zulu beer pots developed in Europe and North America. Old pots were often selected for particular marketable features, for instance patterns formed out of small applied nodules of clay, *amasumpa,* which were regarded as the hallmark of Zulu beer vessels. The large, unburnished and undecorated *izimbiza*, on the other hand, and many pots decorated with incisions were left in the field.

Provenances were not preserved; indeed, many dealers purposely withheld information in order to prevent others from discovering their sources. These pots were largely acquired by private collectors in Europe and the United States of America.[21] Most dealers maintained workshops to 'restore' pots to make them more marketable. They filled in and coloured chips in the rim and other broken sections, repaired cracks and waxed the surface.

Imbiza from Msinga (pre-1964).
H: 707 mm, elliptical cross-section
D: 705/620 mm, capacity about 170
Umancishane from Melmoth (1920s).
H: 129 mm
PHOTO: Ian Carbutt

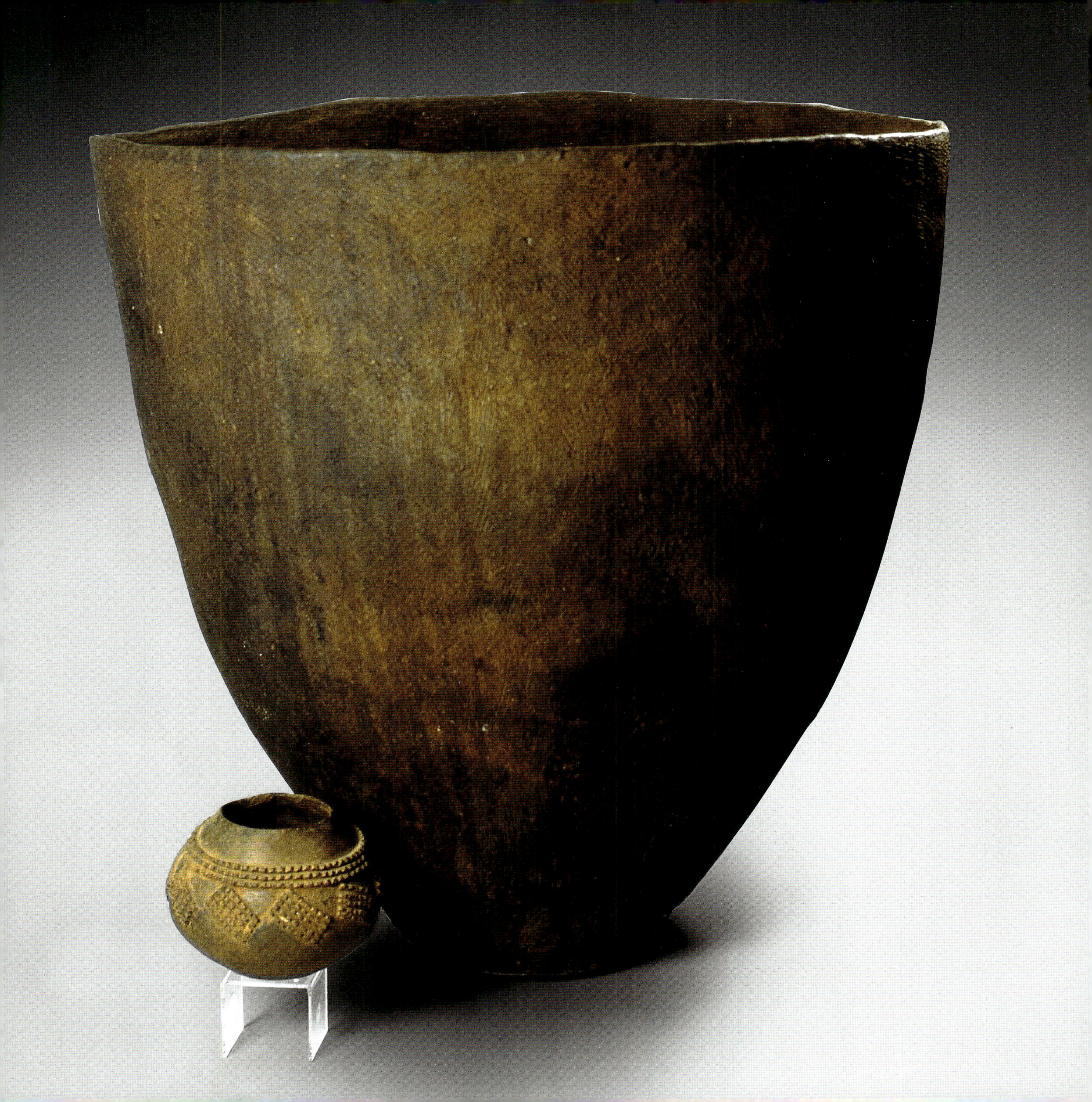

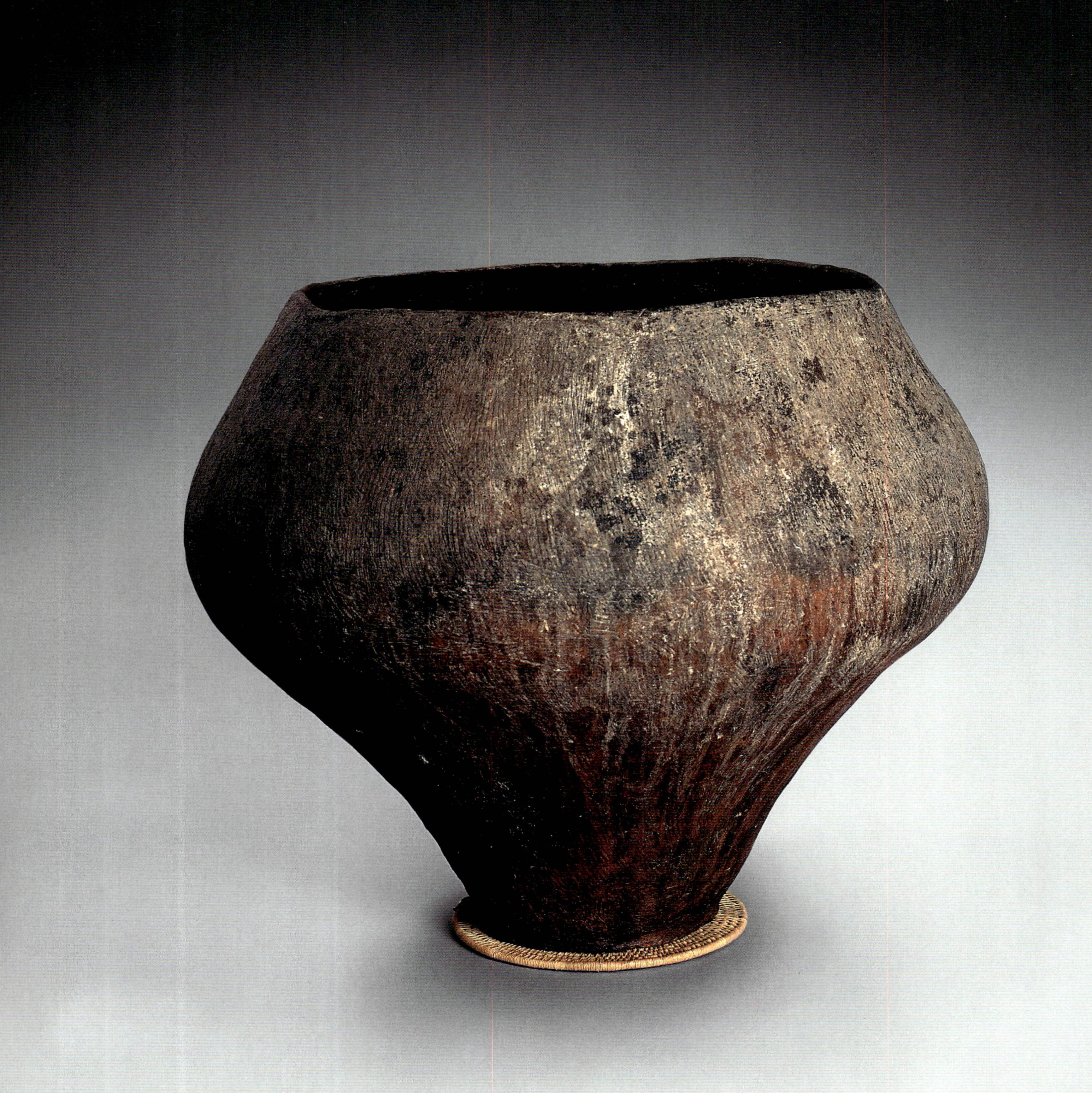

Apart from the reduction of authenticity, a great deal of information was lost through the process of selection and the disposal of pots that were deemed unsaleable. South African public collections do not hold comprehensive collections of Zulu ceramics. The museums did not pursue a systematic collecting policy, as ceramics were not highly regarded at the time that they would have been available. As a result, most of the pots in local museum collections stem from bequests. As such, they do have acquisition dates but are rarely provenanced beyond that. In more recent times, lack of resources and competition from dealers and their 'runners' in the field have made it impossible for South African museums to acquire representative collections. At the time of writing there are still a few large *izimbiza*, but hardly any other old pots left in their original homesteads.

The current survey is based mainly on some 900 beer pots in public and private collections in South Africa and the United States. Many were collected and provenanced between 1992 and 2003. However, in spite of this relatively large database, the survey cannot, unfortunately, be regarded as comprehensive. In particular, some important areas, such as Nkandla, had been depleted before they could be recorded.

Identification and classification of Zulu beer vessels

Beer vessels are embedded in a wealth of information. This includes specific information from primary sources, such as potters and owners of particular vessels, as well as more general economic, social and cultural aspects, which have a bearing on our understanding of the vessels. Given that the aim of this survey is to describe and classify the pottery in its development and distribution, it can limit itself to addressing questions of form, function and ethnicity. Form, in this context, is defined as the totality of physical features in the sense of Gestalt, 'an organised whole in which each individual part affects every other, the whole being more than the sum of its parts'.[22] Function includes not only the basic utilitarian use of the artefact, but also its wider social and religious implications. Within this framework form and function are interdependent, describing the same object from different perspectives.

So, in the first place, the description of twentieth-century ceramics must address a number of general issues including:

- The meaning of Zulu in the context of pottery (regional; tribal; identity).
- The general taxonomy of Zulu pottery (functional typology, size, shape, treatment of the surface: burnishing, blackening, decorations, including different patterns and techniques, etc).
- The origins of Zulu pottery.

Having established the wider perspectives the examination can proceed to the specifics of style, including:

- Regional, and within the regions, chronological variations.
- The categorisation of the main regional styles.
- The impact of individual potters and pot-making families within the regional framework.

'Zulu' in the context of pottery

In the context of this survey Zulu is defined in regional, political and linguistic terms as that part of eastern

Imbiza H: 446 mm
REGION: Msinga, KwaMabaso Imbiza, KwaMabaso, Msinga, before 1948. See p. 251 No 704. Characteristic broad-shouldered form tapering or very narrow base.
PHOTO: IAN CARBUTT

South Africa comprising the former Colony of Natal and the former Kingdom of Zululand, in which Zulu is spoken as the main language. The two defunct political entities, the Colony of Natal and the Kingdom of Zululand, enjoyed an afterlife throughout most of the twentieth century. It found expression above all in the rural settlement pattern: white farmlands offset by Shepstonian locations for the indigenous population. From the narrow perspective of the craft of beer-pot making in the twentieth century, the regional basis of the term 'Zulu' can be reduced to those locations in Natal and the corresponding reserves in Zululand in which the customs and 'thought patterns'[23] of the past still regulated the daily lives of most people.

This definition seeks to forestall the concept of a distinct 'Zulu identity' as a determinant of style formation. As the consequences of the settlement of 1879 – the break-up of Zululand into rival chiefdoms – clearly demonstrate, the Kingdom of Zululand was never a 'nation state' in the European sense (although some of the settlers of that time may have chosen to regard it as such). Instead it consisted of a central polity with a number of client polities, some more dependent than others, grouped around it. However, Adulphe Delegorgue, an astute observer who travelled in southern Africa between 1838 and 1844, nevertheless recognised that there was such a thing as a Zulu sense of national identity: 'The Zoulou is born proud and possesses to a high degree a sense of nationhood.' He compared them to the French.[24] It was characterised by internal rivalries overridden by the loyalties engendered through the centralised *amabutho* institution of military service. Or, more famously in the words of Sir Theophilus Shepstone: 'The Zulu nation is a collection of tribes, more or less autonomous, and more or less discontented; a rope of sand whose only cohesive property was furnished by the presence of the Zulu ruling family and its command of a standing army.'[25]

It would be wrong to suggest that a 'Zulu identity' was the determinant of the styles of Zulu pottery; rather, the main features common to all Zulu pottery emerged throughout a region settled by a group of clans sharing a common system of customs and beliefs but not integrated into a unified political order. This is not to deny that the centre of political power exerted a formative influence on the material culture of the area under its immediate control.

Main features of Zulu pottery

Four distinct types of beer vessel according to volume and function can be distinguished: *imbiza*, *uphiso*, *ukhamba* and *umancishana*. *Imbiza* (plural: *izimbiza*) are large storage and brewing vessels that may be up to 90 cm high. In some places they are set into the floors of huts as permanent features. In a few areas small *izimbiza* used to be made. The distinguishing feature of *izimbiza* is that they are fired once only in an oxidising environment producing a reddish to yellowish surface, depending on the iron content of the clay. They are usually covered with a slip applied with a broad circular motion.

Uphiso (plural: *izimpiso*) are medium to large usually round-bodied pots of up to 30 litres capacity, although exceptionally one may come across ones that are considerably larger.

They have a small usually cylindrical neck (typically between ¼ and ⅓ of the diameter of the pot) to prevent liquid from spilling. Their main function is to transport water or beer. They are always burnished and fired twice to produce the familiar black surface.

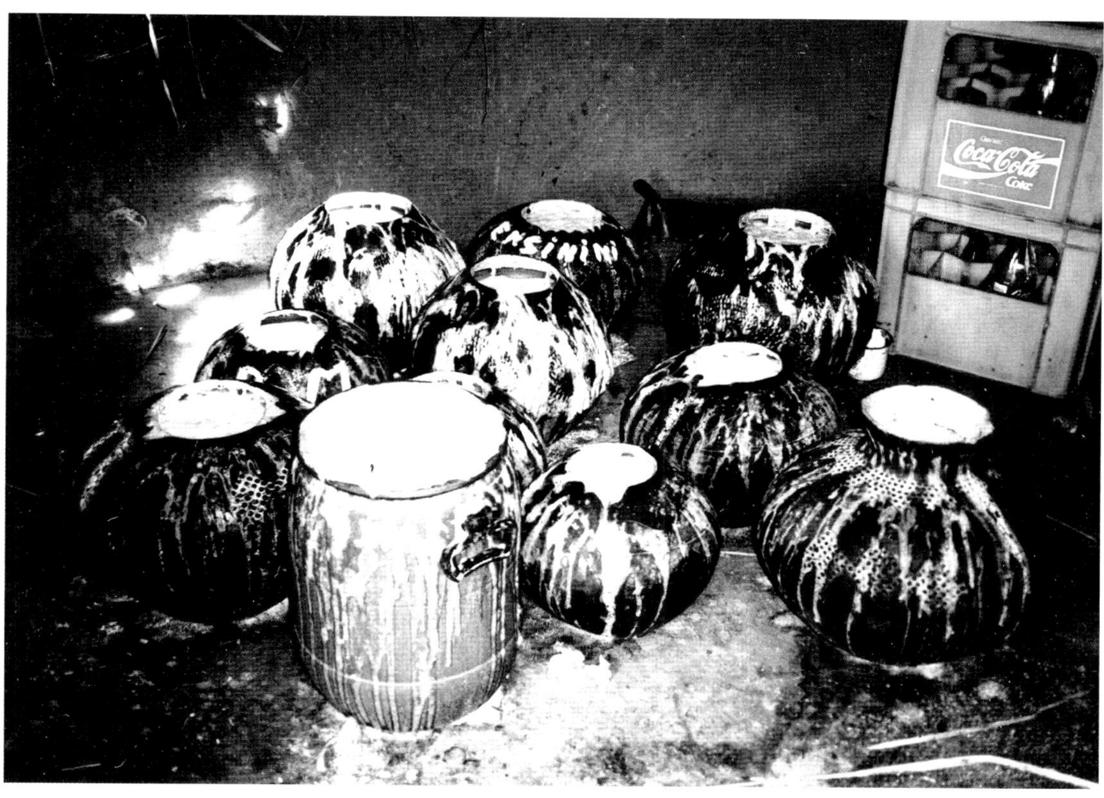

Preparing beer for a ceremony: fermentation. Nongoma region, 1997 or 1998

They are decorated on the shoulders and sometimes on the body of the pot according to region.

Ukhamba (plural: *izinkamba*), also *isikhamba* (plural: *izikhamba*)[26] are used for serving beer. The beer is lifted out of the pot with a ladle made from a bottle gourd (*inkhezo*, plural: *izinkezo*), which holds about 300 ml. The beer is usually drunk directly from the *inkhezo*, which is passed round, but it can also be drunk from the *ukhamba* itself.

Izinkamba come in many sizes, from 1 500 ml to 50 litres and more. In shape they vary from almost conical to bag-shaped, round, shouldered, tapered or squat. Such variations may be regional or the work of particular families of potters. They are usually richly decorated. It has been suggested that the decorations serve to give a grip on the pot when it is slippery with beer.

Umancishana, (plural: *omancishana*) is a small version of the *ukhamba* holding between 500 and 1 500 ml of beer. The name is derived from *ncintshana*, 'to be stingy with, niggardly towards'[27]. It is usually near-spherical, undecorated or decorated in a manner similar to *izinkamba*. In the middle of the twentieth century *omancishana* were sometimes made with a foot. It has been suggested that this was a stylistic transfer from the form of a European chalice (Tim Maggs, pers. communication). They might also be derived from Sotho pedestal cups as illustrated by Barley (1994: 26). They are usually reserved for guests or the spirits of the ancestors. The beer is drunk directly from the pot.

With very few exceptions Zulu pots have a flat base. This is in contrast to the majority of ceramic vessels in many parts of Africa, which have rounded bases. A

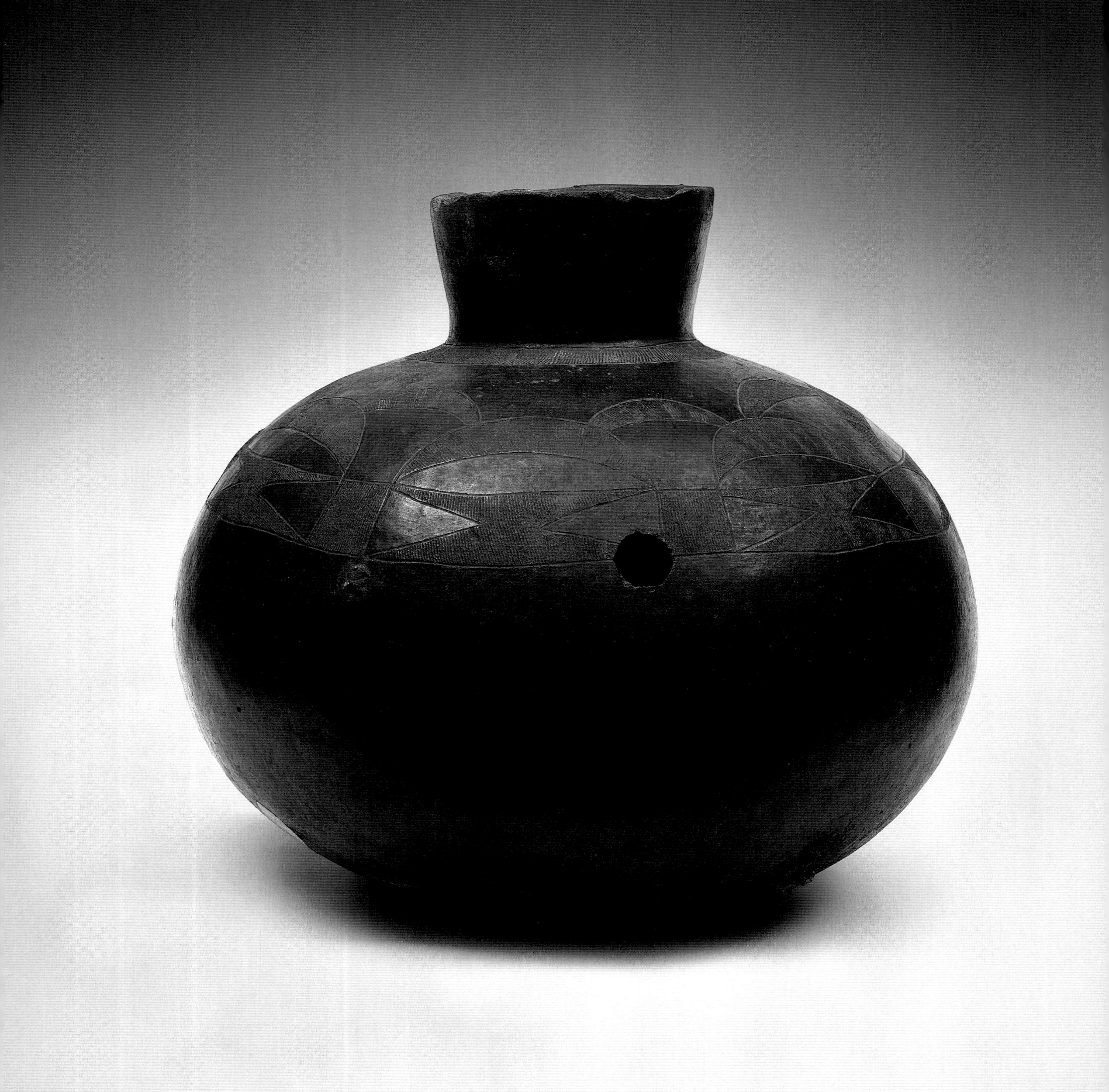

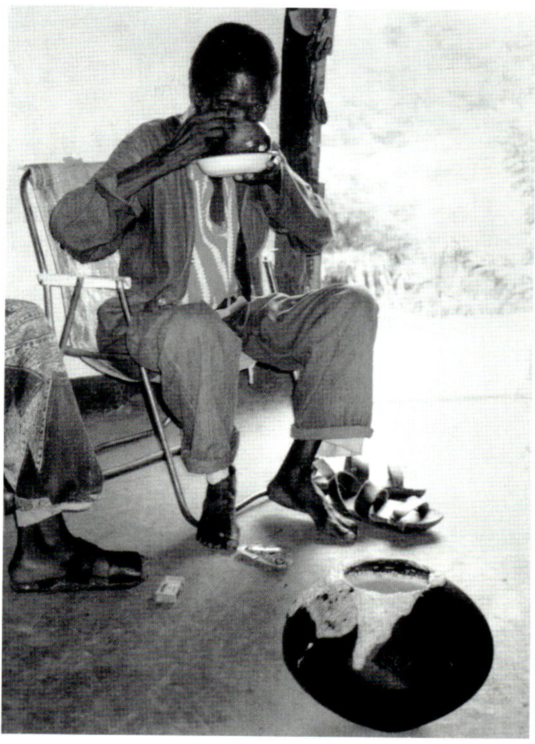

rounded base allows for a better distribution of heat from a traditional hearth, where the pot sits on three stones or directly in the embers. On the other hand pots used mainly for serving or storing liquids need to be able to stand on a level surface. This is the case for most beer pot applications. Twentieth-century Zulu cooking pots are not very common, because most cooking is done in metal pots. They can be recognised by their wide mouths. The bases of the cooking pots are no different from those of serving pots. This may be on account of the technique used in the construction of all Zulu clay vessels by coiling upwards from a flat base.

The treatment of the surface varies with the type of vessel. *Izimbiza* are usually coated with a thin slip of clay mixed with cattle dung applied in a circular motion. The other three types, *izimpiso, izinkamba* and *omancis- hana* are painstakingly burnished at the leathery stage with a small river pebble such as an agate and then fired twice. The first firing produces a red to yellowish bisque

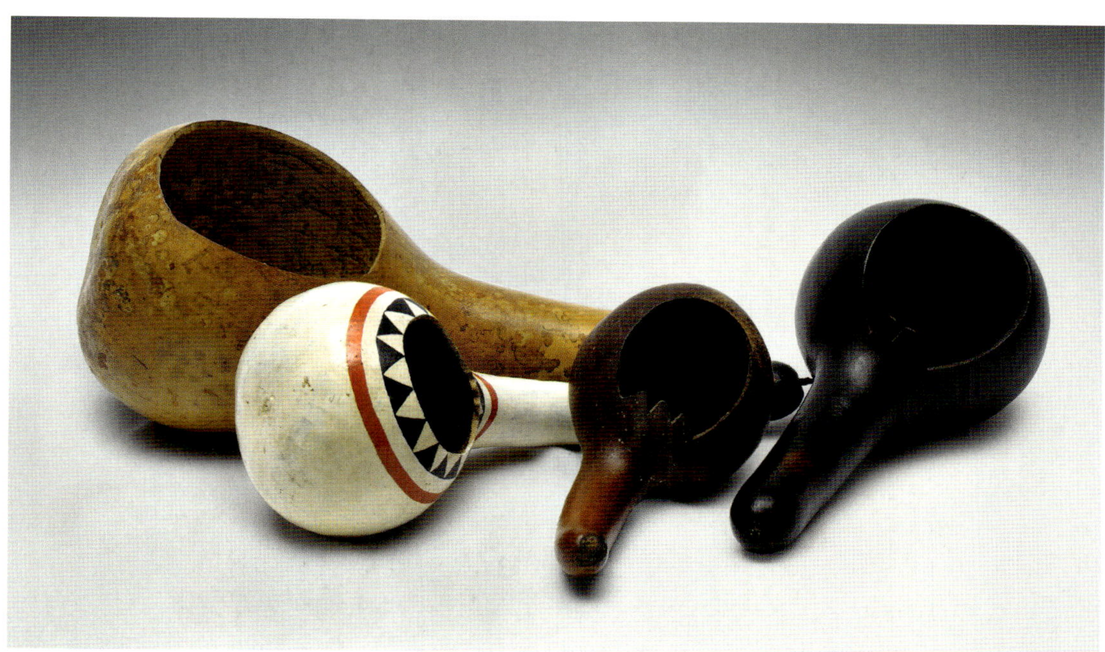

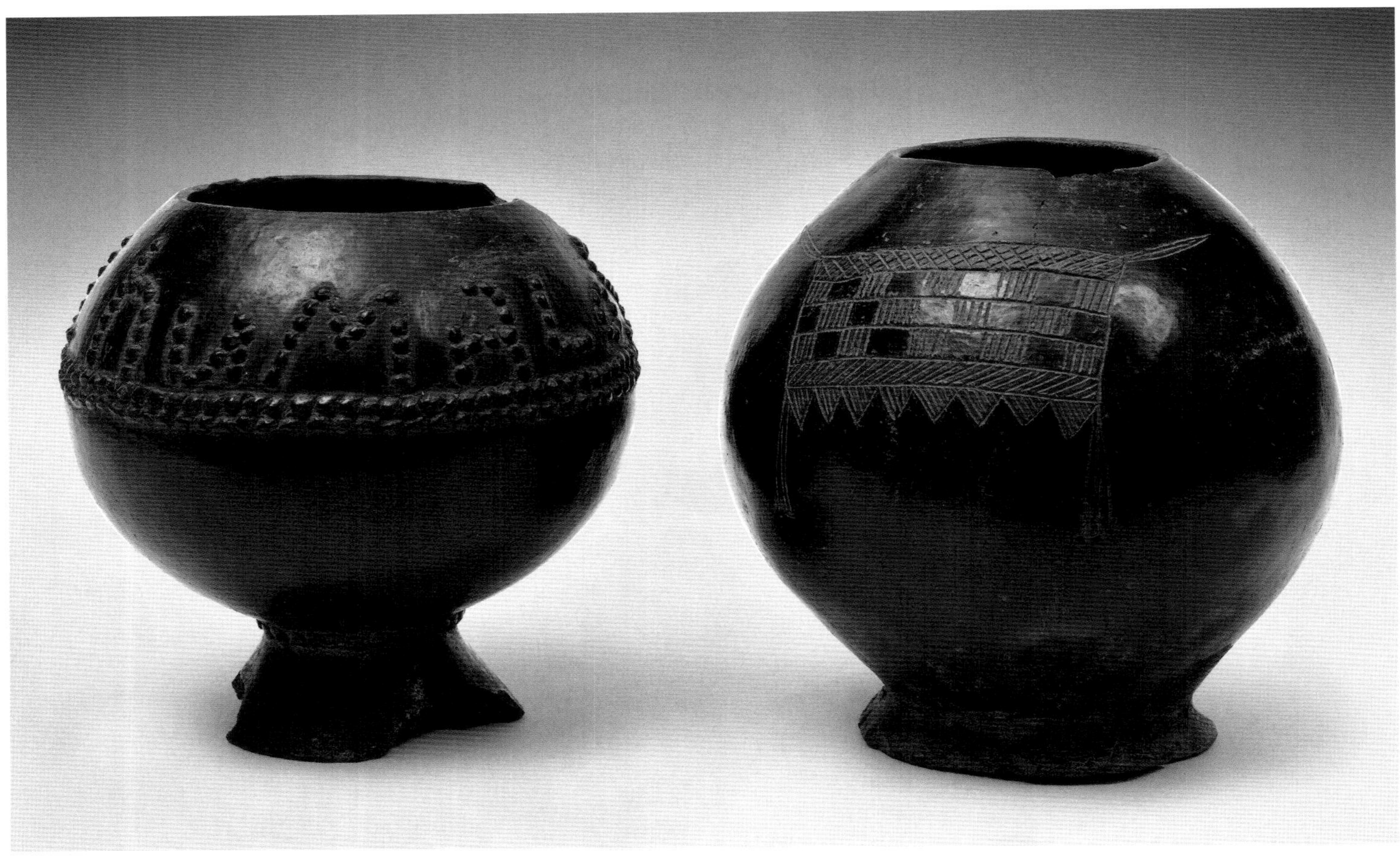

Two old omancishana with feet.

LEFT: H: 182 mm. The text reads: SigidLA LhumALo misspelt for the owner's name: Sigidla Khumalo. The potter was Lesaya Cele. 'She was the first potter in this area. All the others learnt from her when they came here from the farms at Dlomo-dlomo near Ngome.' DATE: 1961

RIGHT: from Phalafini, Msinga (late 1950s)

H: 198 mm. Decorated with an incised *isigege* [pubic apron] in the *umzansi* style.

PHOTO: Patrick Royal

texture. The second firing is done in a reducing environment. This fuses free carbon into the surface of the clay, producing a hard semi-matt black finish.[28]

Izimbiza remain undecorated apart from the shallow circular patterns produced by the application of the slip. *Izimpiso, izinkamba* and many *omancishana,* on the other hand, are highly decorated with a large variety of motifs and patterns. Some of these can also be found on beadwork, wood carvings and scarifications, whilst others are specific to ceramics. A number of techniques are used to create the patterns: incising, impressing, gouging, applying pressure to the inside of the half-dried vessel to force up shallow rounded bumps on the outside, and applying nodules (*amasumpa*), carved plaques and ropes of clay to the surface of the pots. Many of these techniques have regional connotations, as do specific patterns.

The origins of Zulu pottery

The present state of historical and archaeological research would seem to support Laband's assertion that

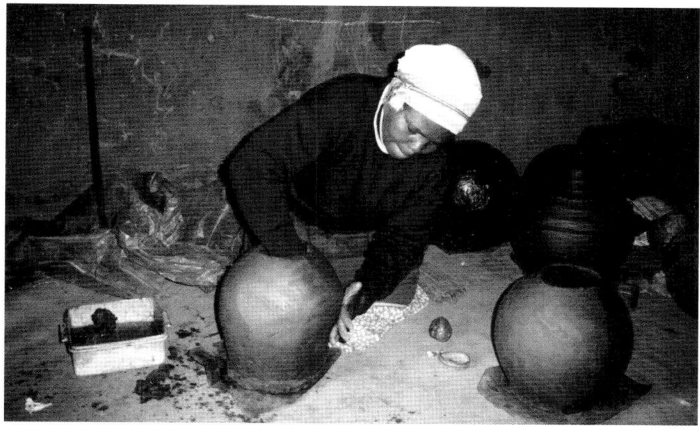

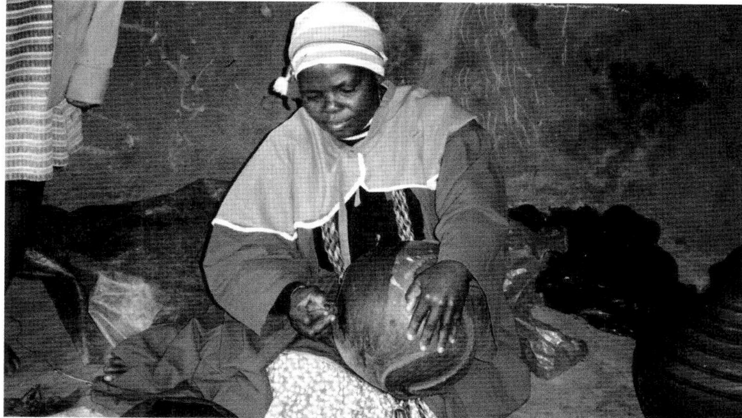

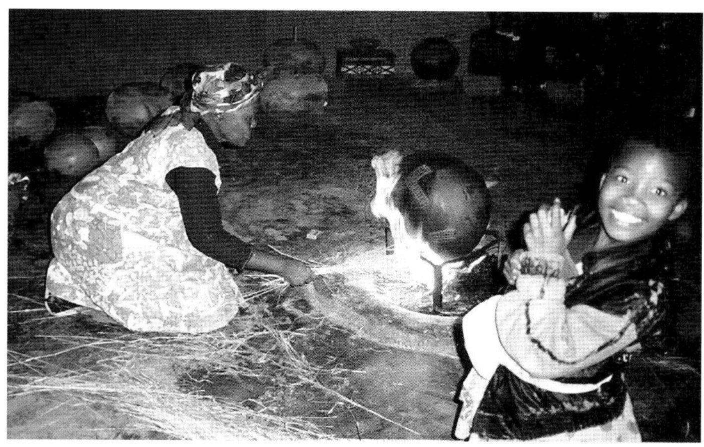

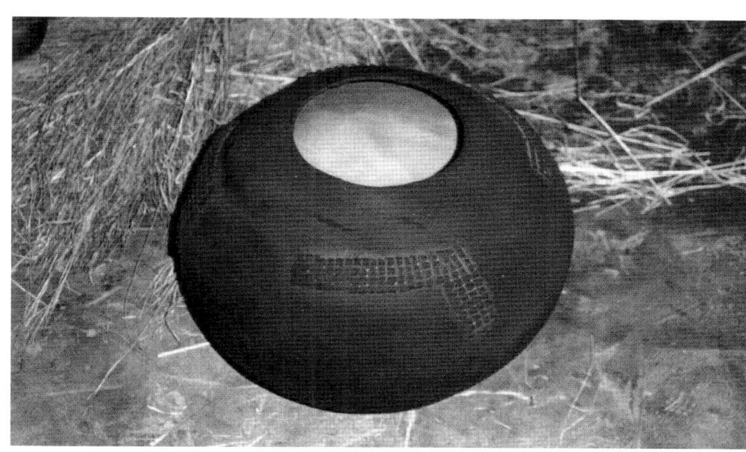

TOP LEFT: Aselinah Mbatha thinning a pot at the semi-dried 'leathery' stage by scraping away clay from the inside. Nongoma, mid-1990s.

TOP RIGHT: Aselinah Mbatha burnishing the surface of a pot with a river agate prior to firing. The stone may be seen lying on the ground to her right in the previous picture.

BOTTOM LEFT: Second firing of new pots with grass over a tripod. Near Nongoma, 1996. The newly blackened pots are rubbed down with raw suet to remove excess soot.

BOTTOM RIGHT: As bottom left: Newly blackened pot before being rubbed down with suet.

after 'about AD 1500 the evidence indicates that the Iron Age people of the Natal-Zululand region were culturally, linguistically and physically the direct ancestors of today's black population'.[29] Despite this, little is known about the origins of pottery with the characteristics described above. Archaeological evidence indicates that from about AD 1700 to 1850 black burnished vessels were much the exception rather than the rule. Decorations are present on a small number of the sherds. They are restricted to lines of fingernail impressions and a few raised elongated lozenges.[30] Hall & Mack report that at eLangeni, the 'capital' of

the Buthelezi chief Phungashe in the late eighteenth century, they found only three black decorated, and 34 black undecorated sherds out of a total of 8 338. They conclude: 'it can be seen that more than 95 per cent consisted of undecorated and unburnished sherds, mostly from the bodies of vessels. The remaining small proportion of sherds does, however, have distinctive characteristics that allow an impression of the pottery industry from this site'.[31]

A similar picture emerges from the excavations at Mgoduyanuka (Maggs 1982), on the Thukela near Bergville, dated to the eighteenth or early nineteenth centuries, and at the similarly dated site of Nqabeni on the plateau between the White Umfolozi and the Buffalo River: 'Only 6,7% of all shards showed any type of burnish, and only 0,3% were decorated … Red ochre had been used on a smaller proportion of the burnished surfaces, while black burnish was still rarer and may represent accidental blackening from firing rather than a deliberate black colouring.'[32]

While Fynn came across burnished pots at the court of Shaka,[33] the evidence from excavations is supported by the pictorial record, the most comprehensive of which is contained in the works of George French Angas (1822–86).[34] Angas visited Natal in 1847. In 1849, after his return to England, he published *The Kaffirs Illustrated*, a volume of 30 hand-coloured lithographs, of which 18 depict scenes from Natal and Zululand, and 11 wood engravings, of which six deal with themes taken from Zulu domestic life (Angas, 1974). Eleven of the plates and two engravings depict beer vessels among other utensils of domestic use. They include 27 beer baskets, 22 *izimbiza*, 13 *izinkamba*, including three blackened ones (one of them probably wooden) and two small *omancishana,* either ceramic or basketry. There are also a number of gourds that might have been used for beer. By far the most common drinking vessels were baskets. They came in various shapes and sizes: bottle-shaped (reminiscent of the gourds), spherical, tall and narrow, and open bowl-shaped ones.[35] In one of his accompanying texts Angas describes how King Mpande sent him 'an Induna with a live bullock, an enormous basket of beer ('outchualla' [*utshwala*]), borne by two men, and a jar of Dutch aniseed cordial'.[36] Another historical illustration shows King Mpande watching an elephant's foot being prepared for roasting, with his beer basket beside him.[37]

Baskets were also used in adjoining regions. In Pondoland, for instance, they were in use from the earliest recorded period until well into the second half of the twentieth century (see illustration p. 24). 'He [Faku] ordered 2 baskets of beer to be placed before me', the Rev Francis Owen noted in his diary entry for 8 June 1837, during his overland journey from Port Elizabeth to Durban on his way to Dingaan.[38] However, Charles Rawden Maclean (aka John Ross) recollected that on his first visit to Shaka in 1825, 'every evening a large earthen vessel, containing from three to four gallons of beer, was sent them [i.e. Maclean and his companions] from the king's private brewery'.[39] This was probably an *imbiza* or large red *ukhamba* as shown on the Angas lithographs.

The majority of the pots that Angas illustrated were *izimbiza*, for storage, fermenting and cooking. This usage may also have applied to some of the *izinkamba*, as they have wide openings associated nowadays with vessels used for cooking porridge. In other images only three are burnished and blackened.[40] By the end of the nineteenth century the situation had changed entirely. The photographic record shows that burnished, blackened ceramic beer vessels representing many of the familiar twentieth-century types were in widespread use, whilst the once common baskets had all but disappeared from the scene.

How did this change in usage come about – particularly in view of the far-reaching social implications associated with the drinking of beer?[41] The explanatory models commonly applied to the introduction of new cultural practices are:

1. Cultural diffusion, i.e. borrowing or diffusion from neighbouring communities.
2. Demic diffusion, i.e. importation of new cultural practices through the movement of peoples.
3. Local adaptations to new or changing circumstances.

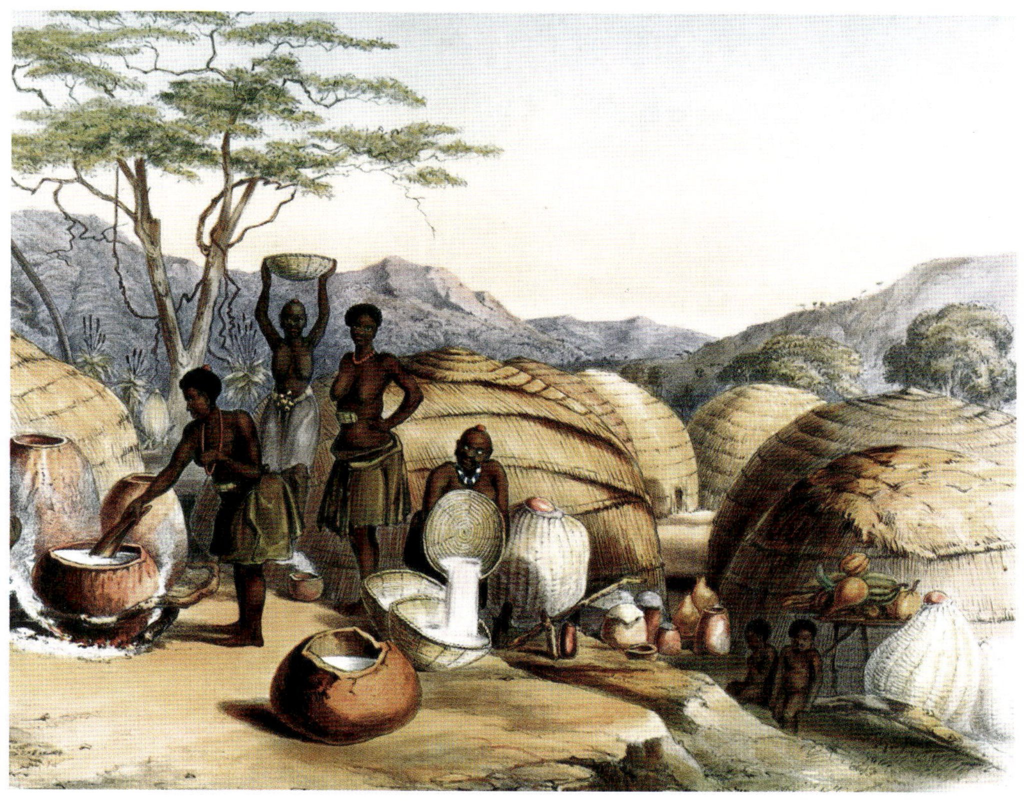

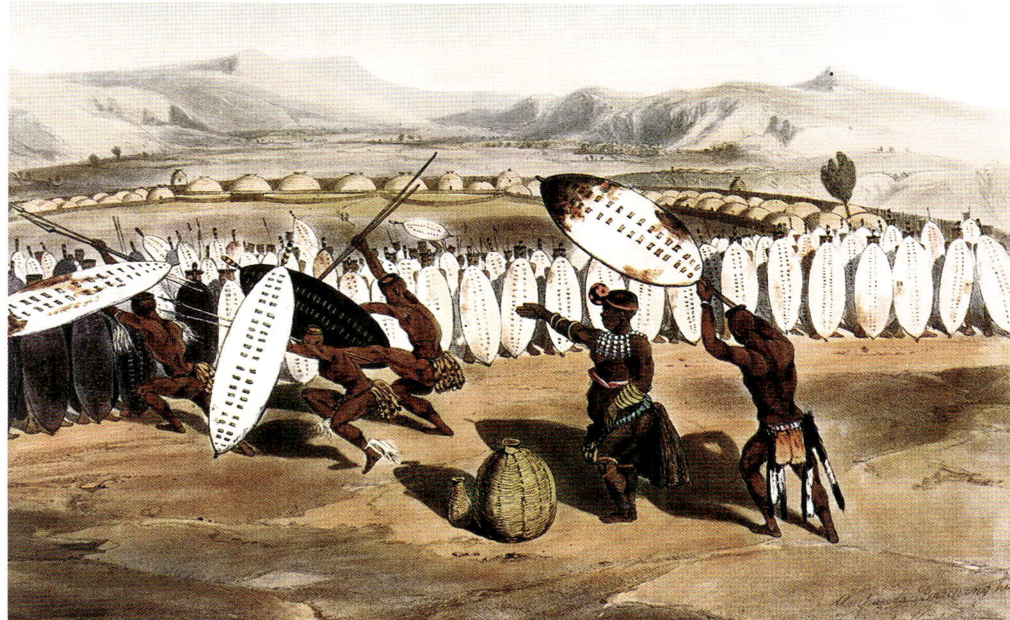

TOP: Angas. Scene of beer making in a Zulu kraal.

BOTTOM: Angas. Mpande directing a dance ceremony of his troops with a large and a small beer basket next to him.

All of these may have played some part: cultural diffusion in the spread of the custom throughout the greater Zulu community from one area to another; demic diffusion through the movement of people due to Shaka's military campaigns and their aftermath; and, finally, adaptations to the new circumstances that arose in both Natal and Zululand during the course of the nineteenth century. Hall and Mack conclude that in the eighteenth century the exogamous patri-local marriage system facilitated the spread of pottery styles across political boundaries from one chieftaincy to the next.[42] Marriages were frequently contracted between parties from different chieftaincies. When the women, who were the potters, married, they took their skills with them from their paternal homes to those of their husbands, enabling the stylistic features of their pottery to spread across a wide area. This would be an example of diffusion. By way of contrast, architectural designs, which were the reserve of men, did not spread, but tended to vary from one chieftaincy to the next. However, the third model, adaptation to changing circumstances, seems to offer the most compelling explanation for the changes.

To varying degrees most of Zululand was suitable both for a pastoral and an agricultural way of life. This held good so long as the population density remained low enough to allow for the more extensive form of exploitation necessary to a pastoral economy (including, for instance, a lower crop yield per hectare, and the seasonal movement of herds in search of better grazing). The mixed economy provided people with the flexibility of food production appropriate to an environment subject to periodic droughts. Transhumance, cattle raiding and, in extreme circumstances, a return to a semi-nomadic condition (with the likelihood of a concomitant reduction in population density) enabled them to survive when crops failed for any length of time.

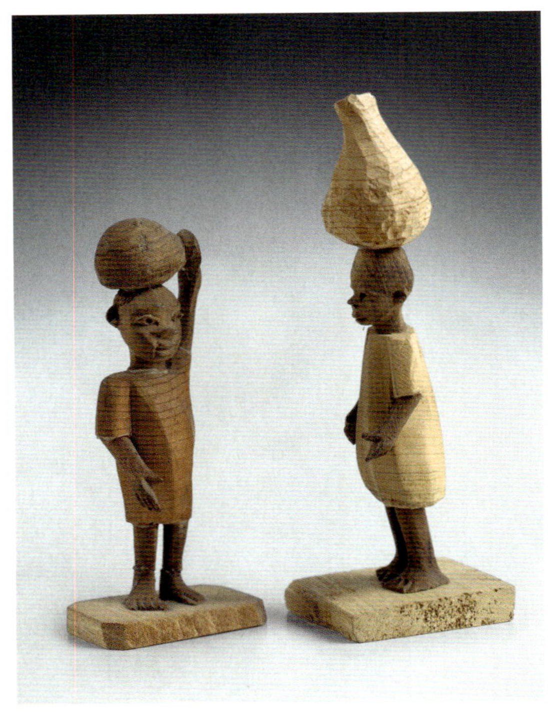

Pots and Gourds
Two Nigerian 'Thorn Figures'
COLLECTION: Robert Niklans, Nsukka.
Anambra State, 1978.
H: 302 mm, 330 mm
PHOTO: Patrick Royal.

The disruption of agricultural activity as a result of the political upheavals and military campaigns of the first quarter of the nineteenth century had an effect that was in some respects similar to a prolonged period of drought. The most urgent consideration for communities under threat was to preserve their cattle from capture and to remove themselves as far as possible from the perceived source of danger. This, in fact, many were able to do successfully. It implied reverting to a nomadic pastoral way of life until a new area to settle in had been identified and cultivation could be resumed. The transitional 'nomadic' period involved a change of diet from one based on grain to one consisting mainly of meat.[43] There was less opportunity for brewing beer and no need for the wide range of heavy and fragile ceramics to do so.

Other factors also played an important role. No doubt the impact of colonialism in Natal and the rever-

Uphiso-shaped beer gourd, *igula,* said to have been in use since the 1930s. Purchased from the owner near Keate's Drift 2004.
H: 250 mm
This cultivar is extinct now.
PHOTO: Patrick Royal

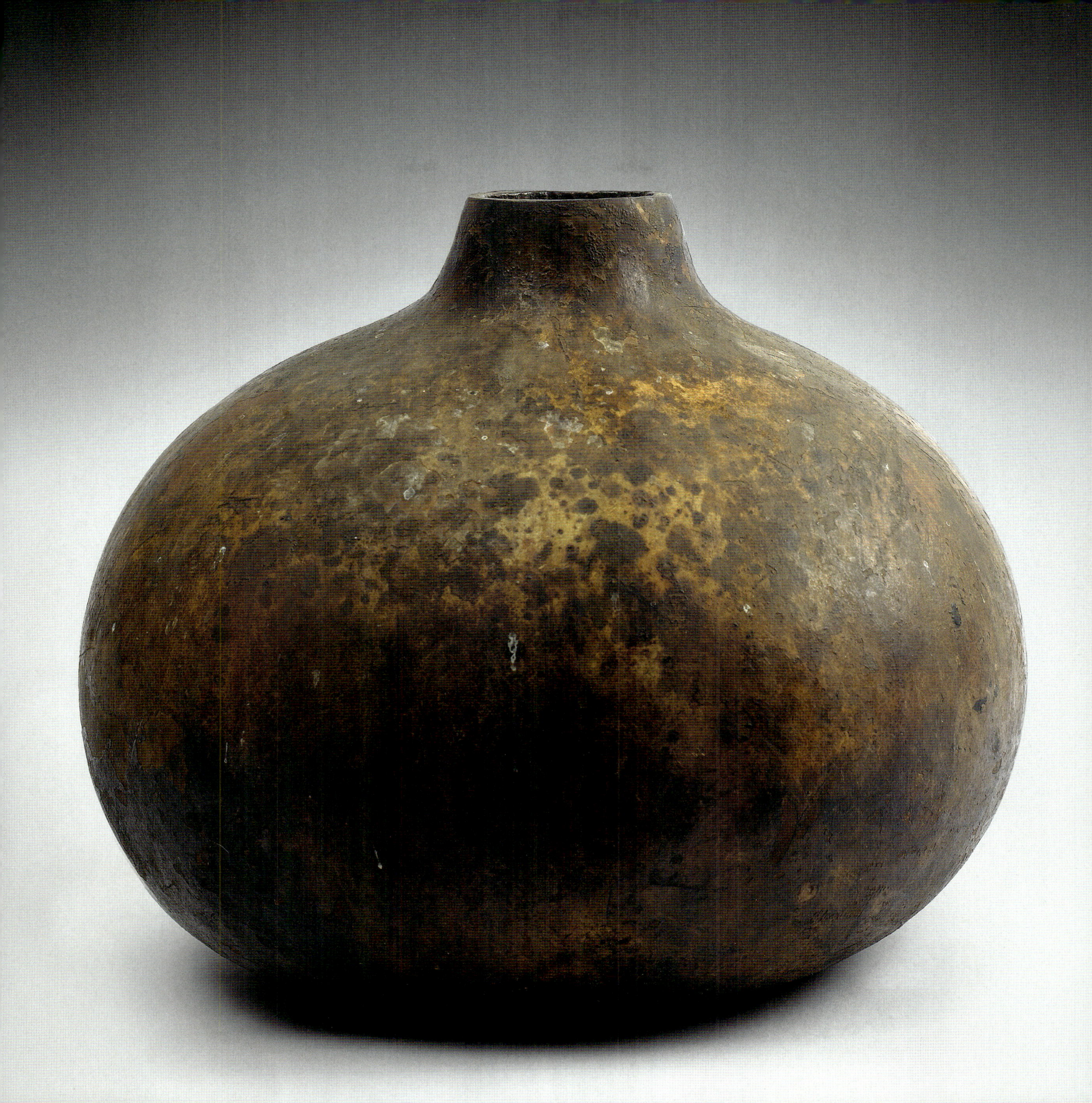

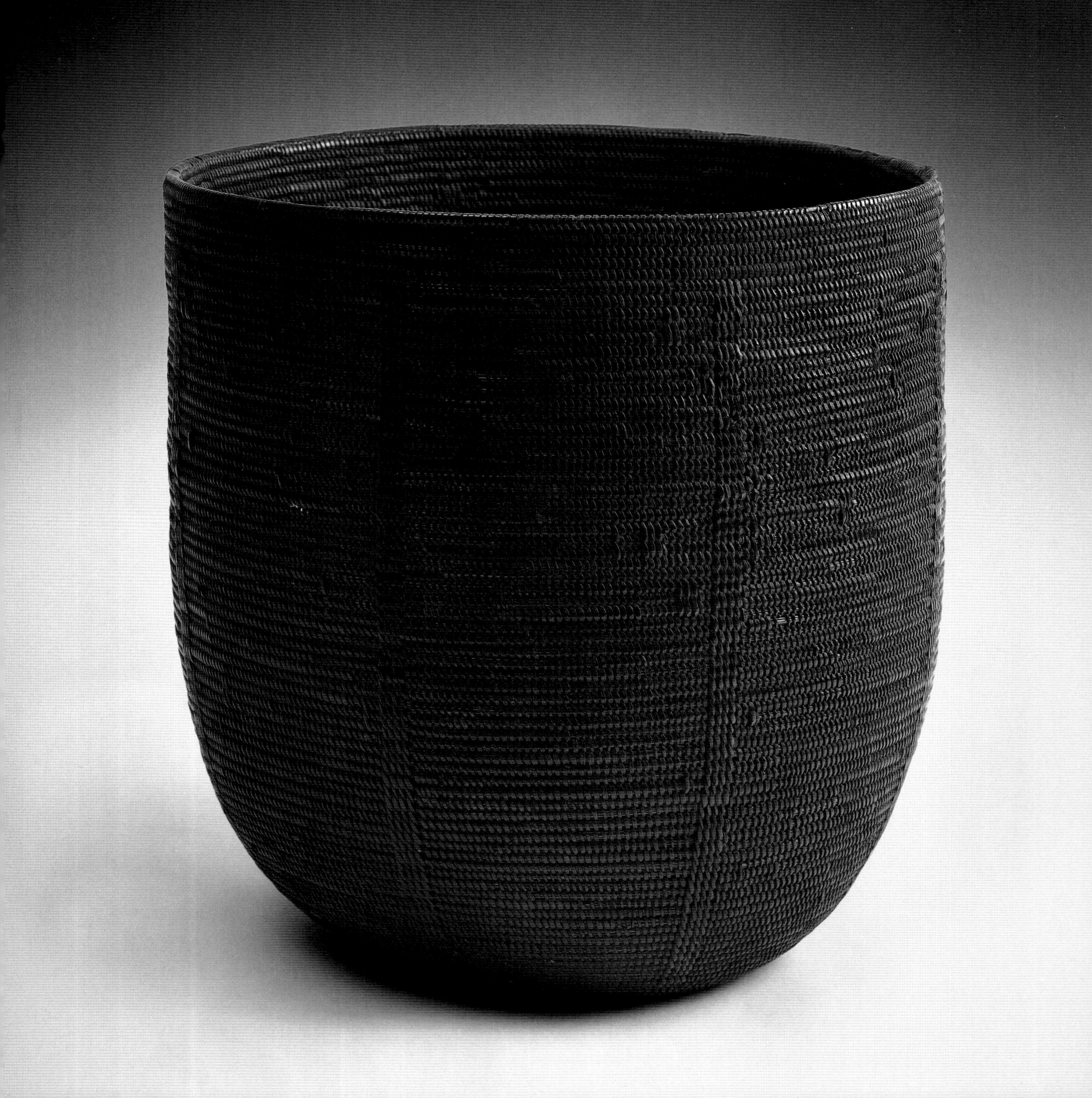

berations of colonialism in Zululand must be counted among them. Furthermore, Natal and Zululand were among the most heavily missionised territories in the world. A plethora of denominations including Catholic, Church of England, Lutheran, Methodist, and even Trappist, from a range of European countries and North America, competed with varying degrees of success for converts. Whereas the impact of colonialism undermined and finally destroyed the authority of the King and the integrity of the Zulu socio-political system, the missionaries had an equally devastating effect on everyday family life.[44] The two main missionary injunctions that affected Zulu material culture were the insistence on the wearing of clothing, or rather the elimination of nakedness, particularly in the case of young women, and the prohibition of beer (*utshwala*) drinking because of its alcohol content (1–2%) and its association with reverence for the ancestors. Both were sensitive issues with deep roots in Zulu culture.[45]

The well-nigh universal shift away from beer baskets and the adoption of blackened ceramic vessels in their stead had important ritual concomitants. The serving of beer was an integral part of most ceremonial occasions in which the spirits of the ancestors were thought to be involved, such as births, marriages and deaths, the ear-piercing ceremony, the Feast of First Fruits, and many family occasions.[46] As the shades were known to shun sunlight and bright places, the blackening of the beer vessels constituted an invitation to the ancestral spirits to be present at the ceremonies and sip their beer in the comfort of darkness.[47] Taken in this context, the introduction of blackened beer vessels in place of the time-honoured baskets could be interpreted as a measure to invoke the assistance of the ancestors in defending the customary way of life against the incursions of the outsiders. This does not necessarily imply that it was part of a new ritual in-

stituted as a result of a conscious strategic decision, but rather an emotional quest for security in a deeply disturbing and threatening spiritual environment.[48] In addition to the above, it could also be argued that the very emphasis placed by the missionaries on the prohibition of beer drinking imbued it with an enhanced ritual significance in the eyes of the people.

Regional variations in pottery styles

The situation described by Hall and Mack (1983) for the late eighteenth century involved a conglomerate of chieftaincies, each of which held a relatively small area of land with contiguous boundaries. However, by the time the turmoil of the first half of the nineteenth century and its aftermath had subsided, most of the original population of Natal had moved to other regions or had been resettled in locations. As has been shown, the process of resettlement was extended to Zululand after annexation in 1887, and completed after the report of the Land Commission of 1904. Where the locations were separated from one another by tracts of white farmlands, any stylistic diffusion through exogamous marriage would, on the whole, have come to a halt at the boundaries of the locations. In the long term one would expect this to encourage the development of location-based styles. In practice the situation was more complex. The institution of chieftaincies – albeit with greatly reduced responsibilities – survived the creation of the locations, and indeed continues to the present day. It is reflected in the system of *izigodi* (singular: *isigodi*, 'district, division of territory'), which has remained the basic unit of administration in the former locations with regard to many everyday matters. Most locations comprised

Pondo beer basket, 1920s.
H: 240 mm. Collected in Bizane by Agnes Dube, (2004). Compare also Natal Museum Accession No. 2399 purchased in 1915.
COLLECTION: Frank Jolles
PHOTO: Patrick Royal

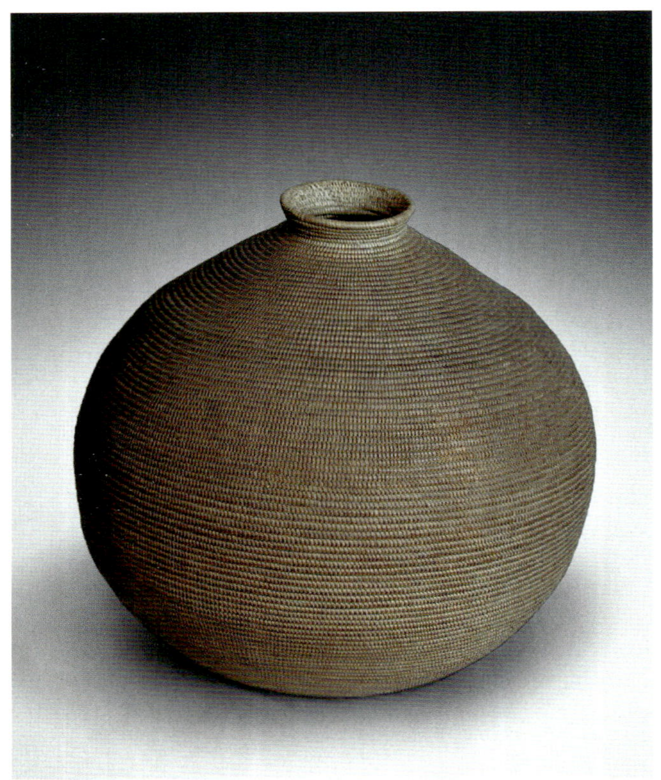

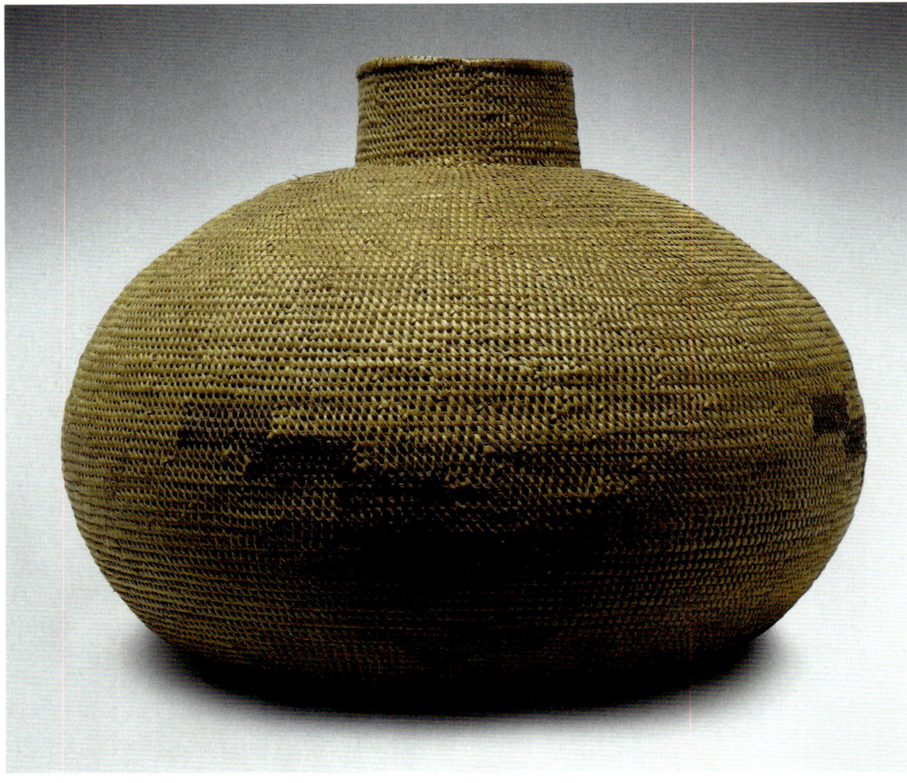

considerable tracts of land, extensive enough to support a number of such diminished chieftaincies. Many also had common boundaries with adjacent locations. A study of the beadwork of the Msinga area, based on the variations in colour combinations ('colour conventions') and patterns, has shown that distinctive location-based colour conventions did indeed develop. However, they were not static but subject to an ongoing process of modification brought about by migration and changes in the social environment of the makers and wearers of beadwork.[49] It remains to be seen whether similar processes determined the evolution of pottery styles.

Most of the information in this section is derived from field research. In addition to the approximately 800 pots collected and documented between 1990 and 2003, a number of pots collected by the African Art Centre in Durban for sale at their annual 'Treasures – Amagugu' exhibitions have been included, particularly in those cases for which a good provenance was available. Although many of the beer vessels in South African public collections lack provenance, they are often the only vessels from the nineteenth century and the beginning of the twentieth century for which an accession date is available. They thus form an important addition to this survey. Well documented beer vessels in public collections are held by the KwaZulu Cultural Museum in Ulundi, collected by Nick Penney in the 1980s, and in the South African Museum in Cape Town, collected by

LEFT: Natal Museum No. 6622, spherical beer basket, *isichumu,* acquired 1990 (but probably from an older unaccessioned collection), cultural affinity 'Thonga'. H: 425 mm W: 460 mm
PHOTO: G Naidoo

RIGHT: Uphiso-shaped beer basket, *isichumu.* H: 375 mm. Probably from Msinga, 1950s.
COLLECTION: Frank Jolles,
PURCHASED: at auction 2004
PHOTO: Patrick Royal

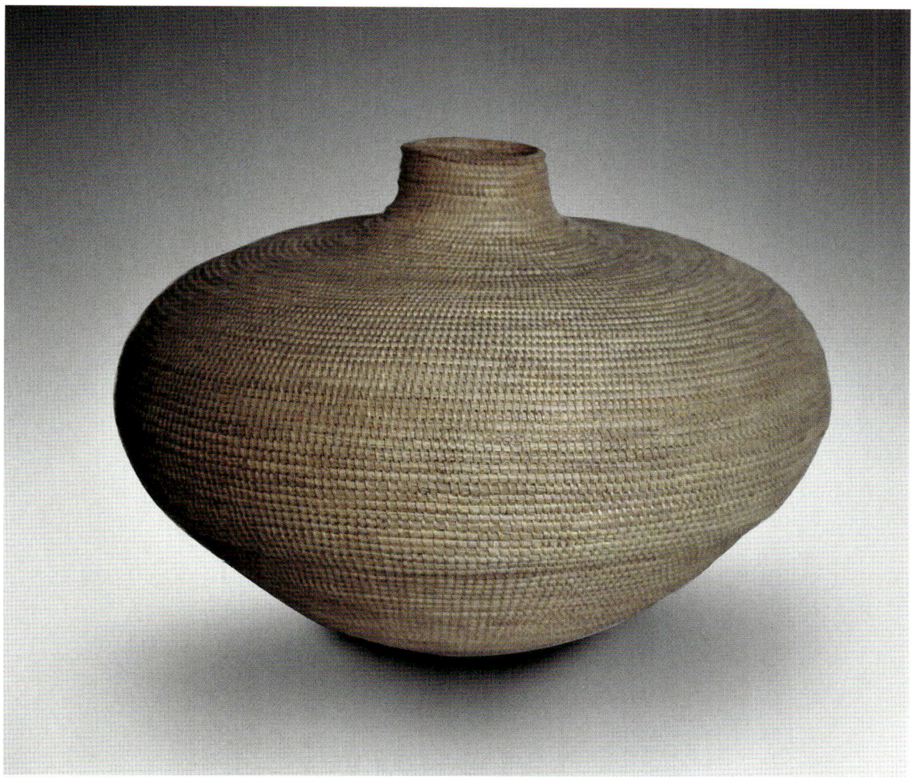

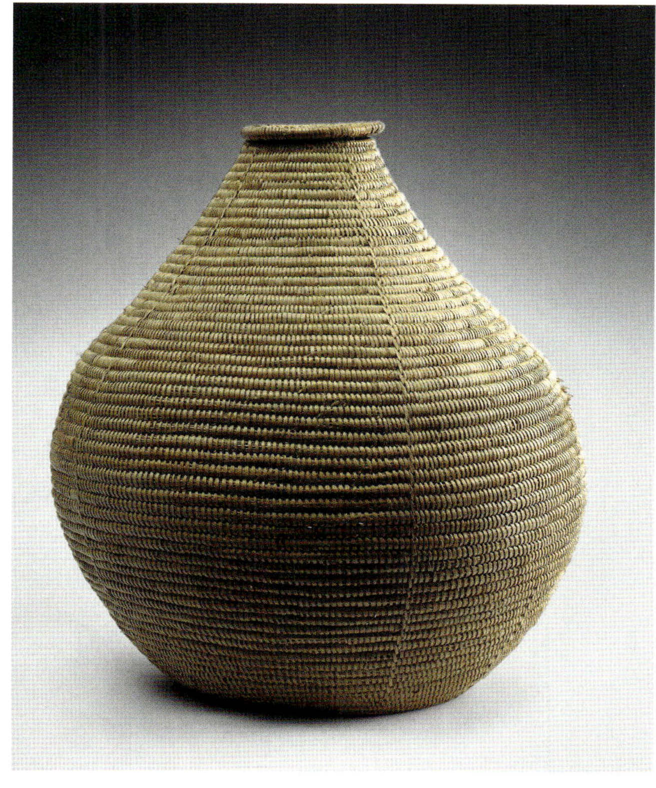

LEFT: Uphiso-shaped basket. Natal Museum No. 6624.
H: 295 mm W: 415 mm
PHOTO: G Naidoo

RIGHT: Bag-shaped beer basket with lid. Probably from Msinga, 1960s.
H: 410 mm
COLLECTION: Frank Jolles, acquired 2005

Margaret Shaw and Anne Lawton in the 1960s. The main constraining factor in compiling a comprehensive database has been the activity of commercial collectors and their local field agents ('runners') in the period before this survey commenced and whilst it was being carried out. Some regions had been so depleted by the time we arrived that it was no longer possible to obtain a representative sample of their pottery.

During the course of the twentieth century very few changes were made to the distribution of land for reserves and locations and the land allocated to white farms and plantations. Some land was acquired from reserves for the extension of wild life reservations, in particular the 'corridor' between Hluhluwe and Umfolozi. In a number of places white-owned farms were bought back for inclusion in KwaZulu before 1994. More recently some white-owned farms, mainly in areas bordering KwaZulu, have been abandoned under the pressure of incursions. Others have been transferred to black ownership under a government scheme of 'willing buyers and willing sellers'. These changes have not materially affected the distribution of Zulu beer vessels. As the settlement of Natal and Zululand proceeded over a long period of time and in a piecemeal manner interrupted by conflicts and the progressive erosion and final annexation of the Kingdom of Zululand, it is not surprising that the pattern that finally emerged should present such a chequered and seemingly chaotic appearance.

Why has the production of Zulu beer vessels in the twentieth century been largely limited to the locations in KwaZulu and in Natal? One explanation might be the rather obvious one: that traditional crafts (like any others) are a product of their cultural environment. They depend on a functioning infrastructure, in this case the rural infrastructure and the indigenous knowledge that goes with it, and on a socio-economic support system. For ceramics, the former would include the routine of collecting fuel (wood, cow dung, dried aloe leaves, whichever is available), the ability to recognise the right clays and additives, and above all the flexibility of working time required to adjust to the contingencies of pottery, such as weather conditions. All these imply a degree of personal freedom of disposition, which was not characteristic of the life of a wage labourer on a farm.

The socio-economic support system includes the question of a ready market for the product. Here again, the farm tended to be linked to the cash economy of the industrial state which supplied most needs (including metal and plastic vessels to take the place of indigenous ceramics), through a network of farm shops. The rural economy, on the other hand, was largely based on barter, though it too was connected to the larger economy through the operation of markets which sold both local and industrial products and through trading posts. Thus, Phiwayinkosi MaMthethwa Ngobese of Mayakazi, Hlabisa (born 'about 1930' in Vryheid), related how 'a long time ago, in the days before there were any motors', she used to sell pots at the monthly Mona Market. It was a two-day walk each way. She and her daughter Thangithile MaNgobese Mhlongo would carry the pots, spending a night at a friend's house half way. At Mona Market there was a good turnover, better than she could get back home. The pots were sold for cash, whereas at home they were bartered against chickens: two large or three small chickens for one large pot. She said that I could not imagine how many chickens she used to have: 'there were chickens everywhere!' She always brought the money she earned at Mona back home with her. It was used for buying building materials, such as corrugated iron, and also for [sacrificial] goats at R3 to R5 each (interview, 19 October 1998).

The close relationship between producer and customer in the rural economy seems to have encouraged innovation and the development of new styles. The pots that Phiwayinkosi made for her neighbours differ from those she made for sale at Mona Market. Of course, size was a factor: the larger pots were difficult to transport and less economical in terms of unit costs. But apart from this, the medium-sized pots made for Mona Market were more likely to sell when they corresponded to the expectations of the potential (anonymous) buyers. Innovation was reserved for the neighbourhood community. This included the beautiful and technically demanding but impractical squat shape and incised patterns using a comb, which Phiwayinkosi claims she was the first to develop. It is noteworthy that even in cases in which the potter managed to break into the commercial and tourist market, as Nesta Nala did, the driving impetus originated in the rural economy and only the second and third generation of potters moved their production base to the cities. There, their work, divested of its primary function, became decontextualised. Whilst the craftsmanship was preserved[51] and the decorations often displayed a sense of humour (applied animals, football matches, etc), these new beer pots lack the dignity that the best of their prototypes derived from integration into the rituals and daily life of the rural community.[52]

Morphology and regional attribution of Zulu beer vessels

Zulu beer vessels of the four functional types may be classified by their form and decoration according to the following rather broad categories:

- Forms may be squat, bag-shaped, tulip-shaped, spherical, ovoid and with shoulders. They may have large or narrow openings, sometimes with everted lips. They may also have cylindrical or inverted conical necks to avoid spillage.
- Decorations may be applied, impressed or incised depending on whether clay was added to the surface or removed from it. Within the first category are the various types of *amasumpa*, described later, and 'ropes' of clay. In the last the clay may be cut, gouged out, scraped with an instrument such as a comb, patterned with roulette, and combinations of the above.

The beer vessels can be separated into six main regional styles. All but the first of these are large, well-populated areas. The main distinguishing features are as follows:

- Phongolo: bag-shaped to near-spherical form with outward (everted) curvature towards the opening; applied decorations.

- Nongoma: near spherical, sometimes ovoid and bag-shaped forms mainly with applied decorations, but also some incised patterns.
- Hlabisa: often squat form, incised decoration.
- Melmoth-Eshowe: mostly somewhat squat forms with *amasumpa* carved from applied plaques or strips of clay. Some are near-spherical with incised, gouged and impressed patterns making use of different techniques on the same vessel.
- The Thukela and its tributaries from the Manyane and the Nsuze through to the southern bank of the uMhlatuze: near-spherical form with both applied and incised decorations.
- Msinga: older pots have mainly near-spherical forms, more recent ones have pronounced shoulders tapering towards the base, incised decorations. A very old type from Muden preserves the tall, slightly bulging cylindrical form similar to milking pails (*amathunga*).

Areas which were visited with a view to collecting beer vessels but in which nothing of significance was discovered include the Umzimkhulu valley and the region bordering Pondoland south and east of Harding in southern Natal, and areas to the south and west of Bulwer.

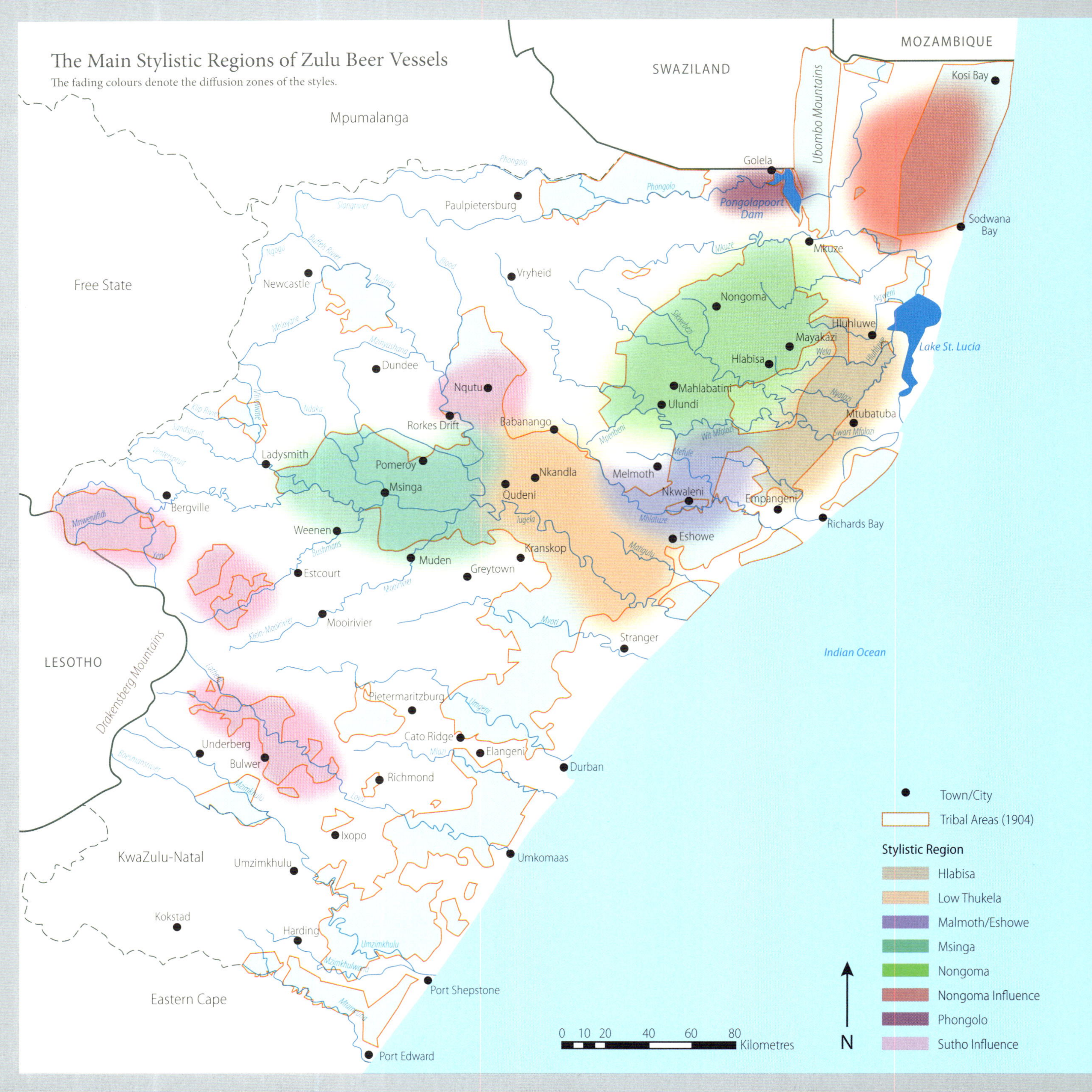

The Main Stylistic Regions of Zulu Beer Vessels
The fading colours denote the diffusion zones of the styles.
MOZAMBIQUE
SWAZILAND
Mpumalanga
Kosi Bay
Ubombo Mountains
Golela
Phongolo
Pongolapoort Dam
Phongolo
Sodwana Bay
Paulpietersburg
Free State
Mkuze
Mkuze
Vryheid
Nongoma
Newcastle
Hluhluwe
Mayakazi
Lake St. Lucia
Hlabisa
Dundee
Nqutu
Mahlabatini
Babanango
Ulundi
Rorkes Drift
Mtubatuba
Pomeroy
Nkandla
Melmoth
Ladysmith
Msinga
Nkwaleni
Qudeni
Empangeni
Weenen
Tugela
Richards Bay
Mnweniiiidi
Bergville
Eshowe
Kranskop
Muden
Estcourt
Greytown
Mhlatuze
Mooirivier
Stranger
Indian Ocean
LESOTHO
Drakensberg Mountains
Pietermaritzburg
Cato Ridge
Underberg
Elangeni
Bulwer
Durban
Richmond
KwaZulu-Natal
Umzimkhulu
Ixopo
Umkomaas
Kokstad
Harding
Eastern Cape
Port Shepstone
Port Edward
Town/City
Tribal Areas (1904)
Stylistic Region
Hlabisa
Low Thukela
Malmoth/Eshowe
Msinga
Nongoma
Nongoma Influence
Phongolo
Sutho Influence
0 10 20   40   60   80 Kilometres
N

The six main regional styles of Zulu beer vessels

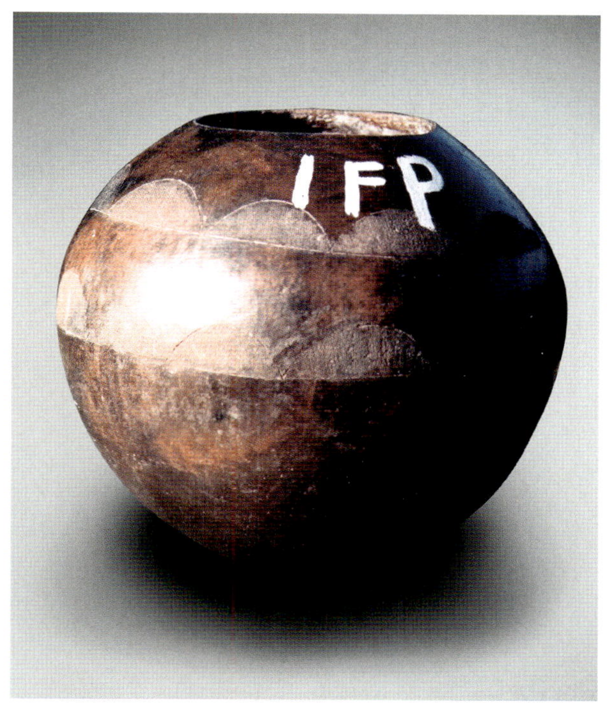

Old Hlabisa beer vessel. The original marker of regional identity, the double wave pattern, has been superseded by the modern political statement of allegiance to the Inkatha Freedom Party (IFP).

I would like to propose that the inception of the six main Zulu regional pottery styles reaches back to the installation of the Shepstonian location system but not beyond, and that they will have been modified through the subsequent encroachments of colonialism. The emergence of a particular style depends on the development of a regional sense of identity. In Natal, chieftaincies based on clan loyalties seem to have arisen shortly after the creation of the original locations, perhaps in the 1850s. In Zululand, on the other hand, continuous instability and warfare reinforced the *amabutho* system with its strong centripetal effect. However, the Wolseley settlement after the conclusion of the Anglo-Zulu War in 1879, which installed thirteen competing semi-autonomous chieftaincies whilst the king was held prisoner in the Cape, created a power vacuum at the centre and strong incentives towards the development of regional identities.

In troubled times clan affiliation was a matter of survival. So by the time the Zululand Lands Delimitation Commission submitted its report in 1904 most of the basic styles of pottery, both of Natal and Zululand, had already been formed.[53] Once a regional style had been established, the balance between retention of the original configurations and newly introduced variants brought about an ongoing evolution. As rural mobility increased, the balance shifted in favour of innovation, leading to a plethora of new motifs (some of which, such as references to beadwork styles, can be used as markers in dating pots). They reflect the ever-evolving situation in which changing circumstances and allegiances are echoed in the material culture of a people.

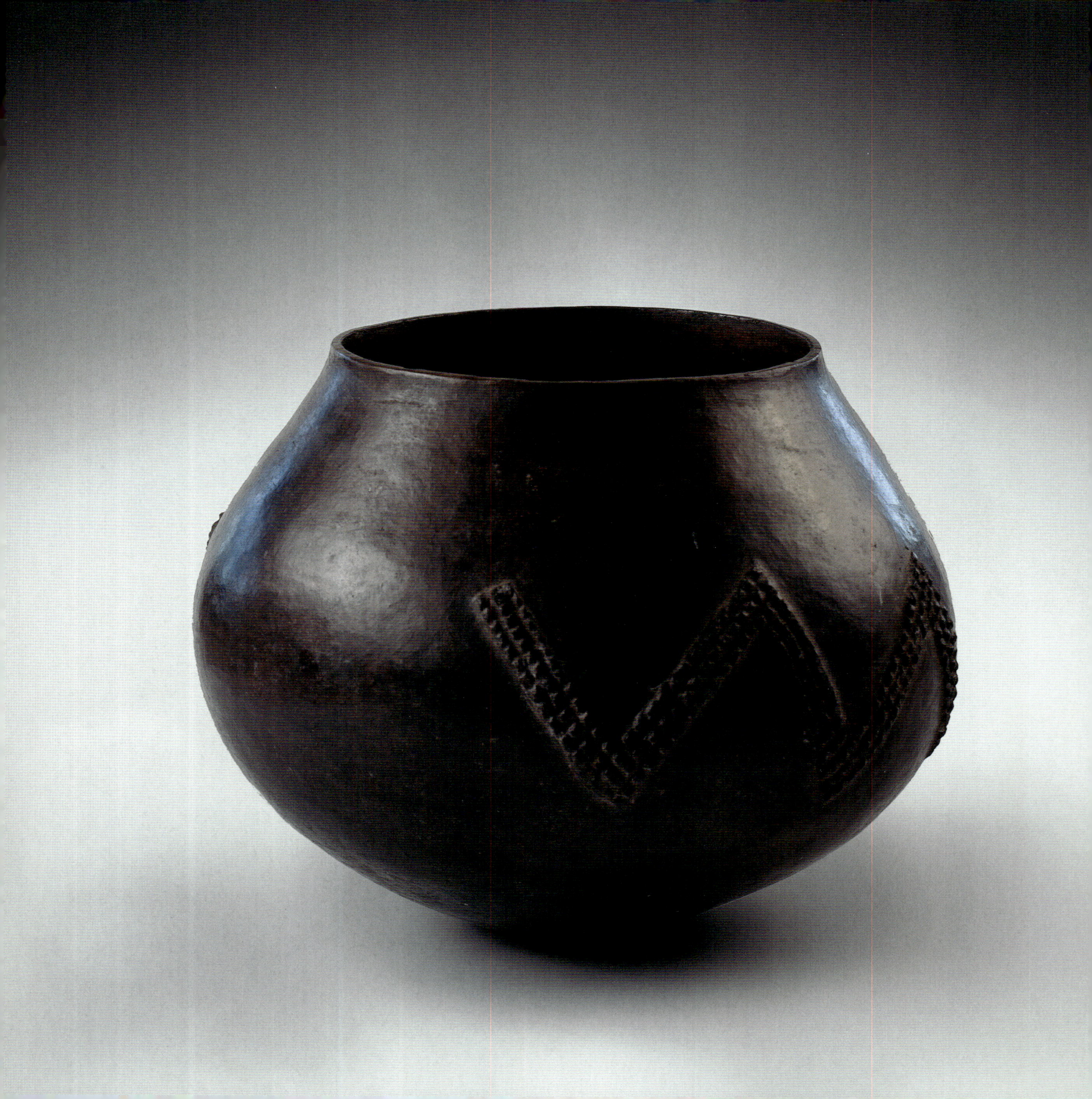

1

The Phongolo region

This is the northernmost stylistic region of Zulu pottery. It covers a relatively small area stretching from west of the town of Phongolo and south of the Swazi border, following the course of the Phongolo River mainly on the northern side to beyond Golela. It is quite distinct from the other regions. The fairly large adjoining area contained by the Lebombo Mountains and the Swazi border on the western side, the Mozambique border in the north and the Indian Ocean in the east does not belong to this region; rather it is inhabited by people related to those of Nongoma, and also relocated people from the Weenen area in Msinga. The pottery there is similar to that from Nongoma.

Before the Anglo-Zulu War of 1879 the territory north of the Phongolo area had been a part of the Swazi Kingdom. In the settlement of 1879 it became a part of a tribal chiefdom, first under Mgojana and then Zibhebhu, the main opponent of the Zulu royal house. After the defeat of Zibhebhu in 1884 it was ceded to the Boers and formed part of the New Republic. On the annexation of Zululand in 1887, it formed no part of the settlement; subsequently it was amalgamated with the Transvaal. It was not a part of the territories ceded to Natal in 1903, which included most of the former New Republic.[54] It was finally assigned to Natal for administrative convenience in 1994.

The Phongolo beer vessels are characterised by their everted rims which are not found elsewhere in Zulu ceramics.[55] Their elegant, gently bulging form tending to-

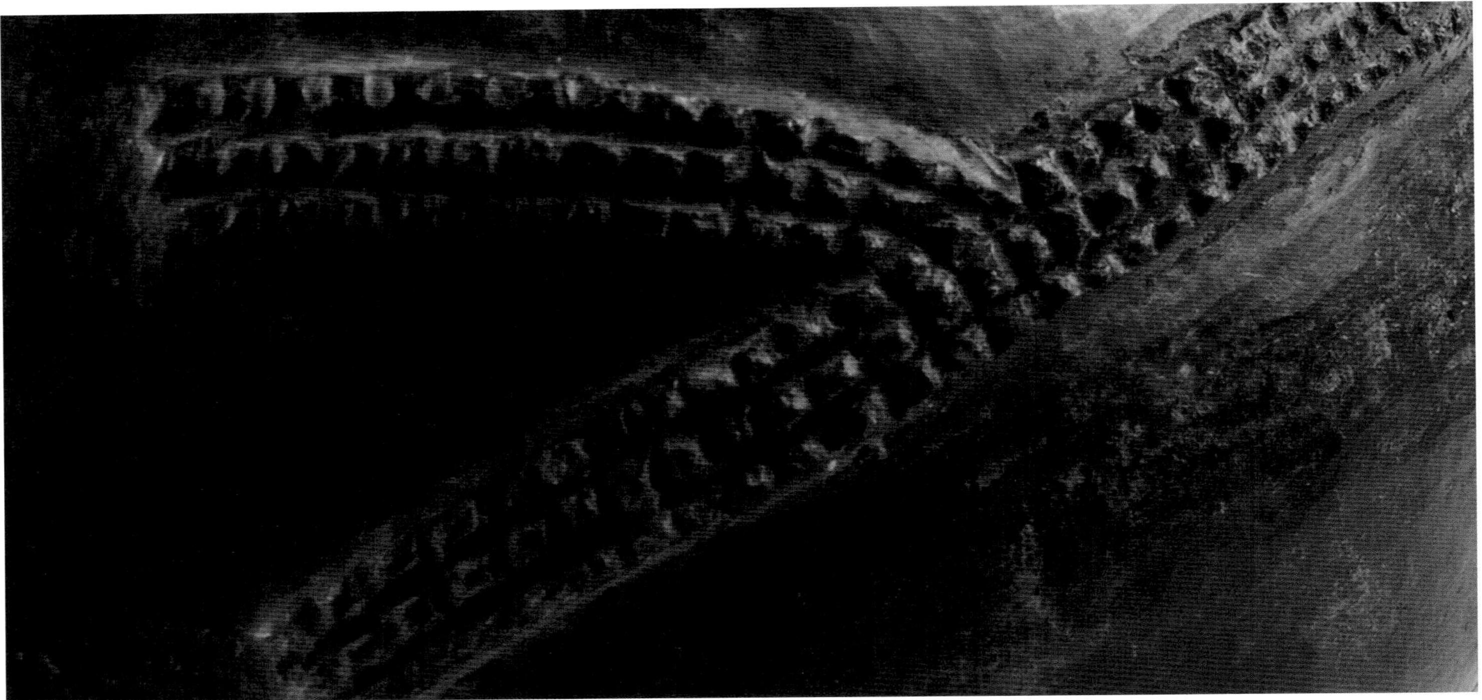

wards the bag-shaped, and their fine, thin-walled, evenly-fired, well-tempered quality, seems to make them less prone to developing hair cracks at the rim than is normally the case. The decoration consists of applied strips of clay divided into very fine *amasumpa* by cutting lengthwise and across and then rounding off the ridges. There are few motifs and these keep recurring: chevrons, Vs, Ws, and short zigs-zags and derivatives of zigzags; long horizontal lines encompassing most of the circumference of the pot; and narrow horizontal or oblique panels (Pots 101–107). These motifs are not necessarily confined to vessels from Phongolo, but the manner in which they are made and applied is distinct and easily recognisable.

The decoration on the oldest pots (Pot number 103, page 36) is more delicate than on more recent examples. Apart from this, there seems to have been little progression in style or decoration since the 1930s, which would be the earliest I have come across. This, in itself, is noteworthy and suggests that further research into the development of the distinctive Phongolo style is indicated. It would be interesting to know more about the formative period. Was it driven by a need to maintain a separate identity in the late nineteenth century, as suggested above? After all, Zibhebhu had been largely responsible for the demise of the Zulu monarchy, and Dinuzulu had protested: 'We cannot live together with the man who killed our king.'[56] What enabled this style to persist for such a long time whilst others to the south were continuing to evolve?

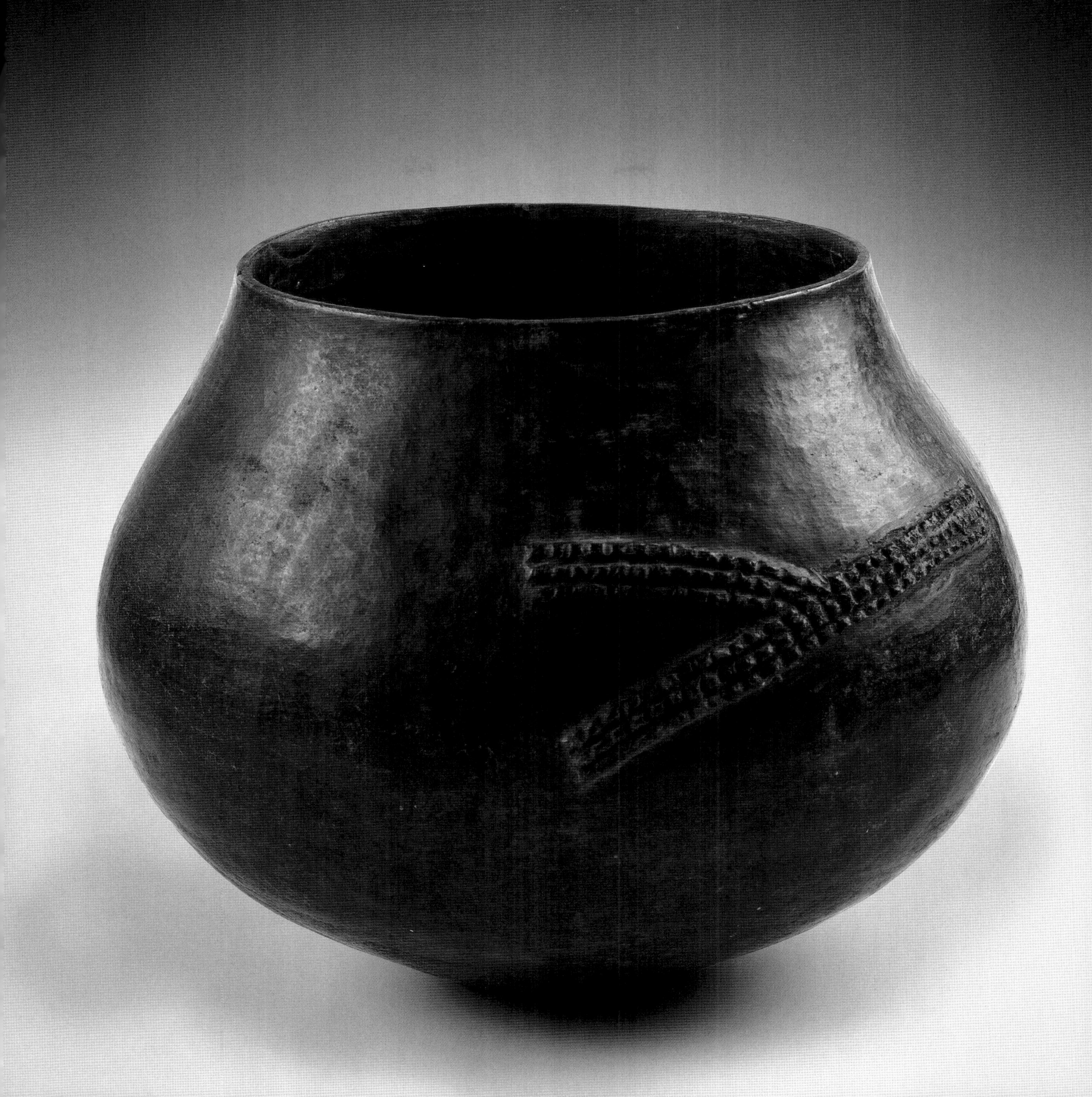

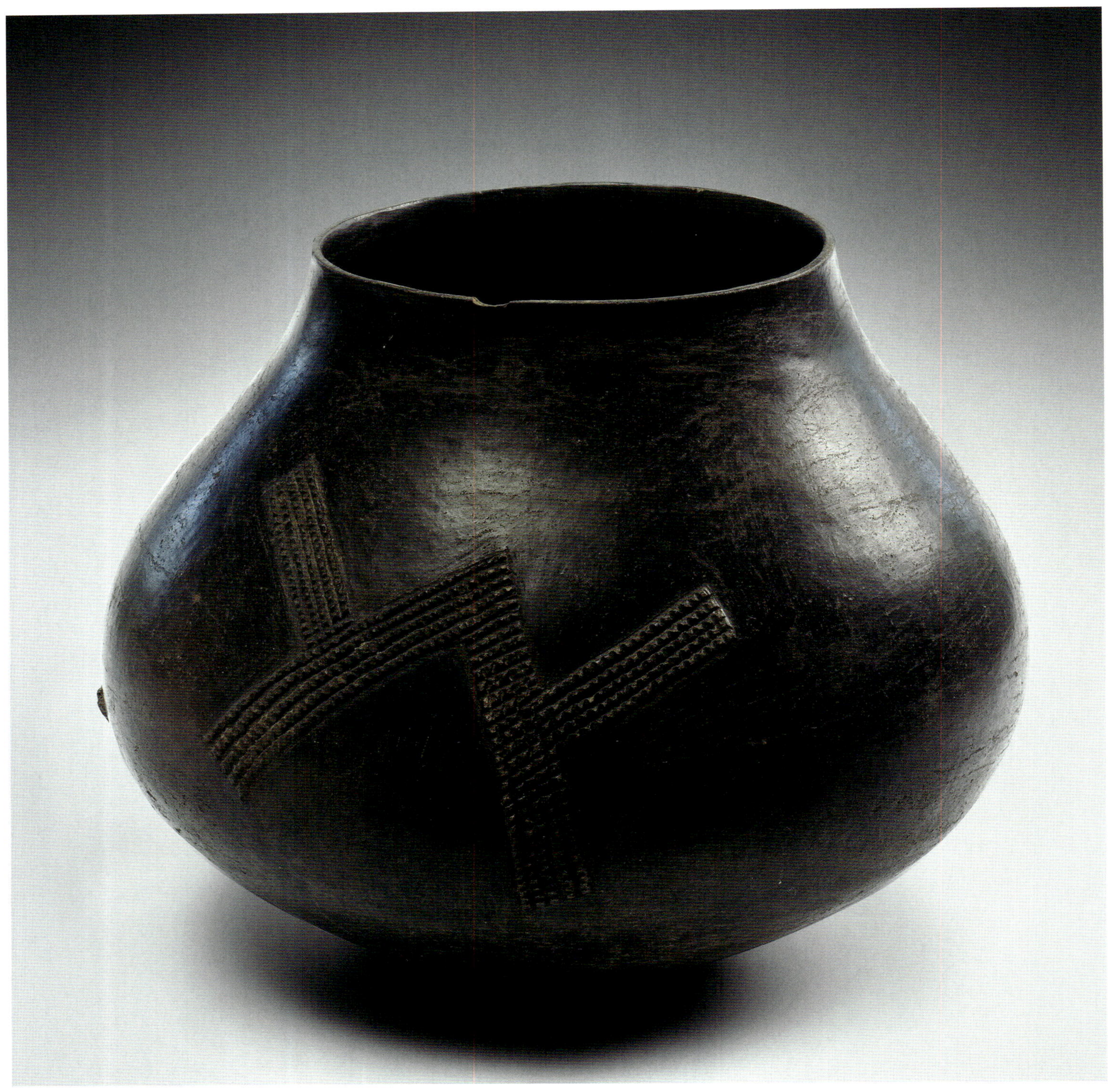

POT NUMBER 103 Ukhamba H: 282 mm Owner said it was 'Very, very, old'.

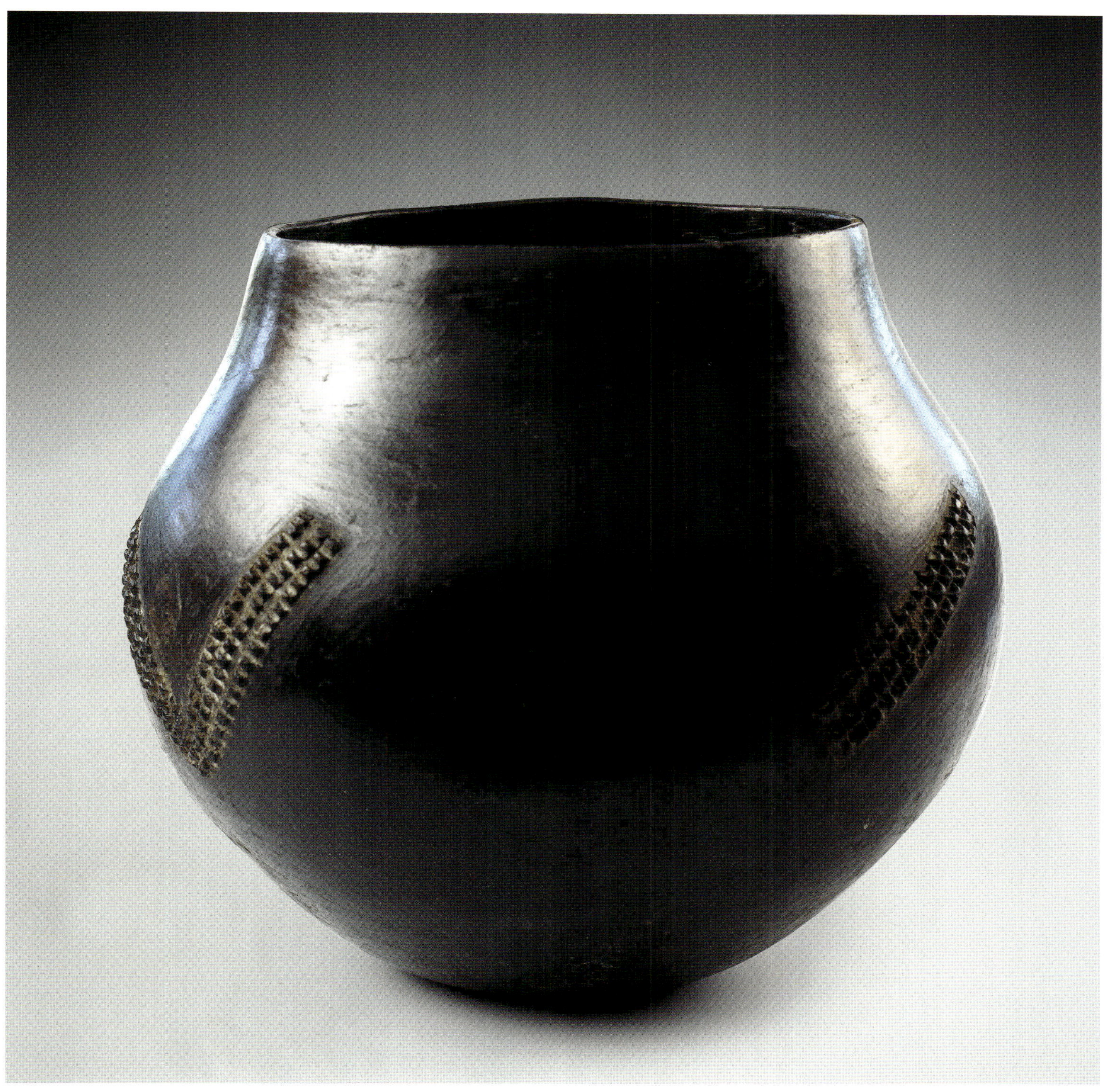

POT NUMBER 104 Ukhamba H: 226 mm

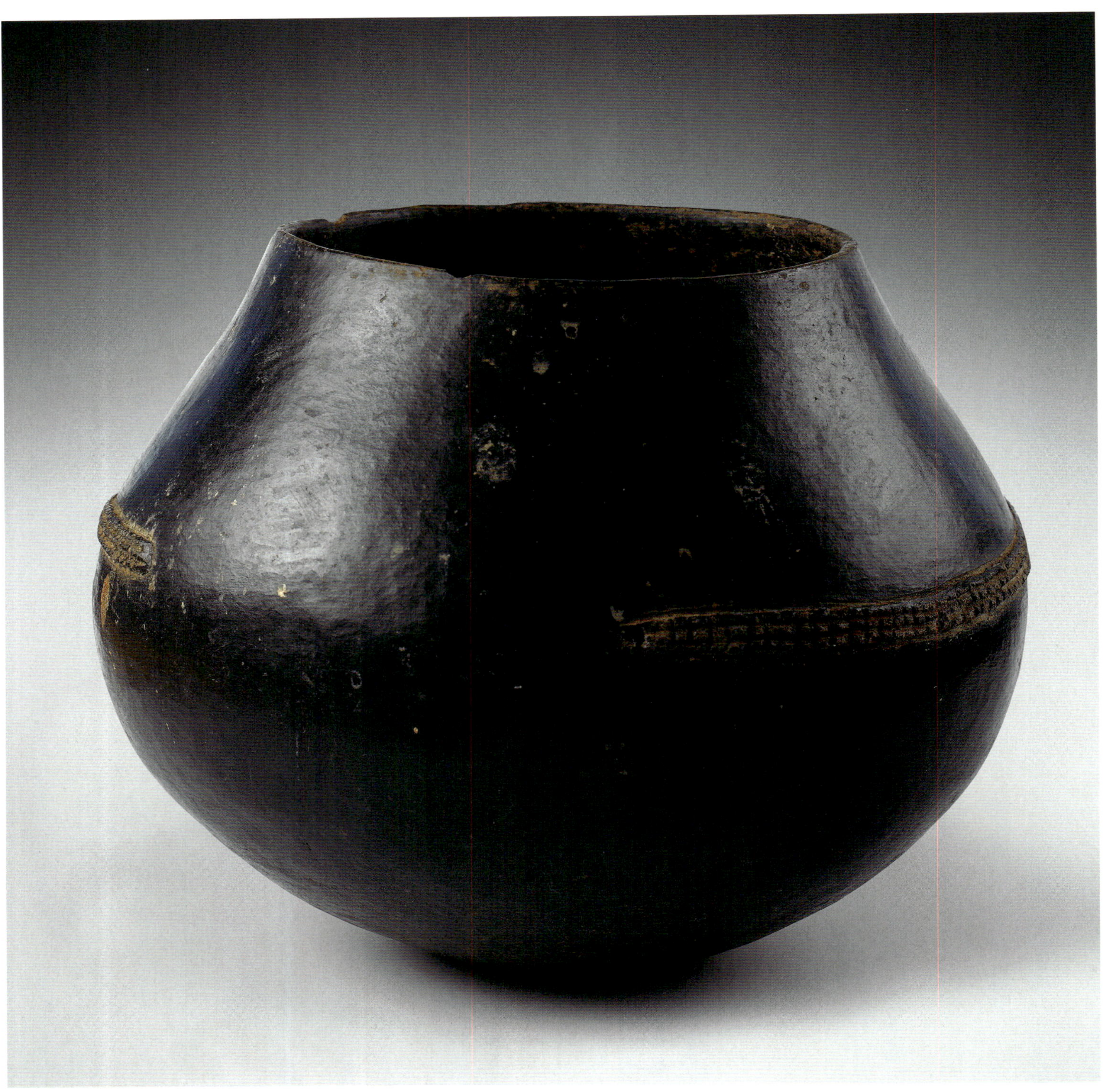

POT NUMBER 105 Ukhamba H: 218 mm

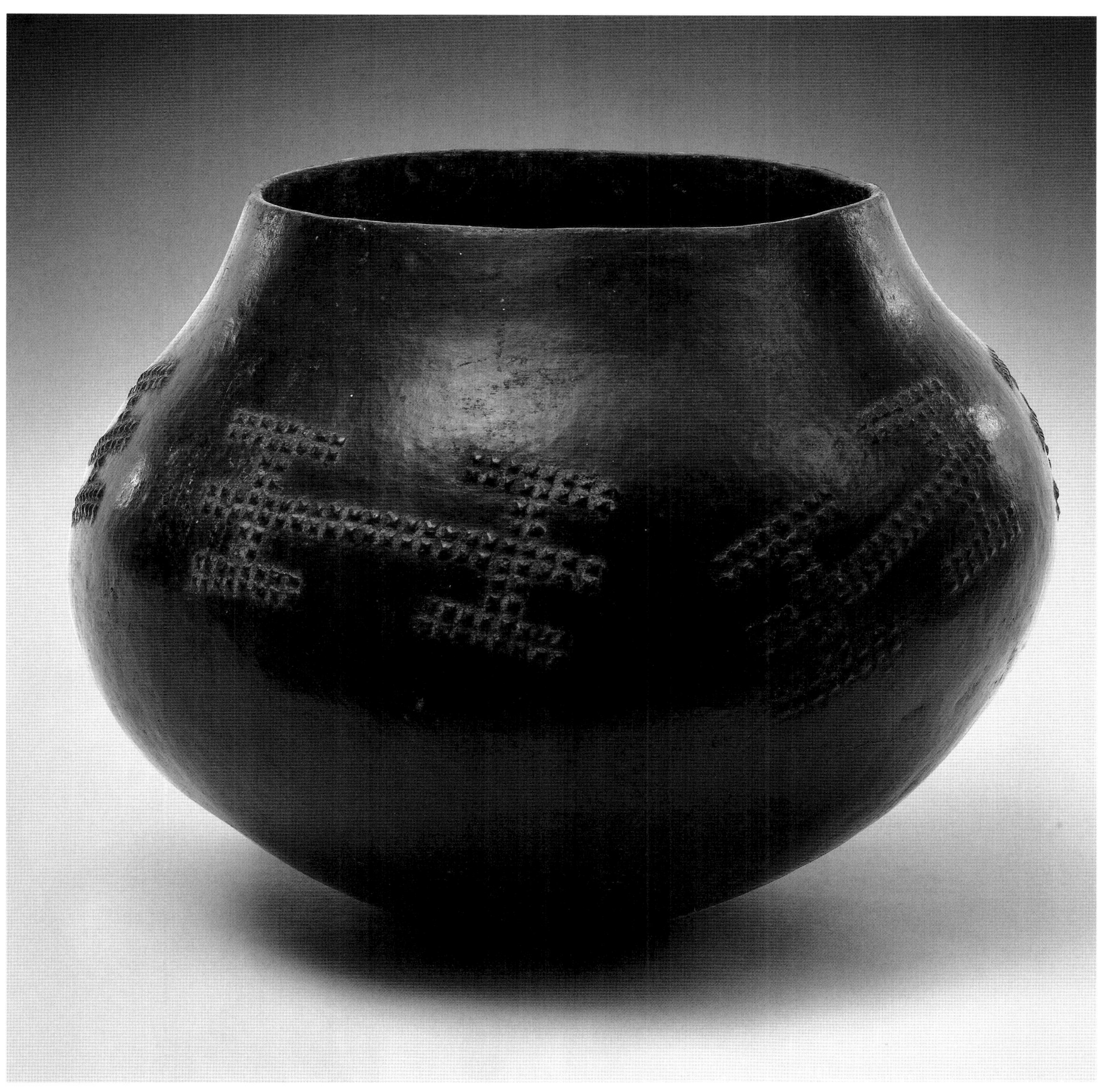

POT NUMBER 106 Ukhamba H: 220 W: 280 mm

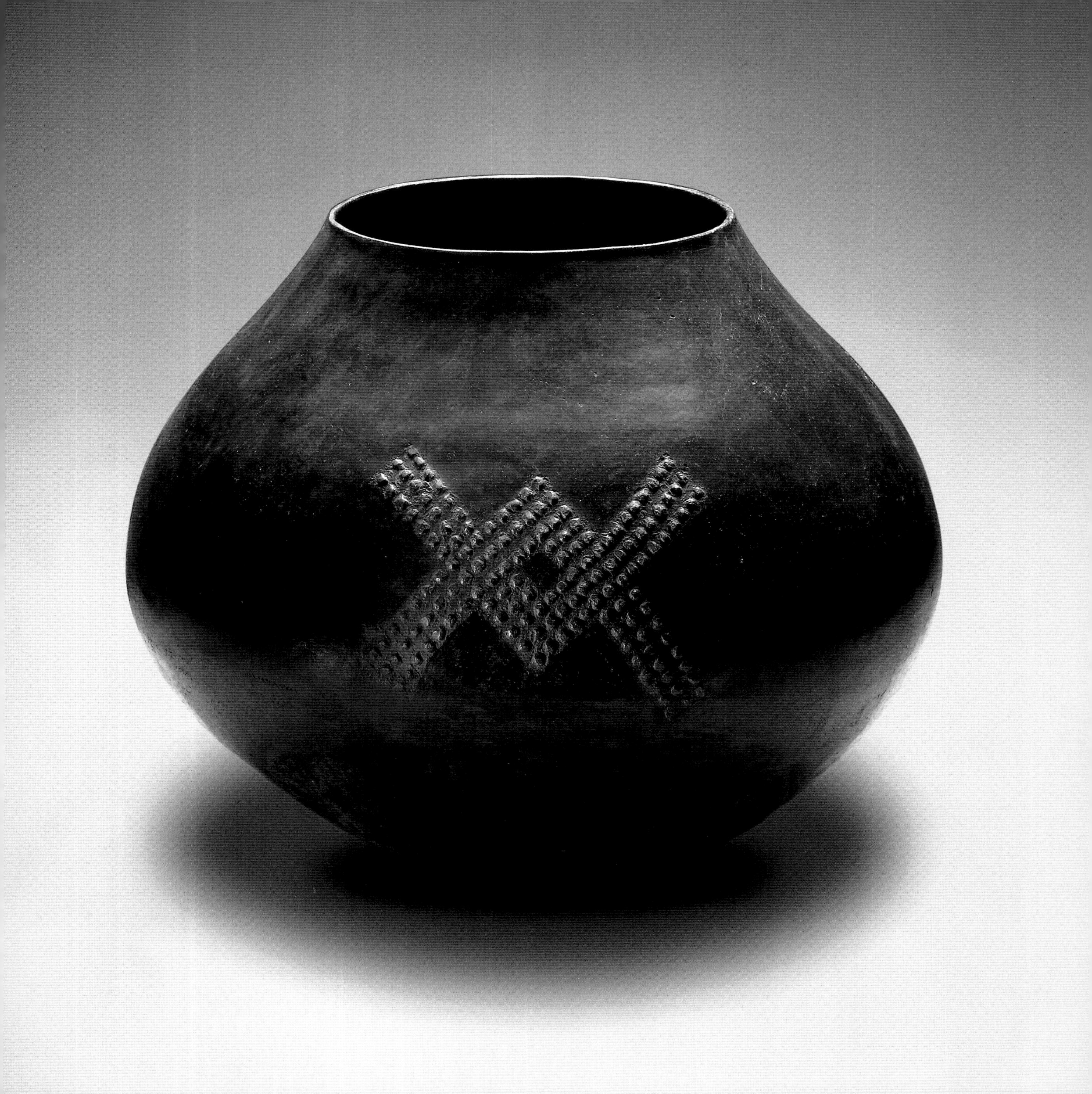

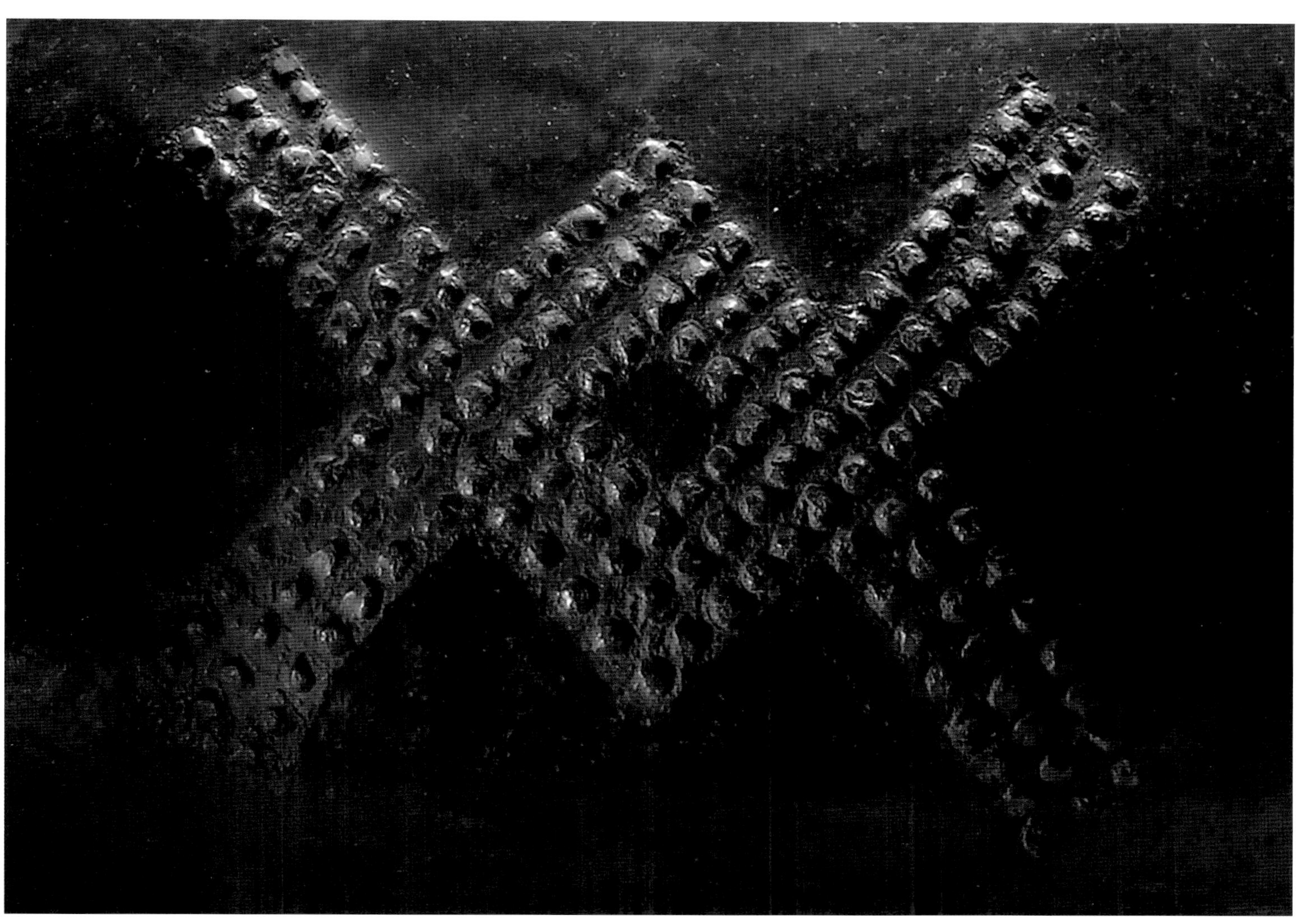

POT NUMBER 107 Ukhamba H:330 mm W: 406 mm (DETAIL)

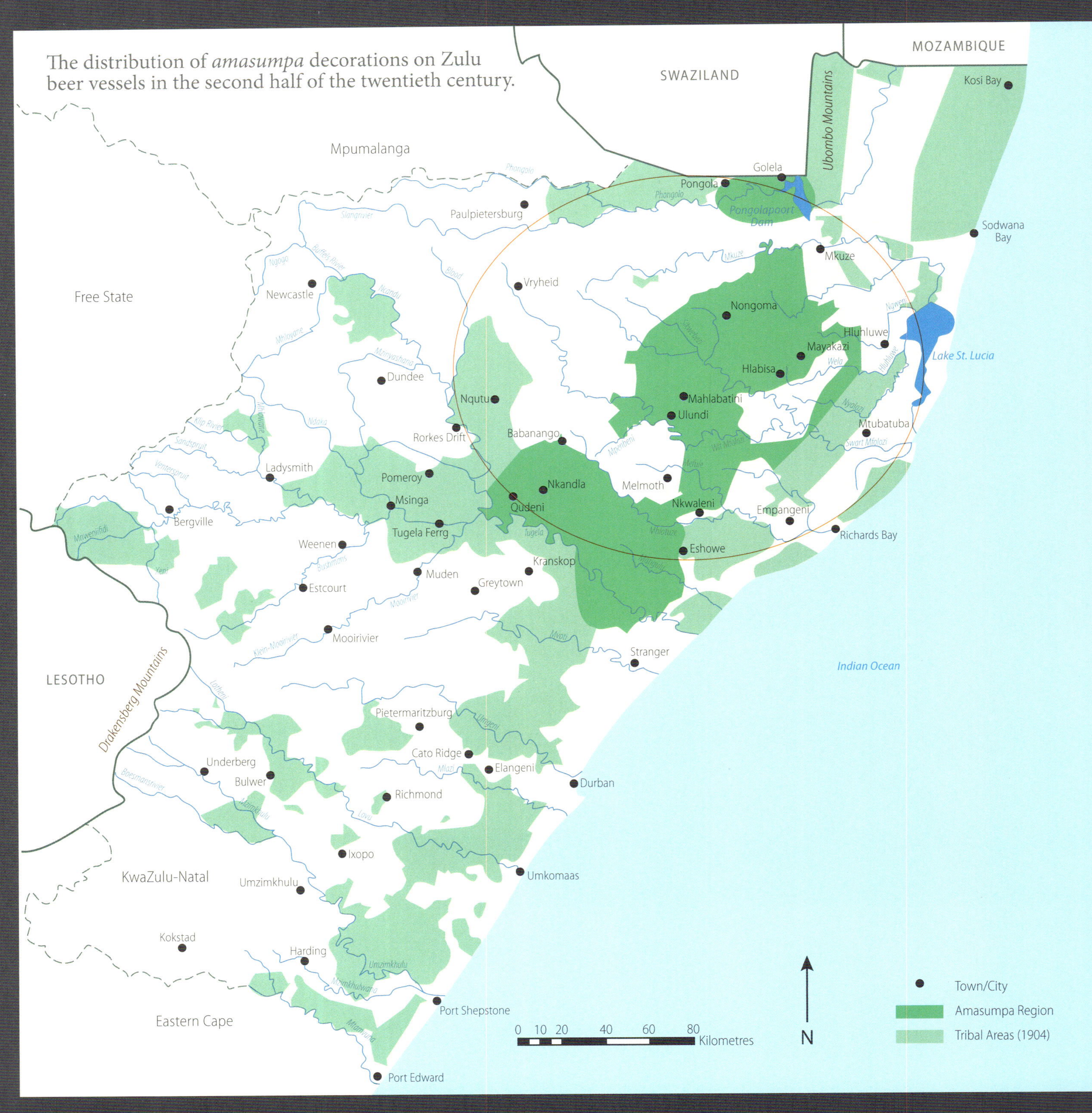

The distribution of amasumpa decorations on Zulu beer vessels in the second half of the twentieth century.
MOZAMBIQUE
SWAZILAND
Kosi Bay
Mpumalanga
Ubombo Mountains
Golela
Pongola
Phongola
Phongolo
Paulpietersburg
Pongolapoort Dam
Slangrivier
Sodwana Bay
Mkuze
Mkuze
Free State
Vryheid
Newcastle
Ncandu
Nongoma
Hluhluwe
Mayakazi
Dundee
Hlabisa
Lake St. Lucia
Nqutu
Mahlabatini
Ulundi
Rorkes Drift
Babanango
Mtubatuba
Pomeroy
Nkandla
Melmoth
Ladysmith
Msinga
Qudeni
Nkwaleni
Bergville
Empangeni
Tugela Ferrg
Weenen
Eshowe
Richards Bay
Muden
Kranskop
Estcourt
Greytown
Mooirivier
Stranger
Indian Ocean
Drakensberg Mountains
LESOTHO
Pietermaritzburg
Cato Ridge
Underberg
Elangeni
Bulwer
Durban
Richmond
Ixopo
KwaZulu-Natal
Umkomaas
Umzimkhulu
Kokstad
Harding
Eastern Cape
Port Shepstone
N
0 10 20 40 60 80 Kilometres
Town/City
Amasumpa Region
Tribal Areas (1904)
Port Edward

2

The Nongoma region

This region lies to the south of the Phongolo area (circled in red) and is separated from it by a wide band of hilly farmland. It is an extensive mountainous terrain intersected by river valleys. It borders on Hlabisa in the east and is connected to the Thukela region in the south by a broad corridor, and by another narrower one with the lowland area between Empangweni and Eshowe. In the southwest and west it is contained by the middle reaches of the White uMfolozi River, which formed a boundary between KwaZulu and the white farmlands around Melmoth and Babanango, and by the farmlands of the Vryheid region.

The Nongoma region has long been considered as the origin of the applied decorations known as *amasumpa*, which are a characteristic feature of Zulu ceramics and carvings. However, applied motifs of various types occur on ceramics in many parts of Africa. In southern Africa they can be traced back several centuries to the beginning of the Blackburn ceramic sequence (associated with Nguni speakers), dating from the early eleventh century near Durban.[57] Similar decorative features are also encountered, though rarely, in the first millennium sequence.[58] The more recent occurrence dates from the nineteenth century. It is likely to be connected to the spread of the influence of the Zulu royal house.

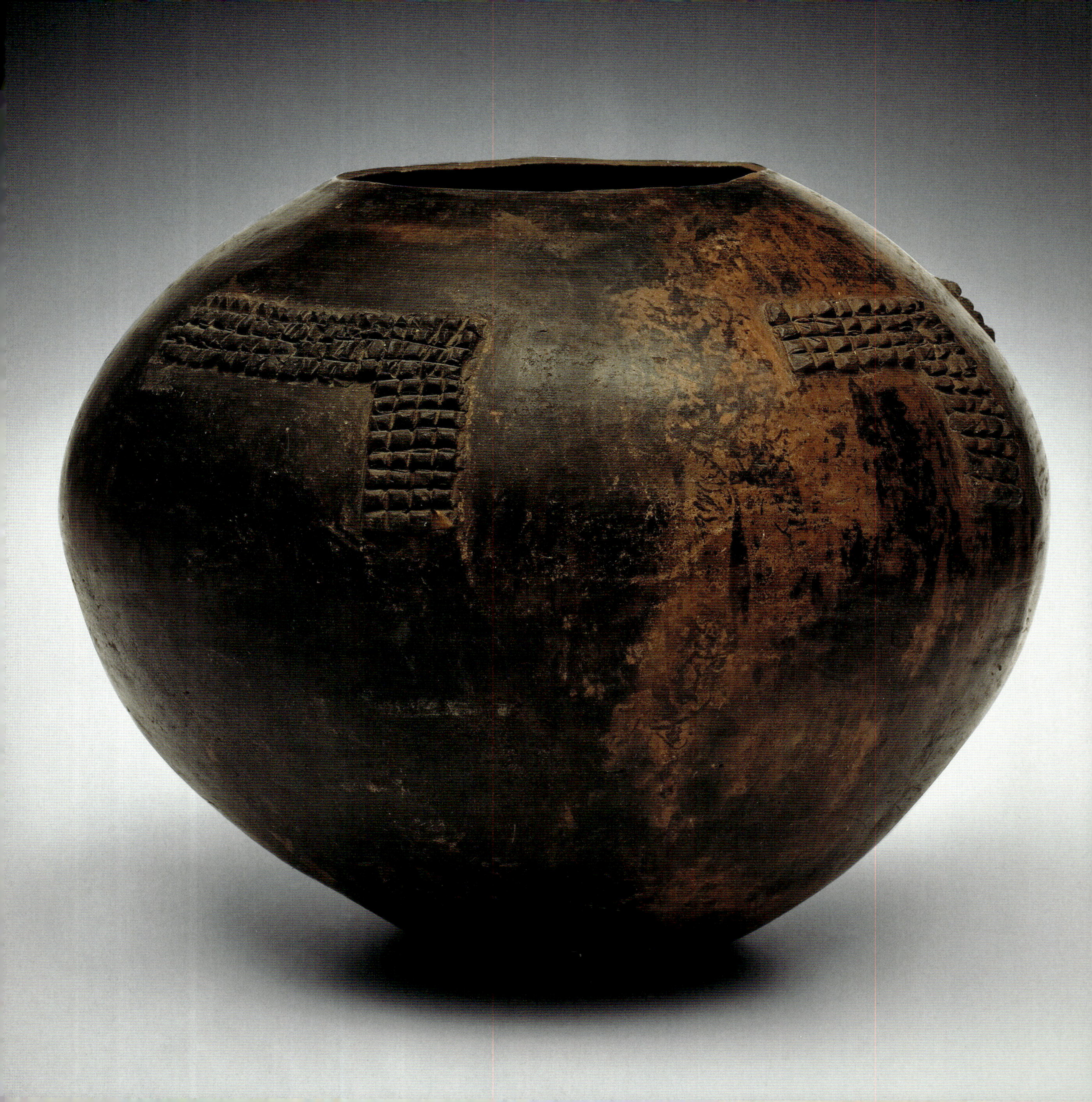

1. *Amasumpa* carved out of
applied panels of clay, which are
the most common.

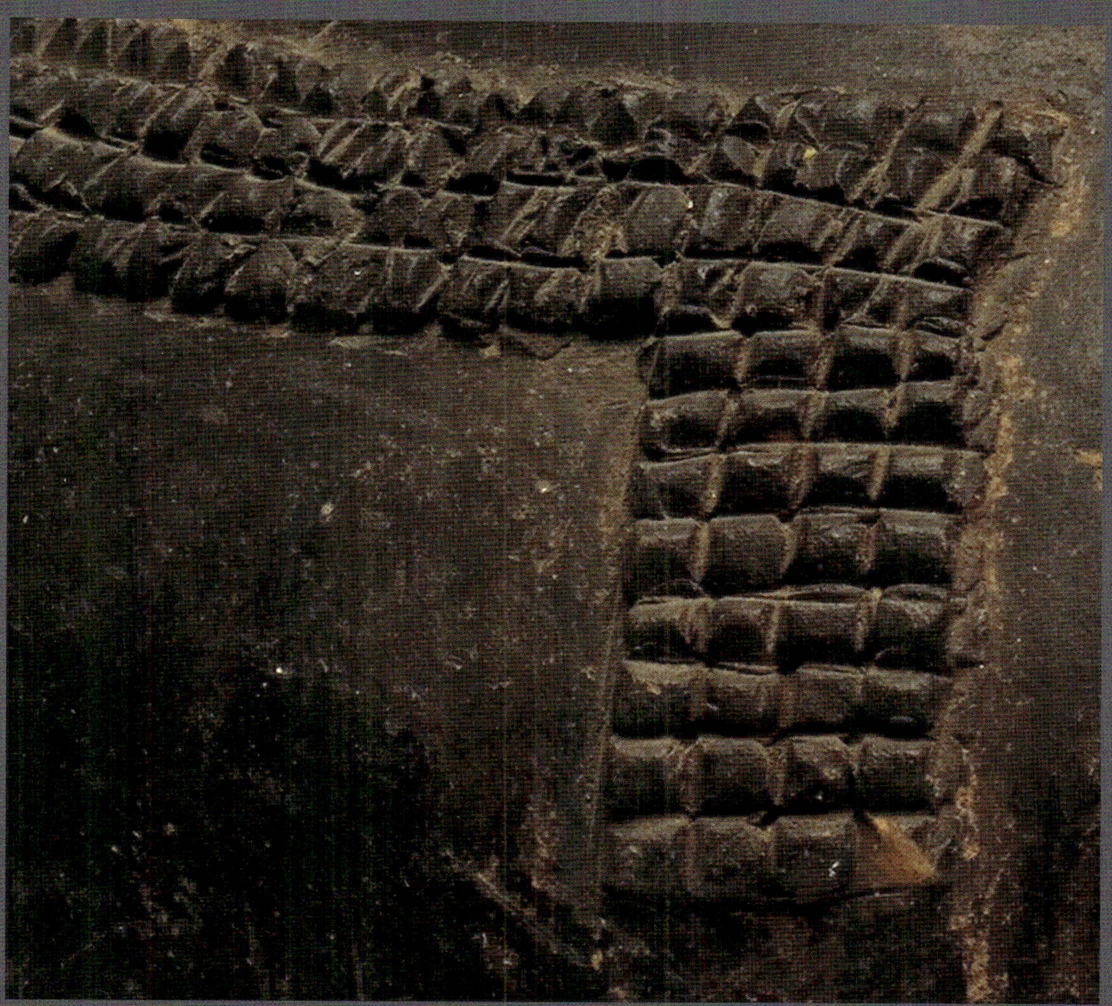

POT NUMBER 211 Ukhamba H: 299 mm Four right angles on a
curved surface.
The fact that they are slightly obtuse frustrates the viewer's
expectation of perfect right angles. This, and the fact that they are
not uniform, is responsible for the disorienting effect of reduced
symmetry, which enhances the aesthetic appeal of the pot.
Amasumpa carved from panels of applied of clay.

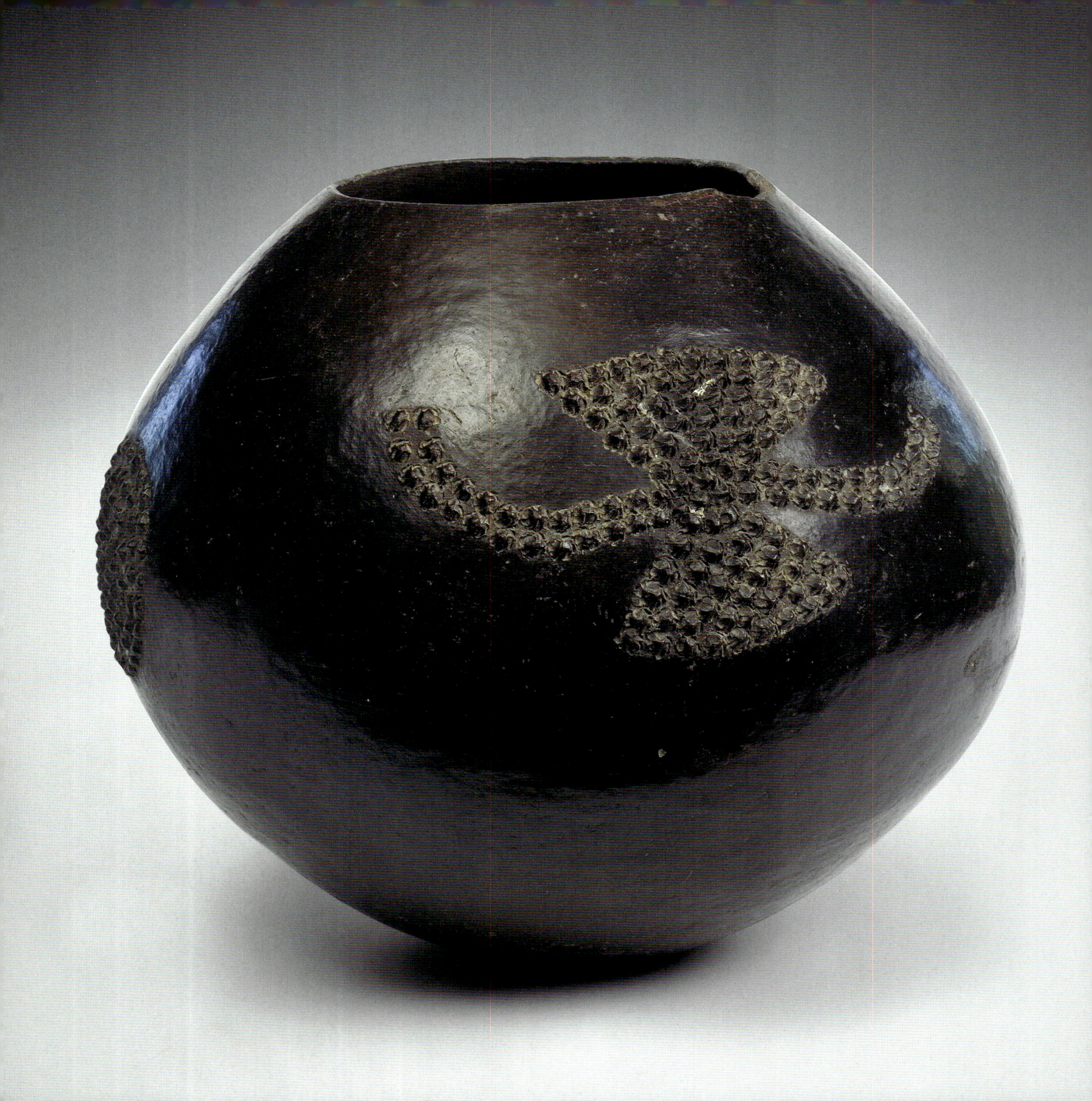

2. *Amasumpa* 'pinched' and
applied singly.

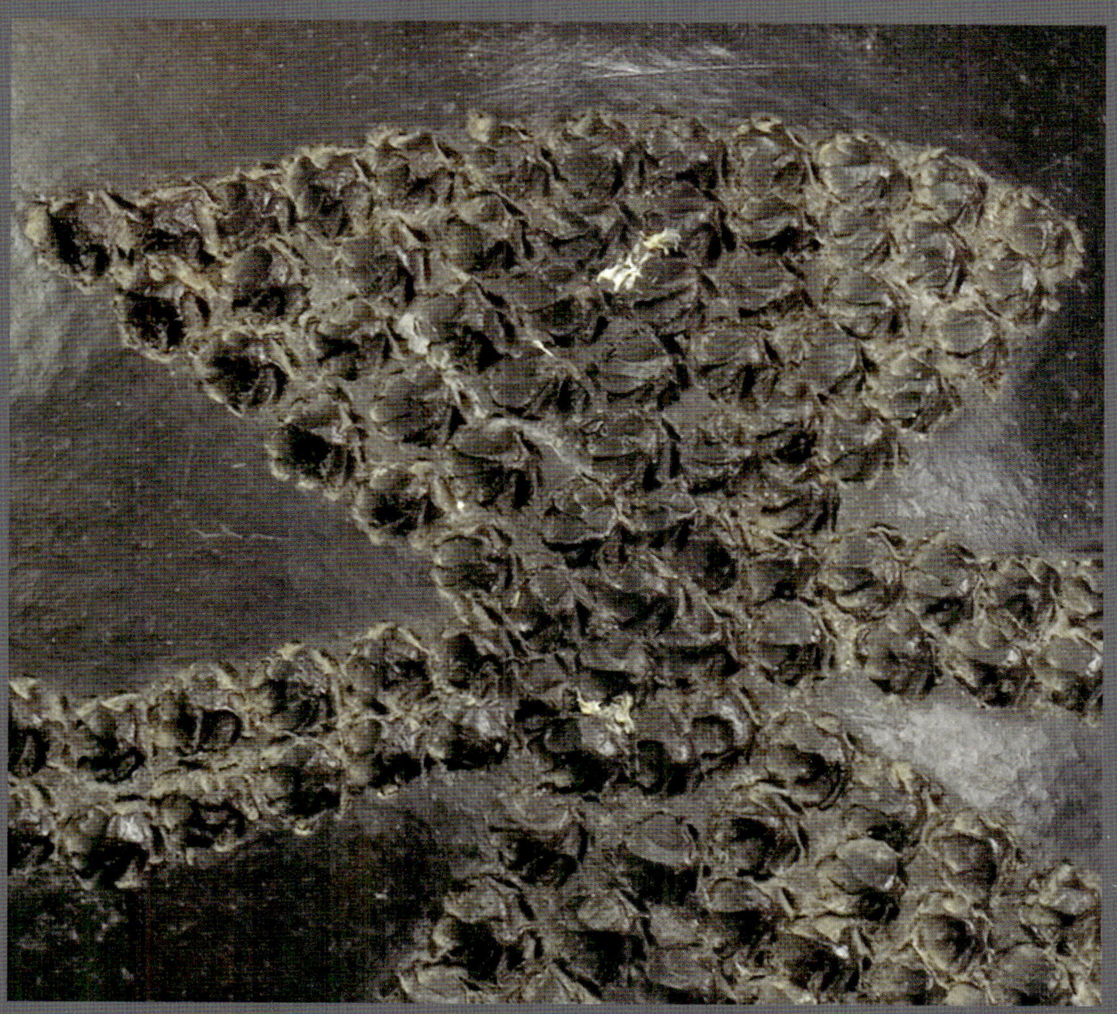

POT NUMBER 216 Ukhamba H: 279 mm Alternating large motifs in
amasumpa, including the circles characteristic of the Nongoma region,
and human figures based on the widespread hourglass motif. In the latter
case creative modification of traditional material.

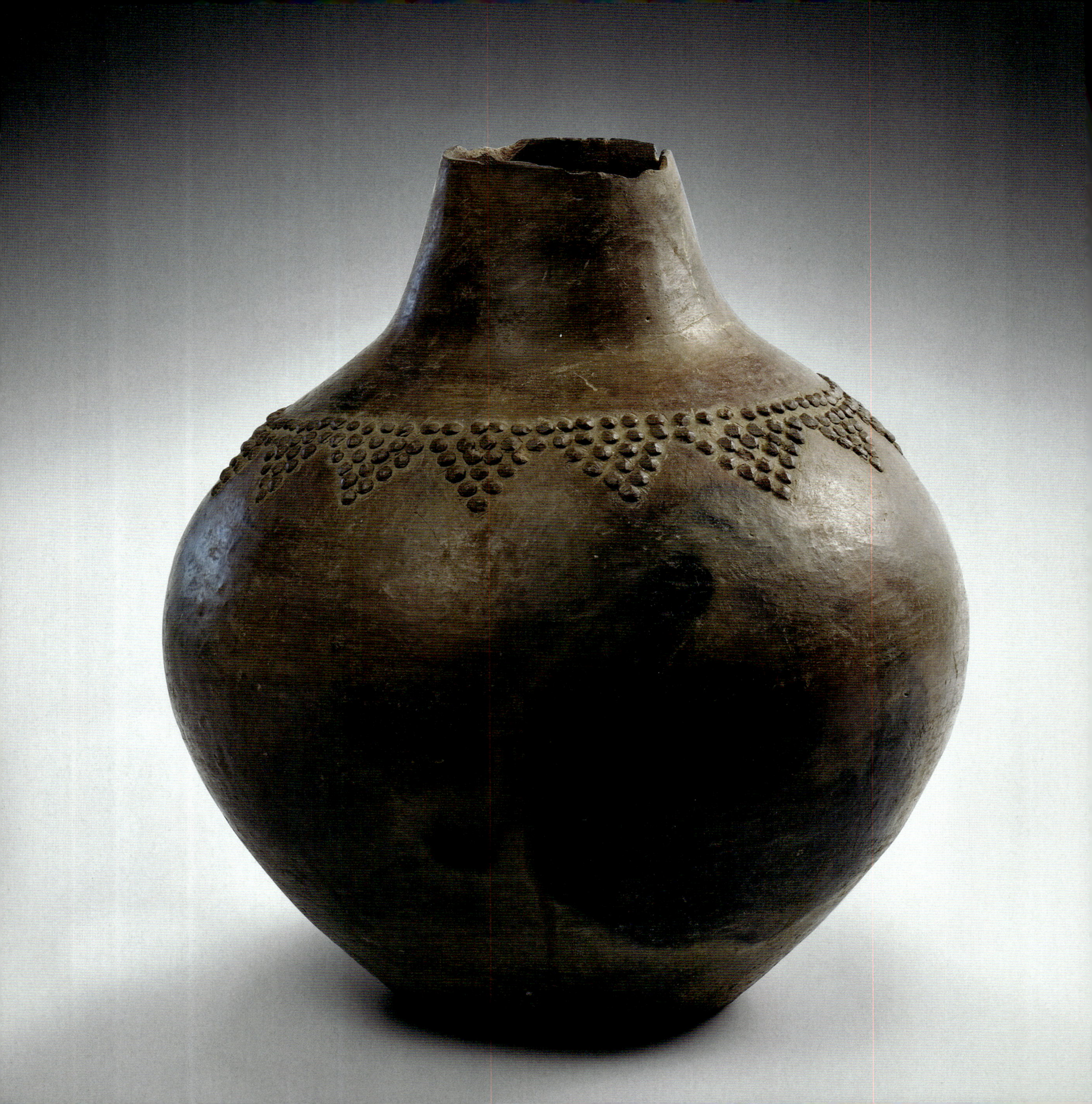

3. Small rounded *amasumpa*
(like 'Smarties' chocolates) also
applied singly and flattened.

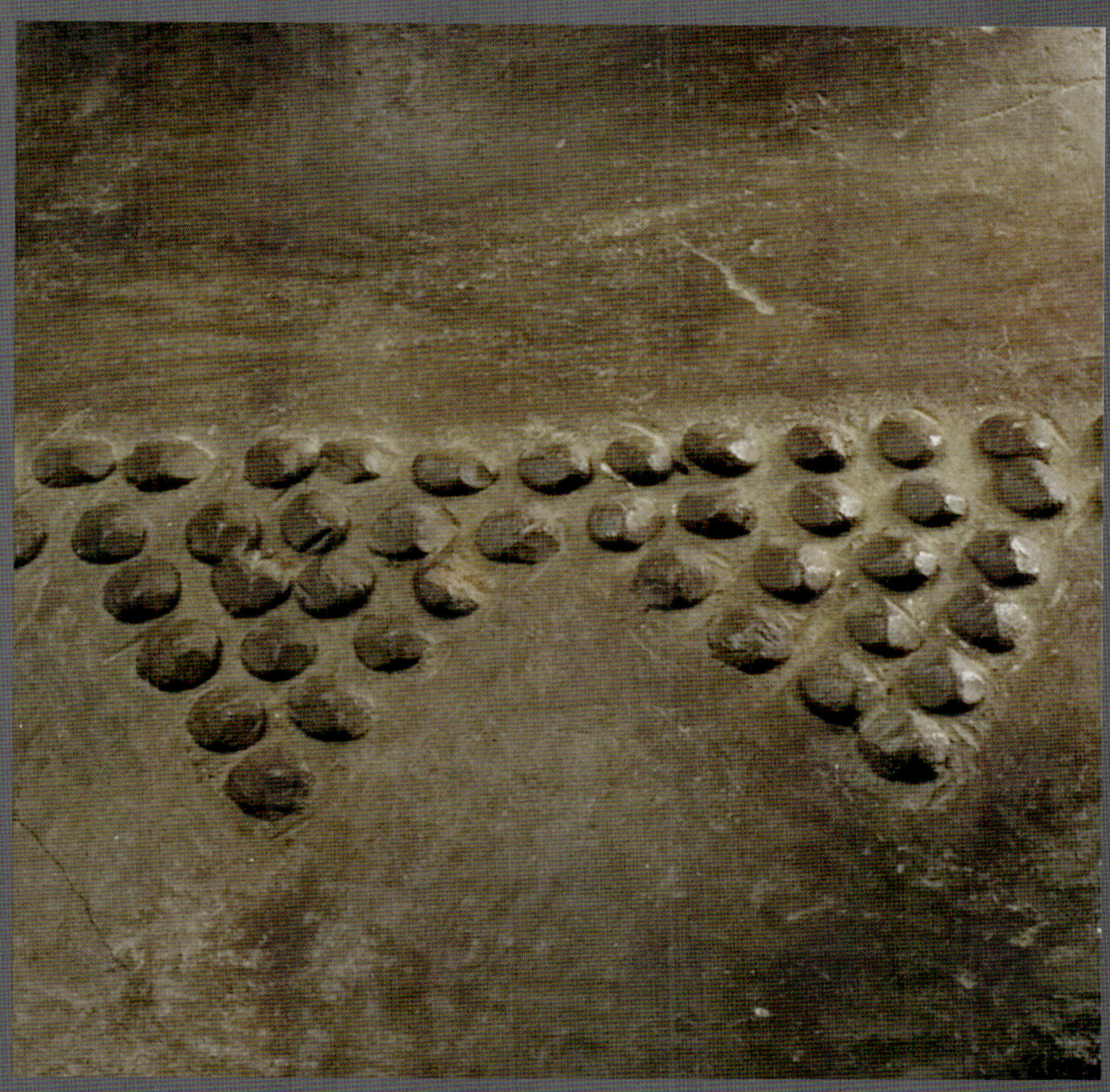

POT NUMBER 207 Uphiso H: 349 mm An old style *uphiso* with a ring of
small facetted *amasumpa* in the pendant triangle pattern below the neck
(cf. 206). Fired only once. Small repair to rim.

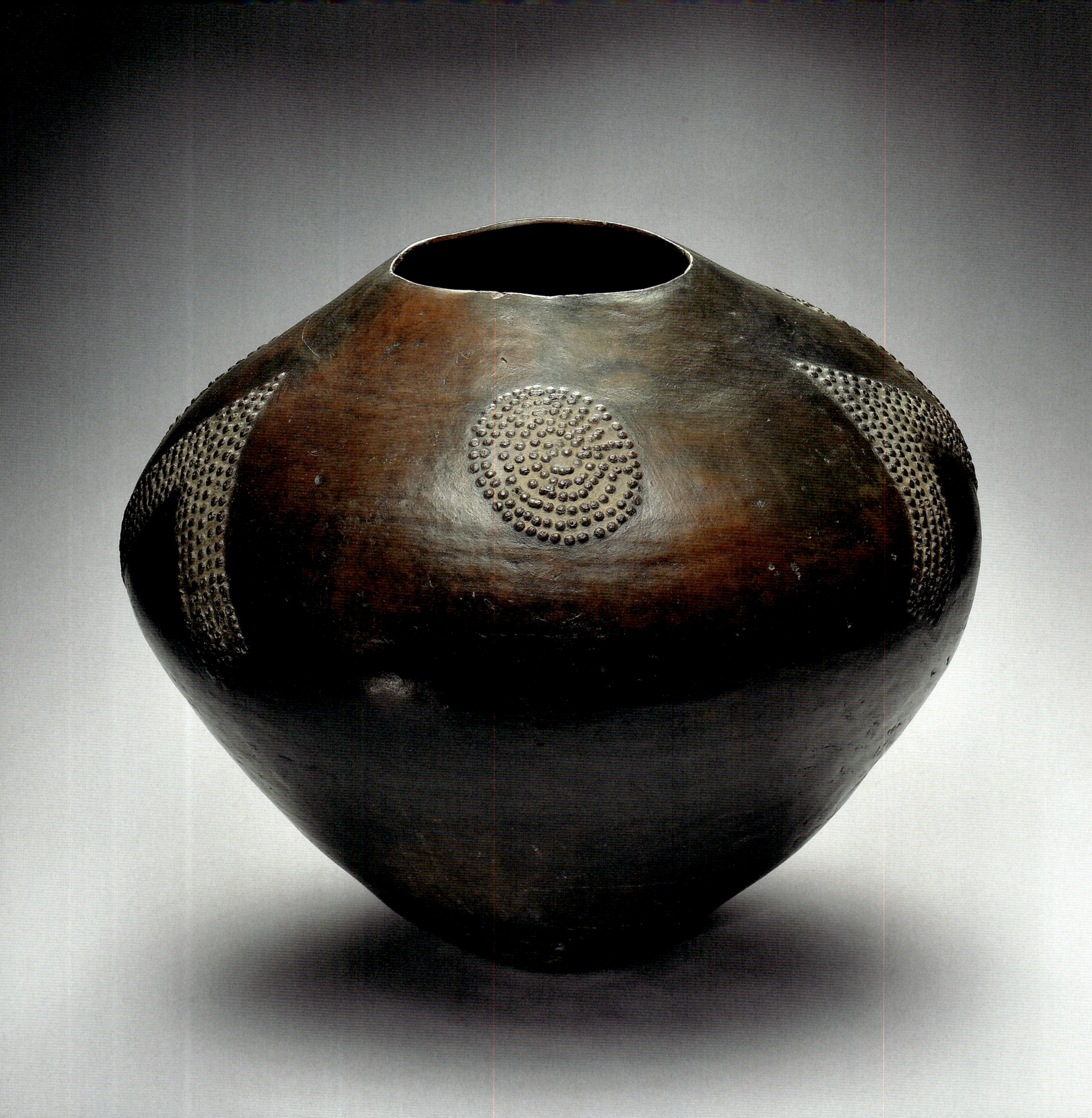

4. *Amasumpa* pressed out from the inside
of the pot and made good again whilst the
clay was still pliable, which tend to be large,
shallow and rounded yet they can also be
small, similar to pot 207.

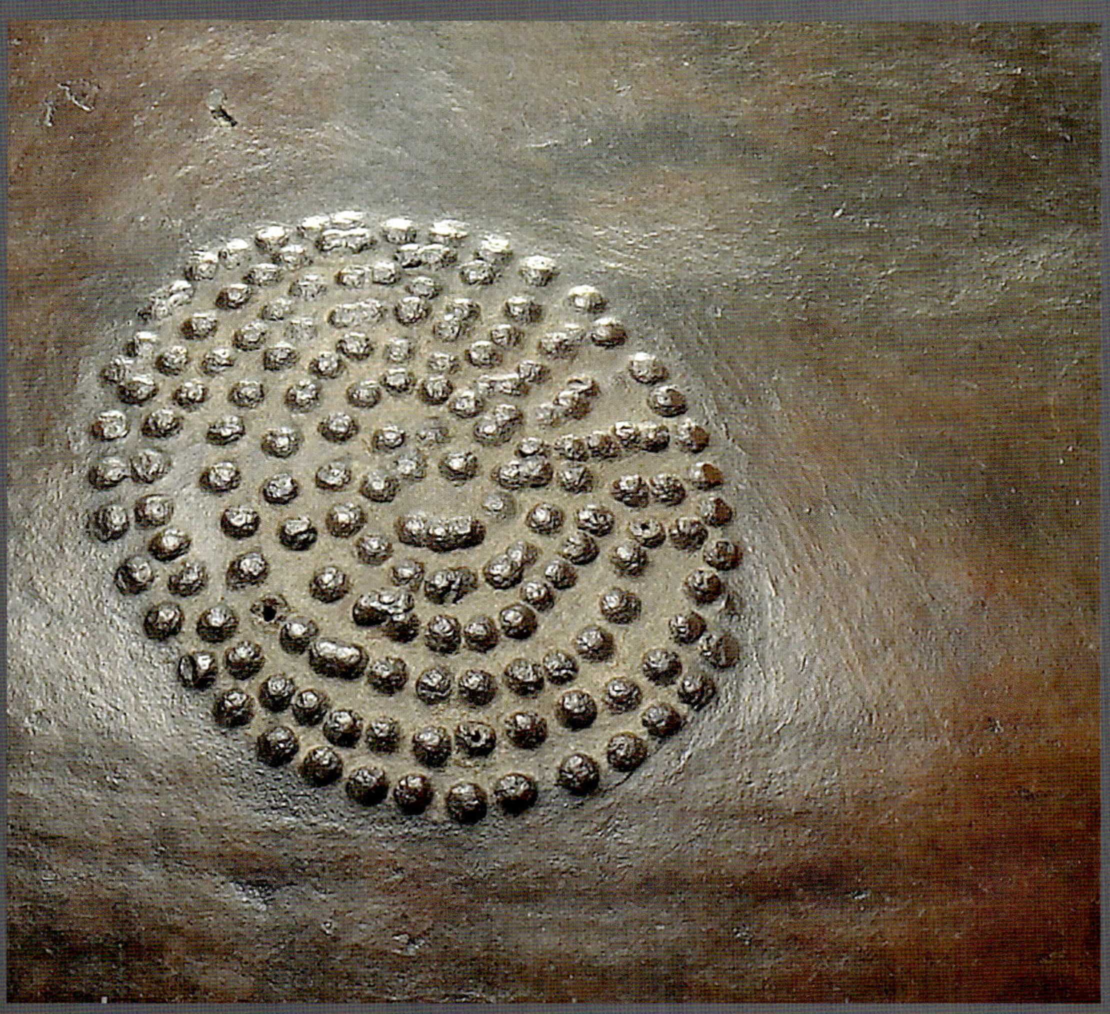

Classification of the Nongoma Styles

There are broadly five Nongoma styles. The most useful general classification in the case of the Nongoma region is one based on *amasumpa* patterns. However, I have included the sub-dominant decorative technique of removing clay by means of incisions and gouging (rather than adding clay as in most of the variations of *amasumpa*) as a fifth category (Nongoma Style 5).

Nongoma Style 1

Small applied panels of carved *amasumpa*. Examples: Pot 201 page 52, Pot 202 page 54, Pot 209 page 55.

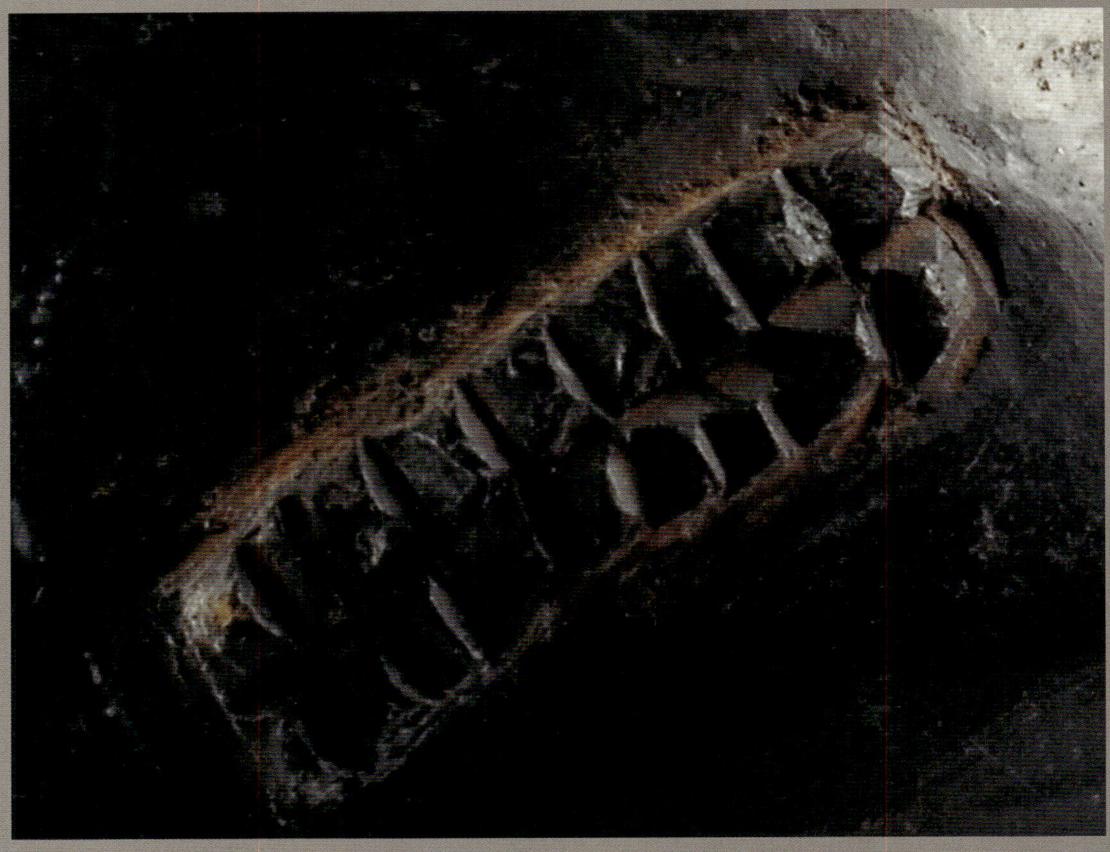

POT NUMBER 201 Umancishana H: 150 mm
Applied panel of *amasumpa* roughly carved.

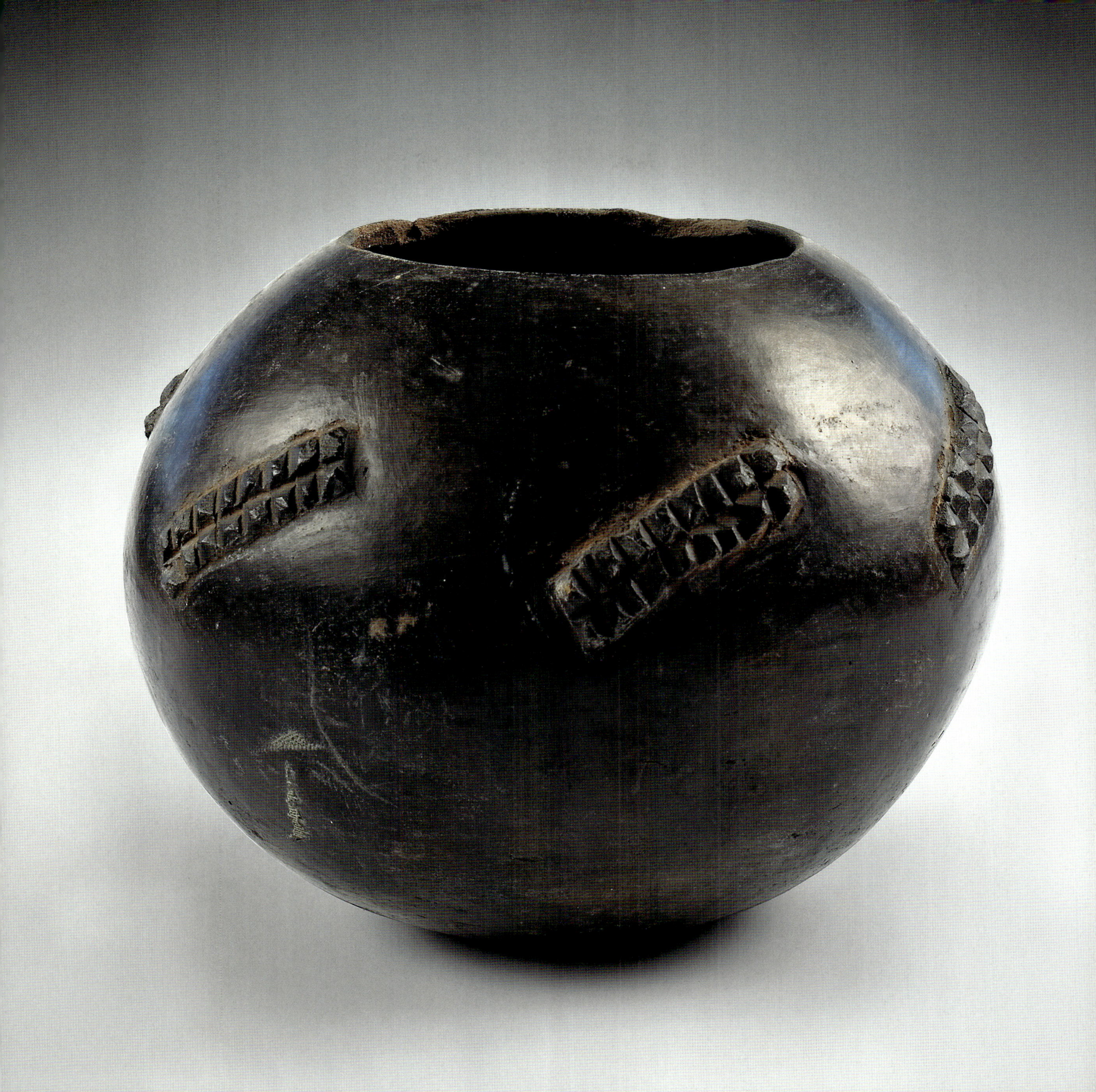

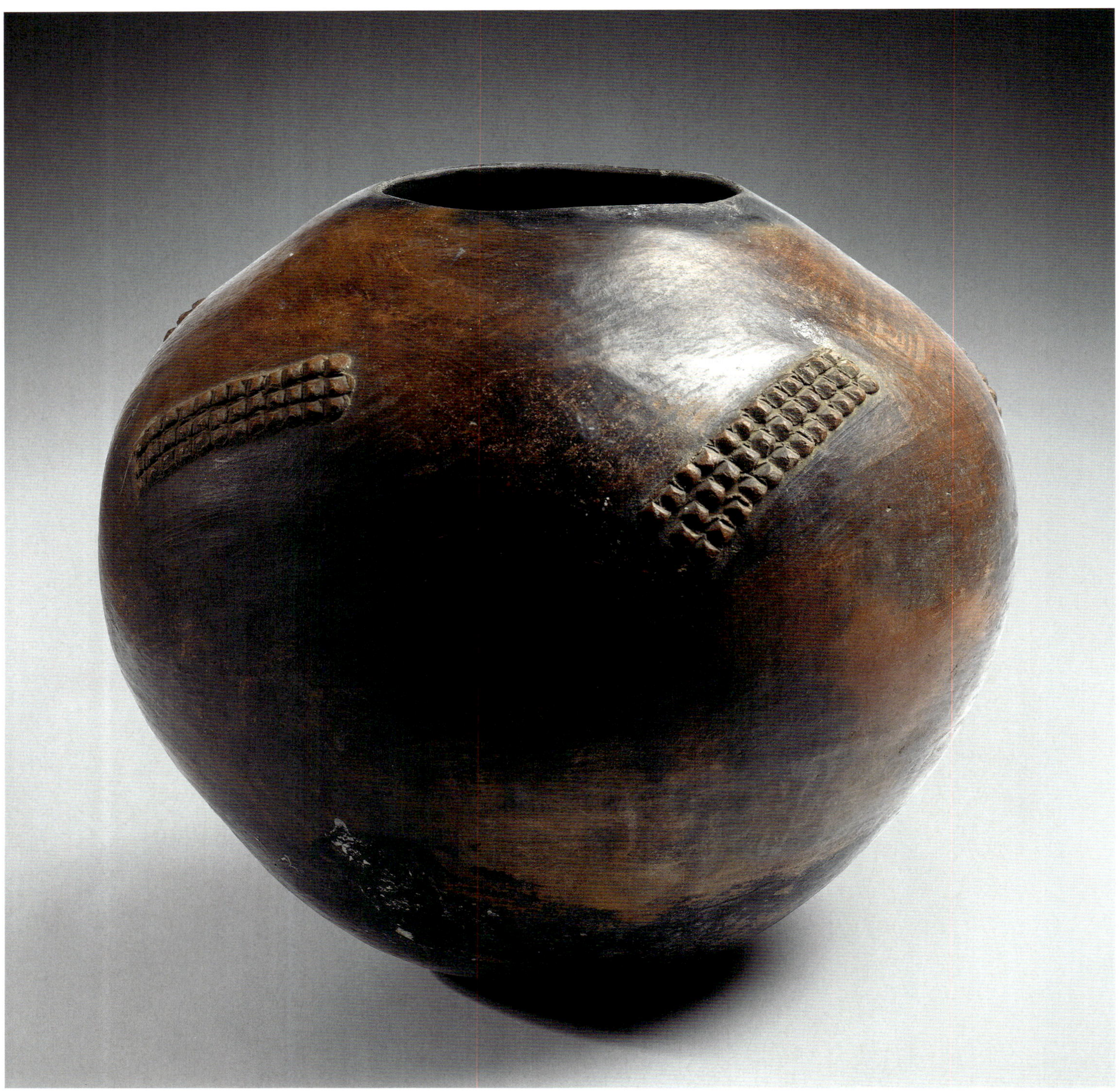

POT NUMBER 202 Ukhamba H: 300 mm panels of *amasumpa* carefully applied.

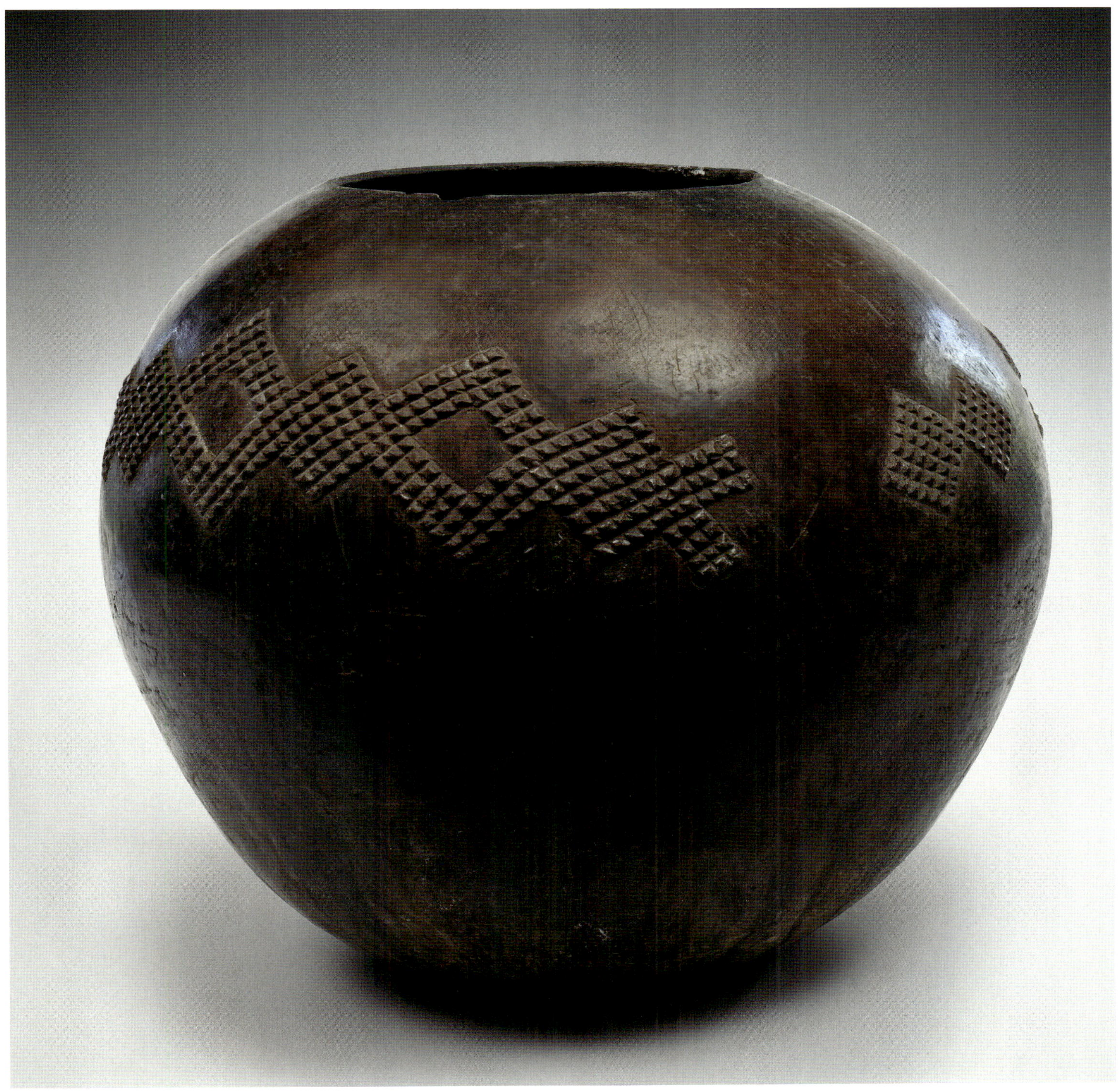

POT NUMBER 209 Ukhamba H: 319 mm Partially superimposed regular zigzags made of *amasumpa* carved from panels of clay. Combinations of zigzags, in parallel or as here in opposition, are characteristic of the Mahlabatini region. They figure on beadwork and basketry as well as ceramics (cf. Jolles 2004).

Nongoma Style 2

Circles of mostly 'pinched' *amasumpa*.
Examples: Pot 203 page 56, Pot 204 page 57

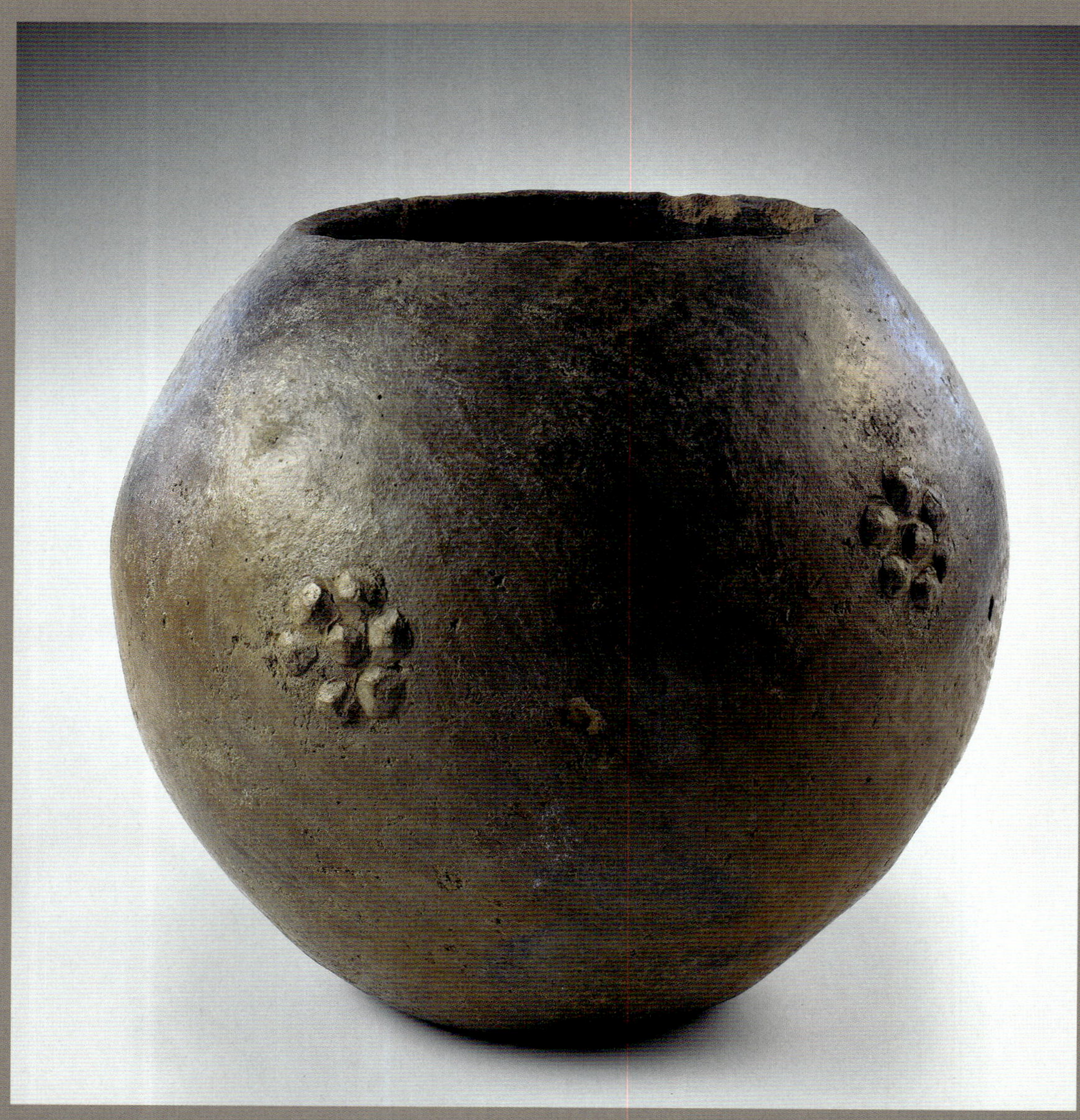

Pot number 203 Ukhamba H: 190 mm
Circle of *amasumpa* applied singly, pot-fired once only. Wide opening, probably for porridge.

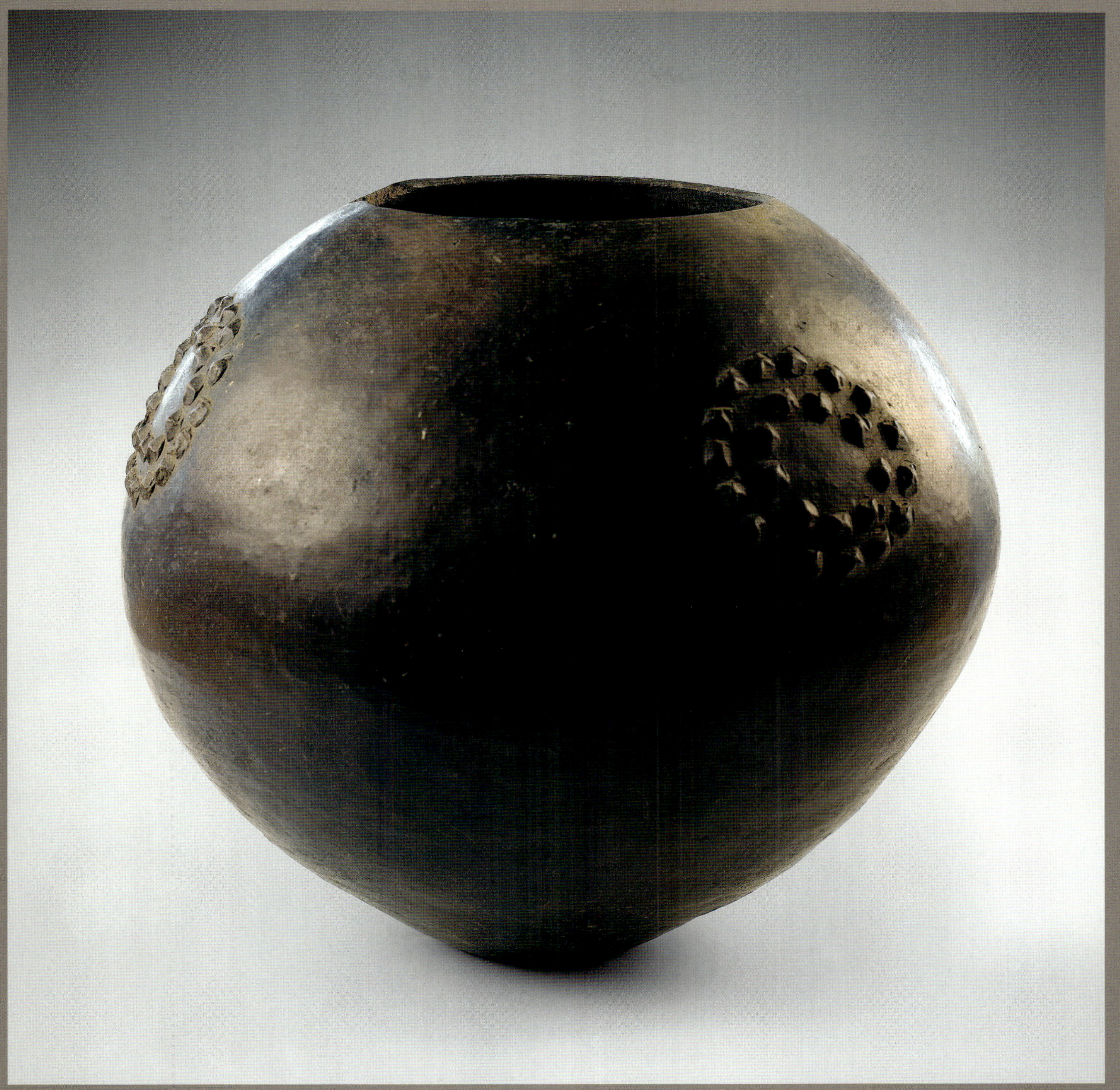

POT NUMBER 204 Ukhamba, H: 265 mm Large ukhamba with pinched *amasumpa* in a circular motif.

Nongoma Style 3

Other motifs in *amasumpa*, including chevrons, zigzags and pendant triangles. These are often in the 'Smarties'-type *amasumpa*, but also occur as carved applied plaques. Examples: Pots 205, 207 (page 48), Pots 208, 209 (page 55), Pots 210, 211 (page 44)

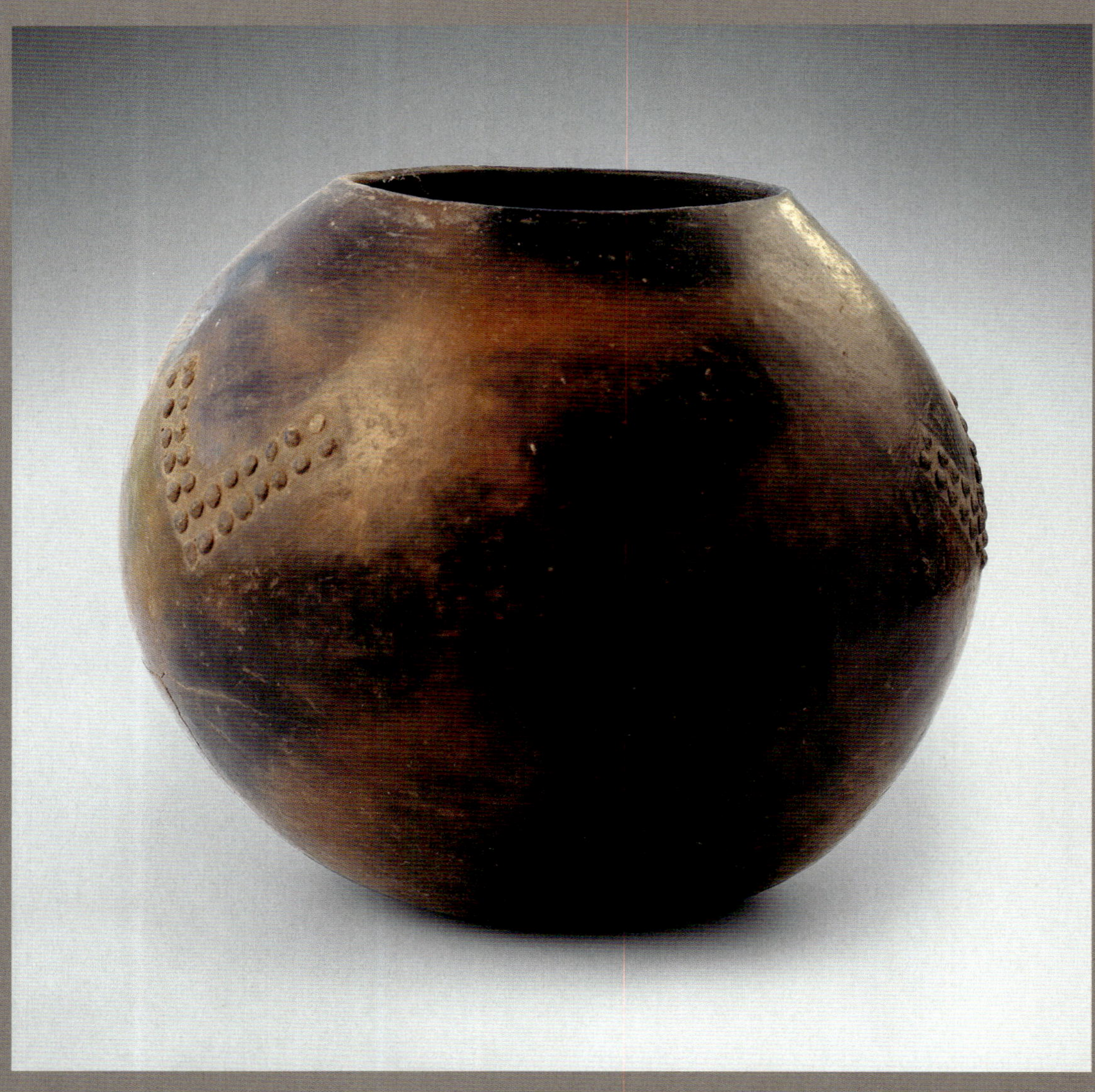

POT NUMBER 205 Ukhamba H: 210 mm
Small *amasumpa*, chevron motif, worn black patina allows underlying red of the fired clay to show through.

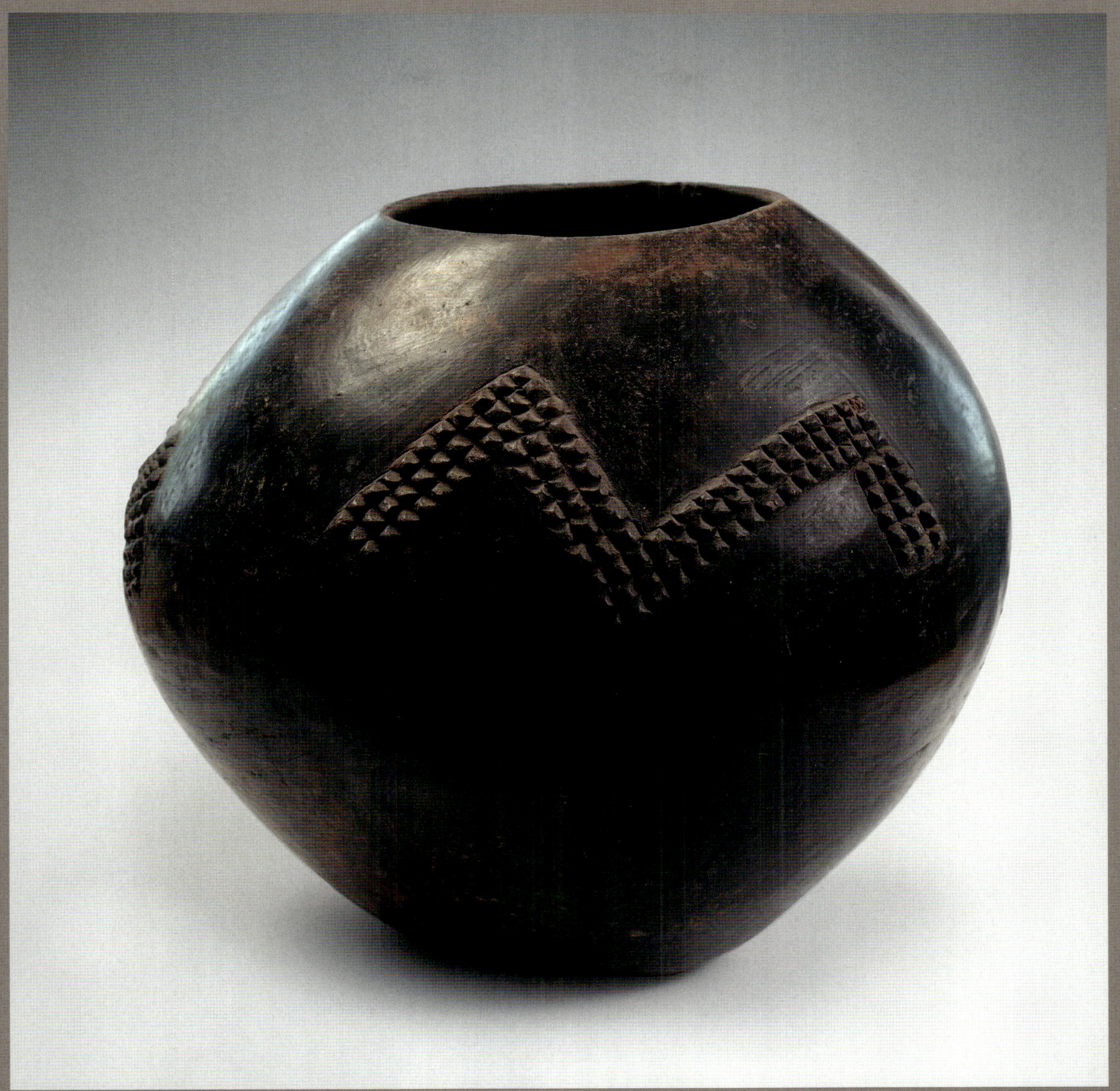

POT NUMBER 208 Ukhamba H: 280 mm Inverted 'W' motif, *amasumpa* carved from an applied panel of clay. Straight 'W' motifs are also frequently encountered.

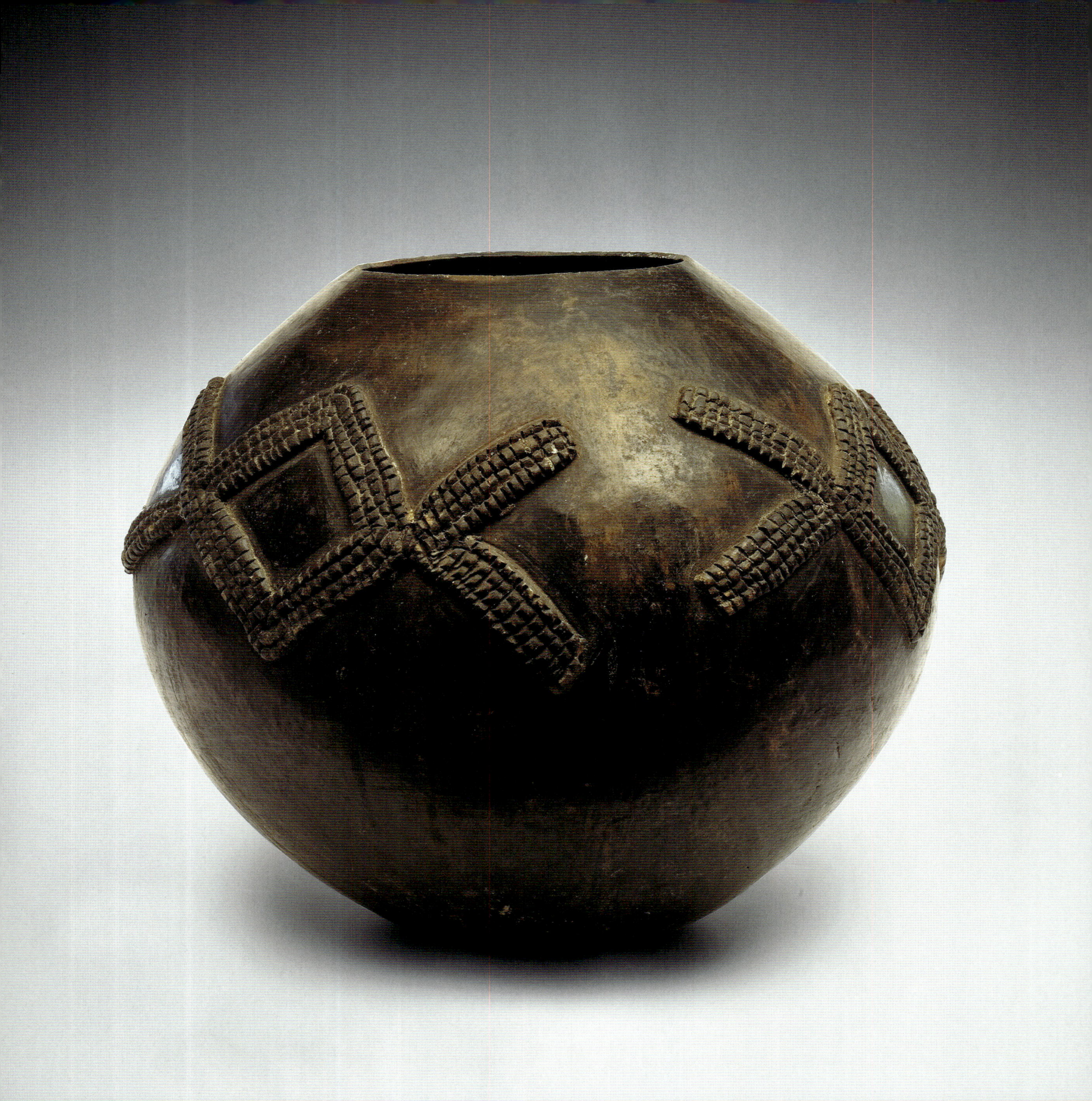

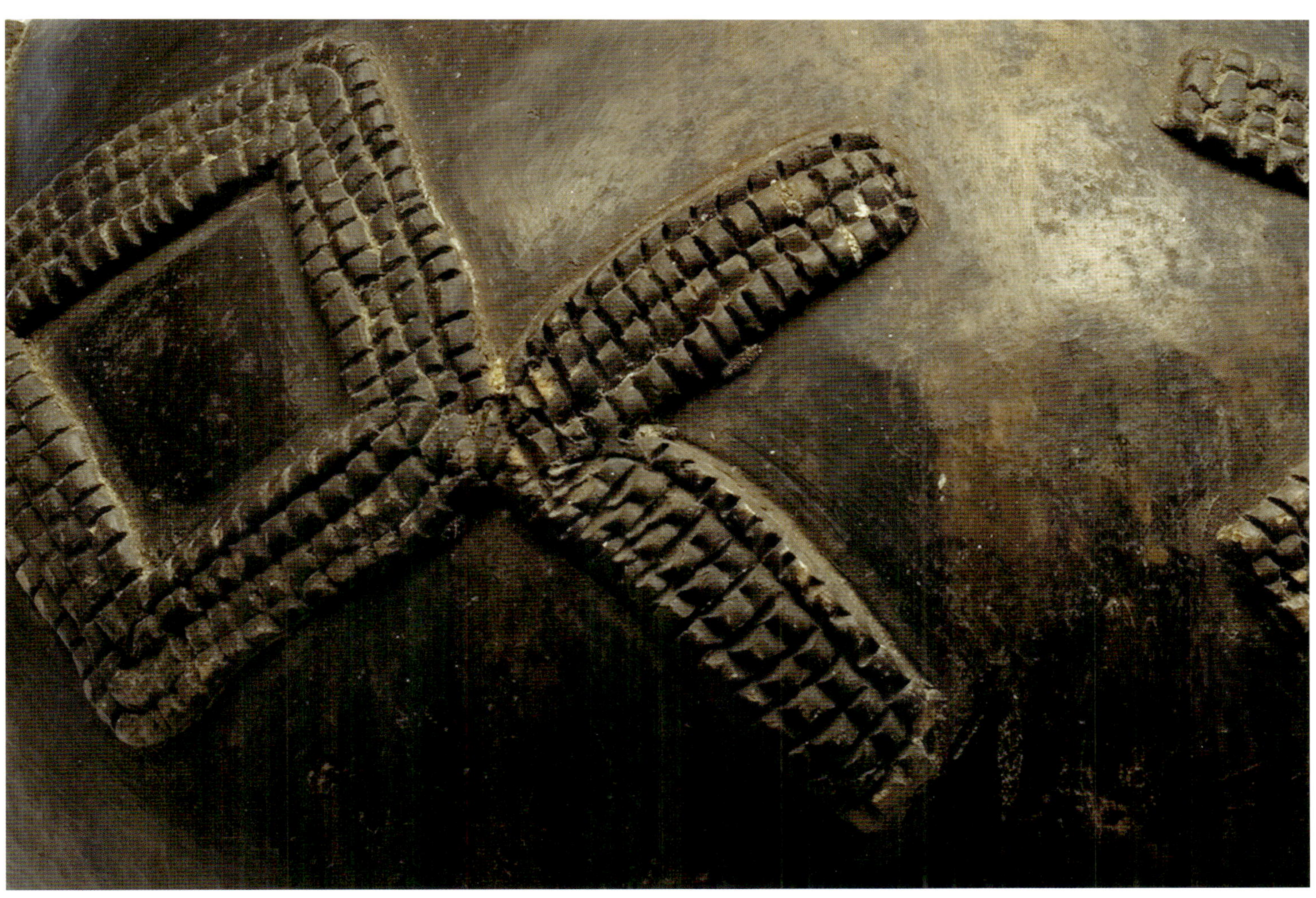

POT NUMBER 210 Ukhamba H: 318 mm Superimposed upright and inverted chevrons made up of several applied panels. The motif is repeated three times. The same motif also exists in small, made up of a single line of *amasumpa*.

Nongoma Style 4

Various large motifs usually in carved panels or strips of *amasumpa*, including alphabetic texts. Examples: Pot 212 page 62, Pot 214 page 66, Pot 215 page 67.

Many of the more expansive *amasumpa* patterns, including those with texts in bold letters, are the work of the potters of ekuShumayeleni referred to below. In the region around Nongoma there is a tradition of incised patterns based on a number of specific motifs, a particularly striking one with a broad spectrum of variations being *amehlo*, 'eyes' (Pot 217 page 72, Pot 218 page 73; Pot 220 page 75). Occasionally several techniques, such as incisions with notches, may be combined on one and the same pot (Pot 221 page 78). This rich palette of styles suggests an influx of people from different regions bringing their own stylistic traditions as would be in keeping with an important administrative centre.

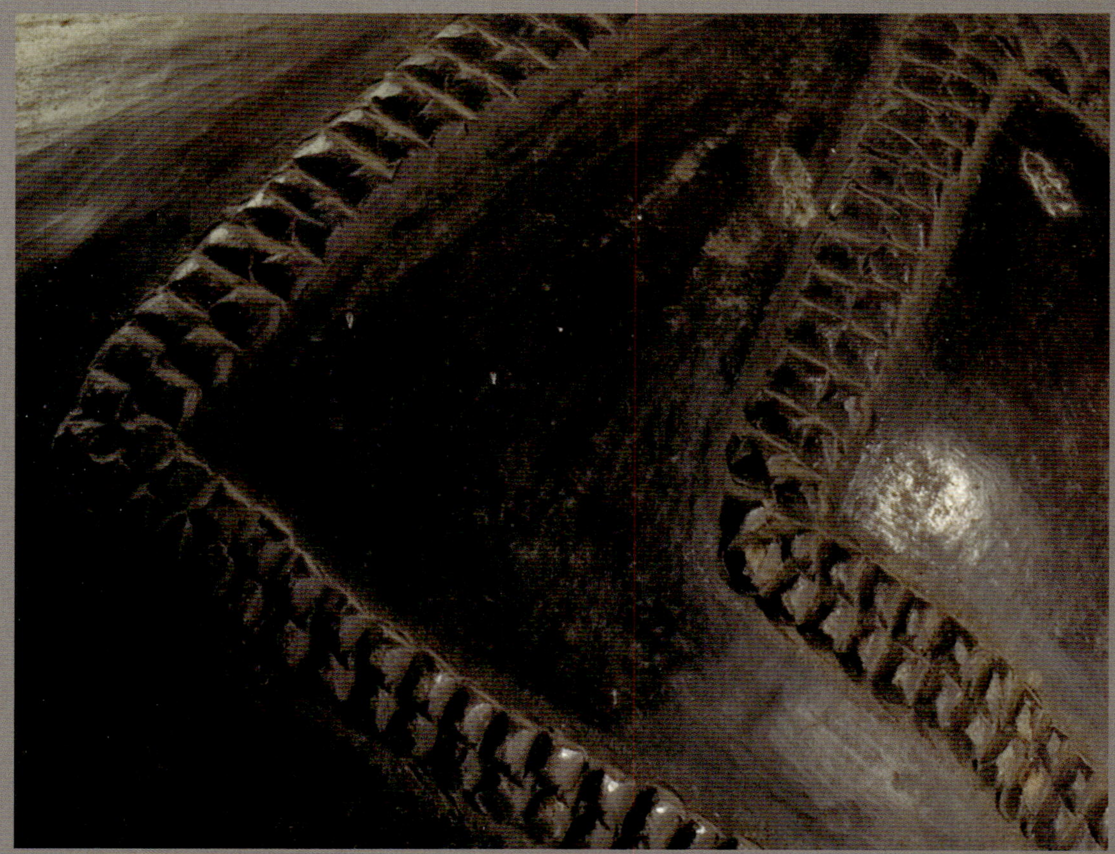

POT NUMBER 212 Uphiso, H: 346 mm Expanded eye pattern with central diamonds. *Amasumpa* from strips of applied clay.

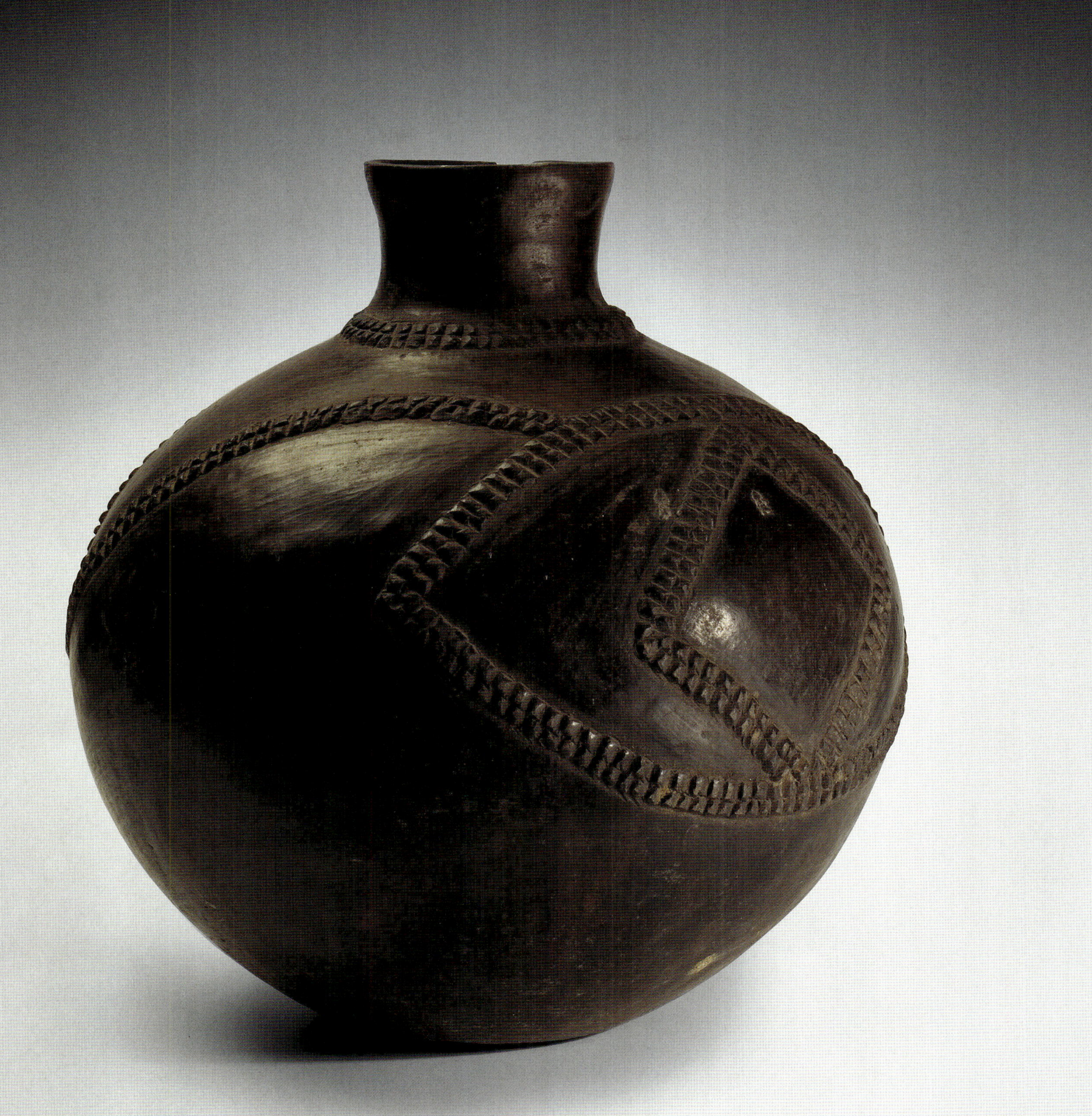

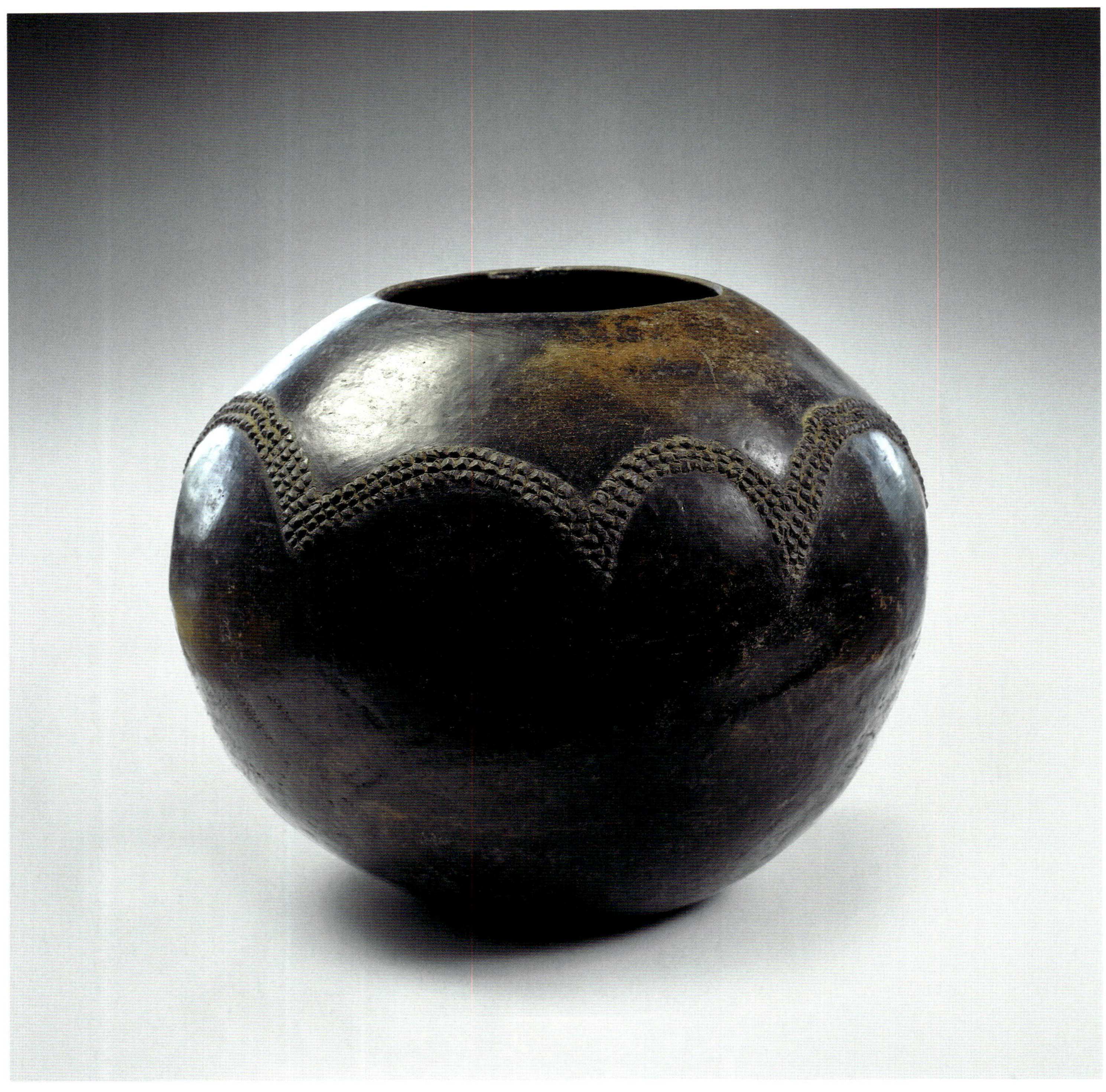

POT NUMBER 213 Ukhamba H: 268 mm Wave pattern: three rows of *amasumpa* from applied strips. In this pattern a small 'wave' frequently completes the sequence. This is another example of reduced symmetry (cf. 211 p. 45).

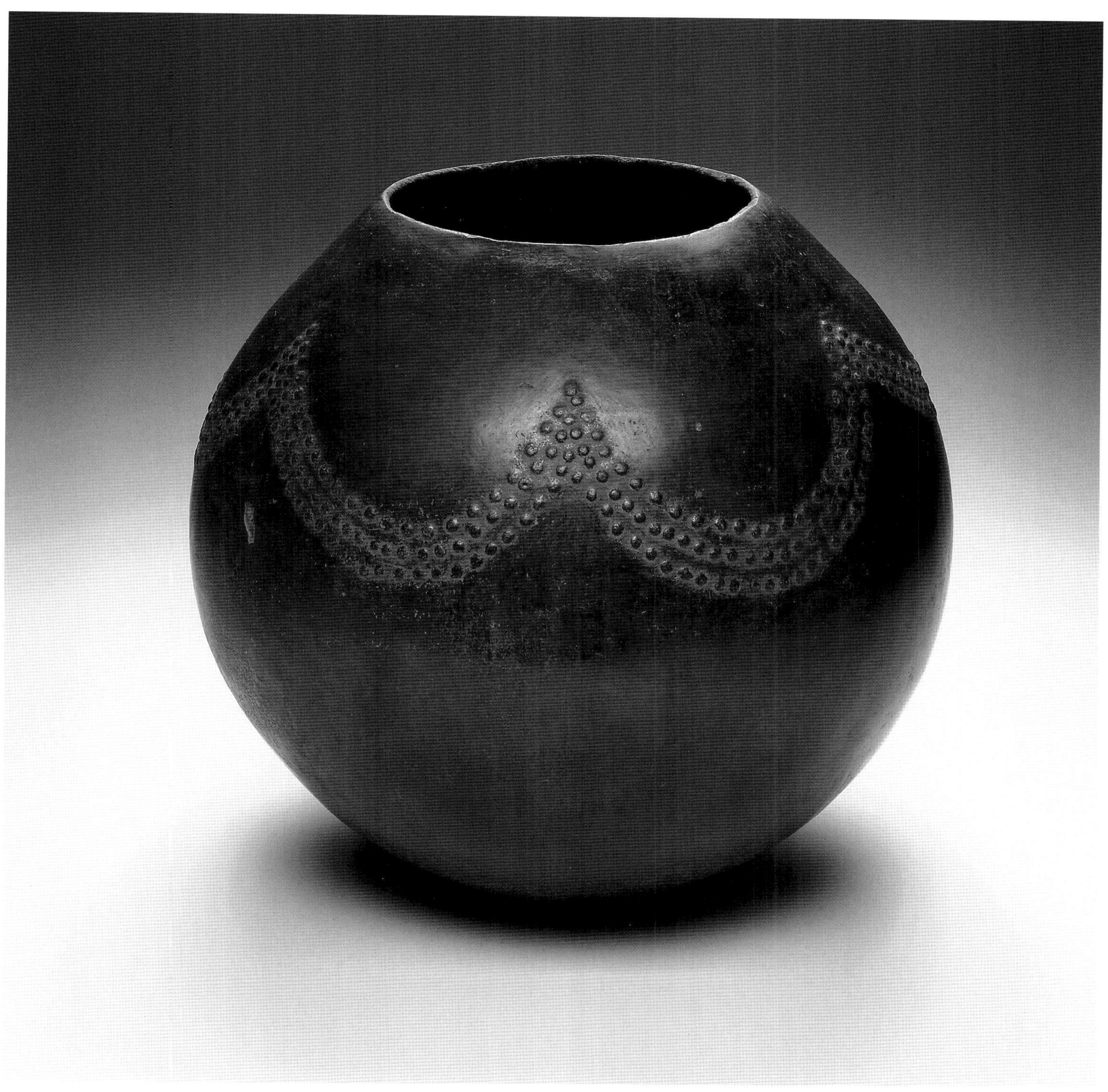

POT NUMBER 227 Ukhamba H: 305 mm, W: 337 mm

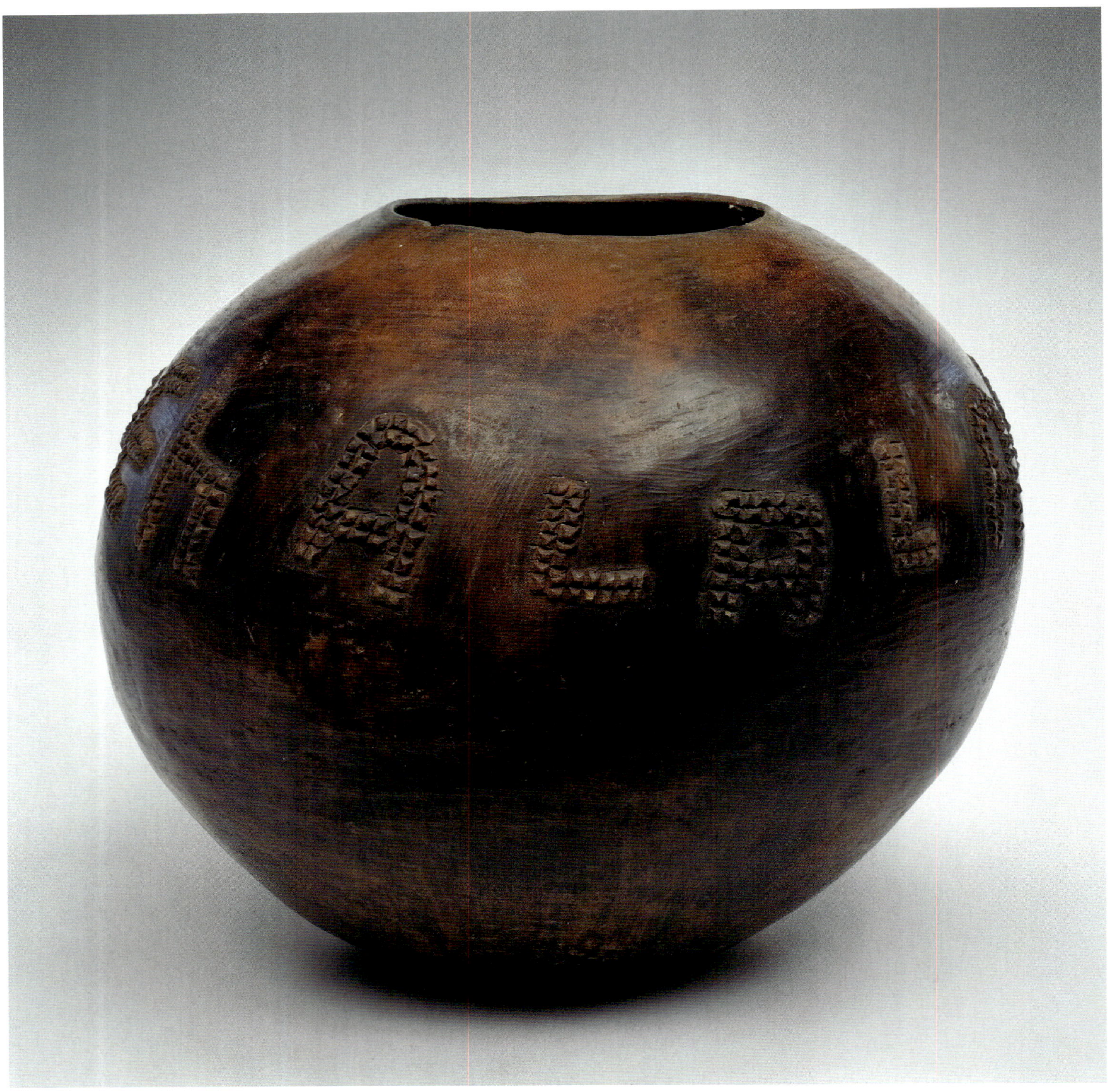

POT NUMBER 214 Ukhamba H: 303 mm Pot with text formed out of strips of *amasumpa*. The text reads: 'ALALA MA O HAMEN'. Such texts are often difficult to decipher, as the illiterate pot makers depended on school children for writing the words. Here there seems to have been some confusion about the use of 'H'. So this text was probably intended to read: 'ALALA MA O AMEN', 'Bravo, Mother, so it's you. Amen' (personal information Jacob Ngwenya, 21.01.2004).

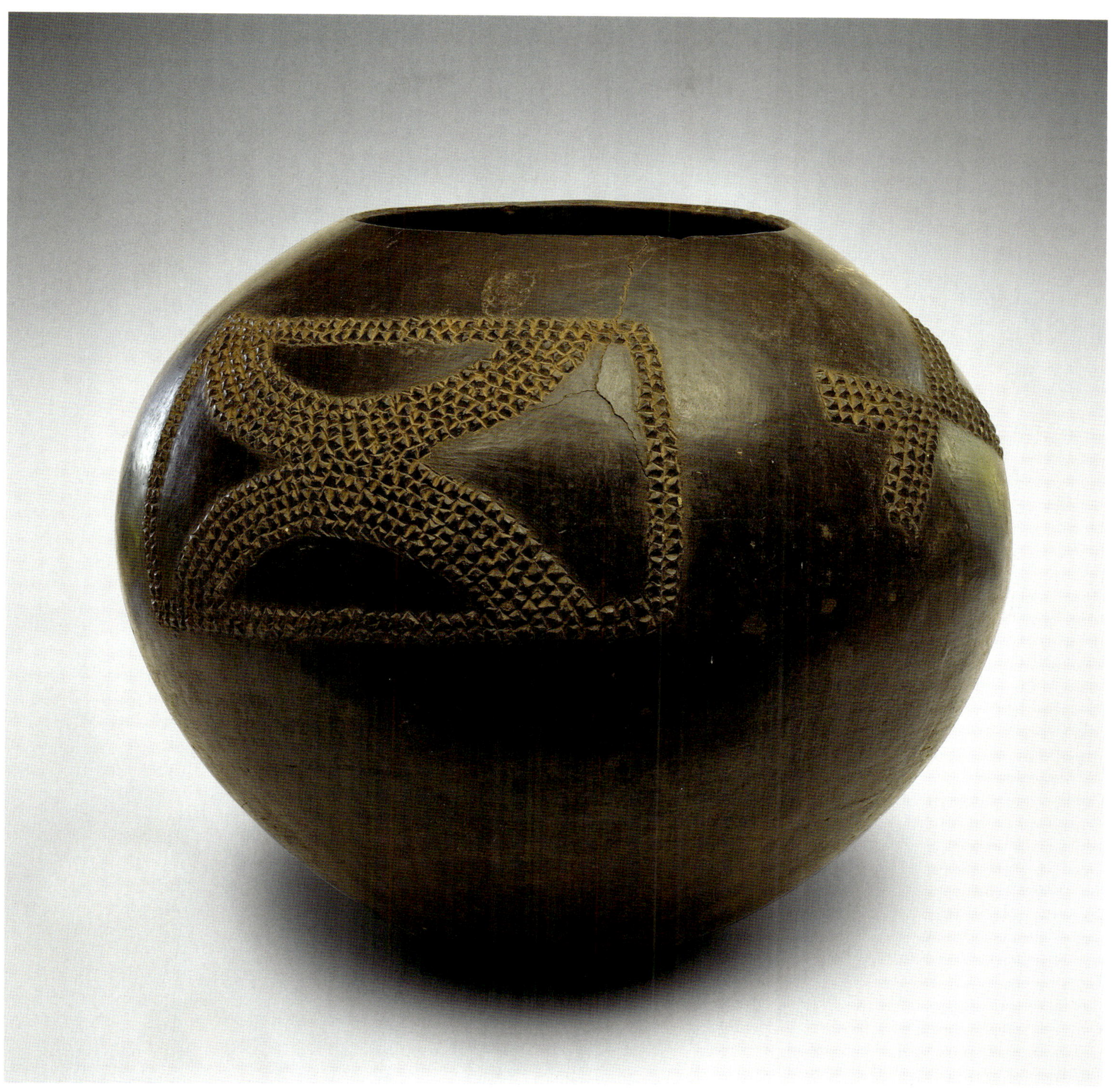

POT NUMBER 215 Ukhamba H: 371 mm Squat form, diameter greater than height (1:1.64, D: 432 mm). Alternating large designs in *amasumpa* on shoulder.

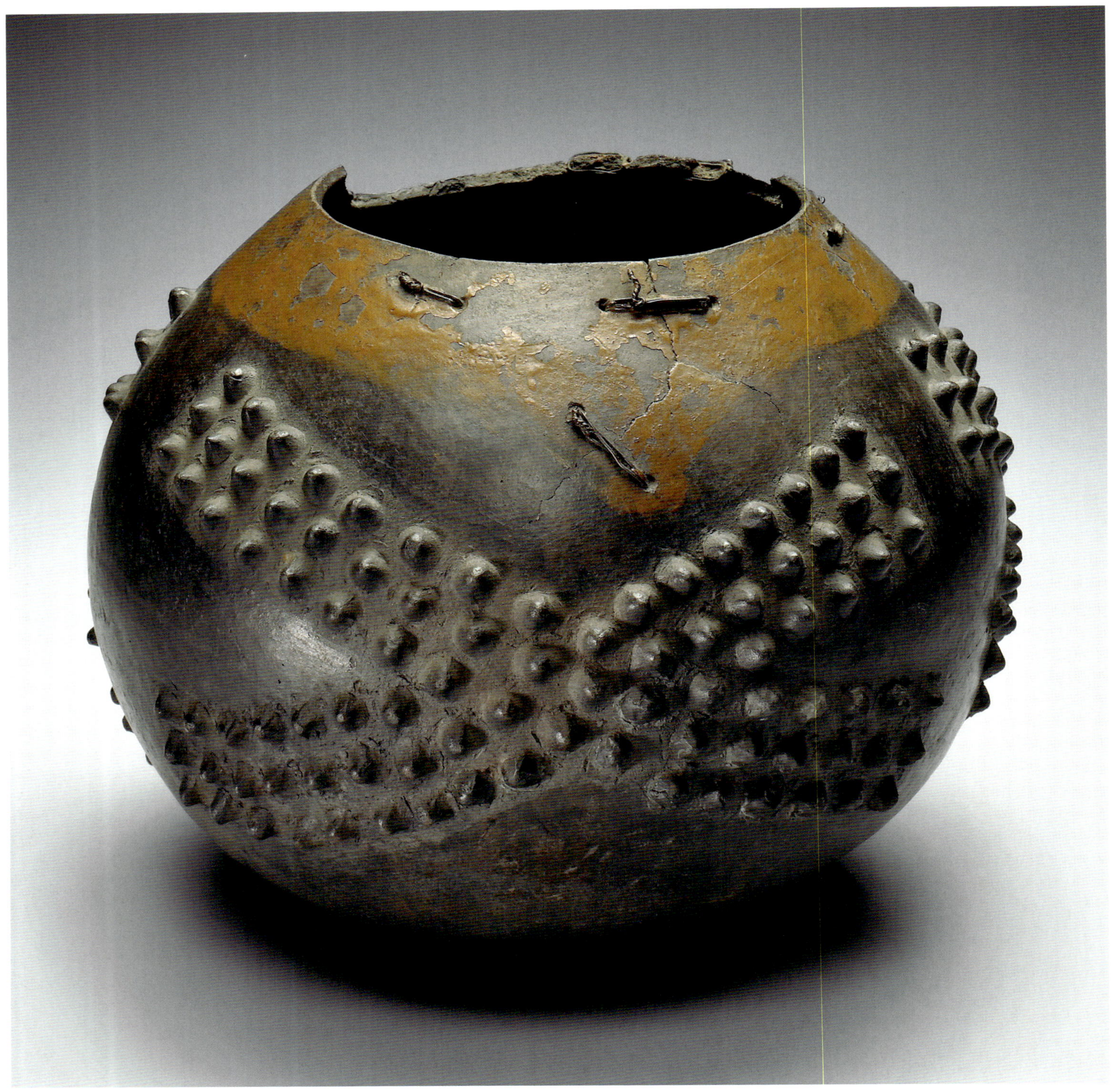

POT NUMBER 228 Ukhamba H:222 mm, W: 279 mm

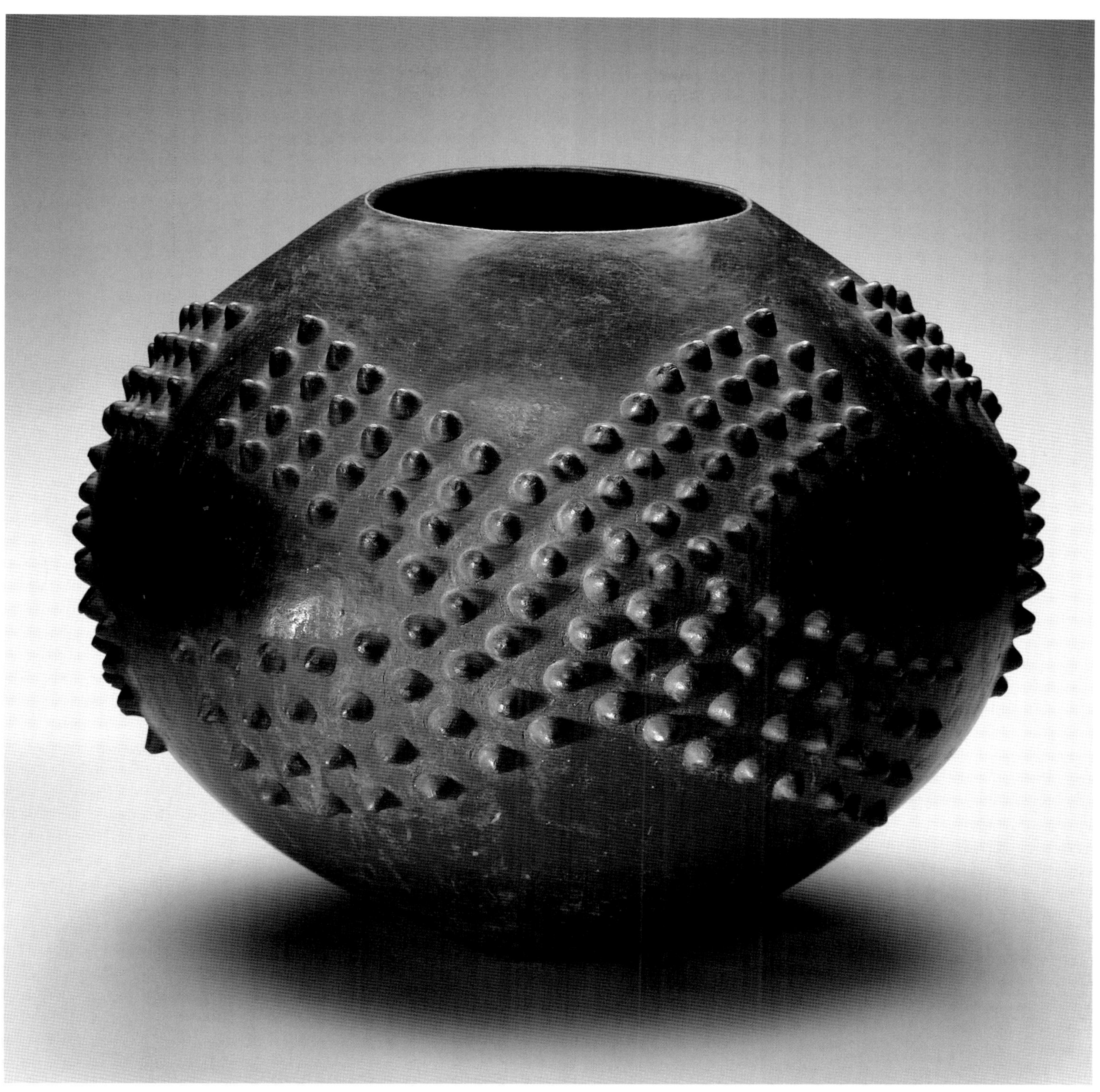

POT NUMBER 229 Ukhamba H: 305 mm, W: 394 mm Note the evenness of the *amasumpa* and the twist to maintain the flow of the pattern.

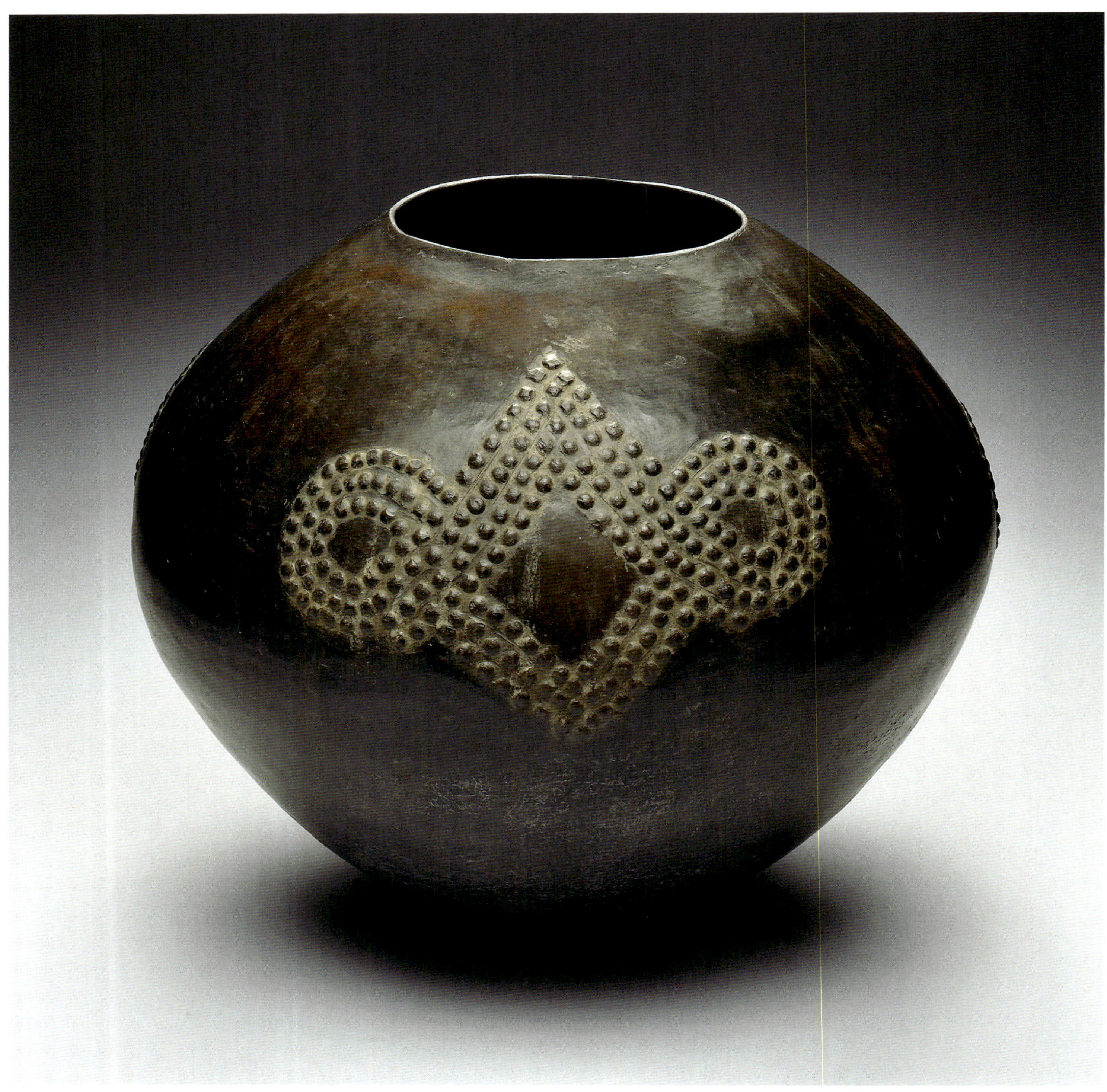

POT NUMBER 230 Ukhamba H: 305 mm, W: 362 mm

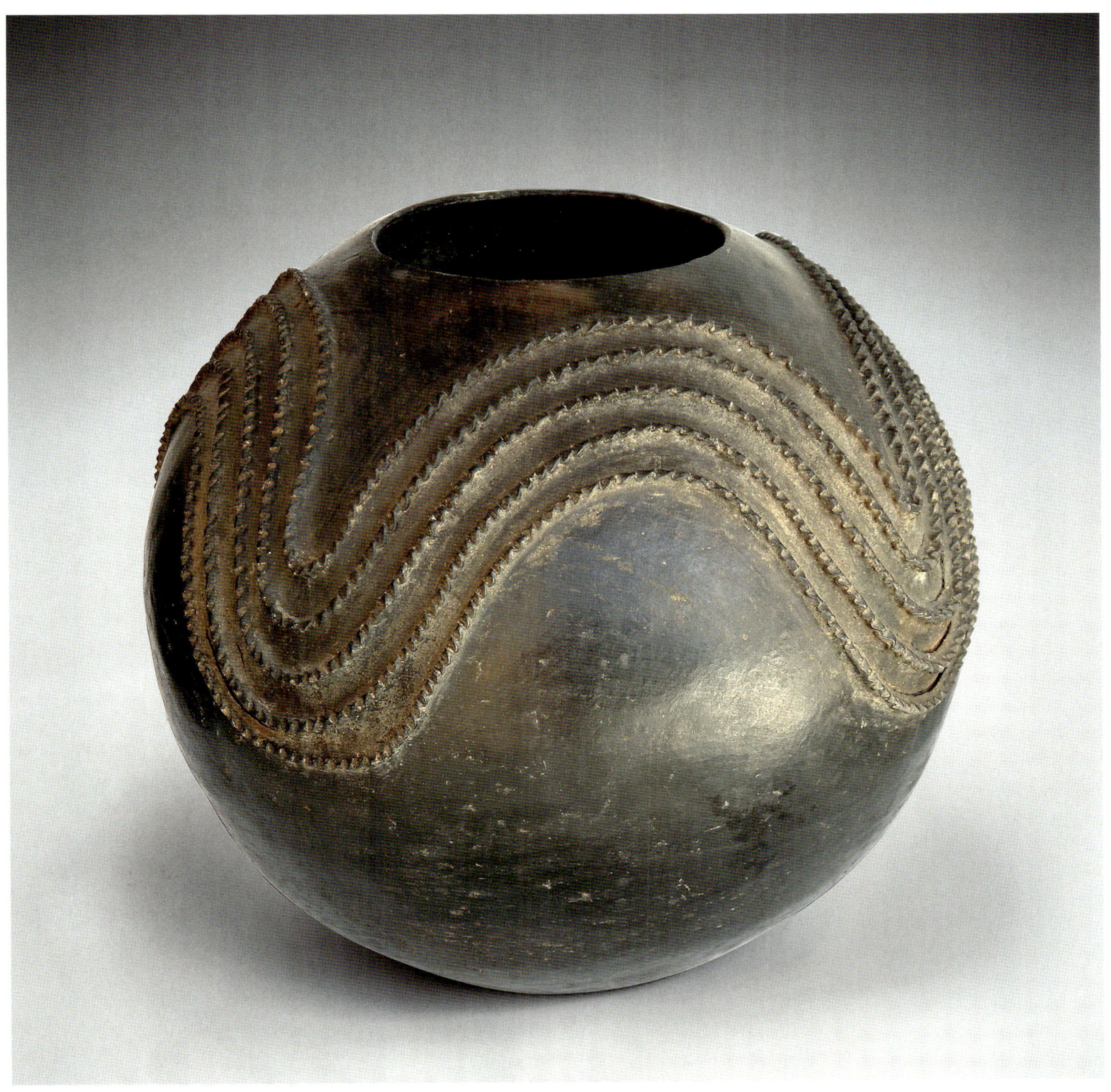

POT NUMBER 232 *Ukhamba* H: 350 mm, W: 390 mm

Nongoma Style 5

Incised and gouged motifs.
Examples: Pots 217–225 pages 72–83.

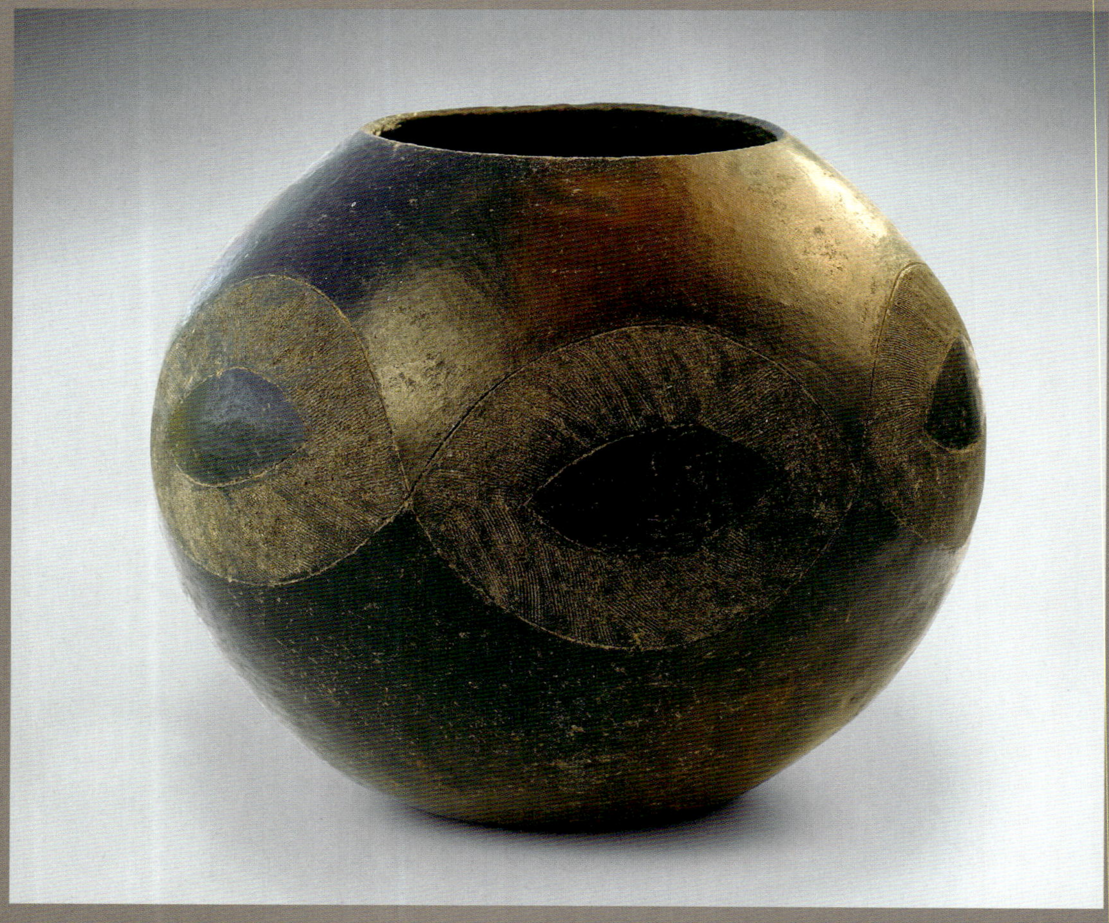

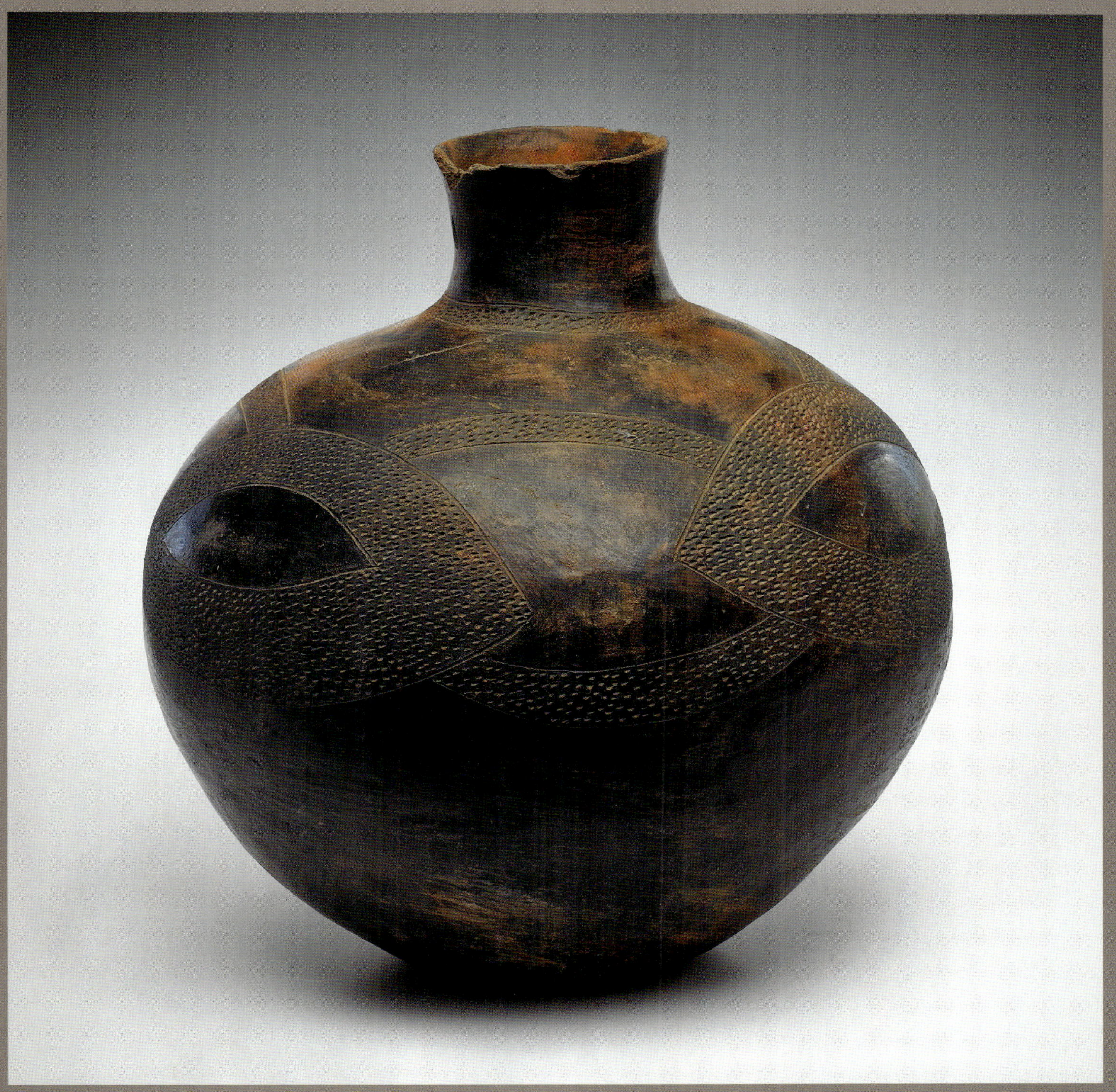

POT NUMBER 218 Uphiso H: 443 mm Incised 'eye pattern' with multiple connecting links.

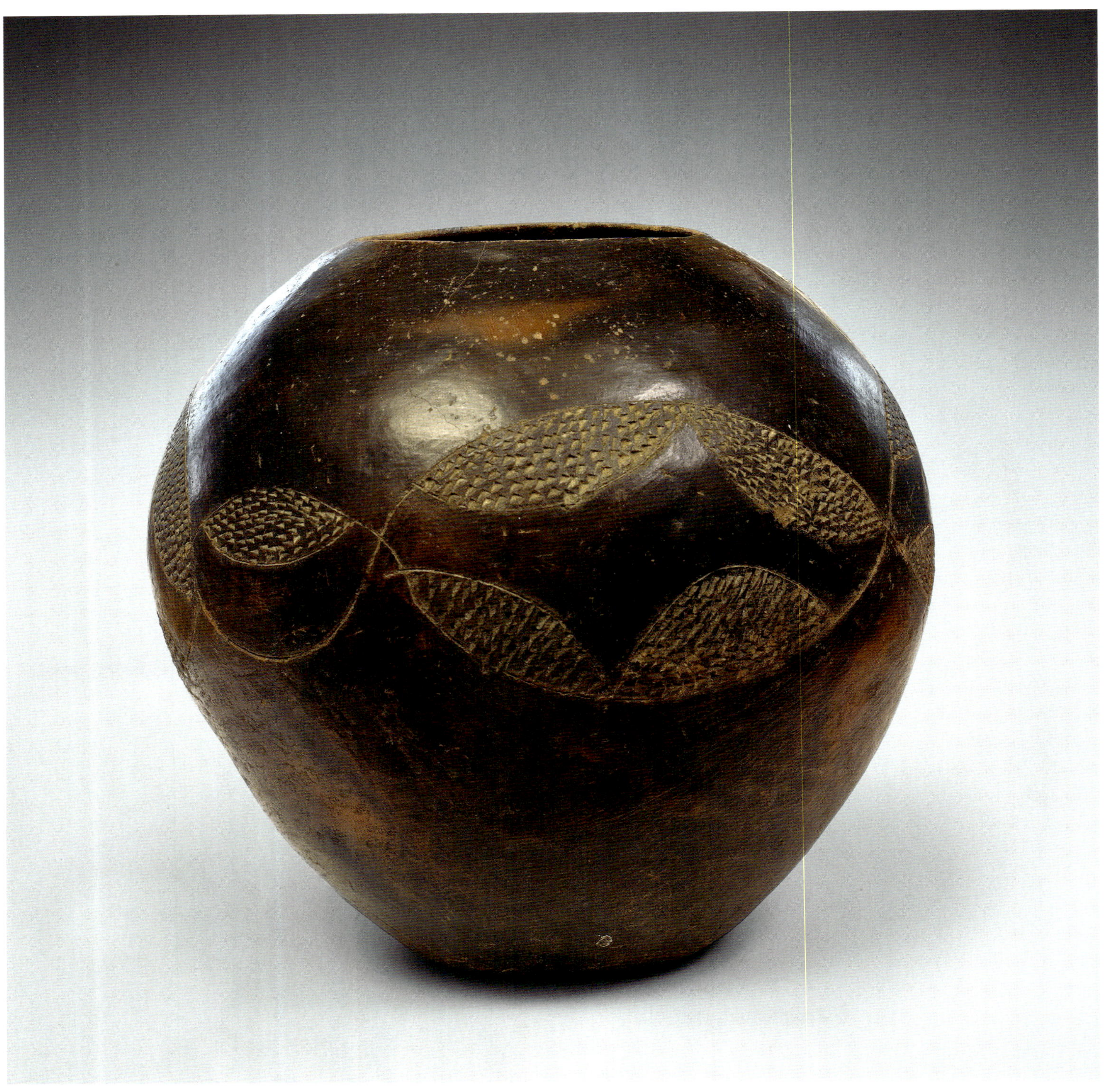

POT NUMBER 219 Ukhamba H: 281 mm Modified 'eye pattern' with broken diamond centres.

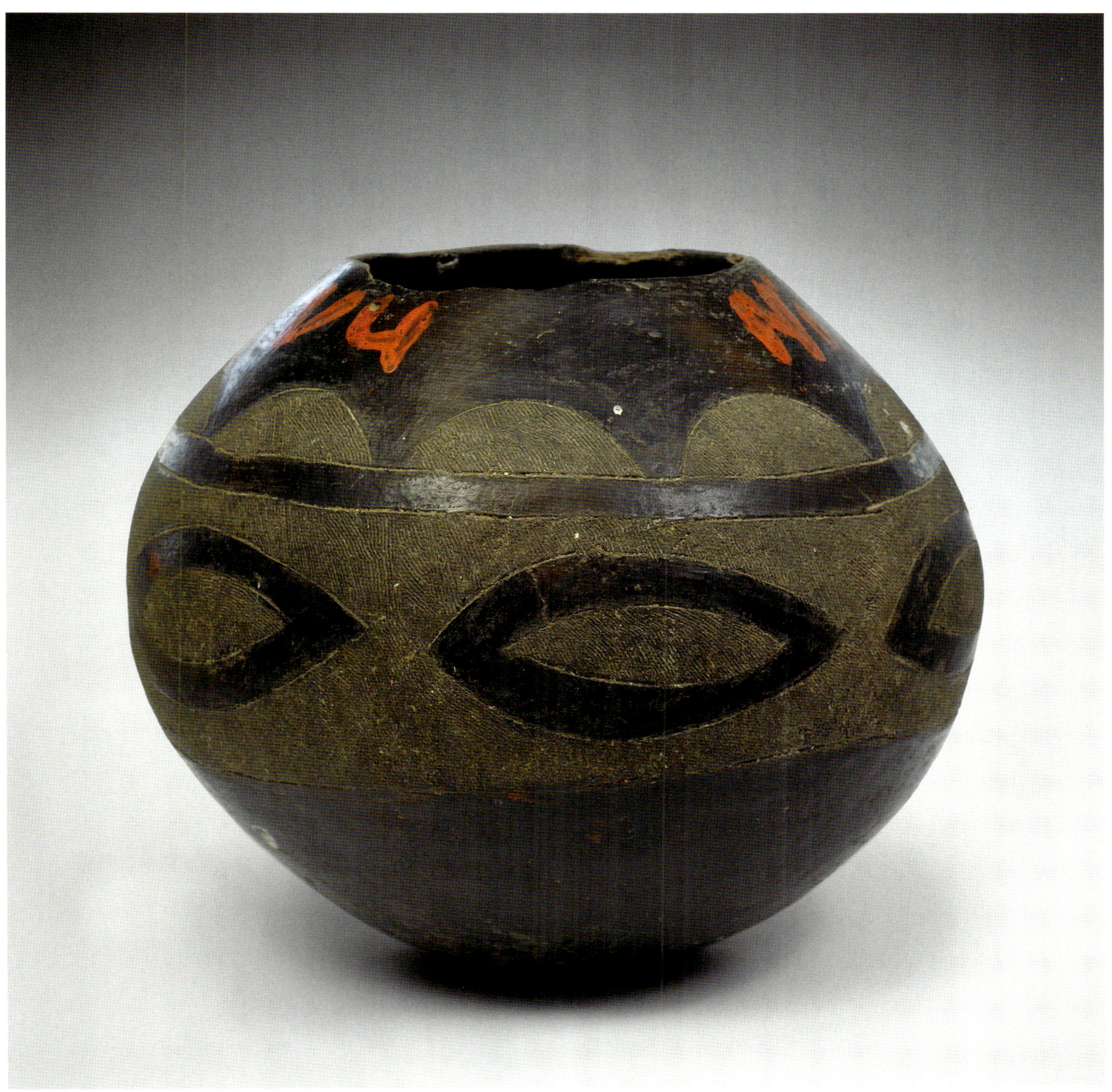

POT NUMBER 220 Ukhamba H: 260 mm Eyes embedded in an incised band, with a wave pattern running along the top.

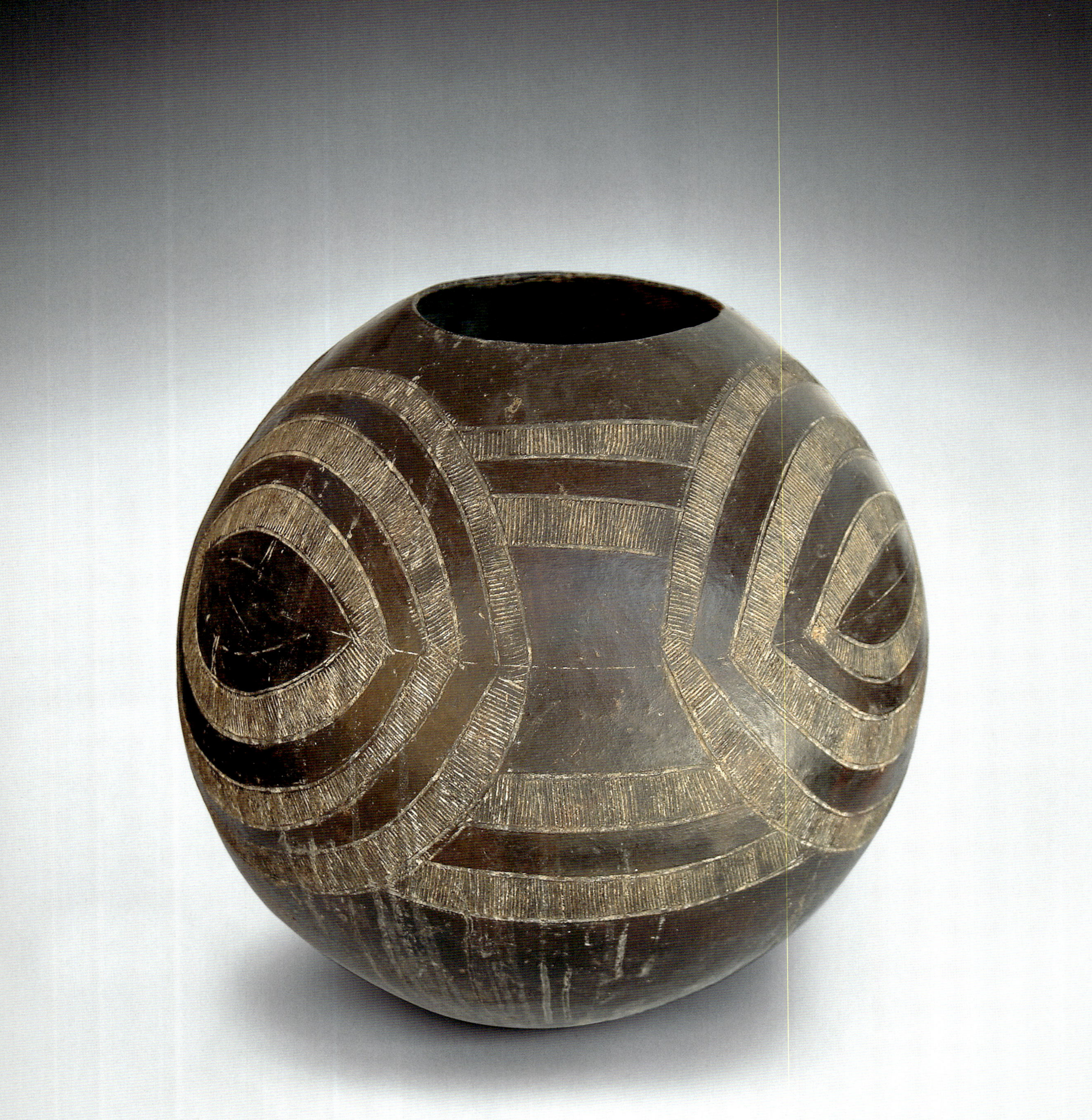

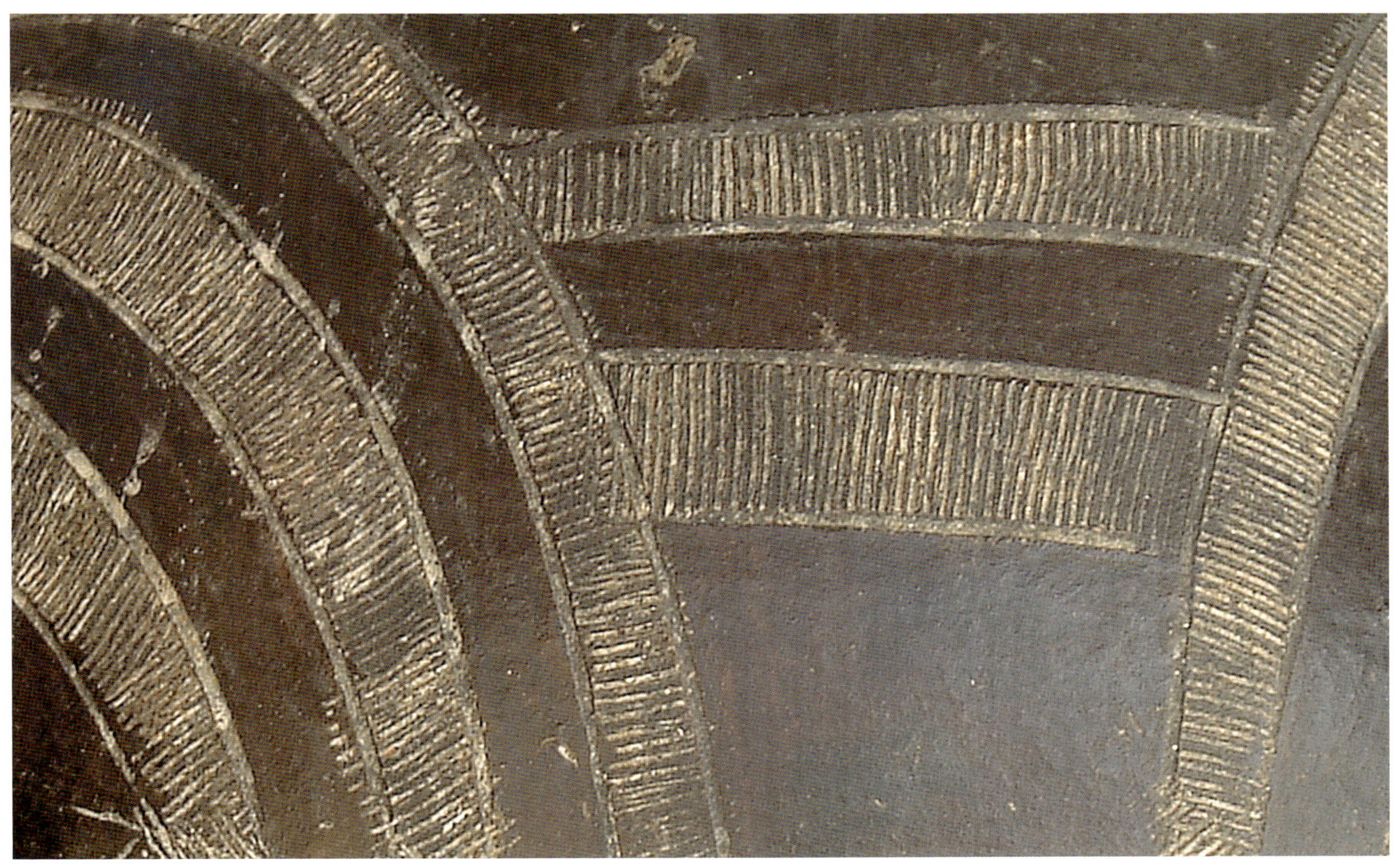

POT NUMBER 231 Ukhamba H: 360 W: 370 mm Imaginative extrapolation of the incised Nongoma eye pattern on a very thin-walled egg-shaped vessel.

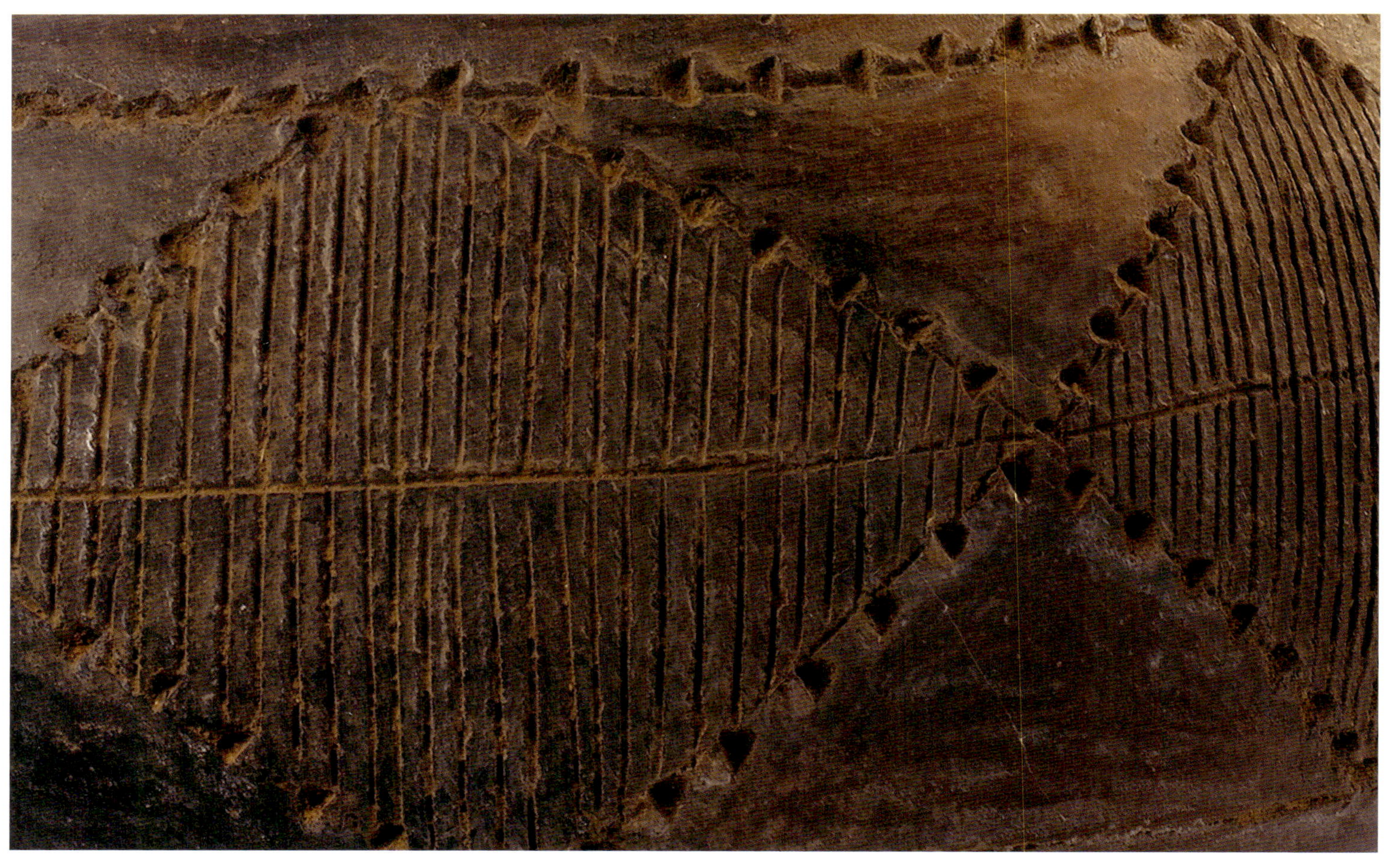

POT NUMBER 221 Ukhamba H: 210 mm Translation pattern of incised diamonds running between two lines.

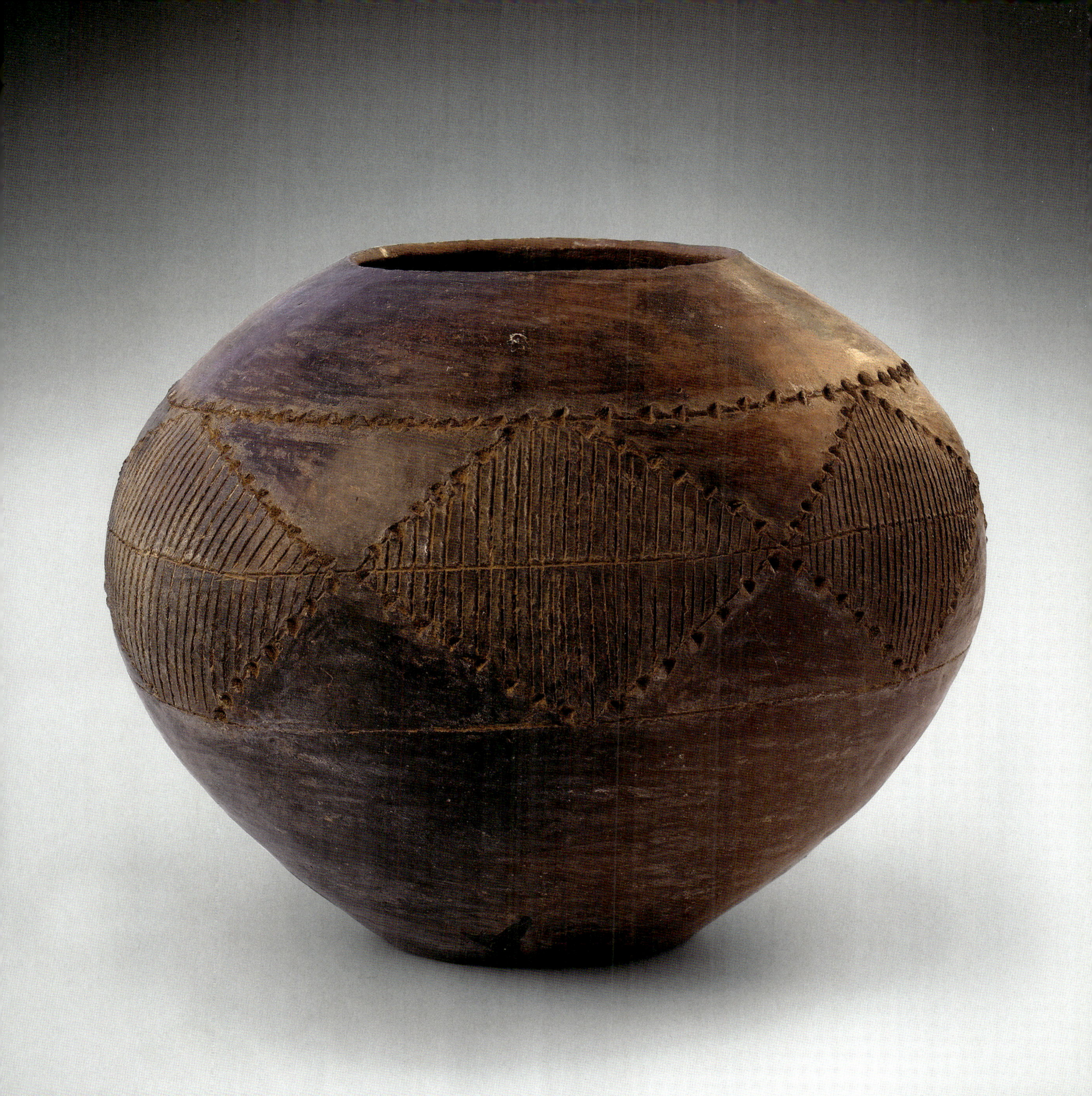

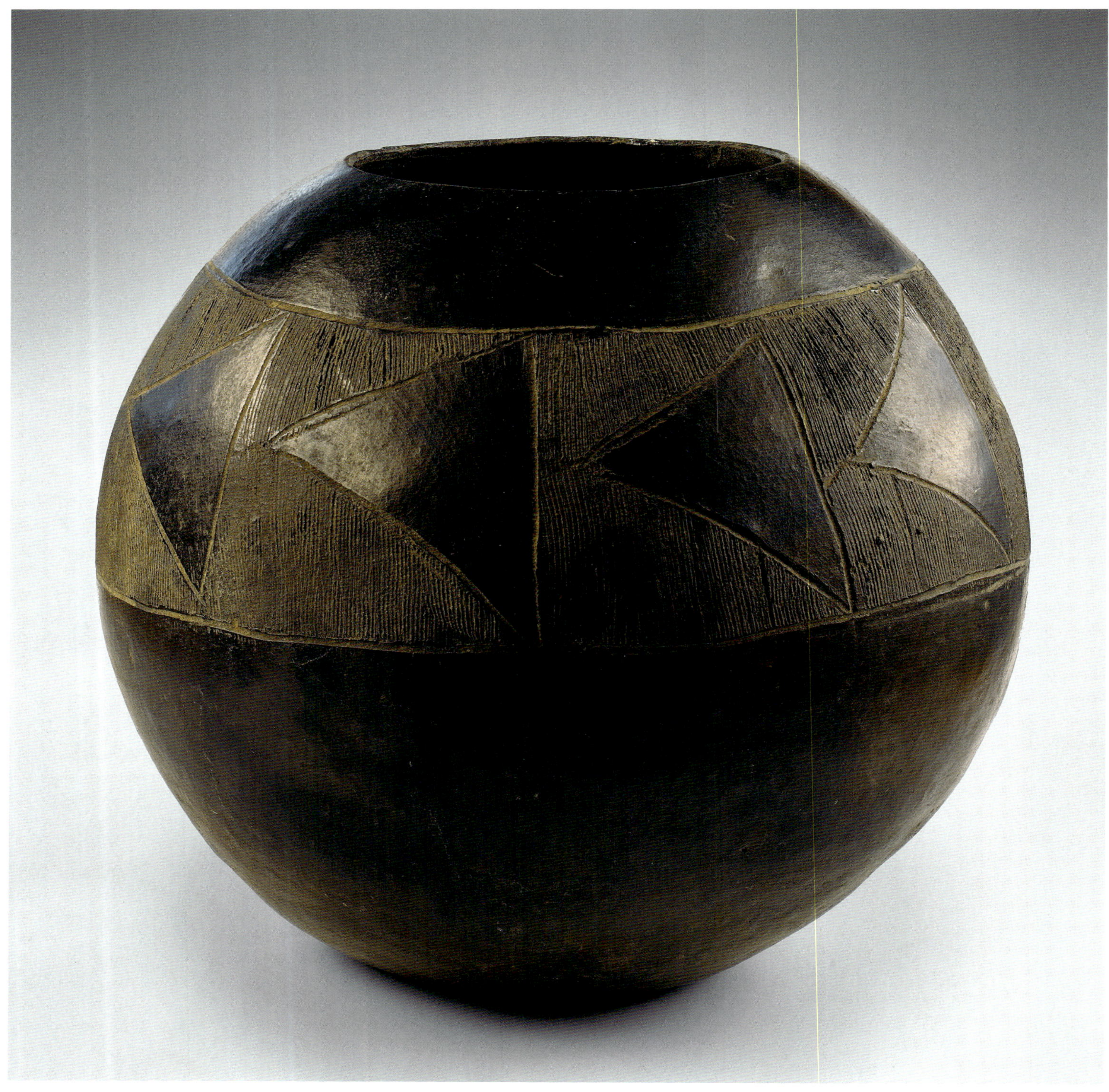

POT NUMBER 222 Ukhamba H: 253 mm Translation pattern of horizontal triangles embedded in an incised band.

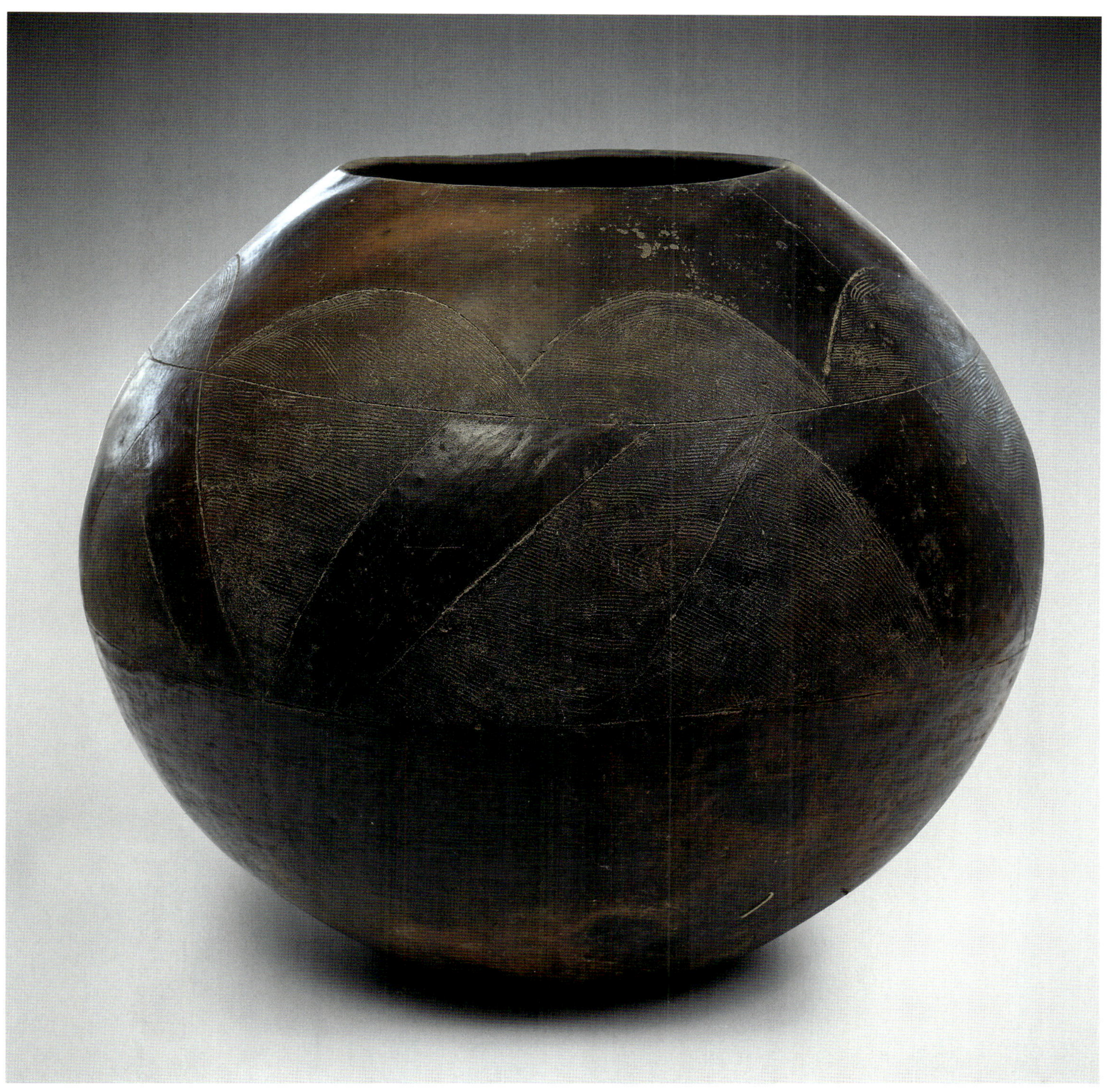

POT NUMBER 223 Ukhamba H: 265 mm Alternating upright and inverted incised triangles with spacers in between in a band surmounted by a wave pattern.

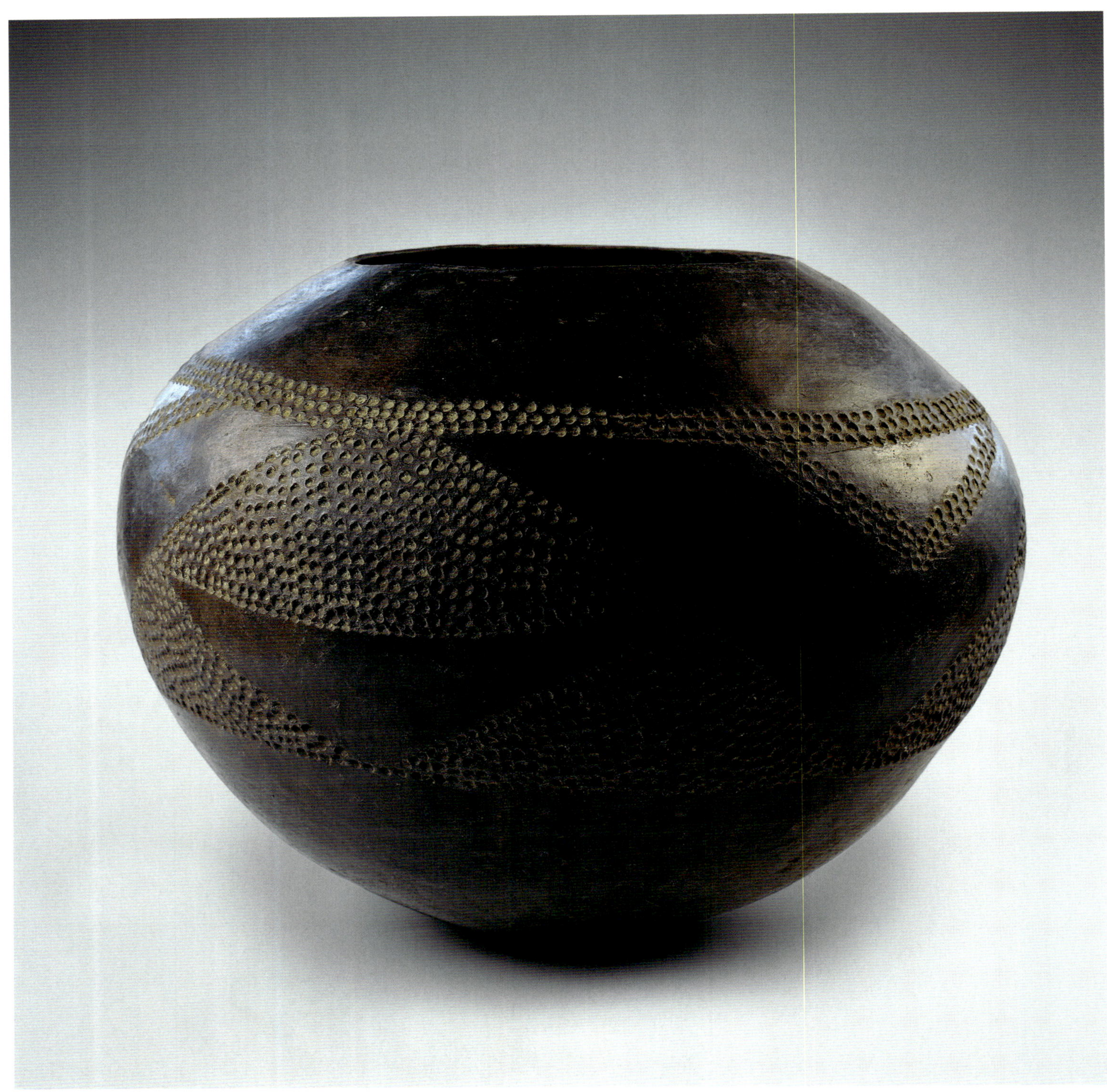

POT NUMBER 224 Ukhamba H: 230 mm A zigzag running between two parallel lines forming alternate upright and inverted triangles each containing a smaller triangle pointing downwards.

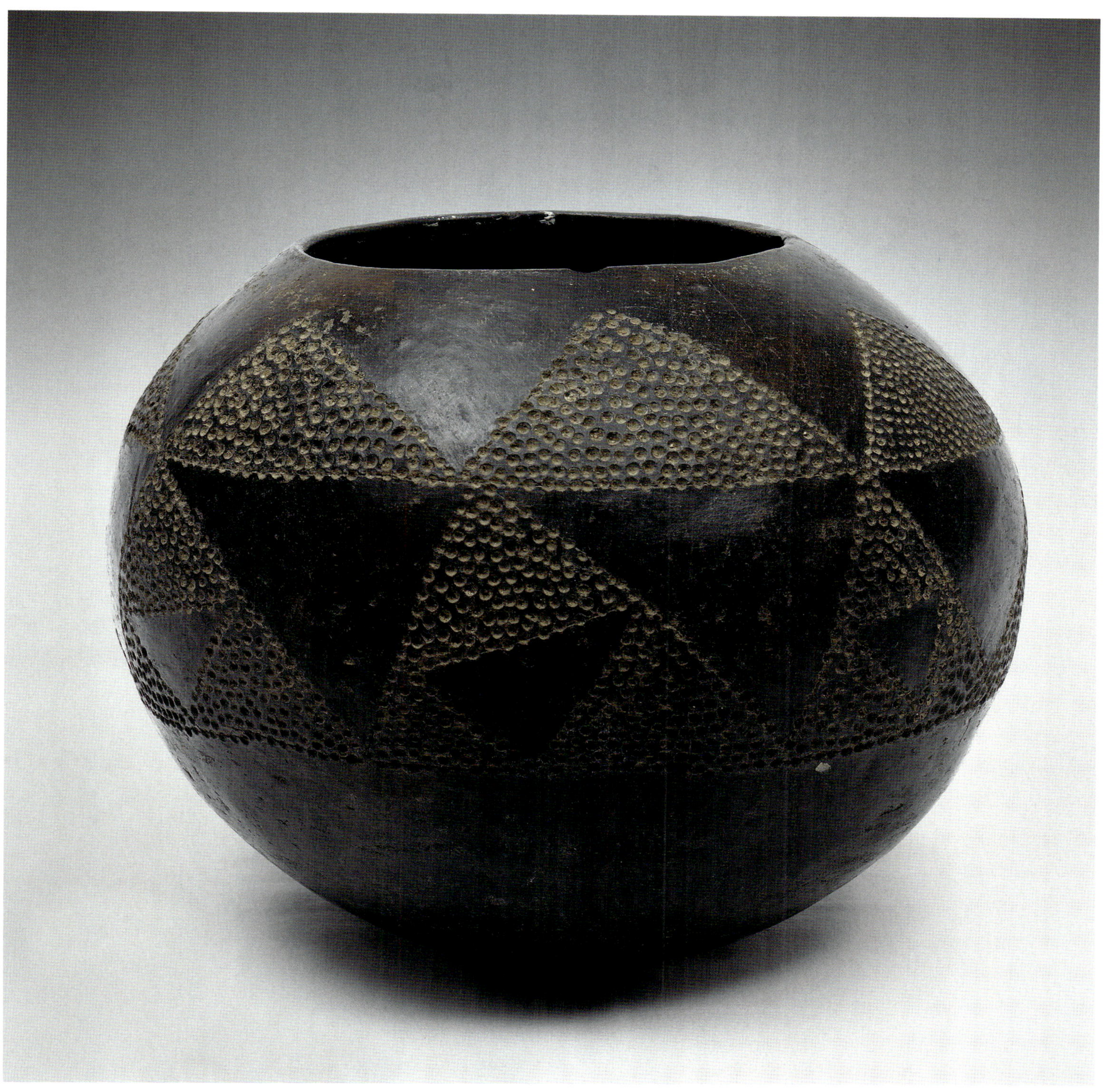

POT NUMBER 225 Ukhamba H 195 mm Though at first sight it does not seem so, this is the same pattern as 224 with the addition of a band of matching triangles running along the top.

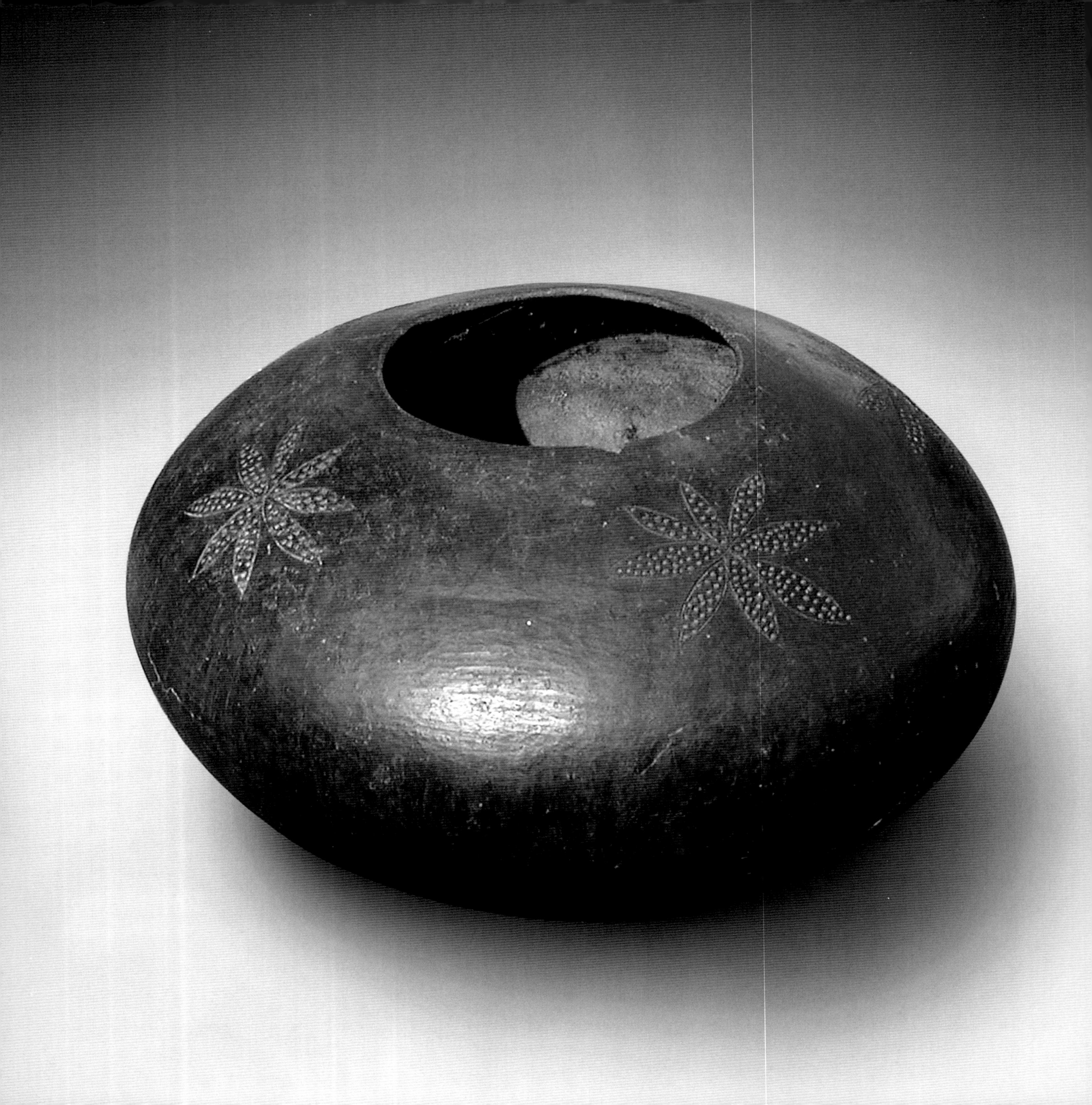

3

The Hlabisa Region

POT NUMBER 325 Ukhamba, from Ndlovu household, Oyaya.

H: 235 mm, max. D: 340 mm. Maker unknown. Though acquired at Oyaya in the Lower Thukela Region this vessel betrays a pure Hlabisa form with a height to diameter ratio of 1.00:1.45. The owner described it as 'very old indeed, from Gogo's (Grandmother's) time or earlier'. The potter Jabulile Nala, daughter of Nesta Nala, who grew up in the Oyaya area was quite unambiguous that it was not a local style (personal communication). The only feature reminiscent of the Lower Thukela Region is the small incised 8-petal wild sunflower, also used by Siphiwe Nala (1914–2003), Nesta Nala's mother. Furthermore the chip broken out of the rim (on the right hand side above the flower) indicates that it was probably brought into the household by a young bride marrying into the family, the chip being retained in her parental home to remind the ancestors of her whereabouts.

It may have been that the potter relocated from Hlabisa to the Lower Thukela Region sometime in the second or third decade of the twentieth century, or that the bride commissioned the pot in Hlabisa with a decorative feature taken from her new home. In either case it illustrates the reach of local styles and their interaction with 'foreign' ones at a time when people were becoming more mobile as a result of migrant labour and the increasing availability of long-distance transport.

In broad terms the Hlabisa region (see map page 30) may be regarded as extending eastwards from the Mona River and its confluence with the Black uMfolozi up to the farmlands of the coastal region. It is truncated by the Hluhluwe-Umfolozi Game Reserve, which in the past has tended to isolate the eastern part of the area from the main body of KwaZulu. The new road through the park, completed in 2008, has mitigated this effect.

From a stylistic point of view, Hlabisa could probably have been regarded as an extension of the Nongoma region during the first half of the twentieth century. But, according to the people I spoke to, it received a steady stream of immigrants from further west, including Vryheid. These were not necessarily relocations resulting from expulsions: apparently word had got round that Hlabisa was a good place to live, and my informants concurred that this was still the case. Some of the potters who came adopted the regional styles for sale at markets, particularly the monthly Mona Market not far from Nongoma. There they were competing with the local potters. They also continued making their own styles for their friends and neighbours.

In the course of time, these imported styles underwent further developments of their own, for instance with the introduction of new techniques such as the use of a comb or matchsticks to make parallel incisions. By the 1960s a distinctive Hlabisa style involving ratios of height to diameter of around 1:1½, with decorative incisions, had gained wide acceptance, for instance Pot 321 page 114. This is particularly true in the case of very large *izinkamba* such as Pot 314 below. This ratio is greater than for most regions, in which the ratio of height to diameter (H:D) would typically vary between 1:1 and 1:1¼. It is also more difficult to make and use, as the upper surface is often close to horizontal. The imported style continued in use well into the 1990s alongside the original *amasumpa* style as in Pot 306 page 88 and Pot 307 page 89, which is related to that of the Nongoma region.

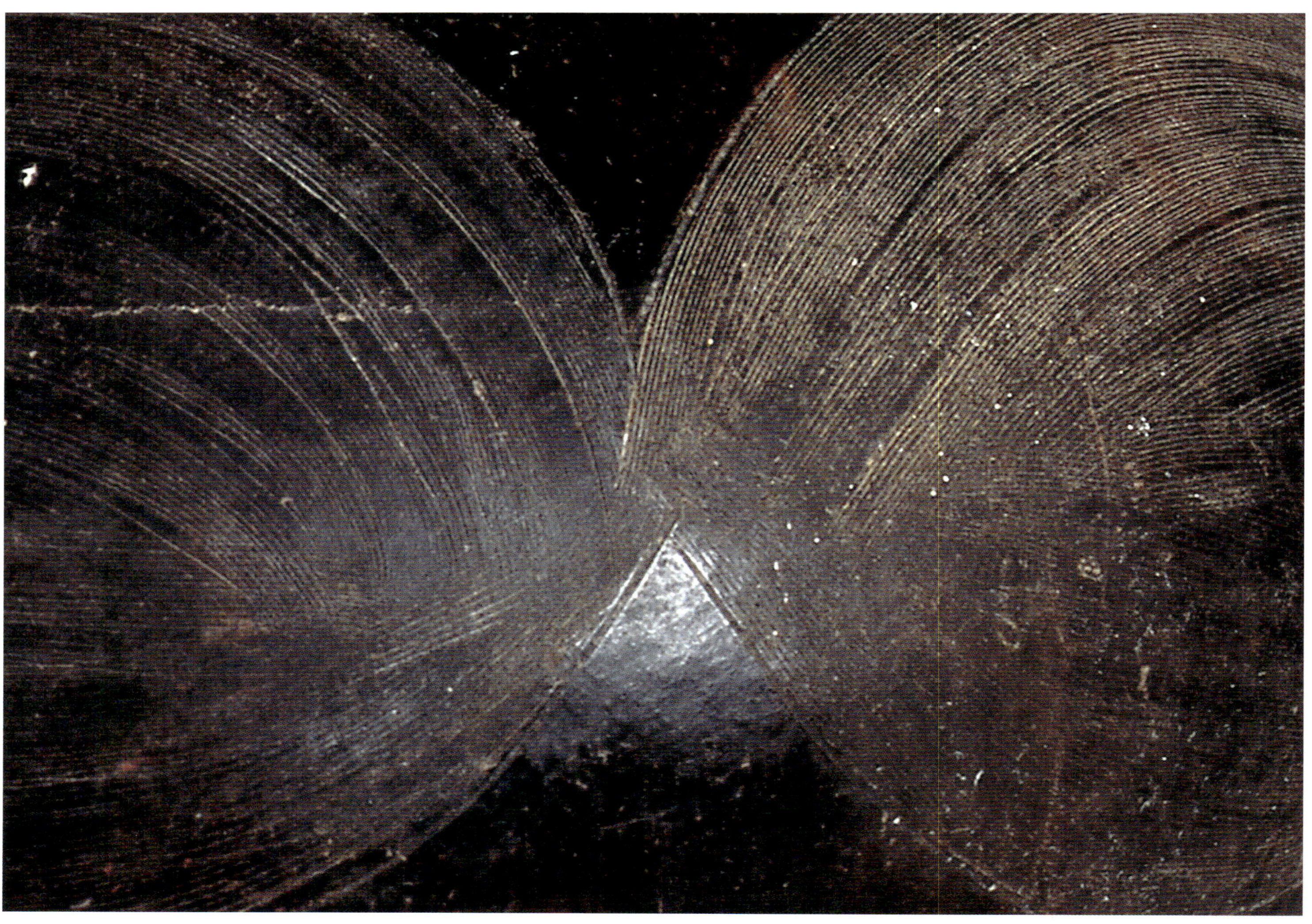

POT NUMBER 314 Ukhamba H: 355 mm Very large ukhamba with the characteristic squat form, H:D: 1:1:58. Opposing waves filled in with combed incisions. Symmetries as for 313, p. 106.

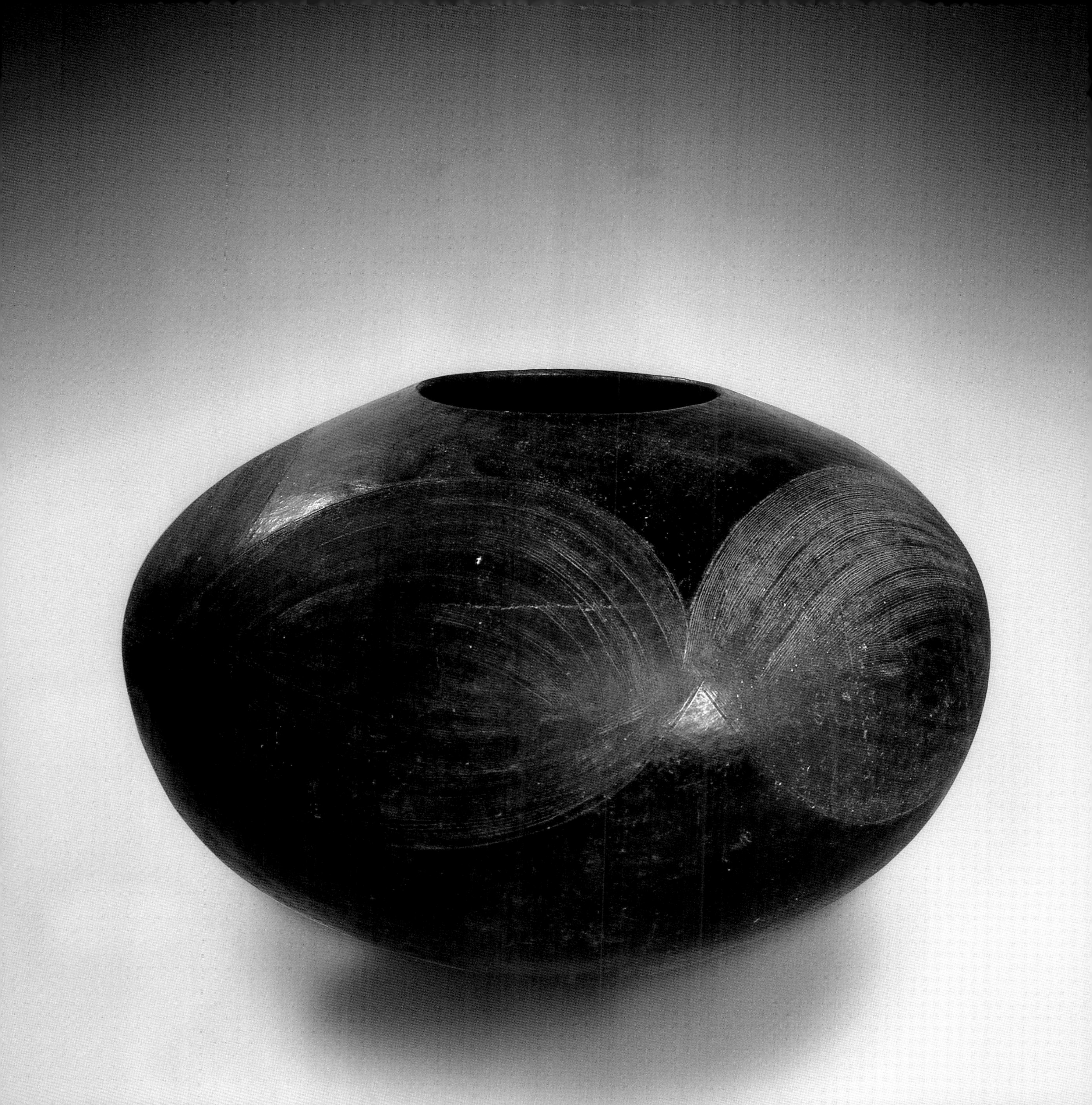

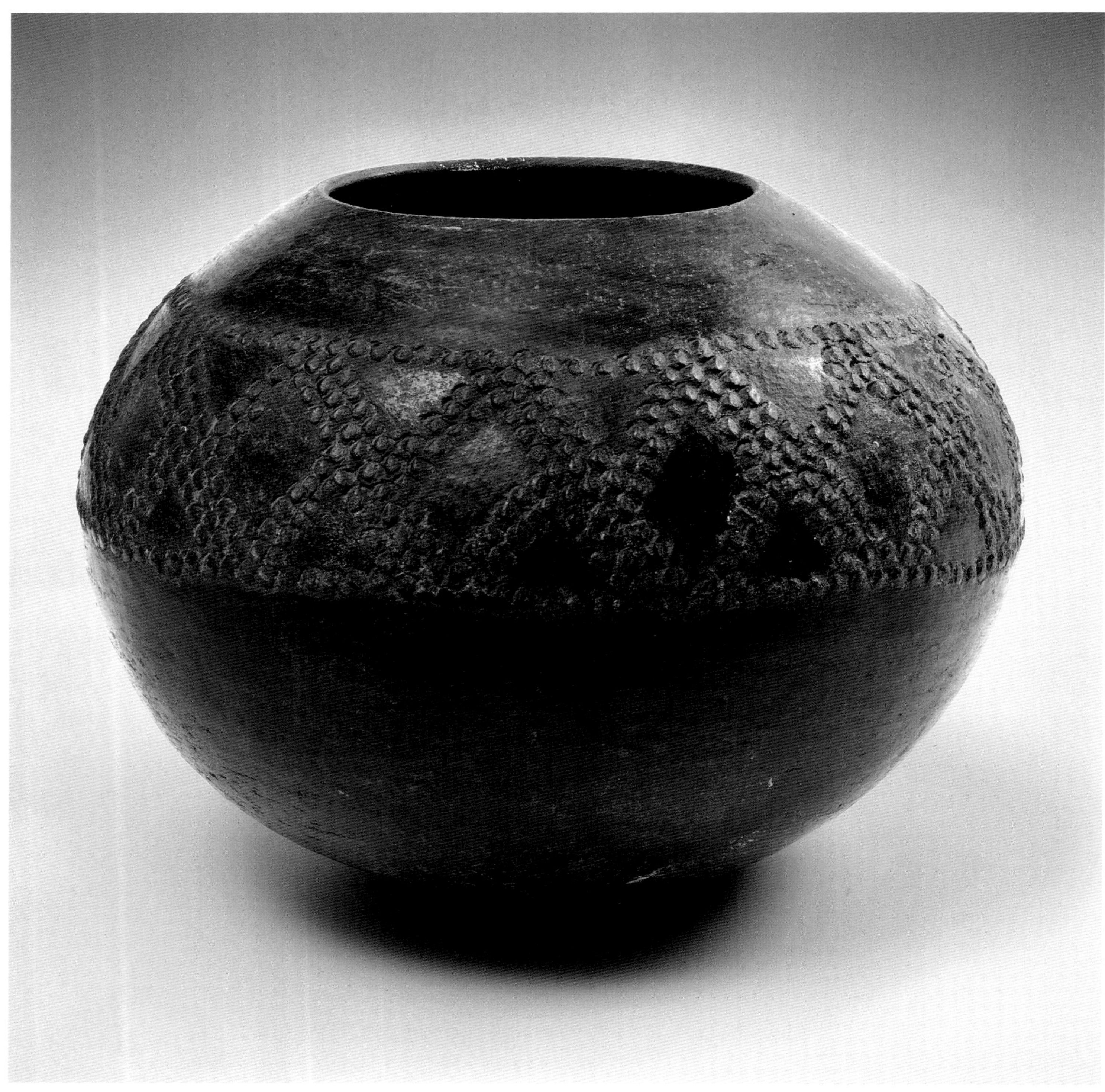

POT NUMBER 306 Umkhamba H: 215 mm Mona Market ware (but not bought on Mona Market) with rather crude *amasumpa*. Double zigzag pattern enclosed in containing lines as in some of the beadwork from this area.

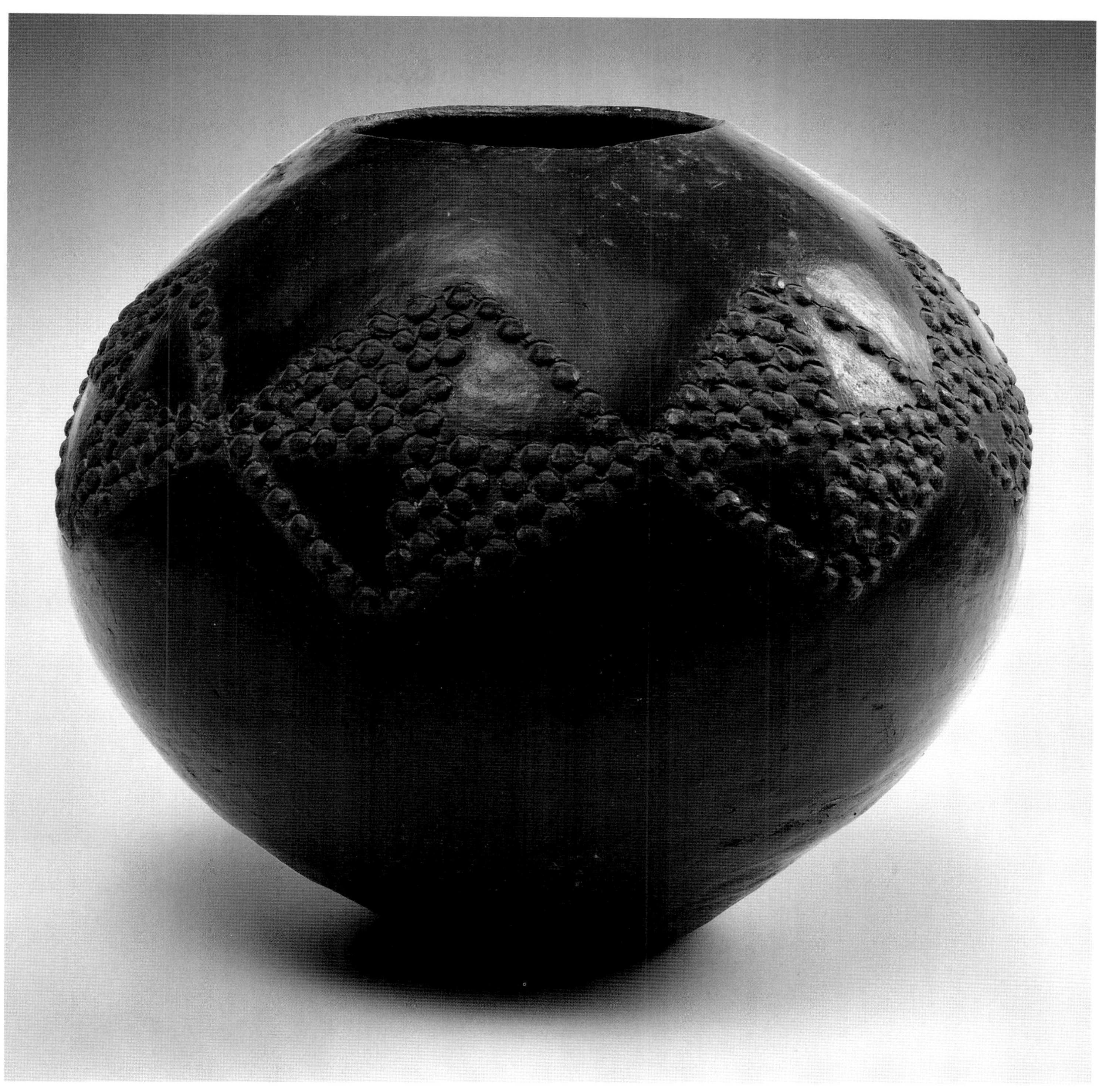

POT NUMBER 307 Ukhamba H: 268 mm Characteristic of Mona Market ware (see 306). Superimposed double
zigzag pattern; the symmetry is translation and rotation through 180 degrees.

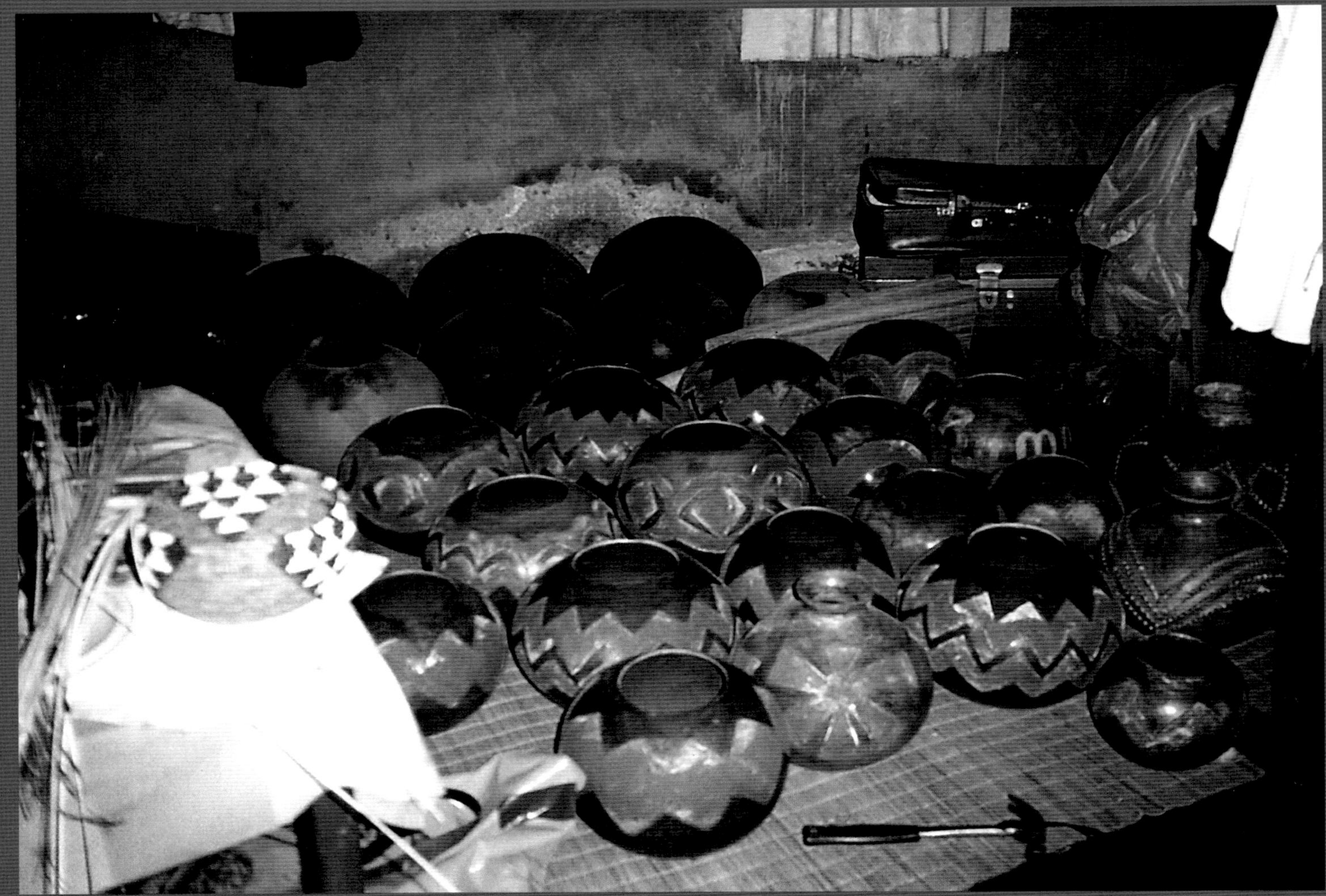

New pots, at Umgangatho, Hlabisa, c.1999.

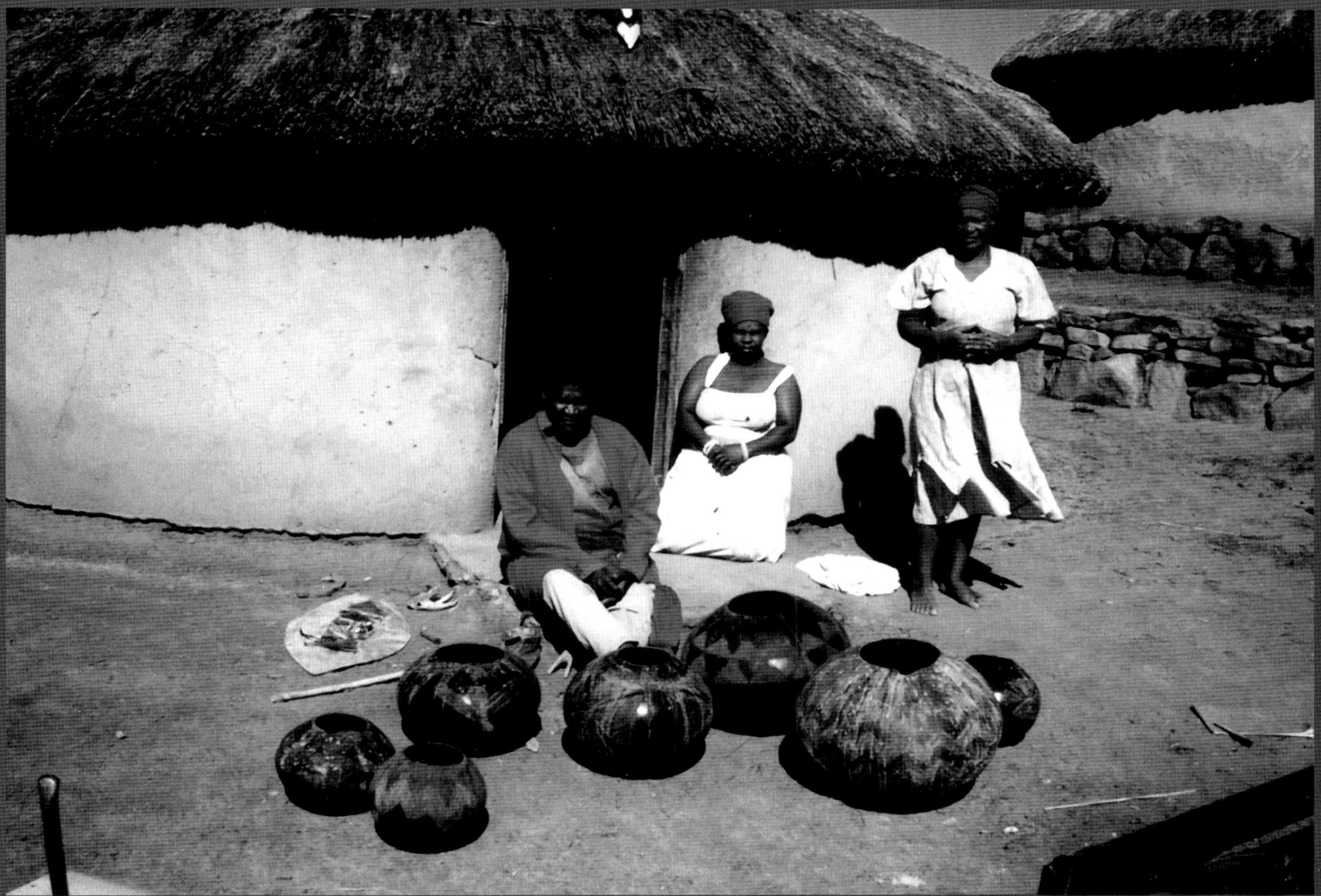

The potter Busisiwe Ngobese and her husband at their home in the hills above the northern bank of the lower Mona River.

Hlabisa Style 1

Zigzags and their derivatives Examples: Pot 303 page 92, Pot 301 page 94.
The characteristic Hlabisa pattern seems to be the zigzag (*imfolozi*, plural *izimfolozi*, *foloza*: 'make chevron or zigzag pattern as on pots'). It occurs widely on beadwork, ceramics and the famous basketry of the region. In the selection of beer vessels illustrated here, it figures as a dominant motif in Pot 302 page 95, Pot 304 page 96 and Pot 305 page 97 and in a number of variations: parallel bands (Pot 301 page 94, Pot 302 page 95), inverted bands (Pot 304 page 96, Pot 303 page 92), bands making use of incisions or roughening to highlight triangles (Pot 305 page 97), diamonds and a combination of both (Pot 306 page 88, Pot 307 page 89). It occurs both in incised patterns and those formed from *amasumpa*.

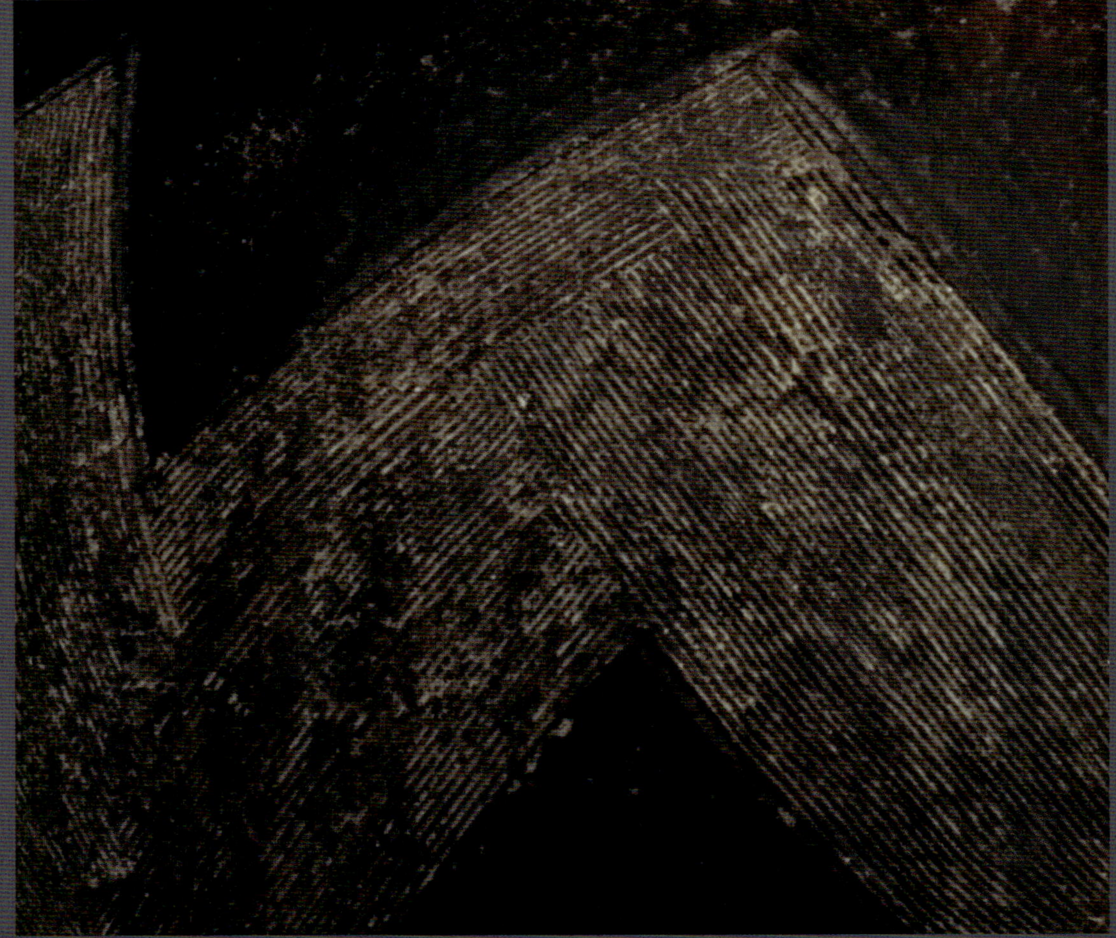

POT NUMBER 303 Ukhamba, H: 268 mm Squat form with two parallel rows of zigzags with space between them incised. In terms of plane pattern symmetry this is an example of 'glide reflection'.

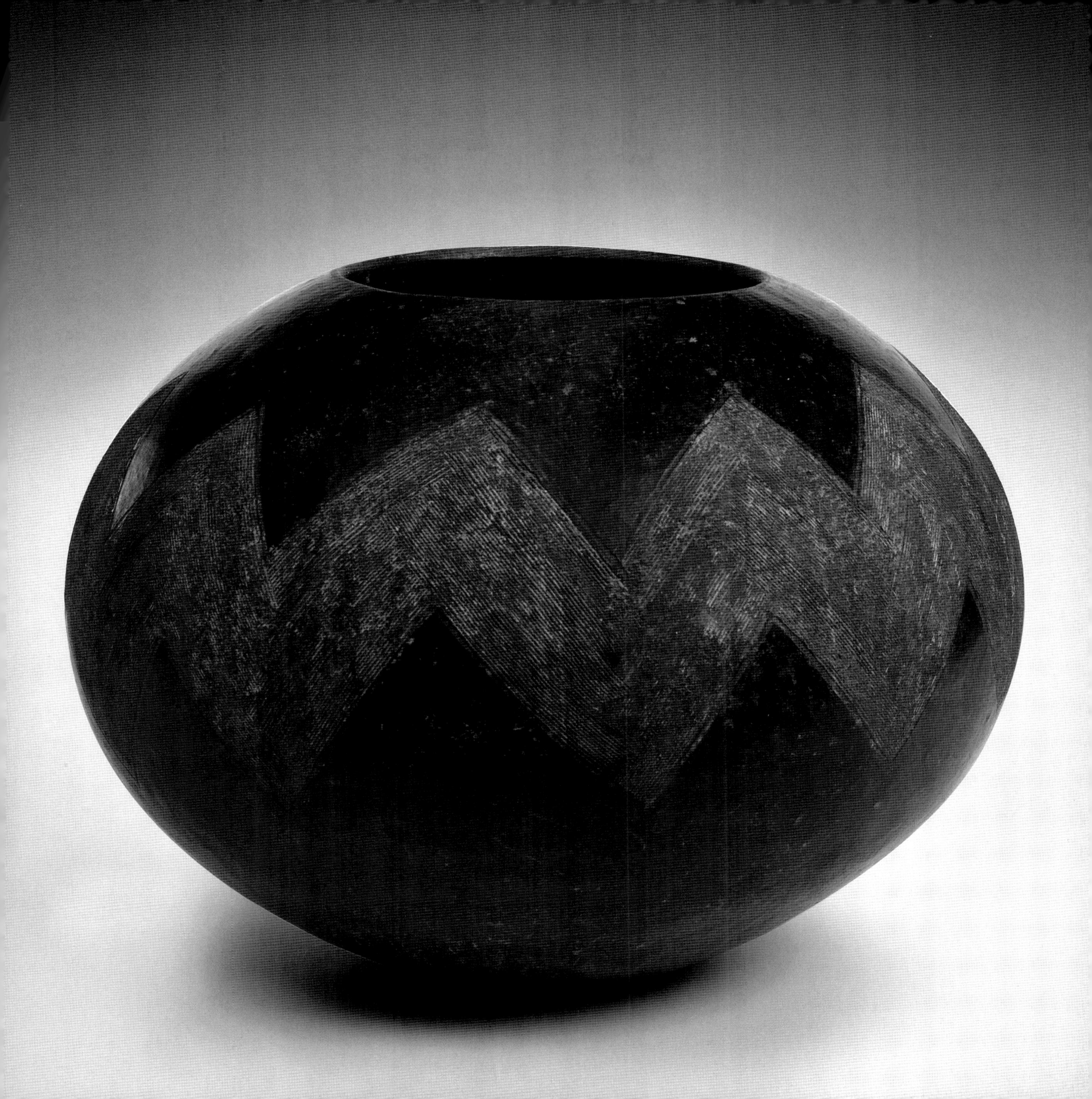

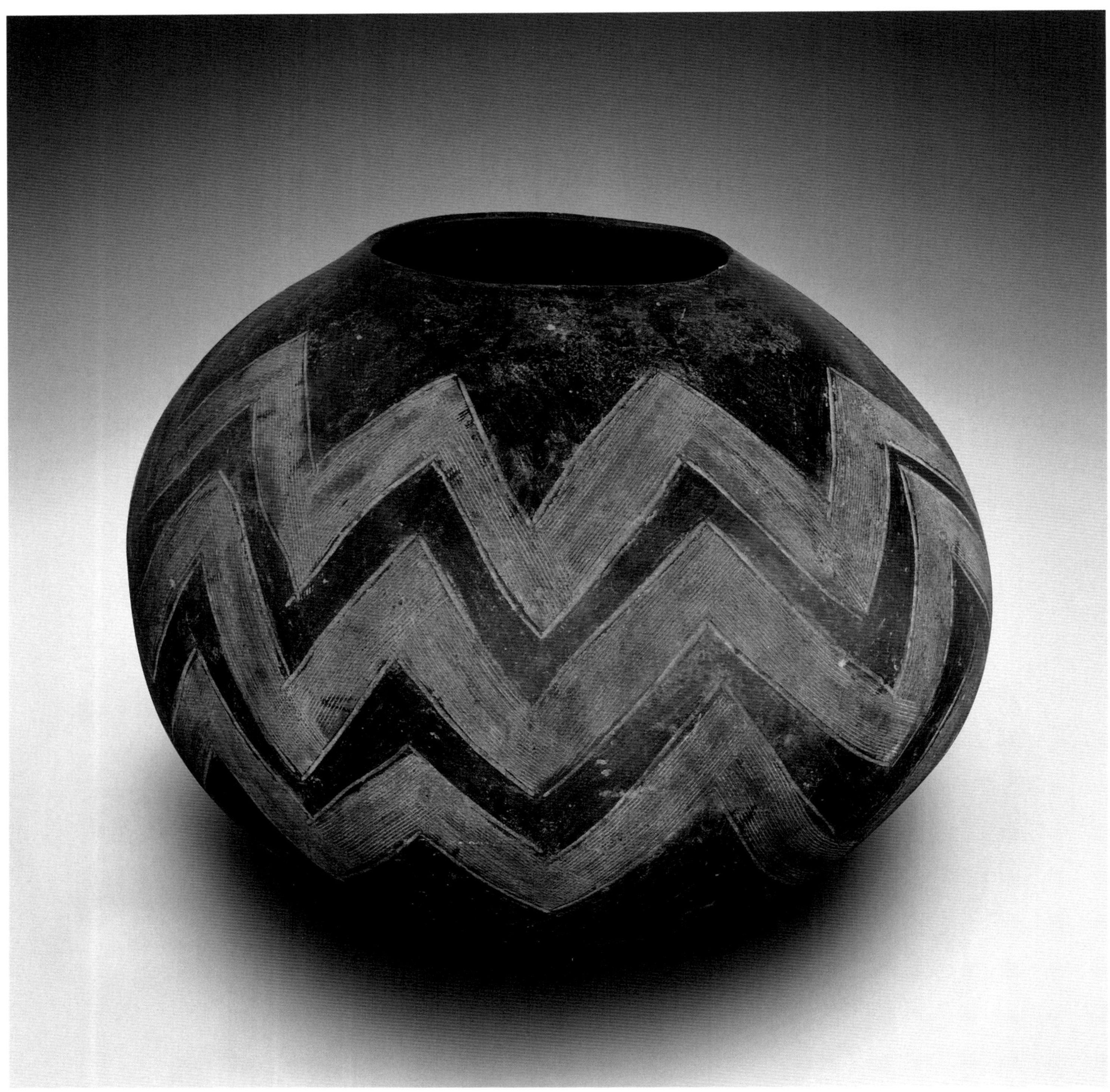

POT NUMBER 301 Ukhamba H: 390 mm Squat form with three rows of parallel incised zigzags. The zigzags and their derivatives are the most widely distributed motifs of the Hlabisa area. They also figure in basketry and beadwork.

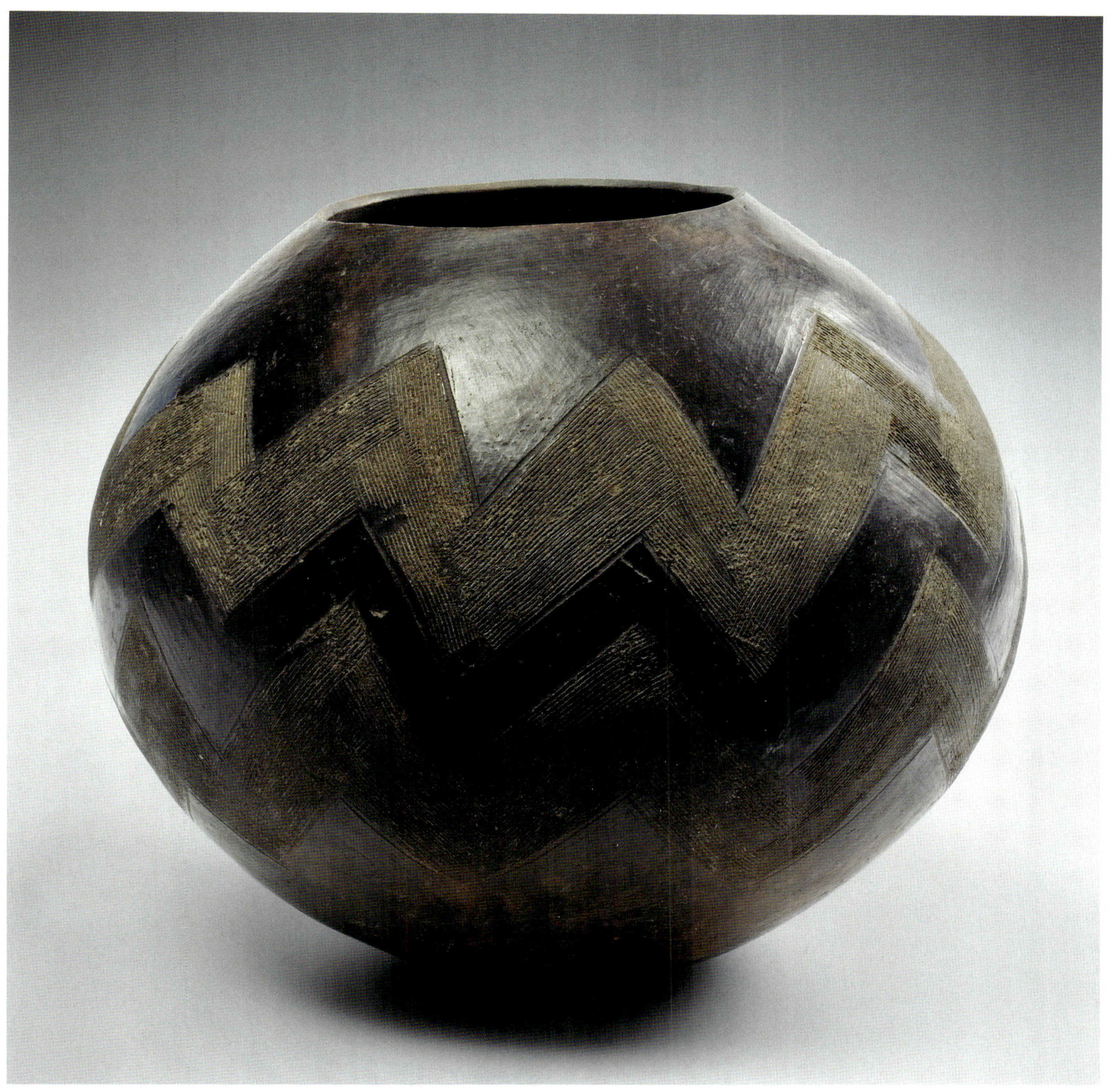

POT NUMBER 302 Ukhamba H: 270 mm Nearly spherical with two rows of parallel incised zigzags.

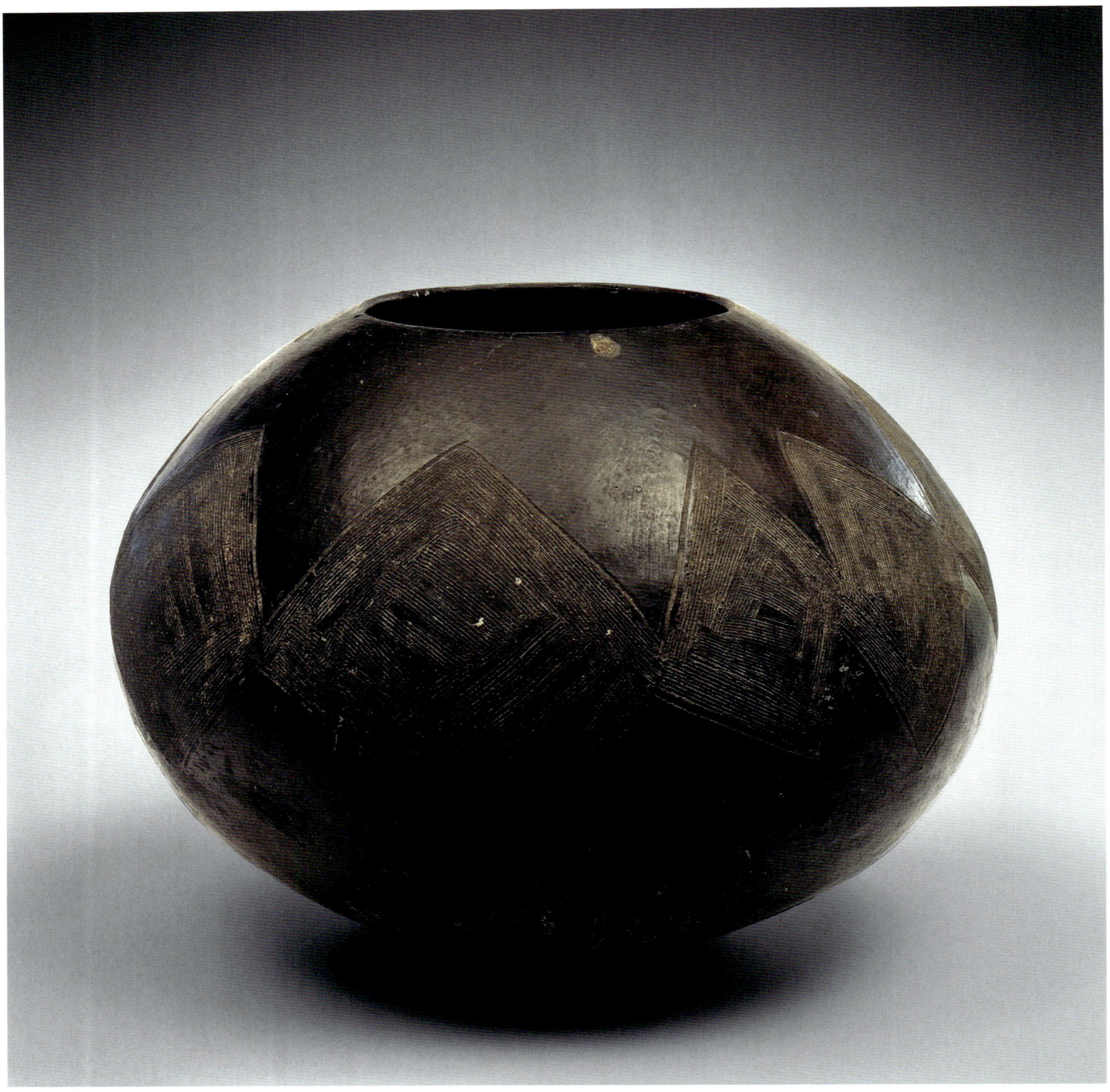

POT NUMBER 304 Ukhamba H: 310 mm Two 'opposing' zigzags (i.e. the lower one is shifted left or right by half a length), with the space between them filled with incisions.
In terms of plane pattern symmetry this is an example of reflection across a horizontal axis passing through the centre of the rhomboids, as well as vertical reflection.

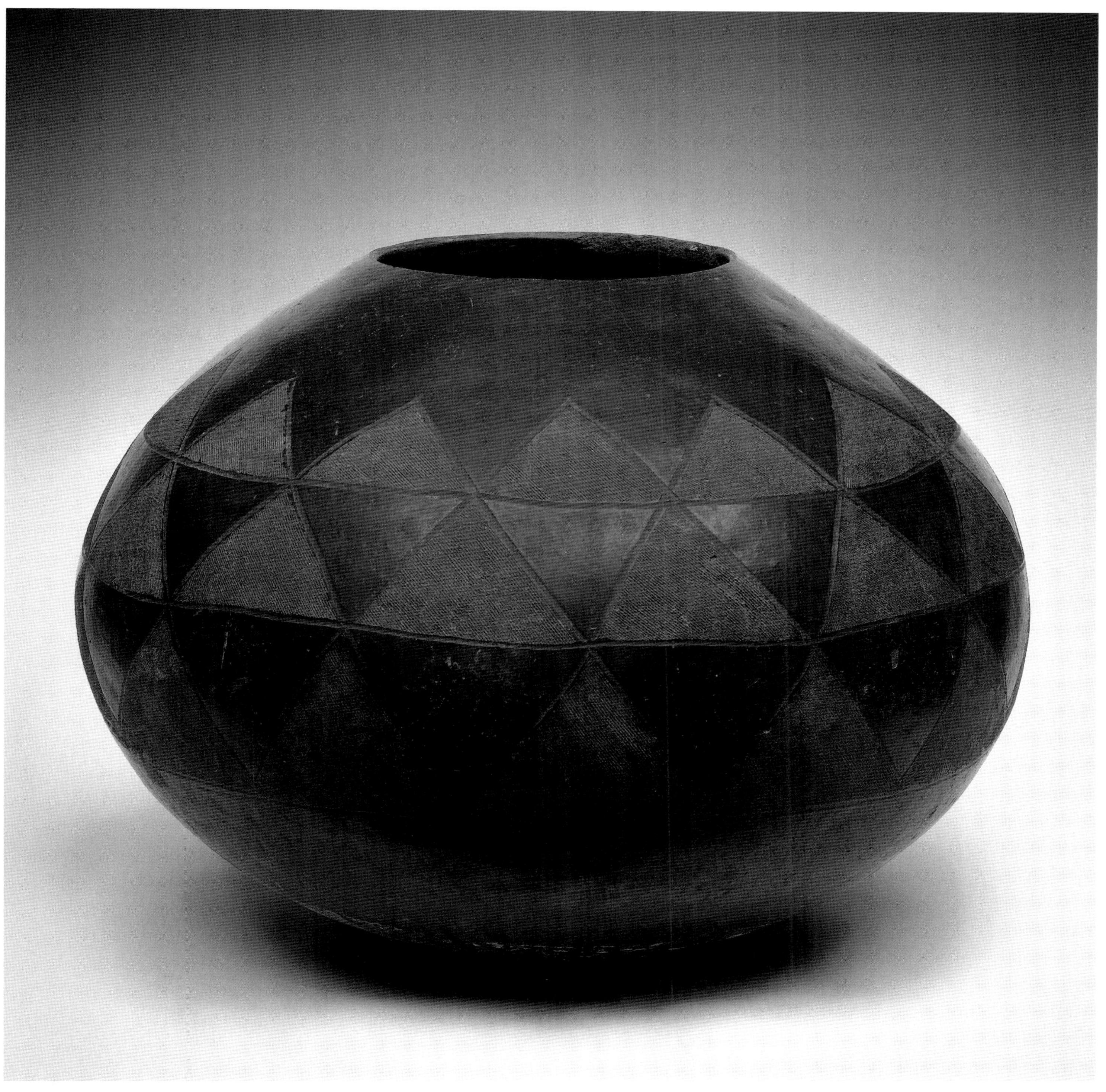

POT NUMBER 305 Ukhamba H: 374 mm The pattern is called *umcijwane* (diamond), but it also refers to playing cards, i.e. 'Diamonds'. Technically it is a two-dimensional pattern consisting of hexagons each formed from six equilateral triangles. It is characterised by reflection through vertical axes and rotation through 60° (Washburn & Crowe, 1988: 163). But it may also be regarded as a derivative of the zigzag motif.

Hlabisa Style 2

Waves and their derivatives

Examples: Pots 308–317 pages 98–109.

Wave patterns occur widely in ceramics, but less so in the media based on weaving: beadwork, basketry and grass weaving, in which it is difficult to produce curved lines. They also have a wide range of variations: parallel waves (Pot 308 page 99), intermittent waves on a base line (Pot 309 page 102), continuous waves on a base line (Pot 310 page 103), opposing waves in a number of modulations with and without a central separator (Pots 311–316 pages 104–108) and superimposed opposing waves in step translation (Pot 317 page 100). Among the opposing wave patterns there are some which are essentially identical to the Nongoma 'eye' motif (Pot 315 page 107 and Pot 316 page 108). This suggests that the incised 'eye' patterns of the Nongoma area may also be imports, and namely from the Vryheid area in the early 1940s (compare interview with Phiwayinkosi Ngobese, described above, and Pot 305 page 97). Where patterns derived from basic motifs are compared with their derivatives the degree of relationship can be expressed through the retention or displacement of the symmetries of the basic patterns. So, in principle, it should be possible to trace the chronology and distribution history of related ceramic artefacts through symmetry analysis, as in the case of beadwork.

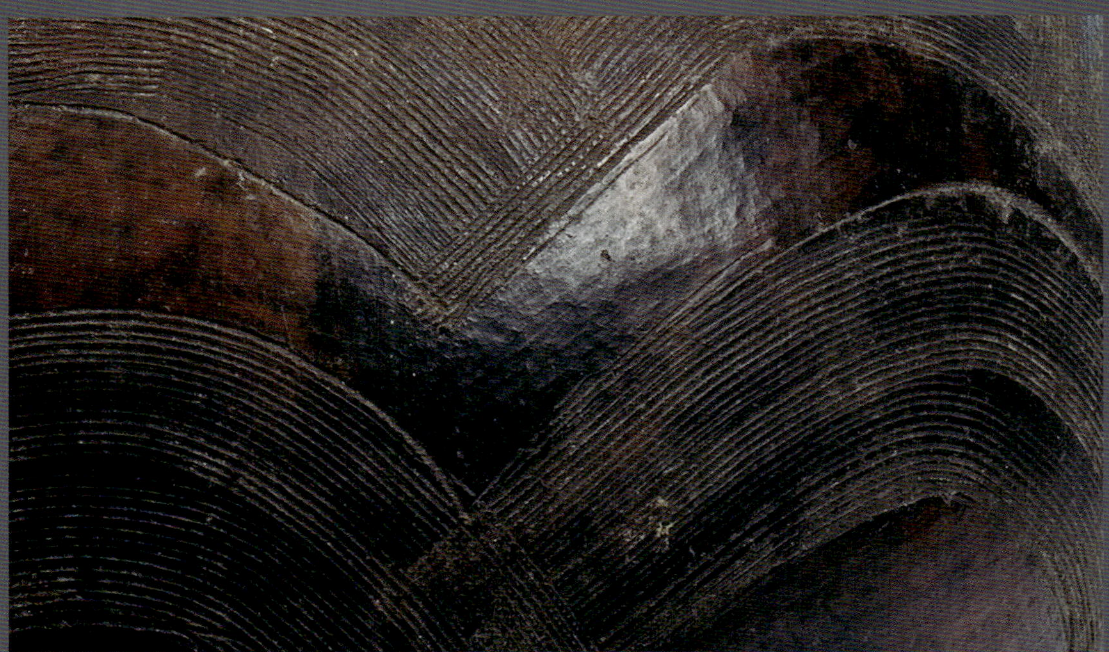

POT NUMBER 308 Ukhamba H: 273 mm
Squat Hlabisa form with double parallel
incised wave pattern.

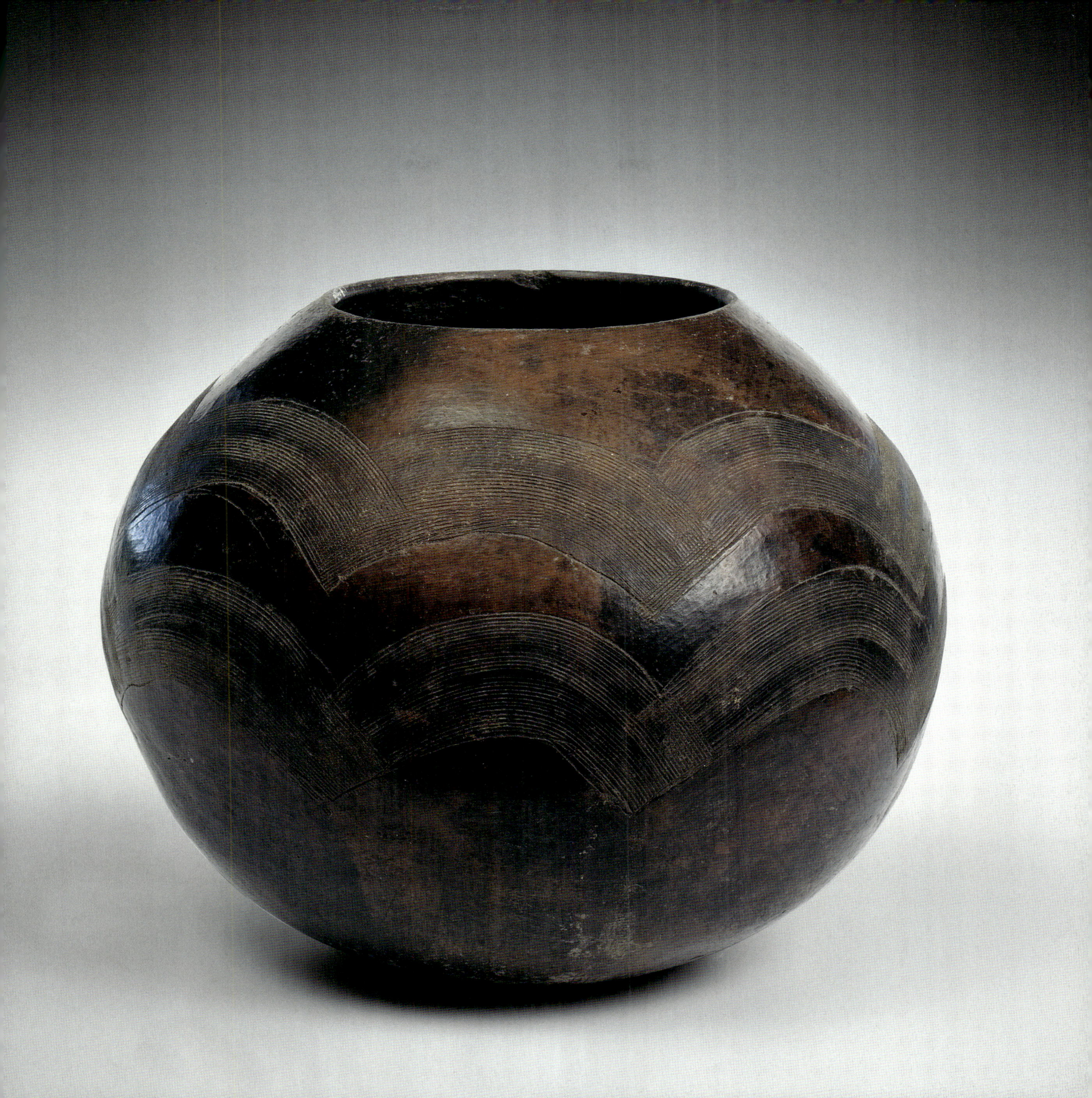

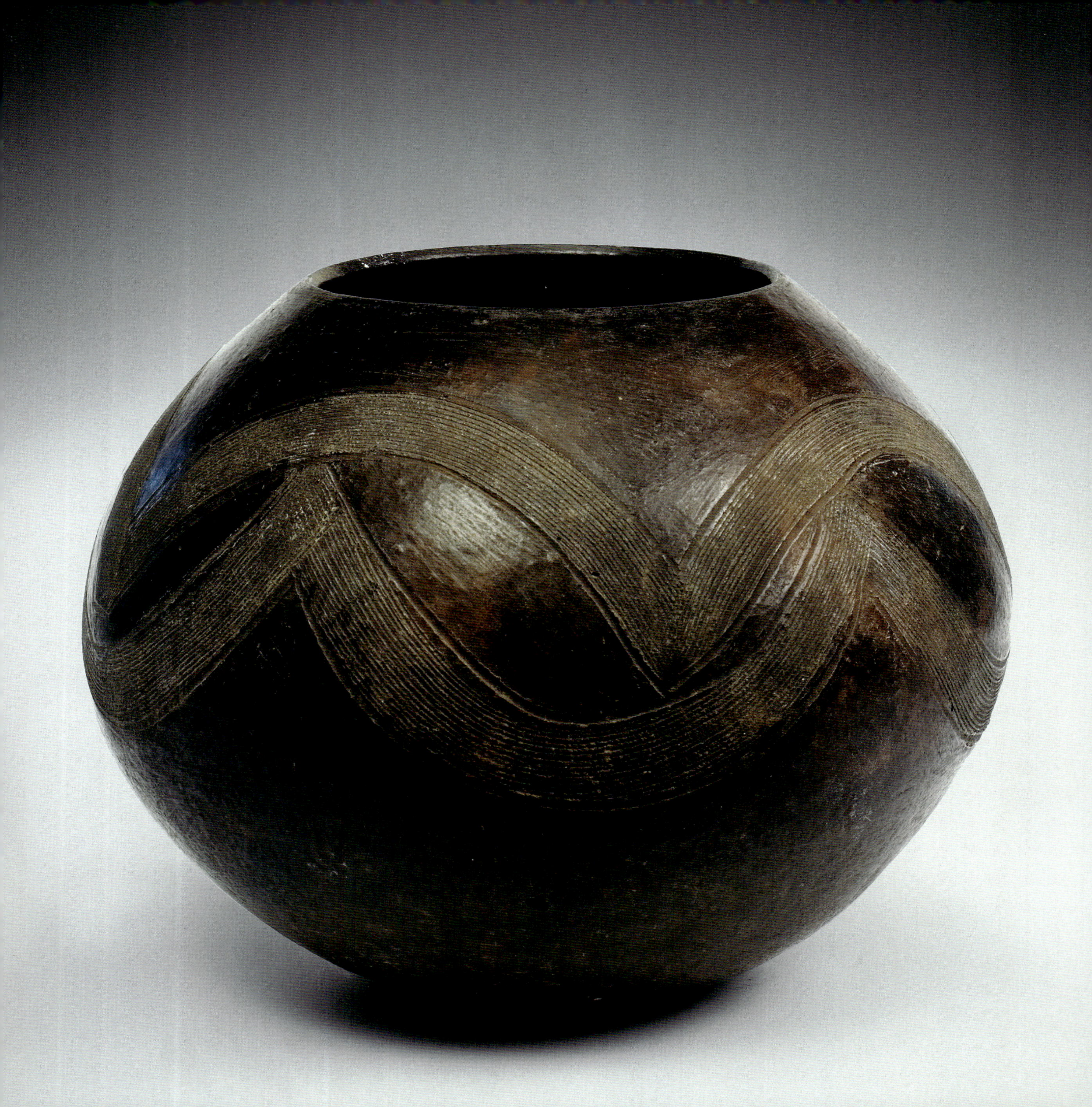

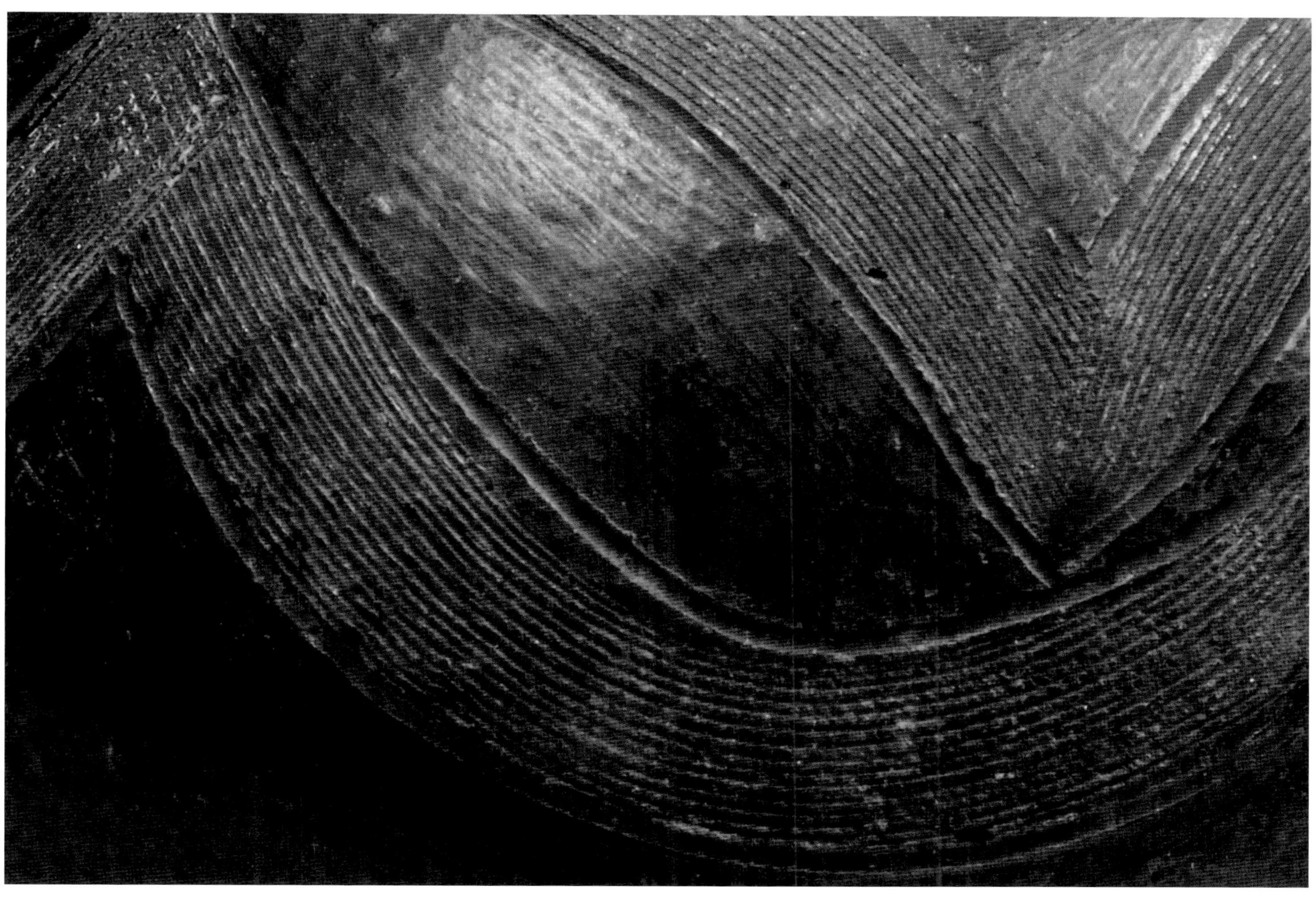

POT NUMBER 317 Ukhamba H: 239 mm Offset opposing waves: symmetries of translation, reflection through vertical axes and glide reflection.

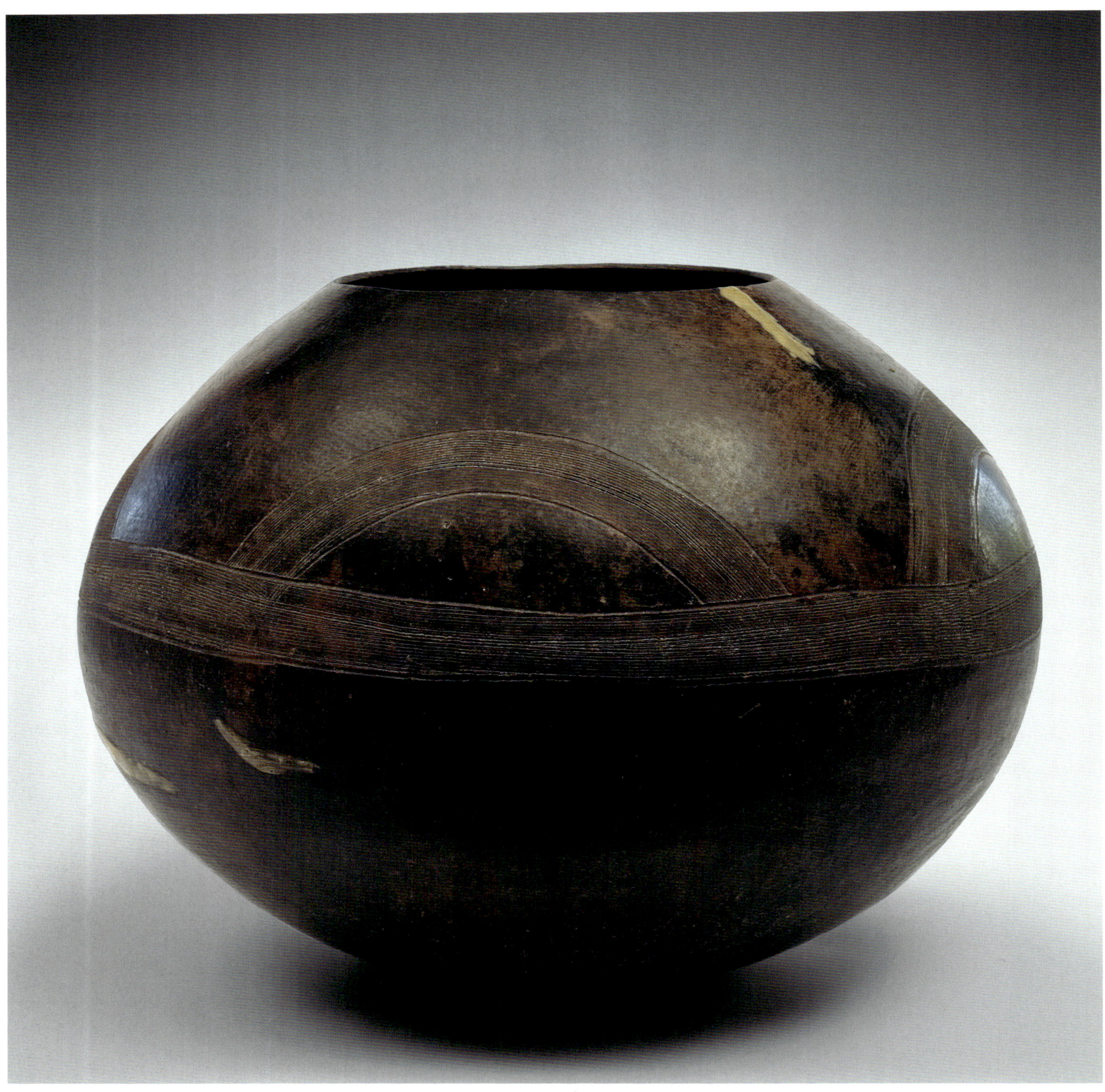

POT NUMBER 309 Ukhamba H: 300 mm Characteristic squat form, variations on single wave pattern.

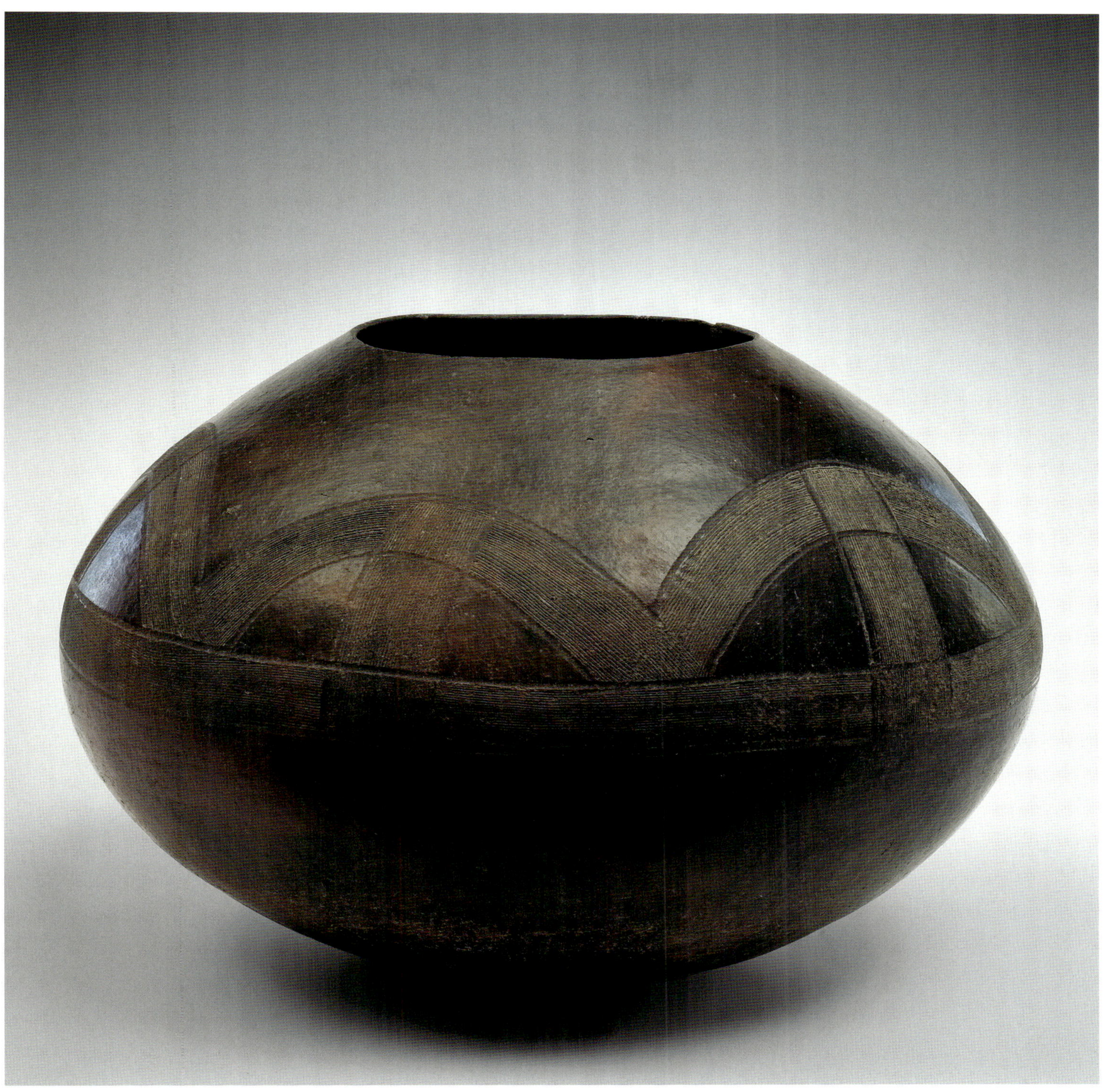

POT NUMBER 310 Ukhamba H: 287 mm Characteristic squat form, variations on single wave pattern.

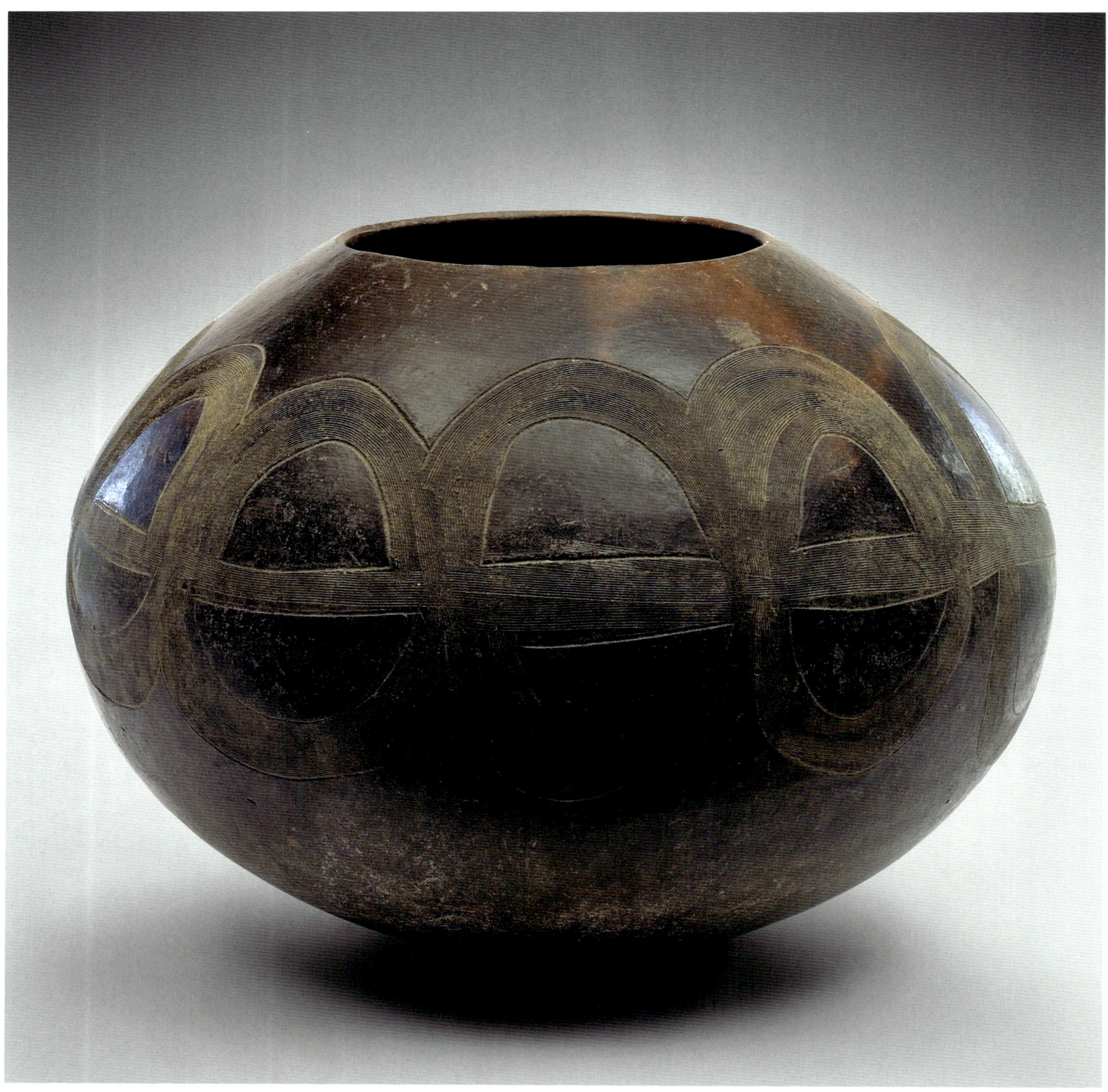

POT NUMBER 311 Ukhamba H: 310 mm Double wave pattern displaying symmetries of translation, vertical and horizontal reflection and rotation through 180°.

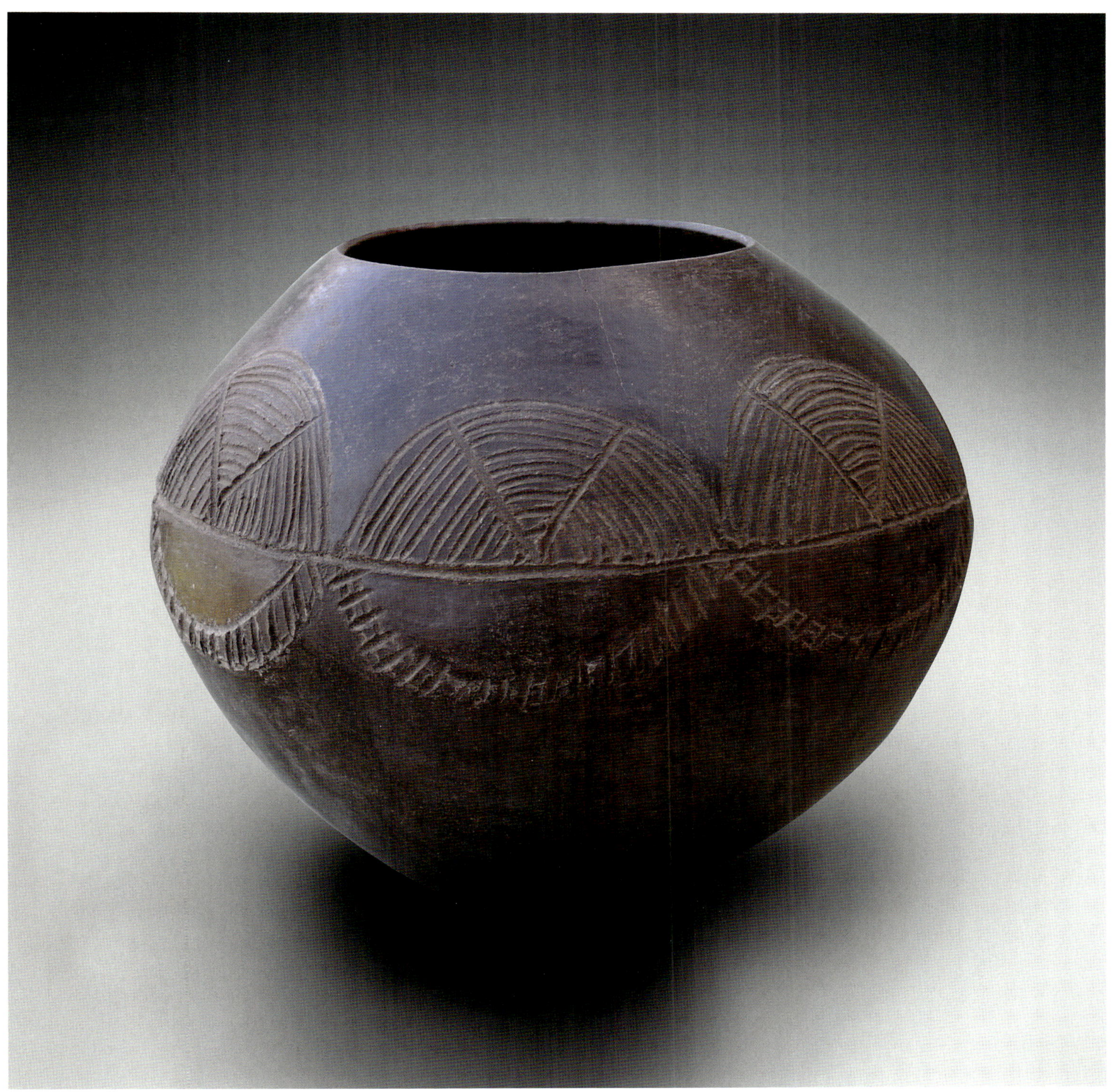

POT NUMBER 312 Ukhamba H: 356 mm The pattern is copied from her mother; it is called *inyanga* (the moon). The symmetries are much reduced compared with the very similar pot by Khunjuliliwe Xulu (311); they are translation and vertical reflection.

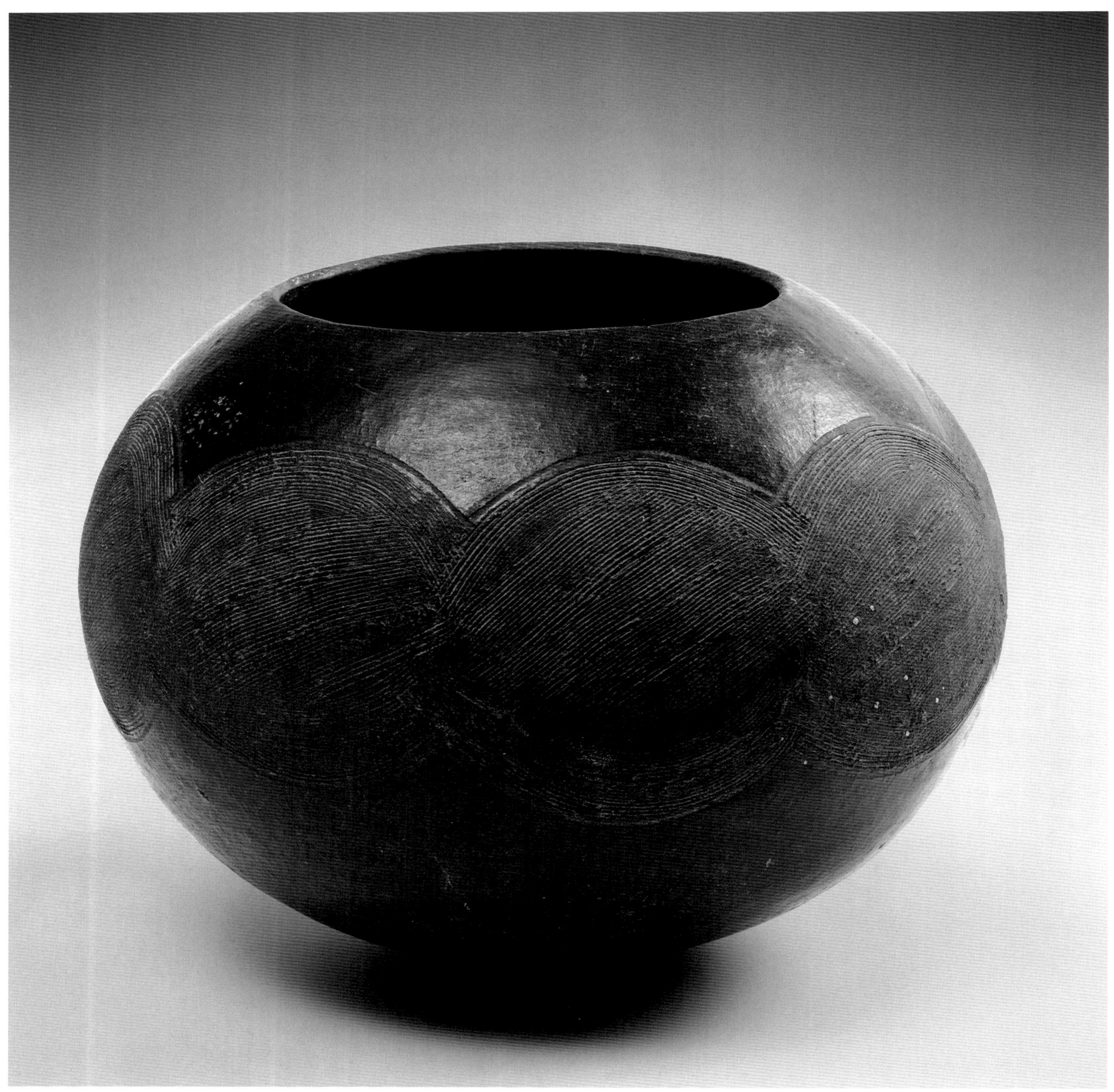

POT NUMBER 313 Ukhamba H: 180 mm Opposing waves with incisions (combed area) between. Symmetries: translation, reflection through vertical and horizontal axes, rotation through 180°.

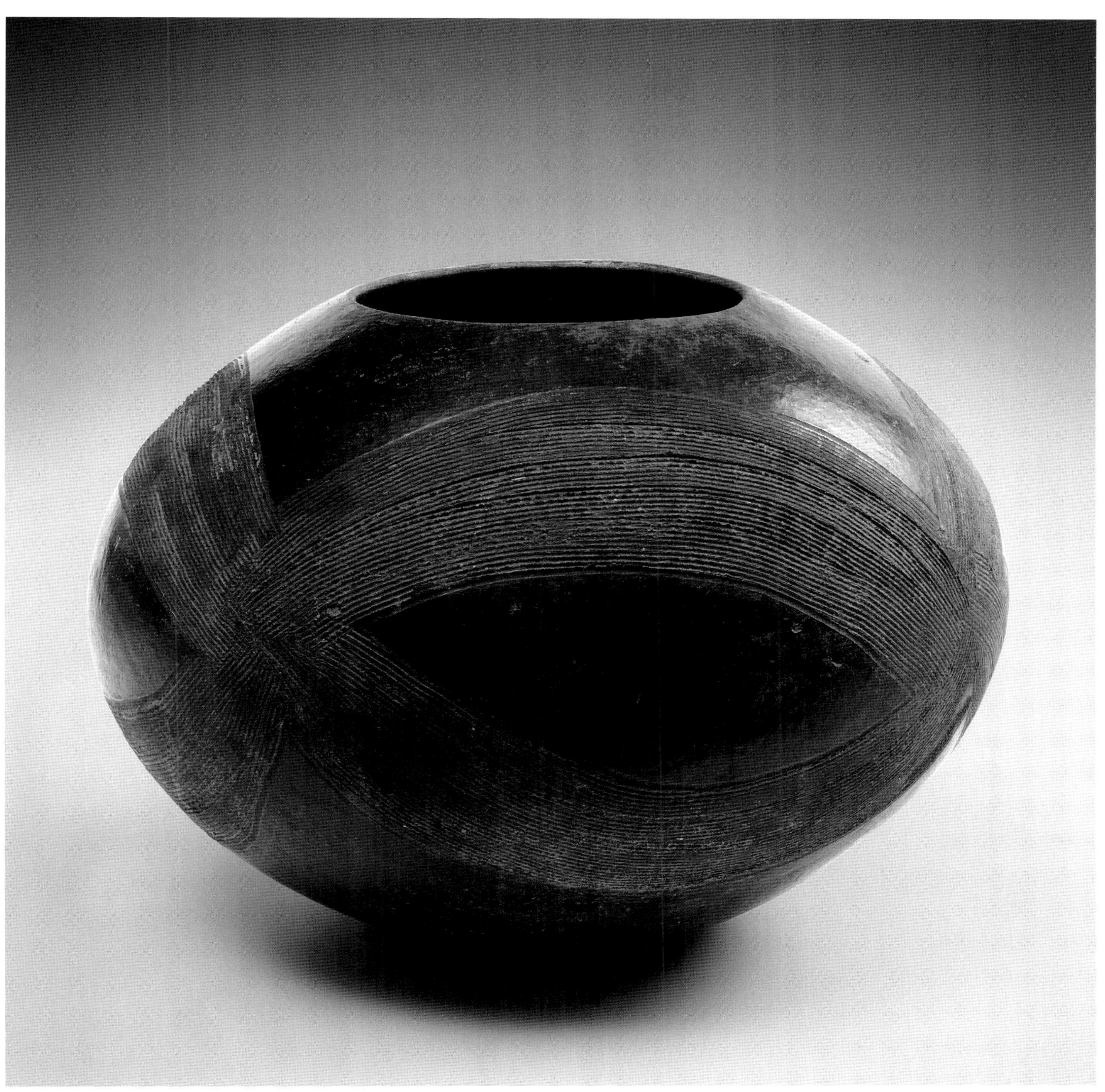

POT NUMBER 315 Ukhamba H: 247 mm Opposing waves making an 'eye pattern'. Symmetries as for 313.

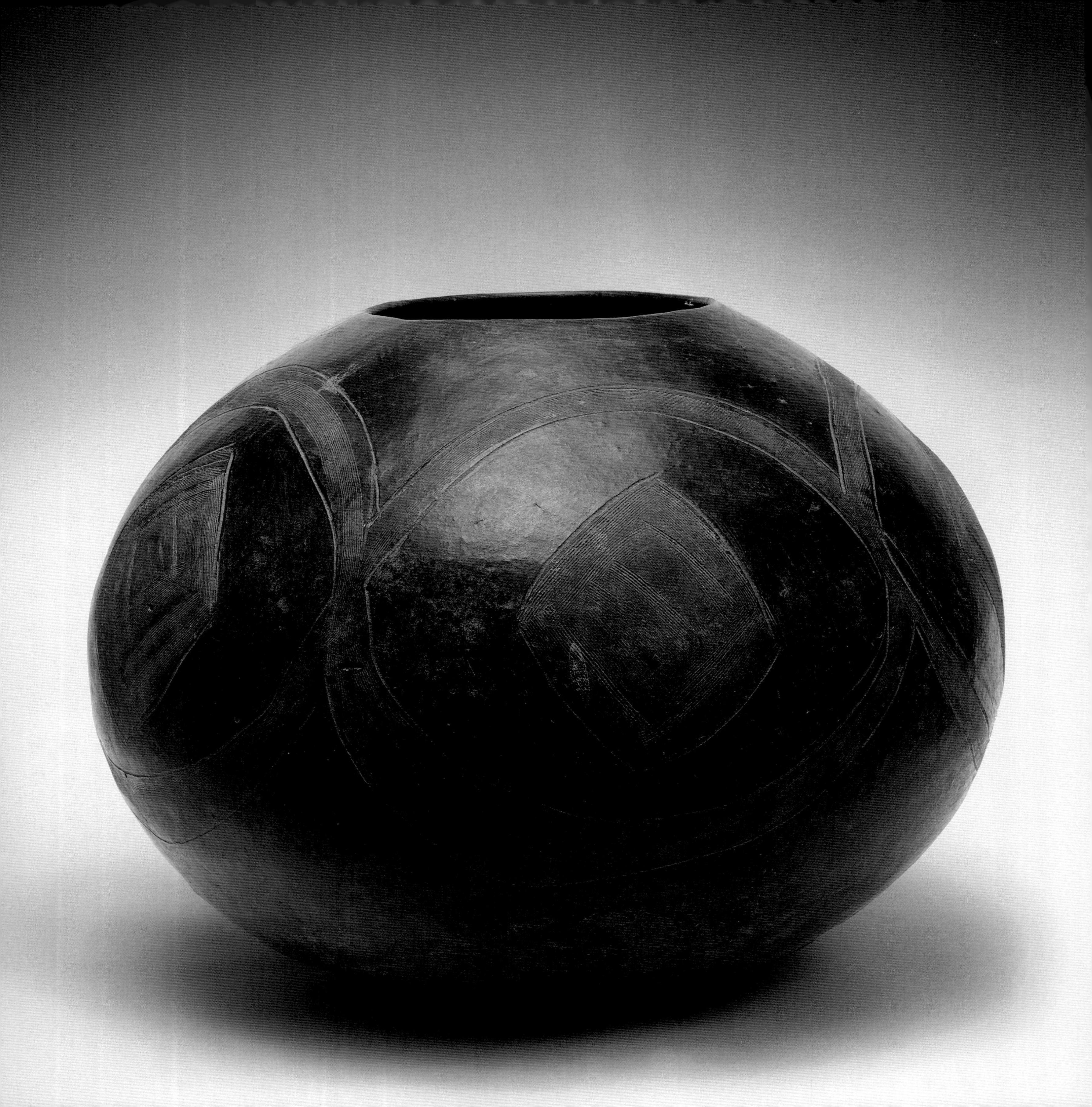

In an interview on 11 March 2000 Phiwayinkosi's daughter Thangithile (born 1946) from Umgangatho, Hlabisa told me how she started making pots when she was ten years old. The family did not come from this area [Hlabisa] but from Ntabankhulu near Vryheid. She learnt making pots from her mother. They fetched the clay from a long way away, from a mountain, Amaphophoma near Mona Market. Some of the designs she made were from her mother, some were her own. She never made pots with *amasumpa*. She started by making 'bag'-shaped pots. Later she turned to making the flat shape. This is very difficult to make. 'You have to build it up little by little, leaving it to harden and then continuing.' She also sketched a number of patterns her mother used compared with her own. It is clear from her drawings that whilst she modified or changed the individual motifs she retained the basic symmetries her mother used: translation with reflection across two vertical axes + reflection across a horizontal axis. This confirms the finding for beadwork patterns that whilst colours and motifs are subject to fashion the underlying symmetries remain constant over considerable periods of time. The diagram opposite is taken from Thangithile's sketches.

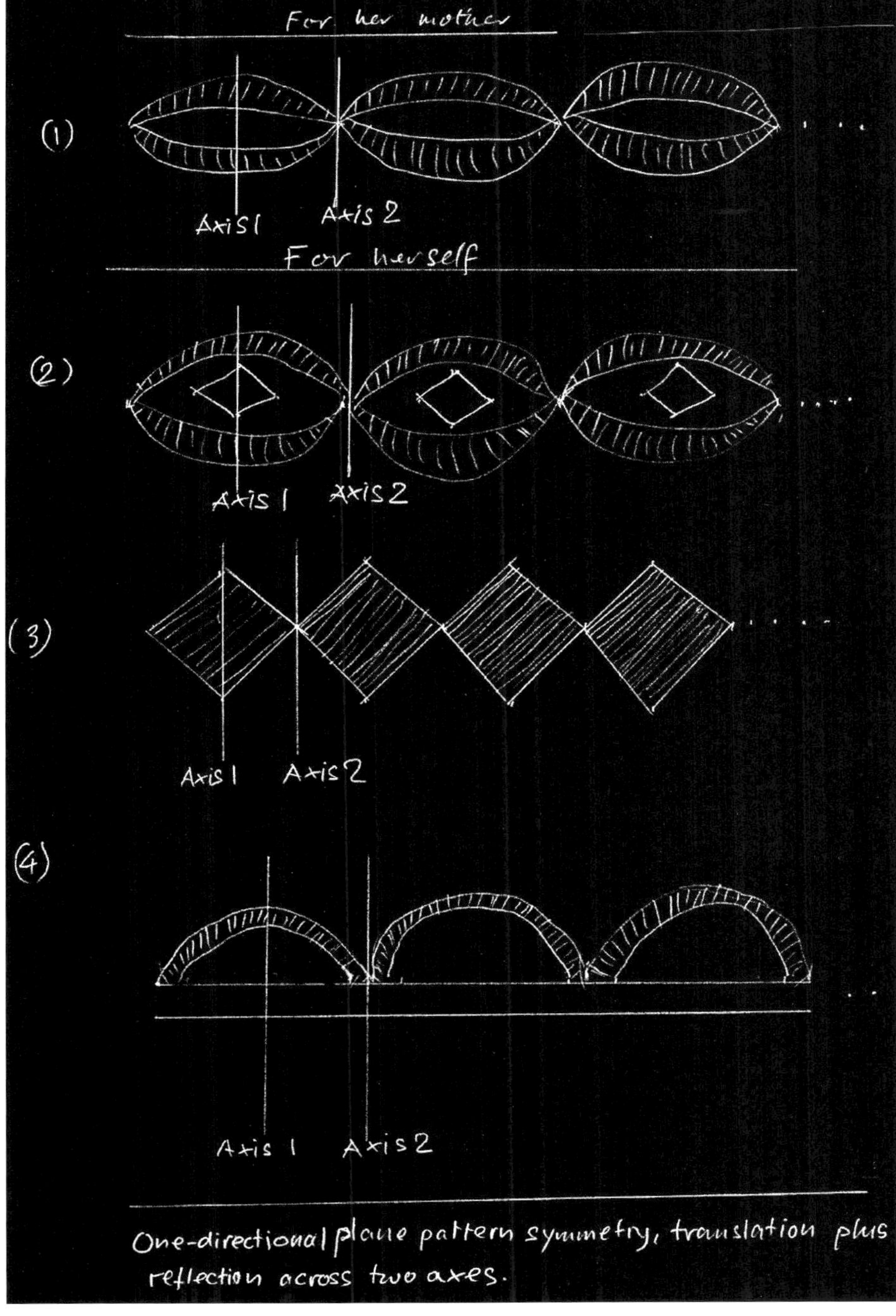

POT NUMBER 316 Ukhamba H: 375 mm
Combination of wave pattern and diamond pattern. The original symmetries are retained.

Hlabisa Style 3

Motifs derived from playing cards
Examples: Pots 318–321 pages 110–115.

The motifs derived from playing cards seem to be specific to the Hlabisa region and are probably the inspiration of a particular family of potters. They go back to the 1950s or earlier, so their origin is lost in the mists of time. This type of decoration is fundamentally different from the two previous ones in that it is based on a number of stand-alone motifs rather than a continuous band. In that regard it is similar to the many patterns based on separate panels of modified surface found in Nongoma, Phongolo and elsewhere, as well as in Hlabisa.

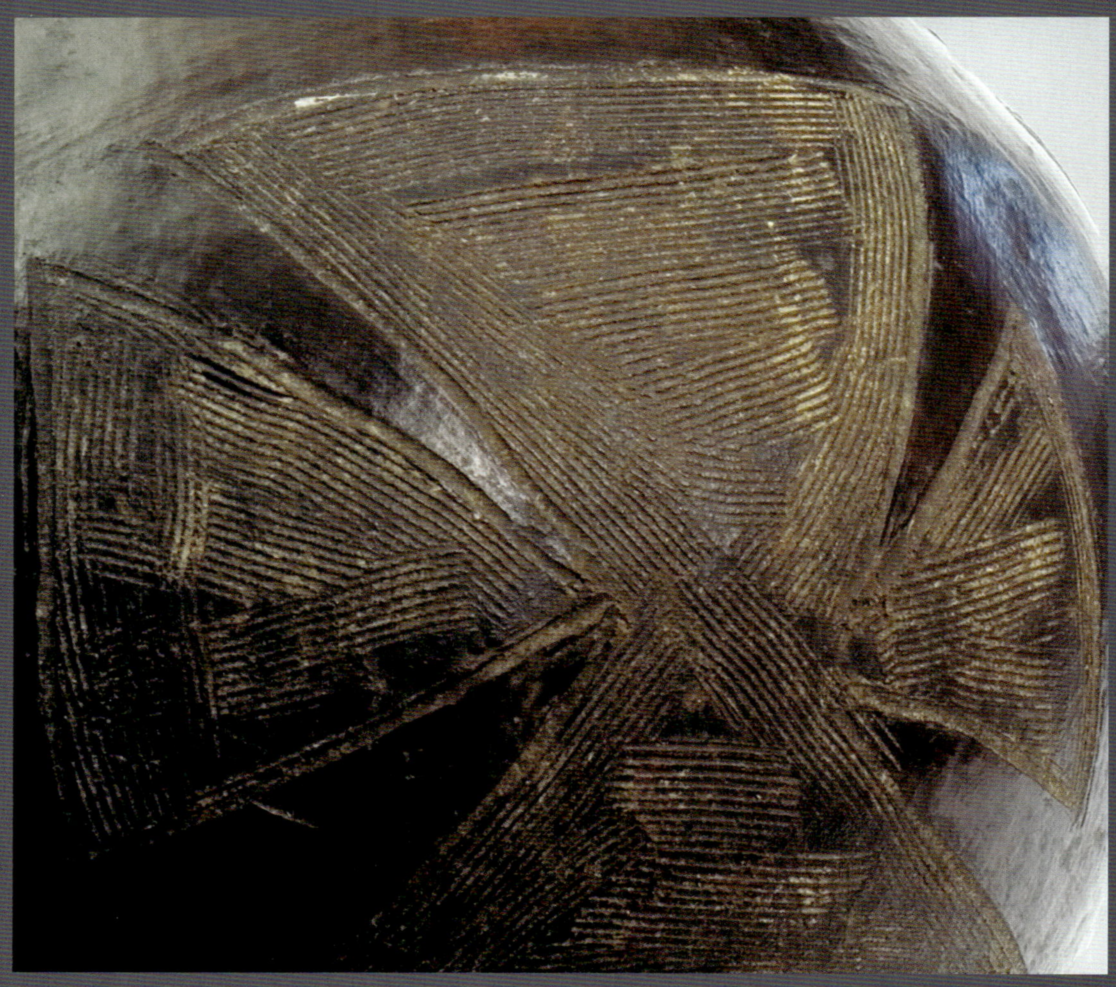

POT NUMBER 320 Ukhamba H: 236 mm
The motif is *ugqebhe* (Spades). Doke et al (1990) for *ugqebhe*, give 'heart-shaped pattern on pottery', and 'playing-card with red heart on it'. Spades is given as *igeja*. So there is some confusion here.

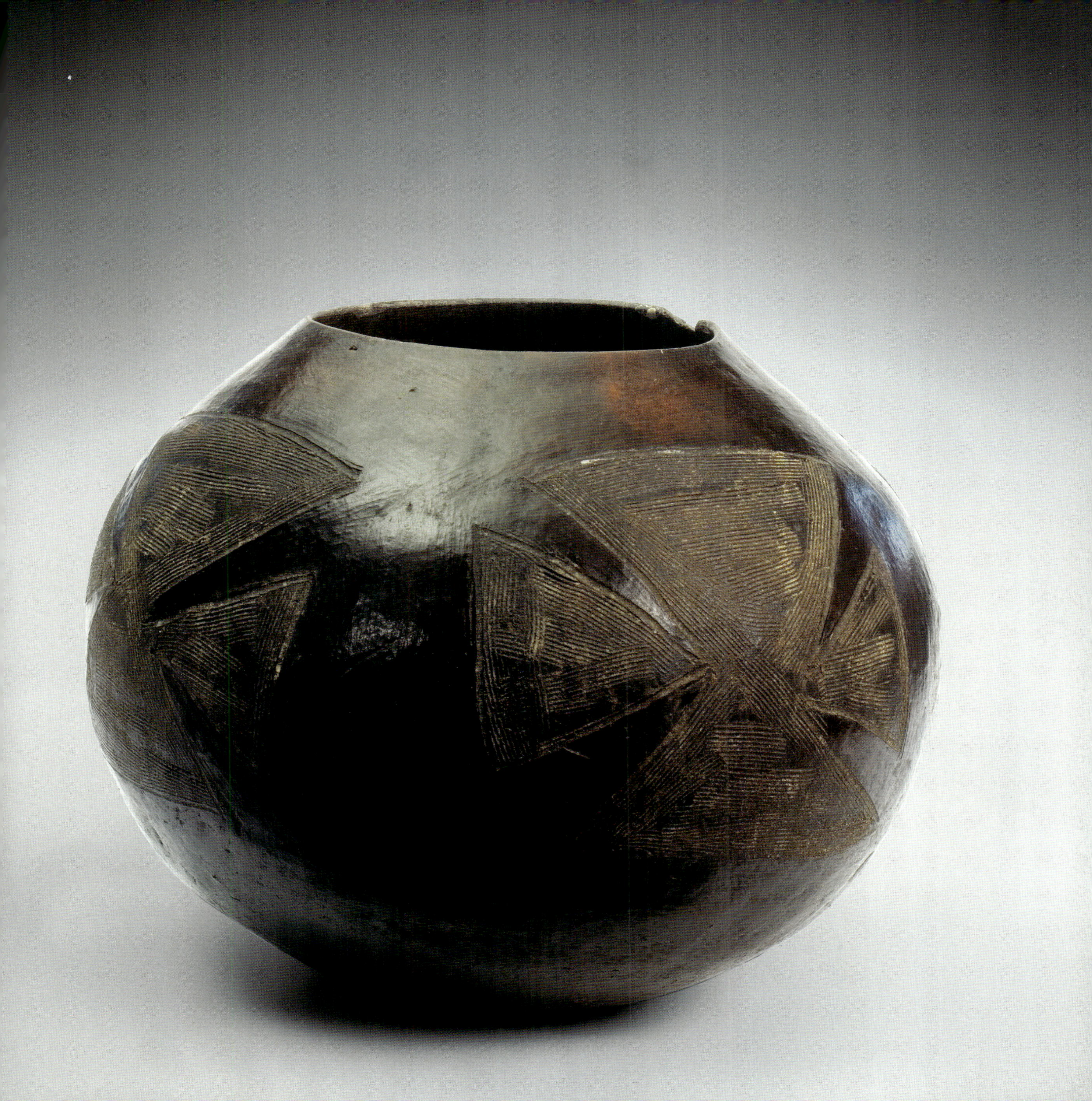

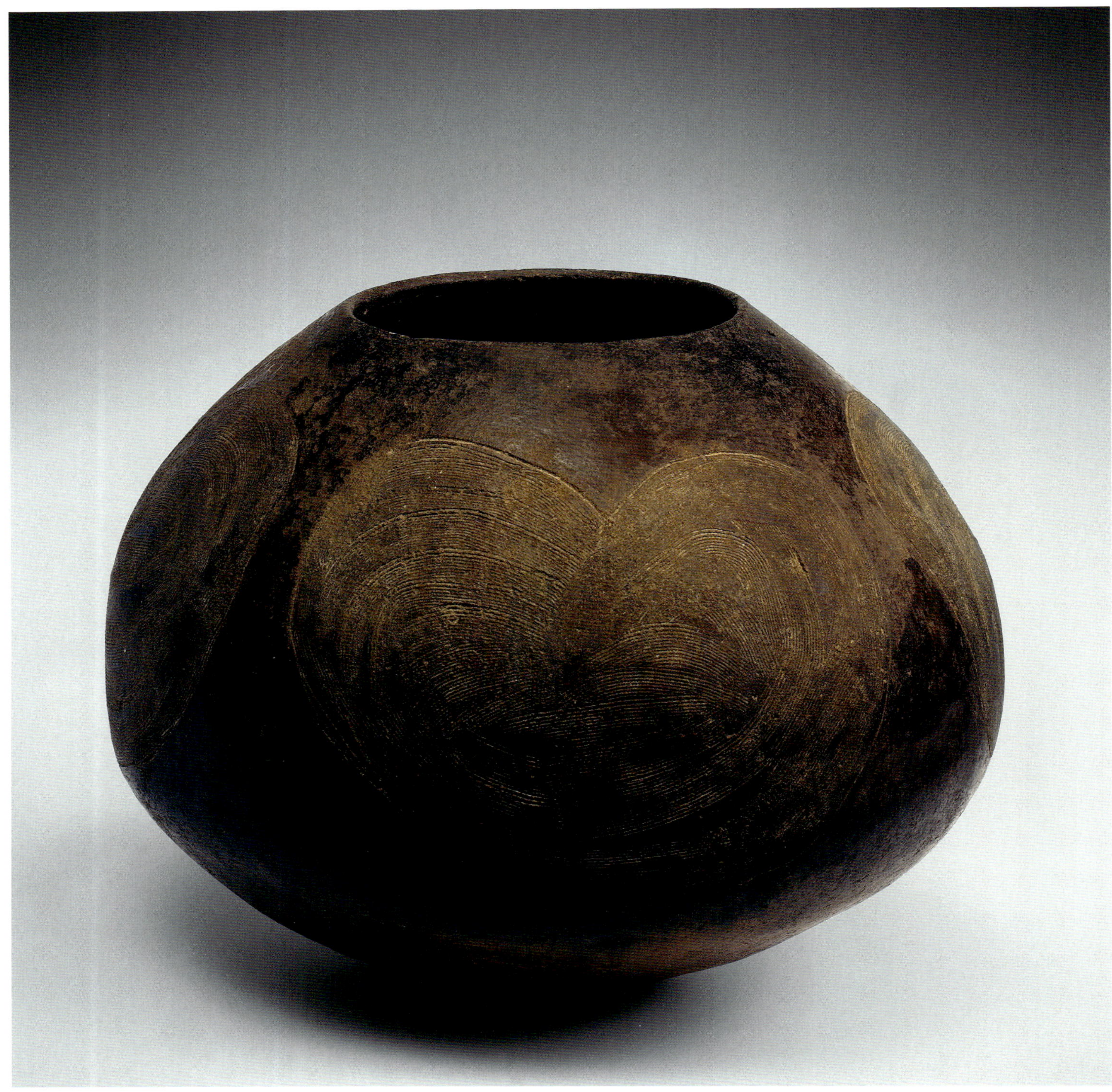

POT NUMBER 318 Ukhamba H: 294 mm Motif from playing cards, 'Hearts'. Very early pot of this type.

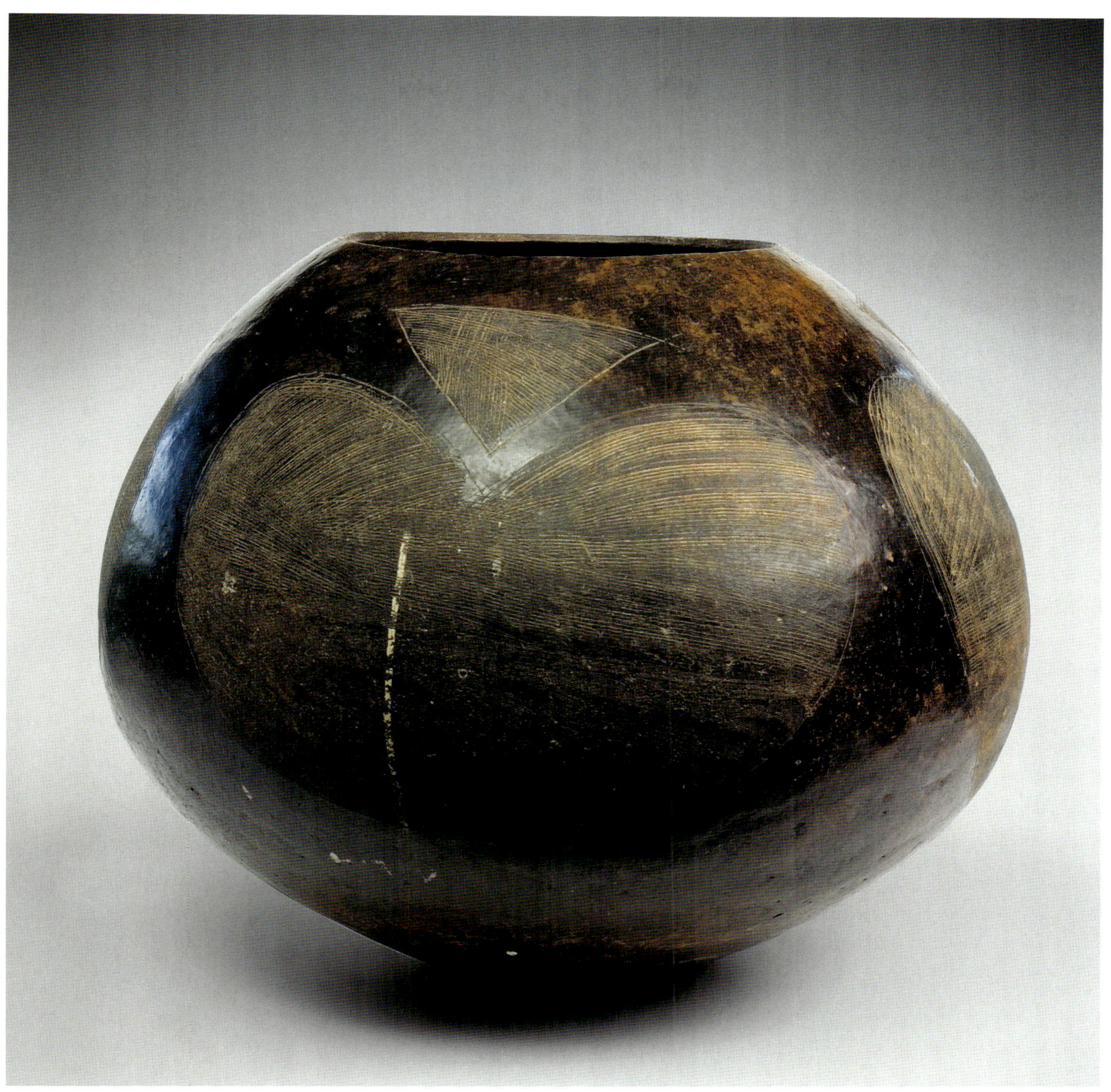

POT NUMBER 319 Ukhamba H: 416 mm A very large ukhamba (about 30 litres) for special occasions. The incised decoration is an elaboration of the 'Hearts' motif.

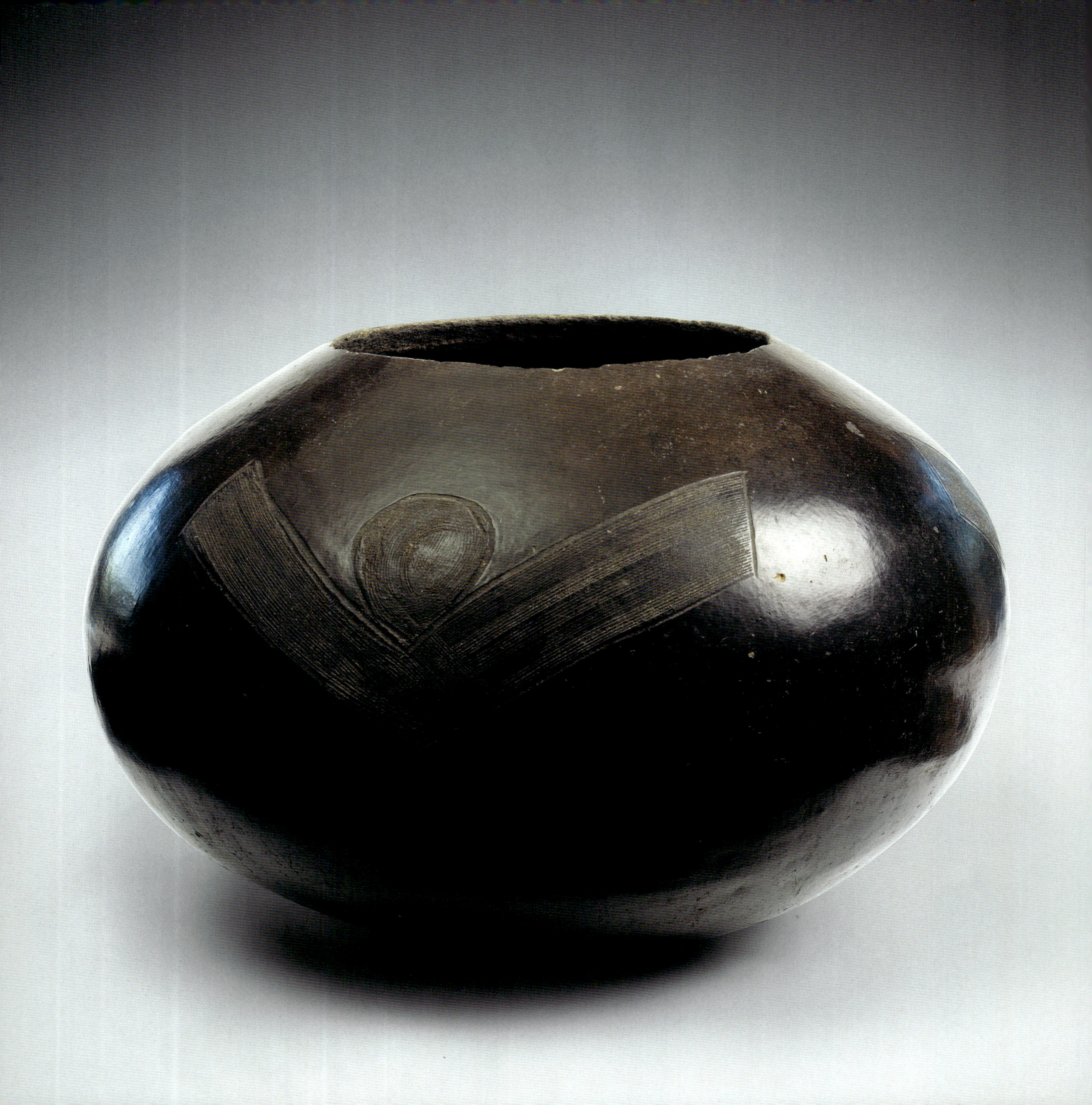

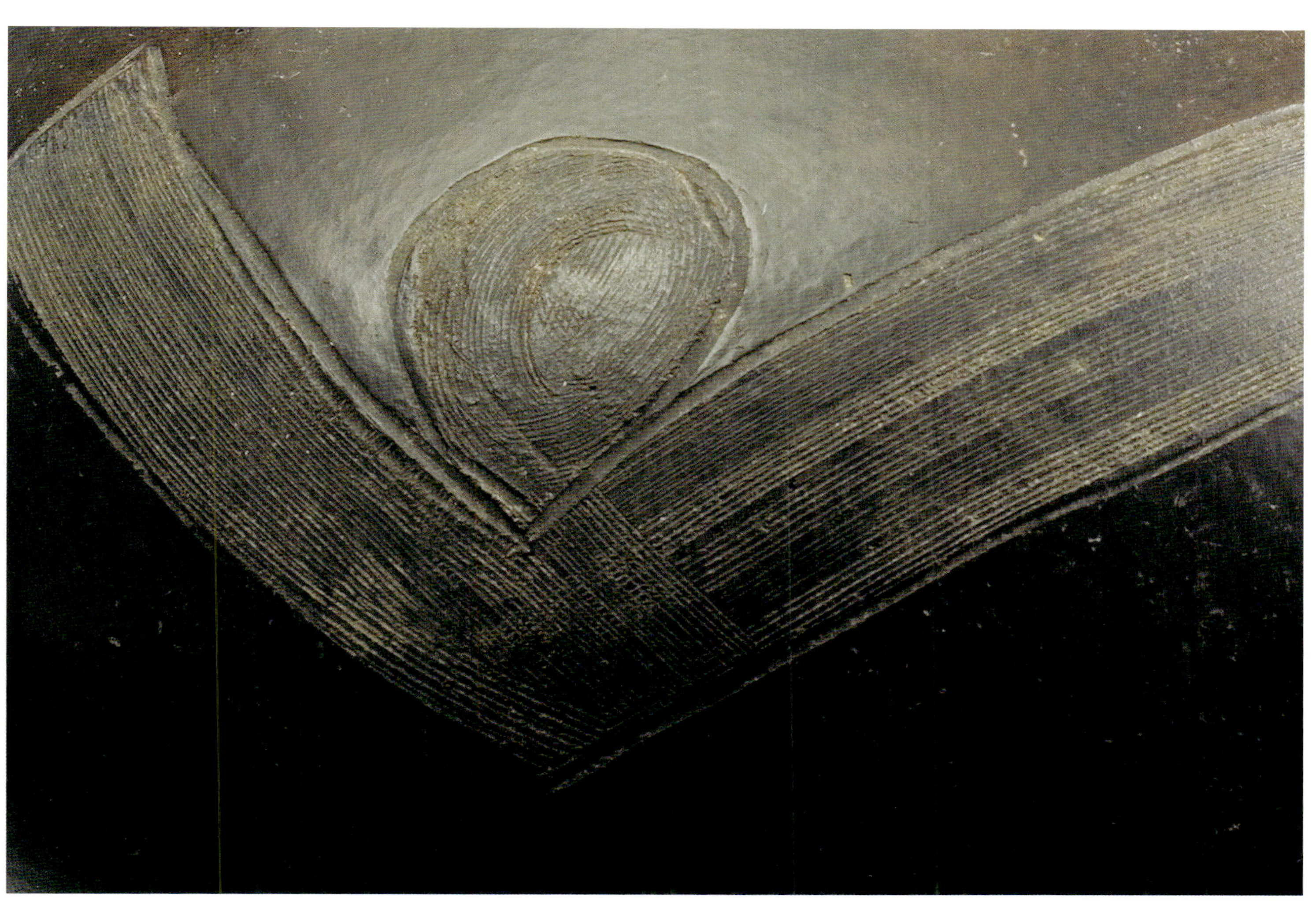

POT NUMBER 321 Ukhamba H: 262 mm Mrs Ngobese said she did not know the name of the pattern, but that it was taken from playing cards. Then someone else said it was called *impukane* (fly).

Hlabisa Style 4

Others

Finally, these two further vessels from the Hlabisa region show the influence of adjoining styles. The second, Pot 323 page 118, is by Phiwayinkosi Ngubane using the slanting rectangles of the Eshowe-Melmoth region but incised with a comb rather than with *amasumpa*.

A number of outstanding pots in US collections hail from the Hlabisa region. Bill Simmons' 'great pot' has already been referred to (pp. 2 and 5). In conclusion I would like to include a most unusual large vessel in which the incised pattern has been heightened by partially over-painting it. It is owned by Carolee Kennedy, of Arlington, VA. Pot 324 page 120.

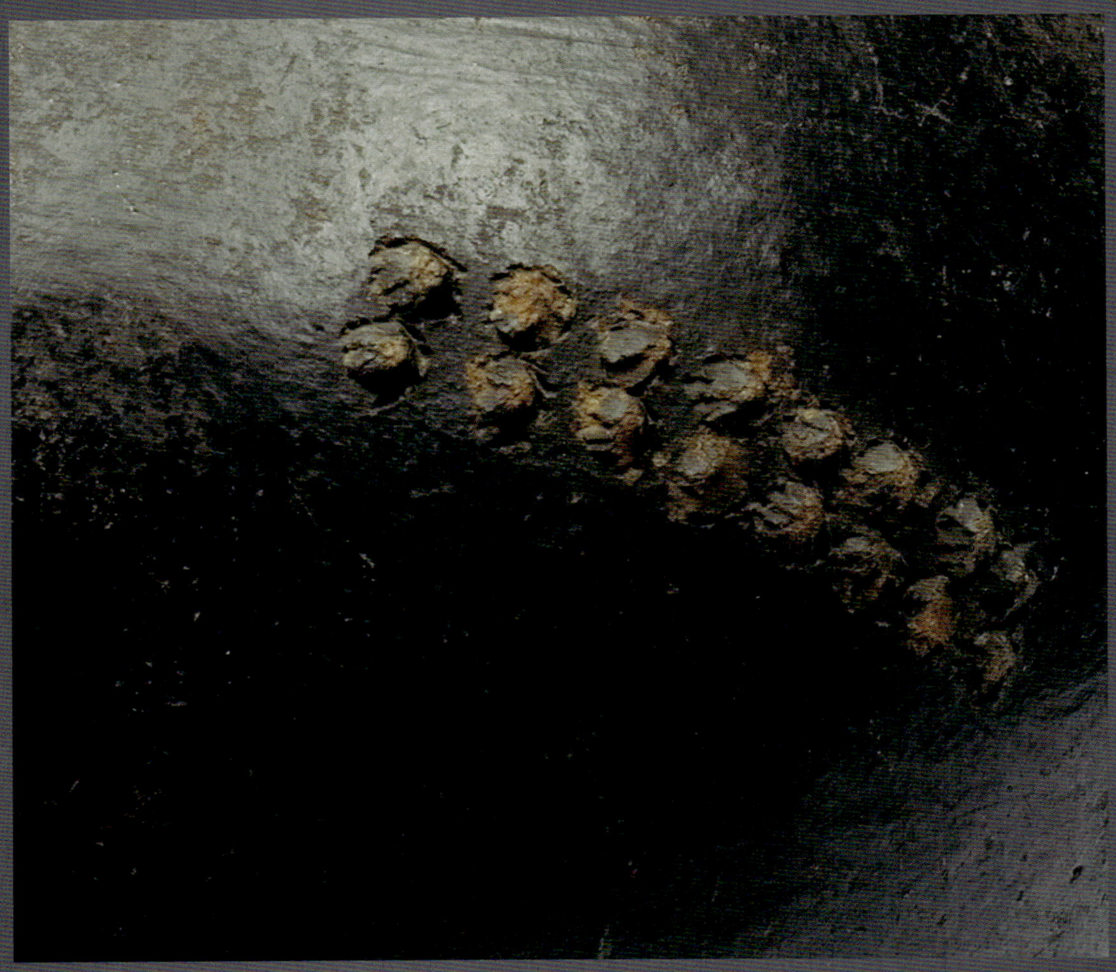

POT NUMBER 322 Ukhamba, H: 216 mm
A characteristic Hlabisa form with Nongoma motifs: two-row panels of *amasumpa*. Despite its narrow opening this pot was used for *amahewu* (fermented maize porridge).

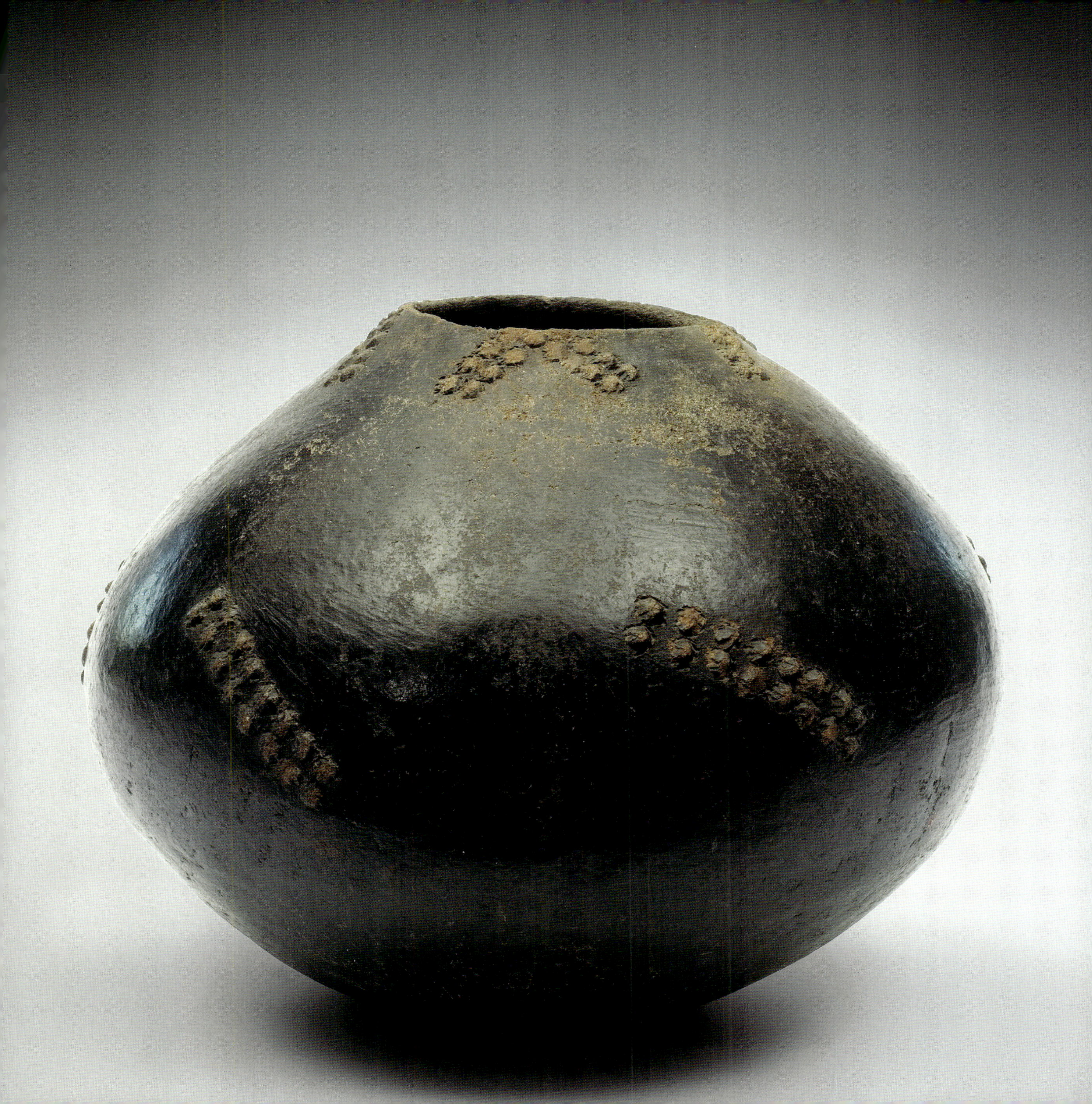

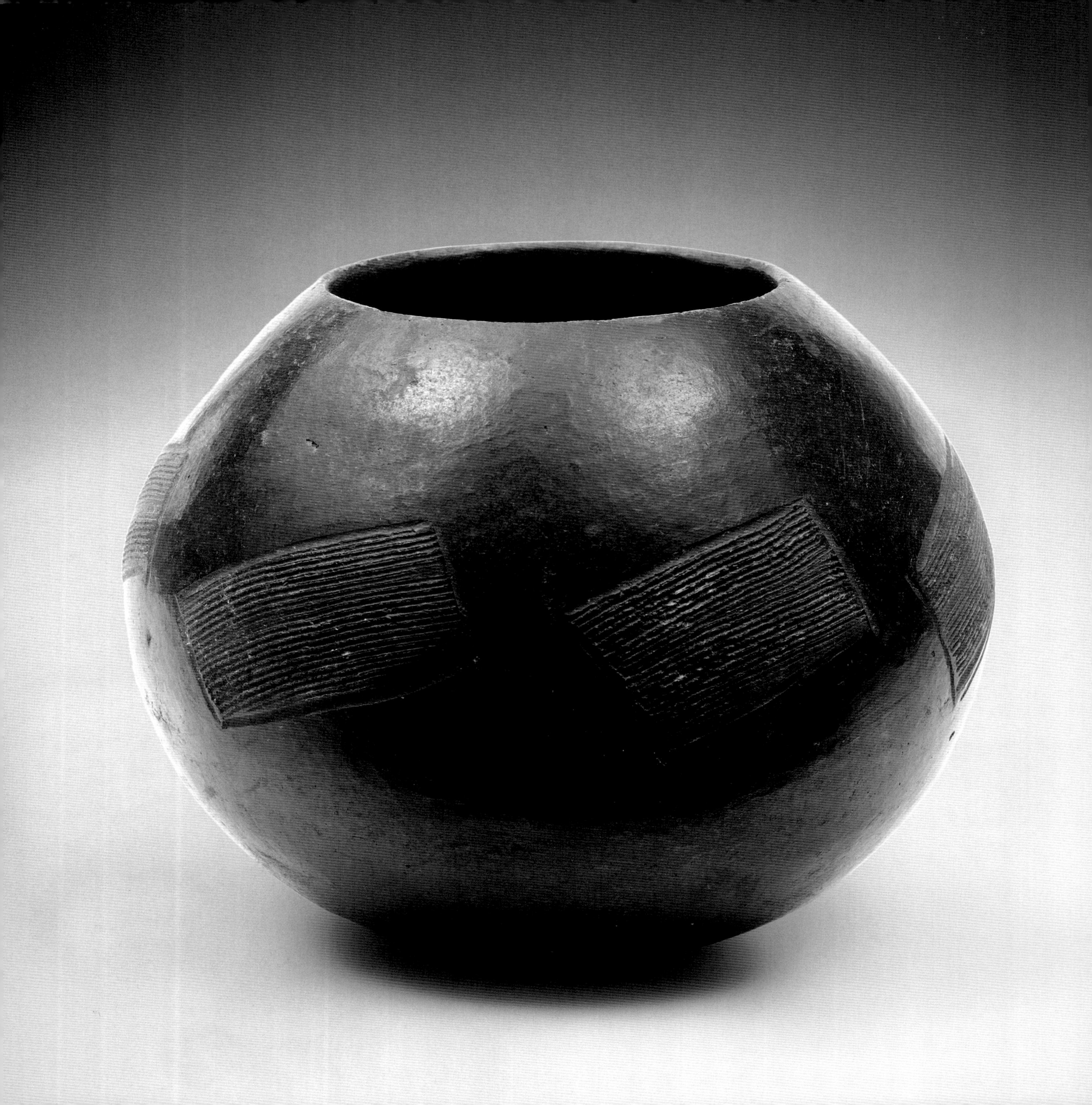

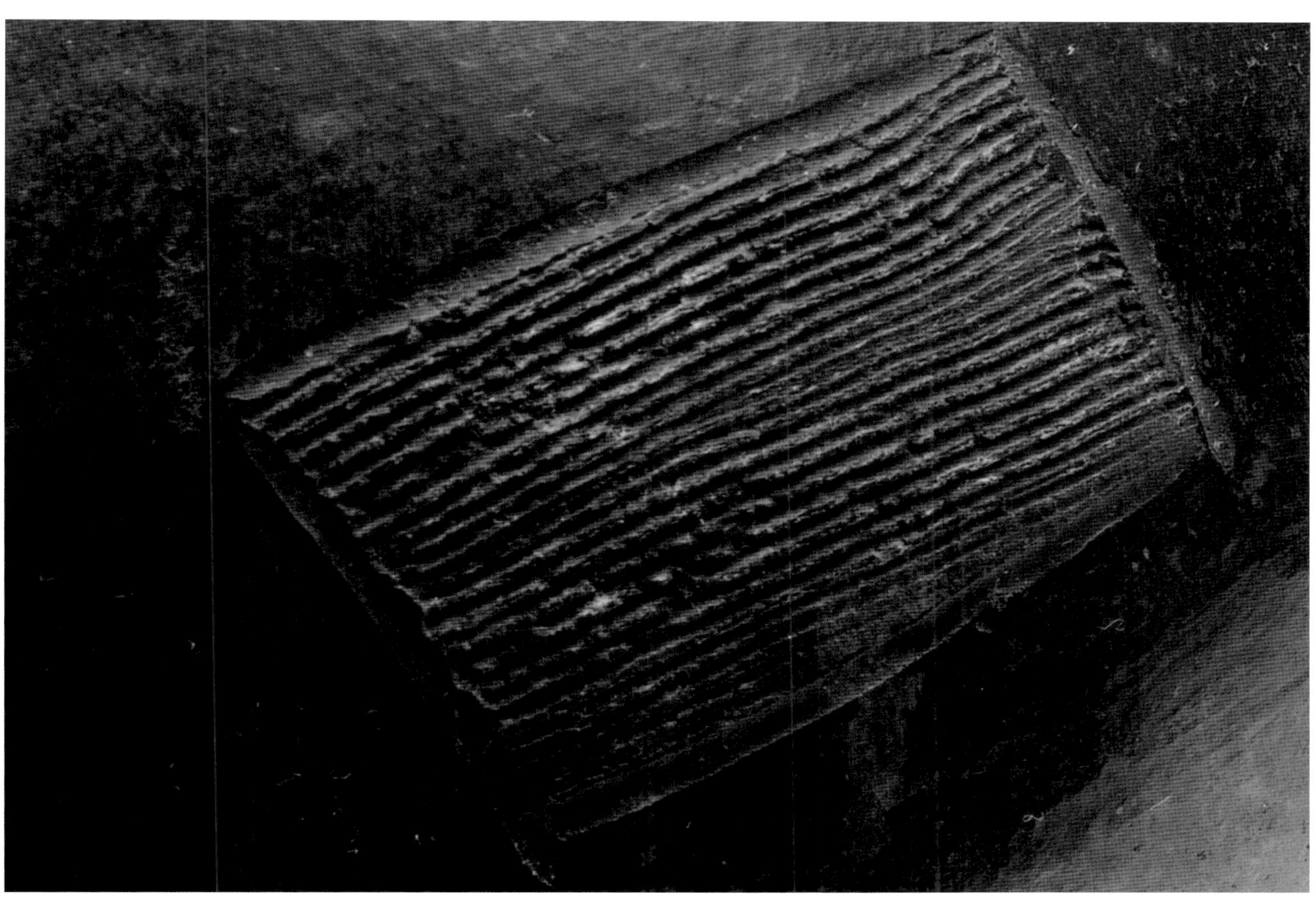

POT NUMBER 323 Ukhamba H: 136 mm Characteristic Hlabisa form (H:D: 1:23) with Nongoma/Melmoth motifs: slanting incised rectangles.

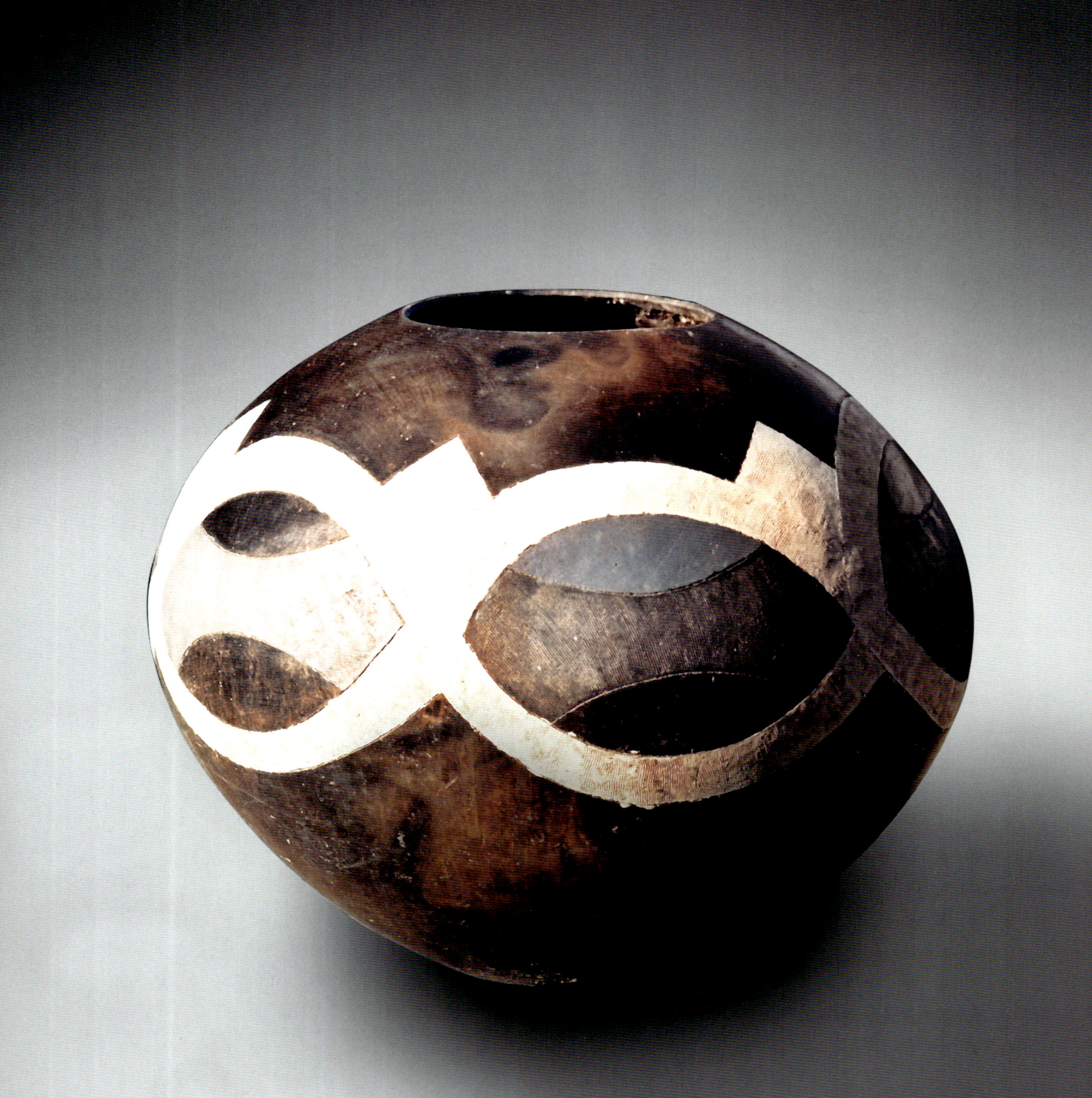

4

The Melmoth Eshowe Region

This comprises mainly the magisterial district Mtonjaneni south of the white uMfolozi through to the uMhlatuze; it also includes some areas north of Eshowe such as the hill country above Nkwalini and the slopes leading down to the uMhlatuze on the southern side (see map page 30). It is an area that has seen quite a lot of movement of people in the course of the twentieth century. Nevertheless, over much of its range a distinctive decorative style, that has its origin in the late nineteenth century or the early years of the twentieth century, is still in evidence: medium to large somewhat squat vessels (typically H:D: 1:1¼) with a well-defined range of motifs in *amasumpa*. Some of the same motifs appear in the archival photograph entitled 'Dinuzulu's drinking vessels and his wives who make his beer', c.1896–1907, (page 123) which shows some 17 beer vessels with four young women posing behind them.[60]

In other respects Dinuzulu's vessels differ from those found today, most of which were made in the second half of the twentieth century. His *izinkamba* were larger and had the wide mouths nowadays associated with cooking pots rather than beer vessels, whilst the two *izimpiso* had much shorter necks. Other vessels from the region tend to be somewhat closer to spherical; many of them are large, with complex patterns executed in a number of incised and impressed techniques.

As far as the forms are concerned there is not much difference between the two groups. However, the decorations tell a rather different story. Those of the first category (i.e., with *amasumpa*) form a coherent group. Many of the basic motifs of Zulu

POT NUMBER 324 Ukhamba, H: 388 mm, D: 483 mm
Incised pattern highlighted with blue and white paint.

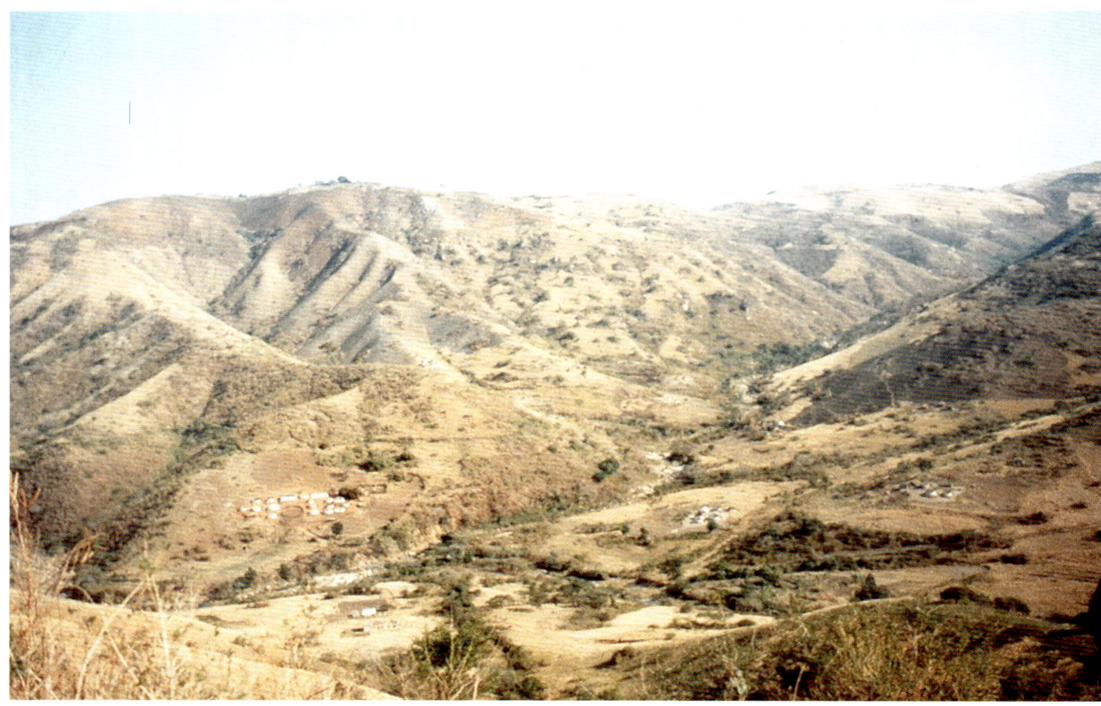

View across the uMhlatuze valley near Nkwalini in winter.

decorative art familiar from beadwork and carvings are represented: single rectangular panels (Pot 401 page 125, Pot 402 page 126), linked rectangular panels (Pot 403 page 217, Pot 404 page 219), continuous bands (Pot 410 page 136, Pot 412 page 138), broad arches (Pot 411 page 137), zigzags (Pot 405 page 132), and a series of derivatives of zigzags not encountered elsewhere (Pot 407 page 133, Pot 408 page 134, Pot 409 page 135). All this points to the formative influence of an important socio-political centre. The Melmoth-Eshowe region had been a showplace of royal activity since the 1850s when Mpande founded the first oNdini, an *ikhanda* (military kraal) for his son Cetshwayo on the southern bank of the lower uMhlathuze, about 25 km southeast of the present site of Melmoth and about the same distance northeast of Eshowe. The *ikhanda* was destroyed on 6 July 1879 during the Anglo-Zulu War,

but the style seems to have survived the subsequent partitionings of Zululand in 1879 and 1883. After the report of the Zululand Lands Delimitation Commission, the region became a reserve.[61]

The vessels with incised patterns (Melmoth II) have affinities with a number of the neighbouring regions: the leaf motifs and the notched technique encountered in Oyaya, Thukela (Pot 414 page 146), incised patterns also found in the Nongoma region (Pot 415 page 143, Pot 416 page 144), a distinctive pattern associated with the region south of Eshowe (Pot 419 page 145), whilst the very old *uphiso* illustrated (Pot 417 page 148) was said to have been brought into the area from the north around Babanango, though the area around the middle reaches of the uMzinyathi (Buffalo River) seems more likely. As in the case of Hlabisa, family migrations from neighbouring areas and far-

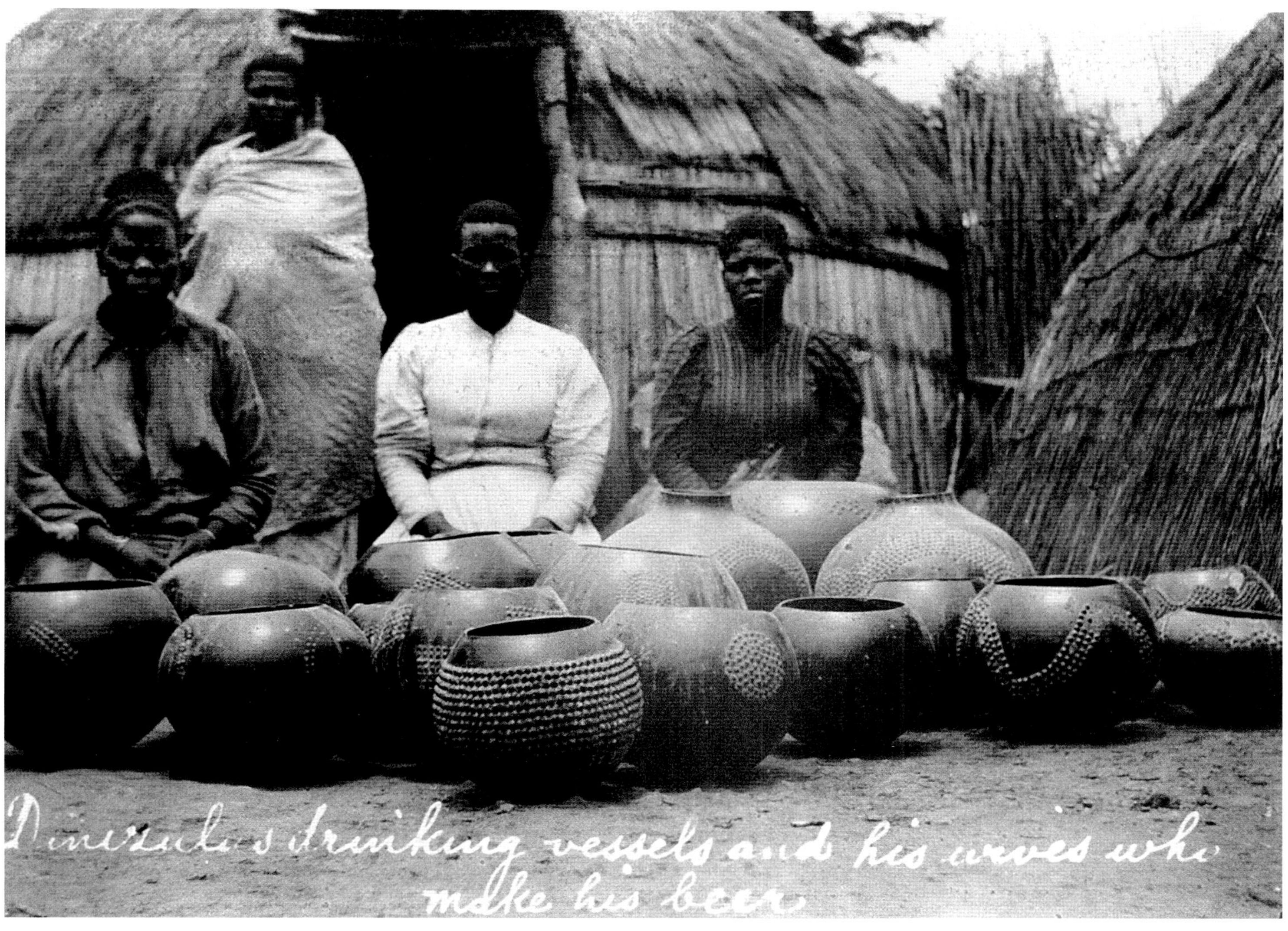

ther afield seem to have imported their pottery styles into Melmoth-Eshowe without actually displacing the original more ancient 'regal' style of the region.

Of the six areas studied, the first two – east and south of Melmoth town and KwaKunzempunga ('The Place of the Grey Bull') – yielded mostly the first type, namely vessels with *amasumpa*. The other four – eFofolozi, uGatsha (from *igatsha,* 'small branch, twig-

branch of a tree'; also a praise name of Chief Mango-suthu Buthelezi), eMatshensundu ('brown stones') and eNdundulu – were found to have vessels with broadly similar forms but a number of decorative features from adjoining areas. The classification is based on these two basic types.

'Dinuzulu's drinking vessels and his wives who made his beer', *c.* 1896–1907.

Classification of Melmoth Style

Melmoth Style 1
Mainly squat vessels with
patterns formed with
amasumpa.

Melmoth Style 2
Vessels with incised patterns
from a number of distinct
regions (*izigodi*) within the
greater area: from eFofolozi
Pot 415 page 142, from uGatsha Pot 419 page 145, from
eMatshensundu Pot 416 page
144 and from eNdundulu Pot
414 page 147, Pot 417 page 148
and Pot 418 page 149.

Melmoth Style 1

Mainly squat vessels with patterns
formed with *amasumpa.*
Examples from the areas east and
south of Melmoth: Pots 401–404 pages
125–129, Pot 406 page 130 and Pot 413
page 131.

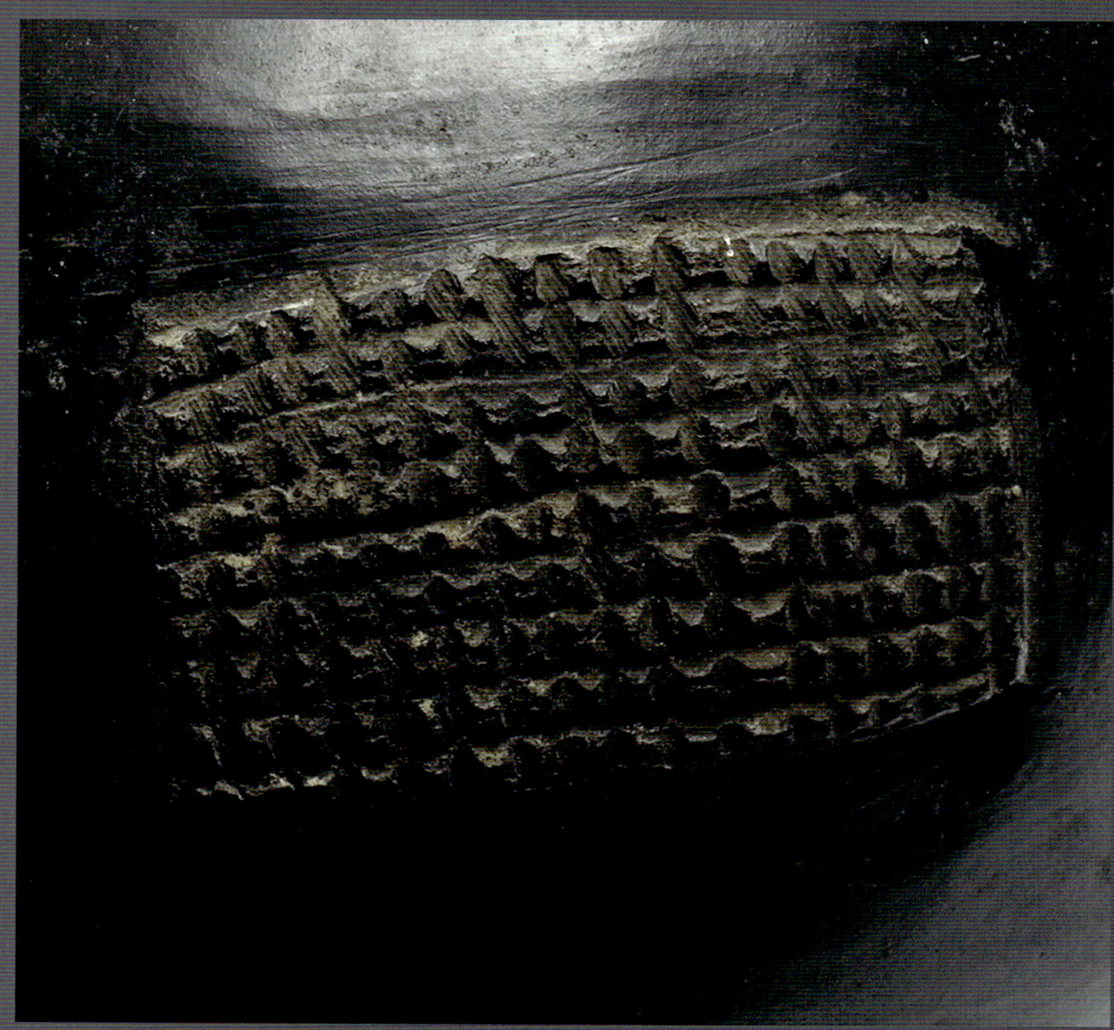

POT NUMBER 401 Ukhamba h: 260 mm
Horizontal rectangles, *amasumpa.*

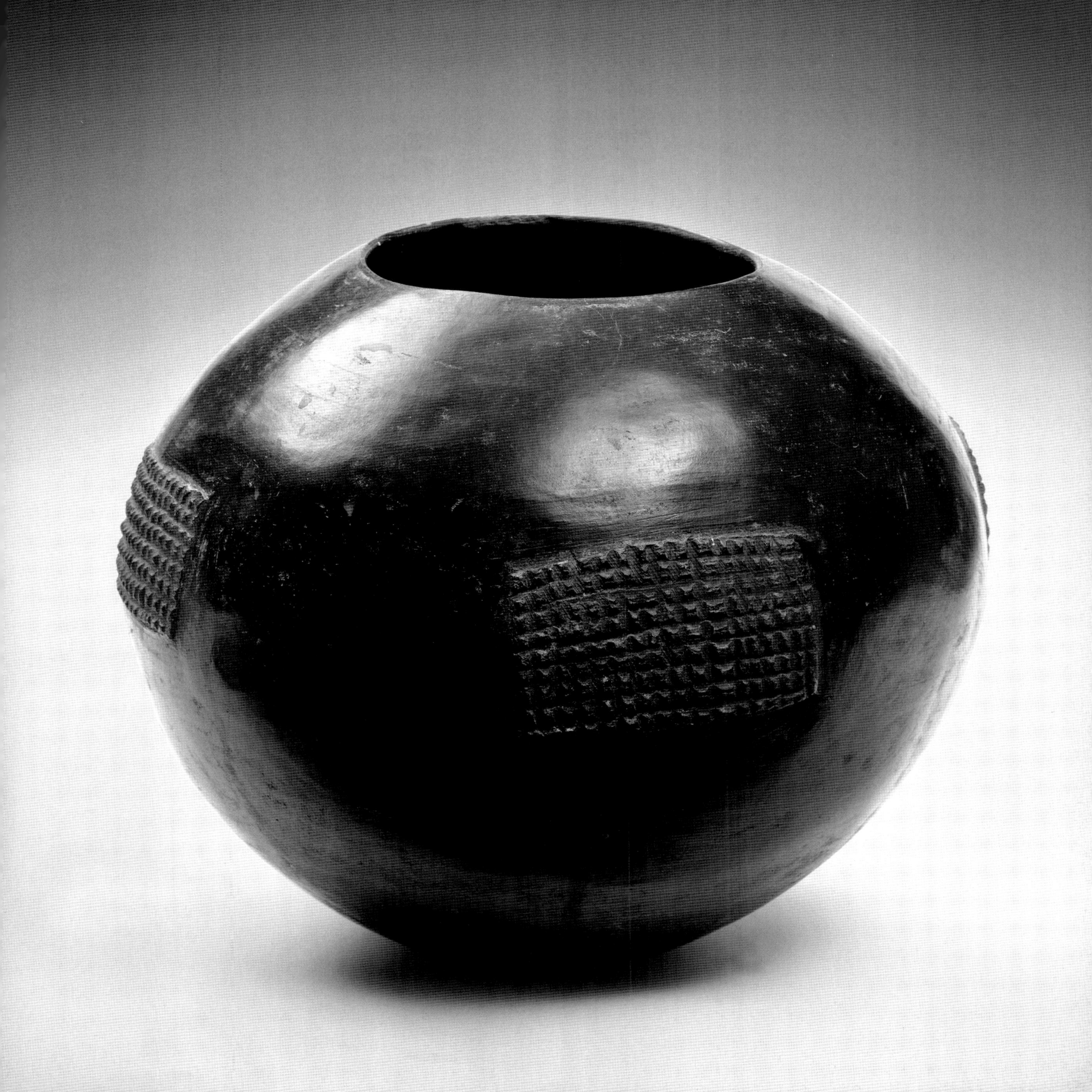

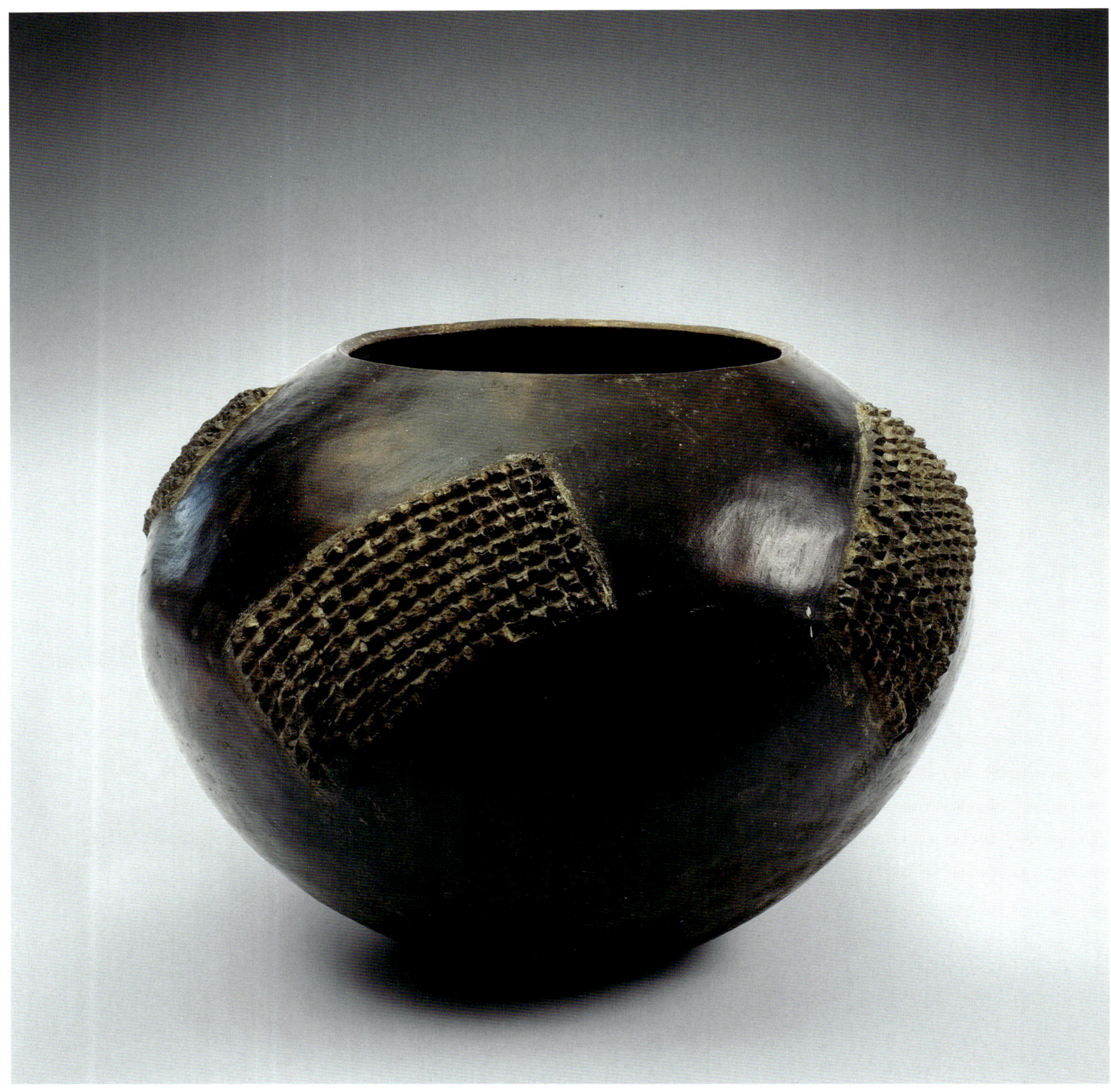

POT NUMBER 402 Ukhamba H: 220 mm Slanting rectangles, *amasumpa*.

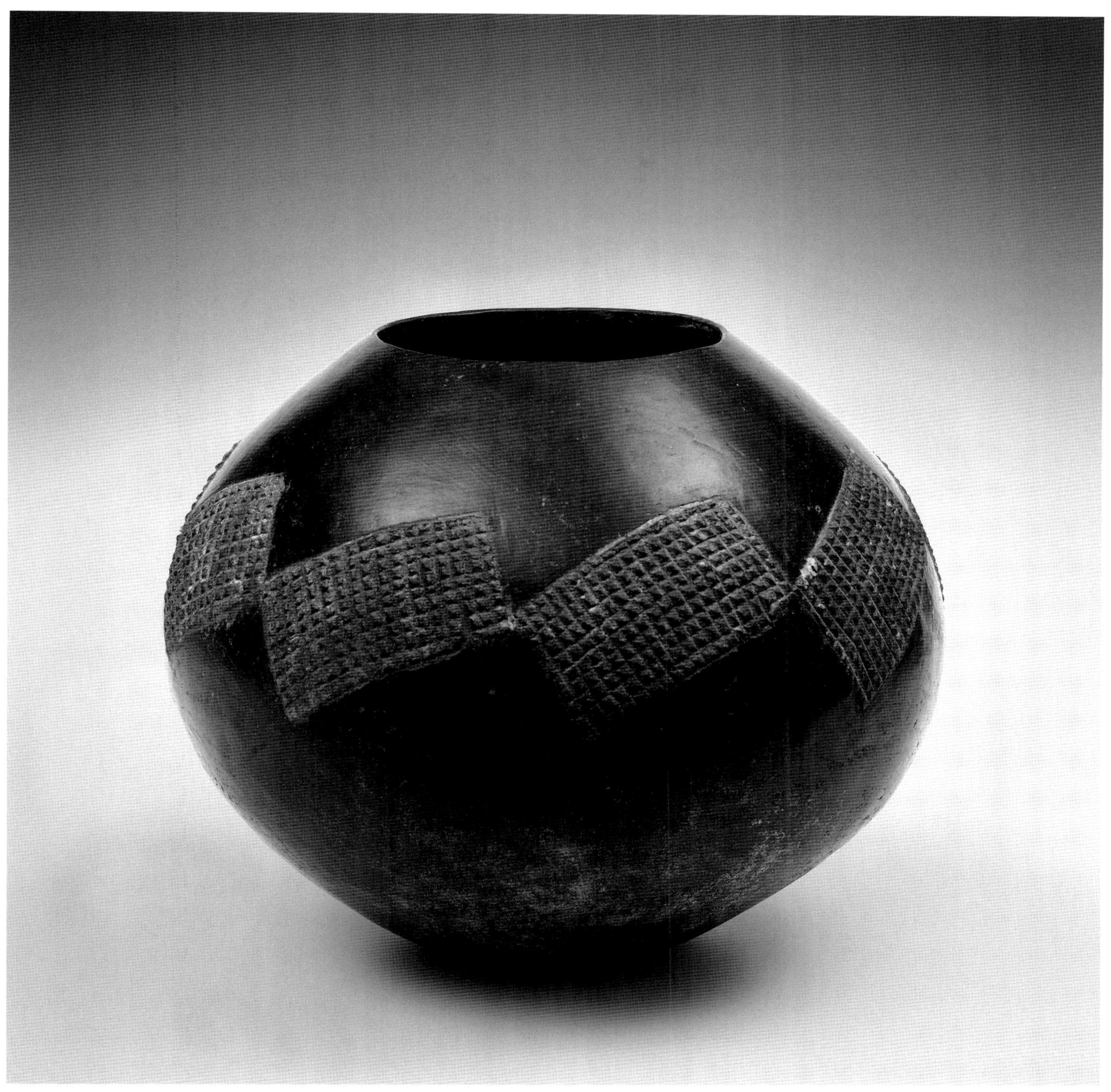

POT NUMBER 403 Ukhamba H: 225 mm Slanting rectangles linked in two groups of four, *amasumpa*.

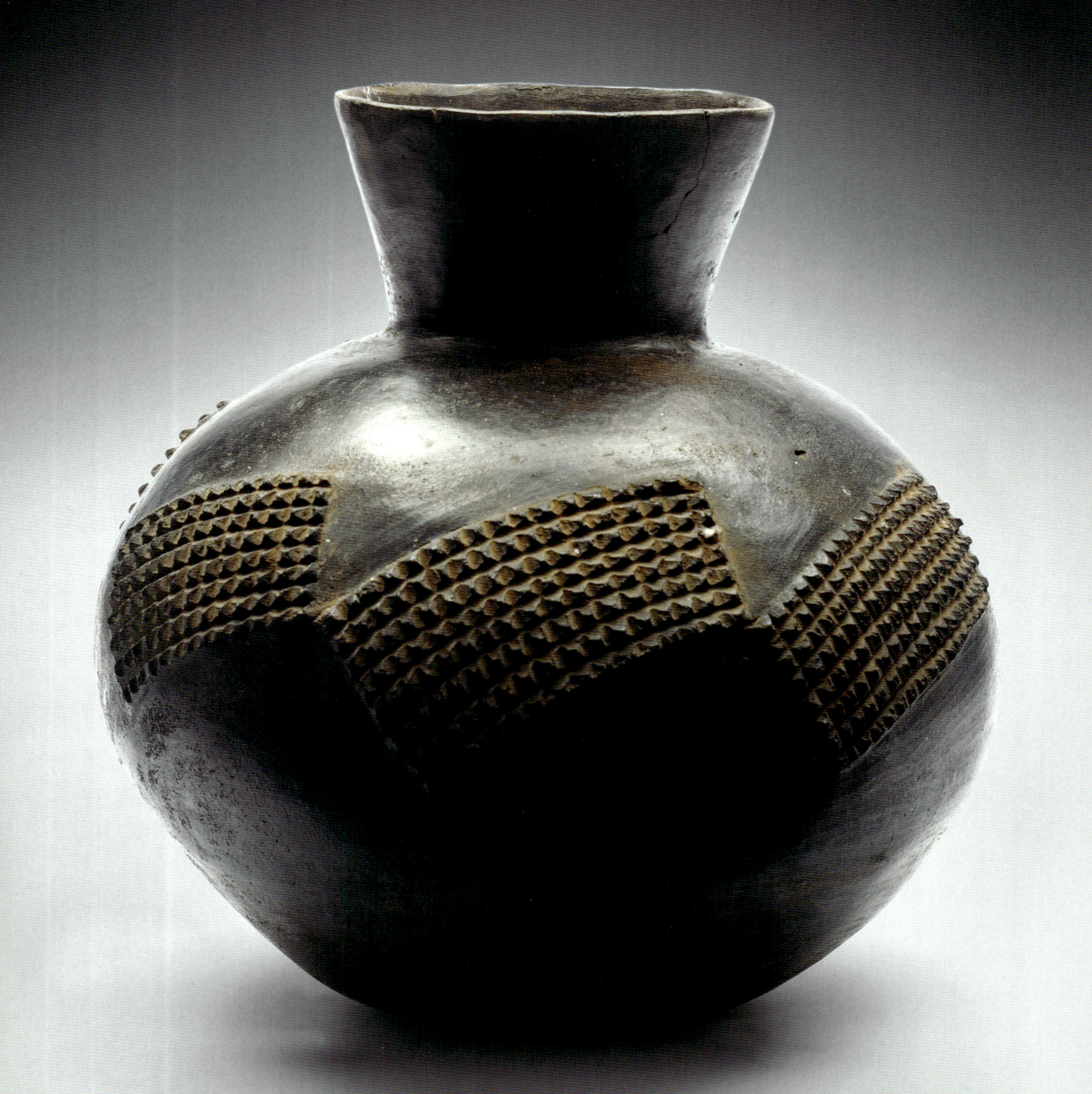

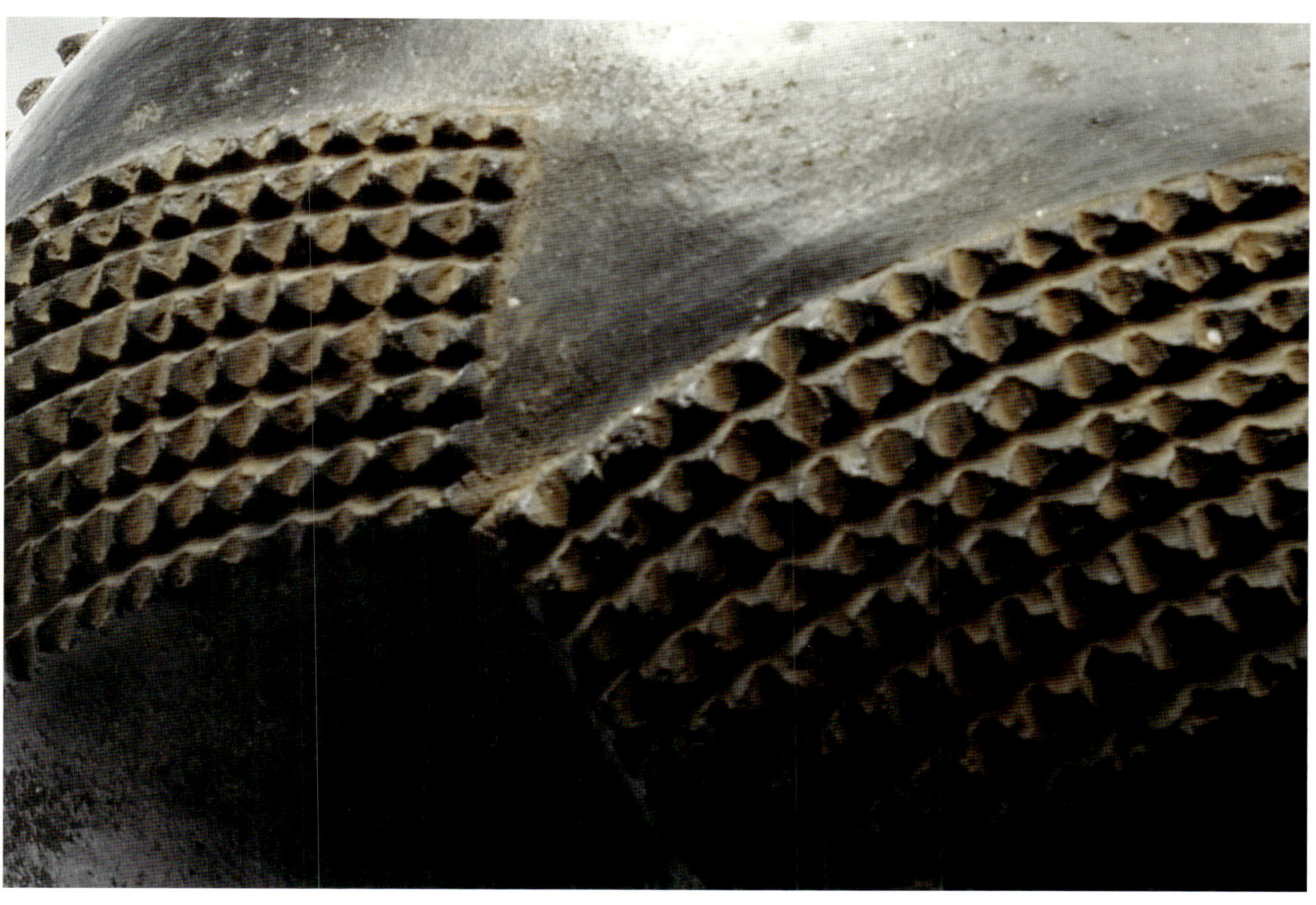

POT NUMBER 404 Uphiso H: 290 mm Uphiso with flared neck. Slanting linked rectangles, *amasumpa*.

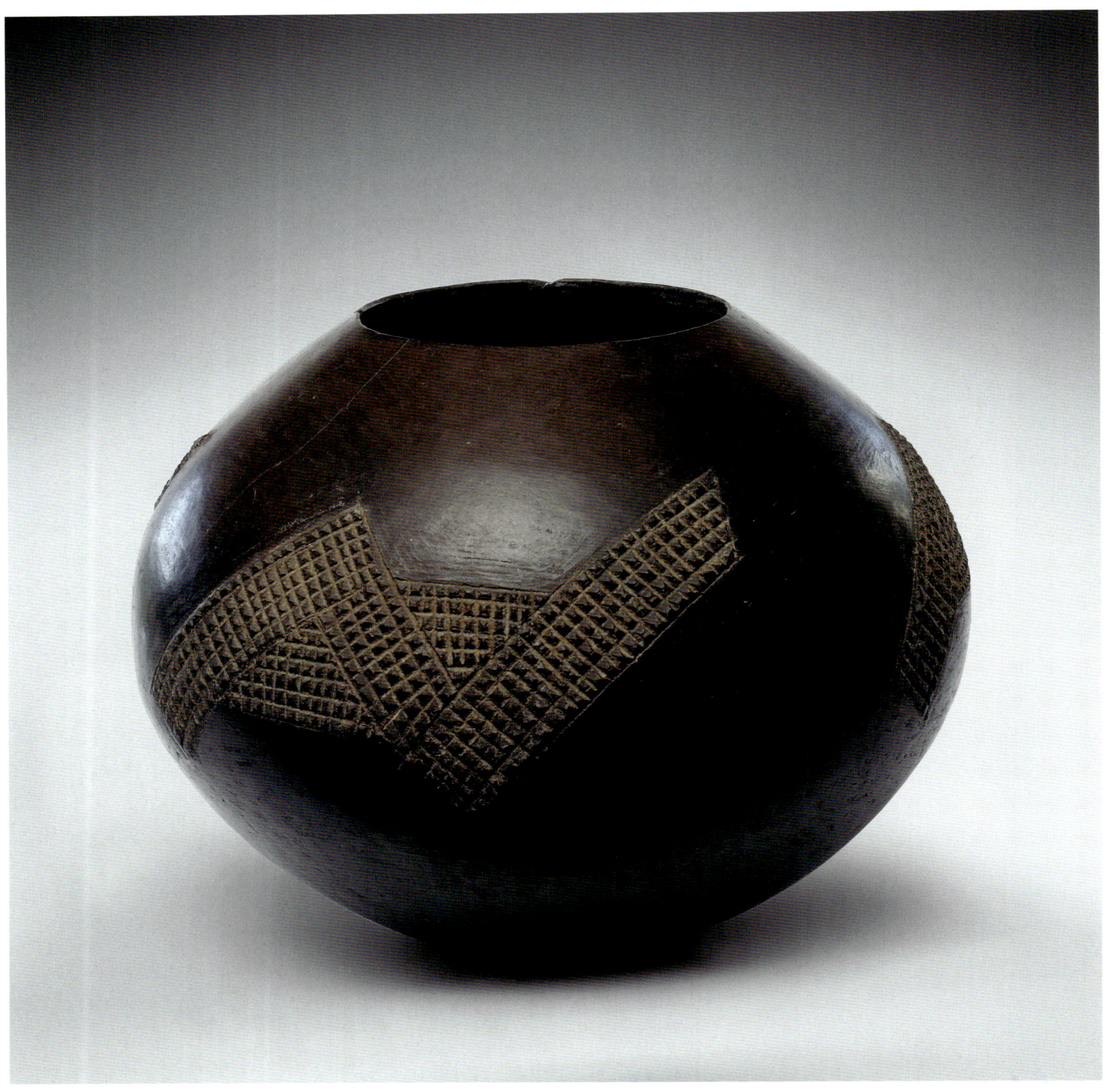

POT NUMBER 406 Ukhamba H: 270 mm Single zigzag motif with filled in apexes, *amasumpa*. As far as I know, this motif and its extensions are specific to the Melmoth-Eshowe region.

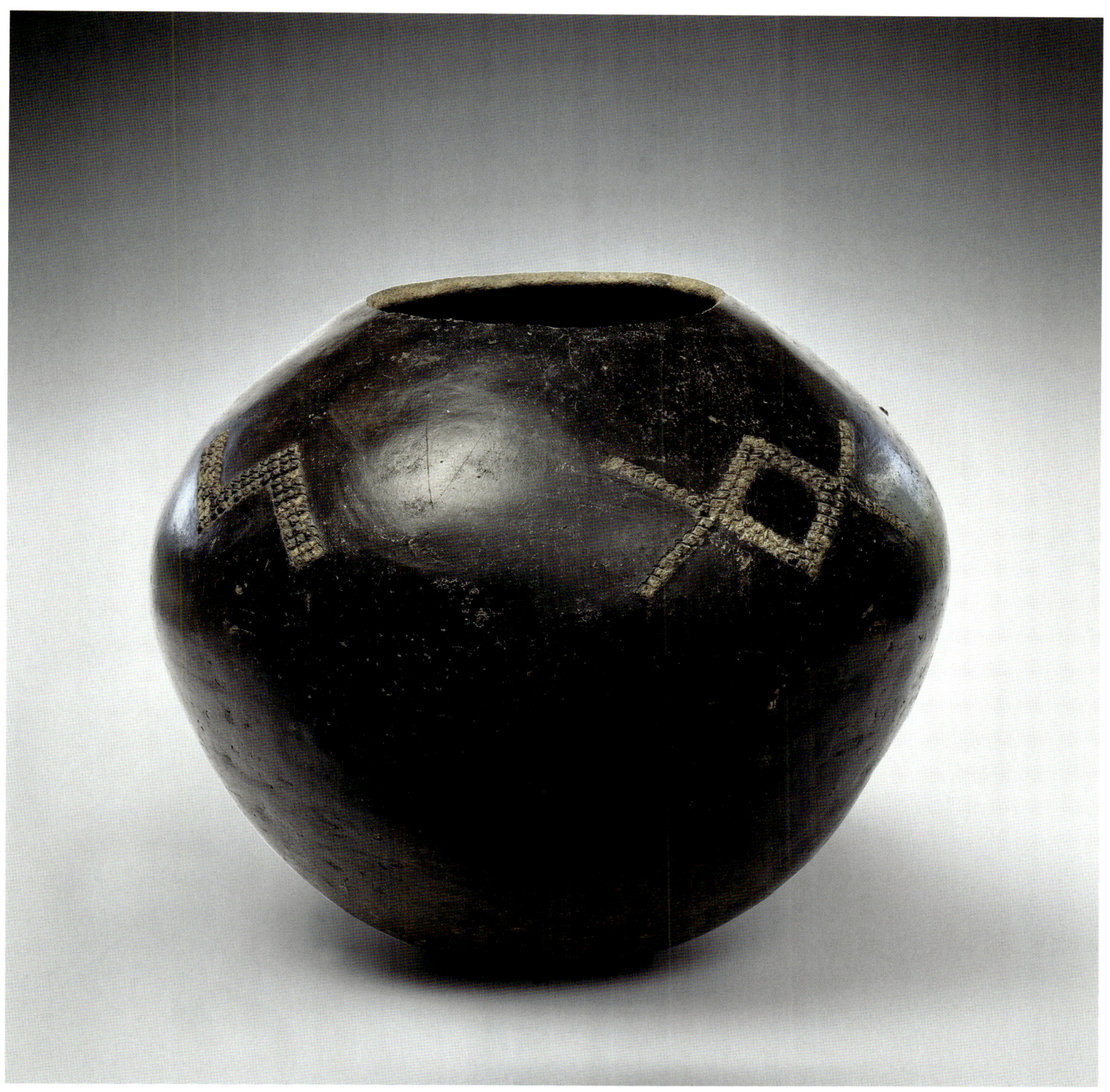

POT NUMBER 413 Ukhamba H: 260 mm Narrow applied single line of *amasumpa* made by incising the applied strip. The two small motifs are both familiar ones reduced in size. In this form they seem to be specific to this *isigodi*. The maker called them *amanunu* (in this context 'insects').

Melmoth Sub-style I – KwaKunzempunga region

Pots 405 page 132, Pots 407–412 pages 133–139

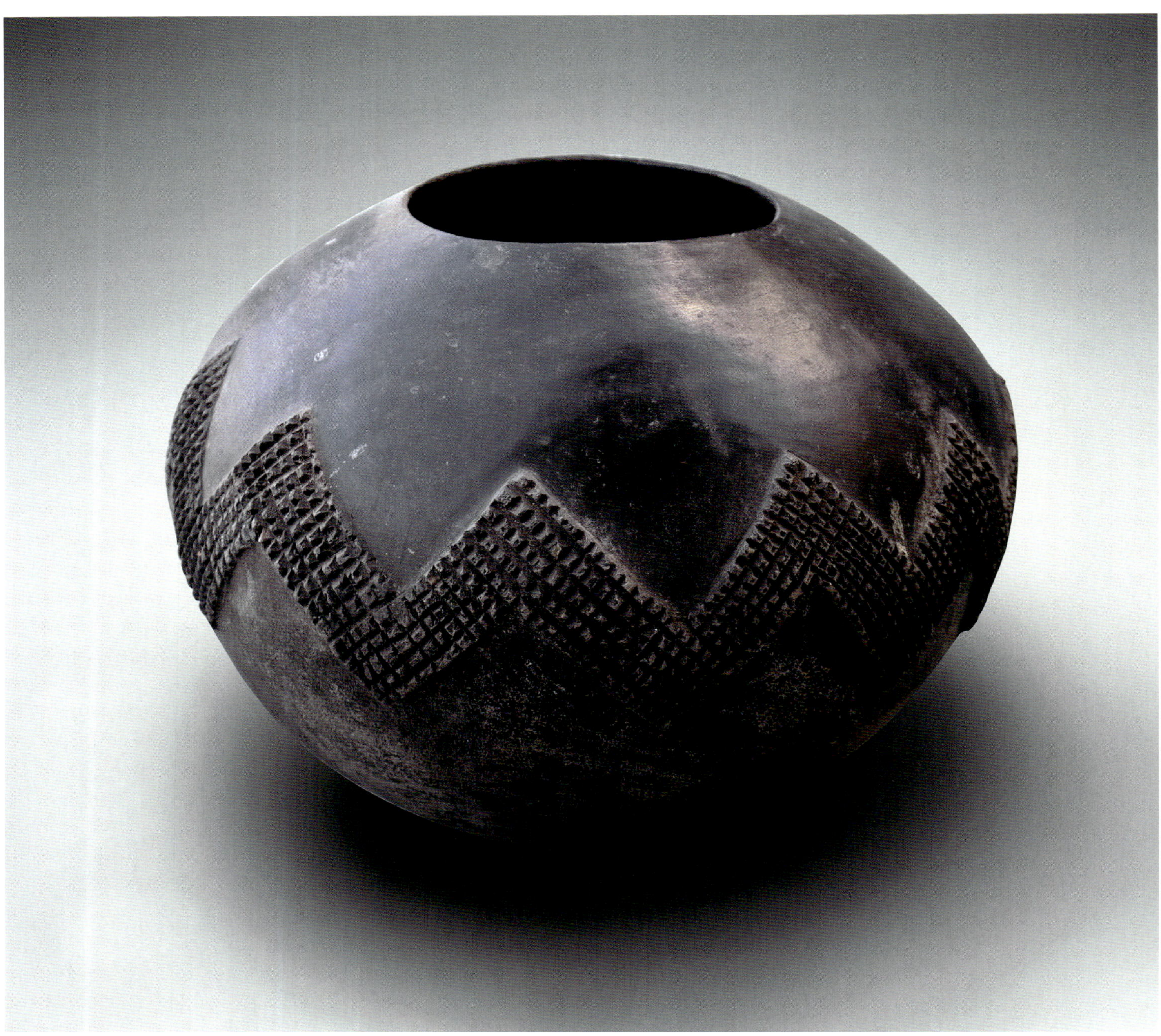

POT NUMBER 405 Ukhamba H: 240 mm Zigzag pattern, *amasumpa*.

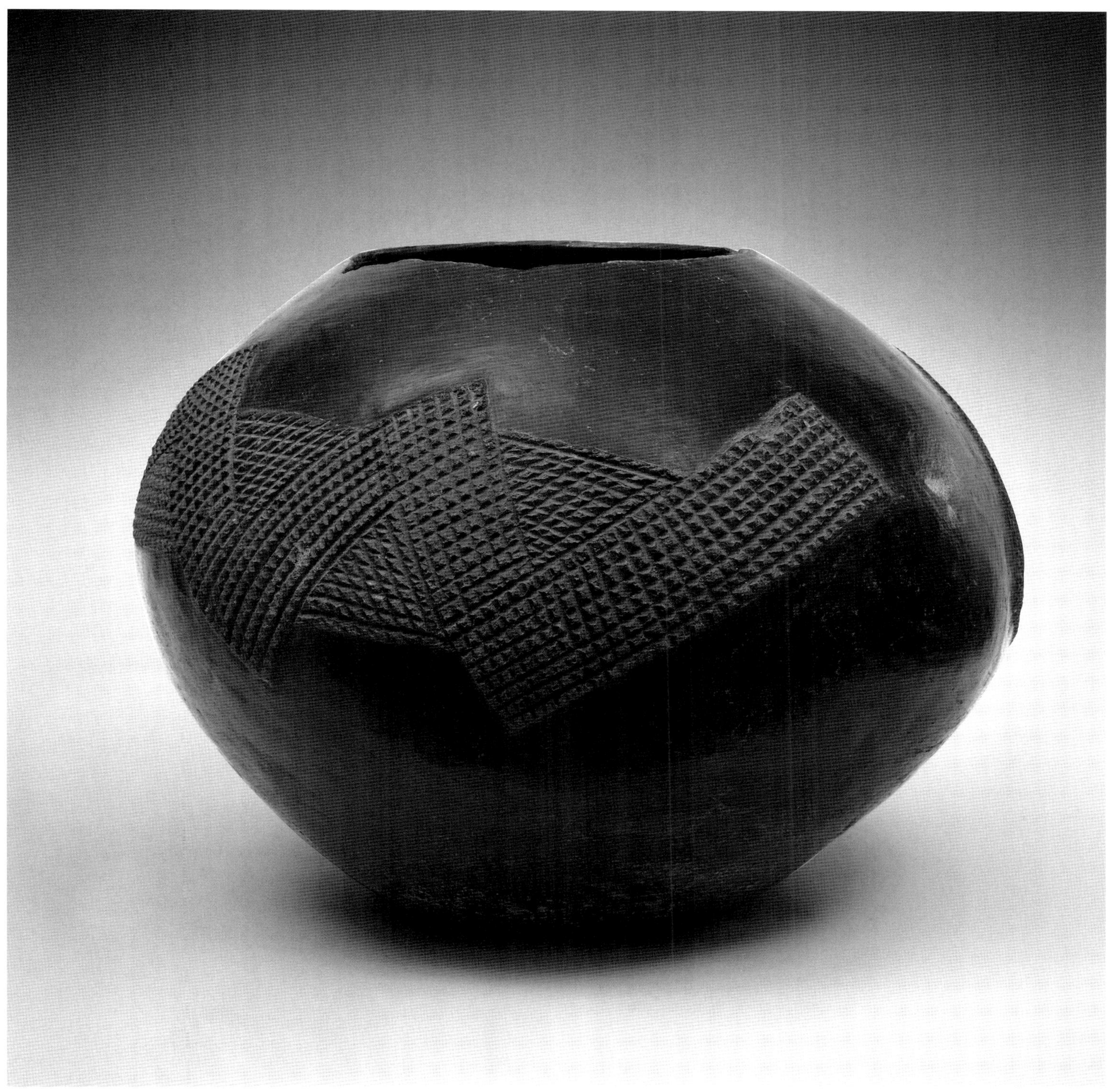

POT NUMBER 407 Ukhamba H: 310 mm Extension of motif of 406.

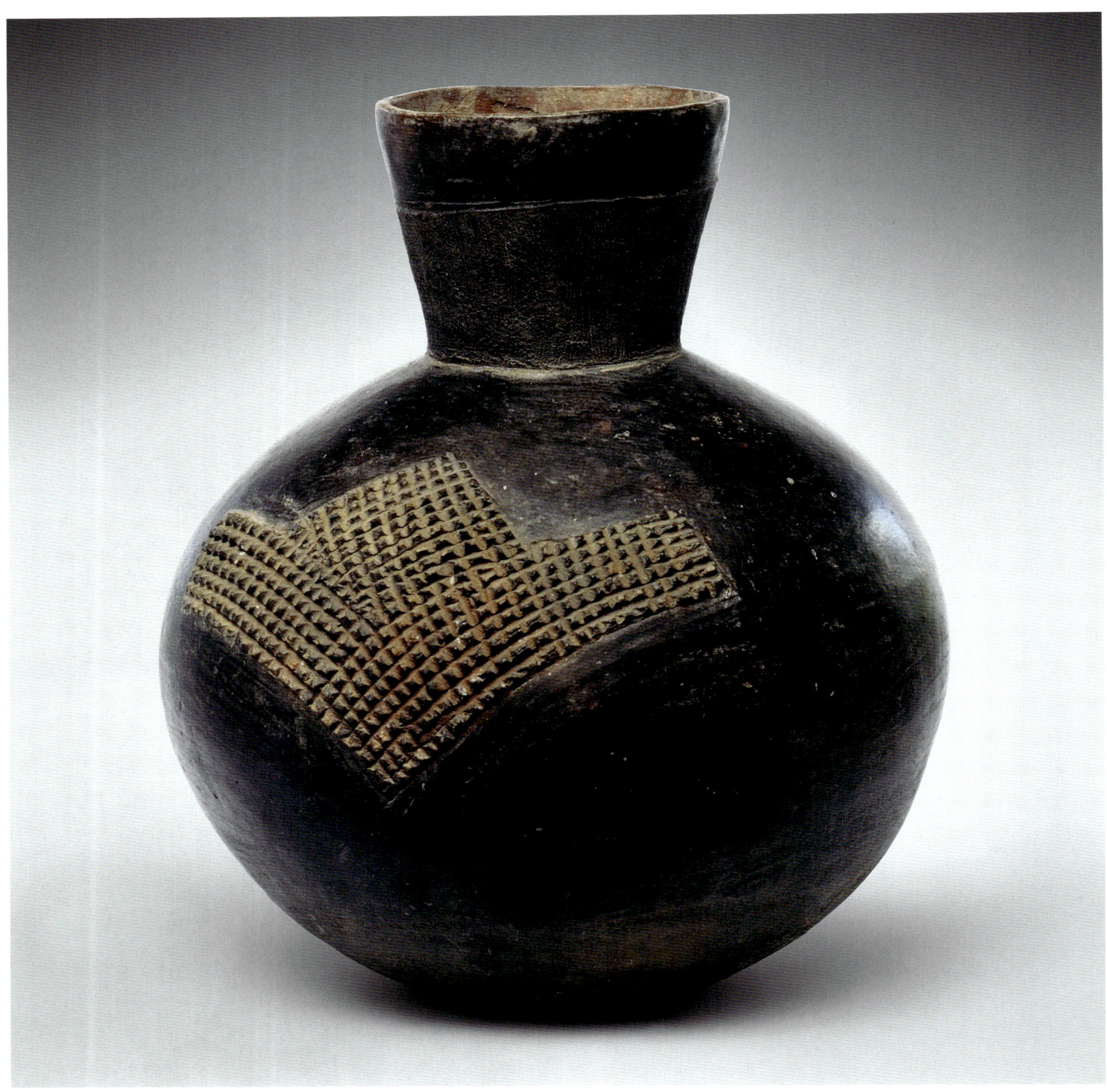

POT NUMBER 408 Uphiso H: 355 mm Half zigzag possibly derived from 406. Another example: Jolles Collection 261 (not illustrated). Neck decorated with light incisions.

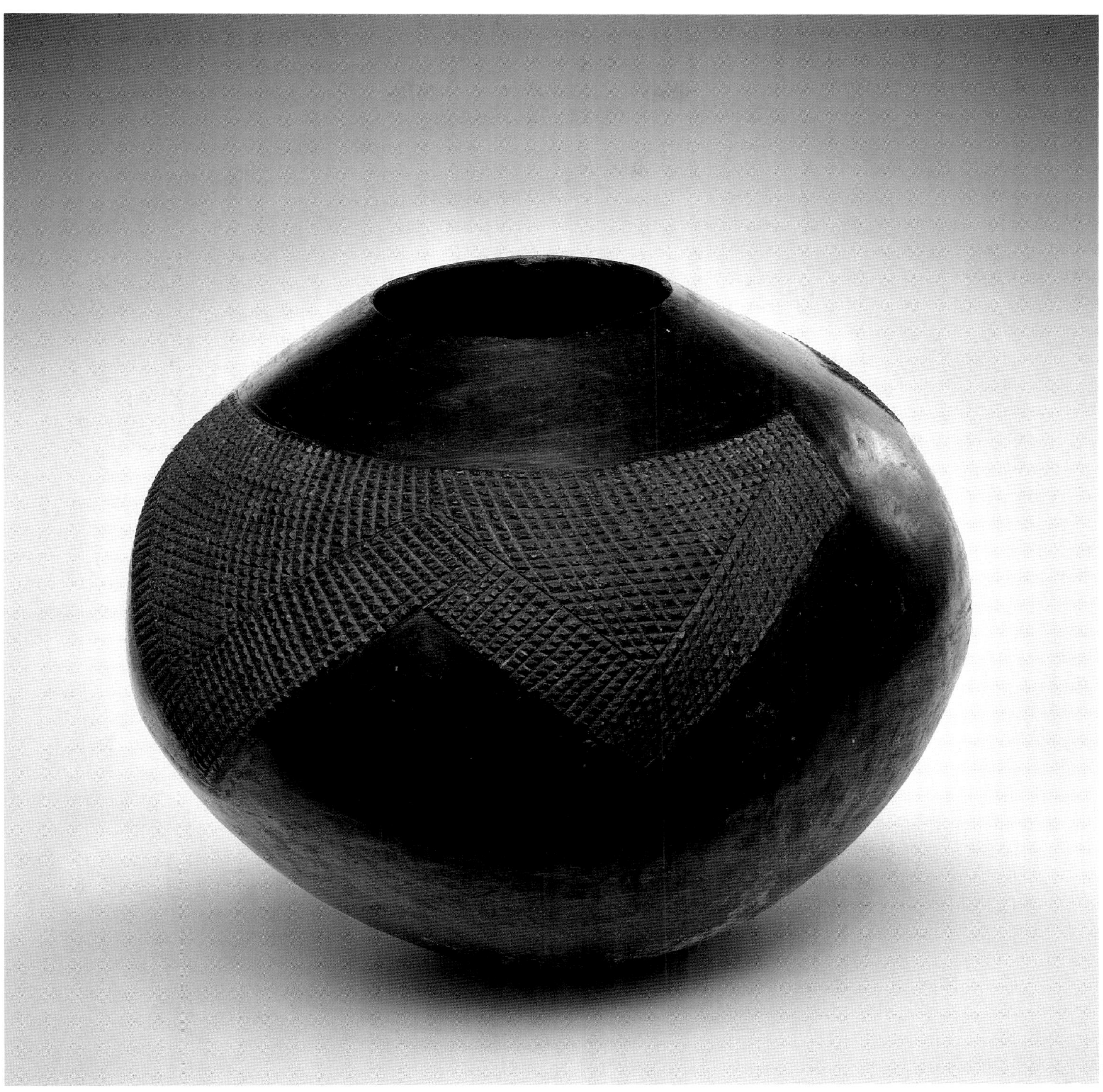

POT NUMBER 409 Ukhamba H: 330 mm Two semi-zigzag motifs, *amasumpa*.

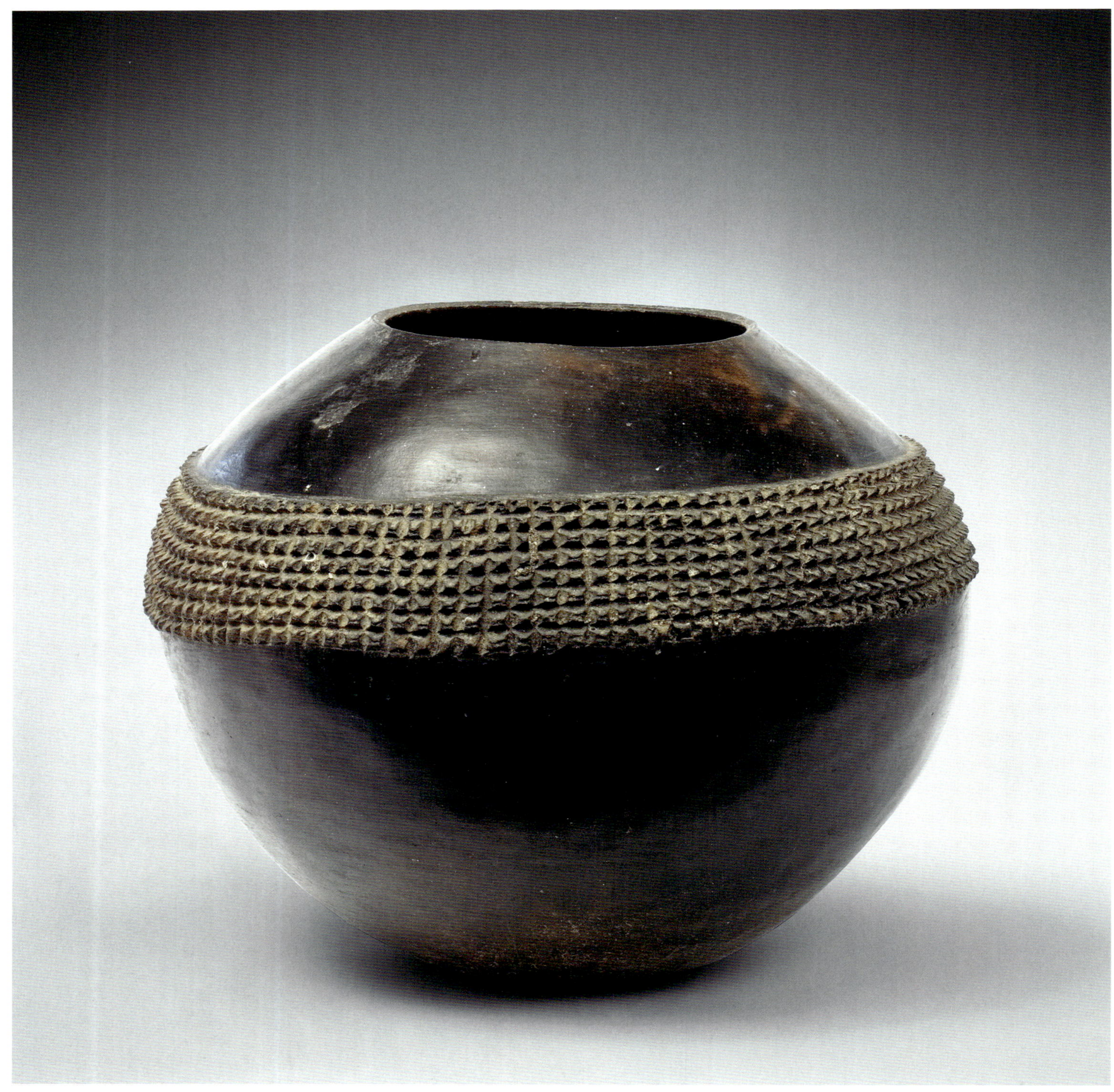

POT NUMBER 410 Ukhamba H: 230 mm Plain belt of *amasumpa* as in the picture of Dinuzulu's drinking vessels, p 123. Compare also Jolles Collection 270
(not illustrated) which has the same motif but with a triangular addition like the fastener of a belt.

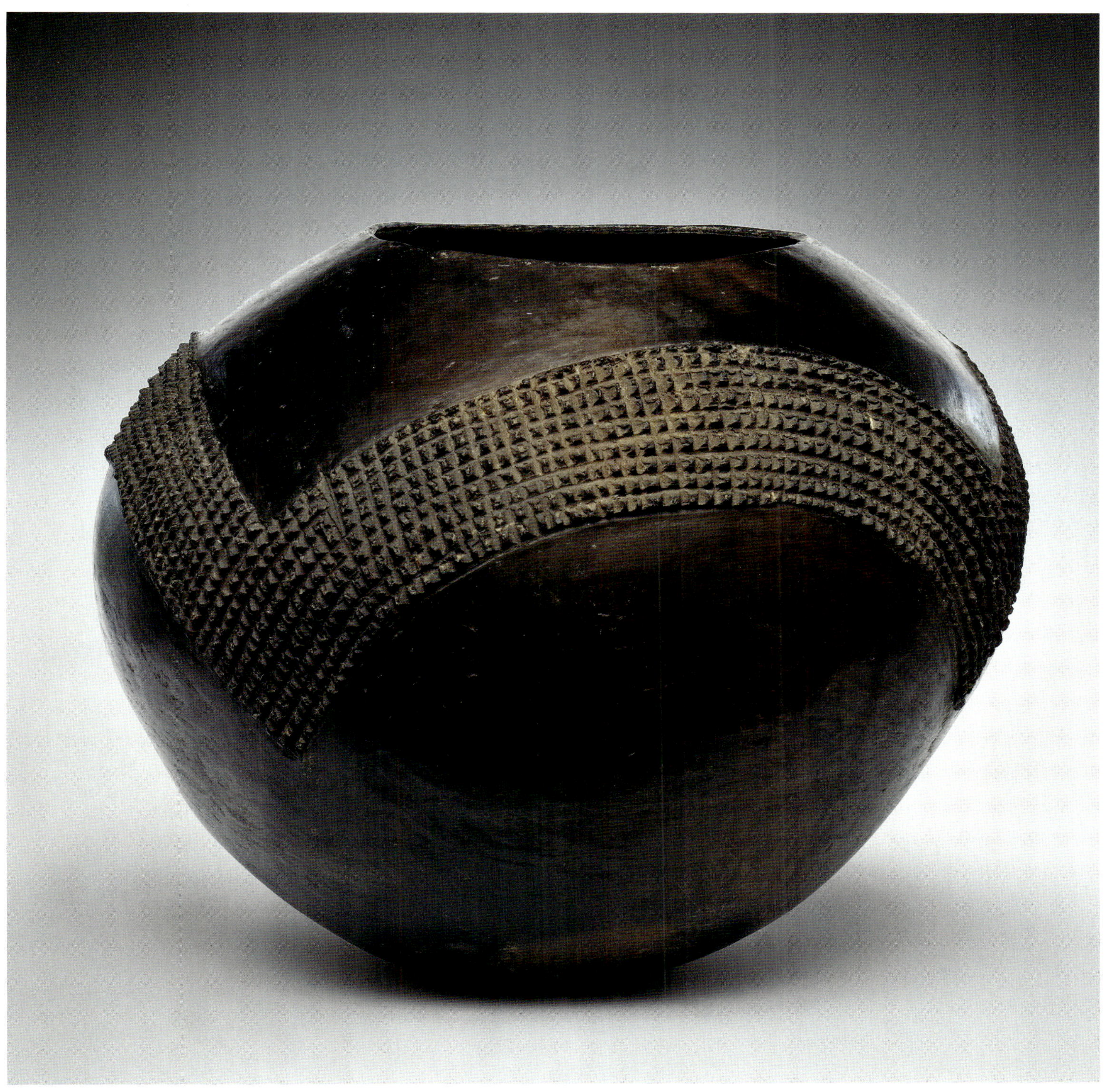

POT NUMBER 411 Ukhamba H: 310 mm Arcs of *amasumpa*.

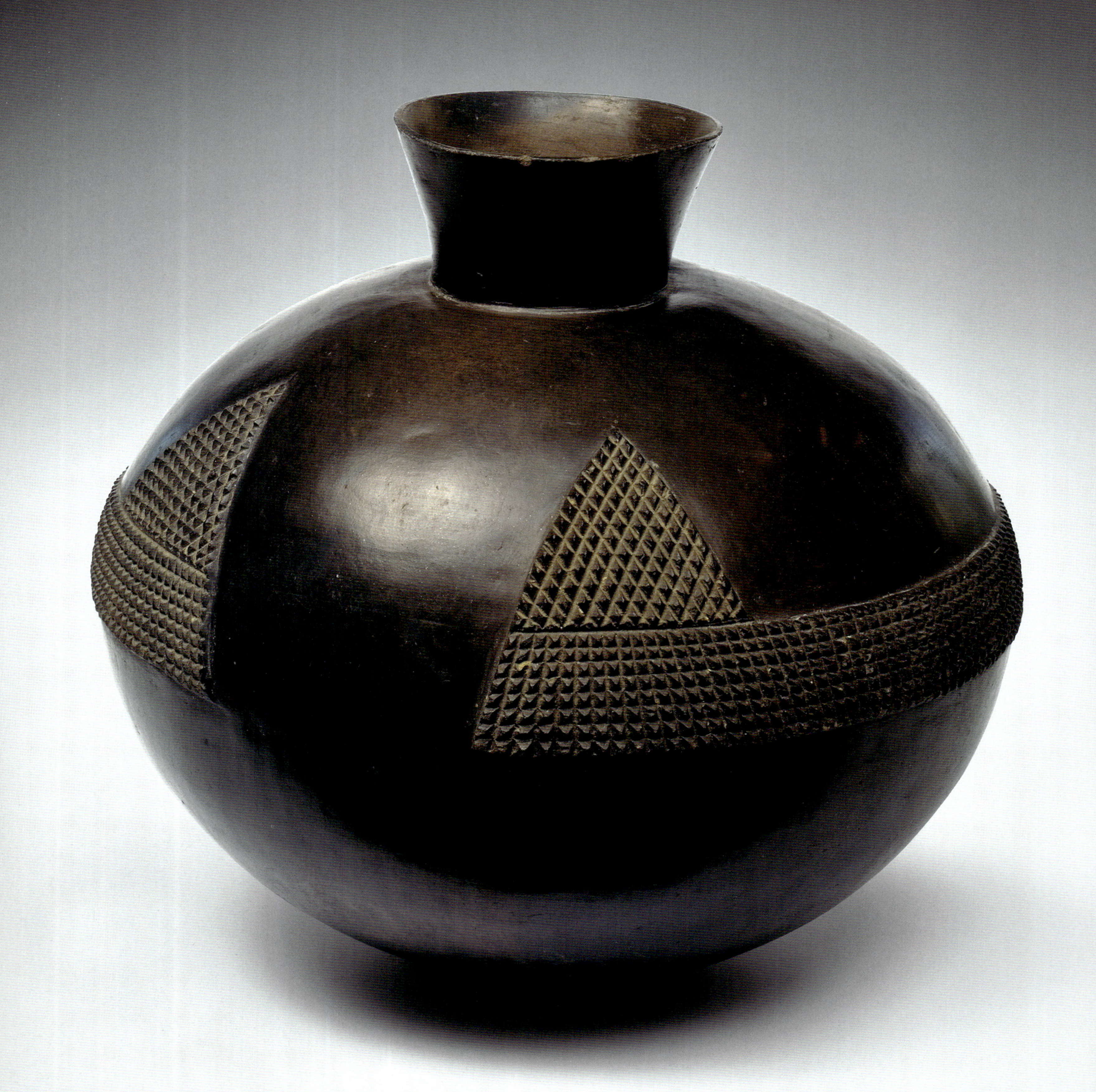

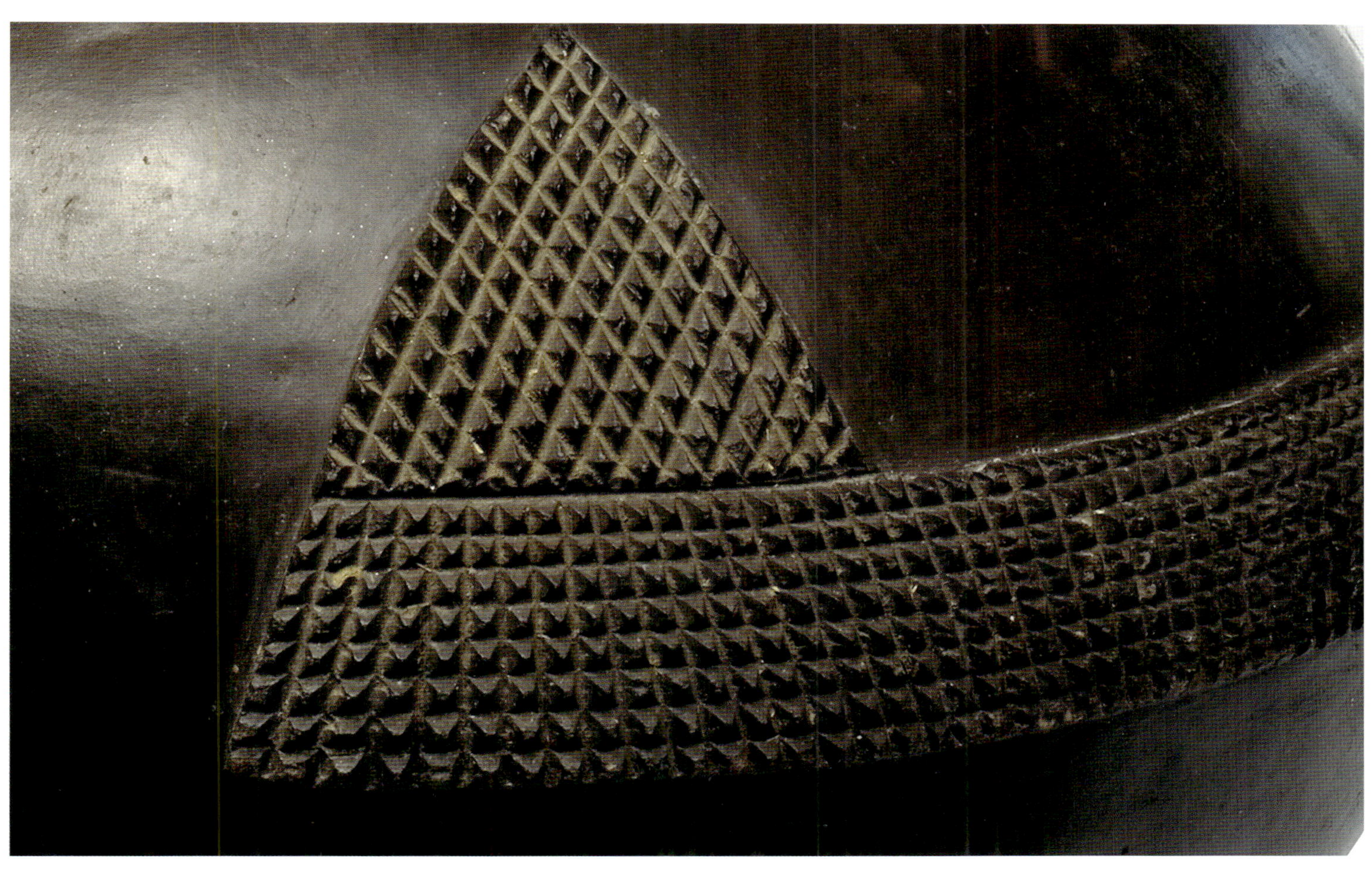

POT NUMBER 412 Uphiso H: 360 mm Two bands of *amasumpa* with upright triangles at their ends. The *amasumpa* of the triangles are set at an angle to those of the bands. Extremely fine regular work. The neck is flared in line with the regional convention; it is very slightly off-centre. Originally the pot had a rounded bottom; later a cement base was added enabling it to stand on a flat surface.

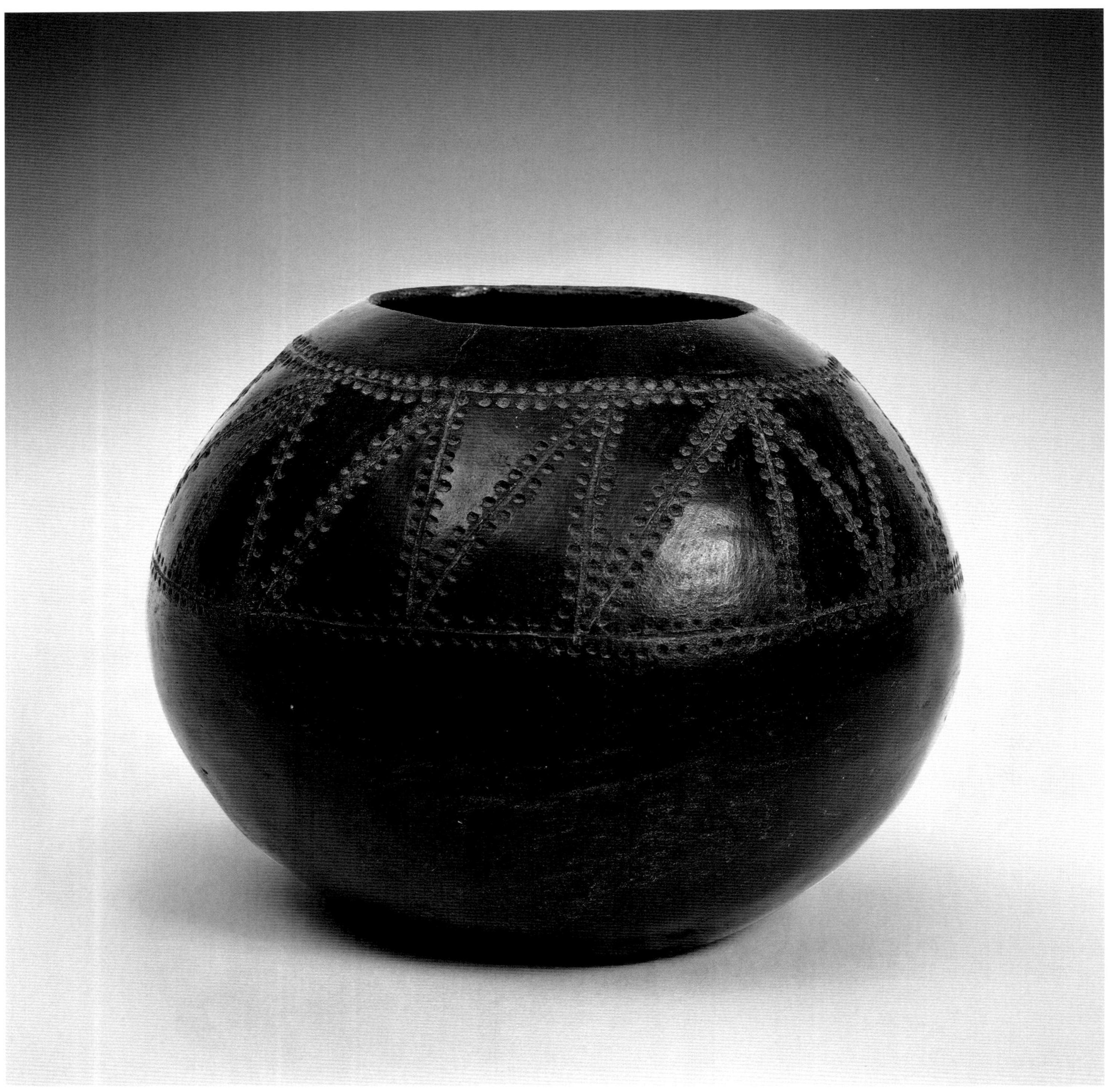

POT NUMBER 420 Umancishana H: 150 mm Incised and impressed on shoulder. Reminiscent of an old Msinga design.

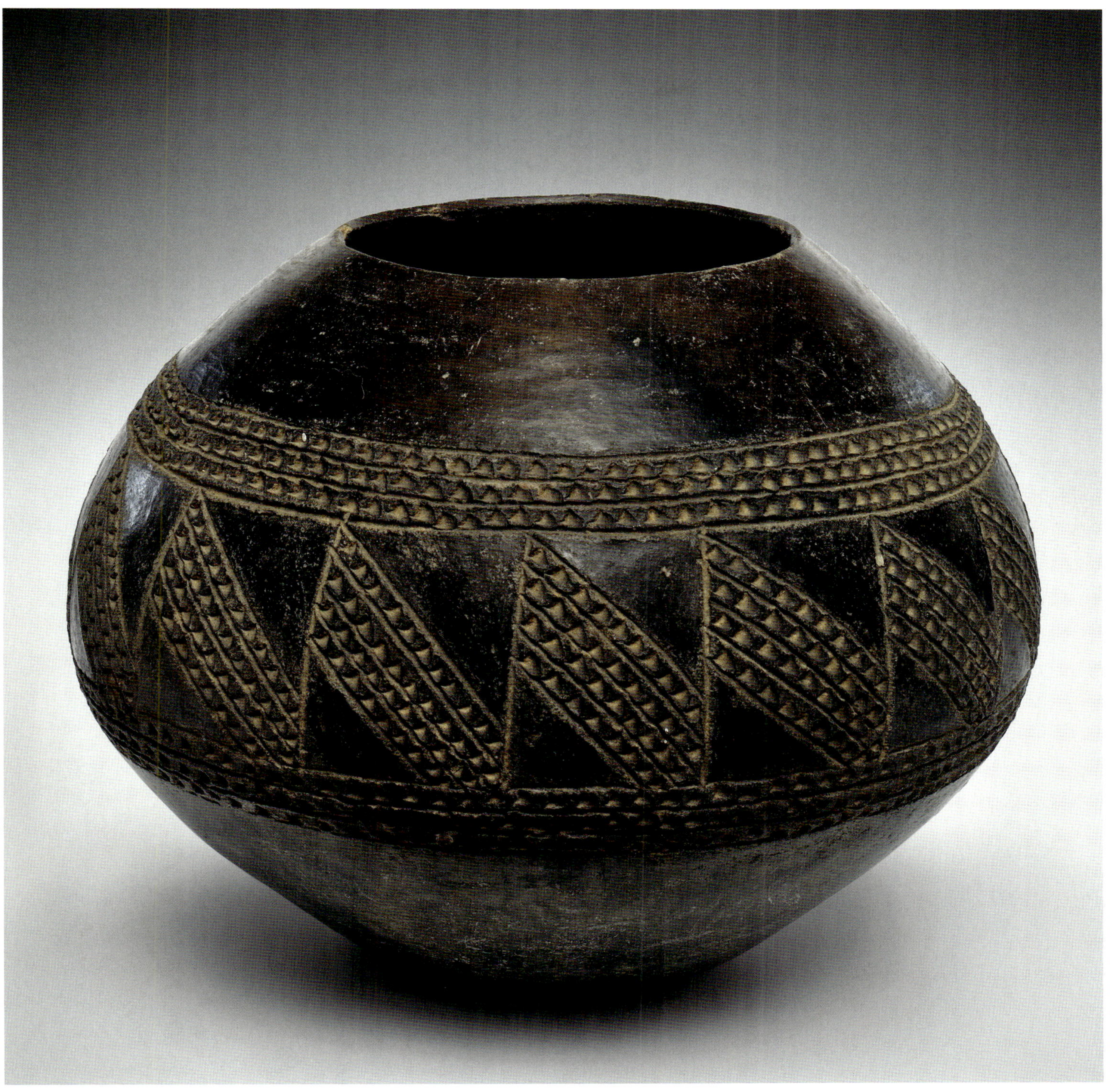

POT NUMBER 421 Ukhamba H: 225 mm Notched

Melmoth Style 2

Vessels with incised patterns from a number of distinct regions (*izigodi*) within the greater area: from eFofolozi Pot 415 page 142, from uGatsha Pot 419 page 145, from eMatshensundu Pot 416 page 144 and from eNdundulu Pot 414 page 146, Pot 417 page 148 and Pot 418 page 149.

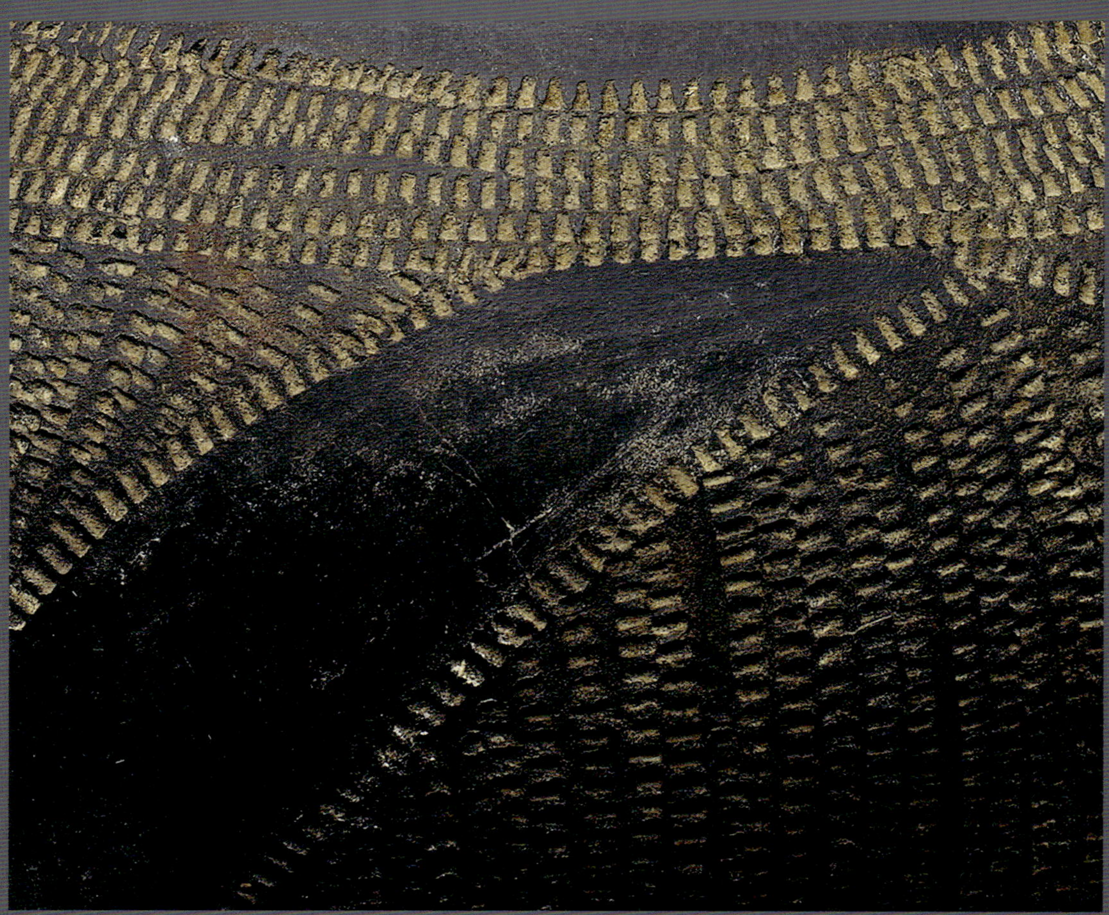

POT NUMBER 415 Ukhamba H: 290 mm
Spaced opposing triangles between bands.

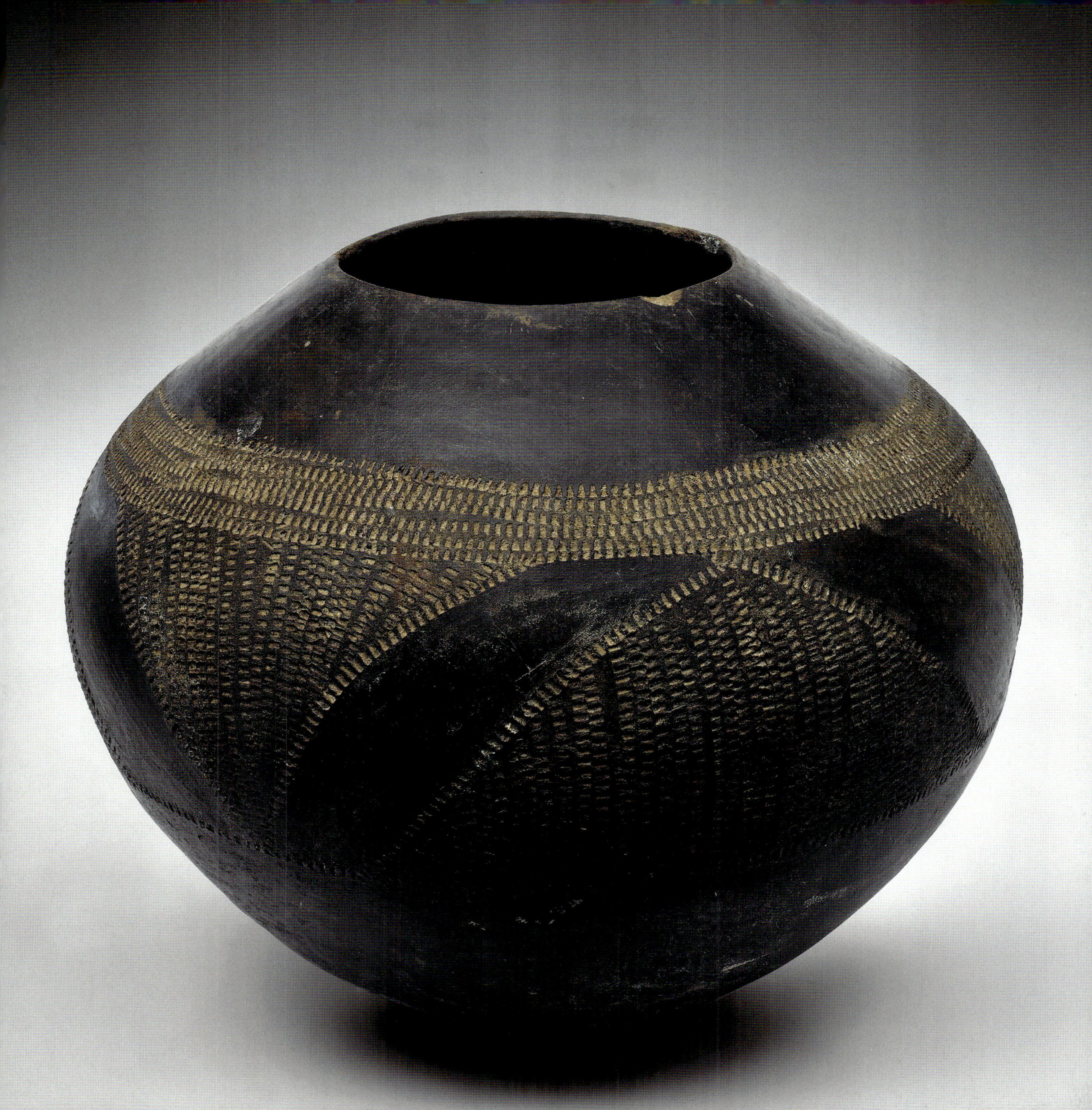

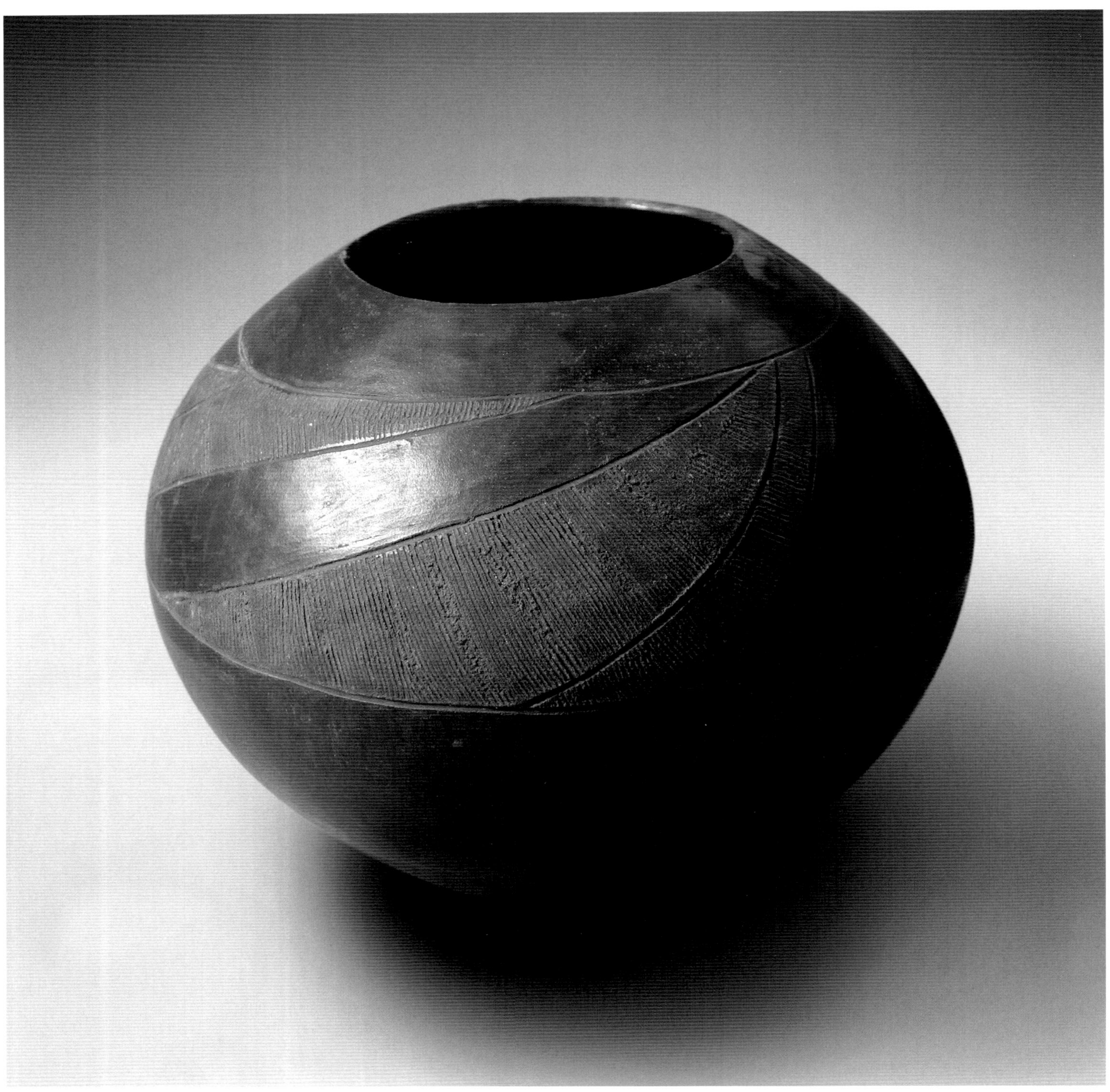

POT NUMBER 416 Ukhamba H: 255 mm Linear incisions, obtuse-angled triangle motif.

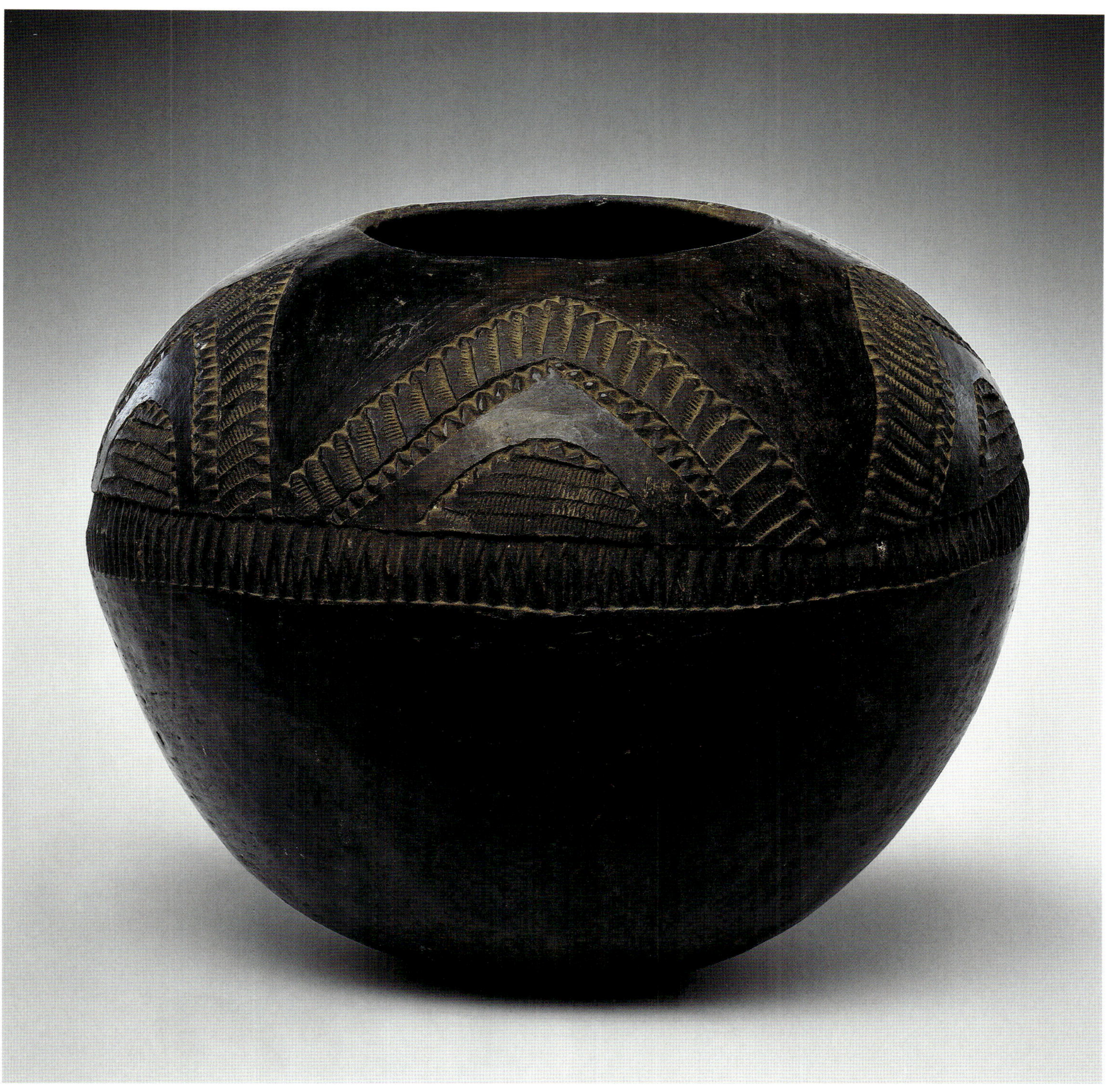

POT NUMBER 419 Ukhamba H: 300 mm Wave pattern, incised and impressed (roller?). This pattern and variations of it are characteristic of the area.

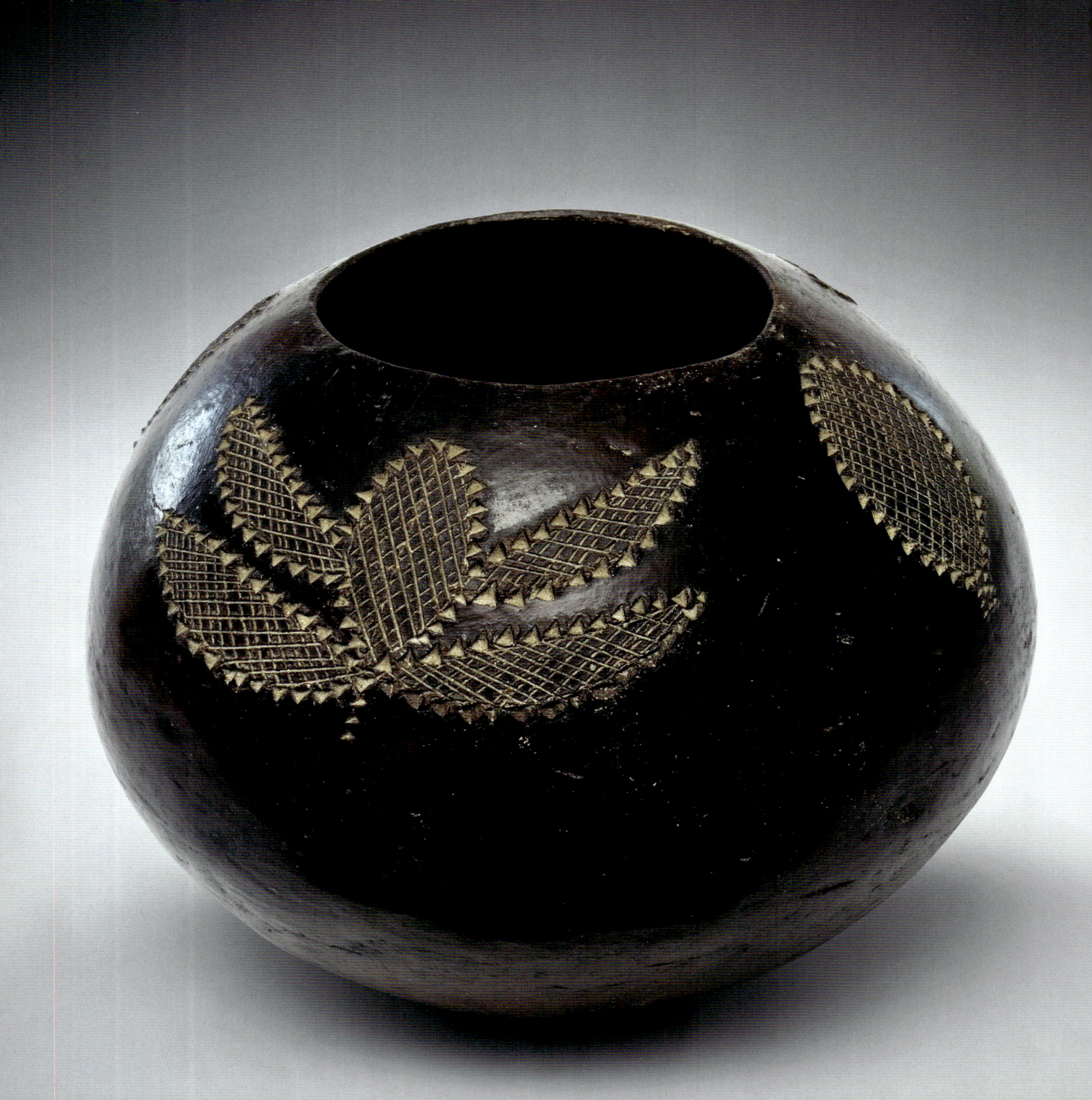

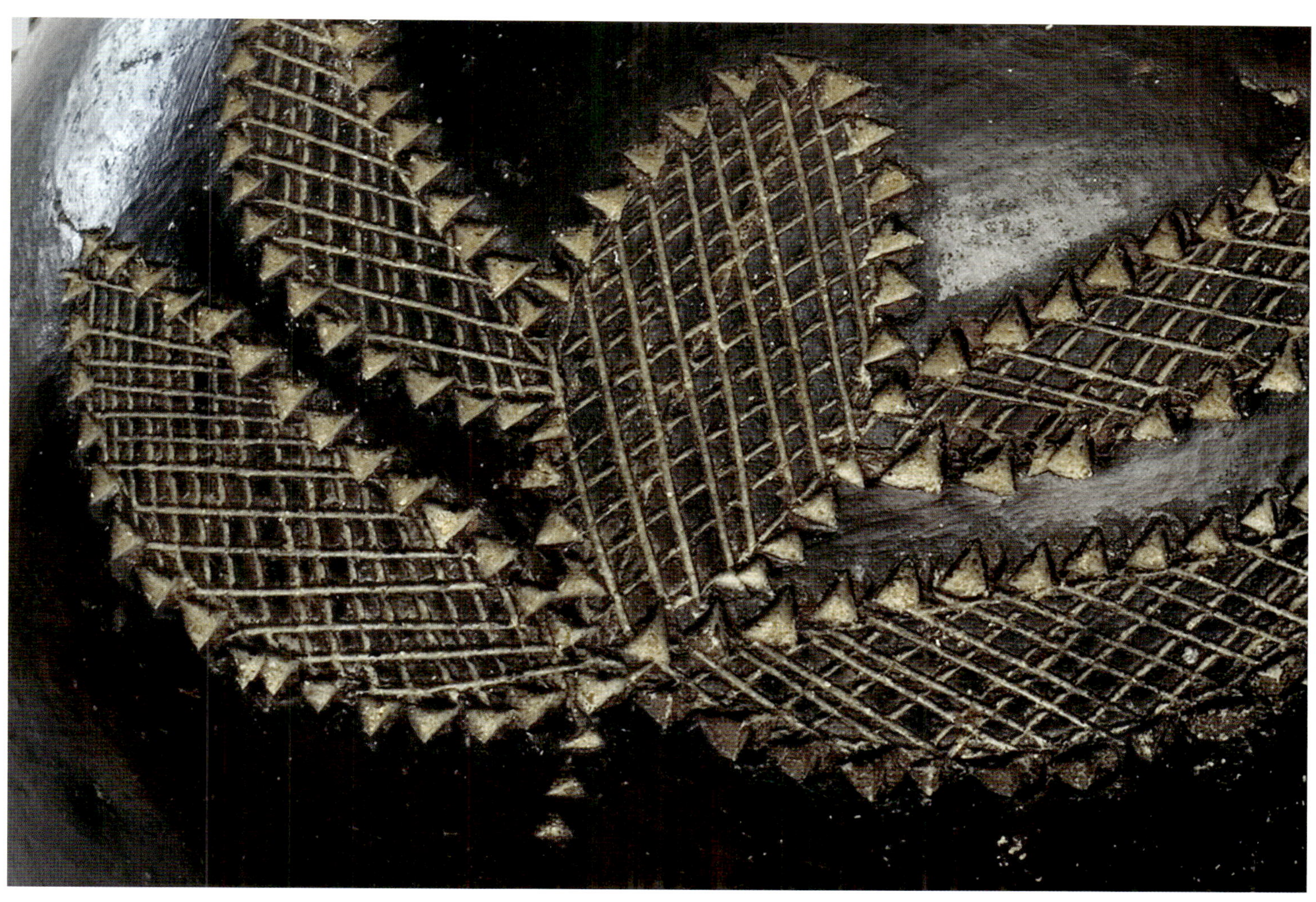

POT NUMBER 414 Small ukhamba H: 195 mm Incised and notched motifs on shoulder, leaf shapes. Said to be an old Eshowe style.

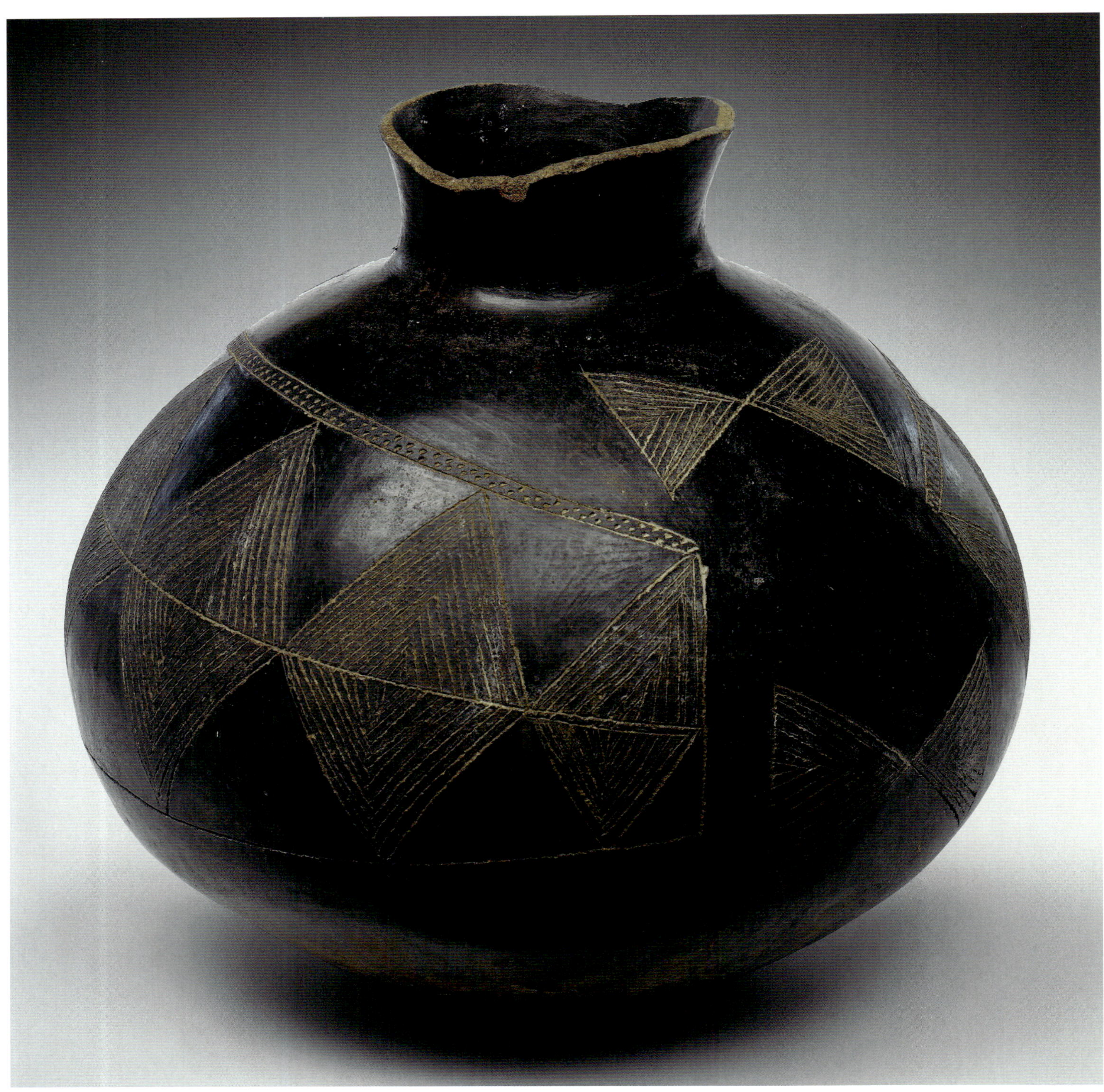

POT NUMBER 417 Uphiso H: 355 mm Linear incisions: slanting groups of rhomboids interspersed with butterfly motifs.

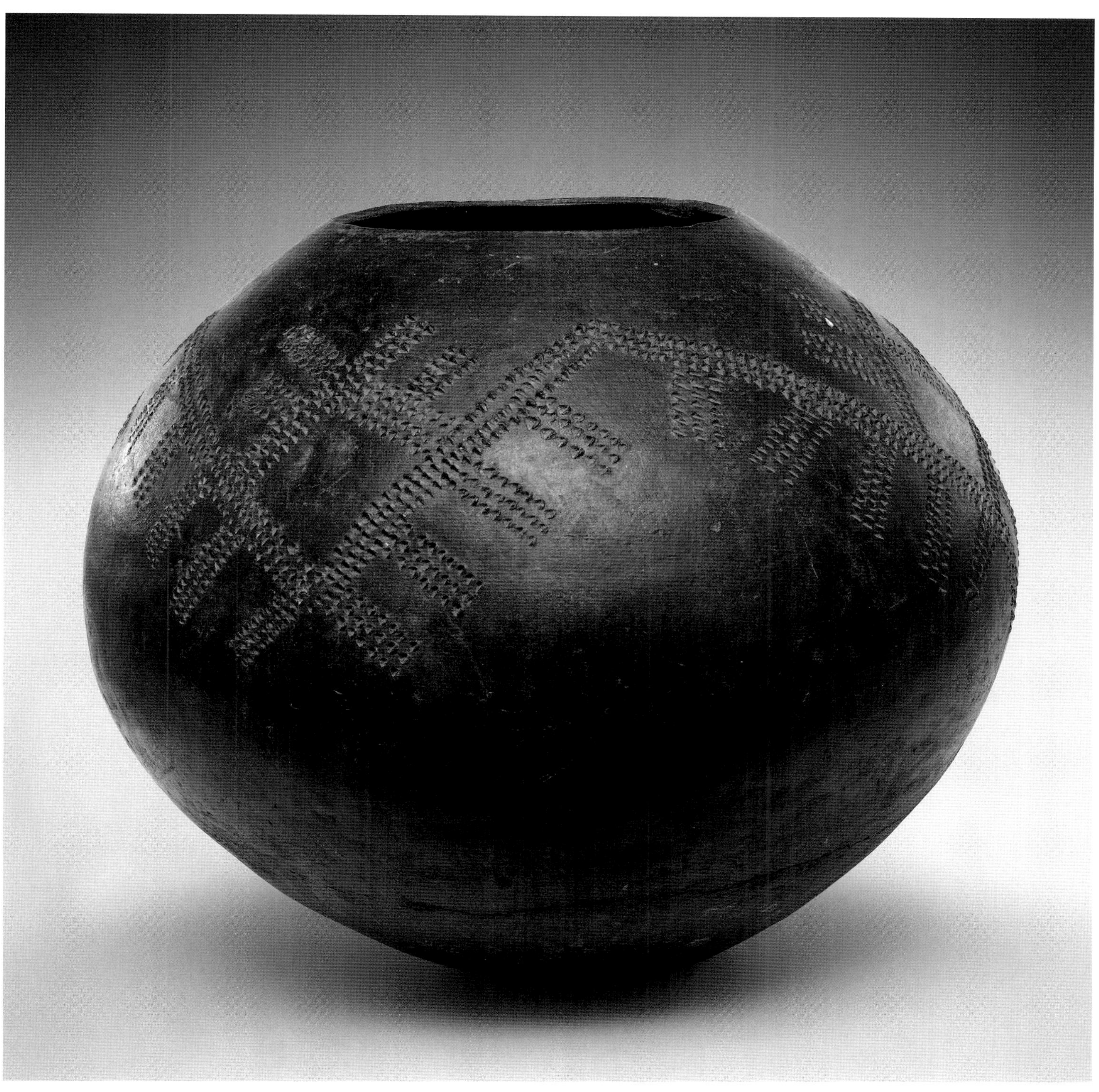

POT NUMBER 418 Ukhamba H: 355 mm Notched.

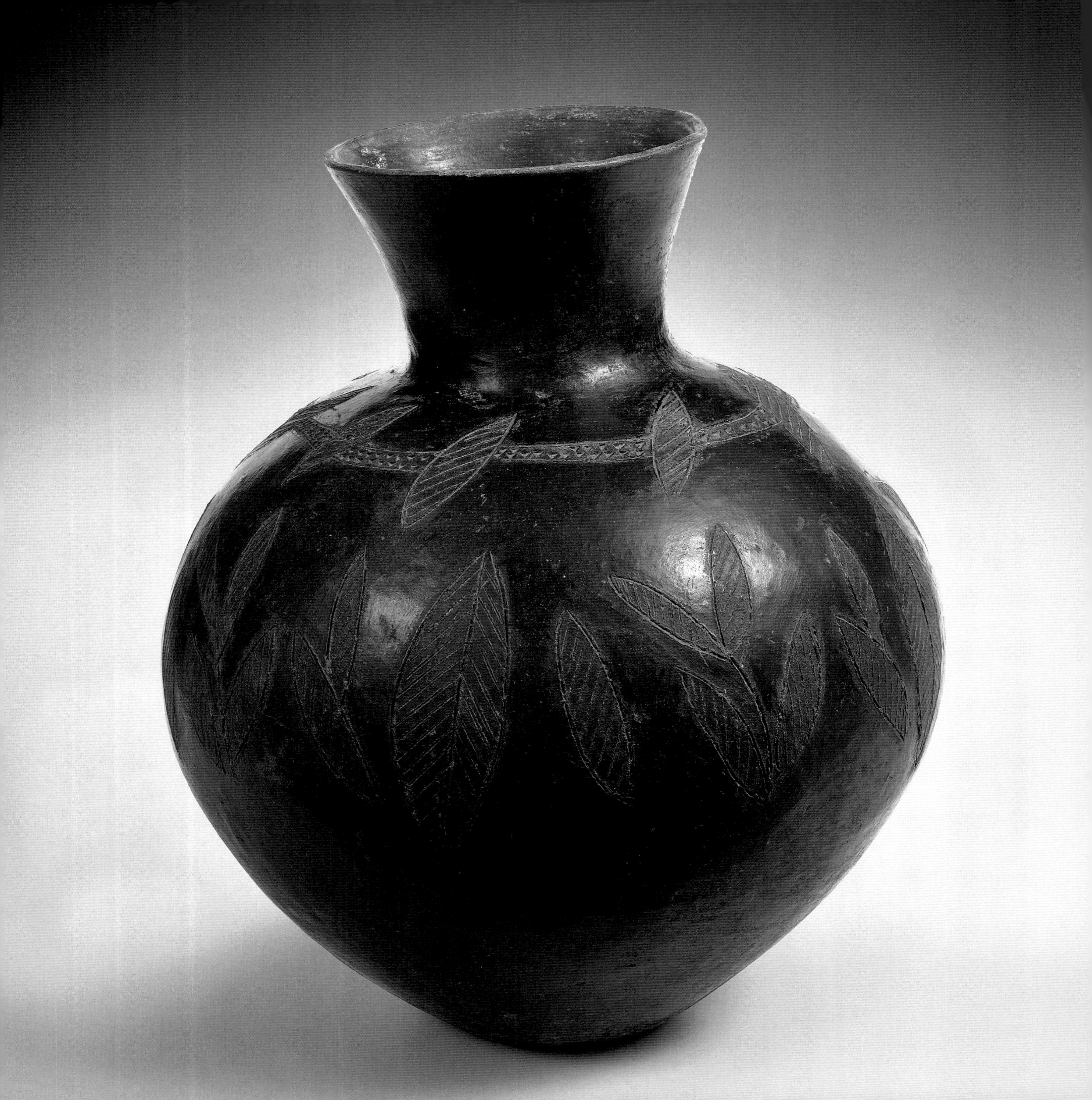

5

The Lower Thukela Region

This encompasses the region south of the uMhlatuze River and east of the uMzin-yathi on both sides of the Thukela (see map page 30). It includes Nkandla and Qudeni in the north, the territory between Eshowe and Kranskop and the tributaries of the Thukela: the Nsuze, the Manyane and the other lesser ones. At first sight it appears to be a transitional region containing pots with decorations based on those of the applied patterns to the north, and ones with the incised patterns of the west. However, on closer examination it becomes clear that the patterns themselves are not directly derived from those of adjoining regions. The similarities that exist, say between patterns employing a motif such as pendant triangles, are more likely to be a part of a common heritage than a direct derivation. There is no obvious 'hier-archy of symmetries'. The same applies to the 'phyto-patterns' of the Thukela valley itself (for example Pot 516 page 150); they cannot be said to be derived from similar designs found upstream.

The pottery of the Manyane valley is known for its complex configurations of *amasumpa* carved from applied panels of clay (compare Pots 501–507 page 157). It was heavily collected by European dealers in the early 1990s, so a representative sample is no longer available. The area marks the southern limit of the *amasumpa* technique. The valley of the next major tributary of the Thukela downstream, the Nsuze, which reaches up into Nkandla, was also heavily collected. Some pots with *amasumpa* pressed out from the inside come from there.[62] The adjoining region

POT NUMBER 516 Uphiso H: 320 mm
Incised and notched leaf pattern characteristic of the region downstream from Tugela Ferry.

to the northwest between Nqutu and the uMzinyathi was settled by Sotho people. I did not find any Zulu pottery.

The Lower Thukela region is also home to a number of families of distinguished potters, such as the Magwazas[63] and the Nalas, who have had a profound influence on the styles of their localities. Of the latter, Nesta Nala († July 2005) is the most well known. She exhibited her work nationally and abroad, winning a number of prizes. In 1983 she introduced patterns into her work from first millennium shards excavated in the Thukela valley by archaeologist Len van Schalkwyk. However, this innovation made little impact on the local market and was not copied by other potters, though it helped to establish Nesta's international reputation.[64] Beer pots made for the local market by members of the Nala family are represented by the following four *izinkamba* (Pot 517 page 153, Pot 518 page 154, Pot 519 page 155, and Pot 521 page 156).

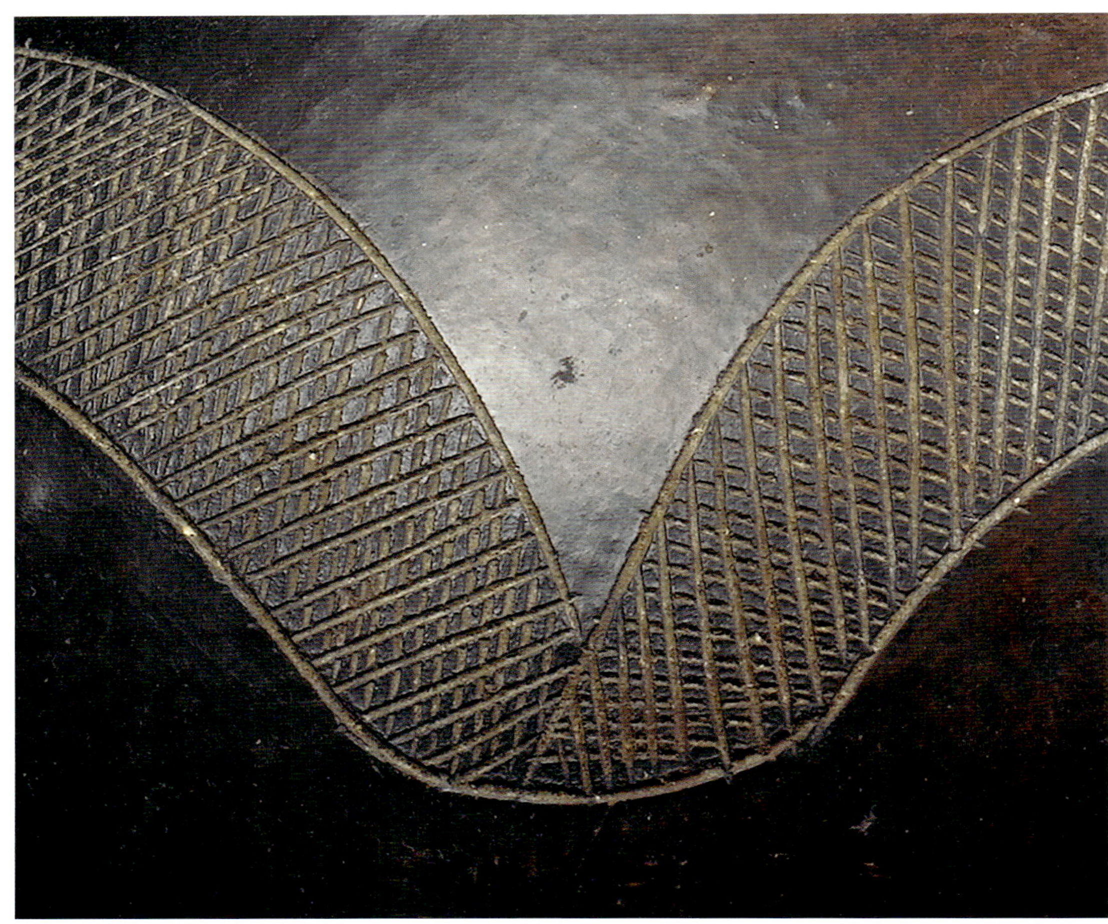

POT NUMBER 517 Ukhamba H: 269 mm
Linear incisions, wave pattern. Siphiwe
Nala's 'old style'. Ratio H:D: 1:1.3

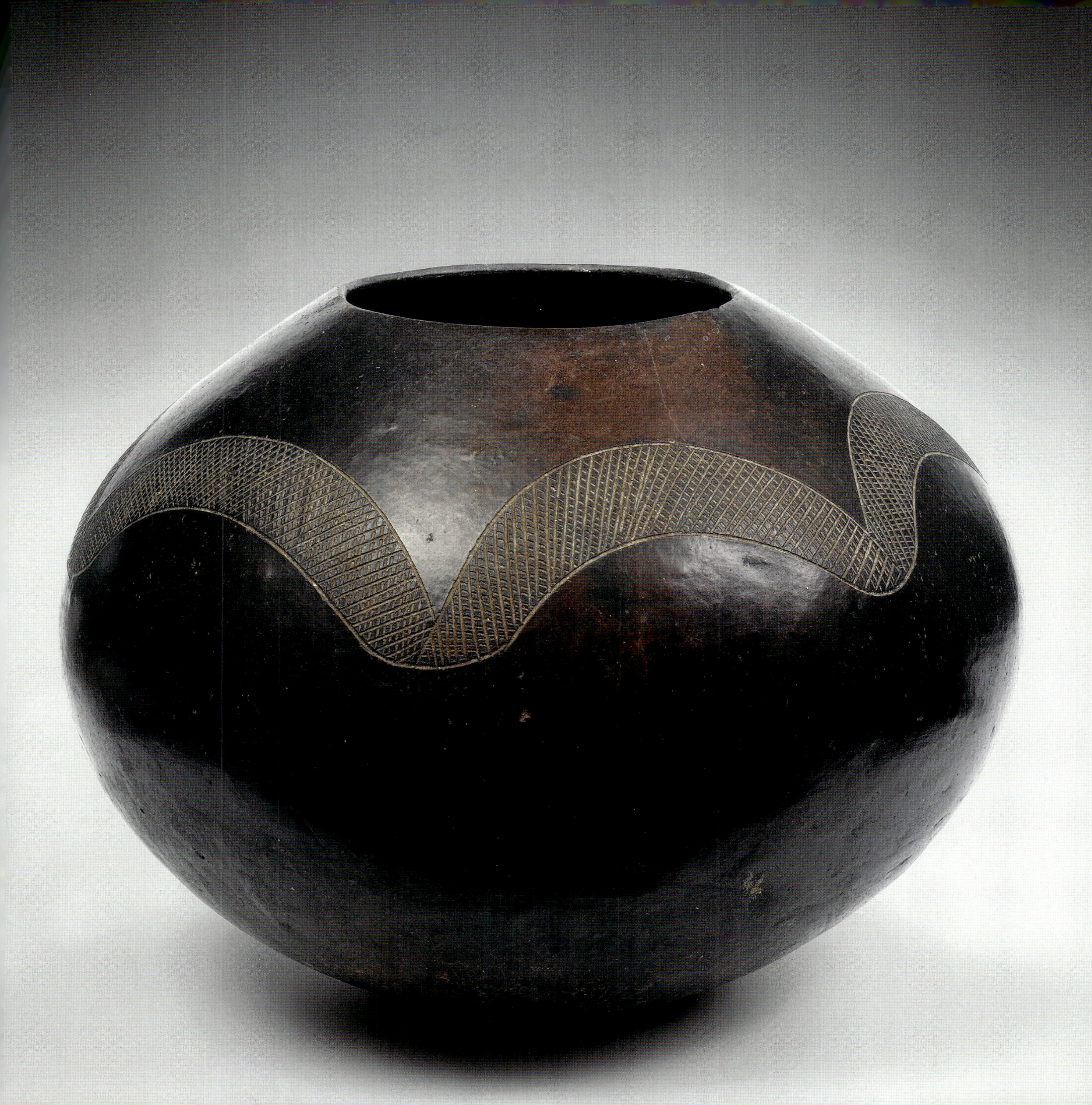

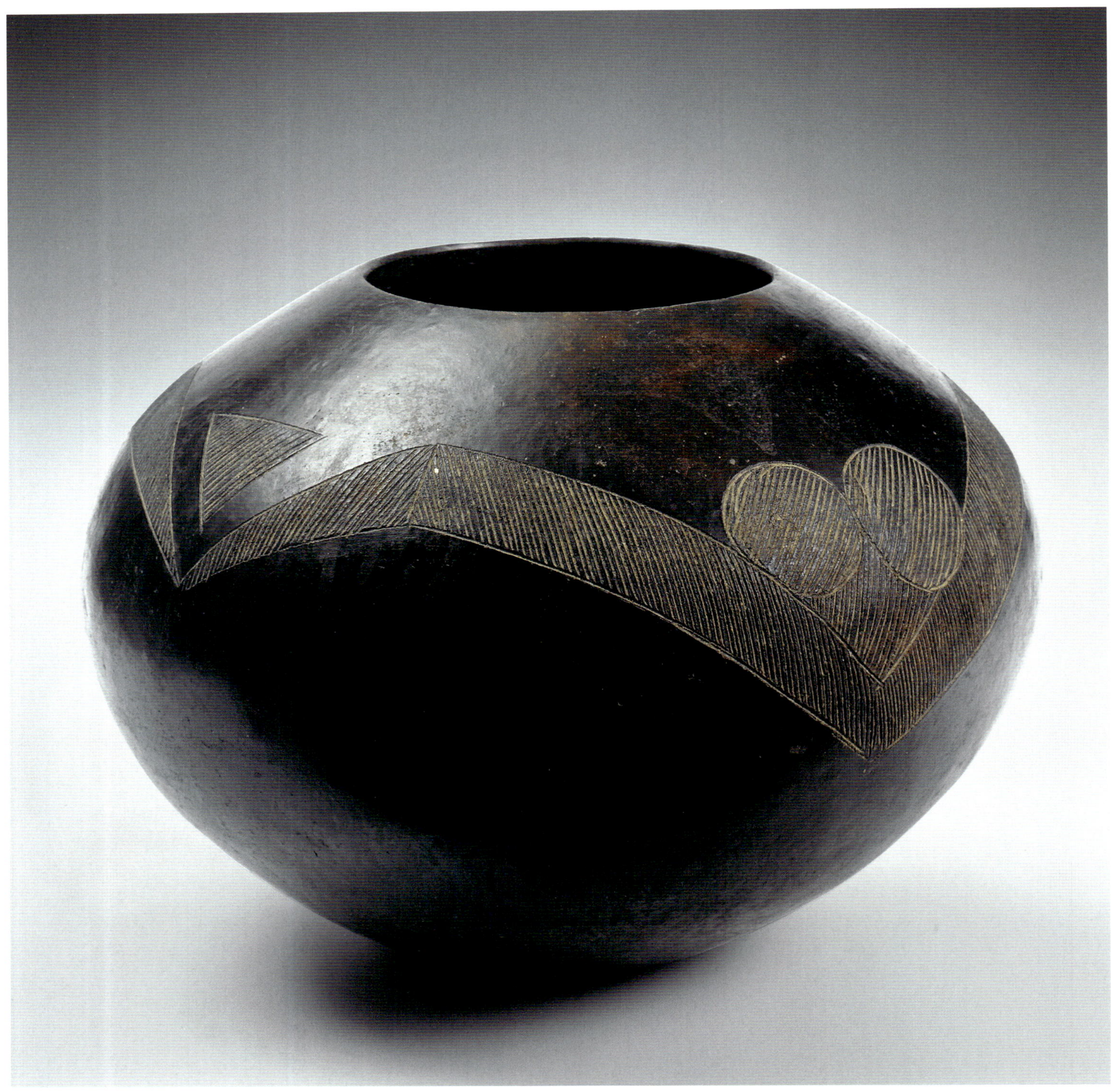

POT NUMBER 518 Ukhamba H: 247 mm Linear incisions, two motifs with triangles and circles (not visible in photo) on wave pattern. For greater detail and interpretation of Pot 517, 518, 519 and 521 see Jolles 2012:15–18.

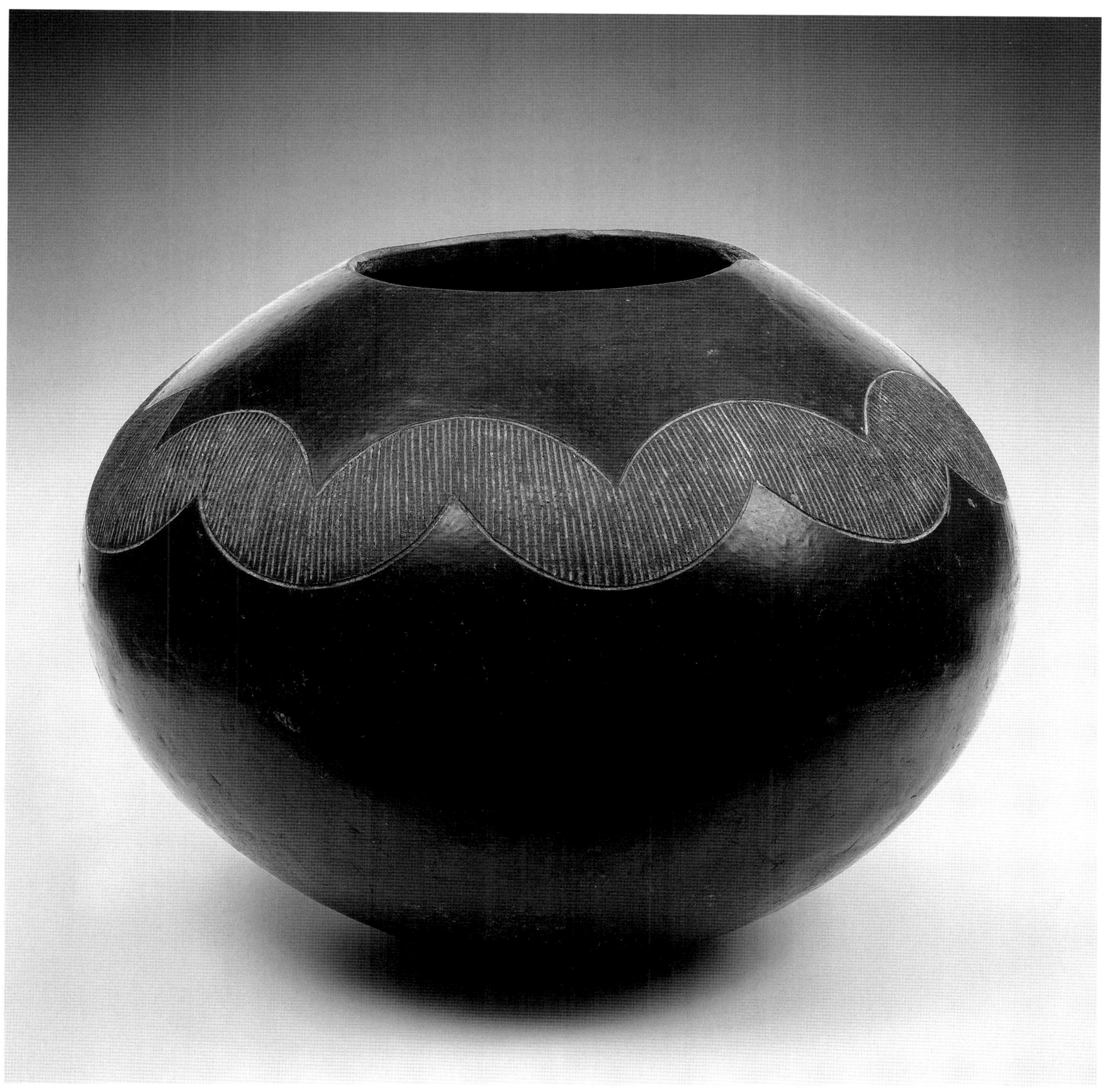

POT NUMBER 519 Ukhamba H: 255 mm Linear incisions.

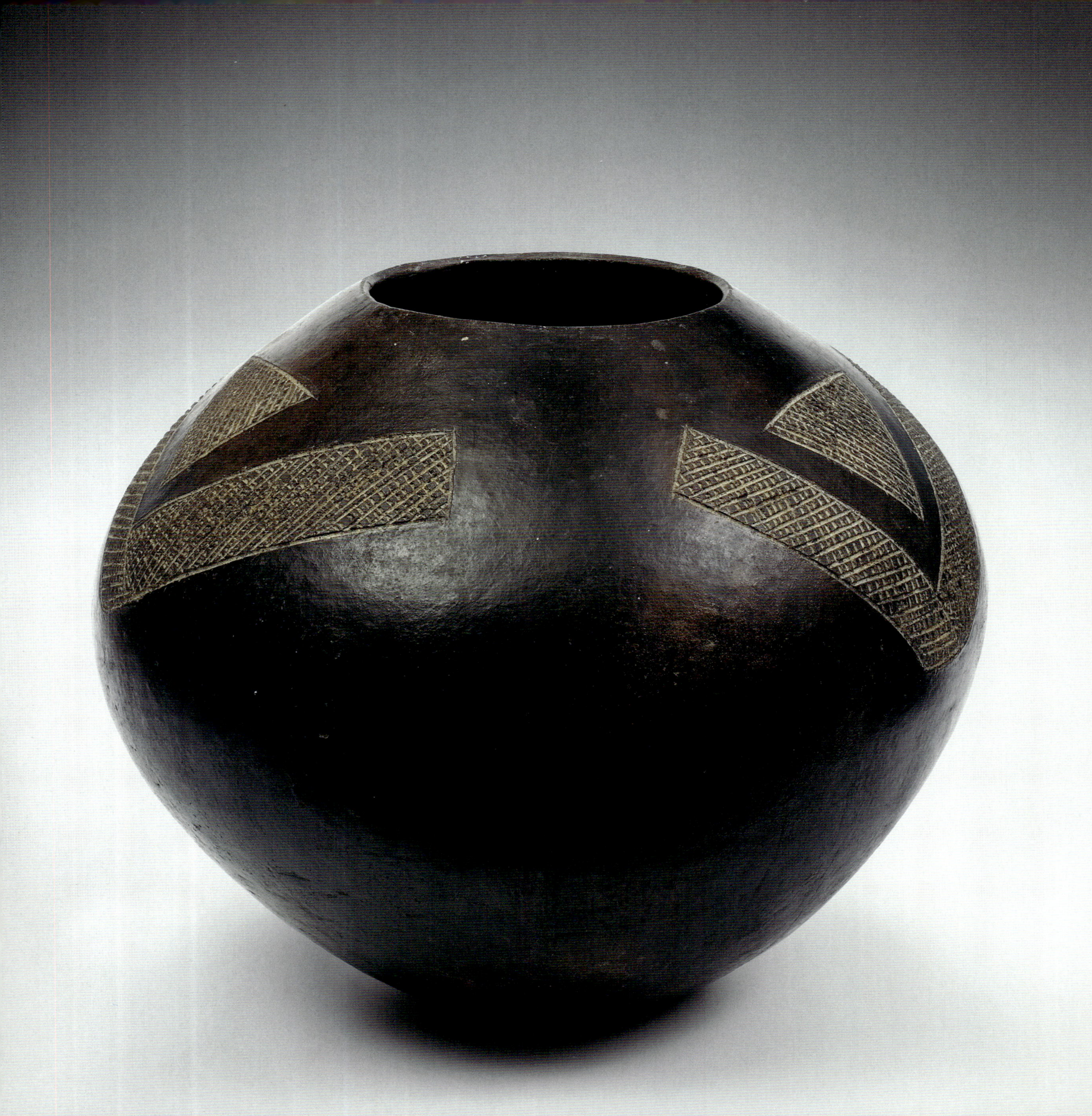

The distribution of styles within the Thukela region is differently structured to that of the previously described regions to the north. It contains the meeting of distinct technical styles: the canonical *amasumpa*-based tradition of applied decorations from the north and the more fragmented clan-based incised patterns from the west,[65] but it is not characterised by an original uniform style overlaid through immigration by styles from adjoining regions. The historical genesis of the Lower Thukela styles would appear to be more complex: the reach of the formative influence of the central kingdom represented by the *amasumpa* style petered out somewhere in Nkandla and the upper reaches of the tributaries of the Thukela.

The lower Thukela region comprises the following areas:

1. Manyane, the valley of the tributary of the Thukela of the same name from its confluence at Jameson's Drift. These pots mainly have applied decoration.

2. eKholwa, the area around Middledrift and the confluence of the Nsuze and the Thukela.

3. Oyaya, a fairly large area downstream from Middledrift.

Areas 2 and 3 have predominantly incised decoration, though some rope-like applications occur in area 3. In this region, there are considerable tracts of country which could not be included in the survey because they were completely collected out.

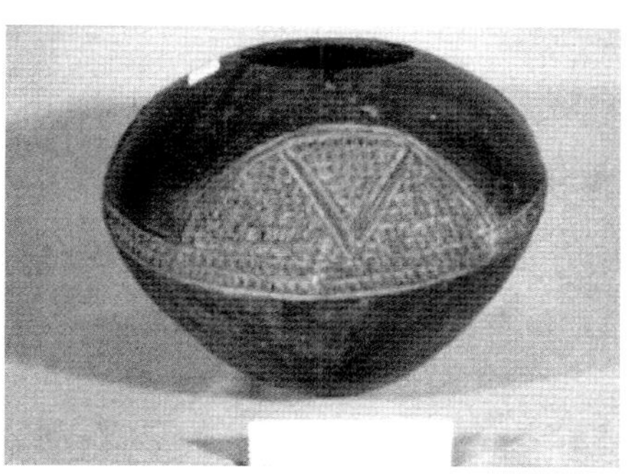

501

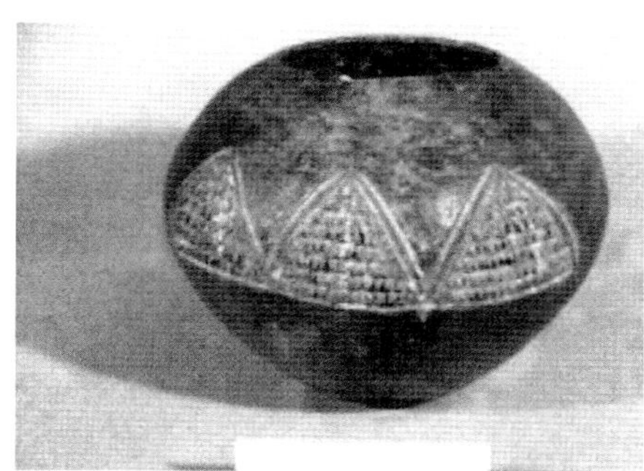

502

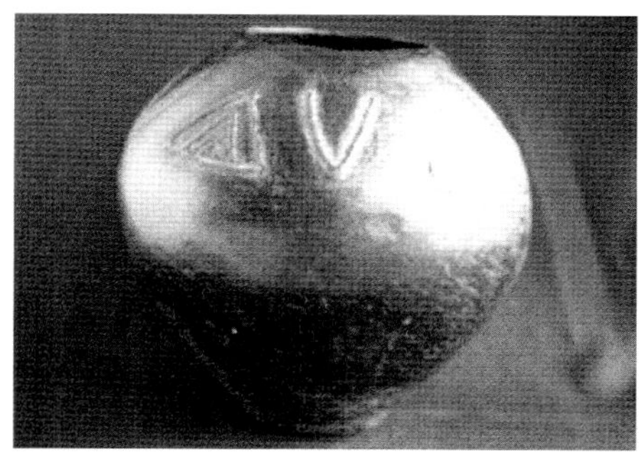

503

Old slides of beer vessels collected in the Manyane valley and exhibited in the Jack Heath Gallery of the University of Natal in 1993. 1970s–1980s Nos. 501–505

505 COLLECTION: Marilee Wood

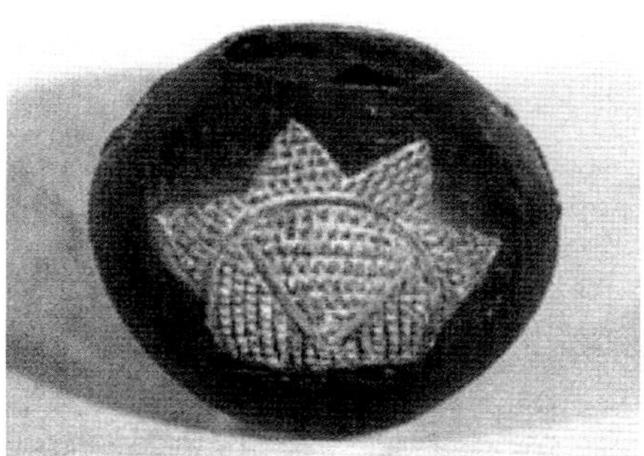

504

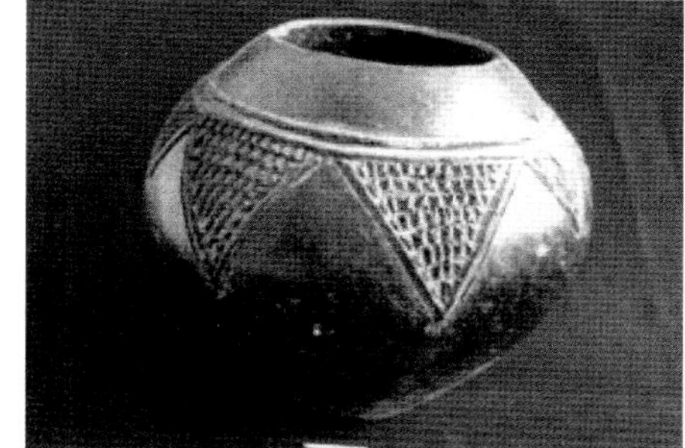

505: see also p. 158

POT NUMBER 521 Ukhamba H: 279 mm ‹
By Siphiwe Nala. Linear incisions.

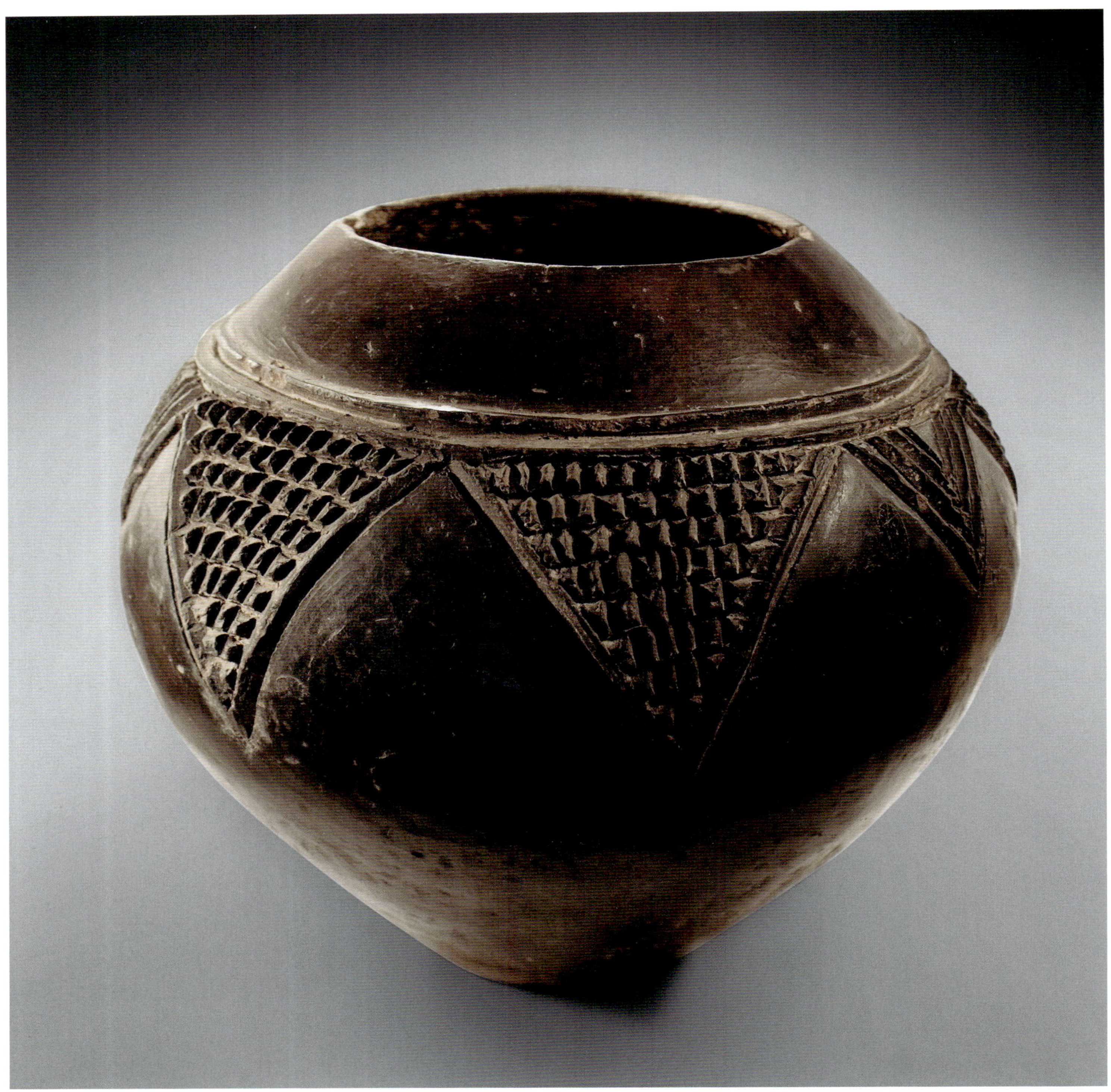

POT NUMBER 524 Ukhamba H: 260 mm Applied pendant triangles alternating between *amasumpa* and engraved ridges. COLLECTION: Marilee Wood.

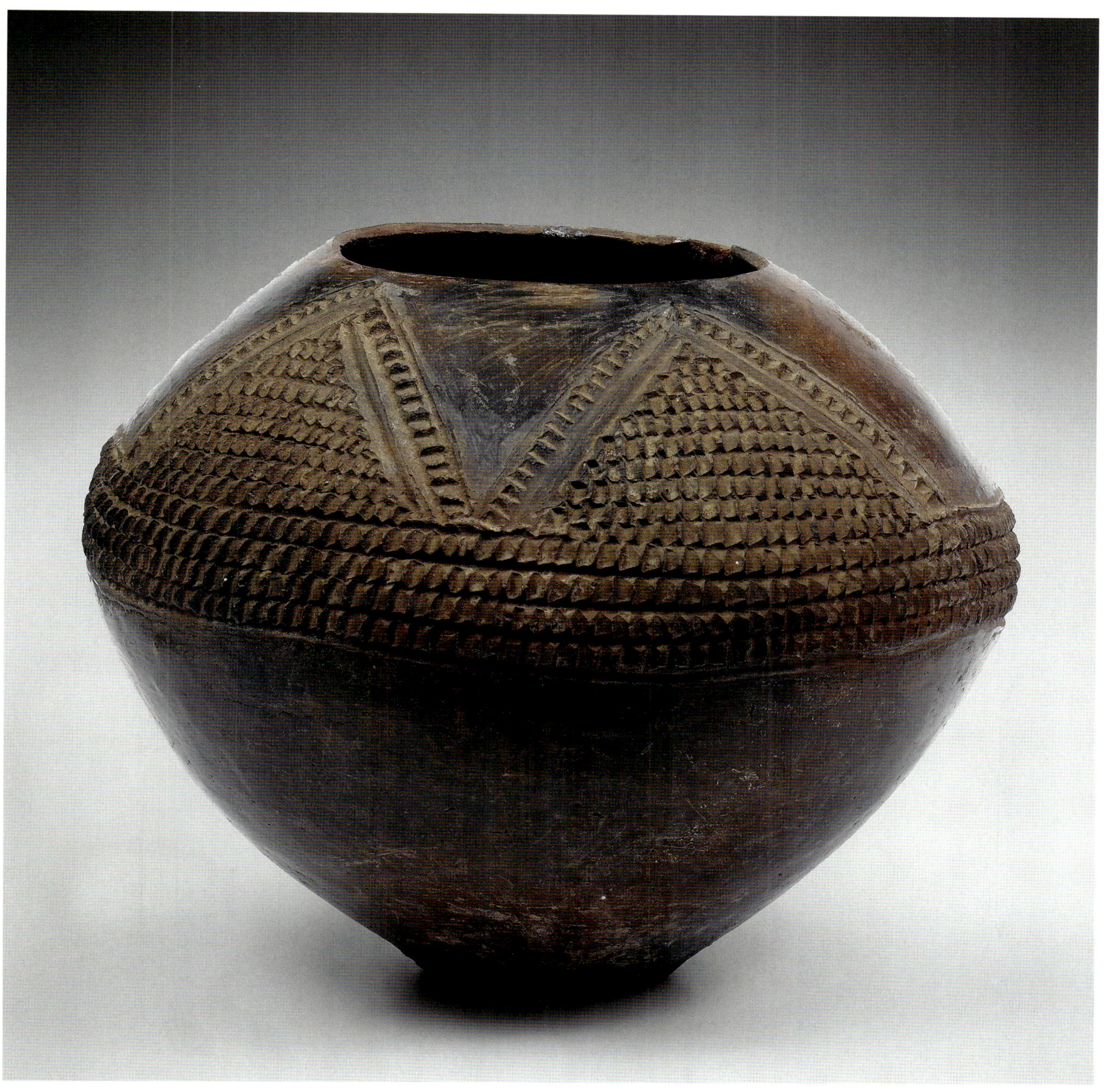

POT NUMBER 505 Ukhamba H: 230 mm Double triangle motifs on band, *amasumpa*.

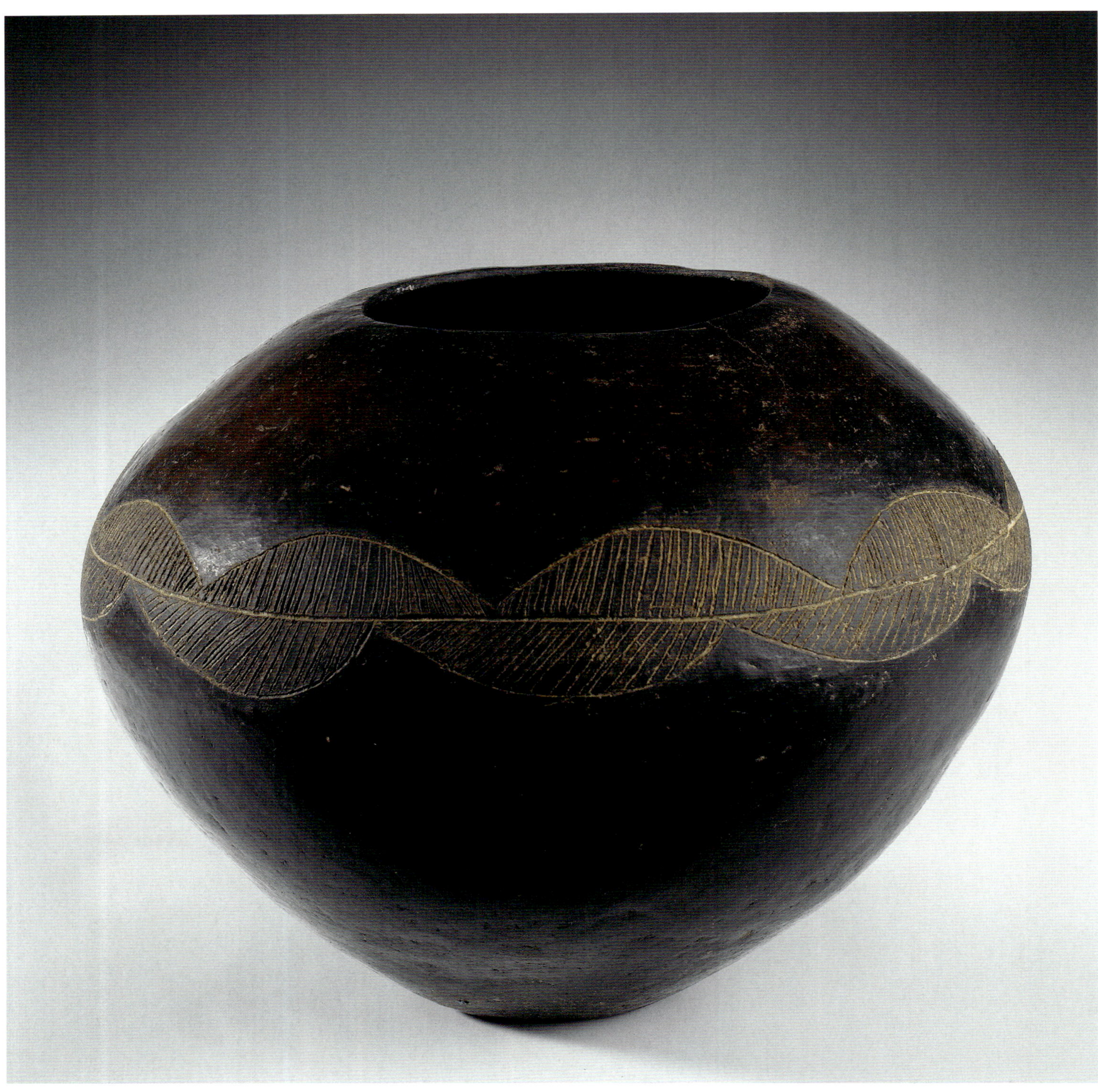

POT NUMBER 509 Ukhamba H: 250 mm Linear incisions, offset double wave pattern.

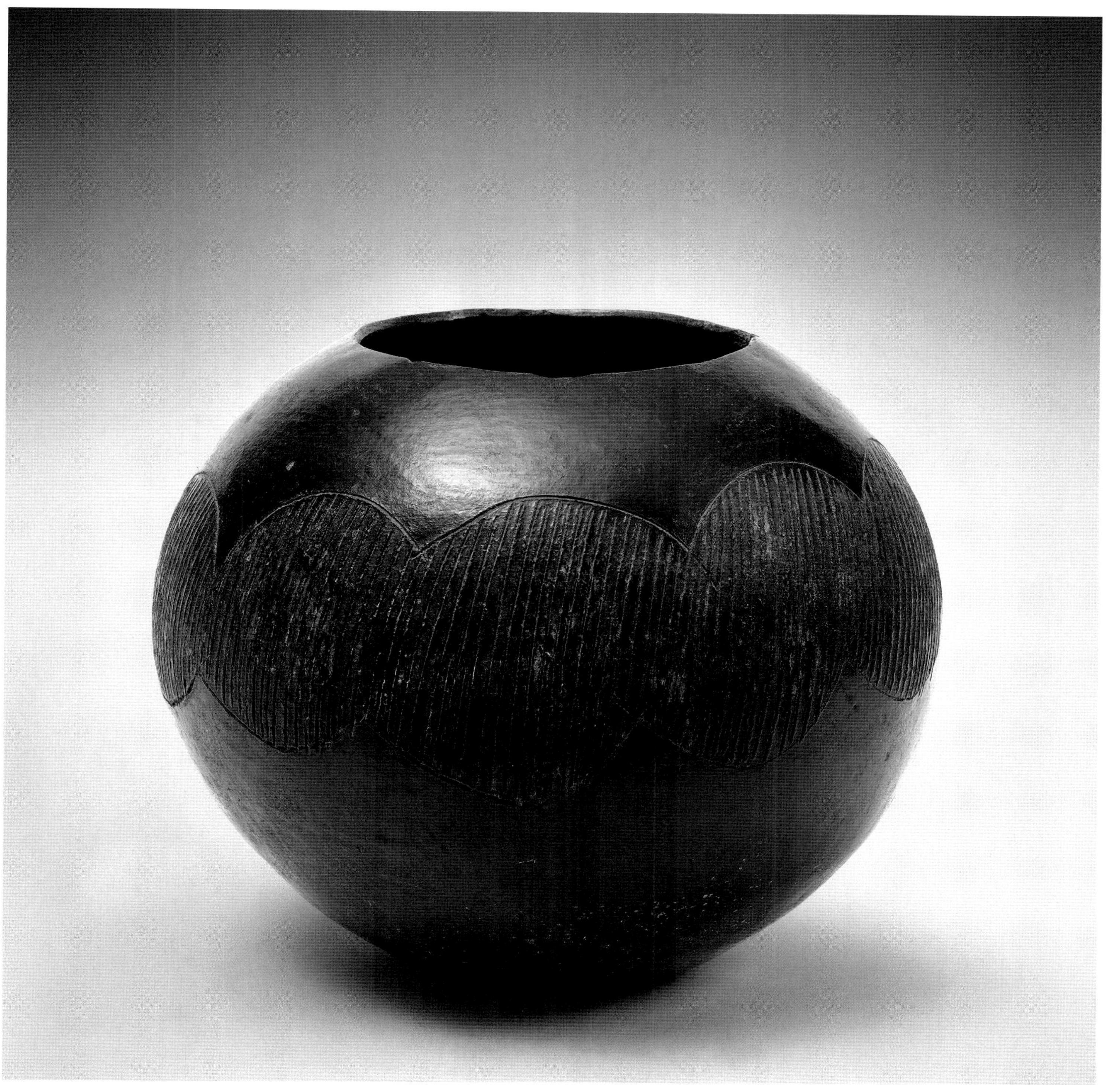

POT NUMBER 510 Small ukhamba or umancishana H: 170 mm Linear incisions on shoulder, offset double wave pattern (cf. 313).

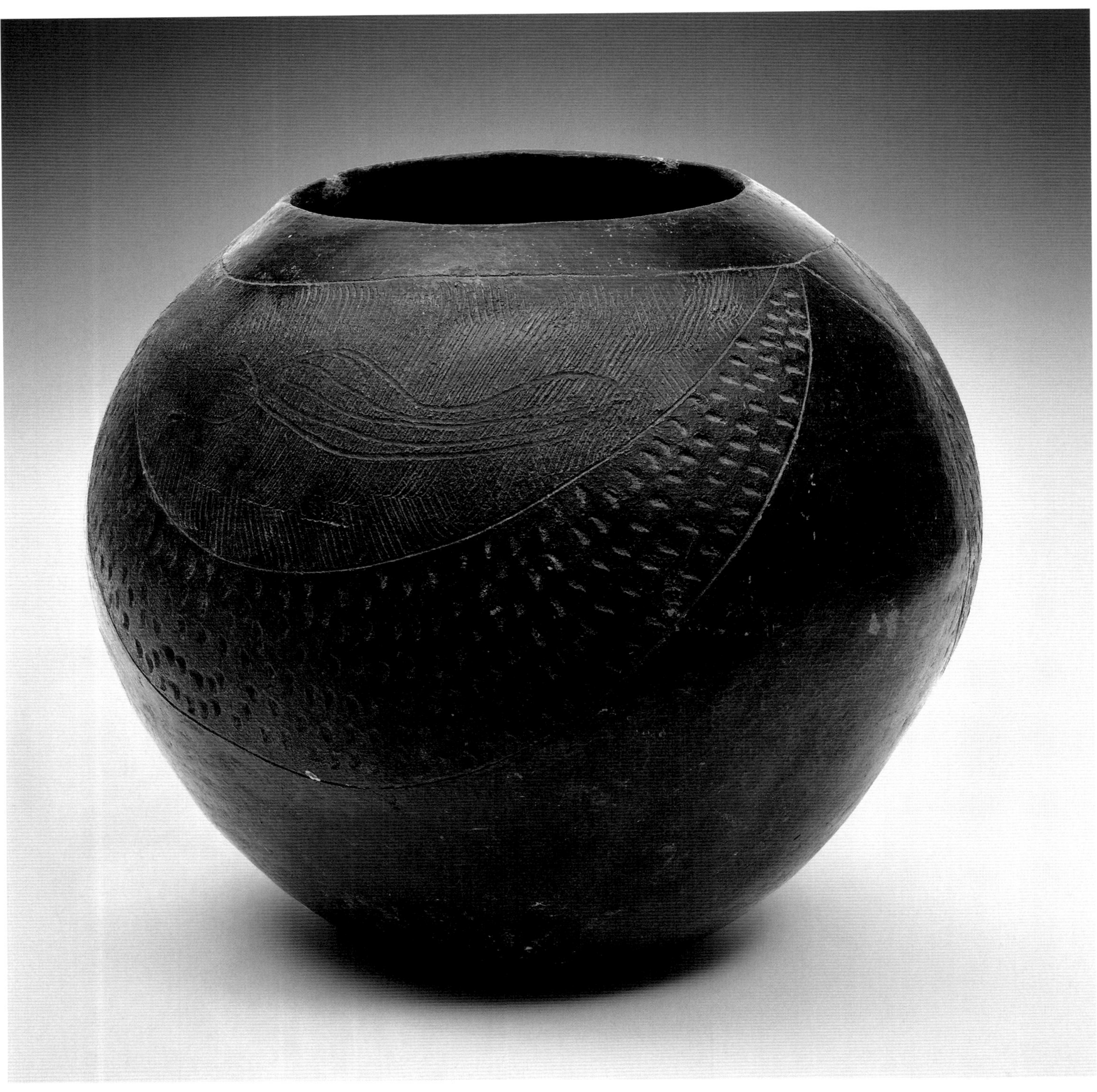

POT NUMBER 511 Ukhamba H: 245 mm Three motifs, incised and carved.

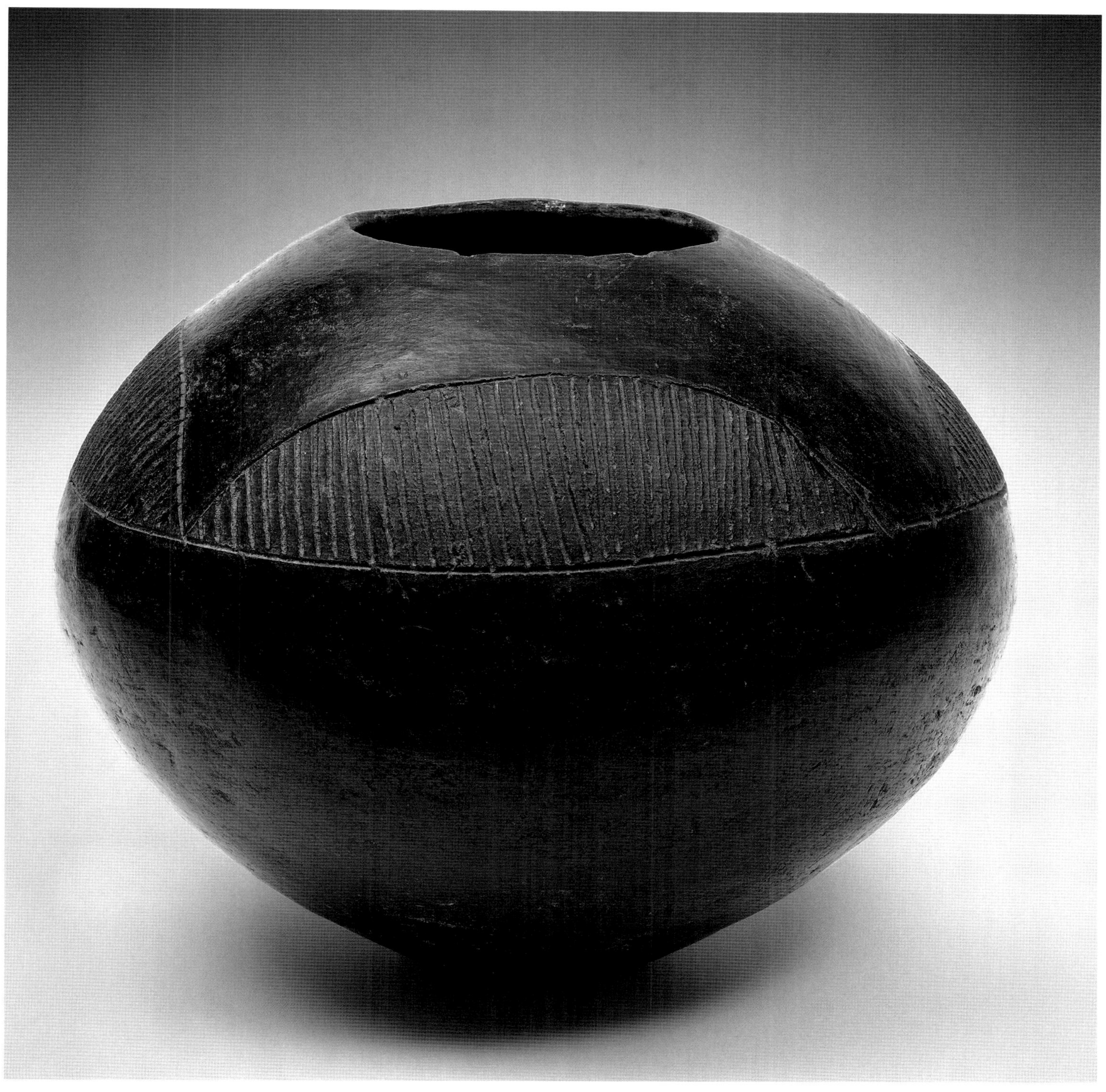

POT NUMBER 512 Ukhamba H: 220 mm Linear incisions on shoulder, separated wave pattern.

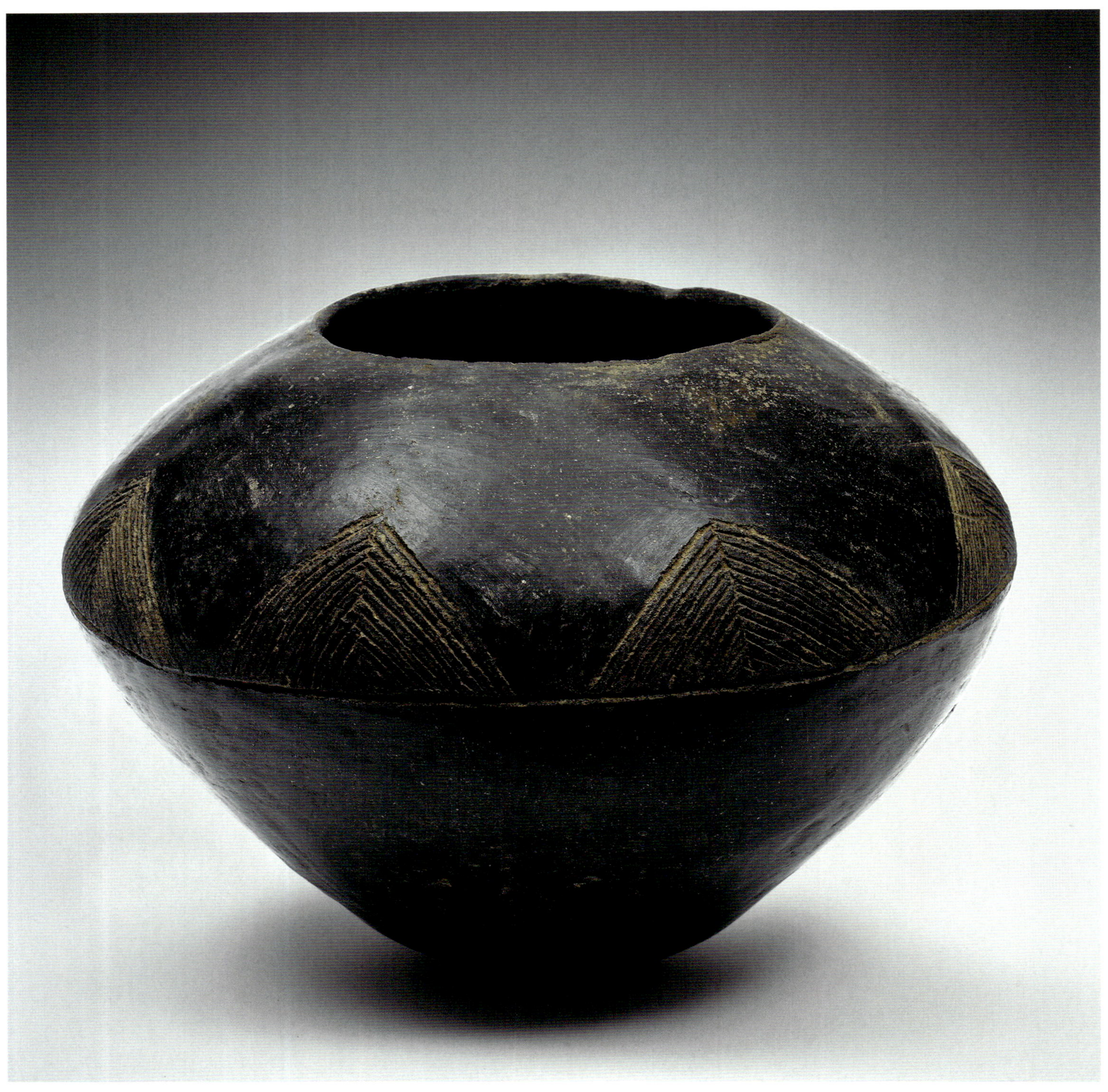

POT NUMBER 513 Ukhamba H:200 mm Linear incisions, upright triangles.

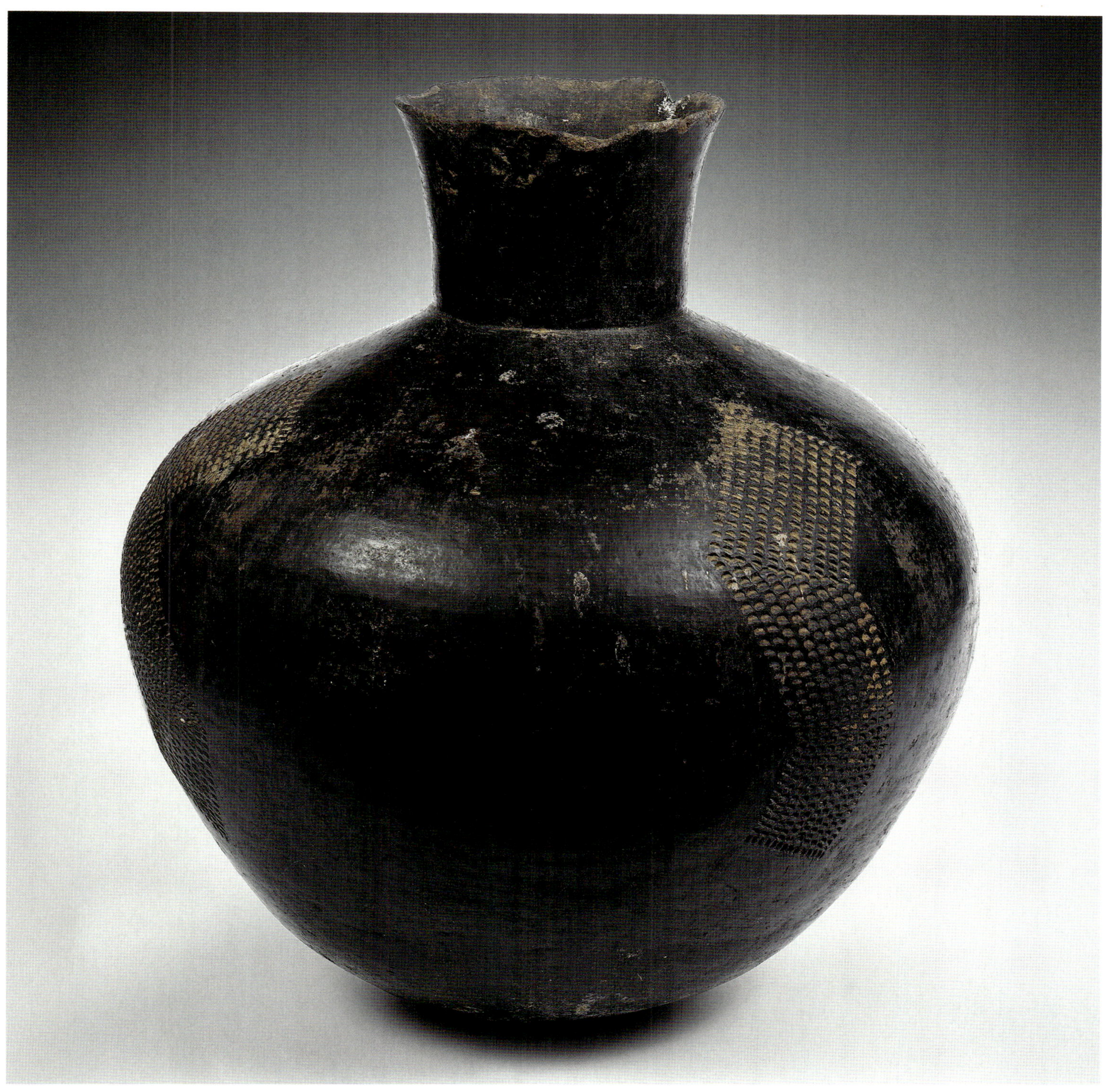

POT NUMBER 514 Uphiso H: 380 mm Notched, vertical zigzag.

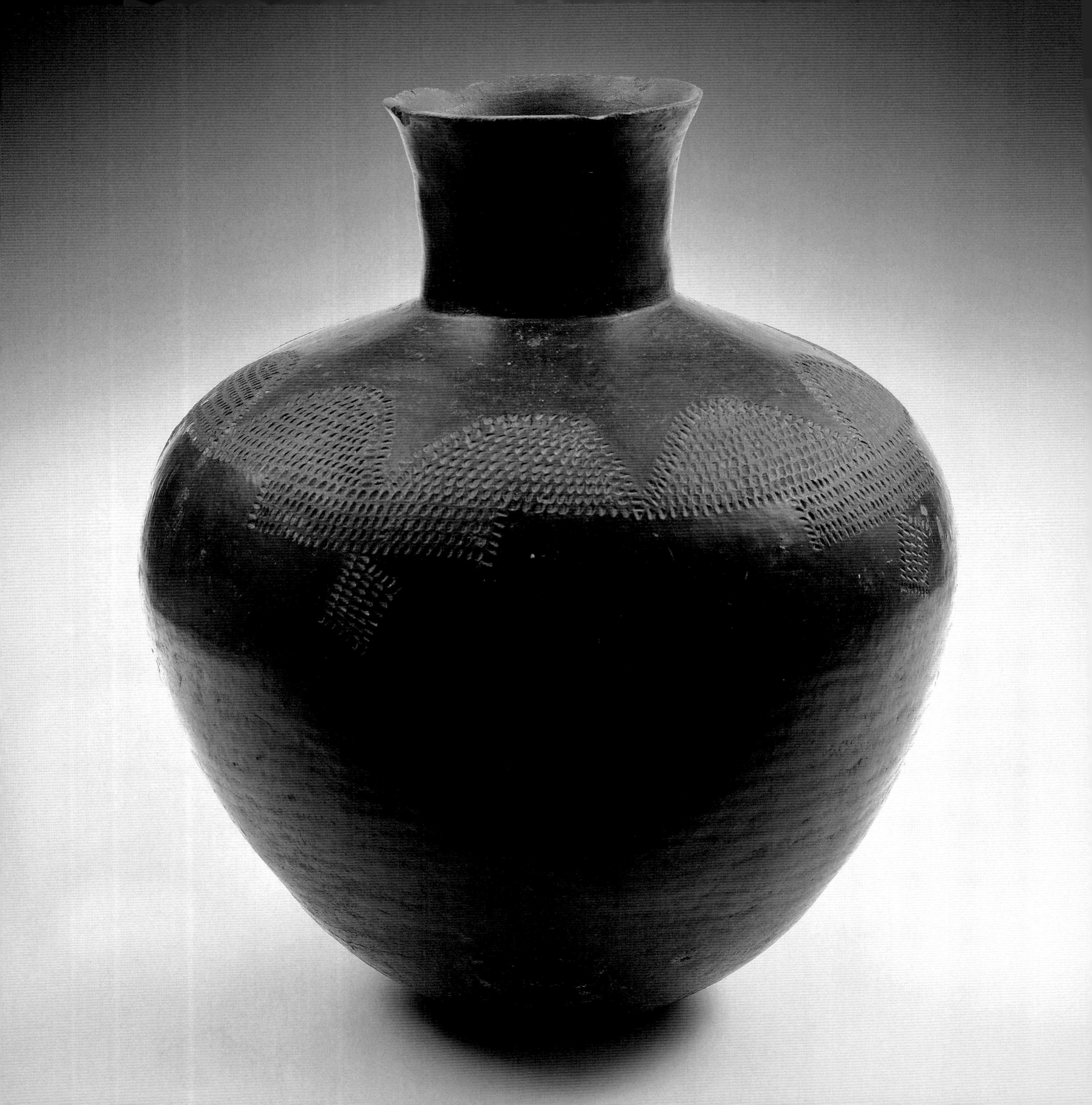

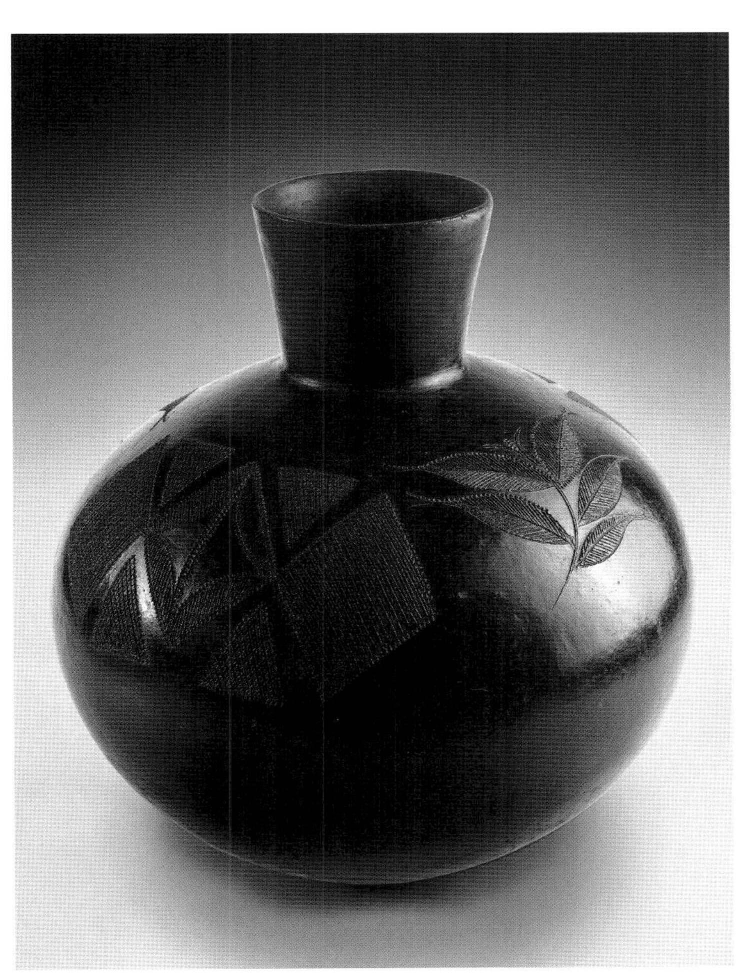

507 Uphiso H: 343 mm Maker Nesta Nala. Pattern based on rhomboids and Thukela phyto-motifs.

POT NUMBER 515 Uphiso H: 380 mm
Notched, single wave with 'pendants'.

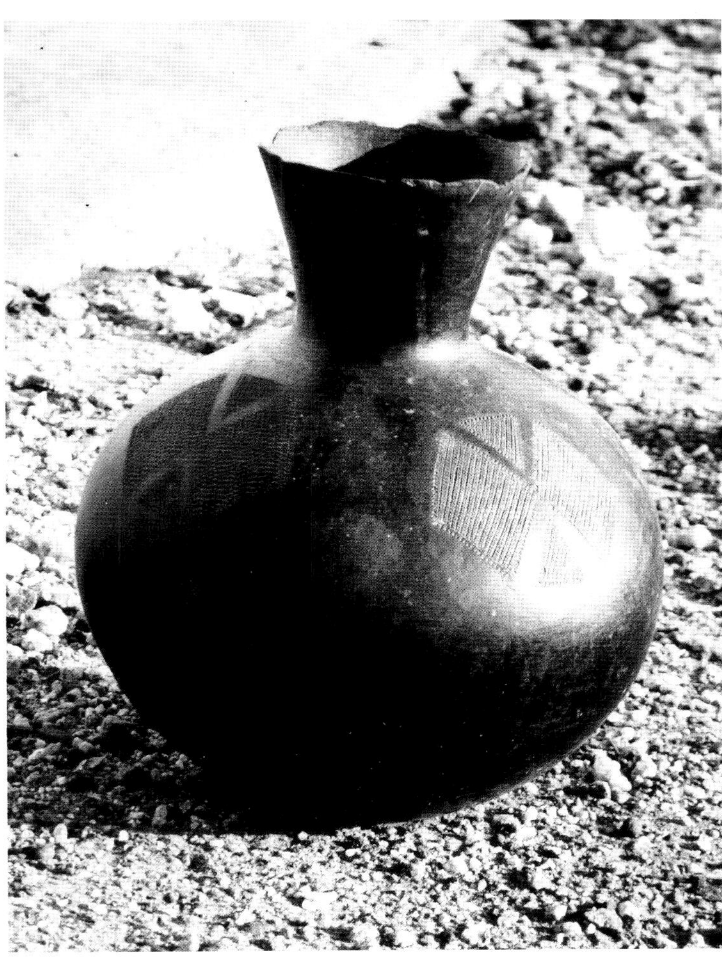

Middledrift: Old *uphiso* that the owner did not want to sell because of the special association with her husband's ancestors. The stand-alone motifs bear a striking resemblance to ones used by Nesta Nala later when she was making vessels for sale on the international art market. (Jolles 2012:19)

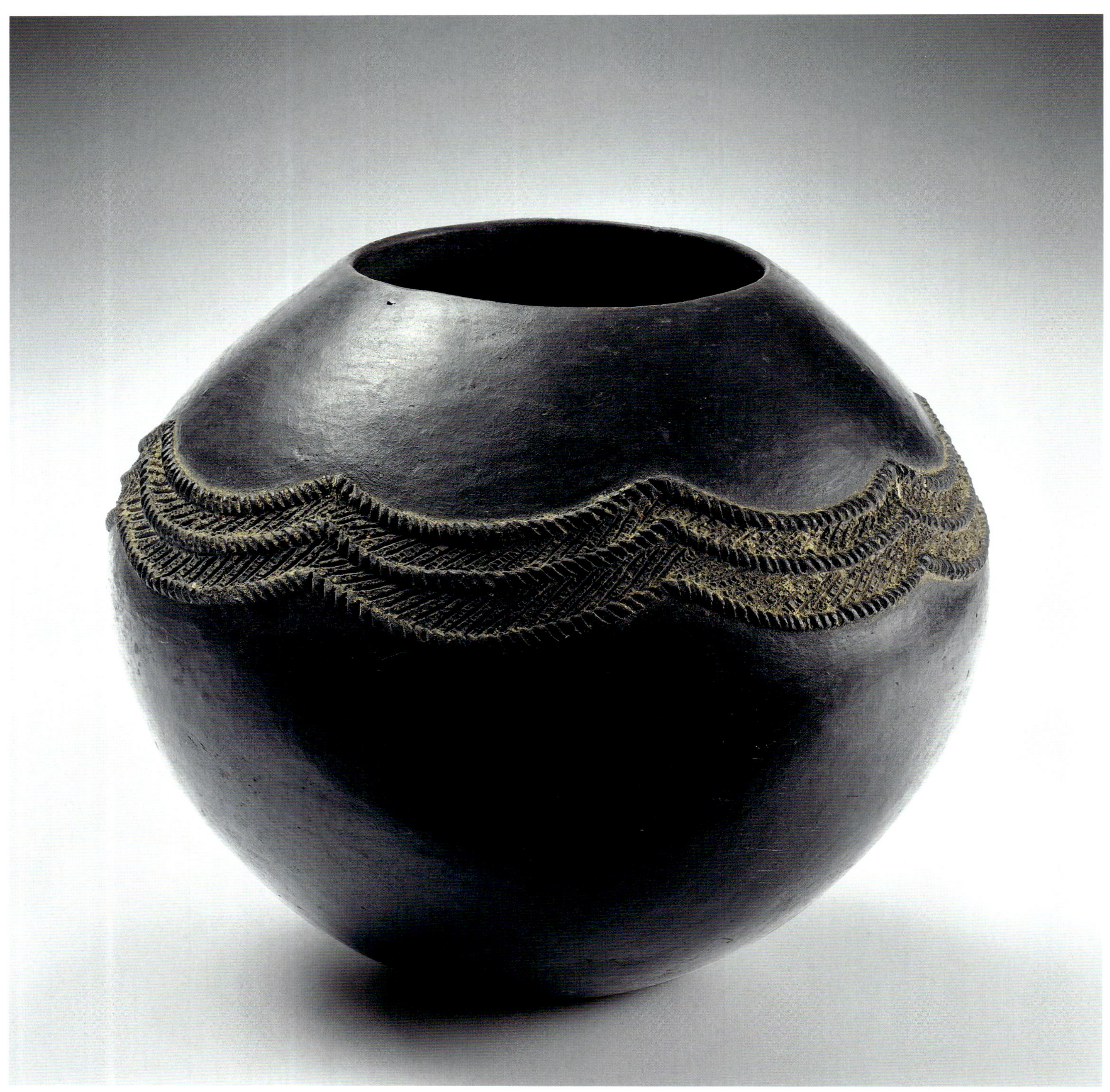

POT NUMBER 520 Ukhamba H: 230 mm Applied waves with incisions. Ratio H:D: 1:1.174

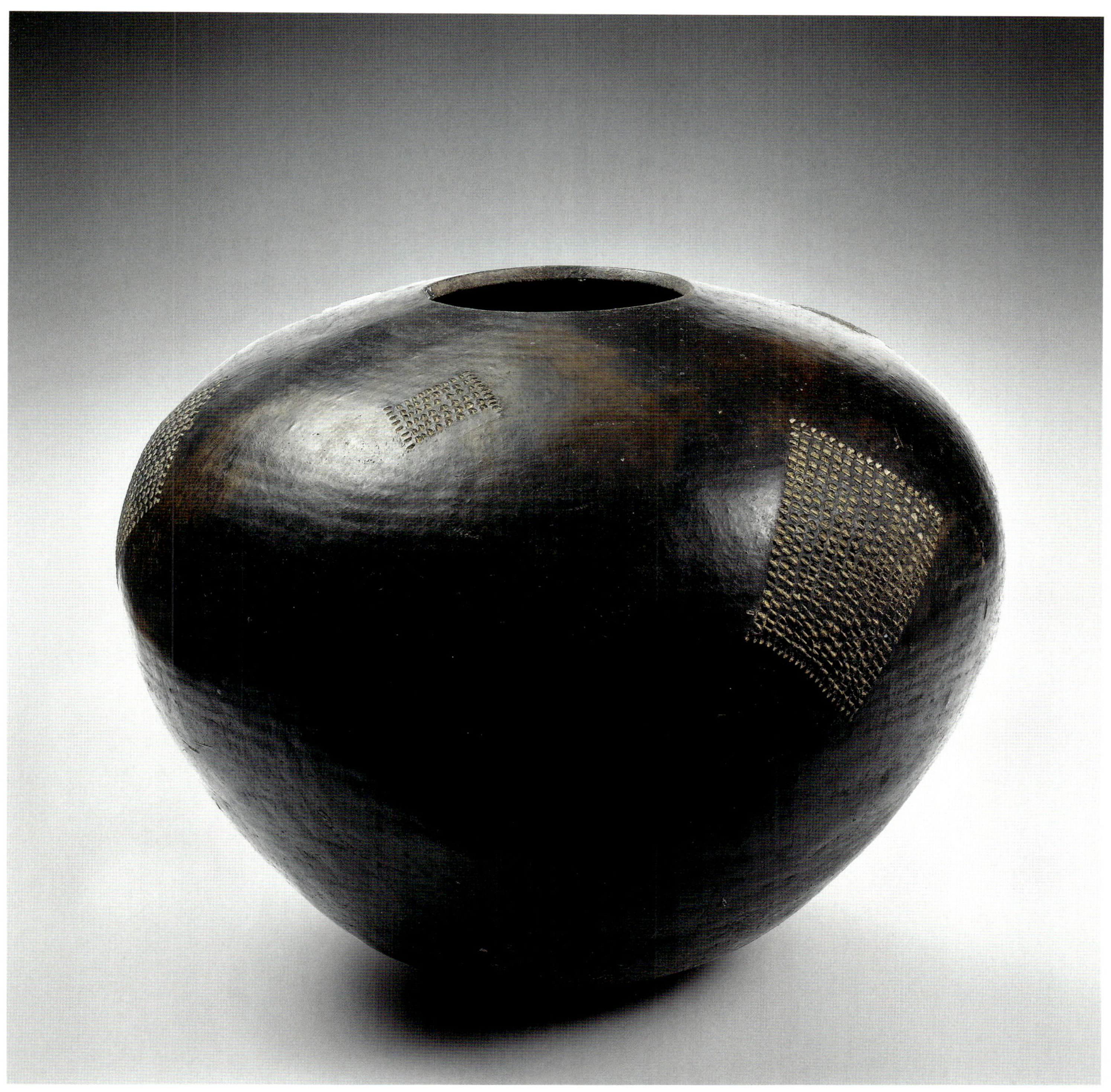

POT NUMBER 522 Ukhamba H: 360 mm Style of *uphiso* but without the neck. Notched rectangles. Note the attractive texture due to accurate coiling.

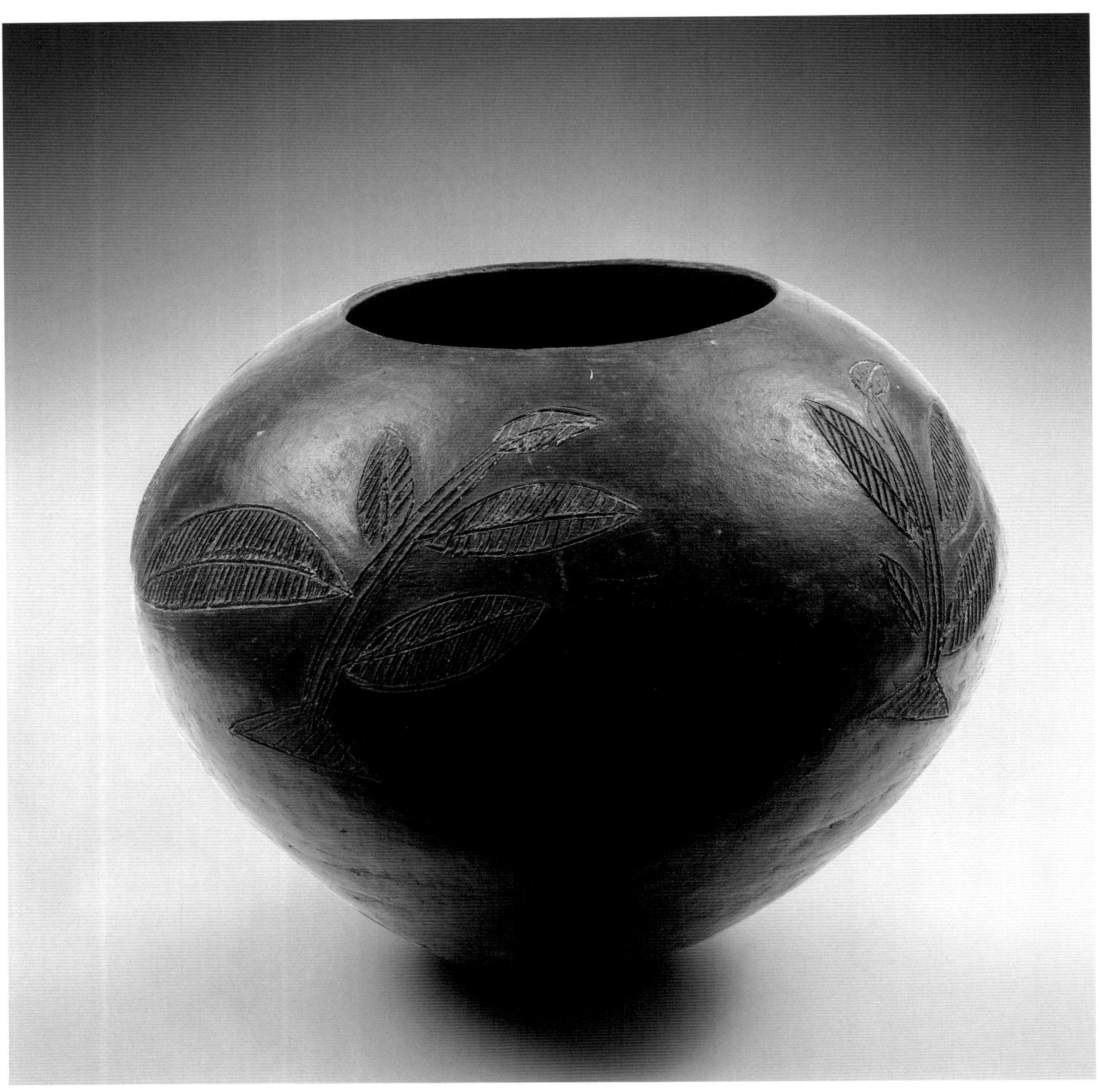

POT NUMBER 523 Ukhamba H: 235 mm Thukela plant motifs, incised, cf. 516.

POT NUMBER 524 Ukhamba H: 305 mm, D:356 mm.
PROVENANCE: Collected David Roberts <1999>, Pophini [?], just north of Kranskop [?].

Taking the road from Kranskop village to Middledrift one descends steeply for about 1000 m. from the farmlands to the valley of the Thukela, leaving the far-famed 'Kop' (1154 m.) on the left hand side. Bearing right (South) before reaching the bridge along a secondary road skirting the river for a while and then right again around the base of the Kranskop massif one reaches a number of rough and steep wooded valleys, clefts, so to speak, of the massif itself. Formerly, before roads were built, this must have been a remote backwater, largely isolated from the human traffic along the Thukela valley. It is perhaps on account of this that the style represented by this ukhamba has survived here. It consists of a ring of sloping rectangles created by parallel lines along the lengths of the rectangular spaces. Identical patterns can be found elsewhere, for instance in the Melmoth-Eshowe Region (Pot 402 page 126, Pot 403 page 127 linked) where the lines are formed of incised plaques of *amasumpa* attached to the surface of the vessel, or in the Hlabisa Region (Pot 323 page 118) where they consist of narrow incisions. In the case of the Kranskop style the lines are formed of applied ridges of clay. This technique also occurs in other configurations, for instance on the detail of the uphiso illustrated on page 240, which was collected in 'Mambulo'. The Mambulo is a river which rises in the Kranskop massif and joins the Thukela, it is also the name of an adjoining settlement. Applied ridges occur on some shards excavated in the Thukela valley in the eighteenth century. For further examples see Reusch, D. (1996) p. 128, No. C5, and Bell, B. & Calder, I. (1998) p. 120, No. 15, p.122, No. 27 and p.123, No. 36.

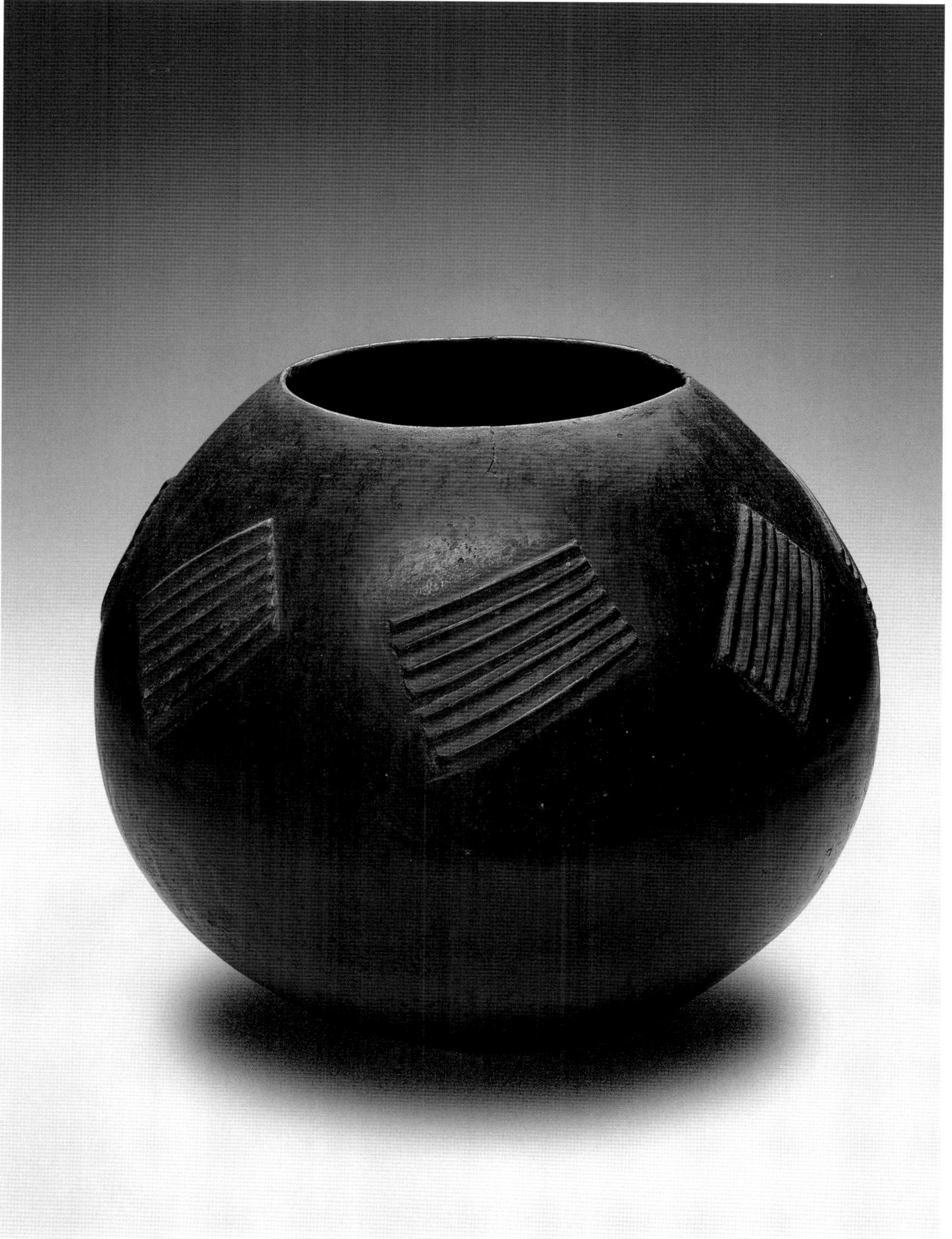

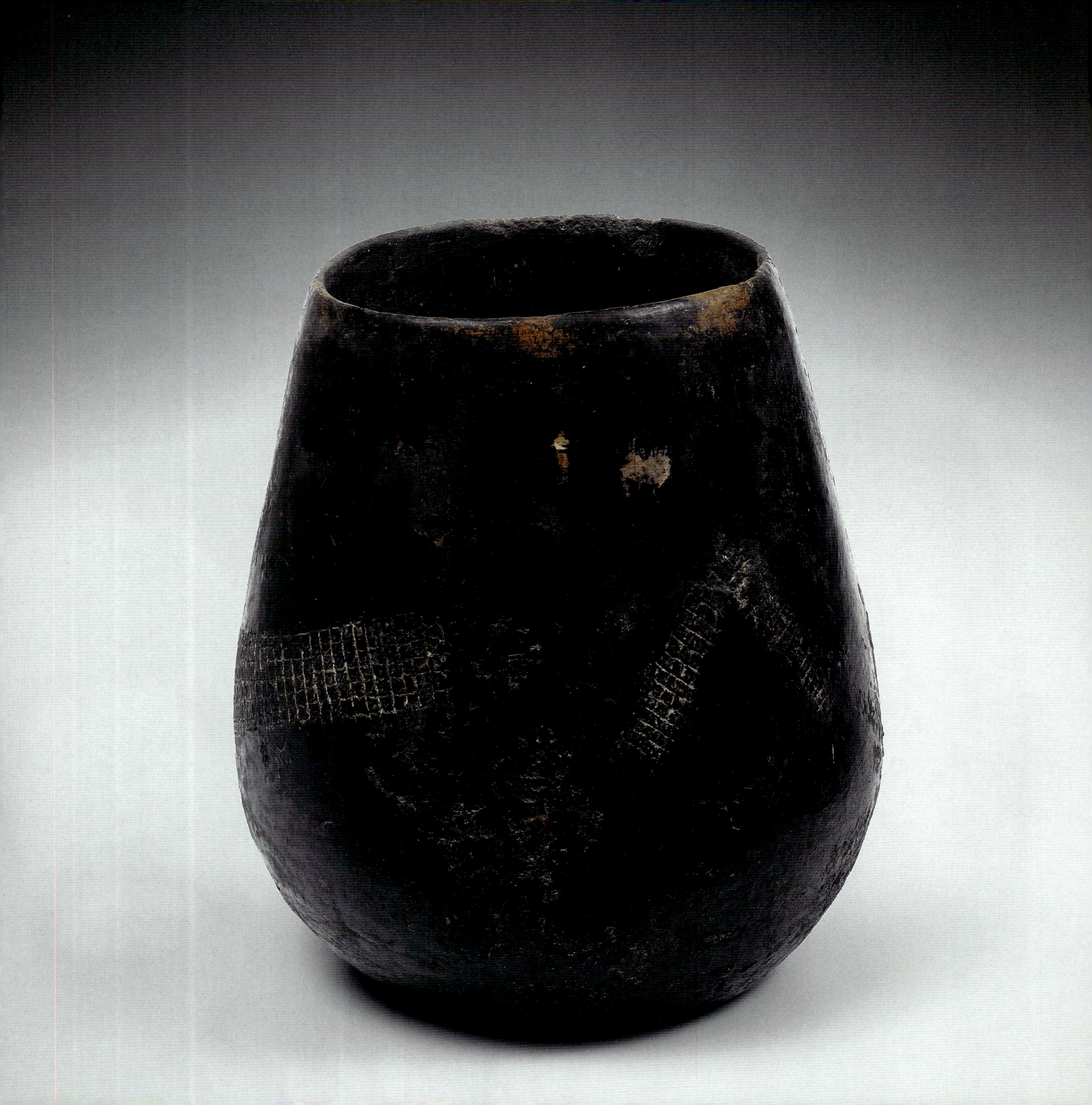

6

The Msinga Region

Named after the Msinga mountain massif, this stylistic region embraces the middle reaches of the Thukela between the Mooi River in the south and the uMzinyathi in the east (see map page 30). In the south it includes some of the farmlands of the Weenen-Muden area that have drawn on local labour for a long time. In the east it extends across the uMzinyathi a short distance, particularly where the river is easily fordable, and in the west it reaches almost as far as Ladysmith. In the north it is bounded by the Ntabankulu and Namkamane mountains and by the farmlands of the Dundee area, some of which (east of Helpmekaar) have been abandoned and are reverting to bush. It incorporates the fertile Thukela basin, but much of it consists of semi-arid eroded mountainous terrain interspersed with hilly country and steep river valleys. As it is a part of the old colony of Natal, the modern local settlement of this region goes back to the 'locations' demarcated by Shepstone in 1846–47. As discussed earlier, a number of regional 'clan-chieftaincies' crystallised out of the medley of peoples that Shepstone had resettled – Mchunu, Thembu, Mabaso and others. This process coincided more or less with the emergence of the blackened beer vessels.

The patterns of this region are all based on incised decorations. A few old pieces from the Mooi River valley retain the *ithunga* (wooden milking pail) form with rectangular incised panels reminiscent of coastal beadwork motifs (Pot 601 page 172). Plant motifs tend to dominate on the pots from the Thukela valley (Pot 608 page 177), whilst further north around Pomeroy and west towards Ladysmith geometrical designs based on triangles prevail (Pot 604 page 174). Sometimes both stylised plant and geometrical themes are combined on the same pot.

POT NUMBER 601 Umancishana H: 223 mm

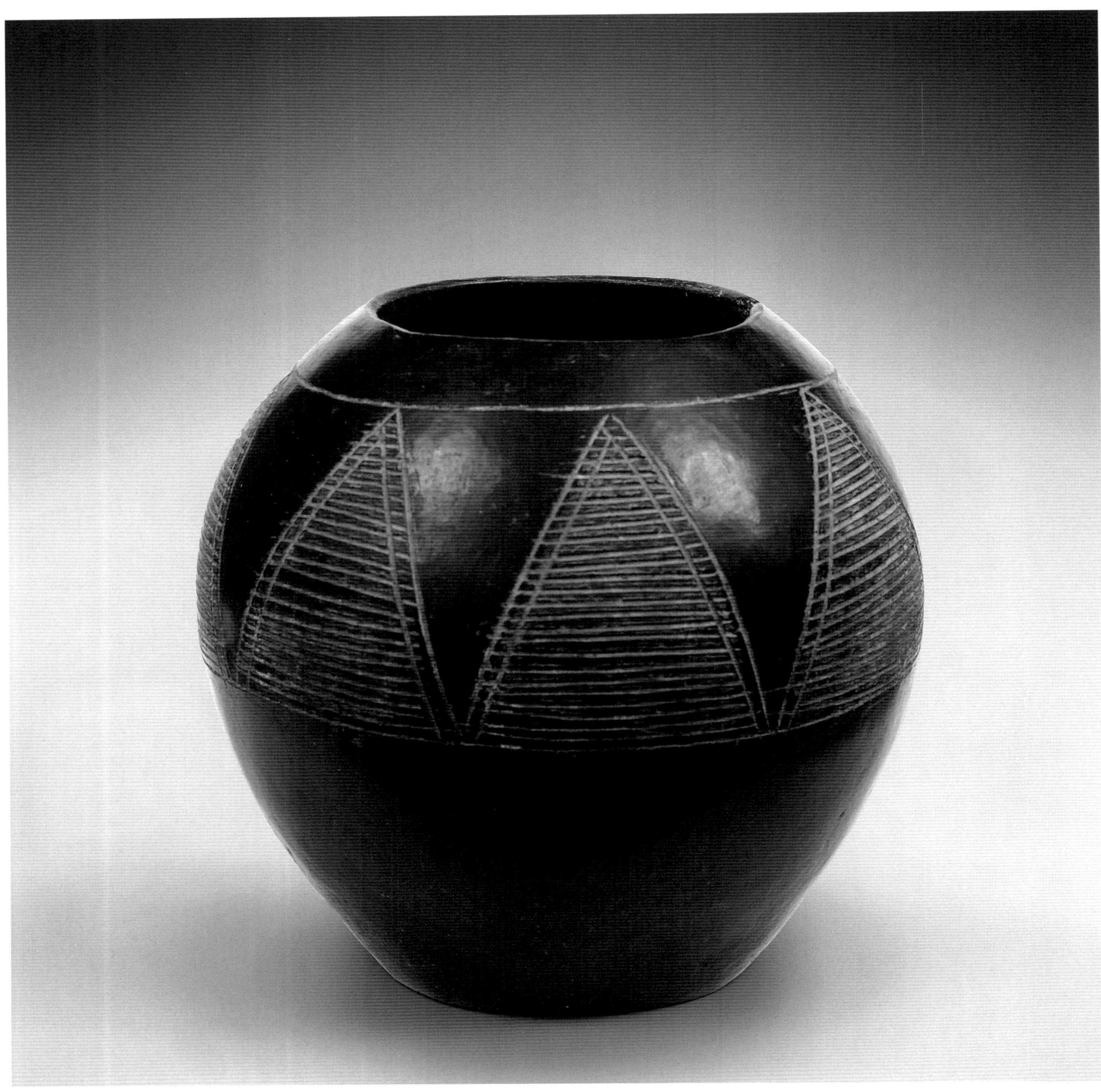

POT NUMBER 604 Umancishana H: 180 mm This linear incised design (upright triangles on a base line) was still fashionable in the Pomeroy area in the 1990s.

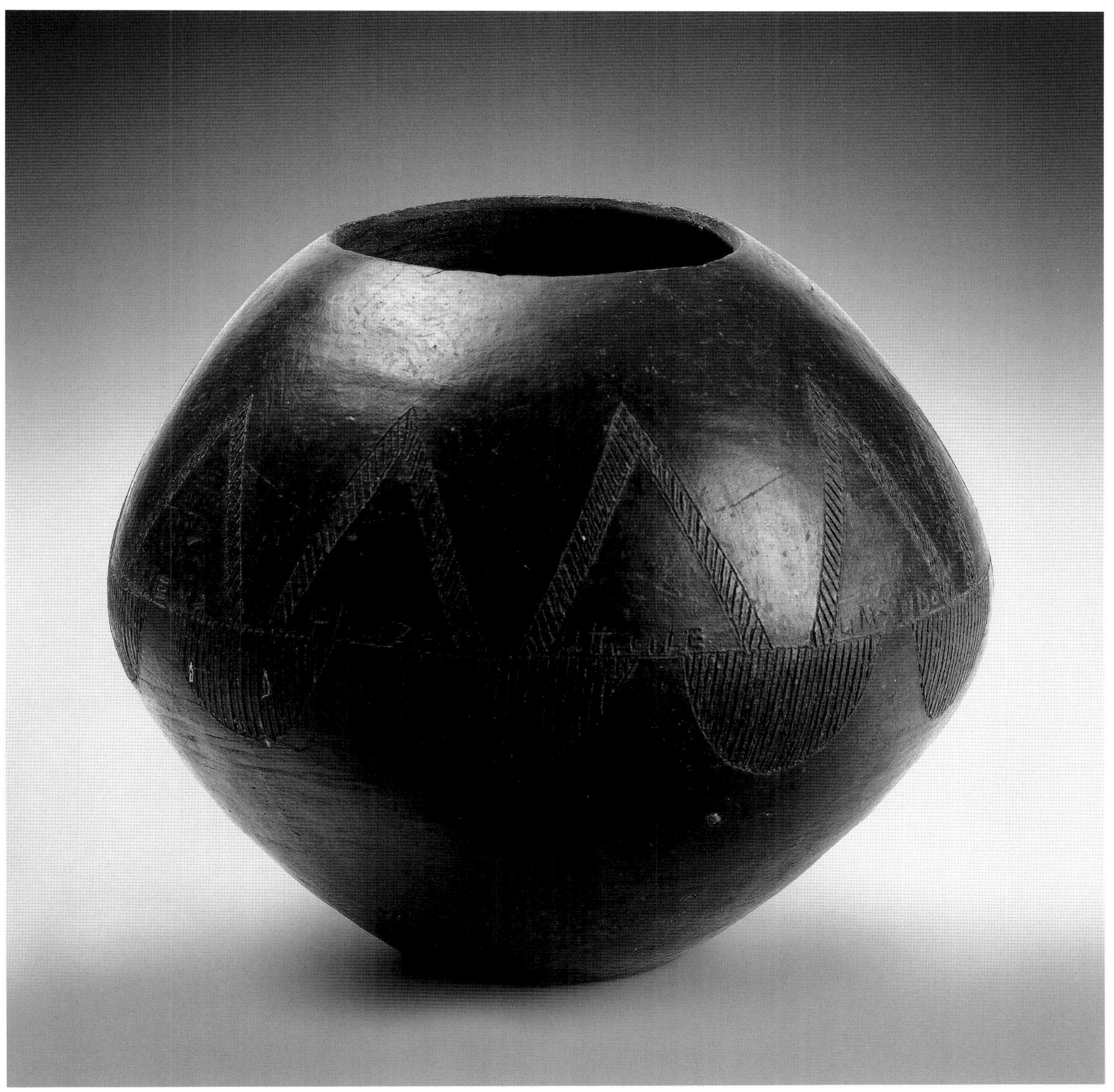

POT NUMBER 602 Ukhamba H: 246 mm The tapered shoulder form with its small base is characteristic of the Msinga region, whilst the design is somewhat reminiscent of the Nongoma-Hlabisa region (however cf. 604). The local people assured me that it was an old Msinga design.

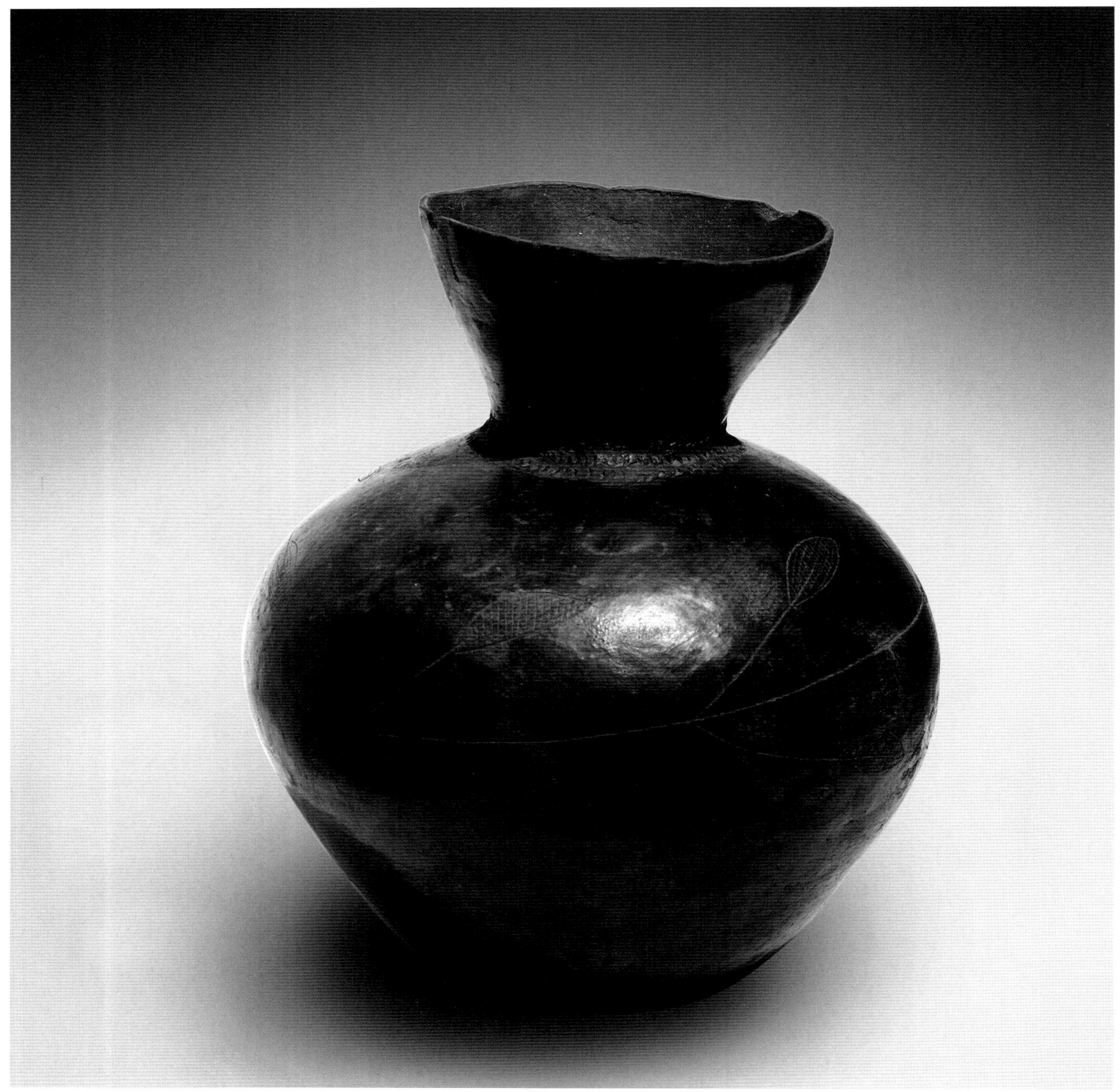

POT NUMBER 608 Uphiso, also termed *ingcazi*: 'narrow-necked water pot'. Note the two small chips in the rim. One was taken before the wedding and was given to the family of the boy she was going to marry. The other was broken out when they got married and was placed in the *insamo* at the girl's home for the *amadlozi* to know that the girl was going to another house, i.e. her husband's home.

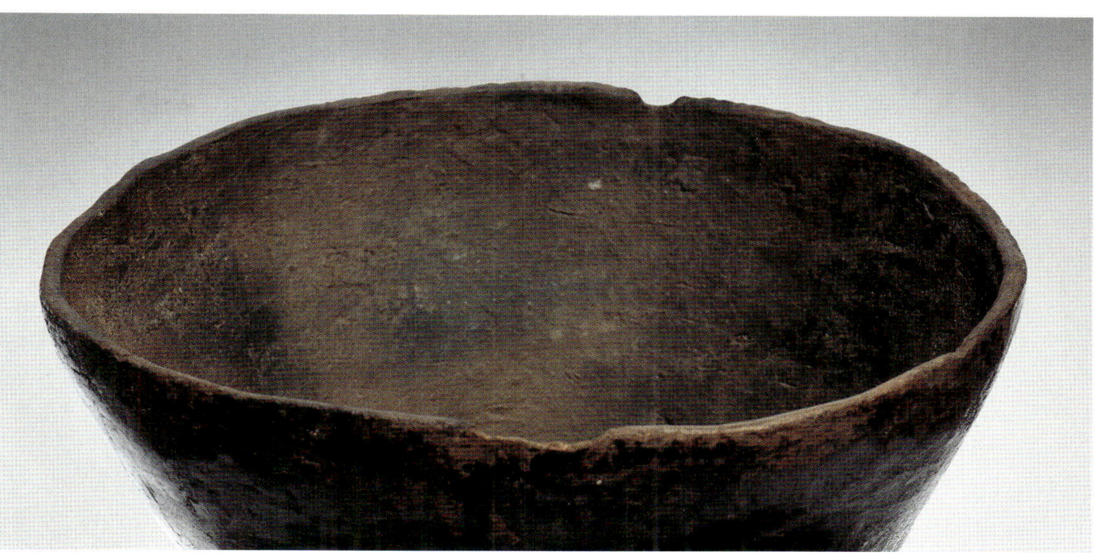

POT NUMBER 608 Uphiso (detail)

The uMzinyathi River south of Rorke's Drift forms a sort of semi-permeable stylistic boundary between Msinga and the adjoining Qudeni region. Whilst the beadwork on the Qudeni side is in the Msinga style, the pottery belongs to the Lower Thukela region (Pot 606 page 179). Some vestiges of an older style from the Muden area occur. Apart from Pot 601 (above), Pot 607 page 180 may also belong to this category. Its owner Mrs Ngubane stated that it was bought in Mtubatuba from a family from near Muden. Relocations from Muden to Mtubatuba took place during the late 1960s and early 1970s.[66] This would indicate that Pot 607 page 180 may have been made during or before that period. Local people said it was an old Msinga style. Another pattern from the 1950s or 1960s involves large semicircular incised arches often alternating with zigzags or butterflies. The pattern is called *inyanga* (moon).[67]

The older pots from Msinga tend to be almost spherical, whilst more recently pots with pronounced shoulders tapering towards a narrow base have be-come popular. The three *izimbiza* (Pot 701 page 182, Pot 702 page 190, Pot 704 page 192, next chapter) demonstrate a similar trend towards a narrow base.

Although it covers such a wide terrain abutting on a number of regions of different historical backgrounds, the Msinga ceramic and beadwork styles have remained clearly demarcated with distinct and easily recognisable regional variations throughout the twentieth century. It remains doubtful whether any of today's patterns can be traced directly to a formative period in the middle of the nineteenth century. But the relative stability and the sequence of fashions in the twentieth century enables one to determine and even to date the movements of people into and out of the area.[68] In this regard the Msinga region is differently structured from the Zululand regions described above. The Msinga styles reflect the social and political consequences of unbroken and hence relatively consistent colonial rule over an extensive region in which the distribution of land and people had been enforced from the outset.

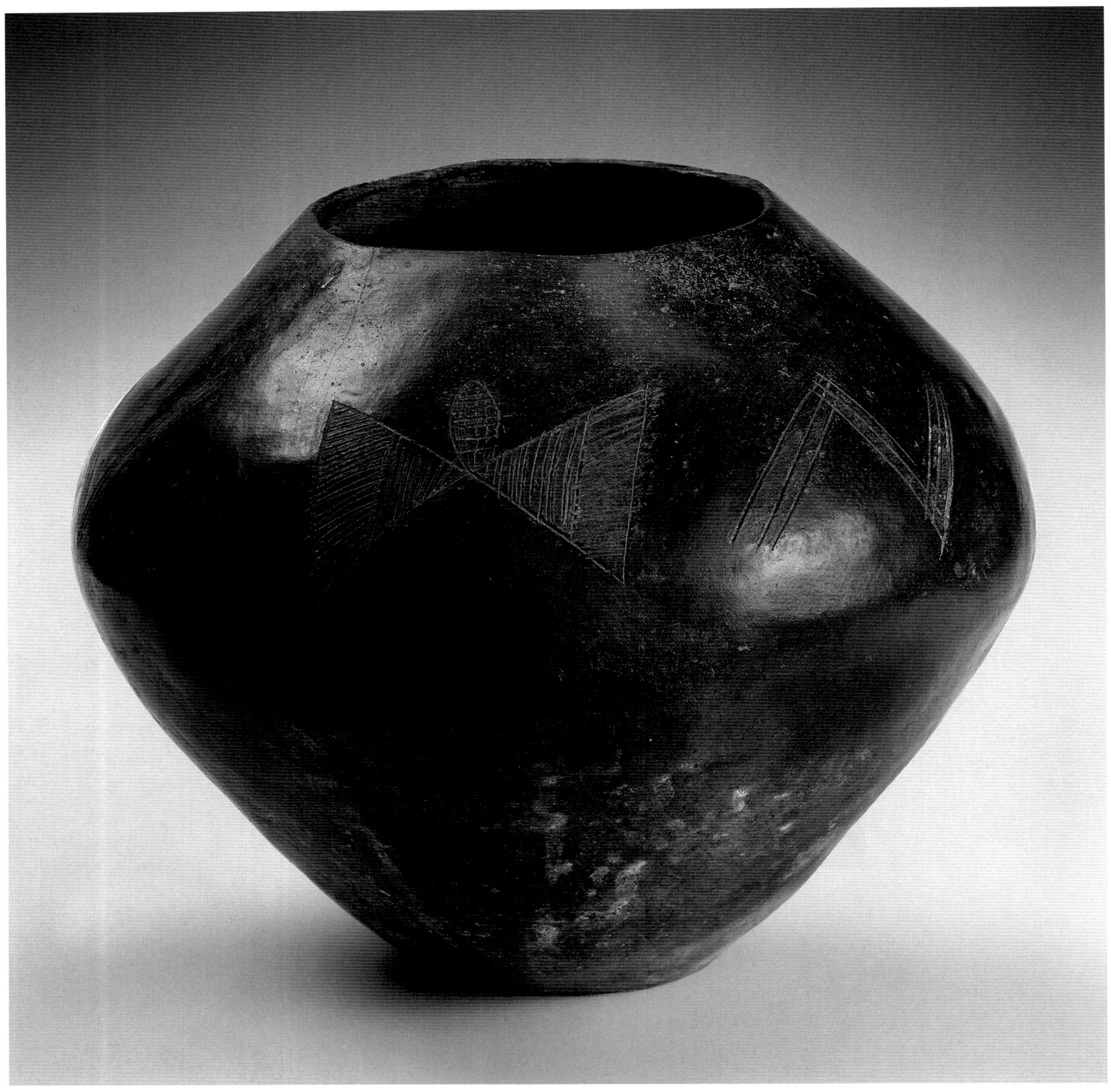

POT NUMBER 603 Ukhamba H: 228 mm Three incised motifs: butterfly, zigzag, and Greek cross – the latter suggests the uMzinyathi area, but it could also be Tugela
Ferry as there was a fair amount of coming and going between the two. The shoulder tapering to a narrow base is characteristic of Msinga vessels.

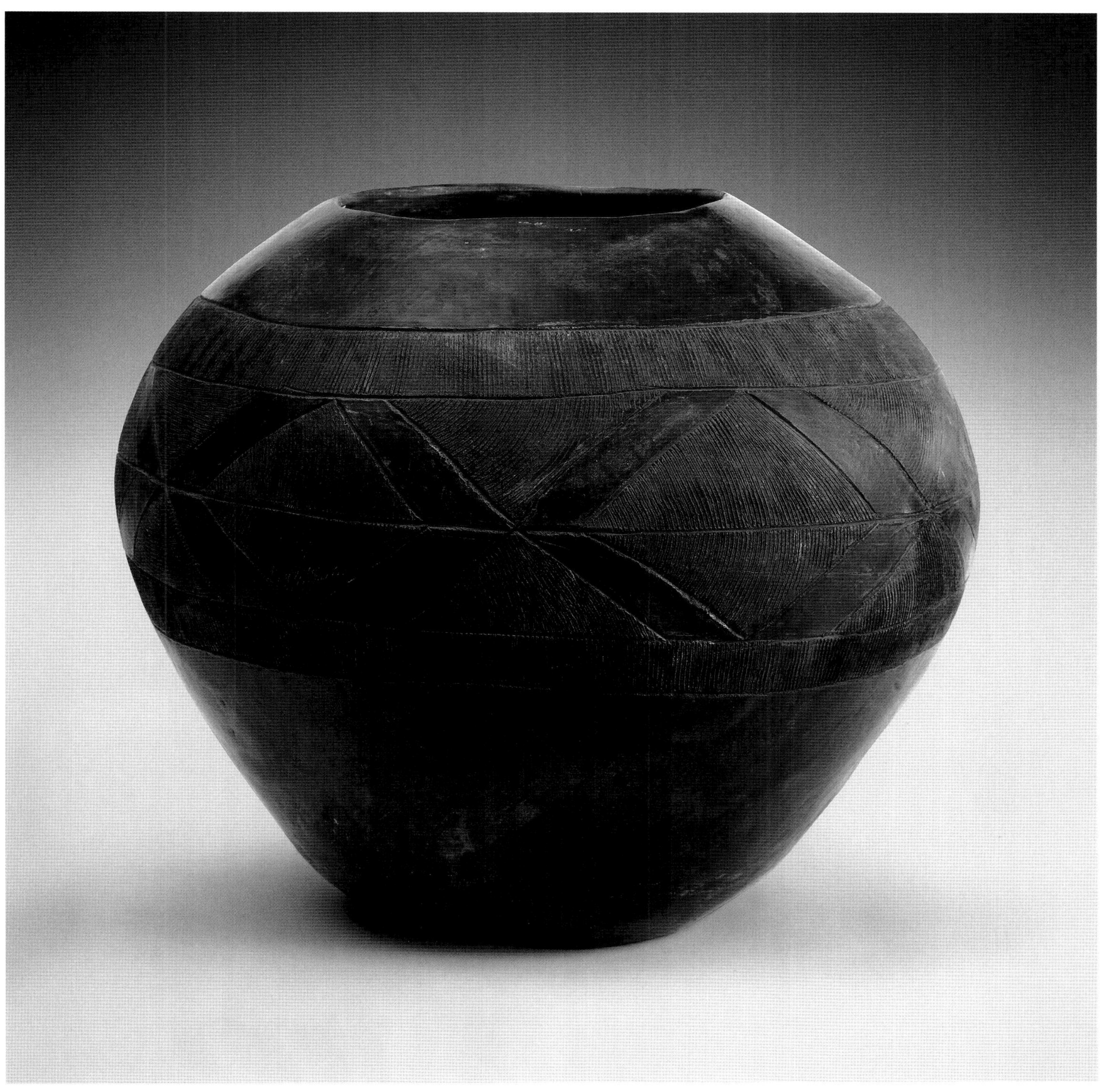

POT NUMBER 606 Ukhamba H: 370 mm Incised band with geometrical motifs.

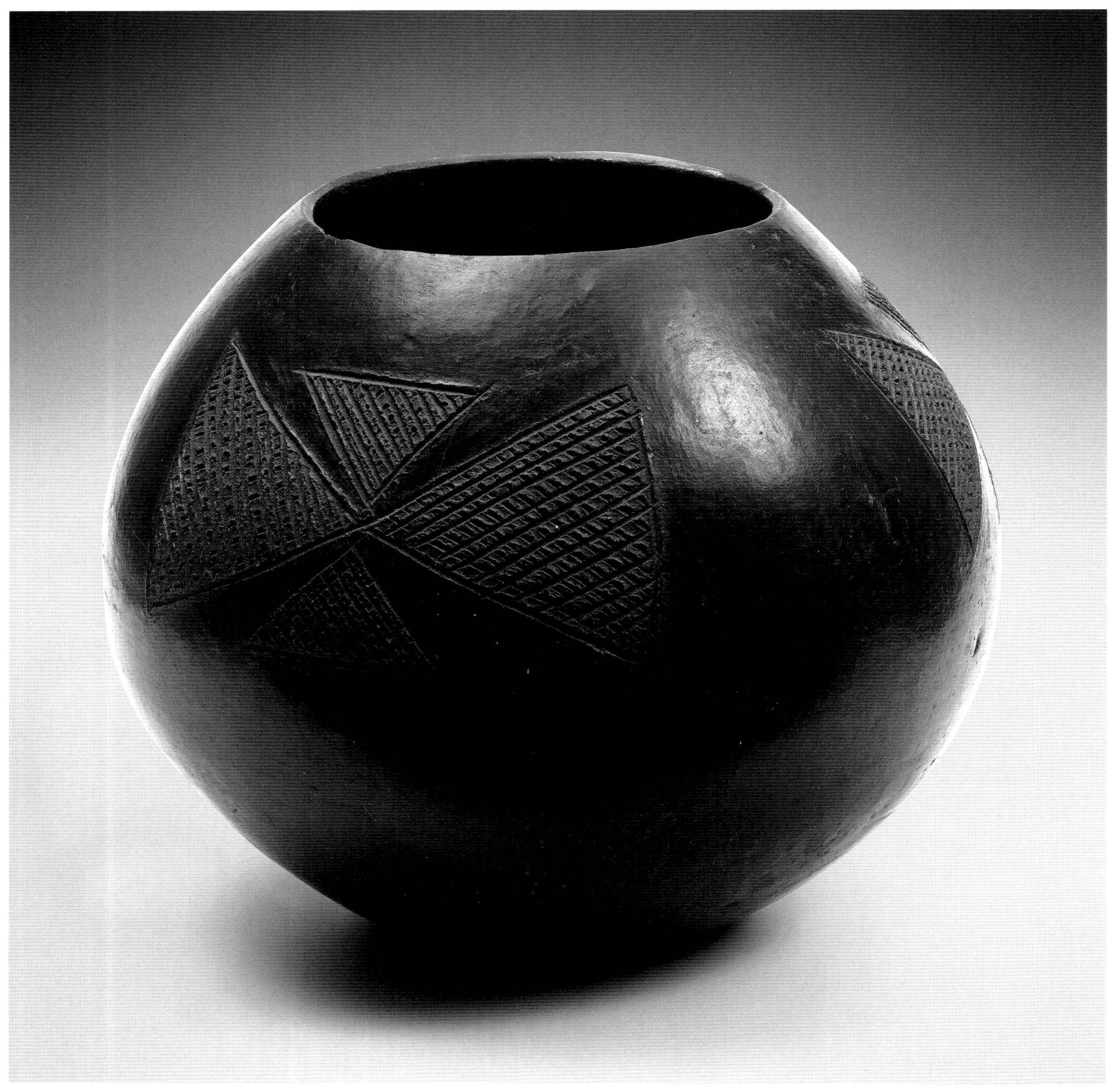

POT NUMBER 607 Ukhamba H: 289 mm Though on the eastern side on the uMzinyathi, this area belongs to the Msinga stylistic region where beadwork is concerned, so I have included it here. It is an area in which very few pots have survived. The incised geometrical motifs bear some relationship to the pots from the uMngeni valley a few miles downstream on the western side of the uMzinyathi.

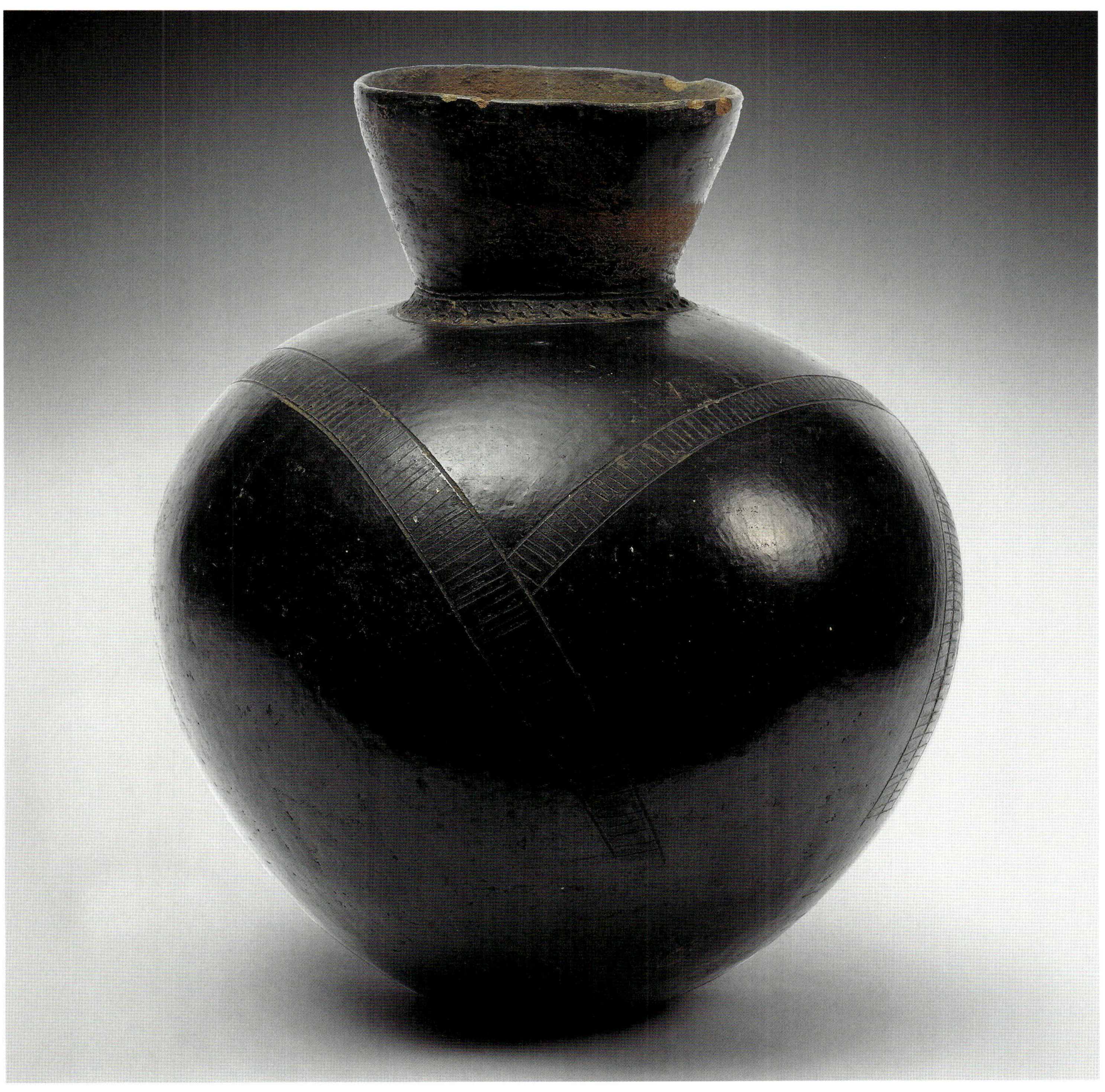

POT NUMBER 609 Uphiso H: 372 mm

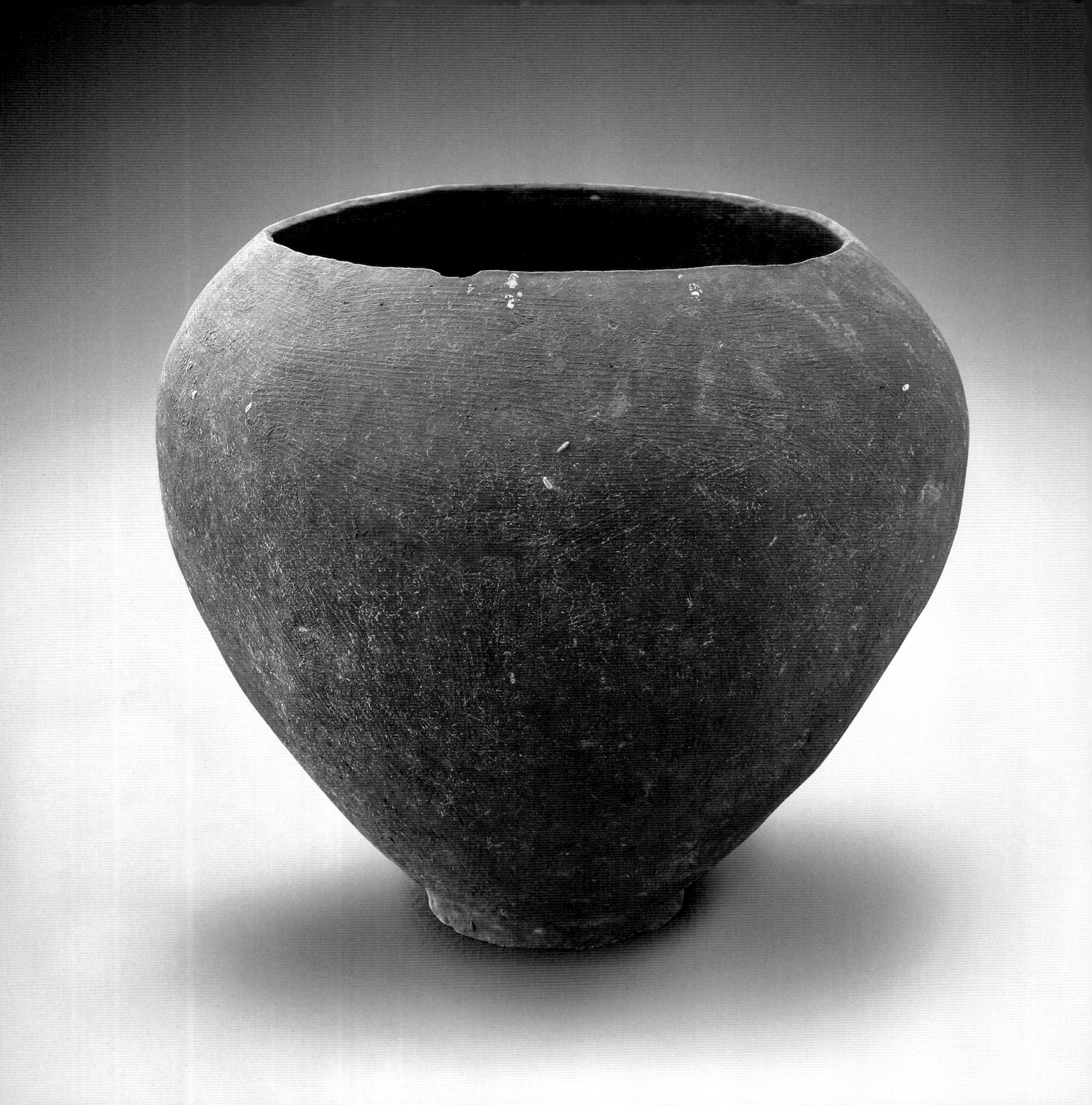

The Art of the *Imbiza*

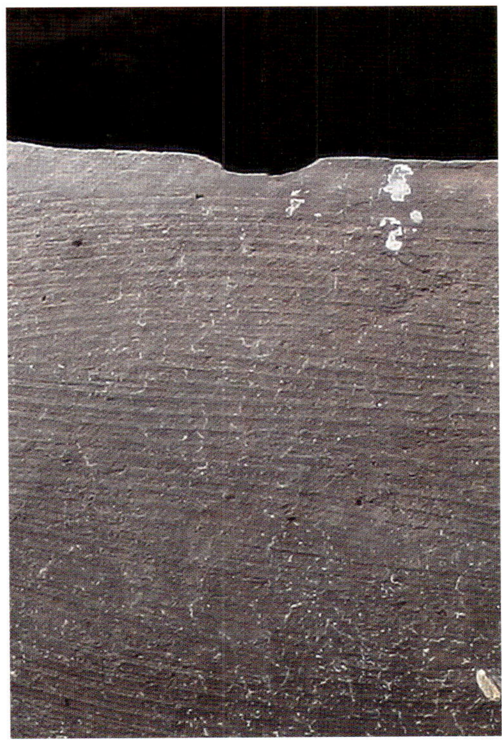

Izimbiza (sing: *imbiza*) differ fundamentally from the other vessels used for brewing, storing and serving beer. As mentioned (pp. 10–11, 14), they are considerably larger, up to 90 cm high with a maximum capacity of nearly 100 litres. They are fired only once: in an open pit with the fuel heaped up around and over them. They are never blackened. The fact that they have no surface ornamentation, apart from a fine slip of clay mixed with cow dung, further sets them apart. Clearly they cannot be assigned to any area on the basis of their decoration. However, some of them do correspond to familiar regional profiles such as a bulging body on a narrow base. This applies to Pot 701 page 182, an *imbiza* from Msinga, with the typical profile of that region. Most of them, particularly the older ones, tend to be slightly taller than they are wide and have profiles approximating to the cylindrical. Despite the limitations imposed on the potter by the size and mode of production – coiling as before coupled with the need to create walls light enough to be handled yet resilient enough to withstand the pressure of the liquid inside them – many *izimbiza* impart an impressive presence, an outstanding sense of balance and harmony.

Maybe on account of the difficulty of transporting them and the risk of breakages *izimbiza* seem to have escaped the attention of dealers. As a result many, including some dating from the turn of the nineteenth century, are still in their original locations: opposite the door in the part of the hut reserved for the ancestors. They are sometimes attached to the floor or enclosed by a low wall, where they form part of the everyday domestic environment. Nowadays they are mostly used for junk storage – grimy and neglected looking, yet their owners are usually unwilling to part

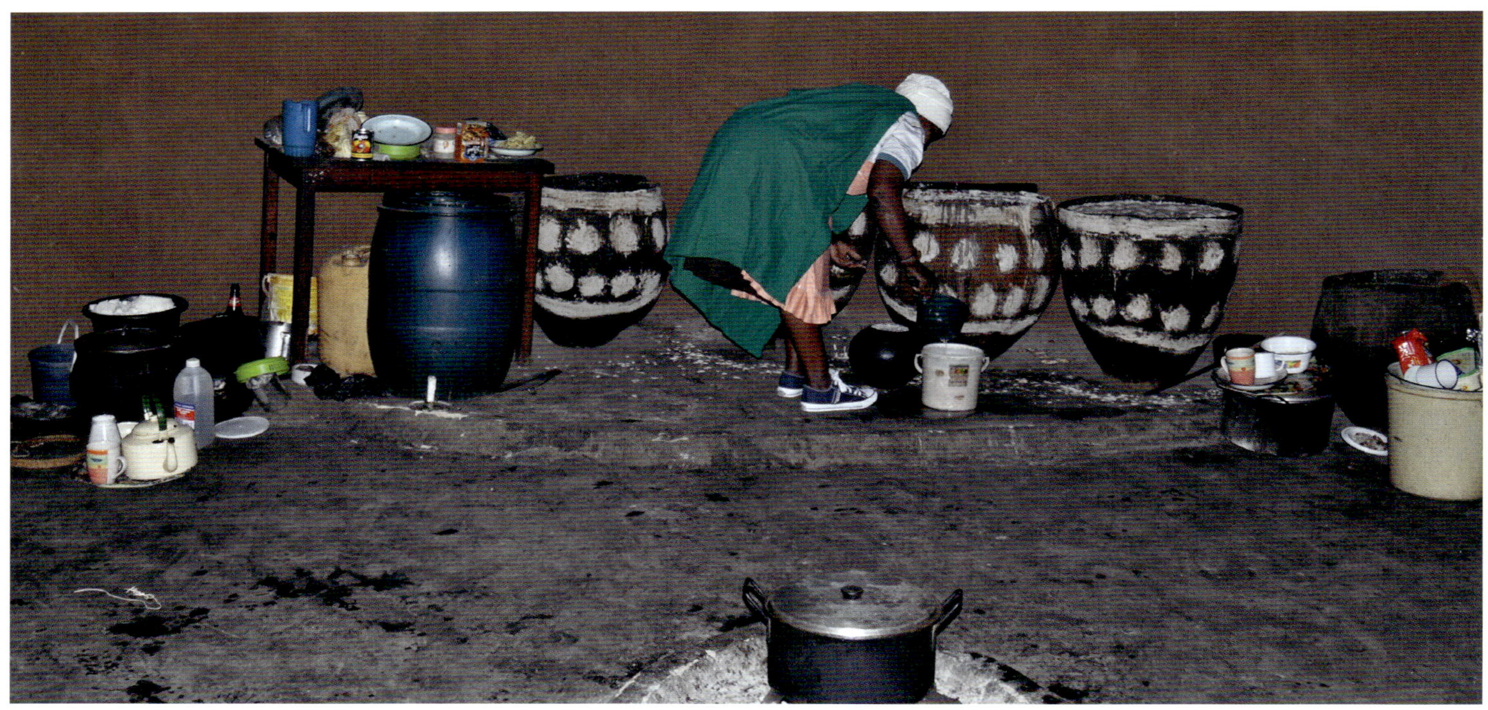

Woman brewing beer for a celebration
in the specially decorated *imbiza* pots at
Manzimhlophe, 26 June 2011.

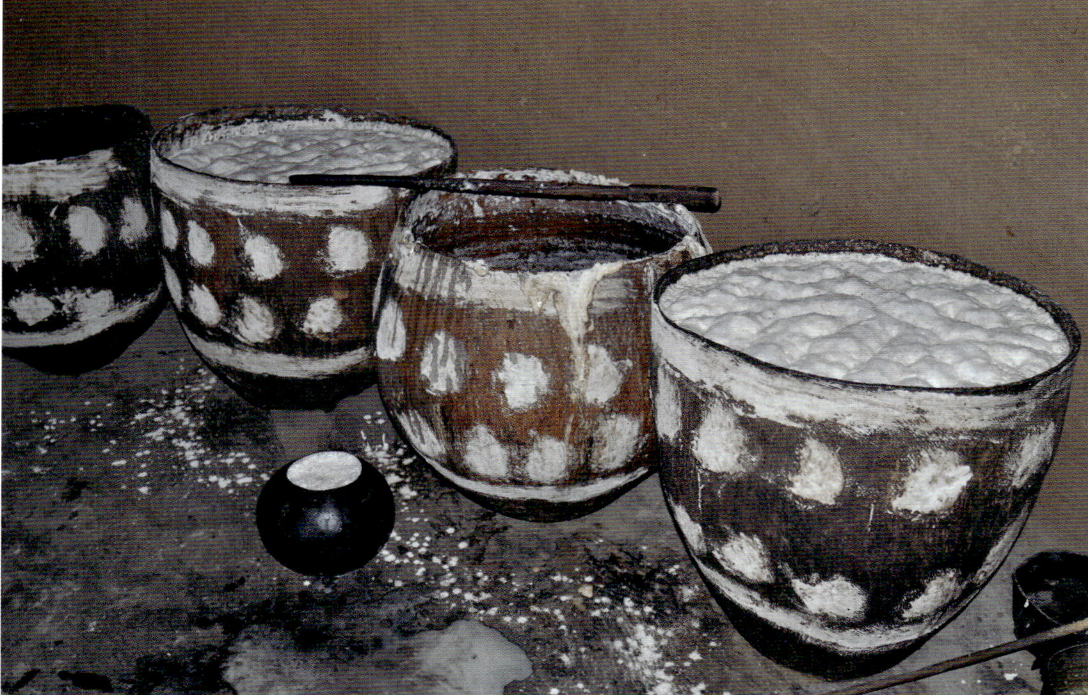

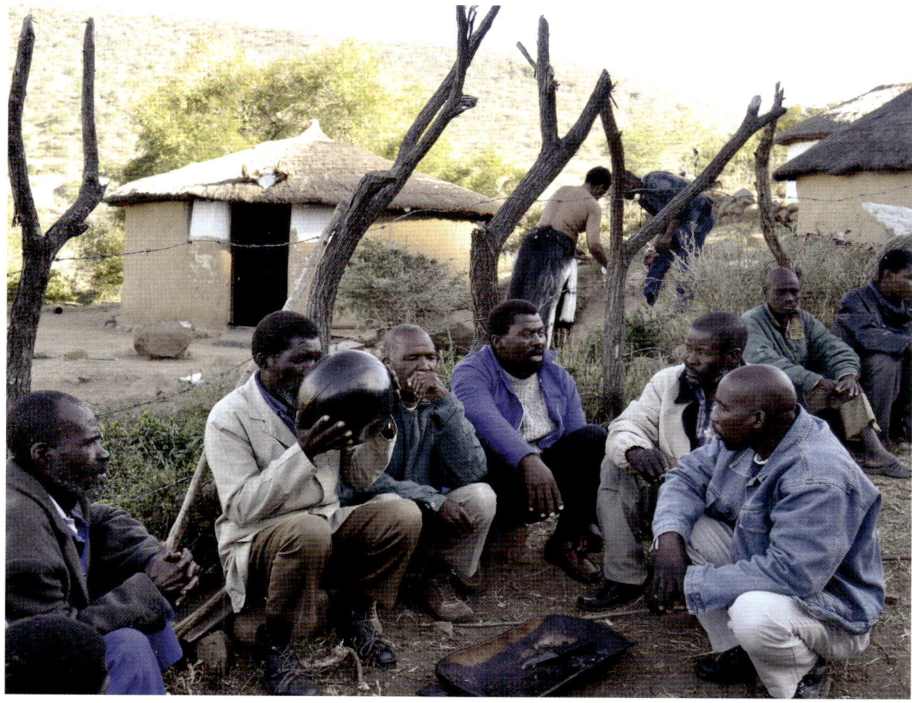

Manzimhlophe, 26 June 2011. Men drinking beer in the cattle enclosure shortly before sunset. The wooden meat tray in the foreground was used for serving roast meat from the sacrificed cow. Cut into small cubes it was nevertheless incredibly tough.

with them. Only on two occasions have I seen them used for brewing, though it seems that in the 1950s they were still the vessels of choice (personal communication, Lettie Mchunu, 16.04.2011).

The most recent of these occasions was a celebration to thank the ancestors for having provided a bountiful year. It took place on 26 June 2011 at Kwa-Manzimhlophe (The Place of White Water), a remote homestead south of Muden. A great many people from the surrounding area came to join in. In the image below it is just visible at the end of the rocky path leading up the mountain.

The *izimbiza* are still in their traditional context: on a raised platform opposite the entrance to a hut also used for cooking. This is the *umsamo*, the abode of the ancestors. The hearth for cooking and heating in winter is at the front centre of the first image. The embellishment of the *izimbiza* with white circles is to enhance the dignity of the occasion; it is purely ornamental. Within the *umsamo* there is also a small blackened pot, an *umancishana* filled with beer. This is specifically for the visiting ancestors to 'sip'. It always remains in that place that is dark and cool the way they like it.

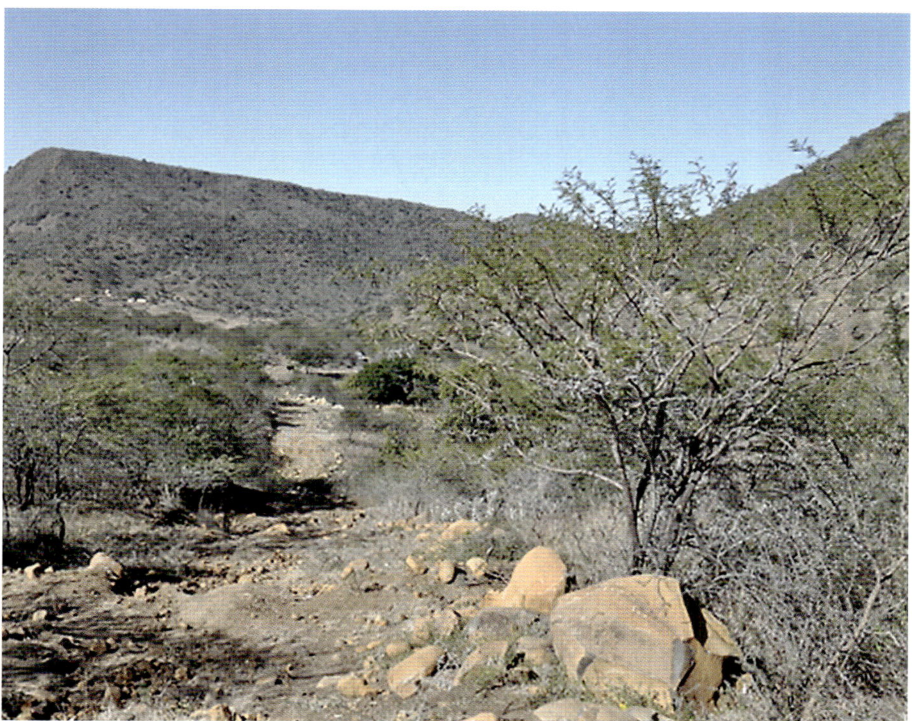

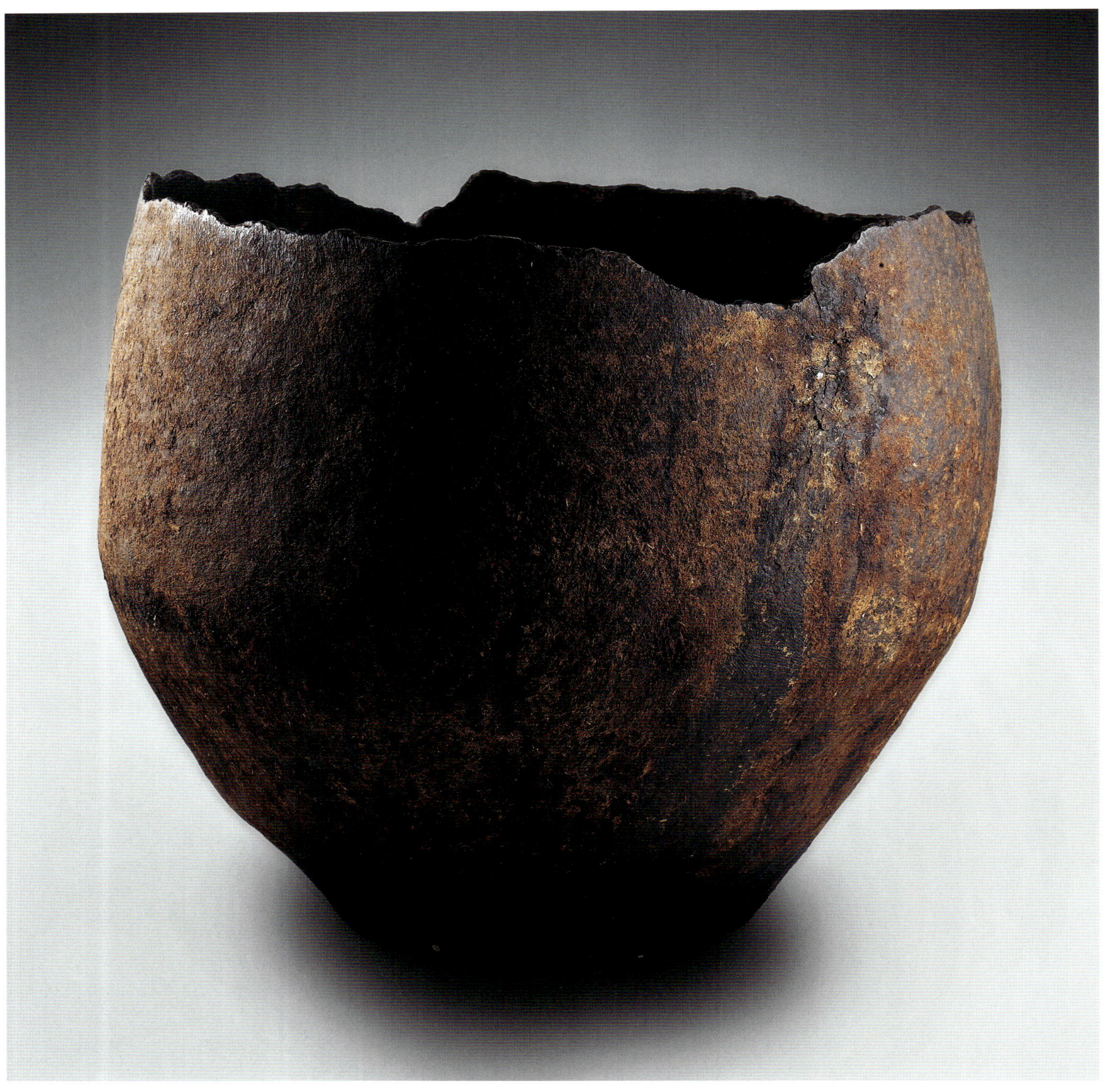

POT NUMBER 706 Imbiza H: 515 mm G: 2100 mm O: 580 mm

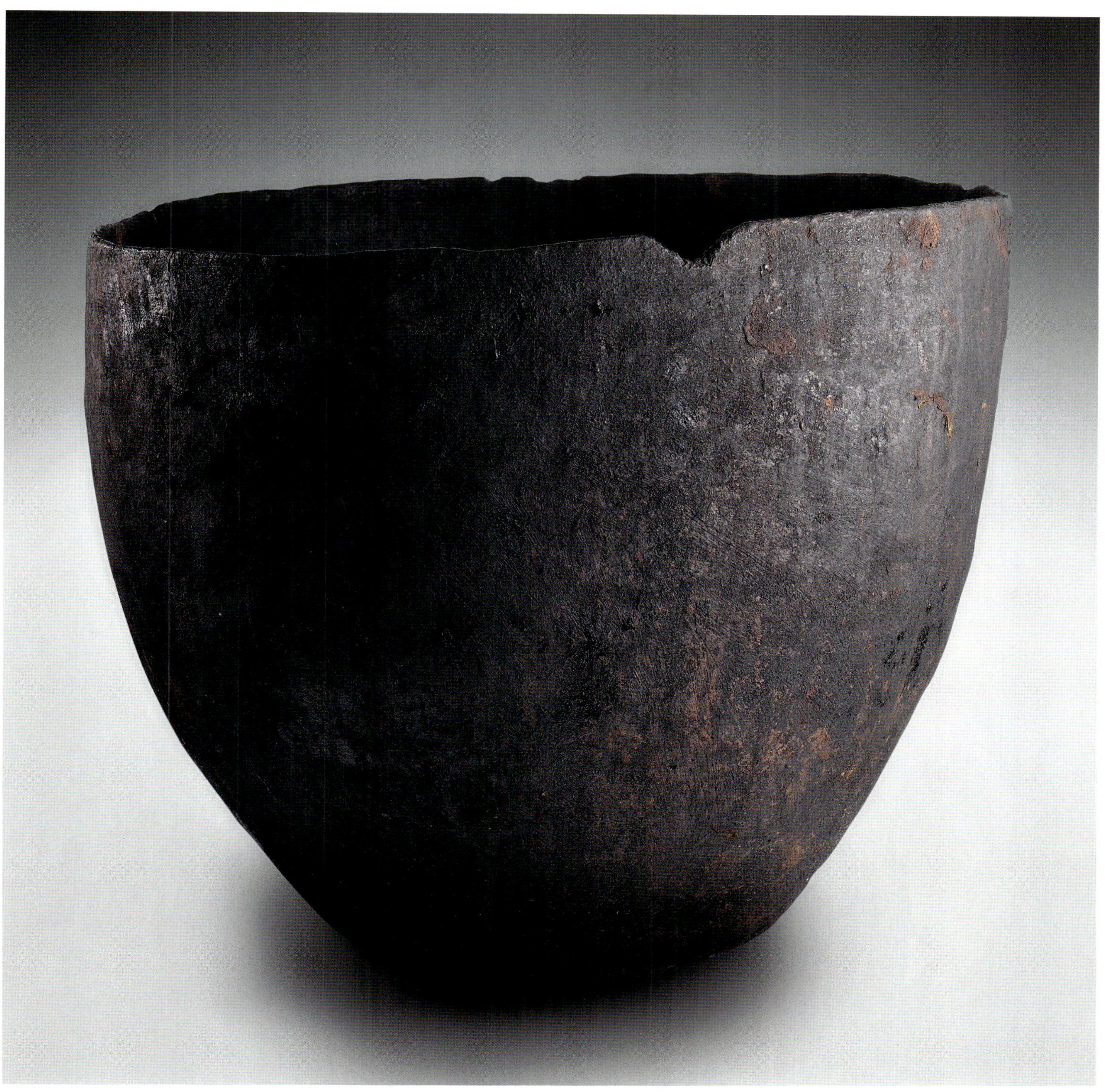

POT NUMBER 707 Imbiza H: 595 mm, G: 2170 mm, O: 660 mm

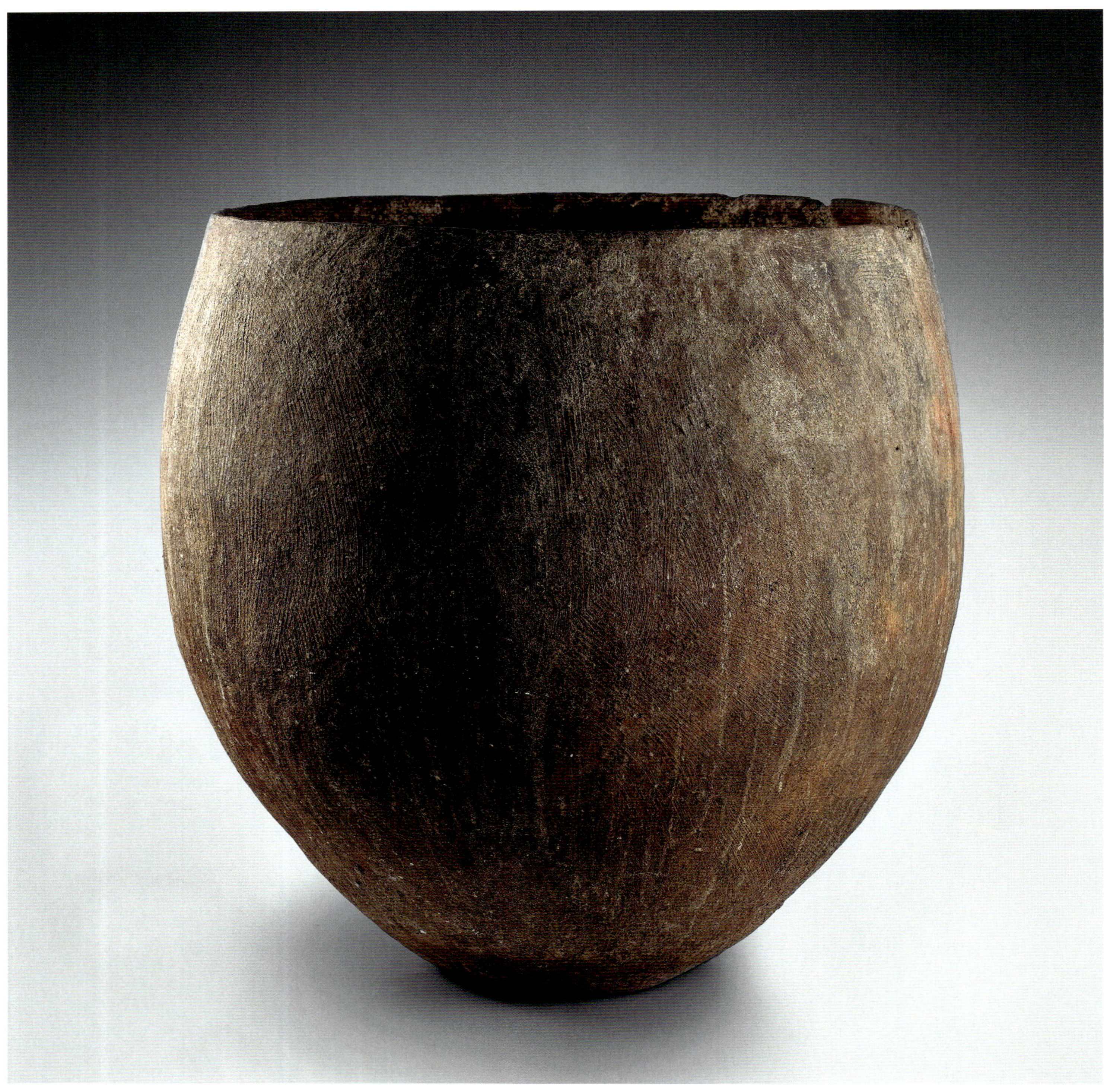

POT NUMBER 708 Imbiza H: 610 mm, G: 2170 mm, O: 500 mm

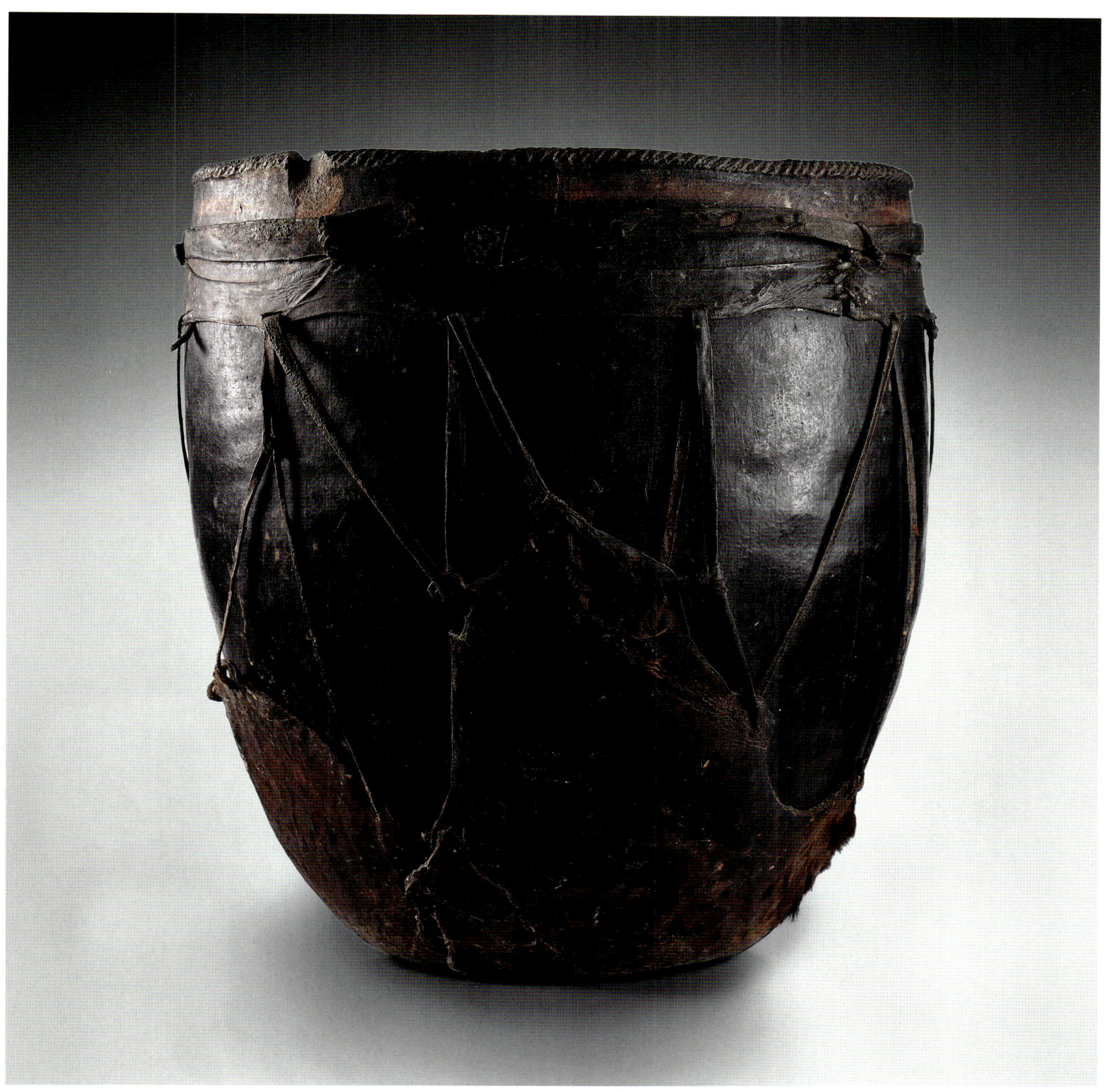

POT NUMBER 710 Imbiza H: 635 mm, G: 1880 mm, O: 550 mm

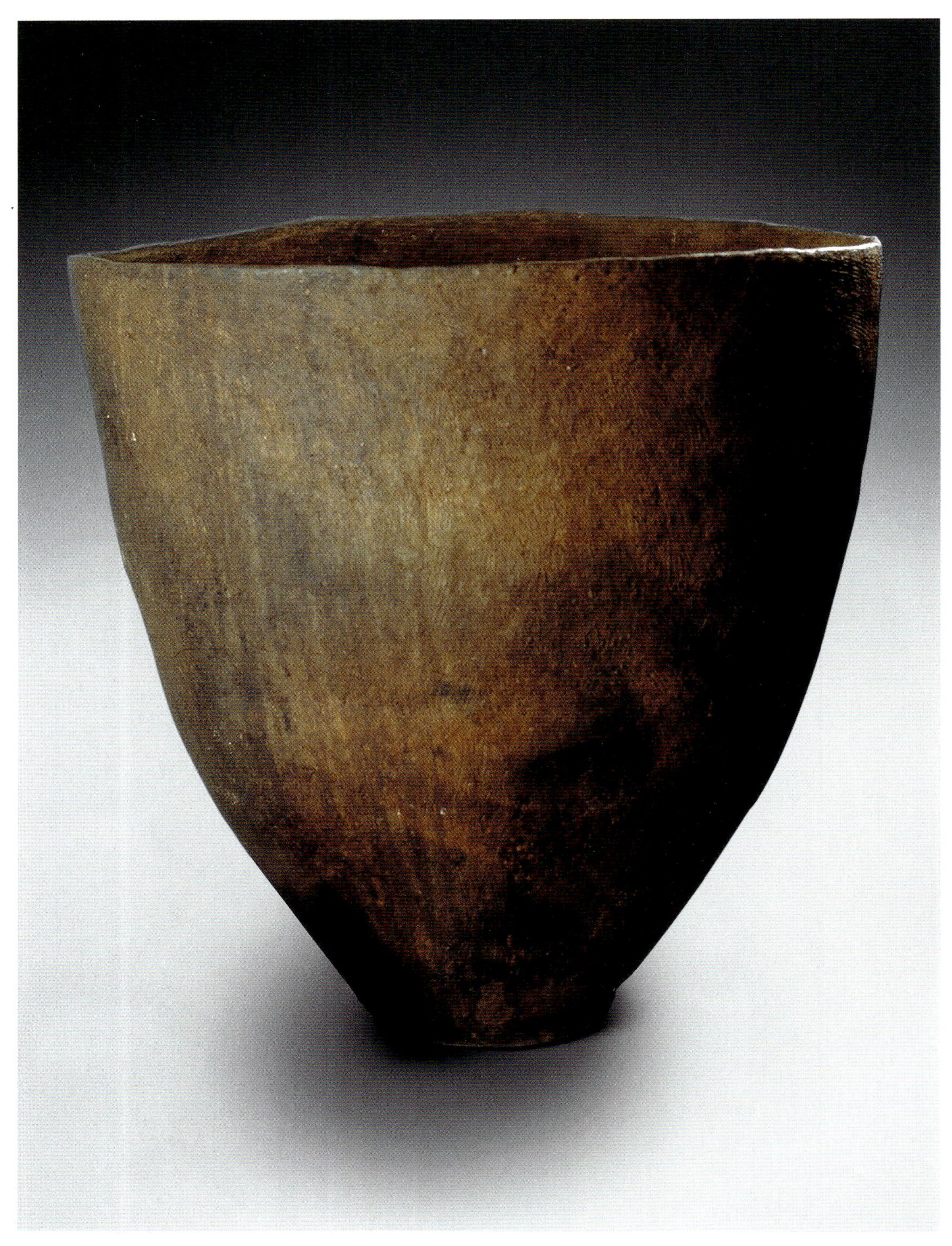

POT NUMBER 702 Imbiza H: 707 mm
The largest imbiza I have found – capacity
over 450 litres – tapering from an
elliptical opening
(D at opening: 705 × 620 mm) to a
narrow base.

POT NUMBER 703 Imbiza H: 412 mm

190

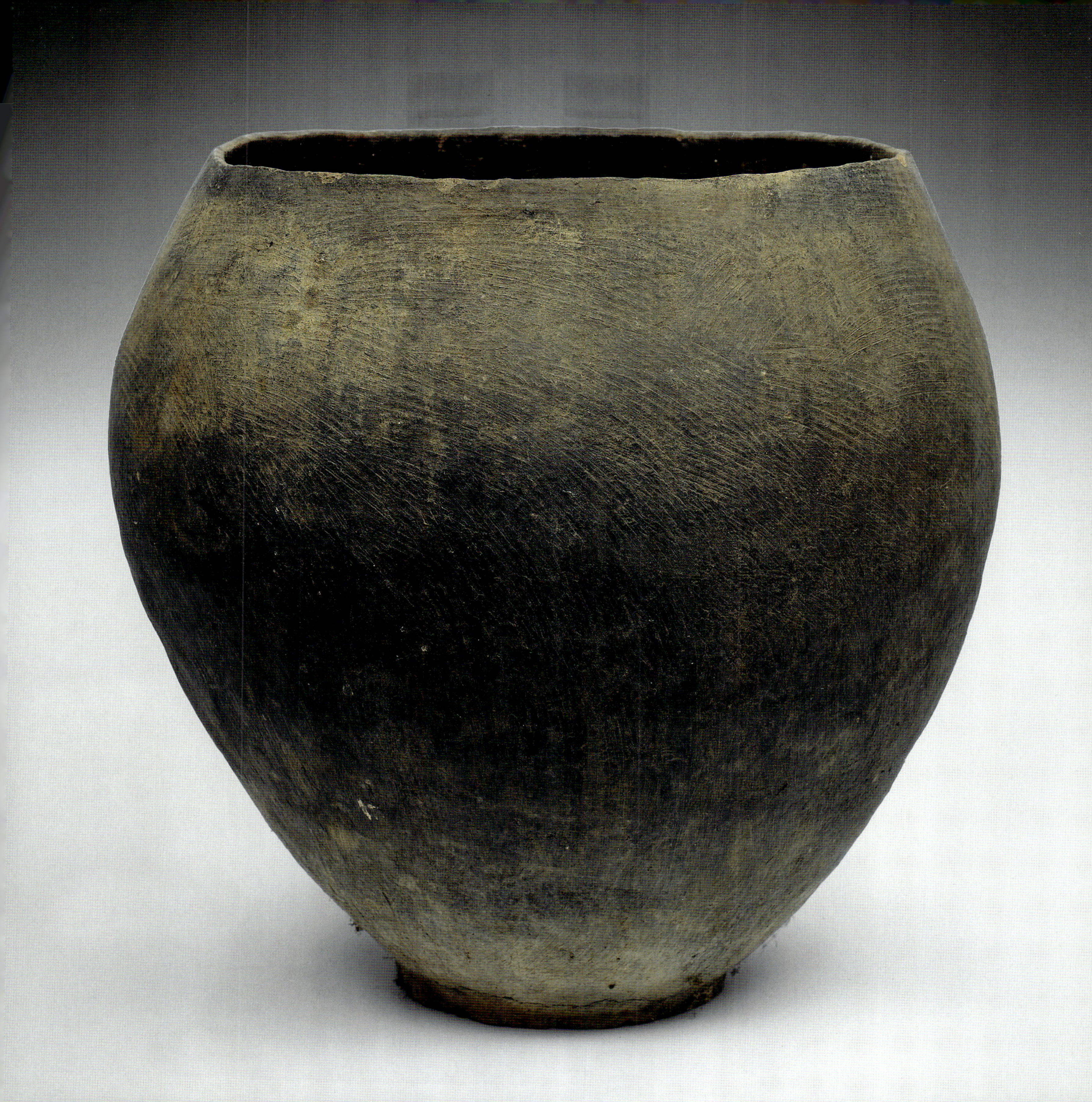

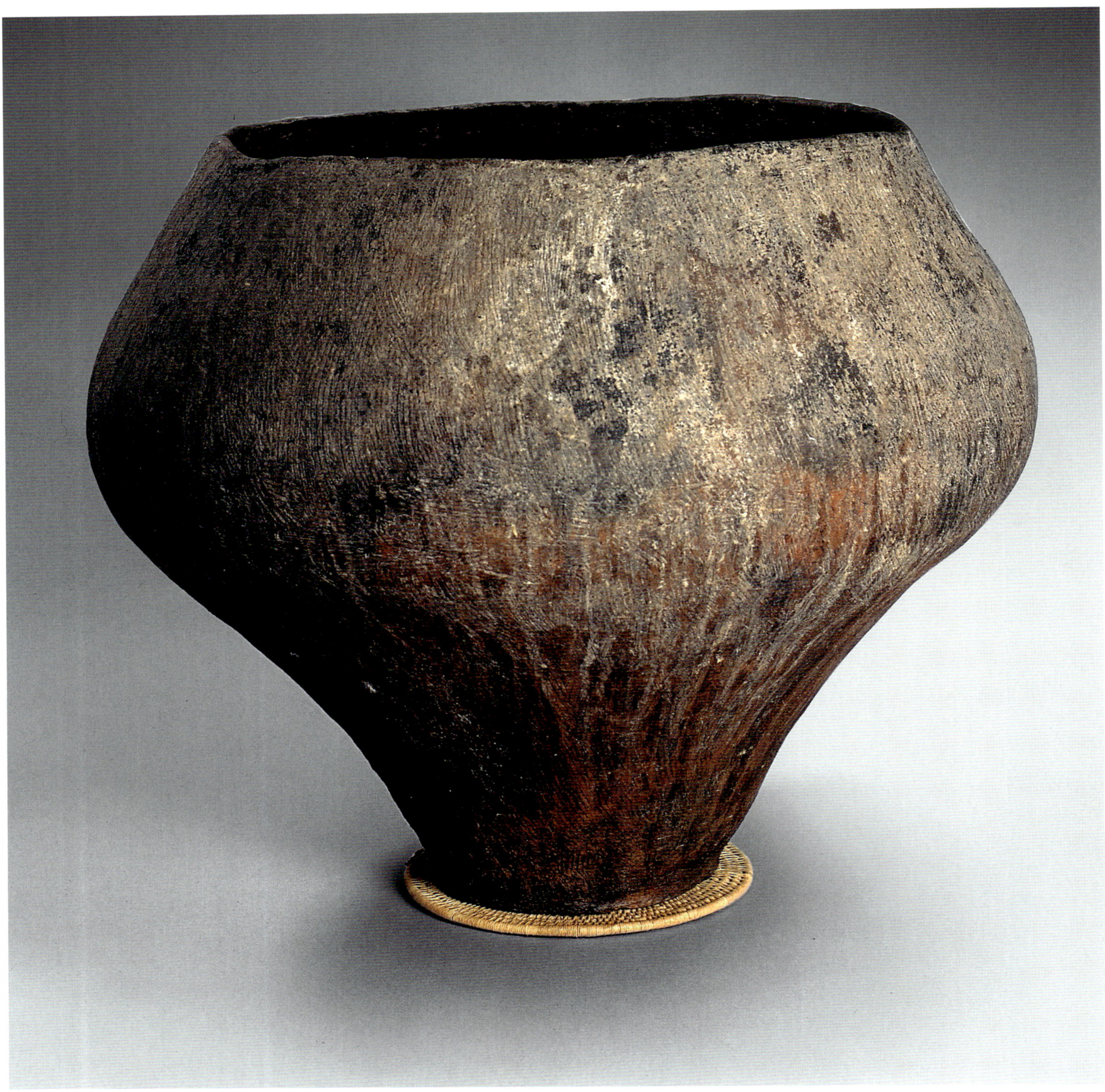

POT NUMBER 704 Imbiza H: 452 mm, W: 510 mm, O: 365 mm Characteristic broad shouldered form tapering to a very narrow base.

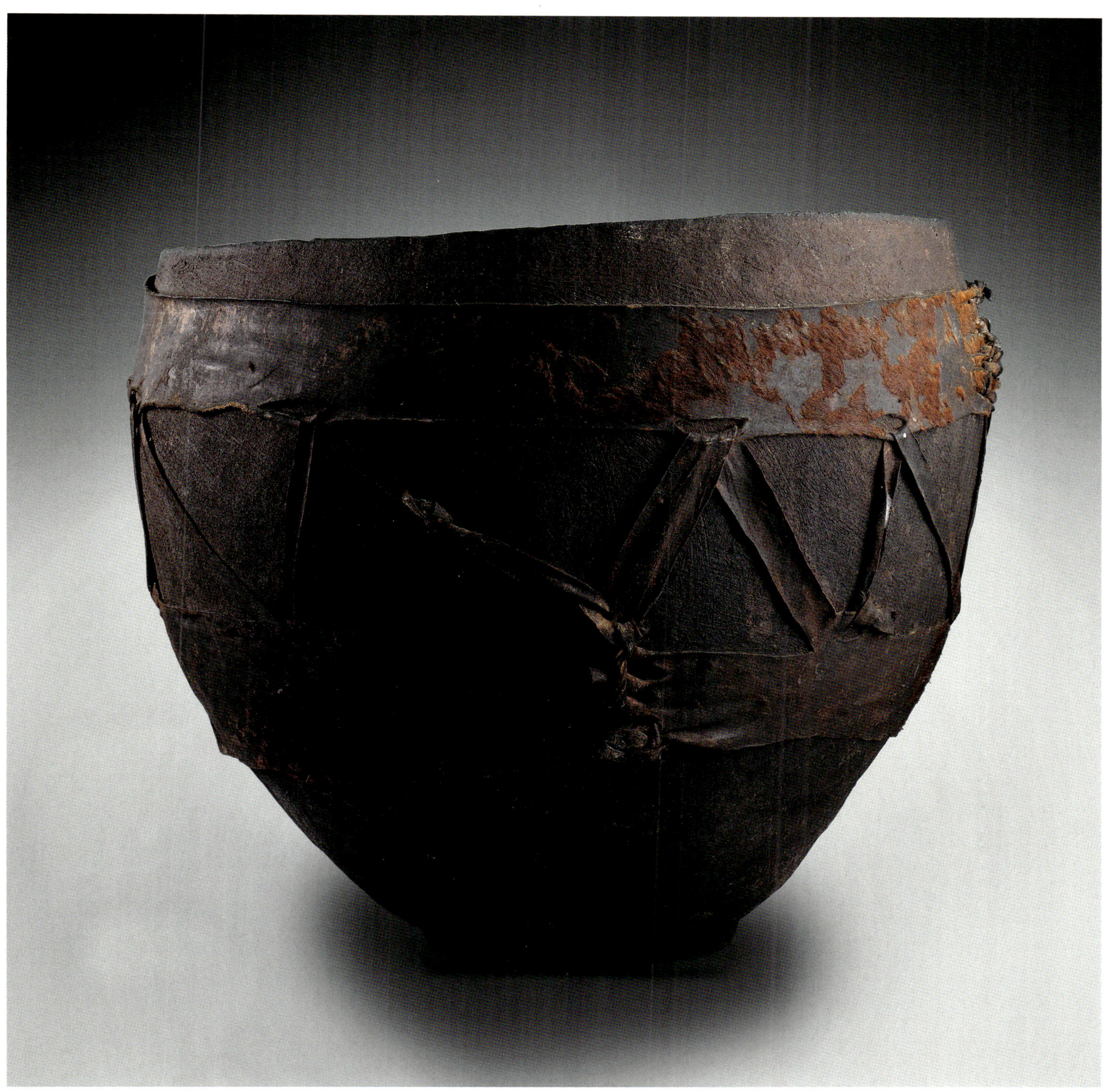

POT NUMBER 709 Imbiza H: 595 mm, G: 1710 mm, O: 670 mm Strapped with leather.

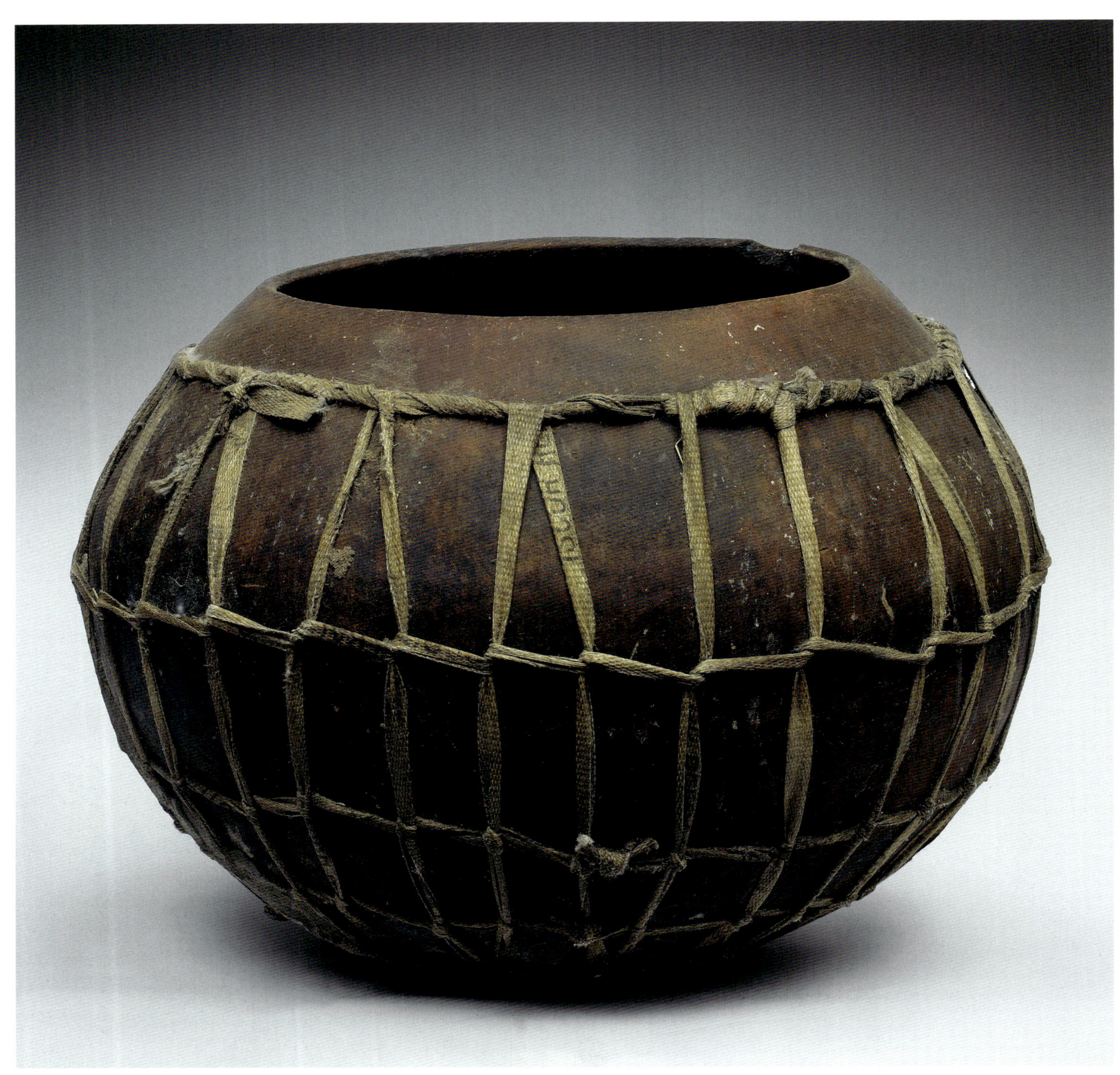

POT NUMBER 705 Imbiza H: 389 mm, W: 535 mm, O: 325 mm ▲ Woven nylon tape used to support the sides of the vessel. Largish chip in the rim may have been taken to leave with the original owners when the vessel moved to another home (cf. p 177). Some mends with cement.

POT NUMBER 711 Imbiza H: 690 mm, G: 2290 mm, O: 550 mm ▶

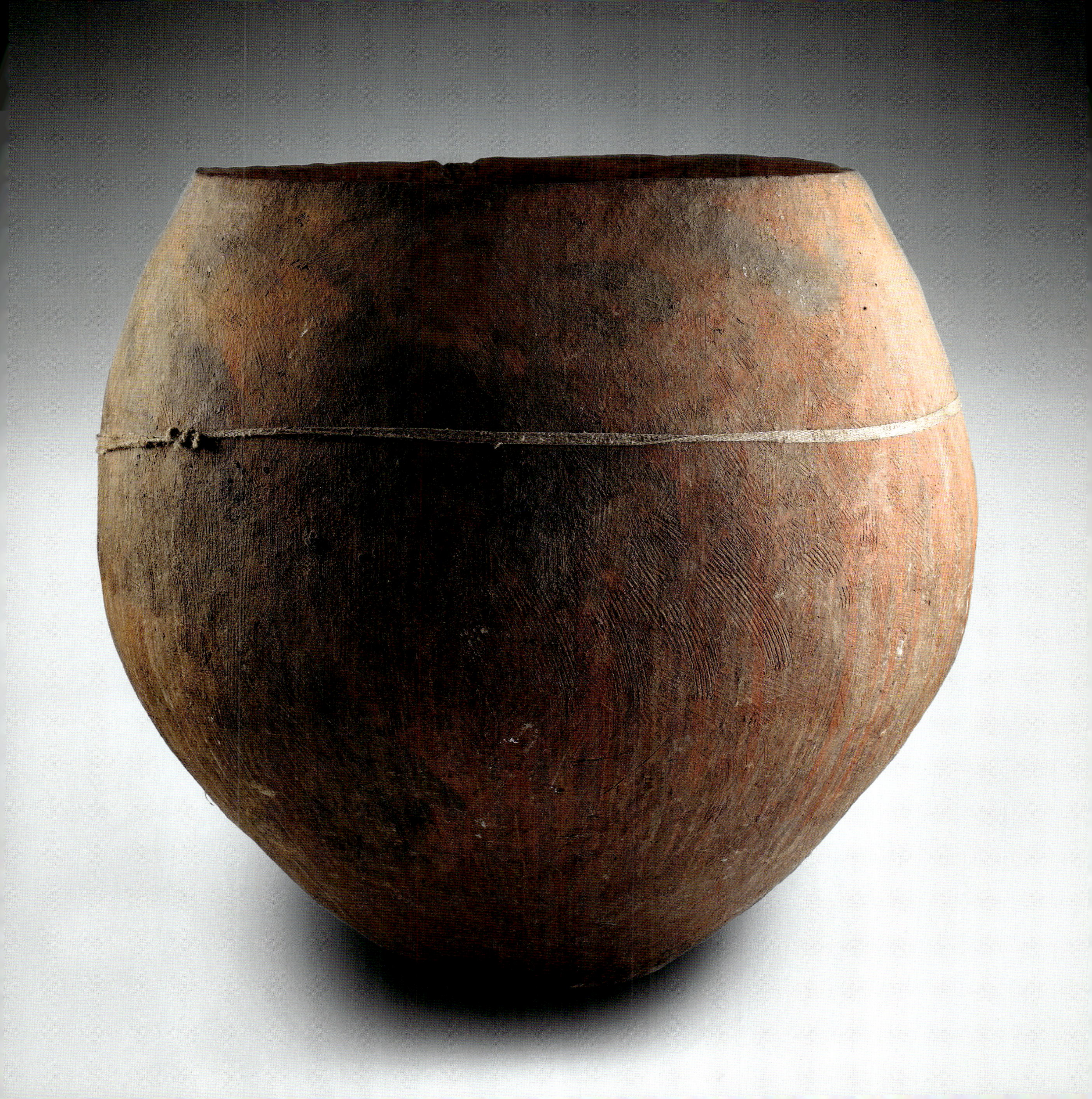

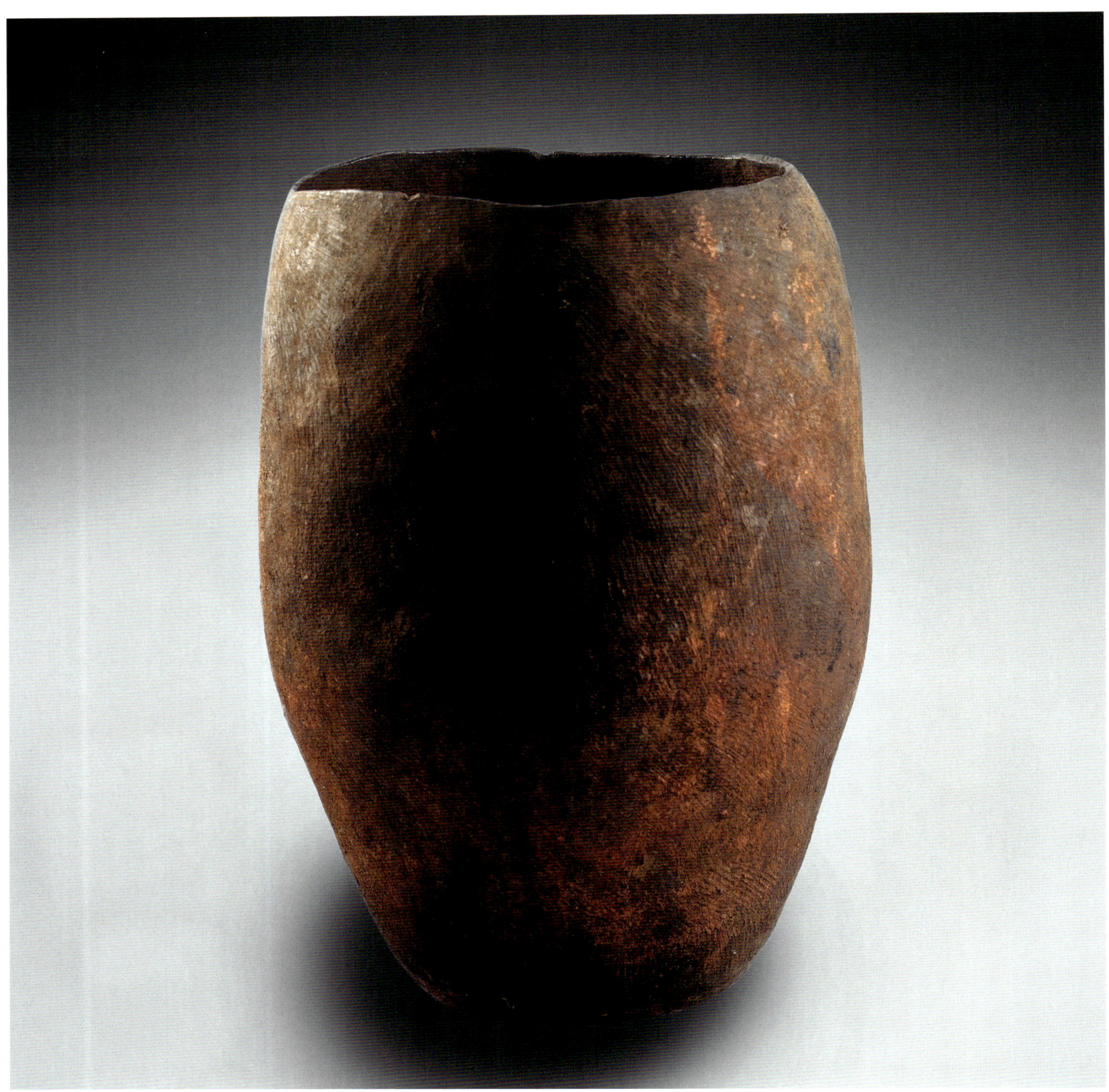

POT NUMBER 712 Imbiza H: 845 mm, G: 1060 mm, O: 280 mm For storing water. Known locally as a 'vase'.

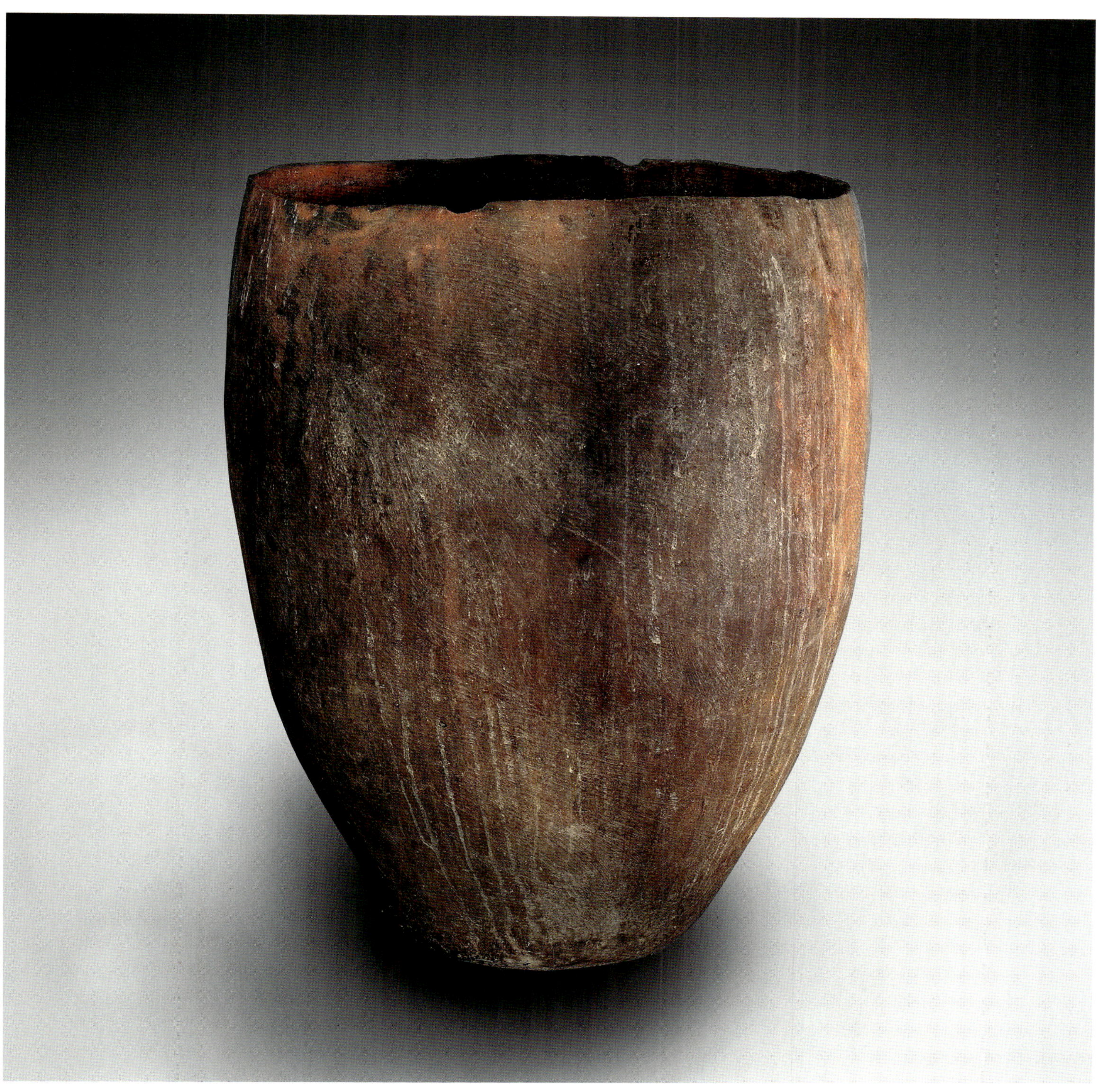

POT NUMBER 713 Imbiza H: 545 mm This one has been used for brewing beer. Two chips taken from rim for the ancestors.

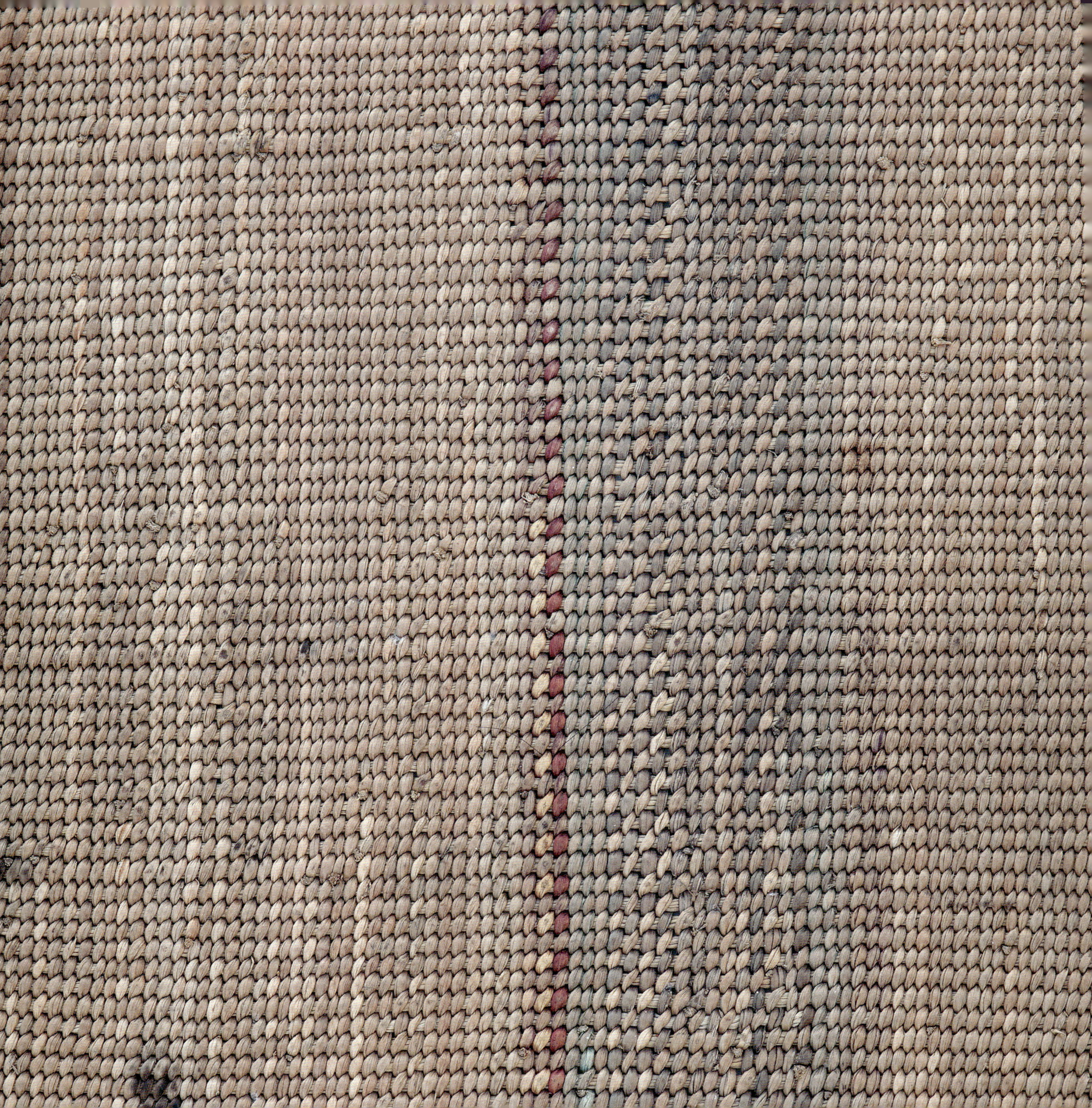

Beer Pot Covers: *Izimbenge*[69]

1. Plain grass *izimbenge*

The *imbenge* is the traditional *ukhamba* beer pot cover used to protect the beer from dust and insects. Technically *izimbenge* are small baskets just large enough to cover the opening of the pots. So there are different sizes according to the type of pot. They are not used for the pots with necks, the *isimphiso*. As the early examples were made of perishable material it is no longer possible to establish when *izimbenge* first came into use. However they were certainly in use by the second quarter of the twentieth century. The association between basketry and beer containers is, of course, much older than that. Up to the middle of the nineteenth century the most widely used beer containers were, in fact, baskets. A number of large beer baskets from the beginning of the twentieth century have survived in museum collections; others seem to have been in use until the third quarter of the century (ultimately they were to give rise to the popular but more loosely woven tourist baskets made of iLala Palm fronds). Such baskets are mostly *uphiso*-shaped but with smaller and shorter necks than their ceramic counterparts. Other types do exist (see pages 24–7). They usually have tight-fitting lids also made of basketry.

The lids of beer baskets may have served as prototypes for the later *izimbenge*, but there was also a transitional stage in which small versions of the familiar grass eating-mats, *isithebe*, were used as beer pot covers and in fact also termed '*imbenge*'. The very

1 Isithebe, grass 1930s, detail
210 x 232 mm
Weave: 5 warp x 9 weft threads of
grass per cm²

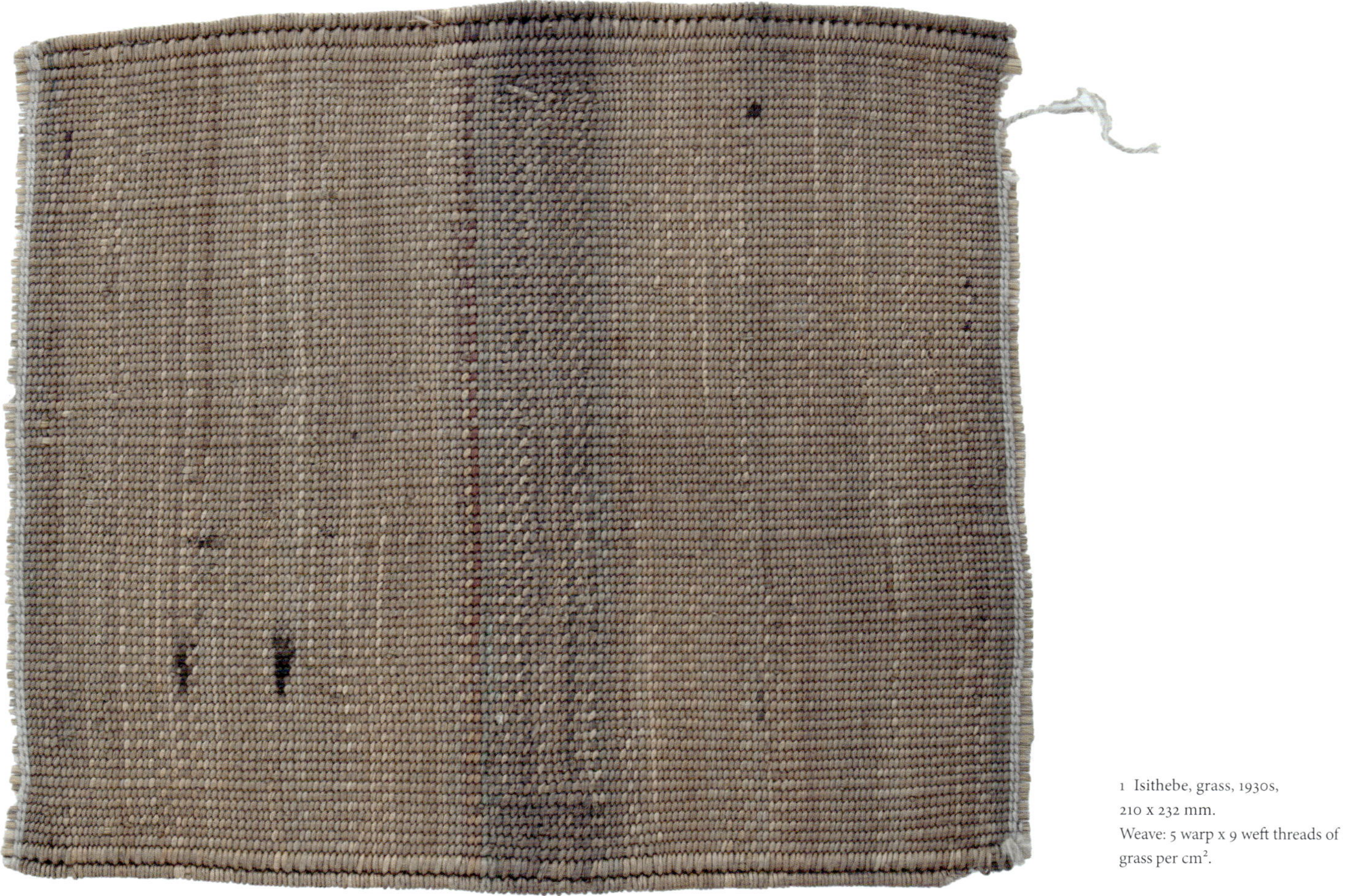

1 Isithebe, grass, 1930s,
210 x 232 mm.
Weave: 5 warp x 9 weft threads of
grass per cm².

finely woven example illustrated above dates from the 1930s or early 1940s. It measures 210 x 232 mm and has 5 warp x 9 weft threads of grass per cm².

The earliest surviving *izimbenge* are of a similar material and weave. Most of them are shallow. They lack decoration apart from variations within the weft and/ or simple motifs woven in grass dyed a darker shade of brown. The following are typical examples. First a plain one, then one with woven decorations and finally one using dyed grass: Nos. 2, 3 and 4.

There was a shortage of imported glass beads from Europe during World War II. In some areas the use of coloured wools replaced beads. The following *imbenge*, No. 5, was said to date from that period, but it could also have been made by a school pupil in the course of crafts lessons at a later date.

2 Plain Imbenge grass, *c.* 1940,
D: 214 mm.
Weave: 7 weft threads per 10 mm warp.

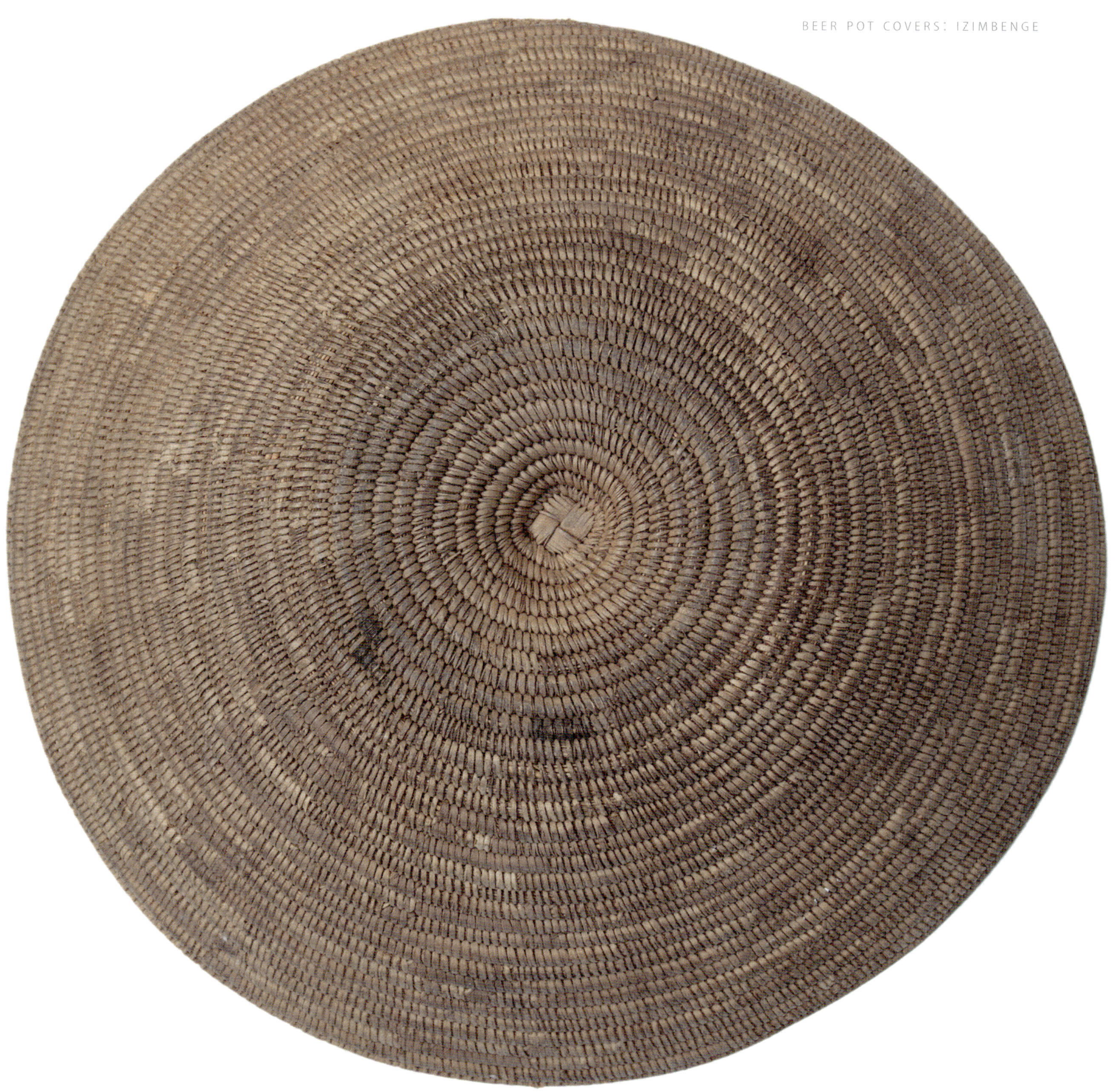

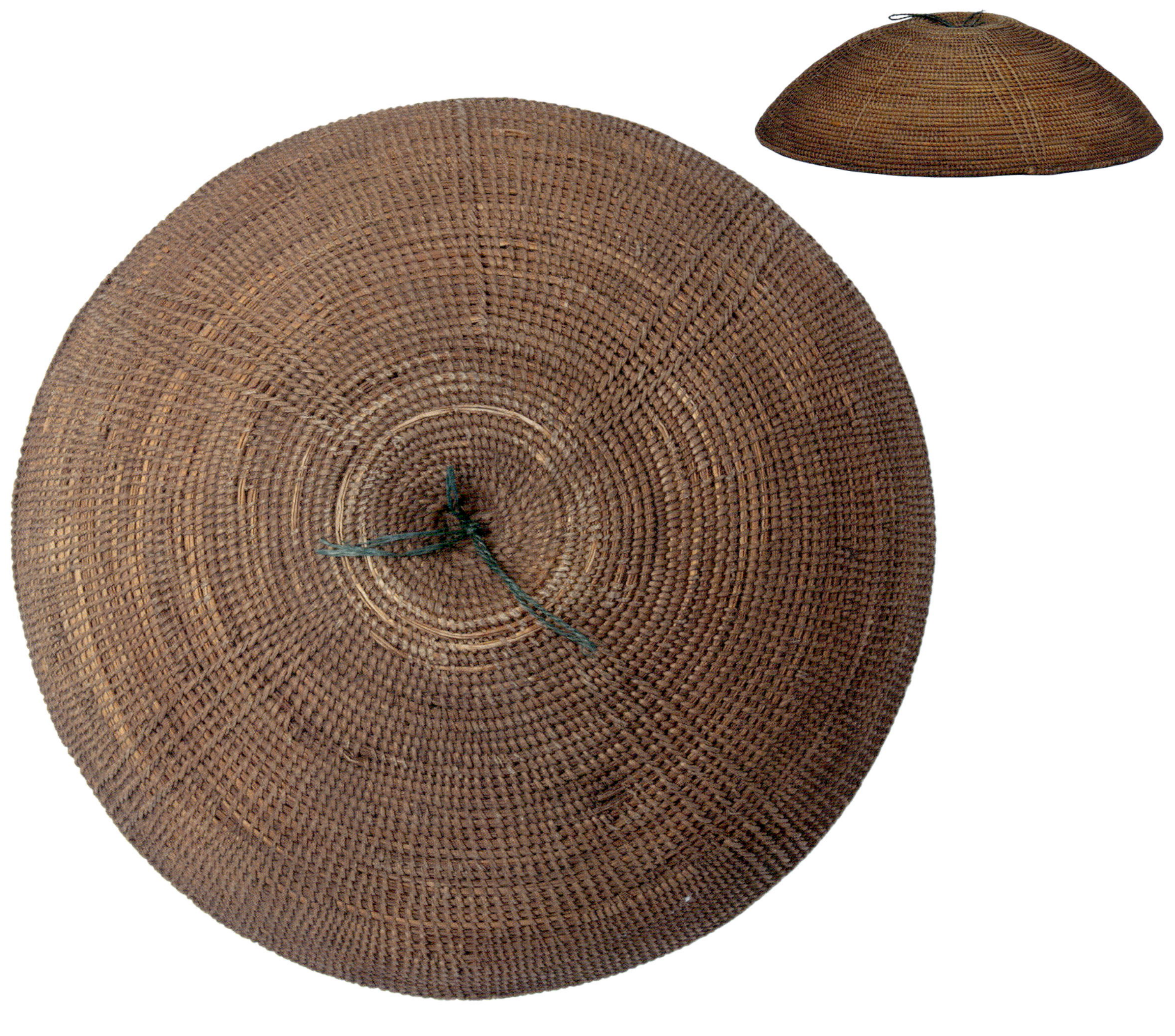

3 Imbenge with woven pattern, grass, 1940s, D: 216 mm. Weave: 4 weft threads per 10 mm of warp. The weft threads are spaced with gaps between them.

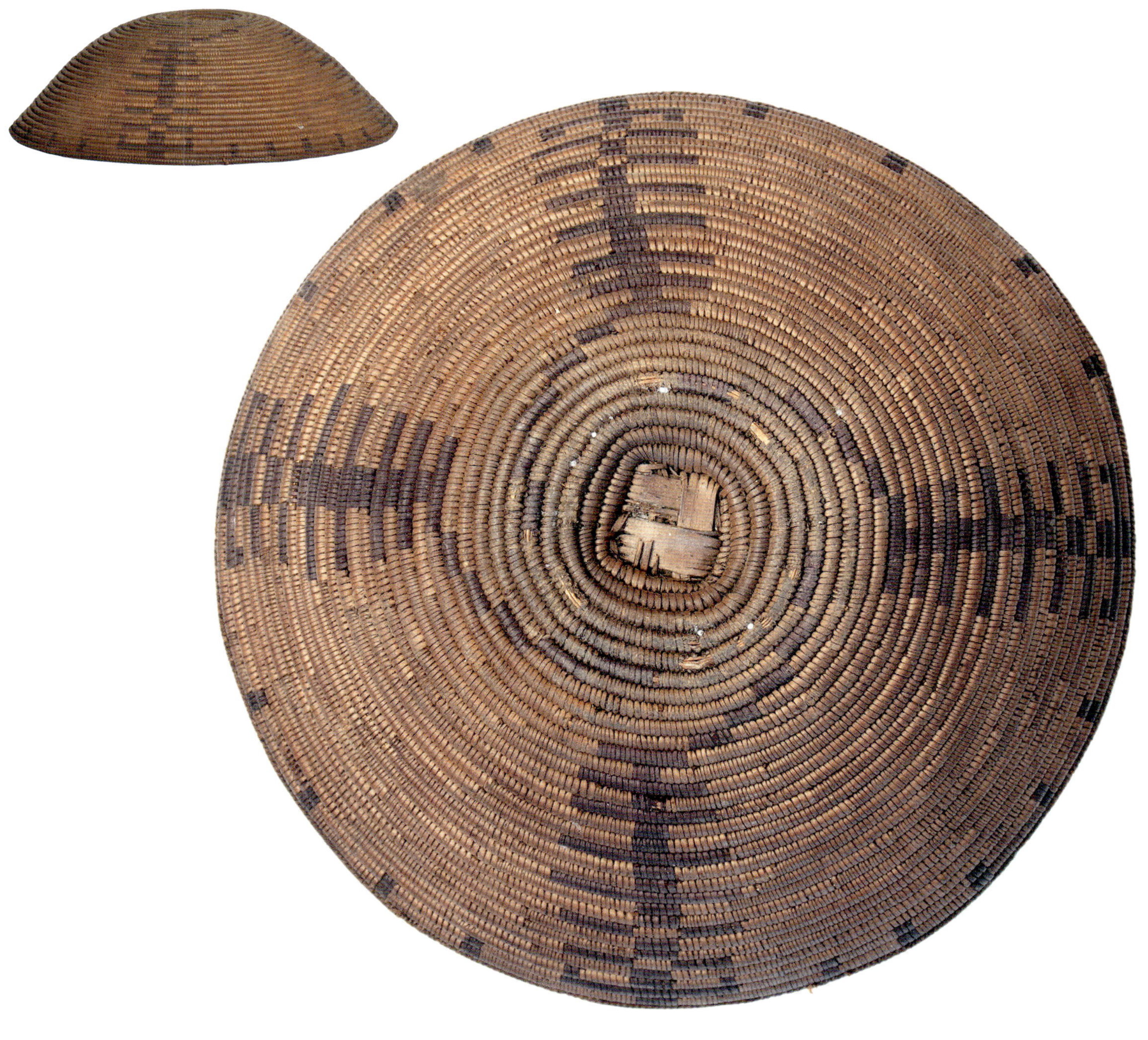

4 Imbenge with dyed pattern, grass, 1940s, D: 205 mm. Weave: 8–13 weft threads per 10 mm of warp.

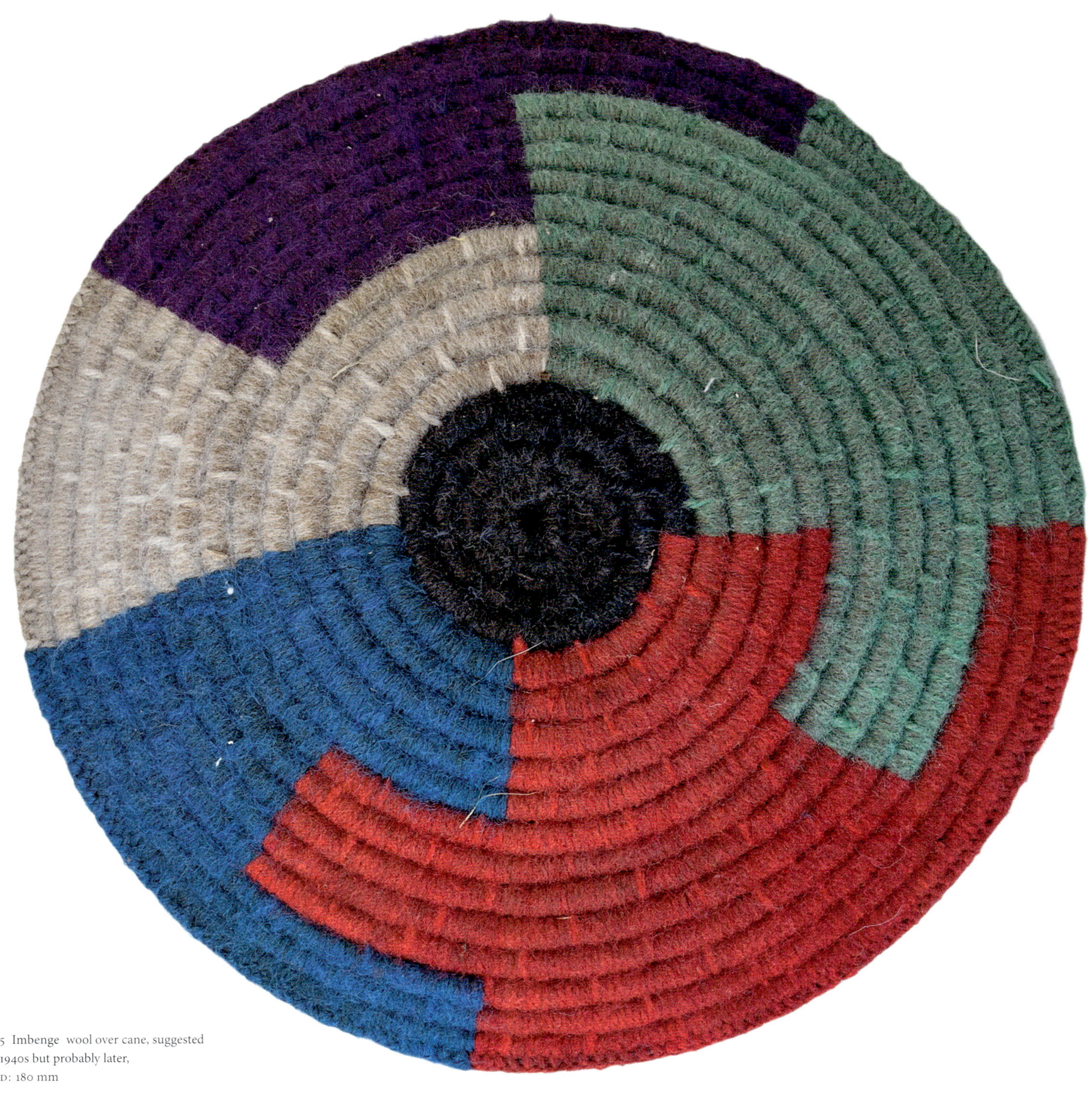

5 Imbenge wool over cane, suggested
1940s but probably later,
D: 180 mm

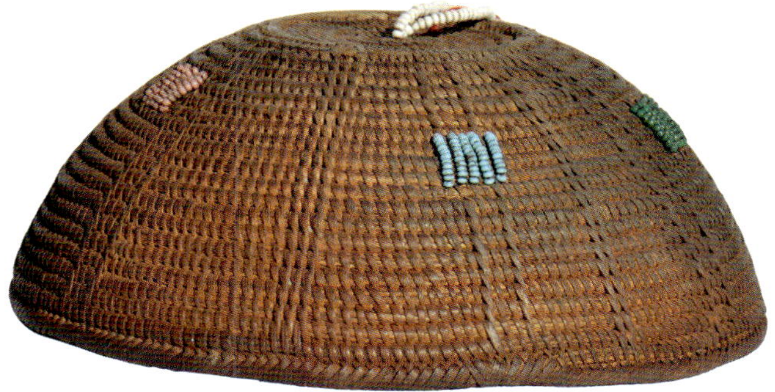

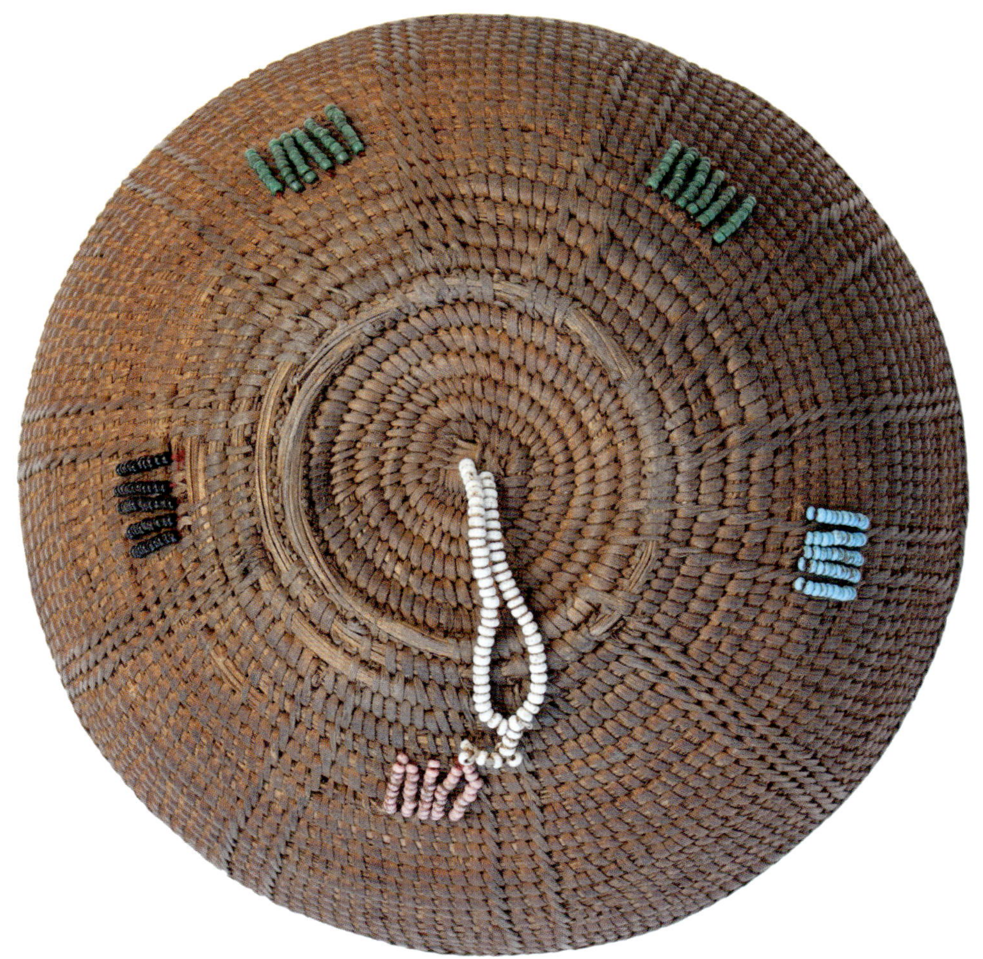

6 Imbenge grass with added beadwork
in the Msinga '*isishunka*' colour
convention, 1940s–1950s
D: 183 mm, H: 77 mm
Weave: 9 weft threads/spaces to 10 mm
of warp. Acquired 8 September 1999 at
Mbangweni (Tugela).

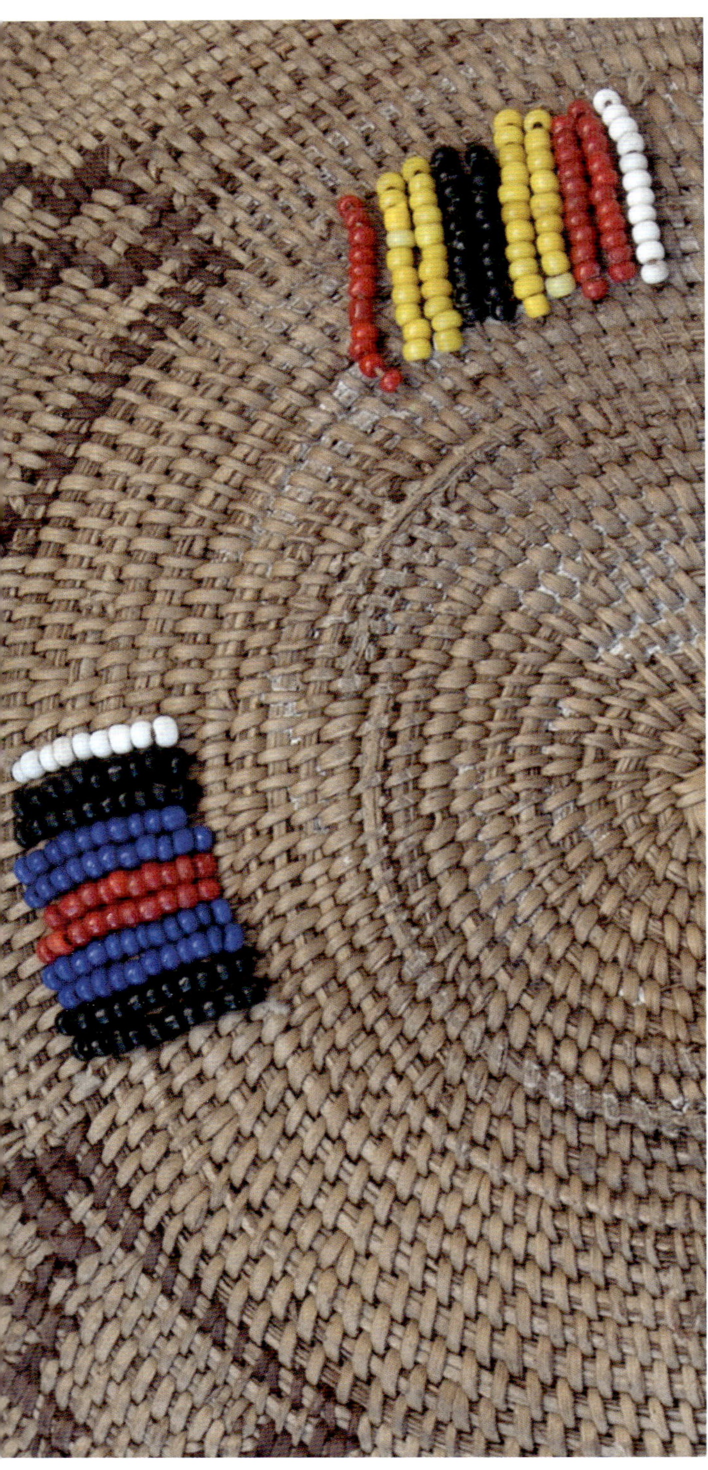

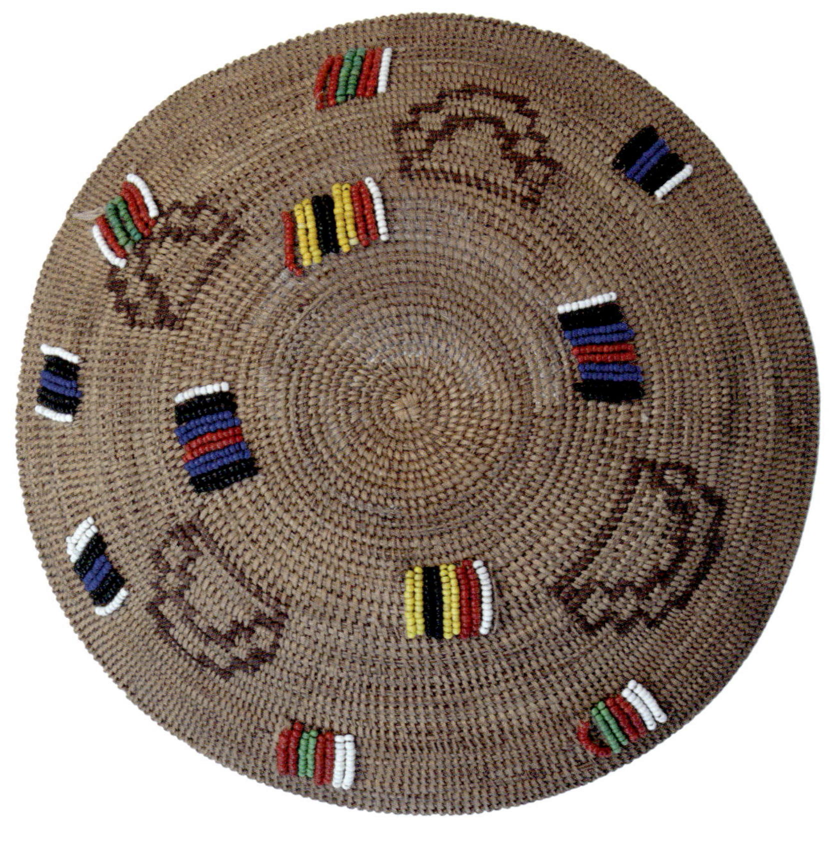

7 Imbenge grass with added beadwork
in the Mthunzini colour convention,
1940s–1950s, D: 200 mm.
Weave: 5 spaced weft threads to 10 mm of
warp (i.e. equivalent to 9 weft threads).

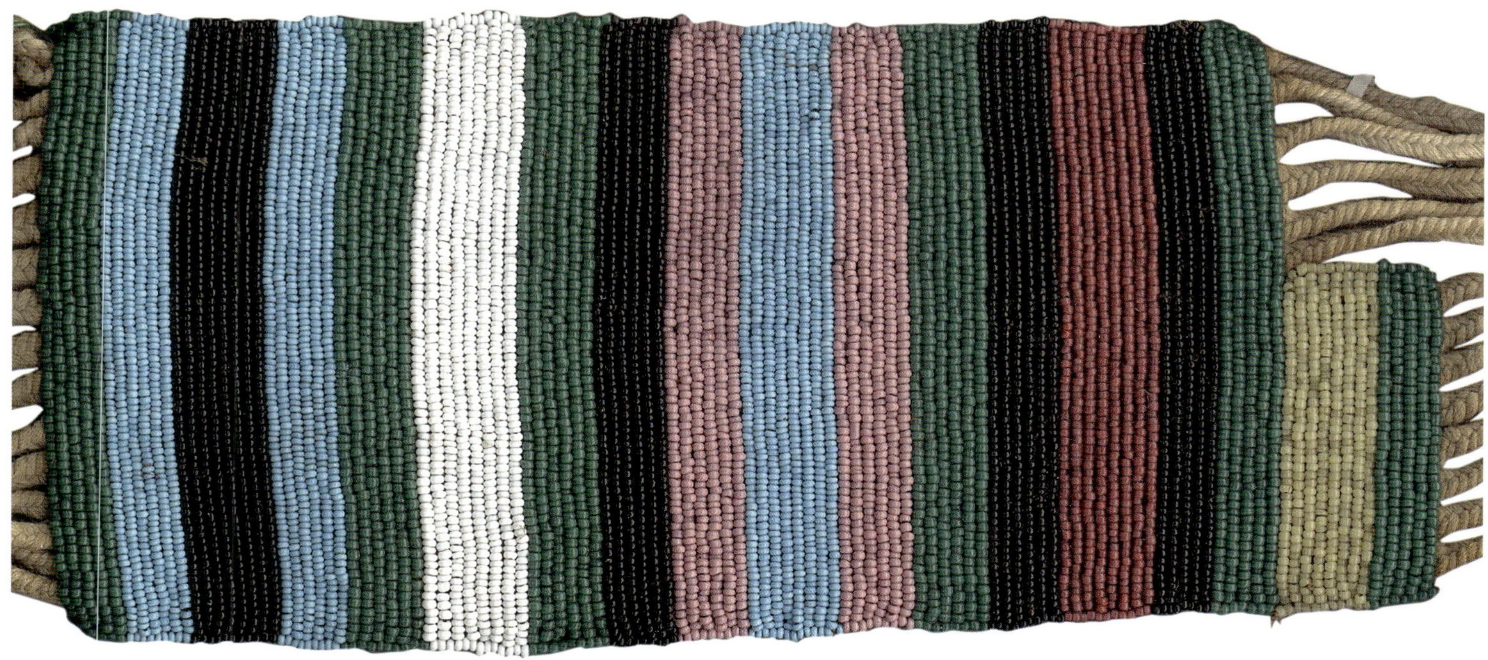

8 Example of isishunka: an anklet dating from the late 1940s or early 1950s.

2. The introduction of beadwork to *izimbenge*

After the conclusion of the war in 1945 there was a revival which led to the great renaissance of beadwork of the 1950s to 1980s. It appears that some of the older plain pieces were reworked with beads. This seems likely because in places the beadwork is superimposed on the original pattern in an unsymmetrical haphazard way: Nos. 6 and 7.

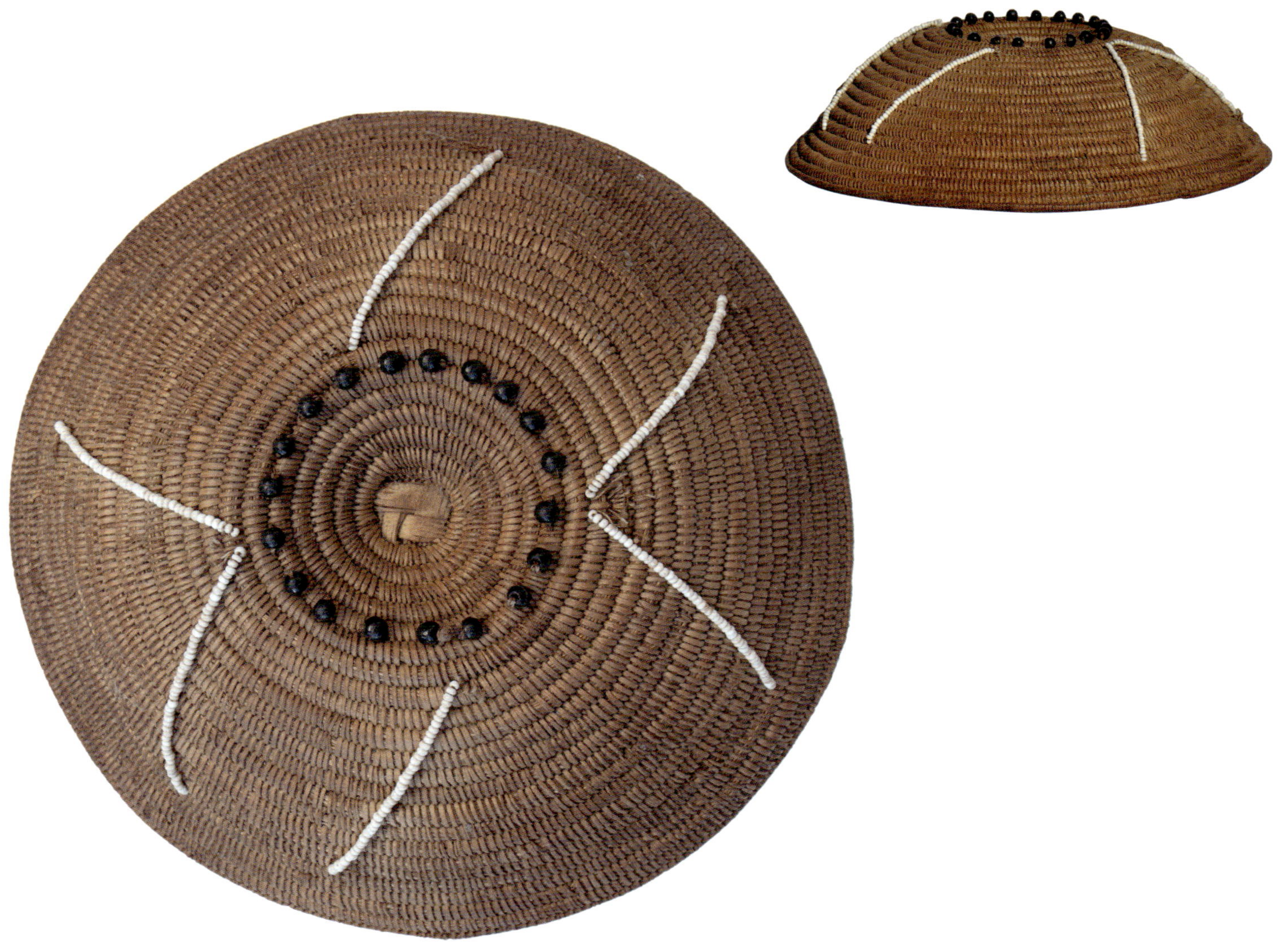

The colours of beadwork usually convey information of some sort. Here, in Nos. 6 and 7, they indicate which area and which clan the *izimbenge* stem from. In No. 7 p. 206, each small panel contains a typical colour sequence from the Mthunzini region. In No. 6, p. 205, the panels themselves are in the Mchunu clan, Msinga, colour sequence. The sequence, called *isishunka*, should read green-black-pink-light blue-pink-green-etc; here the repetition of the pink is omitted in favour of the green (which is the dominant colour) but the sequence remains clearly recognisable to any person familiar with local colour conventions. There is no risk of confusion. No. 6 differs from its predecessors in that it is a deep bowl shape – perhaps intended for a very small pot.

9 Imbenge grass with added beadwork
1940s–1950s, D: 193 mm,
H: 55 mm.
Weave: 10 weft threads/spaces to 10 mm
of warp.

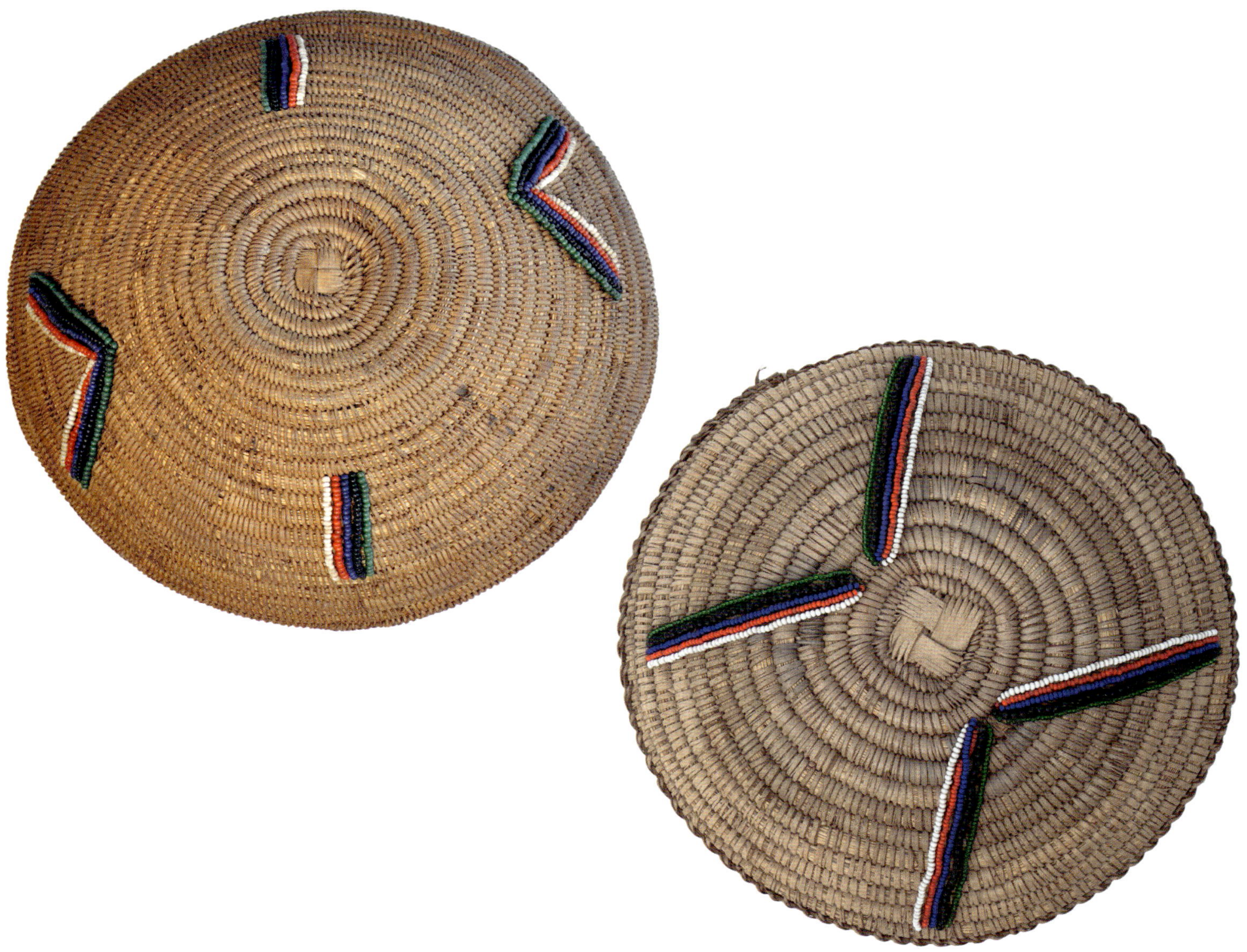

10 Imbenge rye grass with added beadwork, 1950s, Nkandla-Eshowe colour convention, D: 198 mm, H: 51 mm. Weave: 9 weft threads/spaces to 10 mm of warp.

11 Imbenge iLala Palm with added beadwork, 1960s, Nkandla-Eshowe colour convention, D = 199 mm, H: 47 mm. Weave: coarse when compared with rye grass, with some variation in the thickness of 'thread'.

The earlier *izimbenge* are usually tightly woven and sparing in their use of beadwork. They do not necessarily convey a regional colour identity. Instead they are often stunning in the economy of their decoration and their use of symmetry and contrast, as in the following example, No. 9, p. 208, with its black and white beads of different sizes and a simple symmetry of rotation through 180 degrees. Completing the pattern by adding the two 'missing' arms would have produced additional symmetries of reflection and translation but would also have seriously diminished the overall aesthetic impact, which arises from the unfulfilled expectation inherent in the reduced symmetry.

The two following pieces, Nos. 10 and 11, p.209, have similar minimalist tendencies. Both of them display the full set of symmetries in the plane: reflection, translation and rotation, and a clear regional colour convention, namely Nkandla-Eshowe. No. 10 is the older of the two, it is still made of rye grass, whilst 11 is iLala Palm. The dark green beads of the original colour convention were no longer available when the second *imbenge* was made. In this case they were replaced by transparent, so-called 'see-through' beads. In other cases we find them being replaced by a lighter green traded as part of the colour convention of an adjoining region.

The trend towards ever more ornate use of beadwork incorporating complex techniques and patterns continued during the 1960s and 1970s. The following, Nos. 12, 13 and 14, represent a very small selection. The first, No. 12, has 5 panels of raised knots evenly spaced on a patterned iLala Palm base to express the *isithembu* convention from Msinga.

The next, No. 13, is a fuller version of the Nkandla convention with four main motifs and four secondary

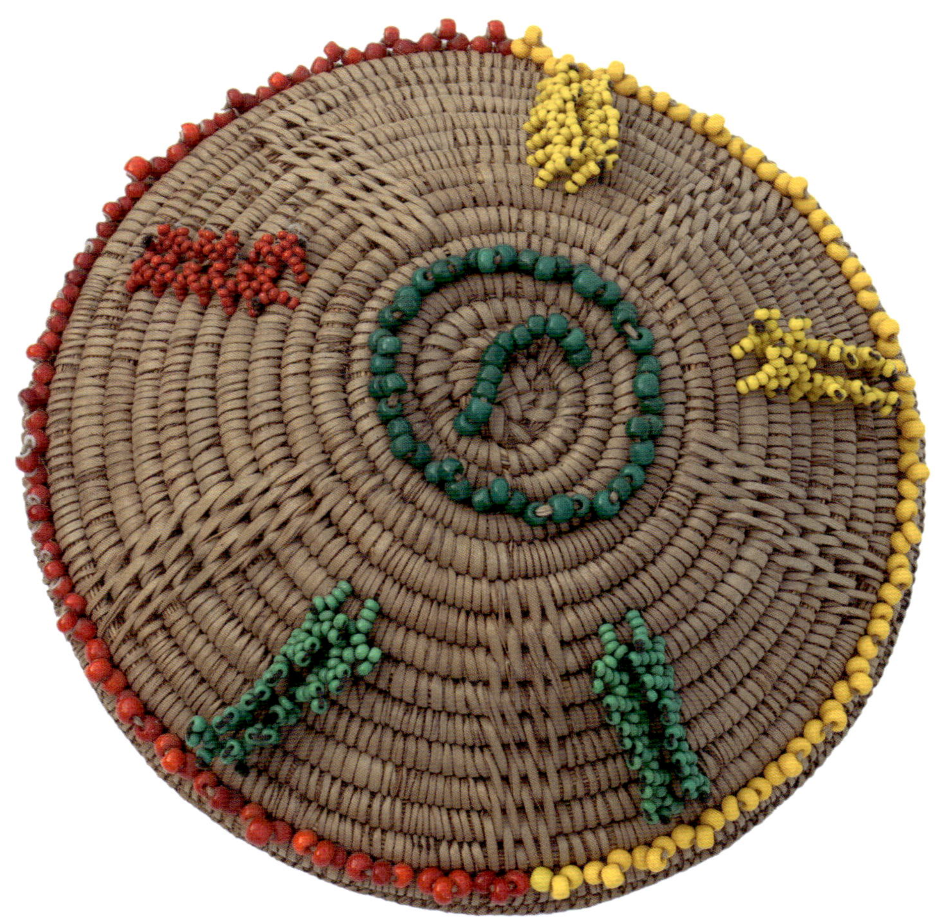

12 Imbenge iLala Palm with added beadwork in the Msinga *isithembu* convention, 1960s, D: 165 mm, H: 53 mm.

13 Imbenge rye grass with added beadwork 1960s, D: 200 mm, H: 56 mm. Weave: 11 weft threads/spaces to 10 mm of warp.

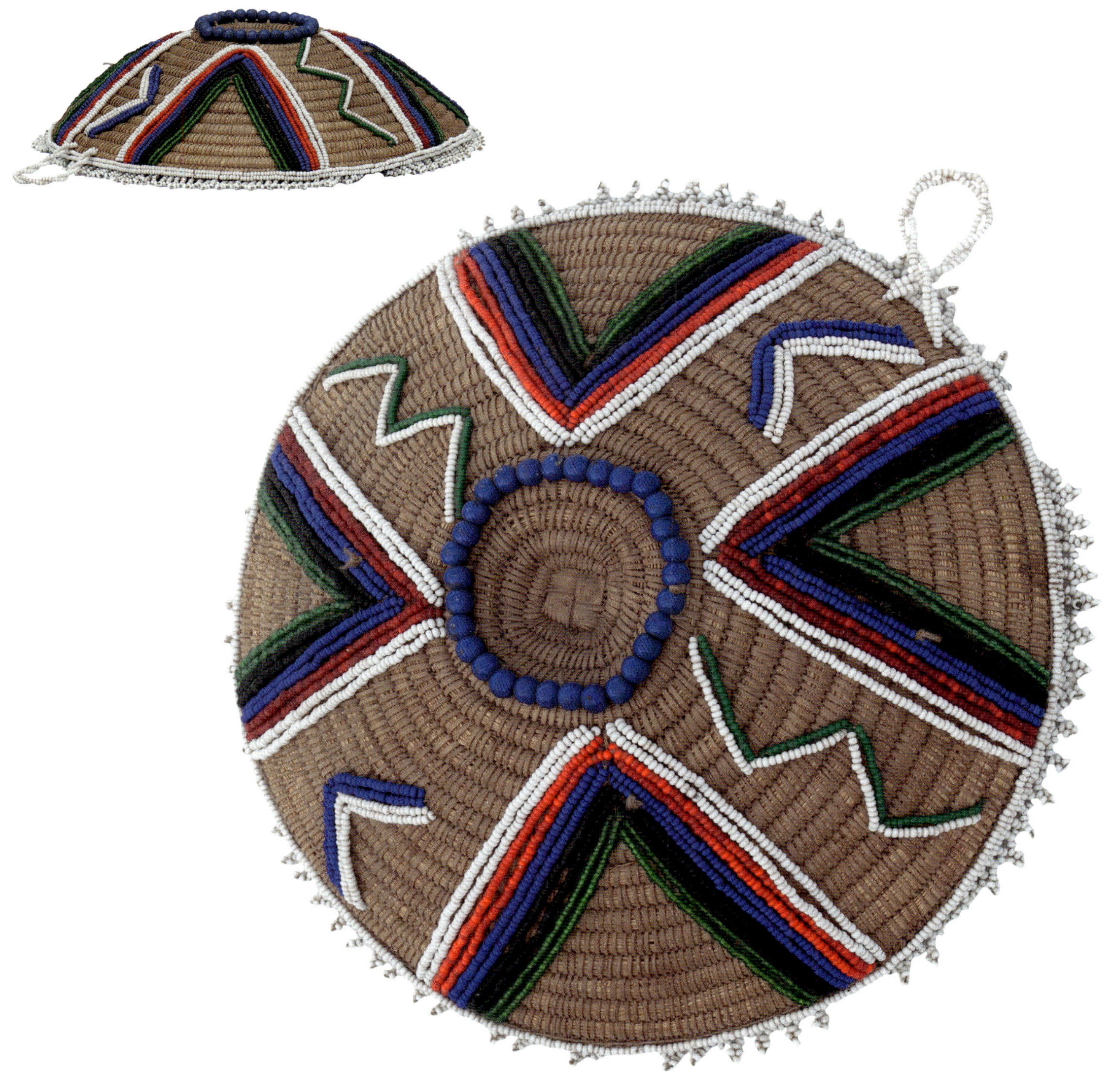

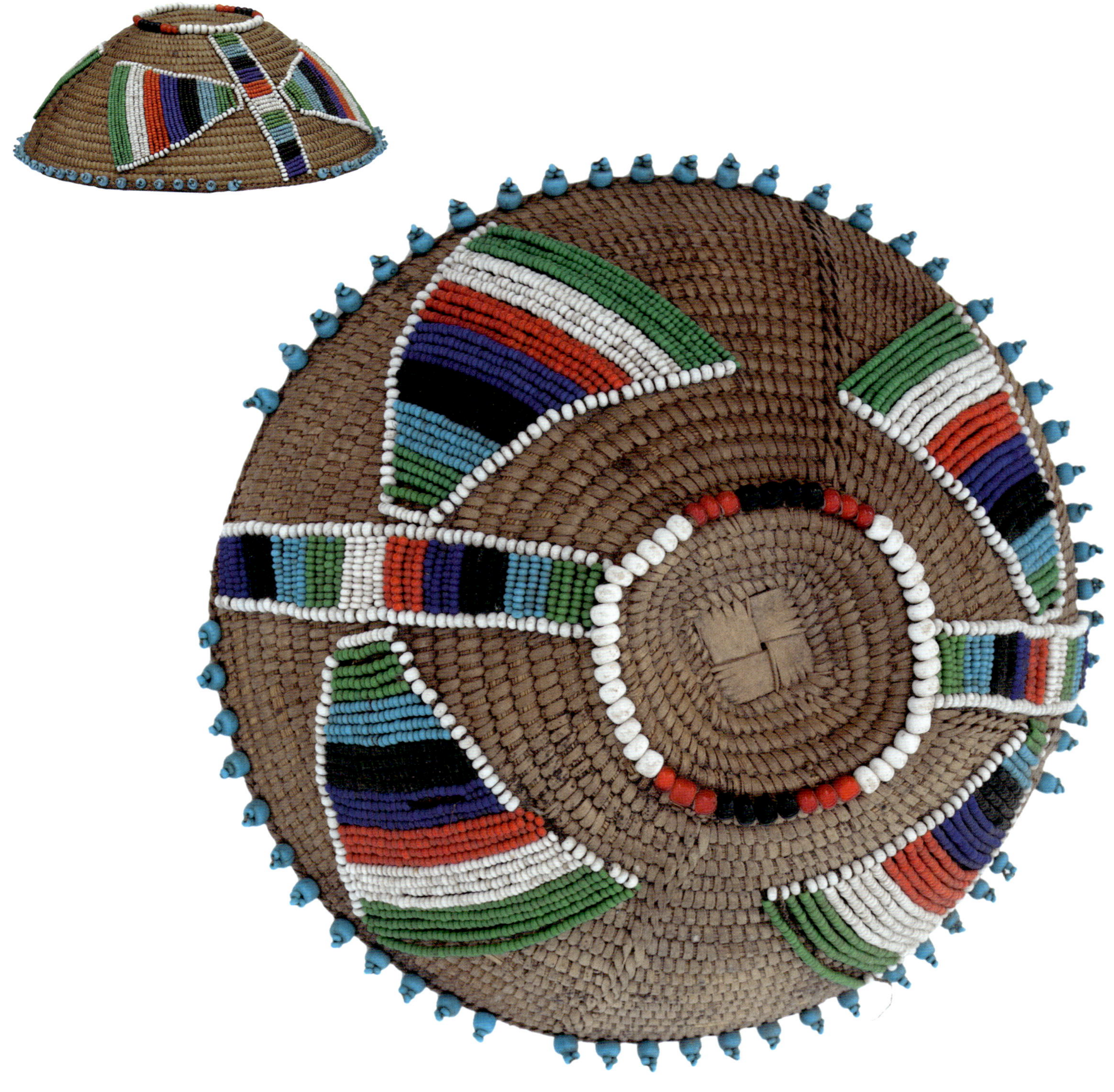

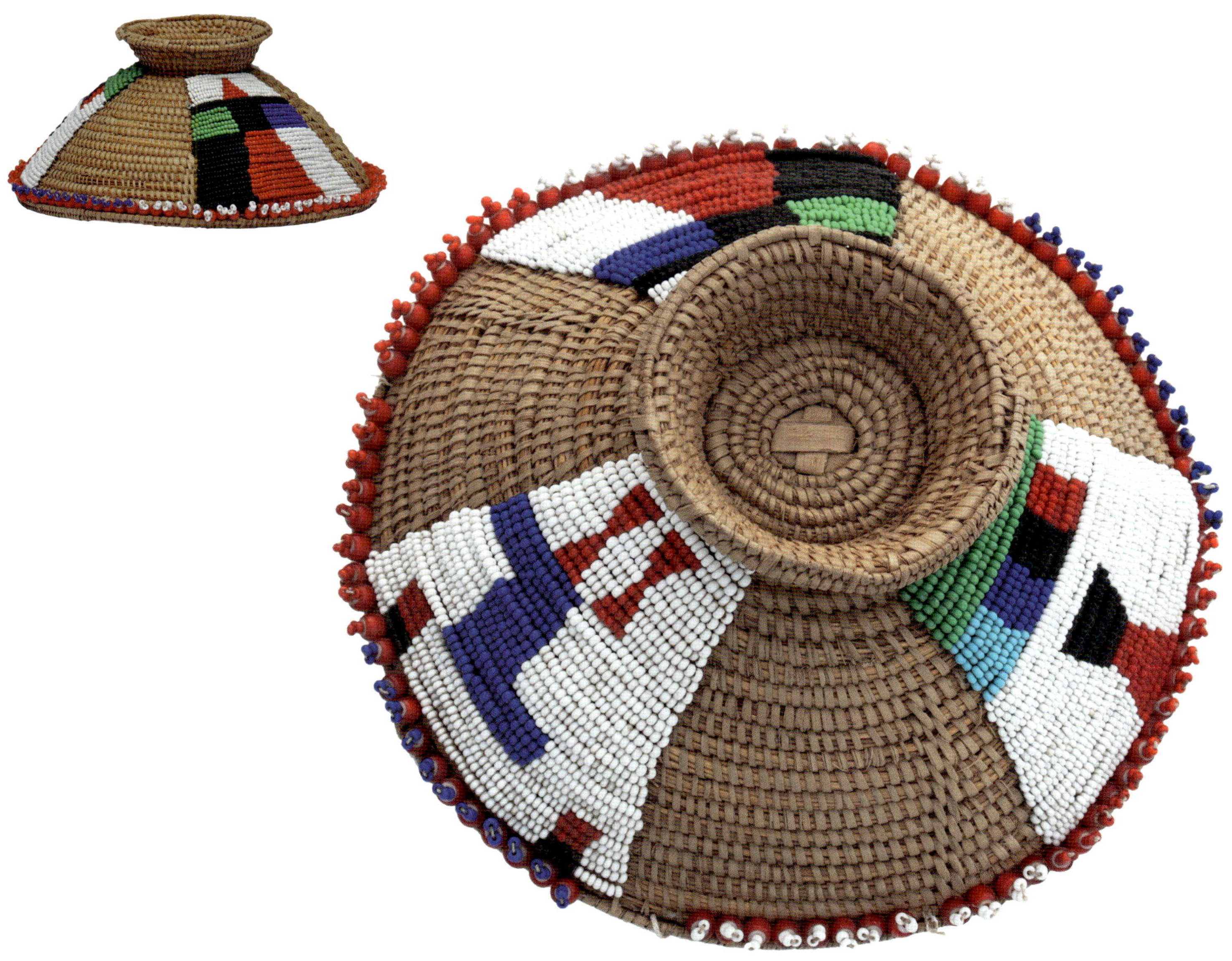

14 Imbenge iLala Palm with added beadwork in a six-colour convention, probably from Muden (Msinga), c.1970, D: 215 mm, H: 81 mm

15 Imbenge provenance *uMqheleni*, iLala Palm with added beadwork in the *isimodeni* convention, 1970s, D: 183 mm, H: 82 mm

motifs so configured that the only remaining symmetry is rotation through 180 degrees. It includes a loop to hang it up by. The third, No. 14, picks up the Thukela butterfly motif in a six-colour version of the *umzansi* ('person from the Low-lands') convention, probably from Muden. It has two such large motifs plus a row of light blue beads along the base and a circle of white ones along the top. The latter include two red-black-red '*uvalivali*' colour sequences which are usually interpreted as expressing a desire for marriage; they also figure in the *isishunka* convention. The red beads are the old so-called 'white hearts' as they are drawn on a white base.

The same colour sequence is picked up again in

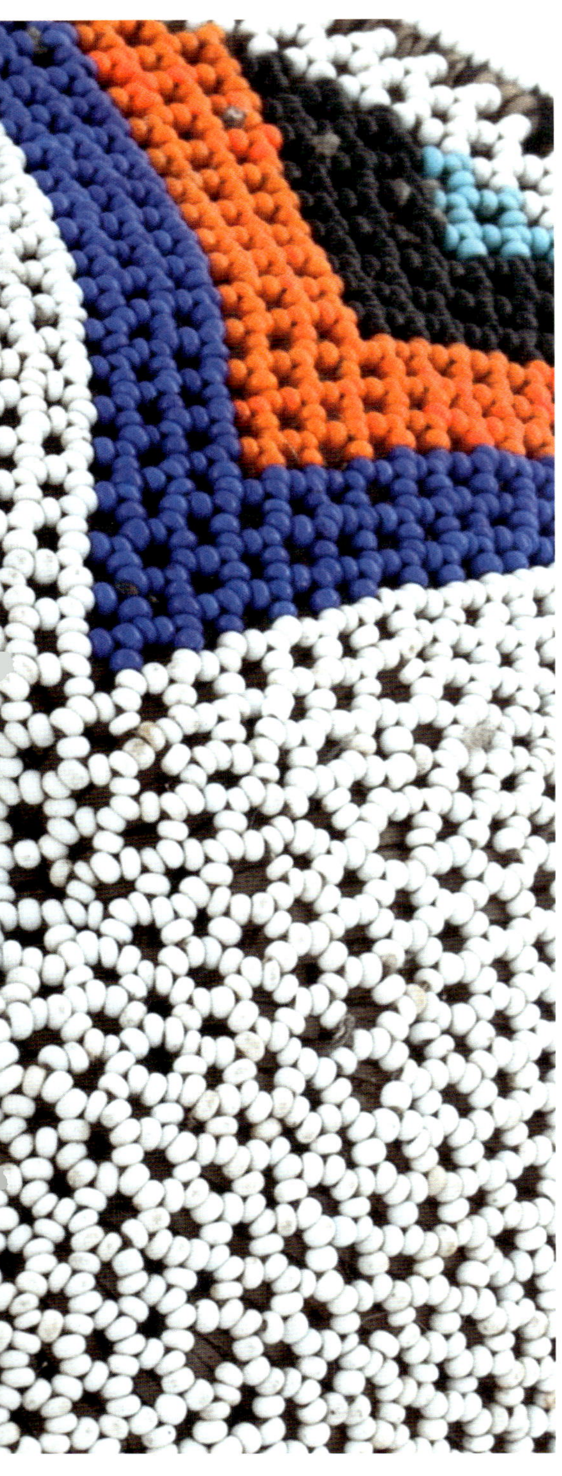

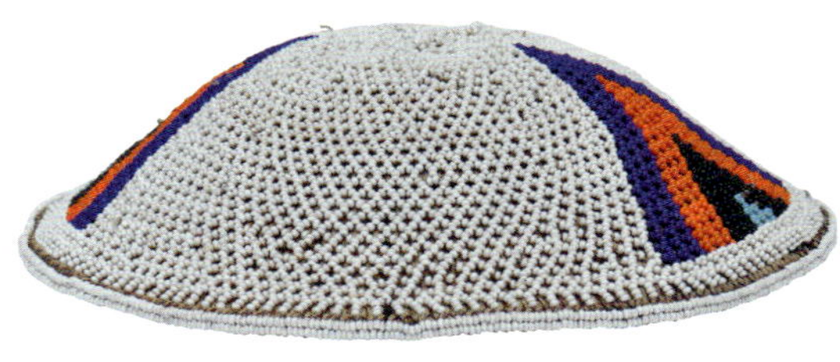

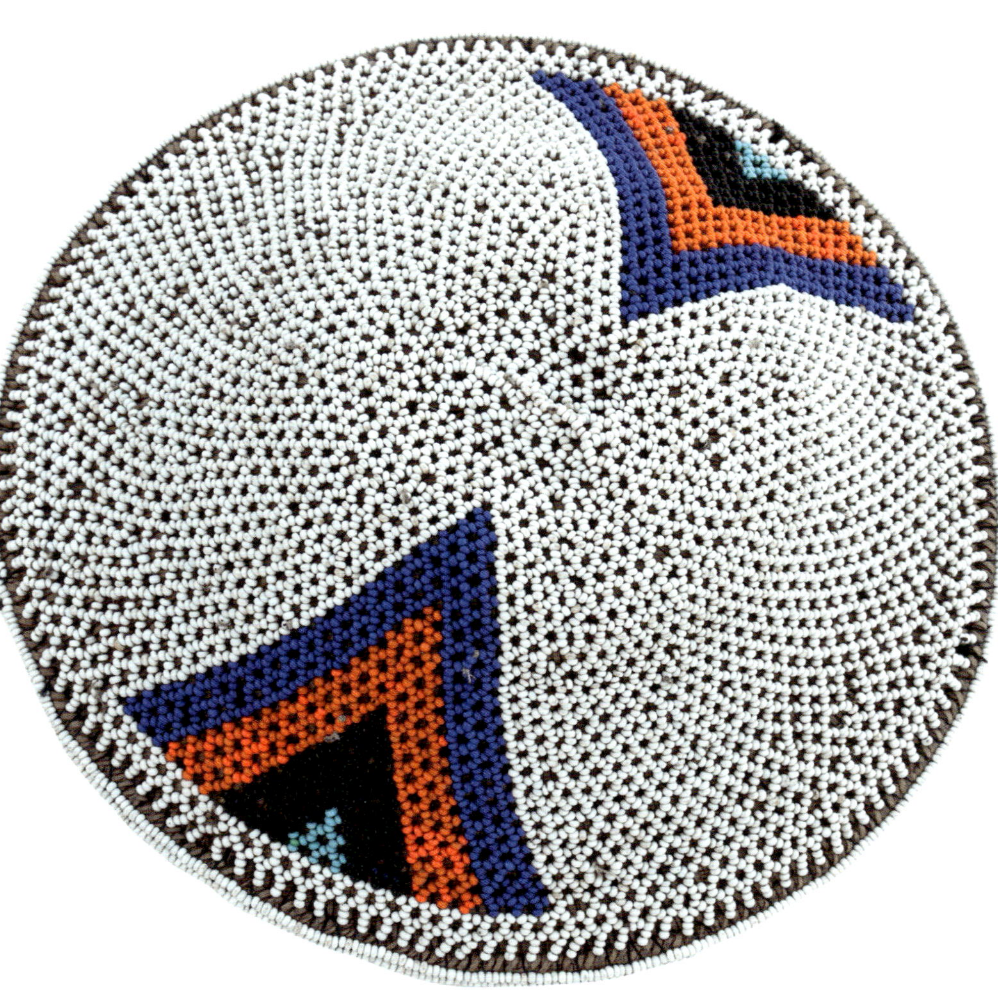

16 Imbenge iLala Palm with added
beadwork, lower Umvoti region, about
1970, D: 208 mm, H: 54 mm.

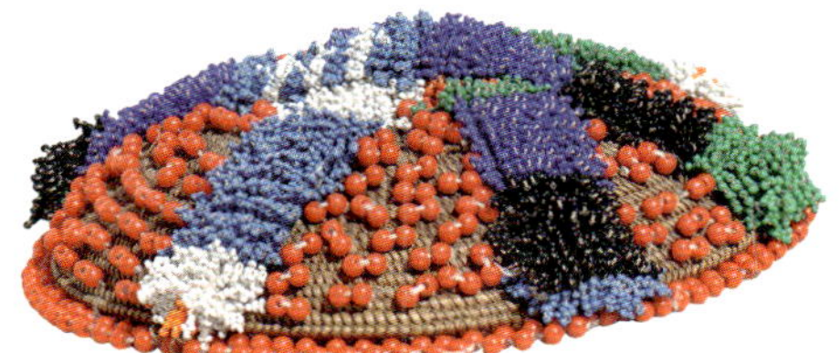

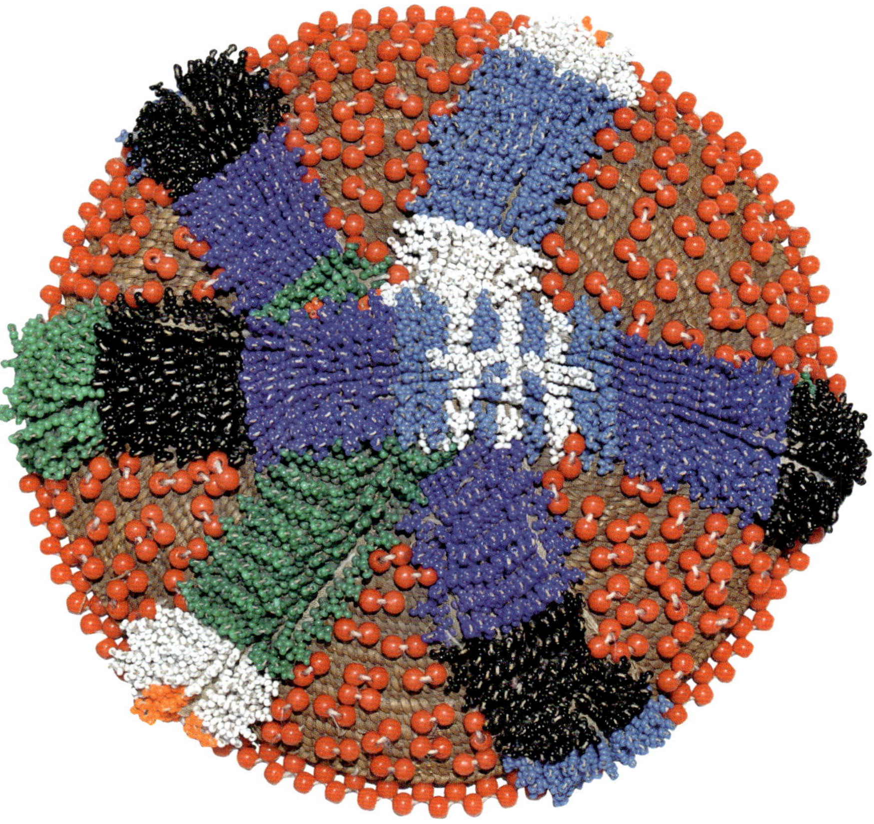

No. 15 but this time in complex irregular configurations reminiscent of the *isimodeni* ('modern') style that was fashionable in the 1970s to 1980s.

No. 16 is an example of a different type: instead of the beads being arranged in the form of longer or shorter strings attached to the base at both ends, the *imbenge* here is completely covered with a mesh of beads which is only attached to the base at the perimeter. The style probably derives from the beaded billycans which were popular among girls in the 1960s. As it is not possible to attach beadwork directly to metal the mesh had to be tight enough to prevent it from slipping off the can.

These latter *izimbenge* (Nos. 6–16) borrowed colours and patterns from beadwork made for personal adornment, i.e. colours and patterns that in other contexts defined a woman's clan affiliation and her social and, in particular, her marital status. This can not have been without some effect on the social and ritual context within which the beer vessels and beer drinking in general operated. From the 1960s onwards there was an increasing migration of labour from the countryside to cities, leaving many rural locations denuded of men. The women who had been left behind had to assume domestic responsibilities and ritual functions that otherwise would have been the prerogative of men. Perhaps the introduction of beaded decorations should be viewed as a visible statement of the growing independence of women in rural society.

17 Imbenge
PROVENANCE: Umvoti region, late 1960s.
Beadwork on iLala Palm.
COLLECTION: Juliet Armstrong.
D: 225 mm, H: 65 mm

The following three examples from the Phansi Museum in Durban demonstrate how once the principle was established that the *izimbenge* could be covered entirely in beadwork there was really no limit to innovation and extravagant development of traditional beadwork designs.

The two zig-zag designs reminiscent of some *Hlabisa* motifs are self-contained pieces of beadwork sown onto the rim at the base of the iLala Palm *izimbenge.* The panel design of the third piece is made up of strings of beads attached individually as in the preceding pieces 13, 14 and 15.

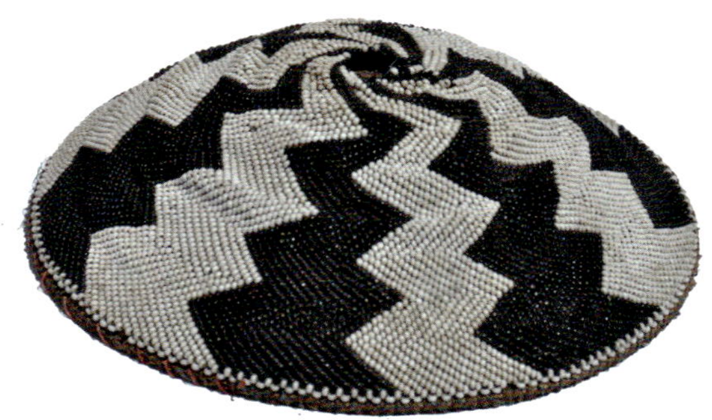

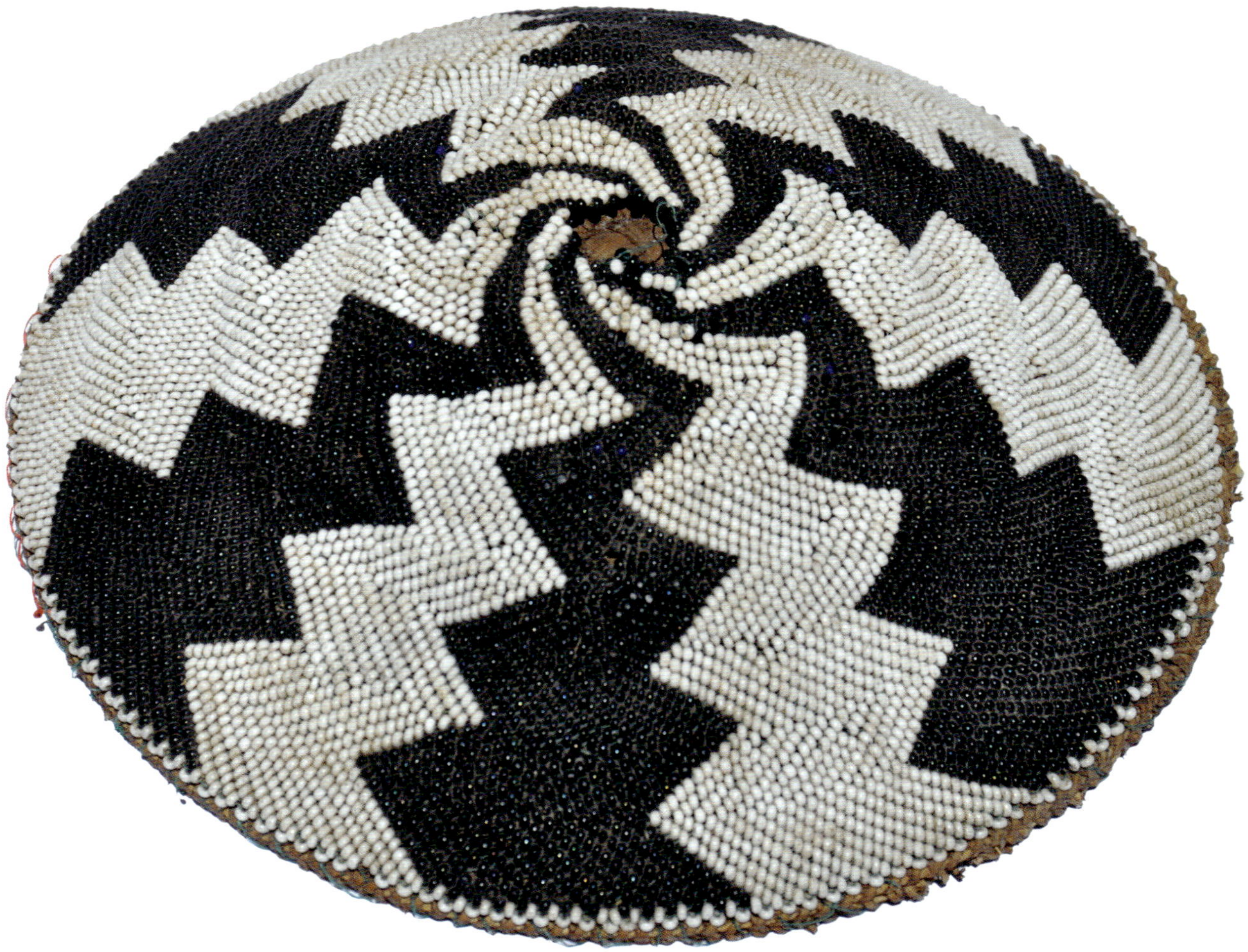

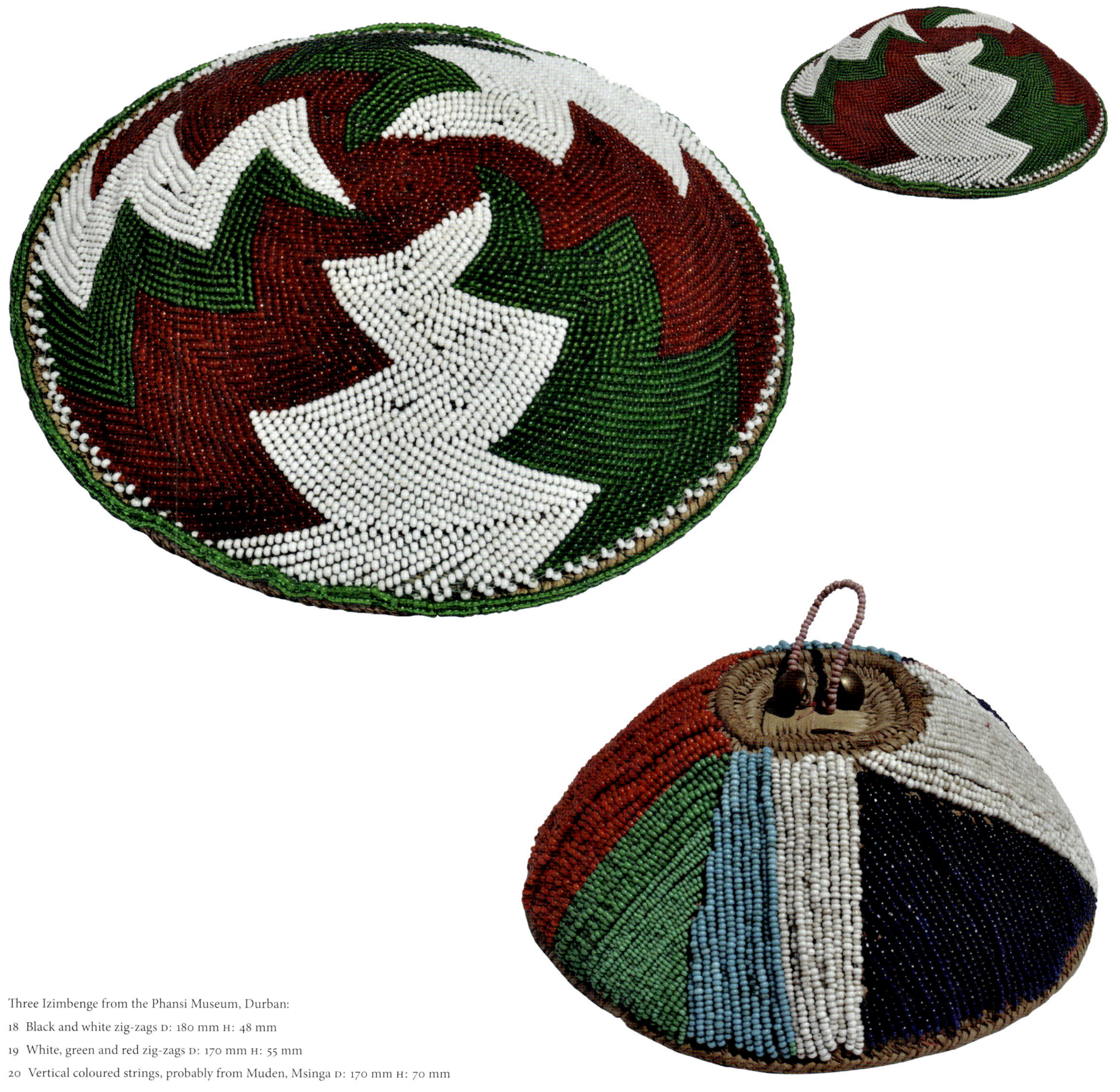

Three Izimbenge from the Phansi Museum, Durban:

18 Black and white zig-zags D: 180 mm H: 48 mm

19 White, green and red zig-zags D: 170 mm H: 55 mm

20 Vertical coloured strings, probably from Muden, Msinga D: 170 mm H: 70 mm

3. *Izimbenge* of woven wire

The renewal and expansion of the South African telephone network in the later 1950s made available a large quantity of discarded cable including colour-coded, plastic-covered, fine-grade copper wire. Unlike beads, the scrap wire was not traded in the countryside. It was primarily available in the cities. As a result the wire woven *izimbenge* were produced by the men who had gone to the cities seeking work (personal communication Paul Mikula, 11.06.11). Wire-woven *izimbenge* (along with wire-covered bottles, sticks, spoons, etc) took their place beside the more traditional beaded iLala Palm ones. This situation continued through the 1970s to 1990s. By then the medium had been taken up by the tourist market and wire-woven baskets, platters and other items were being made specifically for sale to the public through craft outlets. This remains an ongoing cottage industry with ever more ambitious objectives.[70] The techniques of wire weaving enabled the creation of new types of patterns that had not been possible with the pixel-dominated structure of beadwork. In addition the colours that became available did not fit easily into the regional conventions, the latter having been fixed and stabilised by decades of a targeted trade.[71] As the wire was just scrap, the continuity of supply of specific colours could not be guaranteed, apart from which there was a greater range of colours. So, on the downside, the new colours lacked the iconographic associations of the bead colours. Consequently they could not be used to carry information. All these factors contributed to the liberation of the makers of the humble *imbenge* from their traditional constraints. There was a surge of creativity: new colours, motifs and weaving techniques were combined, often to spectacular effect.

Three basic techniques of wire weaving were developed to fashion these small basket-like artefacts:

(1) Open weave with spaced ribs radiating from the centre outwards, woven starting from the centre. The ribs made of heavy 1.0 to 1.6 mm iron wire acting as the warp. This weave does not lend itself to making patterns apart from concentric rings.
(2) A compact single weave with closely packed lighter ribs radiating from the centre.
(3) As in 2, but a double weave allowing for different colours outside and inside.
(4) A heavy circular basket weave, woven from the rim inwards.

The following are some examples shown from above and reverse:

1 Open weave with spaced ribs

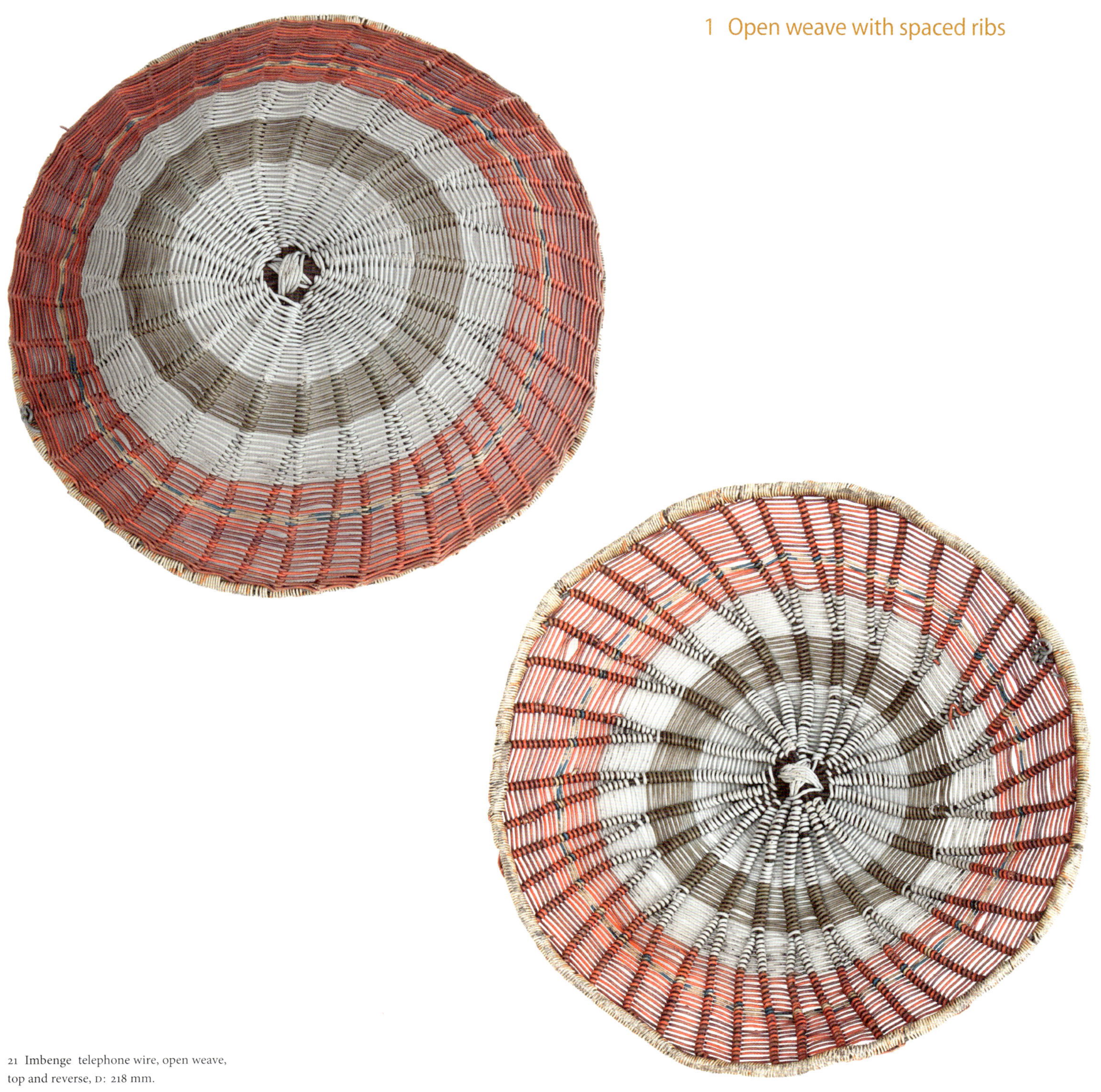

21 Imbenge telephone wire, open weave,
top and reverse, D: 218 mm.

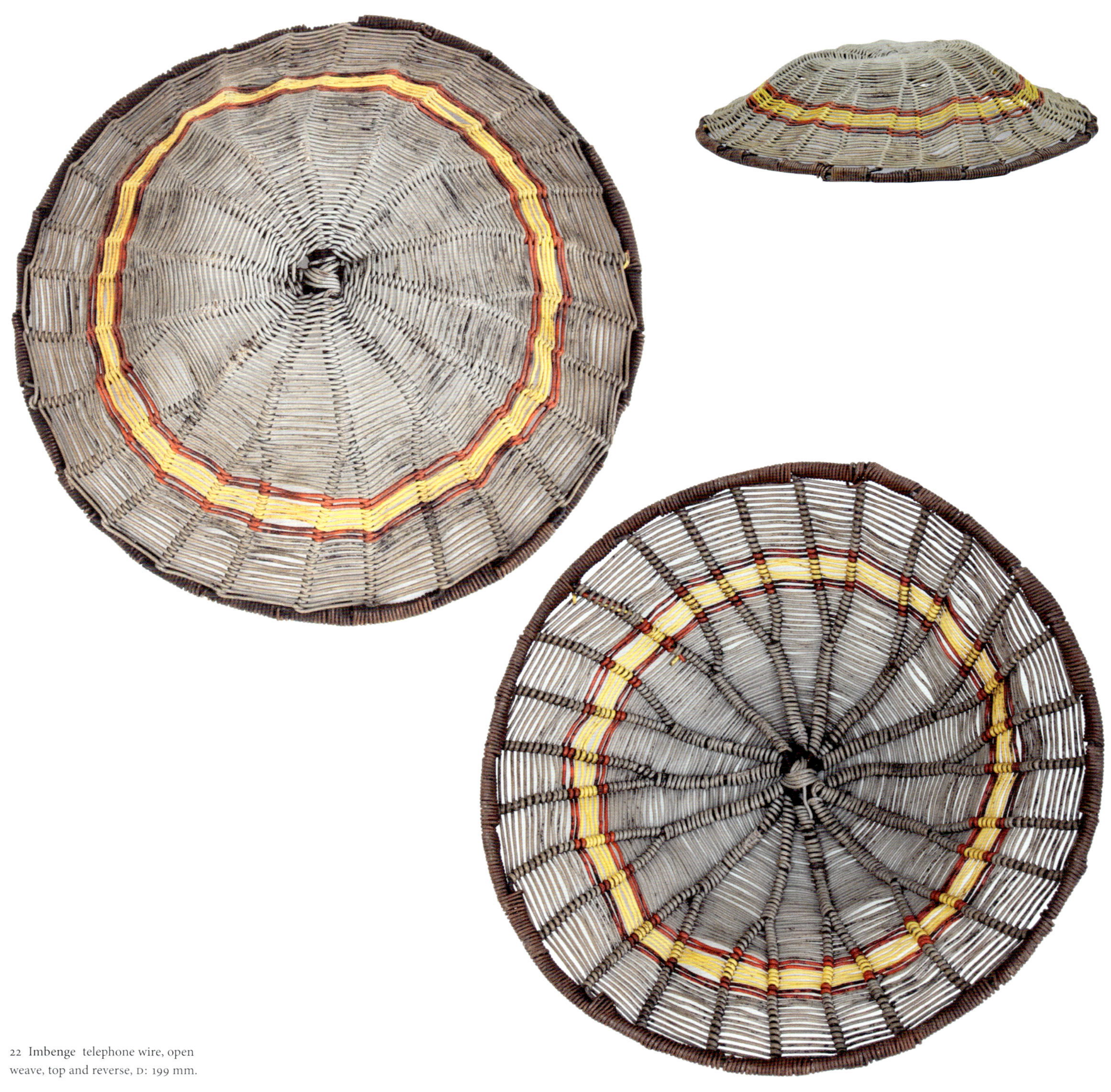

22 Imbenge telephone wire, open
weave, top and reverse, D: 199 mm.

2 Single weave with closely packed ribs

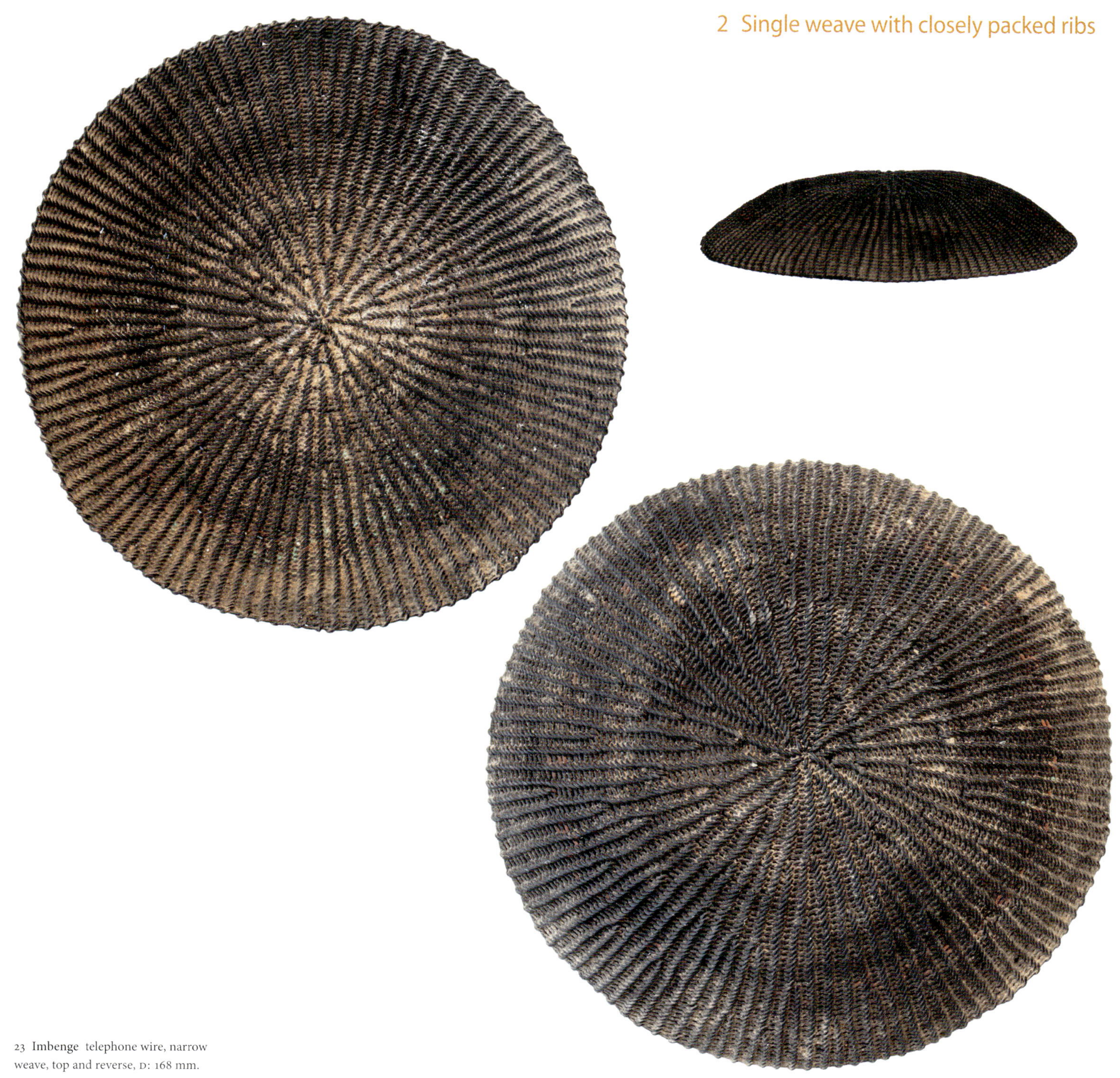

23 **Imbenge** telephone wire, narrow
weave, top and reverse, D: 168 mm.

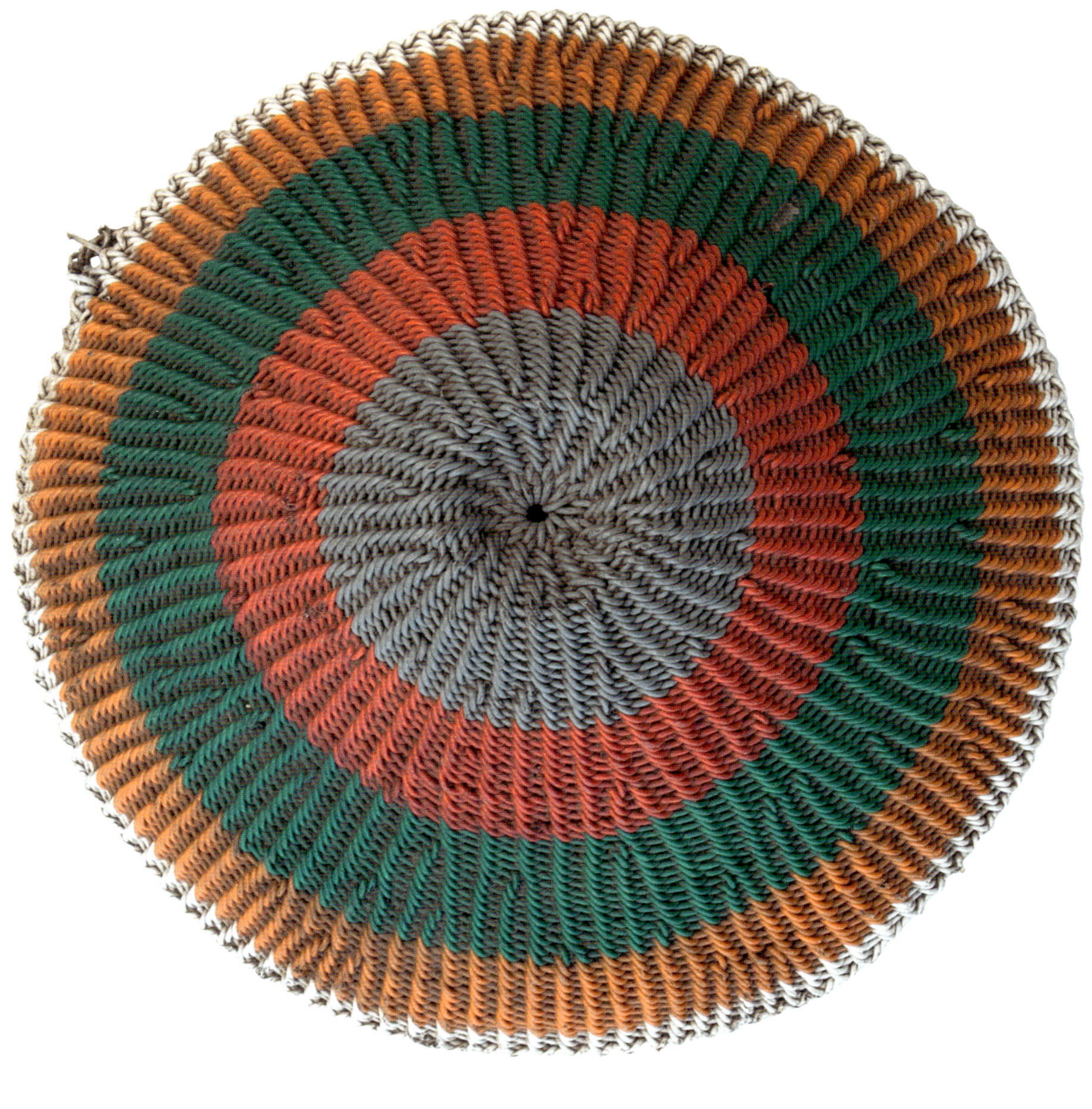

24 Imbenge Telephone wire, narrow
weave. D: 168 mm.

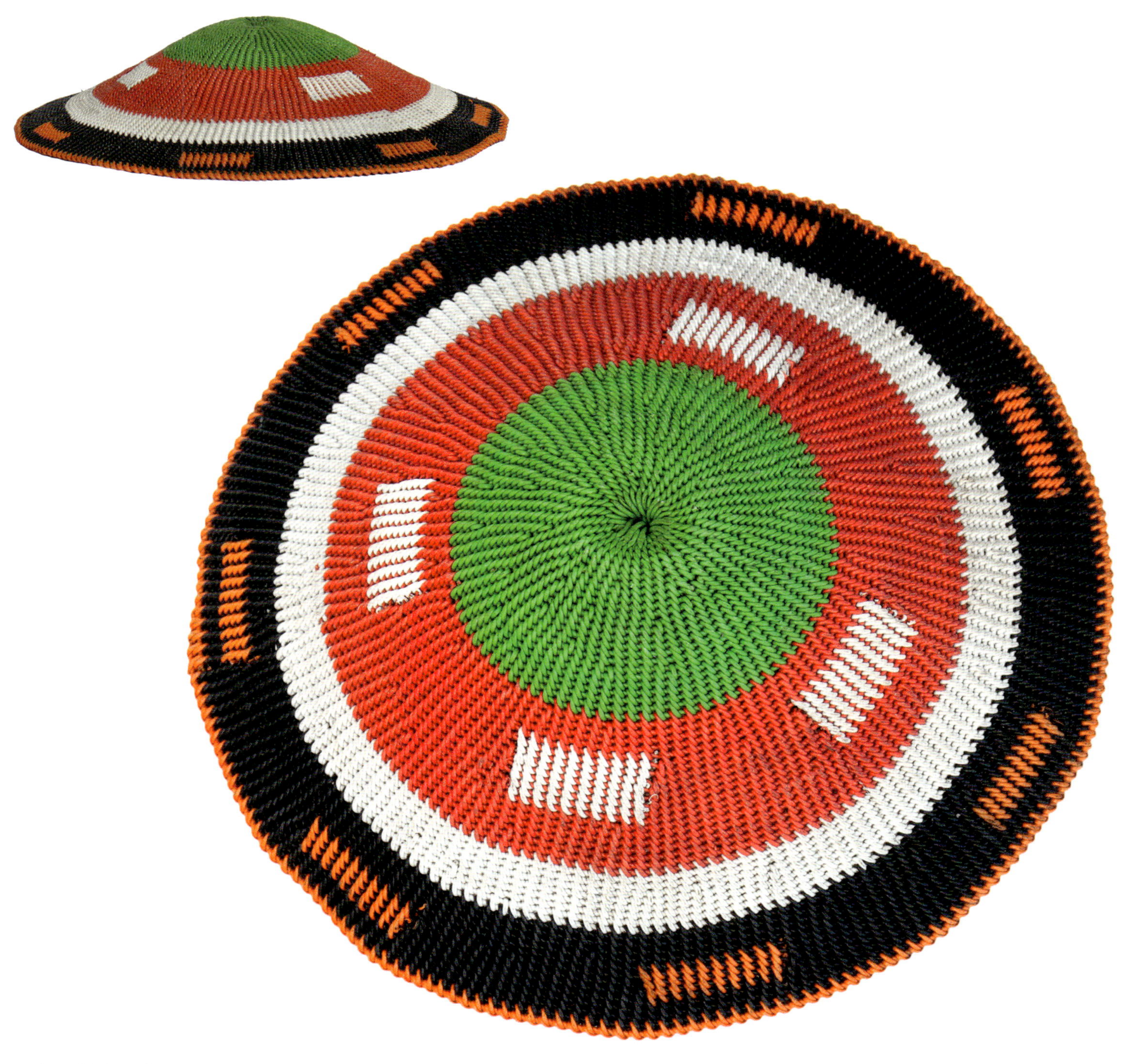

25 Imbenge telephone wire, narrow
weave, top, D: 168 mm.

3 Closely packed ribs, as in (2), but a double weave allowing for different colours outside and inside

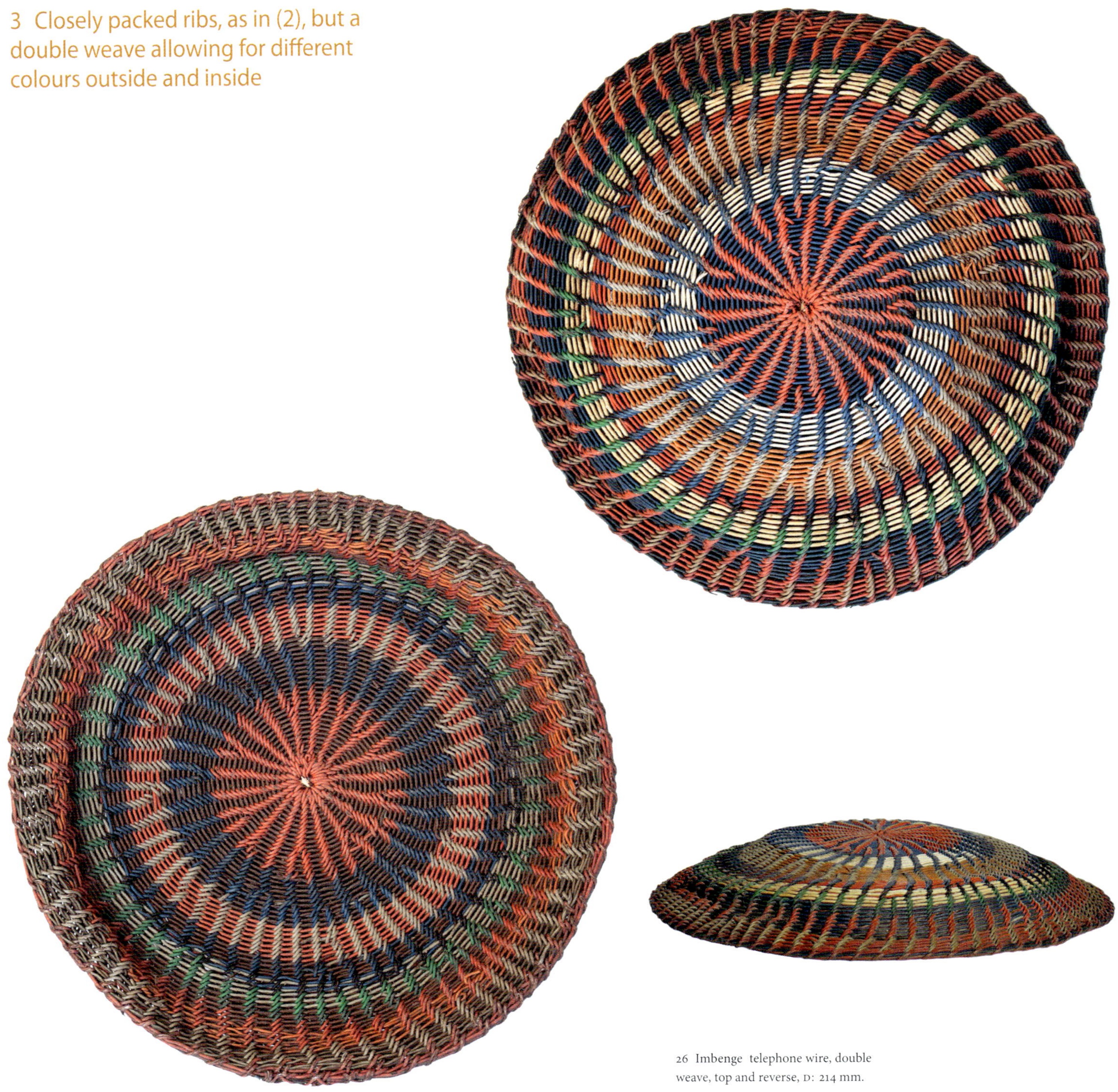

26 Imbenge telephone wire, double weave, top and reverse, D: 214 mm.

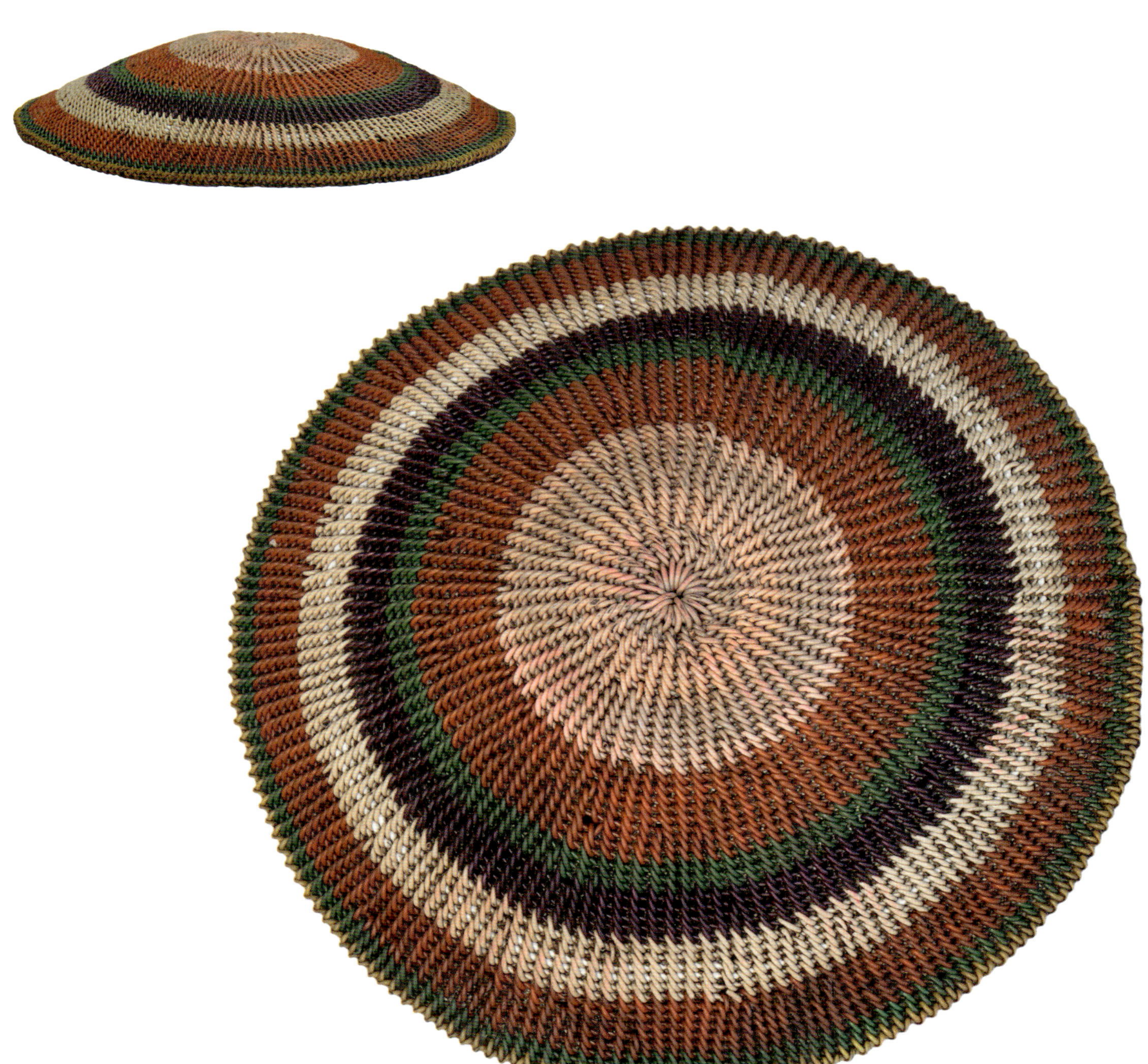

27 **Imbenge** telephone wire, double weave, tasteful combination of pastel colours. D: 165 mm.

4 Heavy circular basket weave, woven from the rim inwards

The majority of *izimbenge* fall into this category. The original colour-coded telephone wire was quite fine, approximately 0.8 mm as measured on woven examples, which may appear somewhat thinner than the original unwoven wire as the plastic will have stretched. The colours were prone to fade when exposed to light. At some stage in the 1980s or 1990s the scrap wire was replaced by new wire. This was considerably coarser measuring about 1.5 mm woven. The difference is clearly visible in the next *imbenge* (No. 24, p. 222) when compared with the following ones). The colours, also, are less faded.

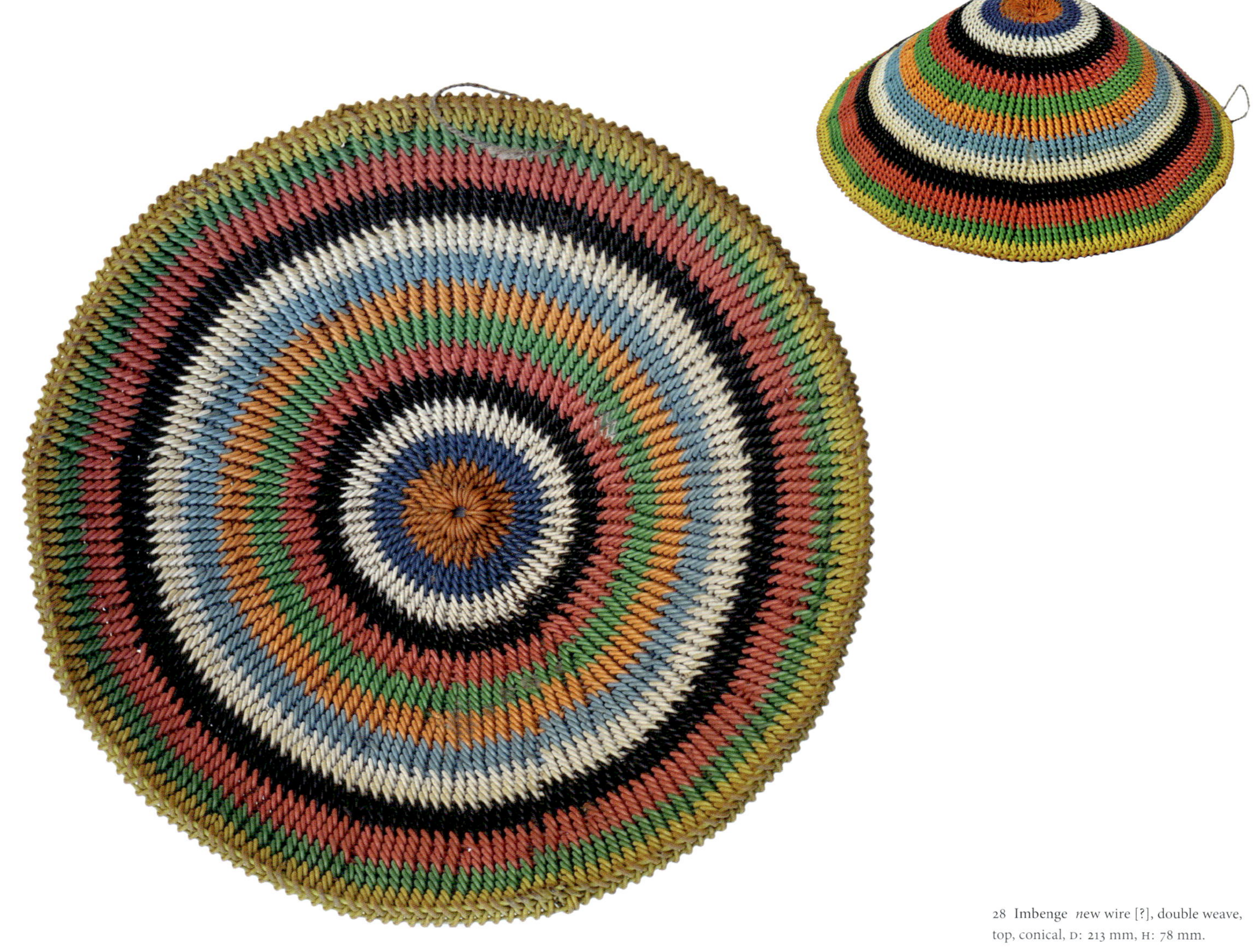

28 Imbenge *new* wire [?], double weave, top, conical, D: 213 mm, H: 78 mm.

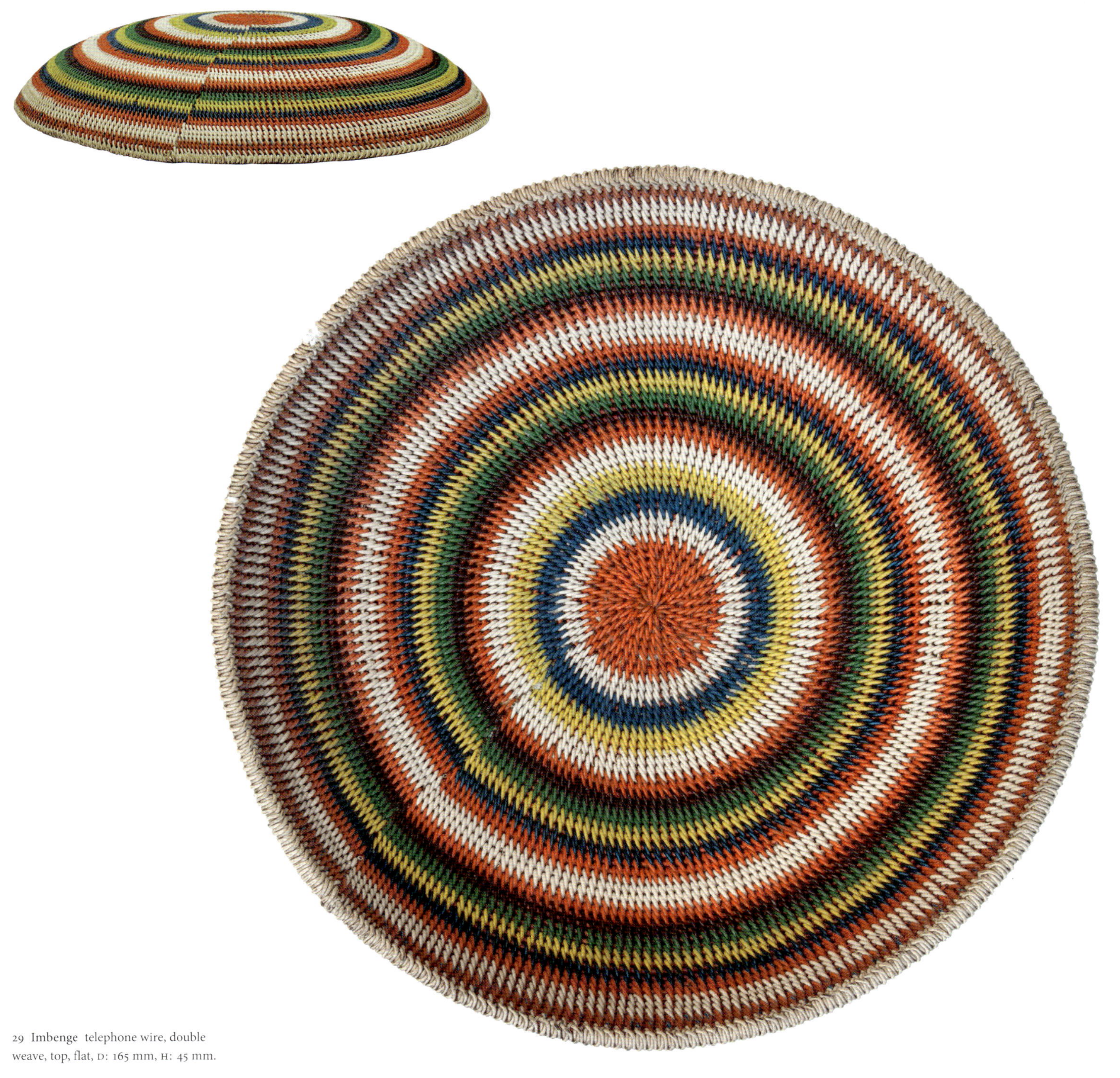

29 Imbenge telephone wire, double
weave, top, flat, D: 165 mm, H: 45 mm.

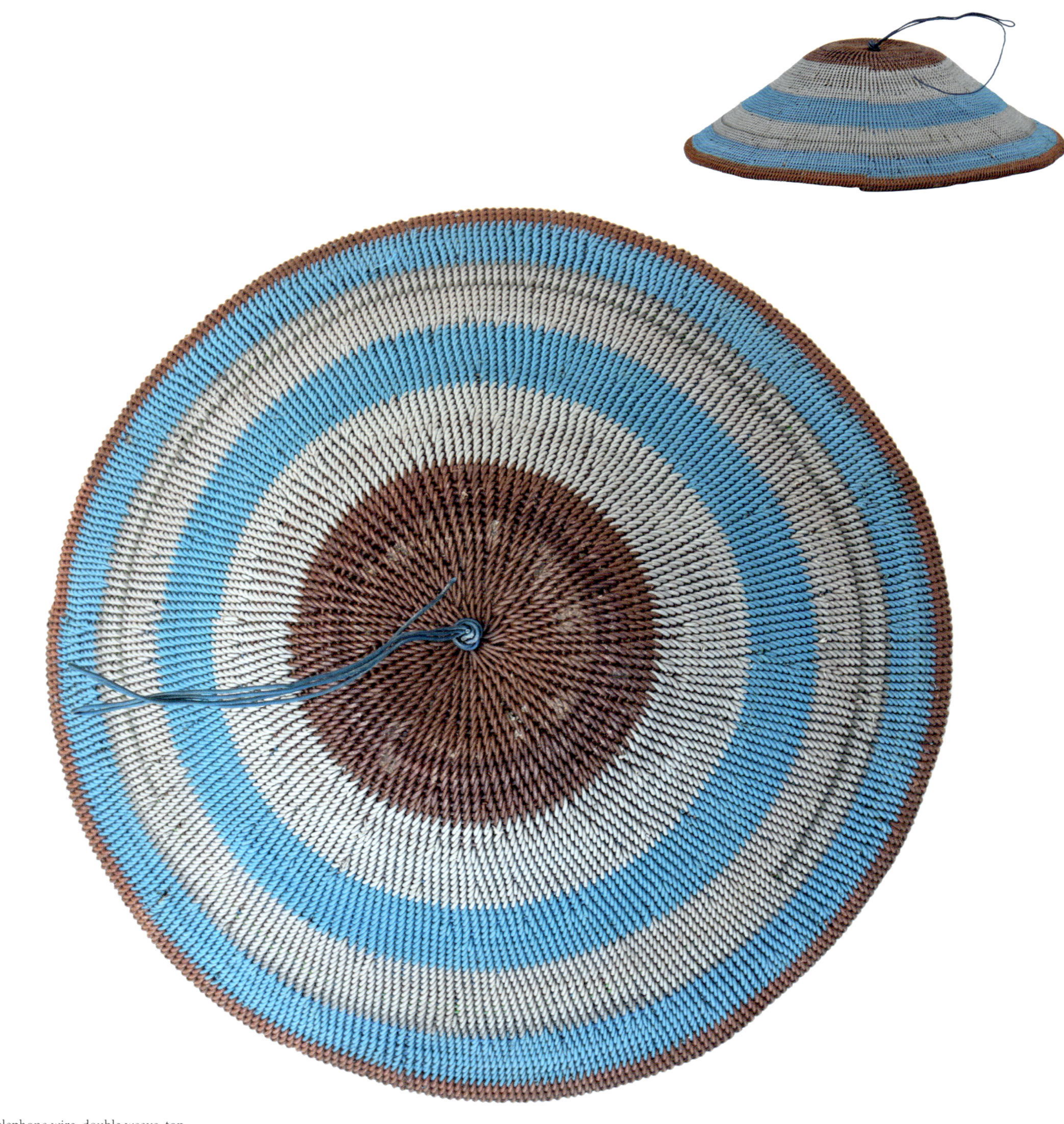

30 Imbenge telephone wire, double weave, top,
conical, D: 215 mm, H: 66 mm.

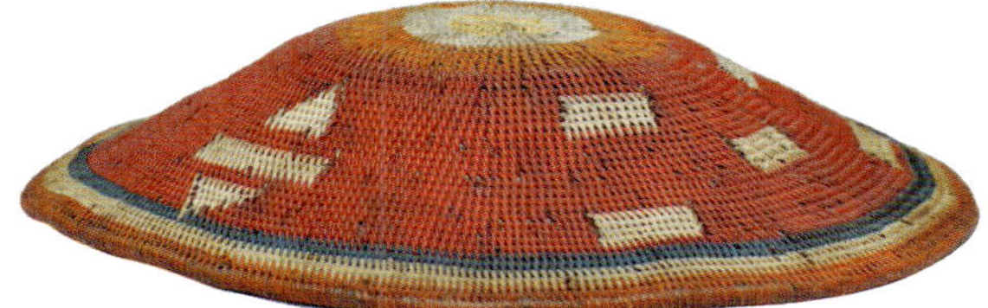

Most wire *izimbenge* have patterns based on concentric rings, and indeed, this is a natural consequence of the circular weave. However, it is not the only possible use of space and colour. In the following example the rings are maintained at the top and the bottom but the space between is filled with rectangular and triangular motifs. These follow the line of the weave but are otherwise irregularly placed so that only a single symmetry is maintained: reflection across an axis which passes through the three triangles. This might be termed a transitional pattern. The three remaining examples are without concentric rings except along their base.

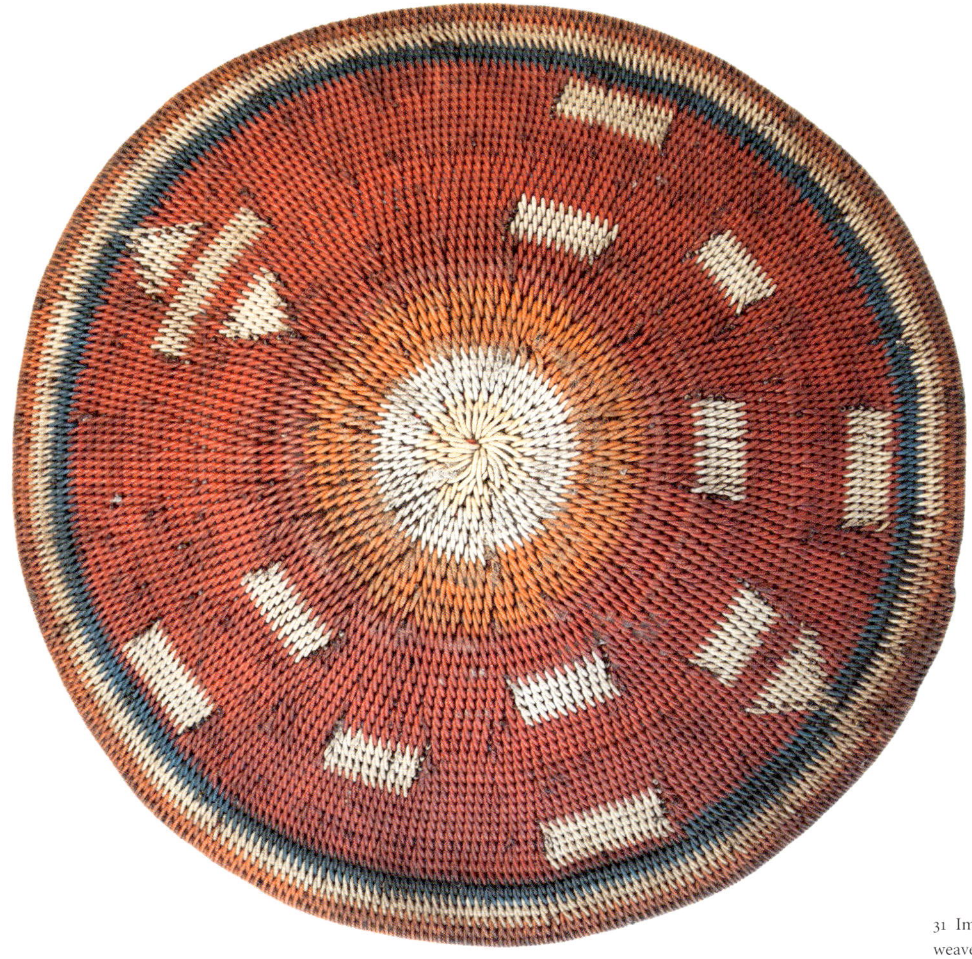

31 Imbenge telephone wire, double
weave, top, D: 188 mm, H: 43 mm.

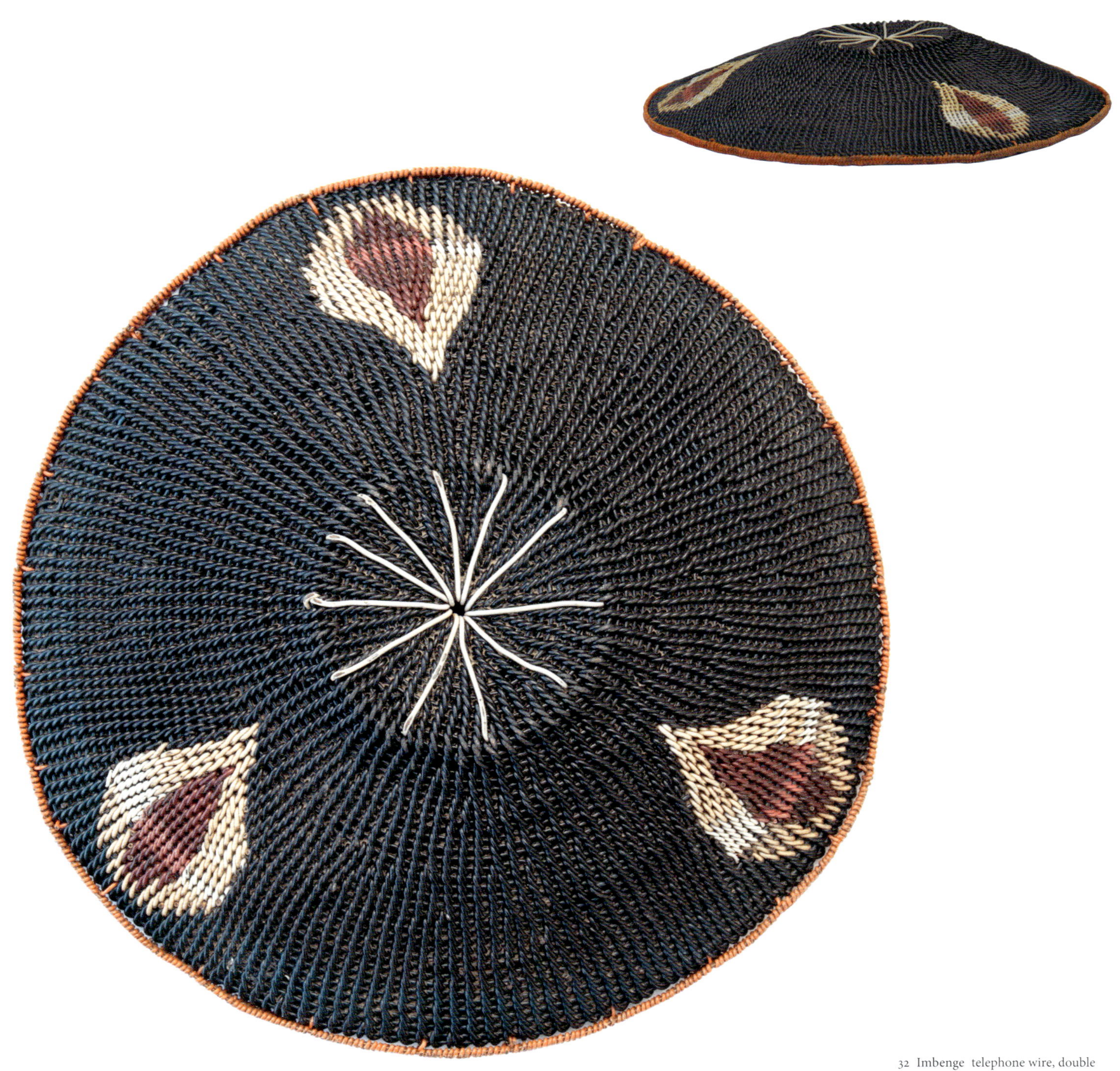

32 Imbenge telephone wire, double
weave, top, D: 190 mm, H: 35 mm.

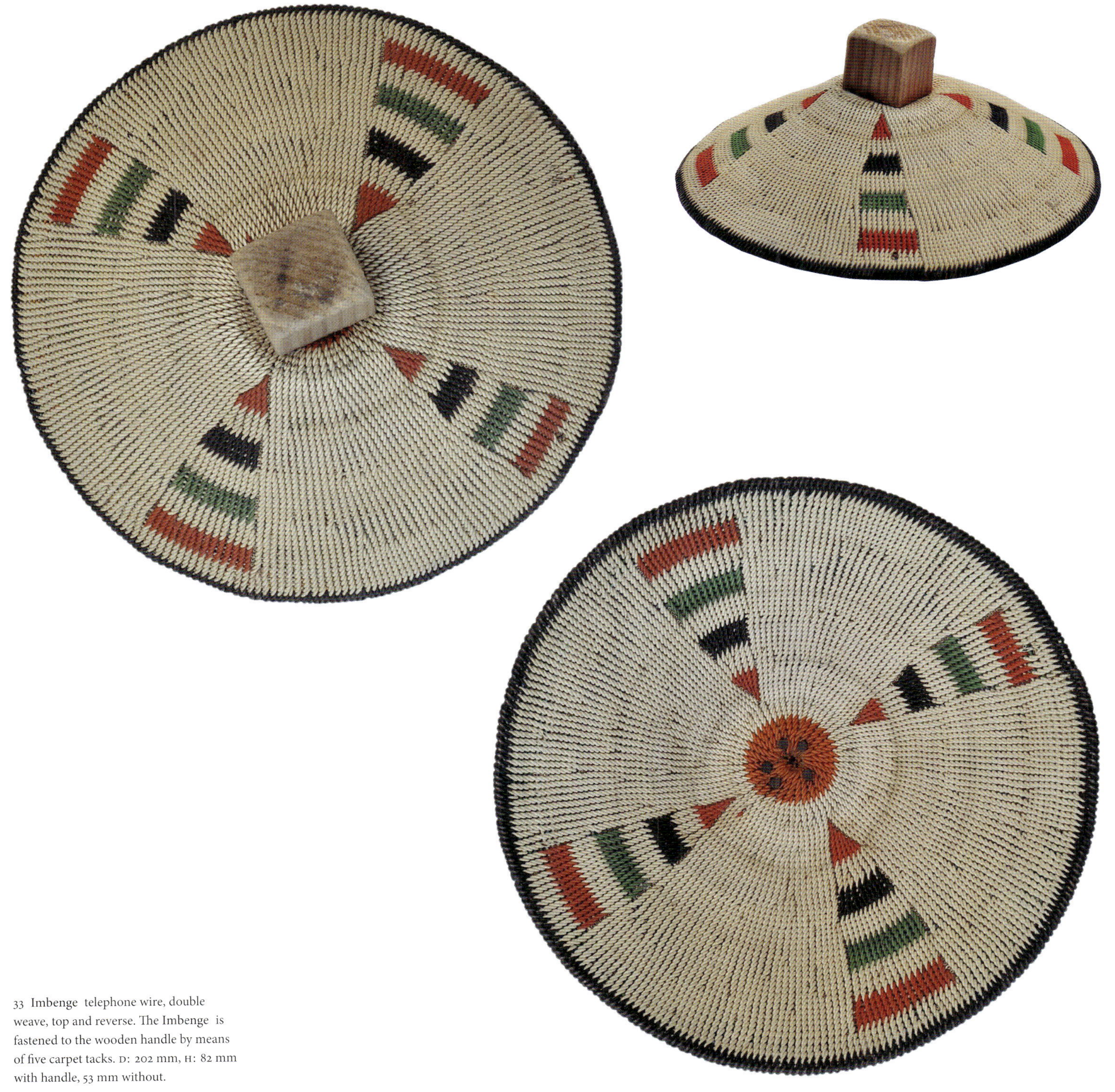

33 Imbenge telephone wire, double weave, top and reverse. The Imbenge is fastened to the wooden handle by means of five carpet tacks. D: 202 mm, H: 82 mm with handle, 53 mm without.

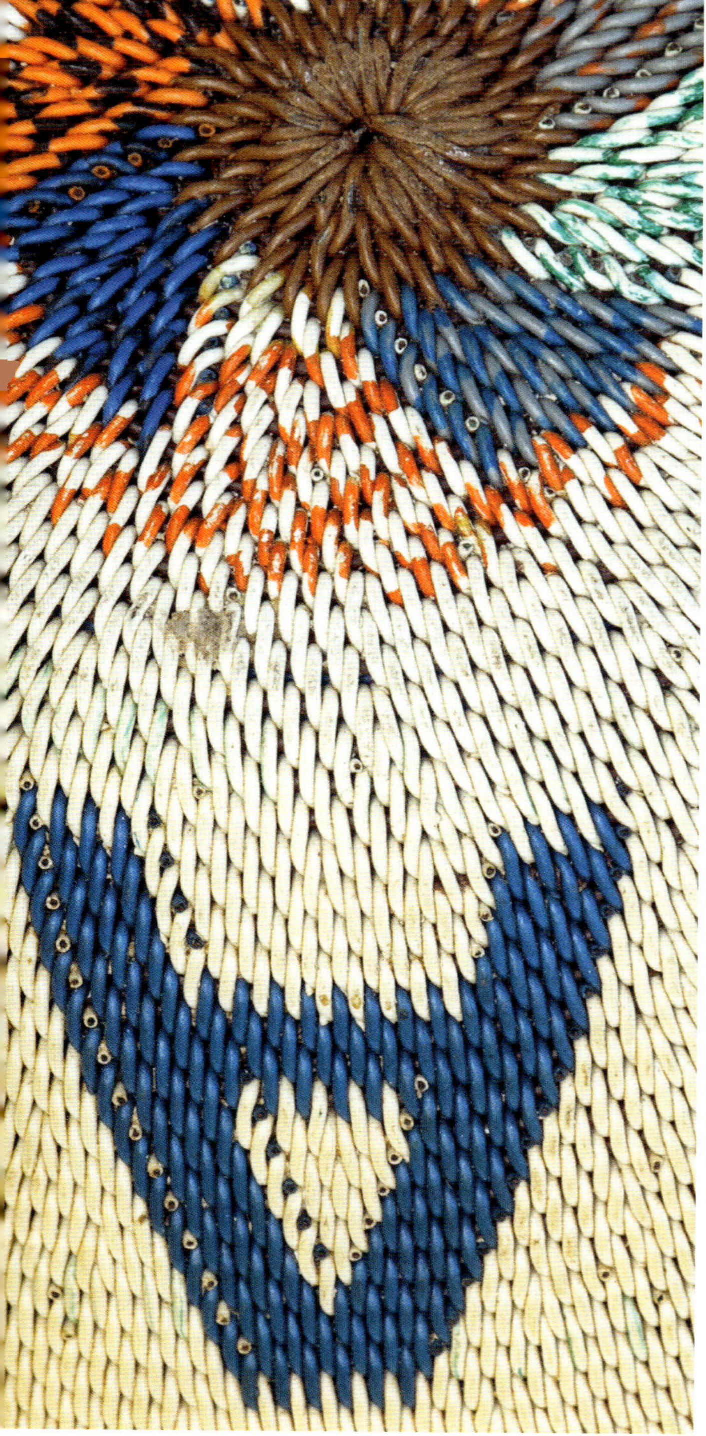

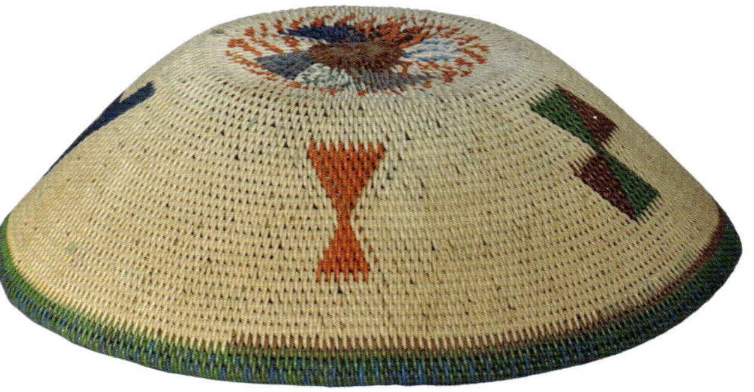

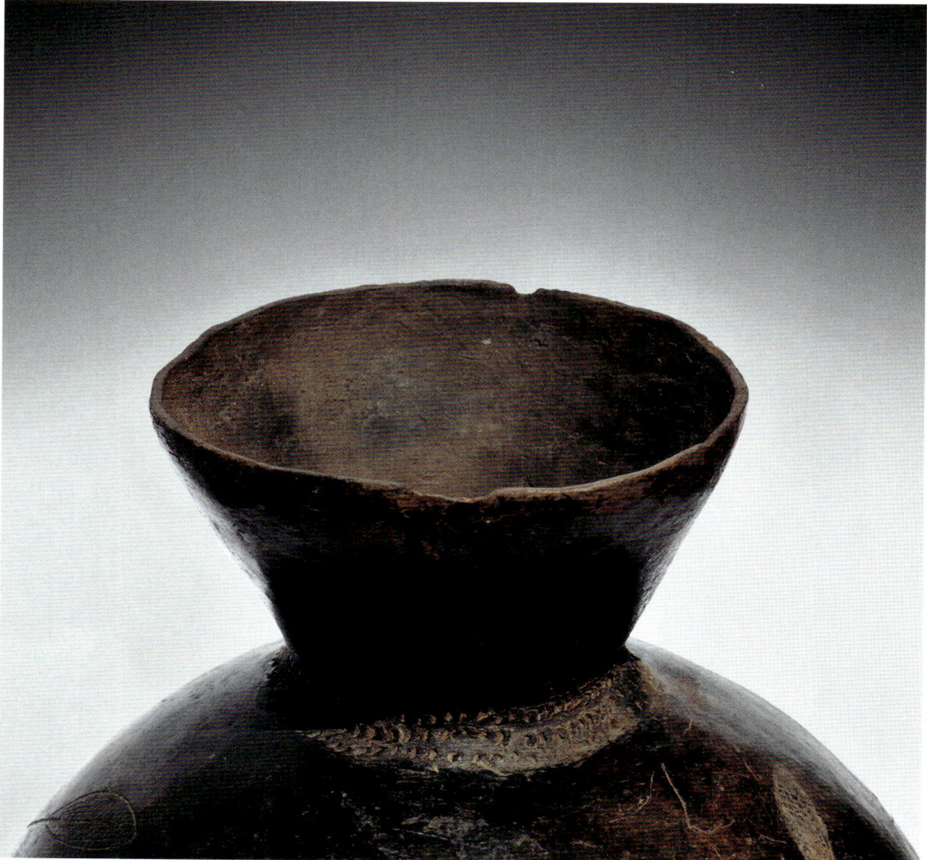

34 Imbenge telephone wire, double
weave, top + detail, bowl shaped,
D: 174 mm, H: 54 mm.

Conclusion

The origins of the great flowering of Zulu pot-making in the twentieth century must be sought in the second half of the nineteenth century, when clay pots replaced baskets as the most common drinking vessels. The spread of the *izinkamba*, the twice-fired blackened beer pots, which represent the main output of Zulu ceramics, probably dates back to the reign of Mpande (1840–72). However, it is doubtful whether any pots have survived from that era. I would suggest that the differentiation of regional styles developed during the period after the Wolseley settlement of 1879, which effectively split the Kingdom into 13 tribal areas.

Wood comes to a similar conclusion. She attributes the diversification of beadwork styles to a diminishing centralised control, which she believes began during the reign of Mpande: 'The combination of lack of centralised control, greater access to beads and, probably, a desire by various groups to build an identity for themselves led to a proliferation of beadwork styles.' She surmises that 'beadwork styles in the early Zulu Kingdom were similar, if not actually uniform.'[72] During the course of the twentieth century the original styles of the post-1879 period became increasingly overlaid by styles imported from adjoining areas by women marrying across tribal boundaries, or whole families moving in search of a better life or evicted from white-owned farms. These 'imported' styles did not necessarily displace the existing ones. In many cases both continued being made side by side, giving rise to the mix of shapes and techniques that could be observed in the later decades of the twentieth century in

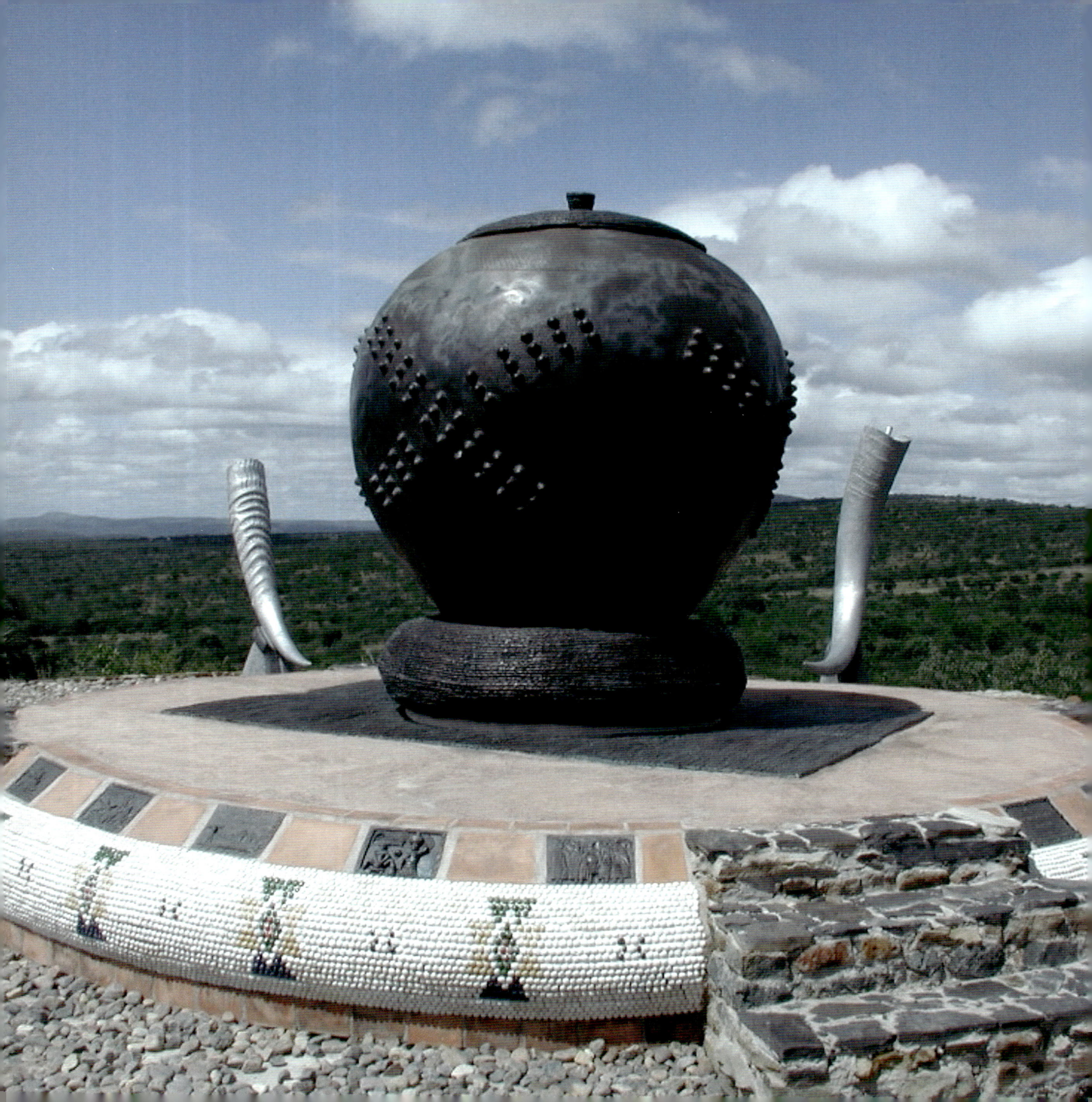

parts of the Nongoma, Hlabisa, Melmoth-Eshowe and Thukela regions. There is additional evidence from the archival and the oral record to support such a view for Hlabisa and Melmoth-Eshowe.

For the period following the report of the Zululand Lands Delimitation Commission it would be inaccurate to speak of stylistic regions with distinct boundaries, but rather of regions in which certain forms, patterns and motifs had emerged as an aesthetic expression, but in which both the boundaries of the regions and the forms and patterns themselves were in a continuous state of flux. In a few instances a more specific case could be made for the continuity of a style from its origins in the nineteenth century. For instance, the distinctive style of the ekuShumayeleni *isigodi* region might hail back to the time when this was a centre of political influence as the ancestral homestead of the intrepid Dabulamanzi, half-brother of Cetshwayo. Similarly the *amasumpa*-patterns from Melmoth might have evolved under the auspices of the first oNdini in the late 1850s. But in general the internal stylistic configurations of the regions differ according to the particular circumstances affecting them, such as internal migrations, migrant labour and the breakdown of social cohesion, the impact of

particular families of potters producing ceramics on a large scale, and so on.

The integration of the consumption of beer as an indispensable part of traditional nourishment with the protective role attributed to the ancestral spirits in Zulu society conferred the status of an icon on the blackened beer vessel. It had its place of honour in *umsamo*, the place of the ancestors in the dwelling hut. The drinking of beer became ritualised in deference to their presence. This icon has been resurrected in the political domain in the shape of the 'Spirit of the eMakhosini' monument (*eMakhosini* is used as another term for *umsamo*) on KwaNkhombo Hill outside Ulundi. It consists of a gigantic beer pot (with rather inaccurately configured *amasumpa*) surrounded by bronze plaques depicting scenes from 'traditional' Zulu life. It is this integral socio-religious function that has ensured the survival of the beer vessels. The extraordinarily innovative new styles and patterns of the migrant labour period in the second half of the twentieth century, coupled with a marked refinement of the potter's art, bear witness to the reawakening pride in a specifically Zulu identity in the face of competing African ideologies in the townships and industrial compounds of the cities.[73]

The 'Spirit of the eMakhosini' – a monument outside Ulundi. 'The beerpot was chosen as the symbol for the monument as across Africa it symbolises people coming together in friendship.' (*Natal Witness*, 21 February 2004, p. 14.)

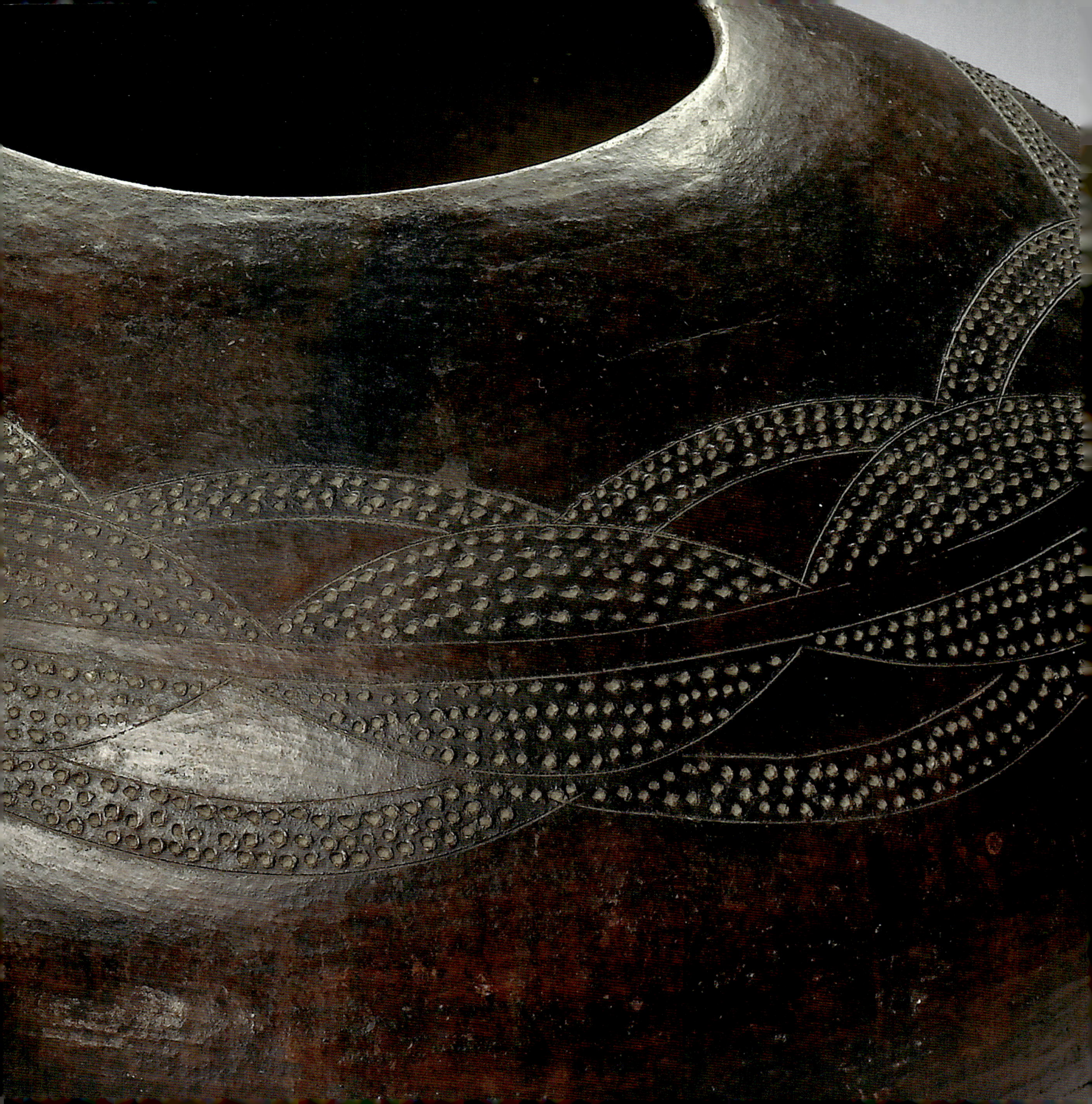

Notes

Introduction

1 That is symmetrical across all vertical sections that pass through
   the centre of a horizontal diameter.

2 Barbara Thompson, 'Namsofueli Nyeki. A Tanzanian Potter
   Extraordinaire.' African Arts, 40/1, 2007, p 58. Barbara
   Thompson shows how the potter who can create a vessel of
   greater aesthetic appeal will have a corresponding advantage in
   the marketplace.

3 Compare Laband: 1995 438f including a map.

4 Laband & Thompson 1989: 223; Meyer 1909: 16, 942f.

5 Lambert 1989: 386f; Duminy & Guest 1989: 429f. It is estimated
   that the population increased from 456 000 to 608 527.

6 Guest 1989: 160.

7 Lambert 1989: 397.

8 Lambert 1989: 383f.

9 Brookes & Webb 1987: 221f; Lambert 1989: 383f.

10 He was released from prison in 1910 by Louis Botha, the first
    Prime Minister of the Union.

11 Lambert 1989: 395f.

12 Jolles 1994 and 2004

13 Jolles 2001: 121f.

14 The term 'Location' was applied to the territories reserved
    for black settlement in the former Colony of Natal in the
    Shepstonian dispensation. In 1902, after the conclusion of the
    Boer War, the Zululand Lands Delimitation Commission was
    set up to demarcate 'sufficient land' for 'native locations', and
    set aside the rest for grants to whites (Laband 1995: 439). In its
    report (1904) the term 'Reserves' was used to describe the land
    set aside for blacks in Zululand. These formed the basis of the
    self-governing homeland of KwaZulu during the apartheid era.
    In this article, the term 'Location' will be used in the general
    sense of land allocated to blacks, and more particularly for such
    lands in the colony of Natal. For Zululand/KwaZulu the term
    'Reserve' will be used. The term 'Reservation' is also used in the
    general sense.

15 Ballard 1989: 124f.

16 Laband 1995: 439

17 Lambert 1989:383.

18 In so far as they were reflected in the beadwork and other
    artefacts these new identities proved relatively stable. They
    could survive transplantation into other regions (including
    Johannesburg) for two generations (Jolles 1994: 58, 1997: 50f).
    This is also well documented in the Erlandson Collection in the
    Natal Museum, Pietermaritzburg.

19 The contrast between life in the cities and the rural areas
    was a recurrent theme in the interviews I conducted with
    woodcarvers. Health problems caused by overcrowding
    and stress, and the inability to come to terms with city life

psychologically were the reasons given by a number of people for returning to the rural areas in the 1970s and 1980s.

20 Compare the map in Lambert 1989: 382.

21 This accounts for the fact that many of the ceramics in public and private collections are without any provenance. A striking example is the two pots included in the prestigious catalogue: *Africa: the art of a continent* (1995), edited by Tom Phillips (p 221, nos. 3.39a and 3.39b). Both are by a well-known potter from Nongoma, Azolinah Mbatha, who, as she told me, sold them personally to a dealer from Belgium. The only provenance given is 'KwaZulu-Natal, South Africa'. Not only has the place of origin been omitted but also the name of the artist. Possibly the commercial value of the artefacts was enhanced by locating them in an anonymous tribal past rather than attributing them to a living artist who made them in the 1970s.

22 Fowler & Fowler 1966: 513.

23 Berglund 1976.

24 Delegorgue 1997: II/120f.

25 Laband 1995: ii, cit *British Parliamentary Papers* [C 5531], enc. in no. 13.

26 I have come across both forms used to describe the same type in different areas. Doke *et al* (1990) distinguish between *ukhamba*, 'earthenware pot, general term', and *isikhamba*, 'open-mouthed pot such as is used for serving beer or sour milk'. They also cite a further form: *umkhamba*, plural: *imikhamba*, 'broad-mouthed earthen pot'. In my experience this type of pot is used for cooking porridge.

27 Doke *et al*, 1990: 531.

28 The Igbo in Nigeria achieve a similar effect by spraying the pot with the sap of a creeper whilst it is still red hot from the firing (personal observation, 1978). Asolinah Mbatha subsequently changed her name to Mucube probably in order to attract the goodwill of the spirits of her paternal anscestors This is a common practice of women growing up with their mothers' surname (personal communication Innocent Mkhize Jan. 2013. Cf. also Perrill 2011: 49.)

29 Laband 1995: 13.

30 The only instance of the survival of pre-colonial motifs into the late nineteenth or early twentieth century is to be found in a number of unprovenanced beer vessels which formed a part of the Old Durban Museum Collection, now in the Local History Museum, in Durban. They are illustrated in Reusch (1996: 128) as numbers C1, C2, C3 and C5. The first three (LHM 95/1444–6) are *izinkamba* shaped like the familiar wooden milking pails (*amathunga*) and might have come from the Muden area,

where similarly shaped vessels survived into the twentieth century. The fourth one is a spherical *uphiso*.

31 Hall & Mack 1983: 179.

32 Hall & Maggs 1979: 170.

33 Stuart & Malcolm 1969: 269.

34 The main repositories of his works are in South Australia. South African collections that hold some of his works are the Africana Museum, Johannesburg; the William Fehr Art Collection, Rust en Vreugd, Cape Town; and the SA National Gallery, Cape Town.

35 Fynn notes in his diary that 'All pottery is made by the women', but whilst 'mats' (the making of which would dominate fibre weaving–sleeping mats, mats for eating) were 'made by the females of almost every family', baskets were 'the work of men, and are of very neat workmanship'. Nowadays, of course, baskets are made almost exclusively by women (Stuart & Malcolm 1969: 269).

36 Angas 1974: 59.

37 Colenbrander 1989: 102.

38 Cory 1926: 17.

39 Gray 1992: 76.

40 One of these (Angas 1974: plate 21) is of the ovoid to cylindrical type similar to an *ithunga* (wooden milking pail).

41 Krige 1950: 58f, 198, 202.

42 Hall & Mack 1983: 192.

43 This is also well attested for armies on lengthy campaigns away from home (which might be considered analogous to a nomadic way of life) in the early part of the nineteenth century.

44 Webb & Wright 2001: 20-22.

45 The removal of *utshwala* from the diet of the rural African population is held to have contributed to widespread mineral and vitamin deficiencies (Tim Maggs pers. communication).

46 Krige 1950: 69, 84, 131, 164, 253, 258.

47 Berglund 1976: 176; Reusch 1996.

48 A similar motive has been attributed to the rise of the characteristic patterns of Ndebele beadwork which can be traced back to the subjugation and dispersal of the Ndebele by the Boers in 1883 (Levy 1990: 26f). Compare also Davison (1985: 19): 'it became imperative both to retain customs and to develop new ways of expressing and defending their identity in alien surroundings'.

49 Etherington 2001: 345; Jolles 1994: 47–52, 2001: 102f; Reusch 1996: 116.

50 For an overview of ceramics in public collections in South Africa compare Perrill 2011: 89–91.

51 In some cases the use of unfamiliar clays in the production

of over-ambitious large pots led to instability with the pots fracturing when exposed to changes of temperature, as in sunlight (Paul Mikula, BAT Art Centre, pers. communication).

52 Jolles 2001: 311f. A striking example of a similar development is the boom and bust of the trade in Ndebele dolls, which became mass-produced curio items in the 1990s.

53 As an example compare the photograph of 'Dinuzulu's drinking vessels and his wives who made his beer' *c*.1896–1907 in the Pietermaritzburg Archive Repository (Ref. No. C611), p. 123

54 Laband 1995: 122, 375, 378, 438.

55 Some pots in an old style from the Pomeroy (Msinga) area show a slight everted curvature of the rim section of an otherwise rather different bag-shaped form. There is an example in the Phansi Museum in Durban.

56 Laband 1995: 391.

57 Davies: 1971.

58 Gavin Whitelaw pers. comm., 2005.

59 Jolles 2004: 127f.

60 Pietermaritzburg Archive Repository (Ref. No. C611), also published as the frontispiece of *Ubumba* (Bell & Calder 1998).

61 Laband & Thompson 1989: map p. 220.

62 The Brooklyn Museum in New York has an outstanding example dating from around 1900.

63 Cf. Armstrong 1998: 41-5.

64 Garrett 1998: 47: 'Van Schalkwyk showed Nala iron-age shards from the site and commissioned her to replicate some of the forms for him. Nala was quick to realise the potential of applying these designs to her work and soon developed a new repertoire of decorative motifs.' I have not encountered any pots with these imported motifs in the field. *Vice versa* the wonderfully refined *izinkamba* that Nesta Nala and her mother Siphiwe made for the local trade did not reach the tourist market. Compare also: Jolles 2001: 314f.

65 The use of applied rope-like waves with incisions by Zungakhohlwa Ndlovu (Fig. 5.20: 437) and some other potters of her neighbourhood might be interpreted as a fusion of the two techniques.

66 Jolles 2004: 128.

67 African Arts Centre, Durban, ref. no.300/72/00, p 16, 2002.

68 Jolles 1994: 58.

69 Unless otherwise stated all examples are from the collection of Frank Jolles and photographed by him.

70 Cf. visit: 'Zulu Telephone Wire Baskets from Kwa Zulu Natal in South Africa' on the home page of Zanzibar Tribal Art, a trading company in Sacramento, California: 'Beautiful and functional, these baskets are every bit as collectable as the traditional iLala palm baskets featured above. Zanzibar works with a cooperative made up of primarily of Zulu men who learn (are taught) to weave these amazing baskets after having been injured working in the gold and diamond mines or oil fields of South Africa. 75% of our retail price goes directly to the weavers. Once Zulus actually downed telephone poles to get wire. Today our cooperative foots 25% of the cost of the raw materials while the South African Government underwrites 25% and the South African Telephone company donates the other 50%!' See also: Arment, A & Fick-Jordaan, M (2005), 'Wired Contemporary Zulu Telephone Wire Baskets', (S/C Editions), Santa Fe, New Mexico.

71 Regional colour cards were in use in the bead trade from the early twentieth century.

72 Wood 1996: 148f.

73 I am indebted to Professor John Wright for his elucidating comments on the revival of a Zulu identity in the twentieth century.

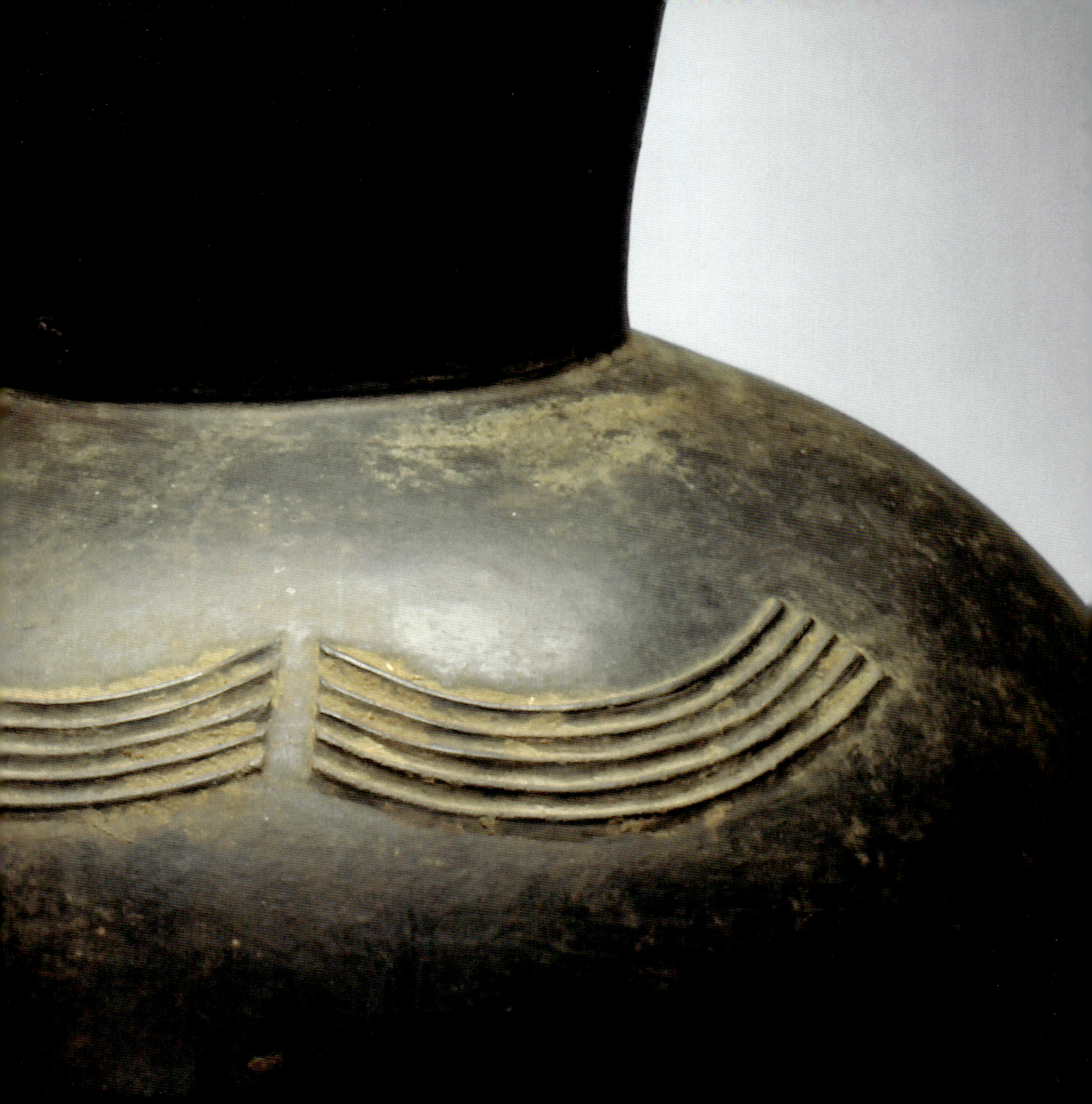

Appendix and references

Systematic review of Zulu beer vessels by region. Unless otherwise stated, all vessels were collected by the author.

Key < >: date of collection   H: height of vessel in millimetres (mm)

The Phongolo Region

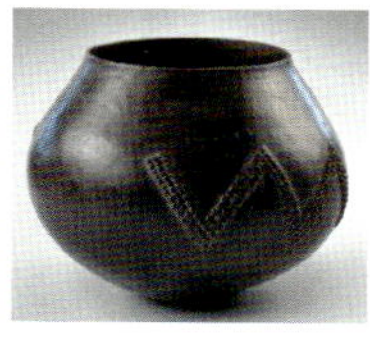

POT NUMBER **101**
Umancishana [or small ukhamba], H: 150 mm
Provenance: African Art Centre, Durban
Collected by Nomusa Dube, 2003. Clan: Phongolo-Shoba.
    [1960s. Patina suggests older. Surface has been waxed.]

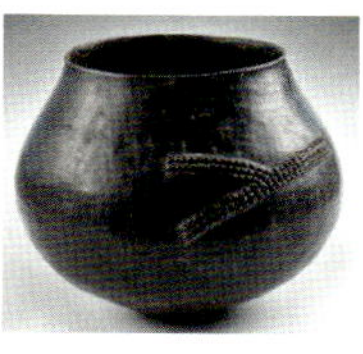

POT NUMBER **102**
Umancishana [or small ukhamba], H: 148 mm
African Art Centre, Durban.
Collected by Jabulani Sibisi, 2003. 'Used by head of
    family to drink beer.' Place of origin: Phongolo. Clan:
    Mzinzangu. Owner: Shabangu family [1960s].

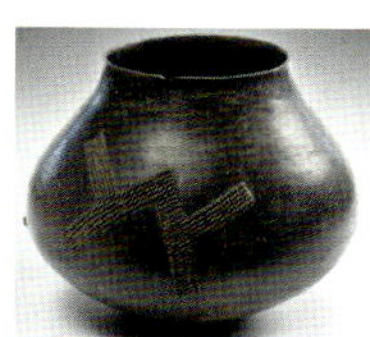

POT NUMBER **103**
Ukhamba, H: 282 mm
Provenance: William Raats.
Collected in the Hlabisa area. Owner said it was 'Very,
    very, old' [1930s].

Uphiso, H: 635 mm D: 597 mm ‹
PROVENANCE: collected David Robers <2003>
MAKER: Mrs Mazibane, Mhlongo household.
Mambulu, Mphise.
COLLECTION: WB Simmons

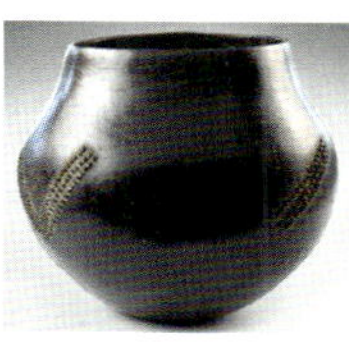

POT NUMBER **104**
Ukhamba, H: 226 mm
Provenance: African Arts Centre, Durban
Collected by P Khumalo, 2003. Place of origin: Phongolo.
    Clan: Mzinzangu, Ndwandwe family [1970s].

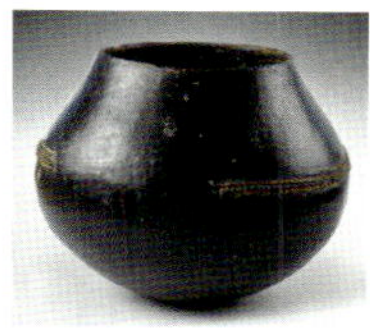

POT NUMBER **105**
Ukhamba, H: 218 mm
Provenance: African Art Centre, Durban
Collected by Nomusa Dube. Place of origin: Phongolo.
    Clan: Shoba, Jali family.

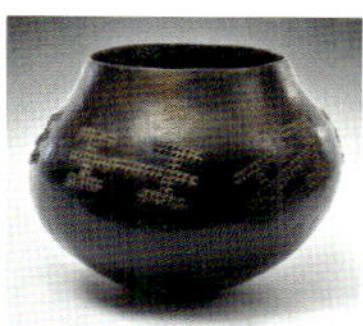

POT NUMBER **106**
Ukhamba,
Provenance: Pongolo.
H: 220 W: 280 mm
Collection: Karel Nel.

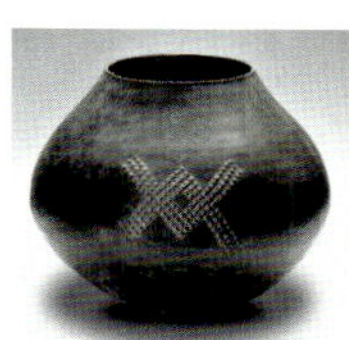

POT NUMBER **107**
Ukhamba, H: 330, w: 406 mm
Provenance: Pongola. W Simmons Collection.
Collected by Mynhardt Bester
Purchased from Kevin Conru, 15.03.1995
Photo: Bruce M White

The Nongoma Region

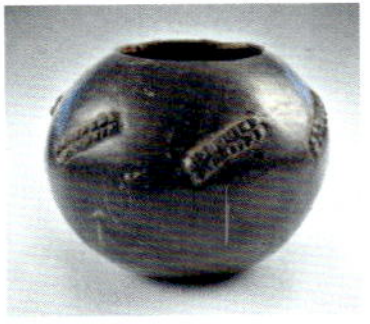

POT NUMBER **201**
Umancishana, H: 150 mm
Provenance: ekuShumayeleni, Nongoma side [c.1980].
<mid-1990s> Applied panel of *amasumpa* roughly carved.

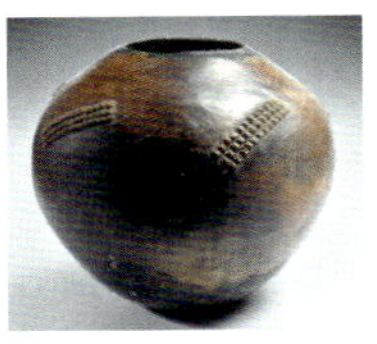

POT NUMBER **202**
Ukhamba, H: 300 mm
Provenance: ekuShumayeleni, Nongoma, [1960s].
<mid-1990s> Detail: panels of *amasumpa* carefully applied.

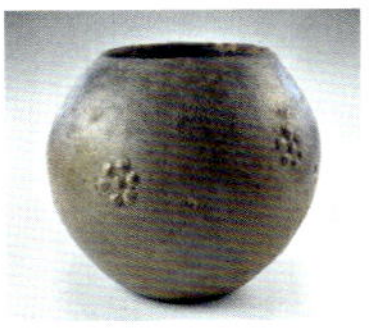

POT NUMBER **203**
Ukhamba, H: 190 mm
Provenance: Nongoma [1960s?]
<c.1996> Circle of *amasumpa* applied singly, pot-fired once
only. Wide opening, probably for porridge.

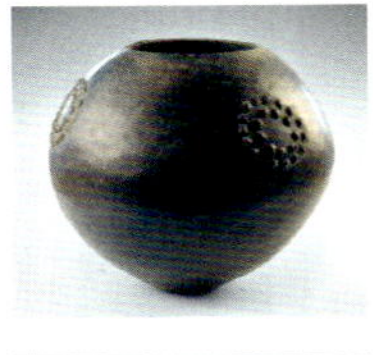

POT NUMBER **204**
Ukhamba, H: 265 mm
Provenance: Nongoma [1960s?]
<1996> Detail of large ukhamba with pinched *amasumpa* in
a circular motif.

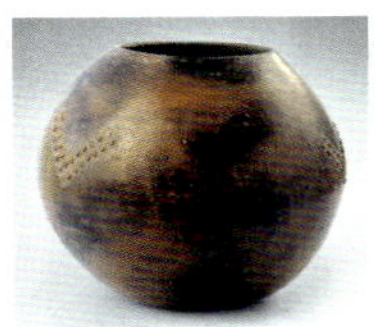

POT NUMBER **205**
Ukhamba, H: 210 mm
Provenance: eSassane, Nongoma [c.1970]
<1996> Small *amasumpa*, chevron motif, worn black patina
allows underlying red of the fired clay to show through.

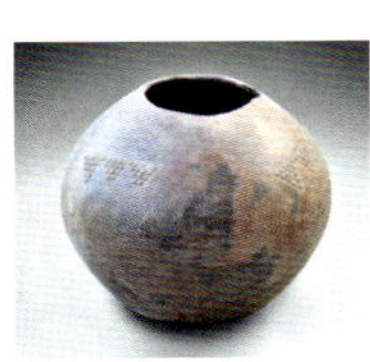

POT NUMBER **206**
Ukhamba, H: 270 mm
Provenance: Khohlokolo, Nongoma. Ndwandwe household
[1960s].
<1996> Pendant triangles of small *amasumpa*, worn patina.

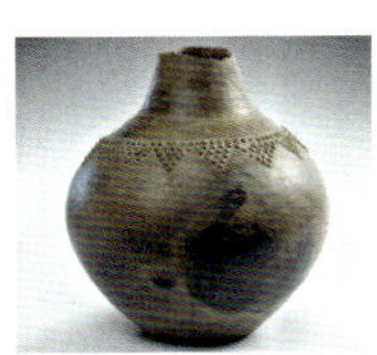

POT NUMBER **207**
Uphiso, H: 349 mm
Provenance: Mahlabatini/Nongoma border region [1940s?].
<1995> An old-style *uphiso* with a ring of small *amasumpa*
in the pendant triangle pattern below the neck (cf. 206).
Small repair to rim.

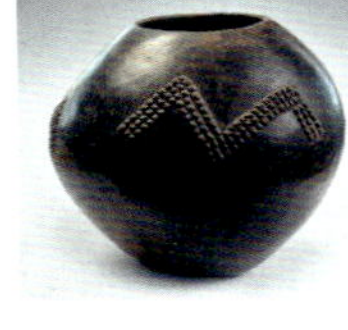

POT NUMBER **208**
Ukhamba, H: 280 mm
Provenance: Nsongweni, Nongoma. Ndwandwe household
[c.1970].
<1995> Inverted 'W' motif, *amasumpa* carved from an applied
panel of clay. Straight 'W' motifs are also frequently
encountered.

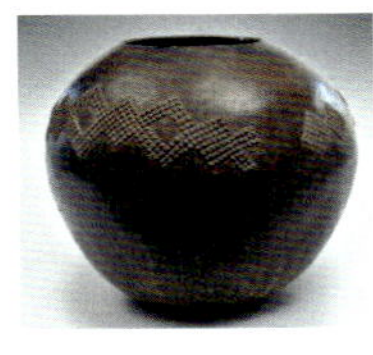

POT NUMBER **209**
Ukhamba, H: 319 mm
Provenance: Mahlabatini [1970s].
<1996> Partially superimposed regular zigzags made of
amasumpa carved from panels of clay. Combinations
of zigzags, in parallel or as here in opposition, are
characteristic of the Mahlabatini region. They figure on
beadwork and basketry as well as ceramics (cf. Jolles 2004).

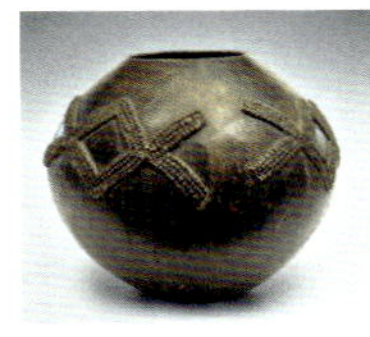

POT NUMBER **210**
Ukhamba, H: 318 mm
Provenance: Nongoma, possibly from ekuShumayeleni
[1970s].
<1996> Superimposed upright and inverted chevrons made
up of several applied panels. The motif is repeated three
times. The same motif also exists in small, made up of a
single line of *amasumpa*.

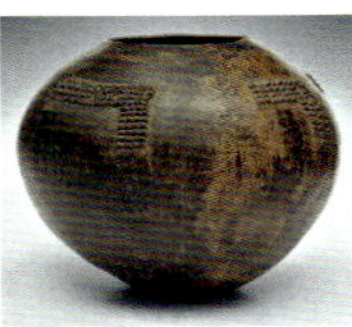

POT NUMBER **211**
Ukhamba, H: 299 mm
Provenance: Nongoma, possibly from ekuShumayeleni
[c.1970].
<1996> Four right angles on a curved surface. The fact that
they are slightly obtuse frustrates the viewer's expectation
of perfect right angles. This, and the fact that they are
not uniform, is responsible for the disorienting effect of
reduced symmetry, which enhances the aesthetic appeal of
the pot. *Amasumpa* carved from panels of applied of clay.

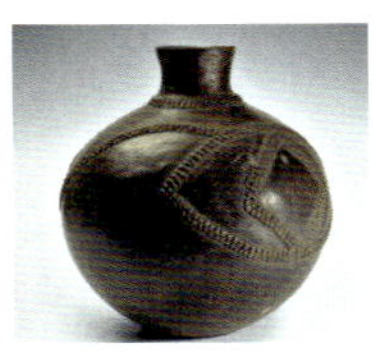

POT NUMBER **212**
Uphiso, H: 346 mm
Provenance: ekuShumayeleni (near top end), Nongoma
[1970s].
<1996> Expanded eye pattern with central diamonds.
Amasumpa from strips of applied clay.

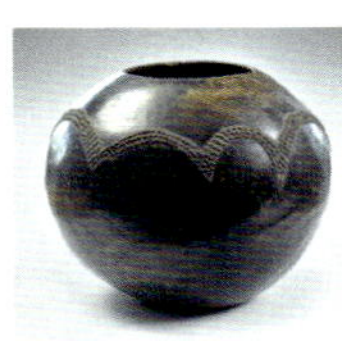

POT NUMBER **213**
Ukhamba, H: 268 mm
Provenance: Nongoma [1970s].
<1996> Wave pattern: three rows of *amasumpa* from applied
strips. In this pattern a small 'wave' frequently completes
the sequence. This is another example of reduced
symmetry (cf. 211).

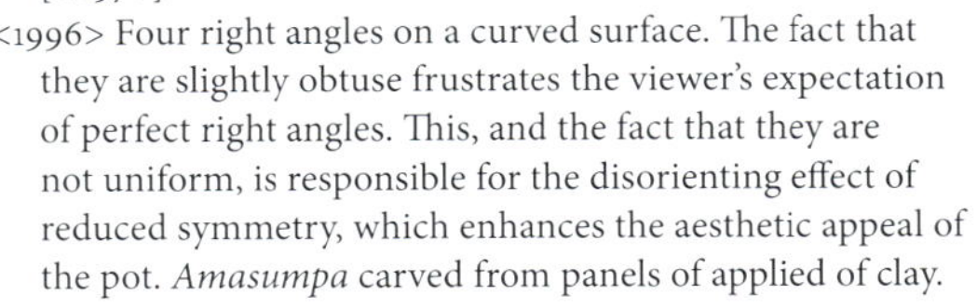

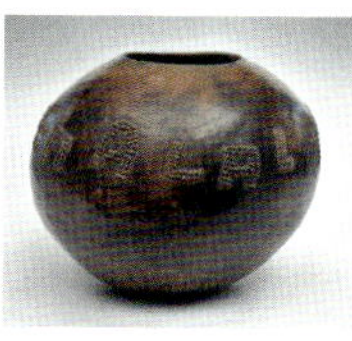

POT NUMBER **214**

Ukhamba, H: 303 mm

Provenance: ekuShumayeleni, Nongoma [1970s].

<1995> Pot with text formed out of strips of *amasumpa*. The text reads: 'ALALA MA O HAMEN'. Such texts are often difficult to decipher, as the illiterate pot makers depended on school children for writing the words. Here there seems to have been some confusion about the use of 'H'. So this text was probably intended to read: 'ALALA MA O AMEN', 'Bravo, Mother, so it's you. Amen' (personal information Jacob Ngwenya, 21.01.2004).

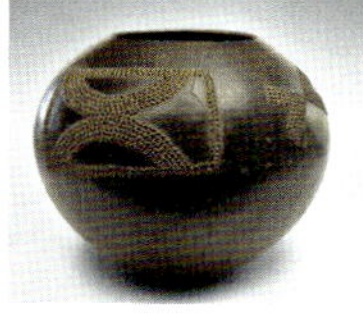

POT NUMBER **215**

Ukhamba, H: 371 mm

Provenance: Qule, Nongoma. Maker: Phozia Shoba, deceased. Owner: Maria Shoba, pensioner, born 1914. She did not want to say when it was made, but all the other people present said it was before they were born [1930s?].

<01.01.1997> Squat form, diameter greater than height (1:1.64, D: 432 mm). Alternating large designs in *amasumpa* on shoulder.

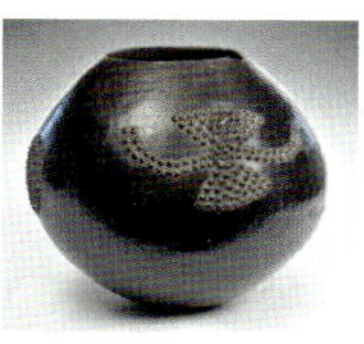

POT NUMBER **216**

Ukhamba, H: 279 mm

Provenance: eMgovuso, Hlabisa. Maker and owner: Emmelina Khumalo, born c.1923. 'She made it before she was old – she is old now' [c.1980?].

<17.10.1998> Alternating large motifs in *amasumpa*, including the circles characteristic of the Nongoma region, and human figures based on the widespread hourglass motif. In the latter case, creative modification of traditional material.

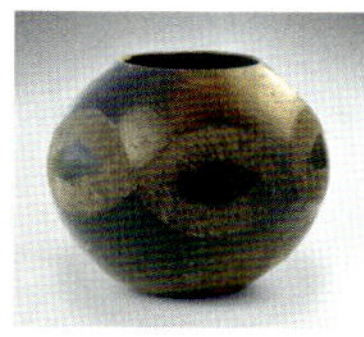

POT NUMBER **217**

Ukhamba, H: 210 mm

Provenance: Nongoma [1970s].

<1997> Incised, plain 'eye pattern'.

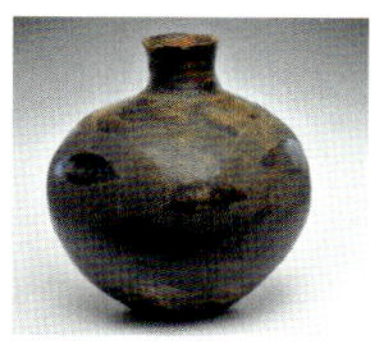

POT NUMBER **218**

Uphiso, H: 443 mm

Provenance: Nongoma [1960s].

<1995> Incised 'eye pattern' with multiple connecting links.

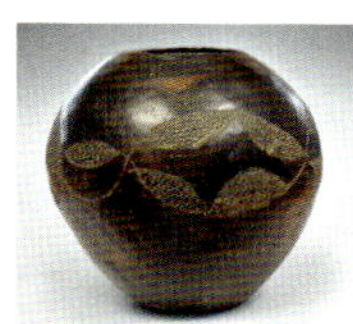

POT NUMBER **219**

Ukhamba, H: 281 mm

Provenance: Nongoma [1960s].

<1995> Modified 'eye pattern' with broken diamond centres.

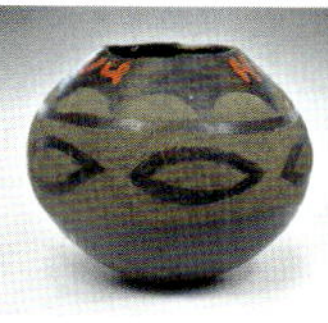

POT NUMBER **220**

Ukhamba, H: 260 mm

Provenance: Nongoma [1970s].

<1994> Eyes embedded in an incised band, with a wave pattern running along the top.

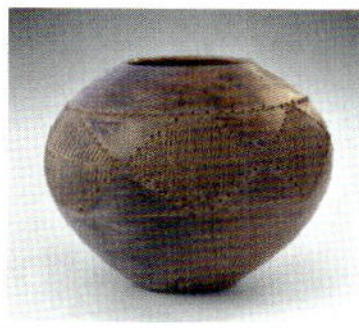

POT NUMBER **221**

Ukhamba, H: 210 mm

Provenance: Nongoma [1970s].

<1994> Translation pattern of incised diamonds running between two lines.

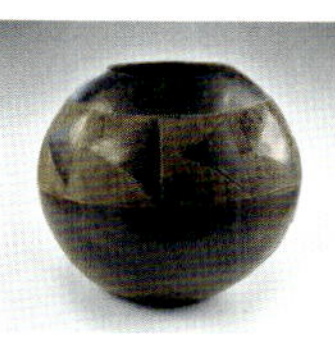

POT NUMBER **222**

Ukhamba, H: 253 mm

Provenance: Nongoma. Maker and owner: Azolinah Mbatha [1970s].

<1997> Translation pattern of horizontal triangles embedded in an incised band.

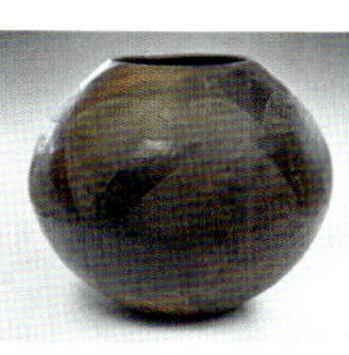

POT NUMBER **223**

Ukhamba, H: 265 mm

Provenance: Nongoma [late 1960s].

<1994> Alternating upright and inverted incised triangles with spacers in between in a band surmounted by a wave pattern.

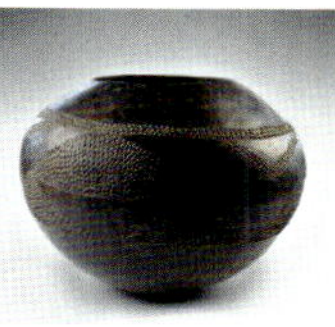

POT NUMBER **224**

Ukhamba, H: 230 mm

Provenance: Nongoma [1980s].

<1996> A zigzag running between two parallel lines forming alternate upright and inverted triangles each containing a smaller triangle pointing downwards.

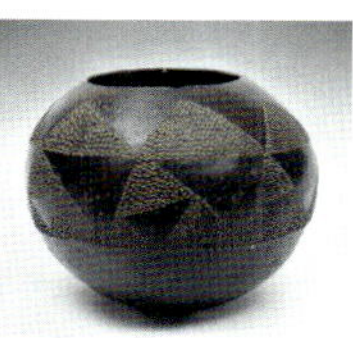

POT NUMBER **225**

Ukhamba, H: 195 mm

Provenance: Nongoma, made for sale on Mona Market [1980s].

<1997> Though at first sight it does not seem so, this is the same pattern as 224 with the addition of a band of matching triangles running along the top.

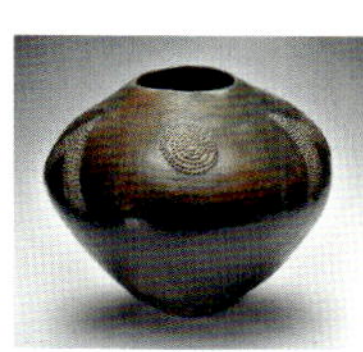

POT NUMBER **226**

Ukhamba, H: 394, W: 464 mm

Provenance: Nongoma. Collection: W Simmons

Collected by Mynhardt Bester

Purchased from Douglas Dawson, 30.07.1997

Photo: Bruce M White

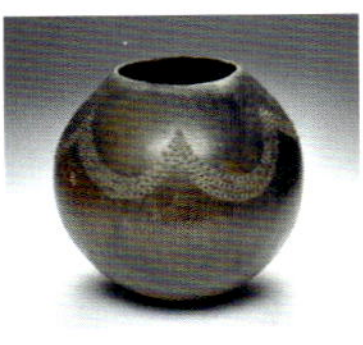

POT NUMBER **227**

Ukhamba, H: 305 mm w: 337 mm
Provenance: Nongoma. Collection: W Simmons
Collected by Mynhardt Bester
Purchased from Pucker Gallery, 25.09.1995
Photo: Bruce M White

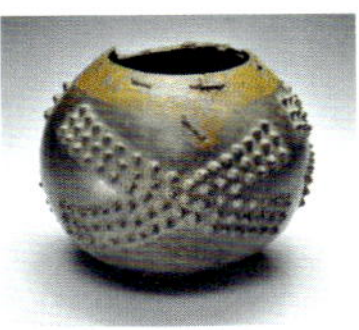

POT NUMBER **228**

Ukhamba, H: 222 mm, w: 279 mm
Provenance: Nongoma. Collection: W Simmons.
Collected by William Raats
Purchased from Frank Jolles
Photo: Bruce M White

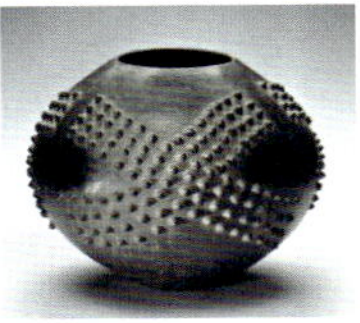

POT NUMBER **229**

Ukhamba, H: 305 mm, w: 394 mm
Provenance: Nongoma. Collection: W Simmons
Collected by Peter Pickford in 1993
Purchased from Steven de Combes, 5.10.2006
Photo: Bruce M White

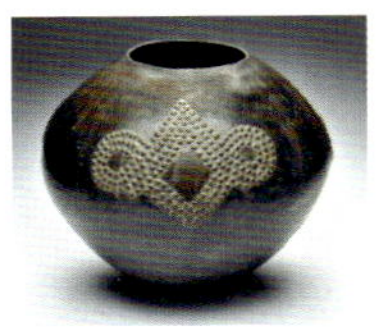

POT NUMBER **230**

Ukhamba, H: 305 mm, w: 362 mm
Provenance: Nangoma. Collection: W. Simmons.
Collected by Kevin Conru, purchased 26.05.1995
Photo: Bruce M White

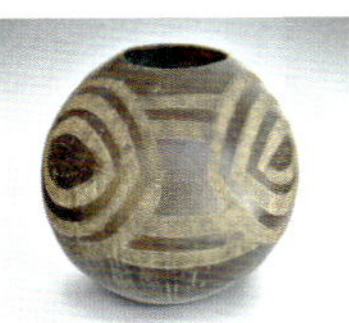

POT NUMBER **231**

Ukhamba, H: 360 w: 370 mm
Provenance: Aselinah Mbatha, at that time living on a hill
    top overlooking Nongoma.
<1996>. See p. 20f. Imaginative extrapolation of the incised
    Nongoma eye pattern on a very thin-walled, egg-shaped
    vessel.
Collection: Karel Nel.

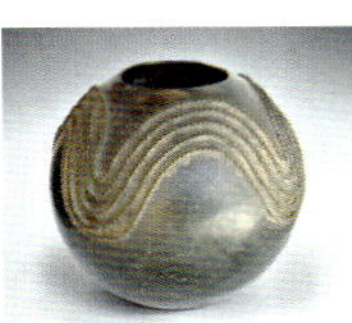

POT NUMBER **232**

Ukhamba, H: 350 w: 390 mm
Provenance: Aselinah Mbatha, at that time living on a hill
    top overlooking Nongoma.
<1996> See Conru, K (ed.), 2002, *The Art of South East
    Africa*, p 115.
Made for her sister's wedding [c.1970].
Collection: Karel Nel.

The Hlabisa Region

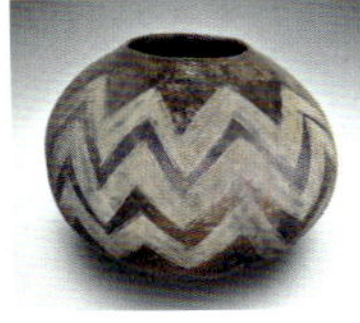

POT NUMBER **301**

Ukhamba, H: 390 mm
Provenance: Hlabisa [c.1970 or late 1960s].
<20.08.1998> Squat form with three rows of parallel incised
    zigzags. The zigzags and their derivatives are the most
    widely distributed motifs of the Hlabisa area. They also
    figure in basketry and beadwork.

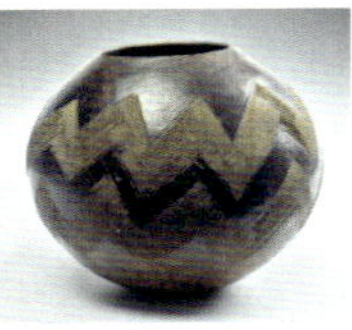

POT NUMBER **302**

Ukhamba, H: 270 mm
Provenance: Hlabisa [c.1970].
<21.08.1998> Nearly spherical with two rows of parallel
    incised zigzags (cf. 301).

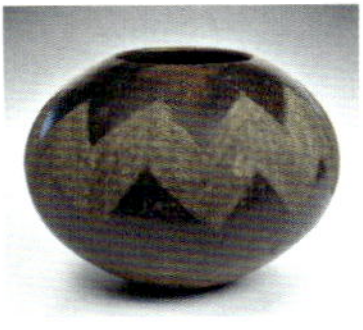

POT NUMBER **303**

Ukhamba, H: 268 mm
Provenance: uMgangatho, Hlabisa. Maker: Phiwayinkosi
    Ngobese. Owner: Jabu Ngobese [1970s].
<17.10.1998> Squat form with two parallel rows of zigzags with
    space between them incised. In terms of plane pattern
    symmetry this is an example of 'glide reflection'. Derivative
    of 302.

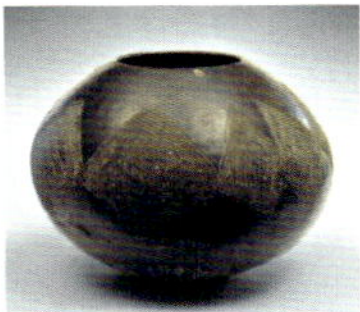

POT NUMBER **304**

Ukhamba, H: 310 mm
Provenance: Hlabisa. [c.1970].
<21.08.1998> Two 'opposing' zigzags (i.e. the lower one
    is shifted left or right by half a length), with the space
    between them filled with incisions. In terms of plane
    pattern symmetry this is an example of reflection around
    an axis passing through the centre of the rhomboids as
    well as vertical reflection.

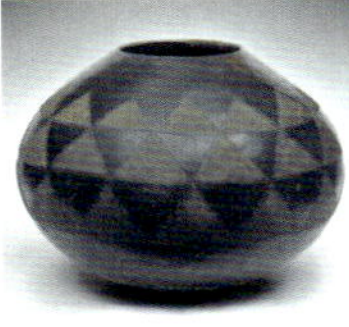

POT NUMBER **305**

Ukhamba, H: 374 mm
Provenance: KwaMayakasi, Hlabisa. This is in the mountains
    on the north side of the lower reaches of the Mona River.
    Maker and owner: Azolinah Ngobese, born c.1928. Her
    family moved to KwaMayakasi from the Vryheid area in
    the 1940s when she was an *itshitshi* (teenager). She learnt
    pottery from her mother. [c.1977].
<17.10.1998> The pattern is called *umcijwane* (diamond), but
    it also refers to playing cards, i.e. 'Diamonds'. Technically it
    is a two-dimensional pattern consisting of hexagons each
    formed from six equilateral triangles. It is characterised
    by reflection through vertical axes and rotation through
    60° (Washburn & Crowe, 1988: 163). But it may also be
    regarded as a derivative of the zigzag motif.

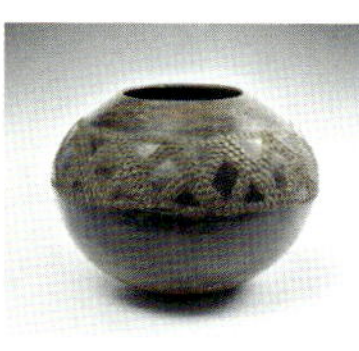

POT NUMBER **306**
Umkhamba, H: 215 mm
Provenance: Qulwane, Hlabisa. Maker: Annie Sishwile [1970s or 1980s].
<17.10.1998> Mona Market ware (but not bought on Mona Market) with rather crude *amasumpa*. Double zigzag pattern enclosed in containing lines as in some of the beadwork from this area.

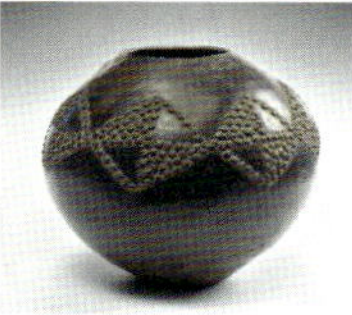

POT NUMBER **307**
Ukhamba, H: 268 mm
Provenance: KwaQule, Nongoma. Owner: Manqele, who said she bought it 'a long time ago' [1970s?].
<01.01.1999> Characteristic of Mona Market ware (see 306). Superimposed double zigzag pattern; the symmetry is translation and rotation through 180°.

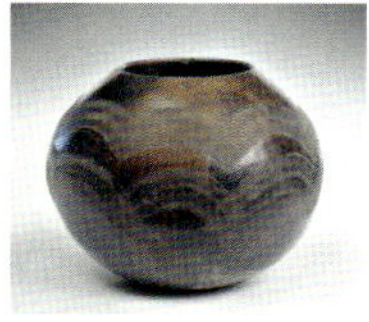

POT NUMBER **308**
Ukhamba, H: 273 mm
Provenance: Bought at KwaSishwile, but from uMgangatho, Hlabisa. Owner Pauline Mhlungu, maker not known. 'It is an older pot' [c.1970?].
<18.10.1998> Squat Hlabisa form with double parallel incised wave pattern.

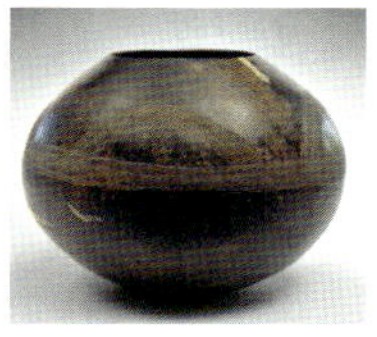

POT NUMBER **309**
Jol 355
Ukhamba, H: 300 mm
Provenance: uMgangatho, Hlabisa. Made by Phiwayinkosi MaMthethwa Ngobese [1970s].
<19.10.1998> Characteristic squat form, variations on single wave pattern.

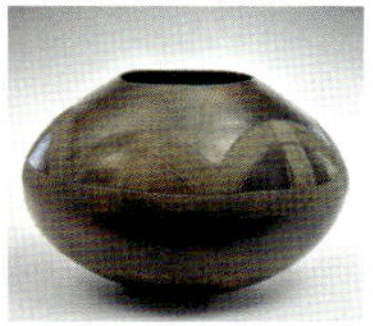

POT NUMBER **310**
Ukhamba, H: 287 mm
Provenance: uMgangatho, Hlabisa. Maker: Phiwayinkosi MaMthethwa Ngobese [1970s].
<19.10.1998> Characteristic squat form, variations on single wave pattern.

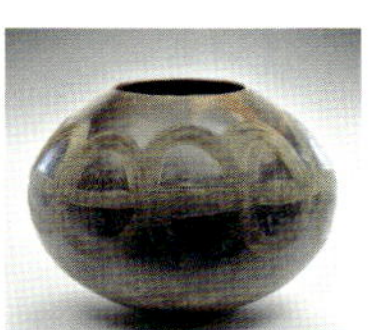

POT NUMBER **311**
Jol 359
Ukhamba, H: 310 mm
Provenance: uMgangatho, Hlabisa. Maker and owner: Khunjuliliwe Xulu [1970s].
<19.10.1998> Double wave pattern displaying symmetries of translation, vertical and horizontal reflection and rotation through 180°.

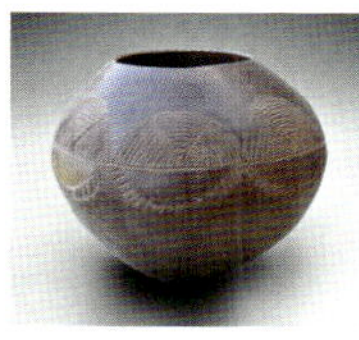

POT NUMBER **312**
Ukhamba, H: 356 mm
Provenance: Qulwane, Hlabisa. Maker: Doreen Sishwili, born about 1928 [1970s].
<19.10.1998> The pattern is copied from her mother; it is called *inyanga* (the moon). The symmetries are much reduced compared with the very similar pot by Khunjuliliwe Xulu (311); they are translation and vertical reflection.

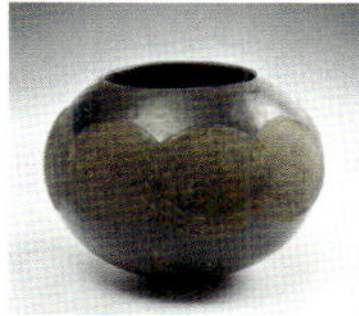

POT NUMBER **313**
Ukhamba, H: 180 mm
Provenance: Hlabisa [1980s?].
<21.08.1998> Opposing waves with incisions (combed area) between. Symmetries: translation, reflection through vertical and horizontal axes, rotation through 180°.

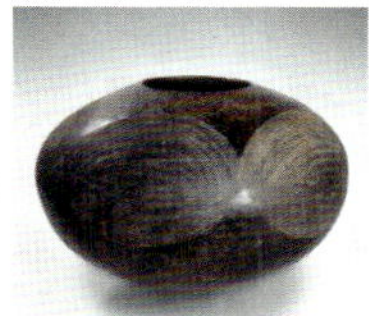

POT NUMBER **314**
Ukhamba, H: 355 mm
Provenance: uMgangatho, Hlabisa. Maker and owner: Trifina Phumlaphi Gamede. She said she did not know the name for this pattern; many copied the design from other people [late 1960s?].
<19.10.1998> Very large ukhamba with the characteristic squat form, H:D: 1:158. Opposing waves filled in with combed incisions. Symmetries as for 313.

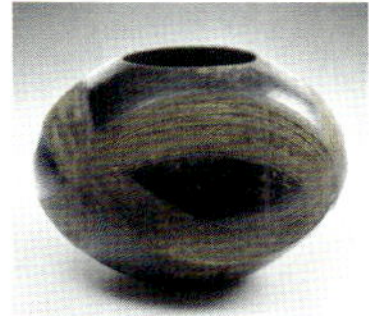

POT NUMBER **315**
Ukhamba, H: 247 mm
Provenance: Hlabisa [1970s].
<1996> Opposing waves making an 'eye pattern'. Symmetries as for 313.

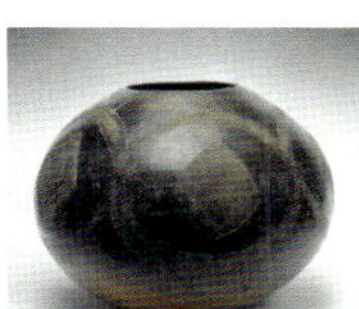

POT NUMBER **316**
Jol 281
Ukhamba, H: 375 mm
Provenance: Hlabisa [c.1970].
<1996> Combination of wave pattern and diamond pattern. The original symmetries are retained.

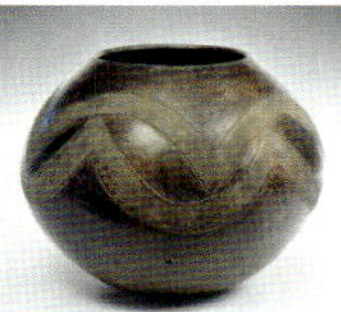

POT NUMBER **317**
Ukhamba, H: 239 mm
Provenance: Hlabisa [1970s].
<1996> Offset opposing waves: symmetries of translation, reflection through vertical axes and glide reflection.

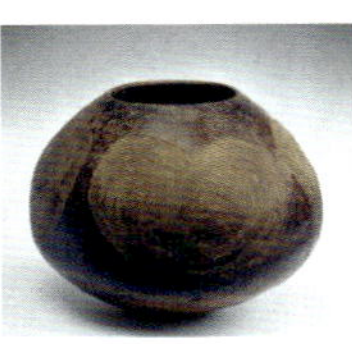

POT NUMBER **318**
Ukhamba, H: 294 mm
Provenance: Hlabisa [1950s?].
<1996> Motif from playing cards, 'Hearts'. Very early pot of
this type.

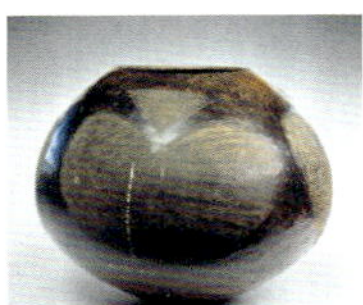

POT NUMBER **319**
Ukhamba, H: 416 mm
Provenance: KwaGwebu, Nongoma, but in Hlabisa style.
Owners: Zulu family [late 1970s]
<12.03.2000> A very large ukhamba (about 30 litres) for
special occasions. The incised decoration is an elaboration
of the 'Hearts' motif.

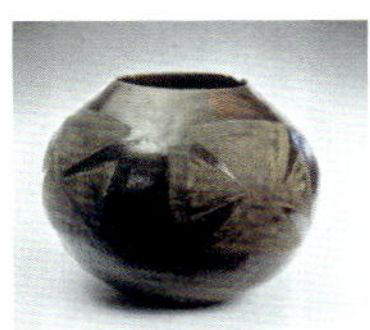

POT NUMBER **320**
H3: 18
Jol 340
Ukhamba, H: 236 mm
Provenance: Mayakazi, Hlabisa. Maker: Busisiwe MaHlabisa
Ngobese, 1982
<18.10.1998> The motif is *ugqebhe* (Spades). Doke et al (1990)
for *ugqebhe*, give 'heart-shaped pattern on pottery', and
'playing-card with red heart on it'. Spades is given as *igeja*.
So there is some confusion here.

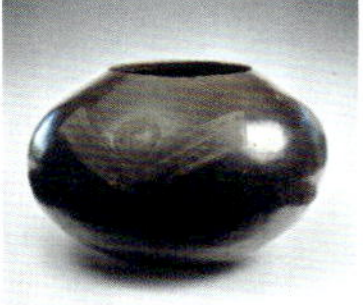

POT NUMBER **321**
Ukhamba, H: 262 mm
Provenance: Mayakazi, Hlabisa. Maker: Azolinah Ngobese,
born c.1930. [1970s].
<18.10.1998> Mrs Ngobese said she did not know the name of
the pattern, but that it was taken from playing cards. Then
someone else said it was called *impukane* (fly).

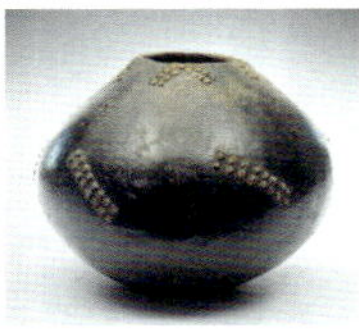

POT NUMBER **322**
Ukhamba, H: 216 mm
Provenance: Qulwane, Hlabisa. Maker: Lesaya Cele, who 'died
long ago' [1960s].
<17.10.1998> A characteristic Hlabisa form with Nongoma
motifs: two-row panels of *amasumpa*. Despite its narrow
opening this pot was used for *amahewu* (fermented maize
porridge).

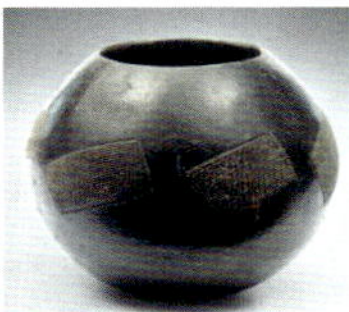

POT NUMBER **323**
Ukhamba, H: 136 mm
Provenance: uMgangatho, Hlabisa. Maker: Phiwayinkosi
Ngobese. Owner: Jabu Ngobese [1970s].
<19.10.1998> Characteristic Hlabisa form (H:D: 1:23) with
Nongoma/Melmoth motifs: slanting incised rectangles.

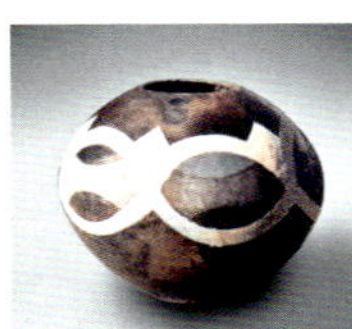

POT NUMBER **324**
Ukhamba, H: 388 mm, D: 483 mm
Provenance: Hlabisa, maker not known. Collection: Phillip A.
and Carolee G. Kennedy. Incised pattern highlighted with
blue and white paint.

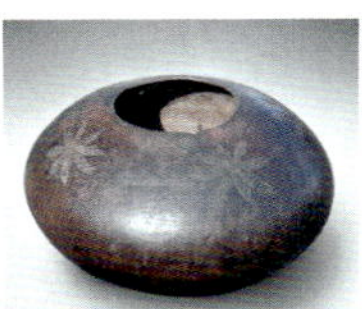

POT NUMBER **325**
Ukhamba, H: 235 mm, D: 340 mm
Provenance: Ndlovu household, Oyaya. Maker unknown.

The Melmoth-Eshowe Region

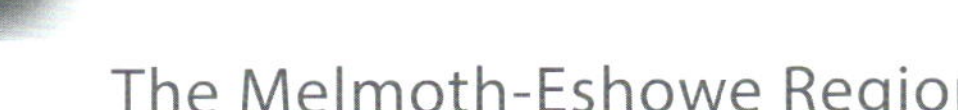

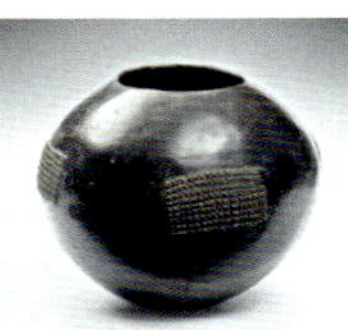

POT NUMBER **401**
Ukhamba, H: 260 mm
Provenance: Melmoth region [1970s or early 1980s].
<21.08.1998> Horizontal rectangles, *amasumpa*.

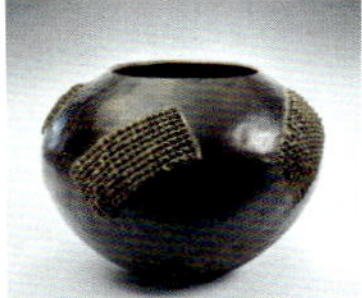

POT NUMBER **402**
Ukhamba, H: 220 mm
Provenance: Melmoth region [1970s or early 1980s].
<21.08.1998> Slanting rectangles, *amasumpa*.

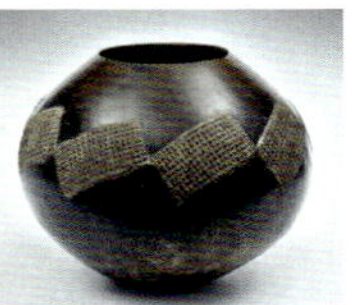

POT NUMBER **403**
Ukhamba, H: 225 mm
Provenance: Melmoth region [1970s or early 1980s].
<21.08.1998> Slanting rectangles linked in two groups of four,
amasumpa.

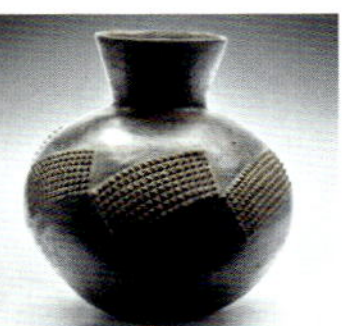

POT NUMBER **404**
Uphiso, H: 290 mm
Provenance: Melmoth region [1970s or early 1980s].
<21.08.1998> Uphiso with flared neck. Slanting linked
rectangles, *amasumpa*.

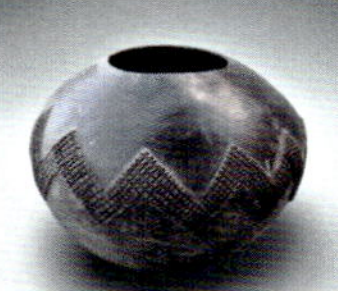

POT NUMBER **405**
Ukhamba, H: 240 mm
Provenance: KwaKunzempunga (approx 28°46'S:31°22'E),
above north bank of uMhlatuze) [c.1990].
<20.08.1998> Zigzag pattern, *amasumpa*.

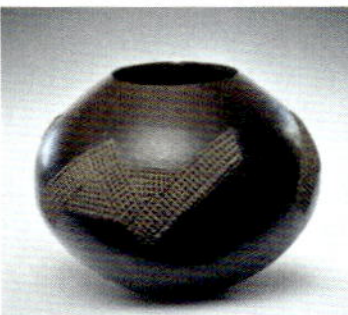

POT NUMBER **406**
Ukhamba, H: 270 mm
Provenance: Melmoth region [1960s?].
<20.08.1998> Single zigzag motif with filled in apexes,
amasumpa. As far as I know, this motif and its extensions
are specific to the Melmoth-Eshowe region.

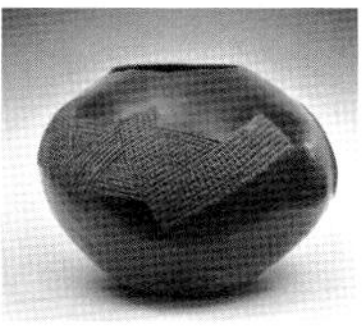

POT NUMBER **407**
Ukhamba, H: 310 mm
Provenance: KwaKunzempunga [1960s?].
<20.08.1998> Extension of motif of 406.

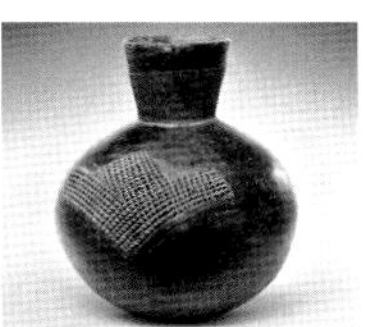

POT NUMBER **408**
Uphiso, H: 355 mm
Provenance: KwaKunzempunga [1980s].
<20.08.1998> Half zigzag derived from 406? Another
    example Jolles Collection 261 (not illustrated). Neck
    decorated with light incisions.

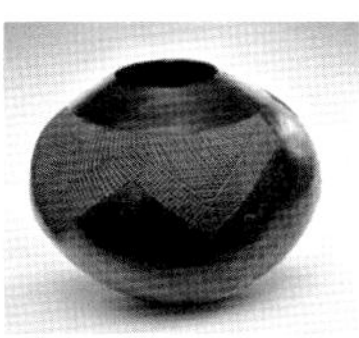

POT NUMBER **409**
Ukhamba, H: 330 mm
Provenance: KwaKunzempunga [1960s].
<20.08.1998> Two semi-zigzag motifs, *amasumpa.*

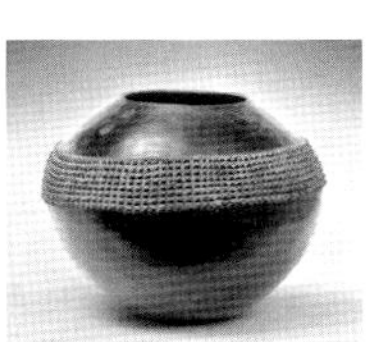

POT NUMBER **410**
Ukhamba, H: 230 mm
Provenance: KwaKunzempunga [1980s].
<20.08.1998> Plain belt of *amasumpa* as in the picture of
    Dinuzulu's drinking vessels, p. 123. Compare also Jolles
    Collection 270 (not illustrated) which has the same motif
    but with a triangular addition like the fastener of a belt.

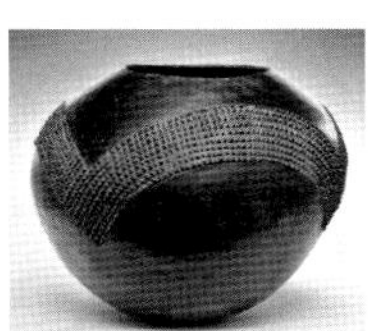

POT NUMBER **411**
Ukhamba, H: 310 mm
Provenance: KwaKunzempunga. Maker: Khoza [1980s].
<20.08.1998> Arcs of *amasumpa.*

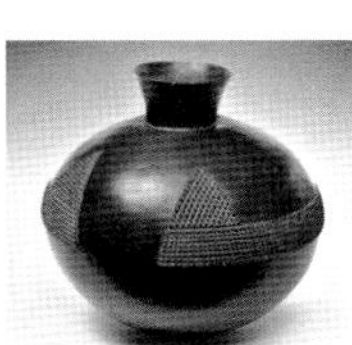

POT NUMBER **412**
Uphiso, H: 360 mm
Provenance: KwaKunzempunga/uMhlatuze, Melmoth
    region [1940s].
<20.08.1998> Two bands of *amasumpa* with upright
    triangles at their ends. The *amasumpa* of the triangles
    are set at an angle to those of the bands. Extremely fine
    regular work. The neck is flared in line with the regional
    convention; it is very slightly off-centre. Originally the
    pot had a rounded bottom; later a cement base was
    added enabling it to stand on a flat surface.

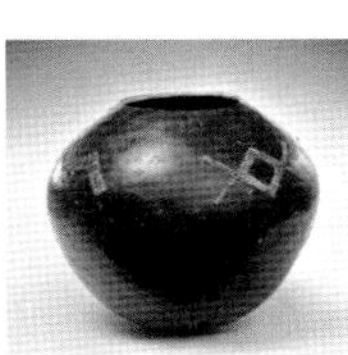

POT NUMBER **413**
Ukhamba, H: 260 mm
Provenance: Entembeni, Melmoth [1970s].
<21.08.1998> Narrow applied single line of *amasumpa* made
    by incising the applied strip. The two small motifs are
    both familiar ones reduced in size. In this form they
    seem to be specific to this *isigodi*. The maker called them
    amanunu (in this context 'insects'?).

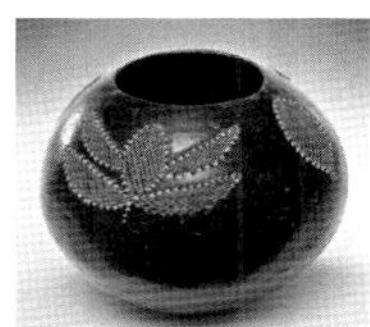

POT NUMBER **414**
Small Ukhamba, H: 195 mm
Provenance: eNdundulu, above Nkwalini [1970s].
<21.08.1998> Incised and notched motifs on shoulder, leaf
    shapes. Said to be an old Eshowe style.

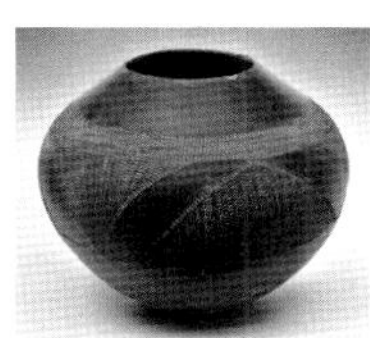

POT NUMBER **415**
Ukhamba, H: 290 mm
Provenance: eFofolozi, above north bank of uMhlatuze near
    Goedetreu Dam. The owner said it came from Eshowe.
    Maker: Nzuzu [c.1980].
<20.08.1998> Linear incisions, spaced opposing triangles
    between bands.

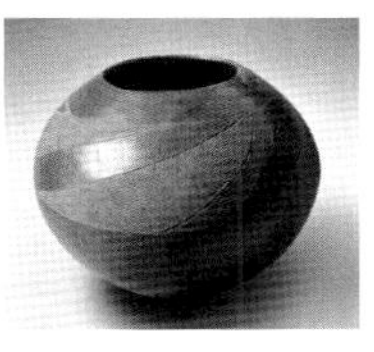

POT NUMBER **416**
Ukhamba, H: 255 mm
Provenance: eMatshensundu (brown stones), Melmoth area.
    Maker: MaMthembu [c.1980].
<20.08.1998> Linear incisions, obtuse-angled triangle motif.
Photo: Gavin Whitelaw.

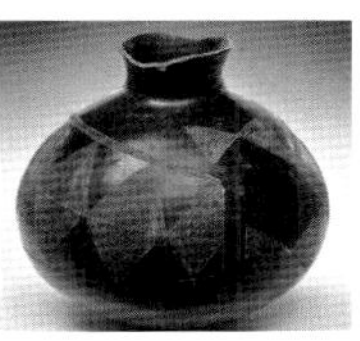

POT NUMBER **417**
Uphiso, H: 355 mm
Provenance: eNdundulu, above Nkwalini [1960s].
<21.08.1998> Linear incisions: slanting groups of rhomboids
    interspersed with butterfly motifs.

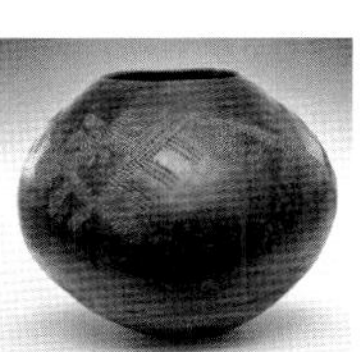

POT NUMBER **418**
Ukhamba, H: 355 W: 440 mm
Provenance: eNdundulu, above Nkwalini. Maker: MaSibiya
    (who referred to it as *isikhamba*) [1970s].
<21.08.1998> Notched.
Collection: Karel Nel.

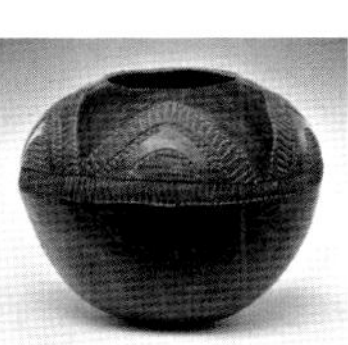

POT NUMBER **419**
Ukhamba, H: 300 mm
Provenance: uGatsha, uMhlatuze, Melmoth area [1970s].
<21.08.1998> Wave pattern, incised and impressed (roller?).
    This pattern and variations of it are characteristic of the
    area.

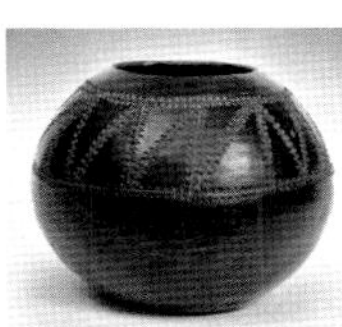

POT NUMBER **420**
Umancishana, H: 150 mm
Provenance: KwaKunzempunga, uMhlatuze, Melmoth area
    [1960s?].
<21.08.1998> Incised and impressed on shoulder. Reminiscent
    of an old Msinga design.

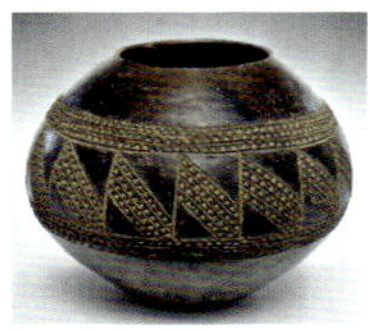

POT NUMBER **421**
Ukhamba, H: 225 mm
Provenance: KwaKunzempunga, uMhlatuze, Melmoth area
[c.1980].
<21.08.1998> Notched.

The Lower Thukela Region

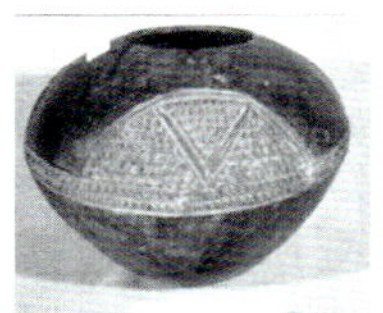

POT NUMBER **501**
Ukhamba
Provenance: Manyane [1970s].
<1993> Applied *amasumpa*: upright triangles.

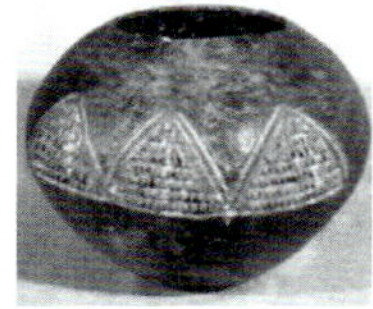

POT NUMBER **502**
Ukhamba
Provenance: Manyane [1970s].
<1993> Detail of *amasumpa*.

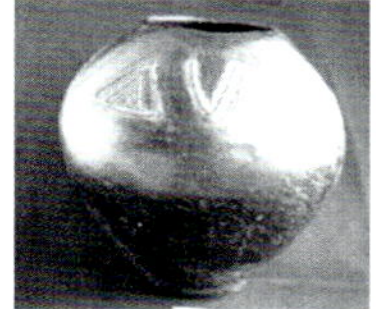

POT NUMBER **503**
Ukhamba
Provenance: Manyane [1960s].
<1993> Collection: Nessa Leibhammer, Johannesburg.

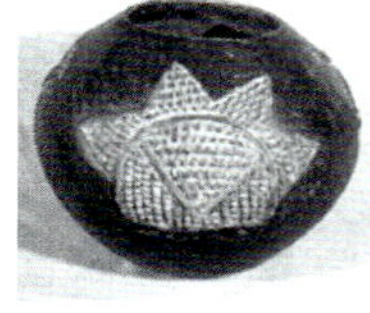

POT NUMBER **504**
Ukhamba
Provenance: Manyane [1970s].
<1993> Pendant triangles, variant of 503

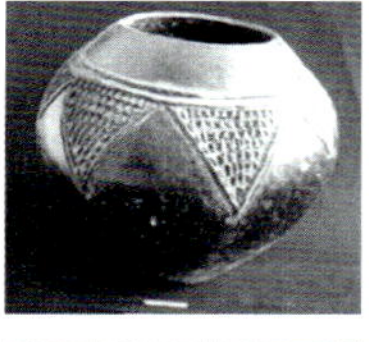

POT NUMBER **505**
Ukhamba, H: 260 mm
Provenance: Manyane valley. Collection: Marilee Wood.
Applied pendout triangles alternatiing between *amasumpa*
and engraved ridges.

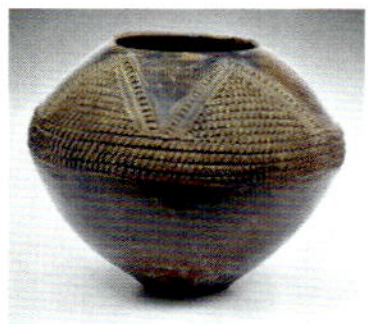

POT NUMBER **506**
Ukhamba
Provenance: Manyane [1970s].
<1993> Derivation of 505

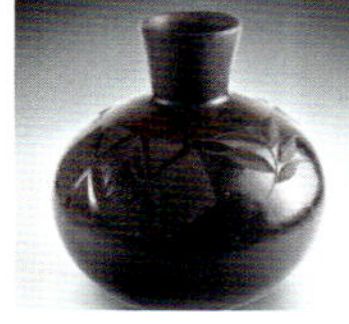

POT NUMBER **507**
Ukhamba H: 343 mm
Provenance: Middledrift, Thukela. Collected by Paul Mikula.
Nesta Nala [c. 1990] Shapes based on rhomboids and
Thukela phytomotifs.

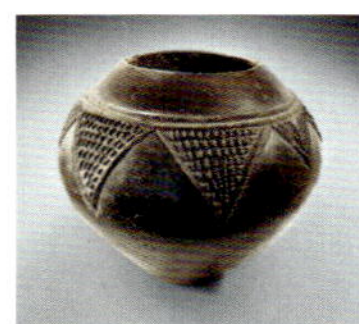

POT NUMBER **508**
Ukhamba, H: 305 mm, D: 356 mm
Provenance: Pophini [?] 'just north of Kranskop.' Collected
David Roberts <1999>. Collection: WB Simmons.

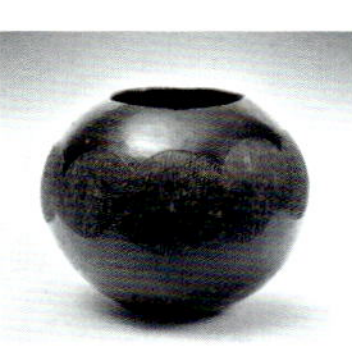

POT NUMBER **509**
Ukhamba, H: 250 mm
Provenance: eKhohlwa, Middledrift, but probably brought
from Oyaya [1960s or 1970s].
<1996> Linear incisions, offset double wave pattern.

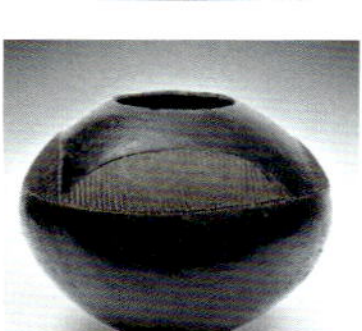

POT NUMBER **510**
Small Ukhamba or Umancishana, H: 170 mm
Provenance: eKhohlwa, Middledrift, but probably brought
from Oyaya [1960s or 1970s].
<1996> Linear incisions on shoulder, offset double wave
pattern (cf. 313).

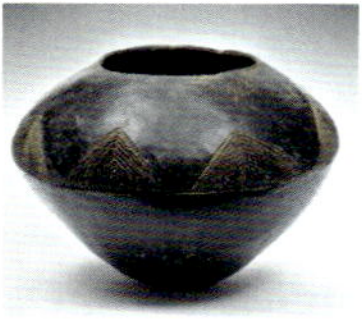

POT NUMBER **511**
Ukhamba, H: 245 mm
Provenance: eKhohlwa, Middledrift [1970s].
<1996> Three motifs, incised and carved (upper motifs not
clearly visible in photo).

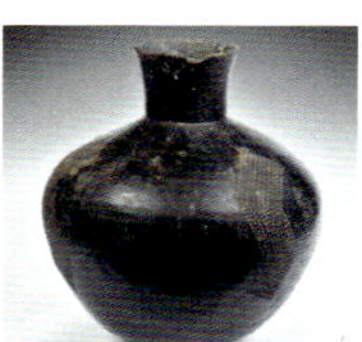

POT NUMBER **512**
Ukhamba, H: 220 mm
Provenance: eKhohlwa, Middledrift [1970s].
<1996> Linear incisions on shoulder, separated wave pattern.

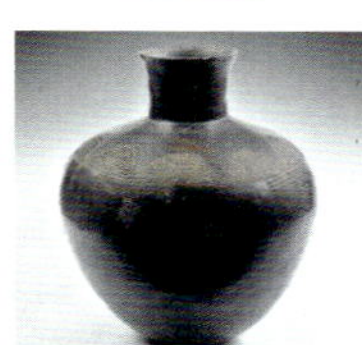

POT NUMBER **513**
Ukhamba, H: 200 mm
Provenance: Middledrift [1970s].
<1996> Linear incisions, upright triangles.

POT NUMBER **514**
Uphiso, H: 380 mm
Provenance: eKhohlwa, Middledrift [1960s].
<1997> Notched, vertical zigzag.

POT NUMBER **515**
Uphiso, H: 380 mm
Provenance: eKhohlwa, Middledrift [1960s].
<1997> Notched, single wave with 'pendants'.

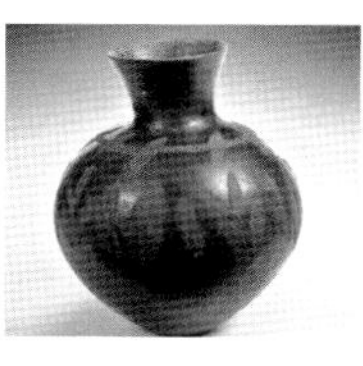

POT NUMBER **516**

Uphiso, H: 320 mm

Provenance: Near Middledrift, on the road to the grave of
King Cetshwayo [1960s].

<1997> Incised and notched leaf pattern characteristic of the
region downstream from Tugela Ferry.

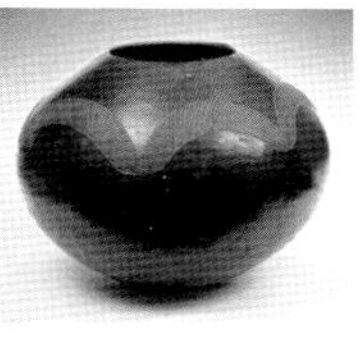

POT NUMBER **517**

Ukhamba, H: 269 mm

Provenance: Oyaya. Maker: Siphiwe Nala. Owner:
Tombinyana MaPhungula [1940s?].

<26.07.2000> Linear incisions, wave pattern. Siphiwe Nala's
'old style'. Ratio H:D: 1:1.3

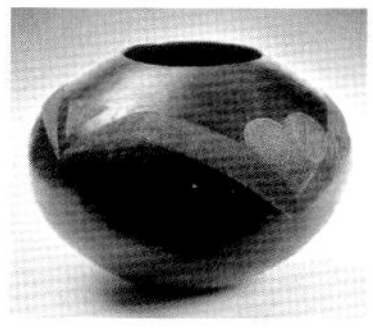

POT NUMBER **518**

Ukhamba, H: 247 mm

Provenance: Oyaya. Maker: Siphiwe Nala. Owner: Ndlovu
household. 'Made long ago when Siphiwe Nala was the
only one making pots.' Her 'old style' [1950s].

<26.07.2000> Linear incisions, two motifs with triangles
and circles (not visible in photo) on wave pattern. See also
Jolles 2012: 15–18. For greater detail and interpritation of
Nos. 517, 518, 519 and 521 see Jolles 2012: 15–18.

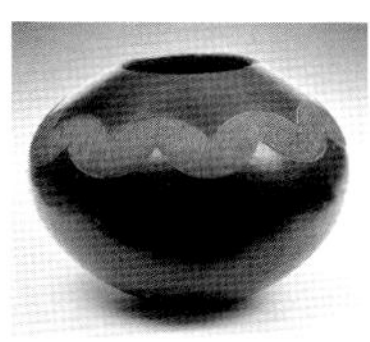

POT NUMBER **519**

Ukhamba, H: 255 mm

Provenance: Oyaya. Made by Siphiwe Nala 'long ago'
[1950s or 1960s].

<26.07.2000> Linear incisions.

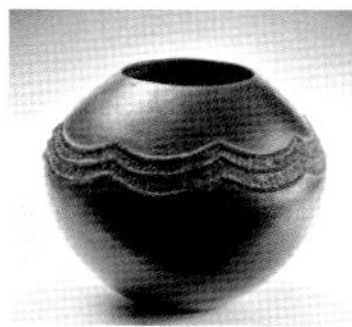

POT NUMBER **520**

Ukhamba, H: 230 mm

Provenance: Oyaya. Maker: Zungakhohlwa Ndlovu (born
1949). Owner Ndlovu household. 'Made four or five years
ago'[mid 1990s].

<26.07.2000> Applied waves with incisions. Ratio H:D: 1:1.174

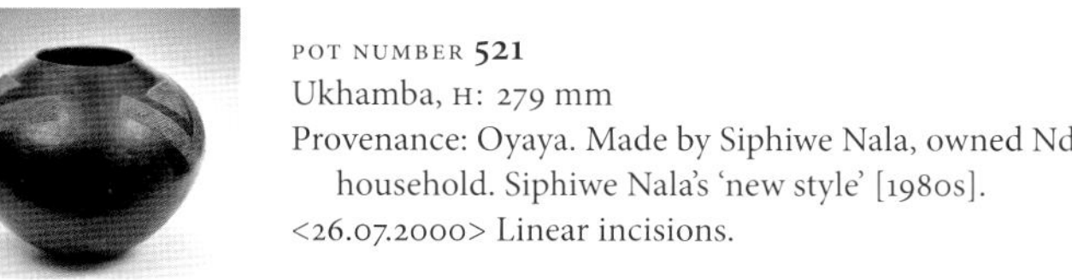

POT NUMBER **521**

Ukhamba, H: 279 mm

Provenance: Oyaya. Made by Siphiwe Nala, owned Ndlovu
household. Siphiwe Nala's 'new style' [1980s].

<26.07.2000> Linear incisions.

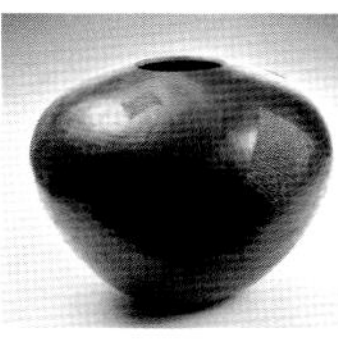

POT NUMBER **522**

Ukhamba, H: 360 mm

Provenance: Oyaya. Made by MaMkhize who 'died long ago'
[1950s].

<26.07.2000> Style of *uphiso* but without the neck. 'Bought
long ago'. Notched rectangles. Note the attractive texture
due to accurate coiling.

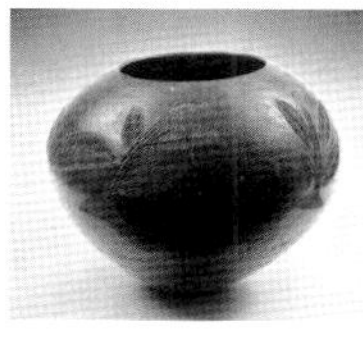

POT NUMBER **523**

Ukhamba, H: 235 mm

Provenance: Oyaya. Maker: MaMkhize Mahlaba, 'who died
long ago'. Owner: Ndlovu household [1960s ?].

<28.07.2000> Thukela plant motifs, incised, cf. 516.

The Msinga Region

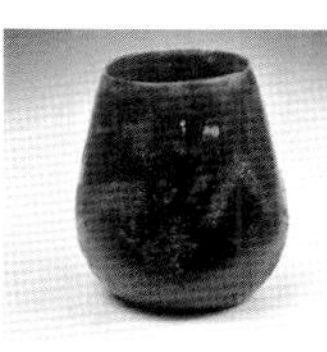

POT NUMBER **601**

Umancishana, H: 223 mm

Provenance: Muden. Owner: Lutile Mchunu [1940s or 1950s?].

<1998> Old Muden style *ithunga* (milking pail) form.
Compare unprovenanced examples in the Local History
Museum, Durban (Wood 1996: 128), but here with incised
rather than applied motifs reminiscent of beadwork
patterns. Further example Phansi Museum, Durban.

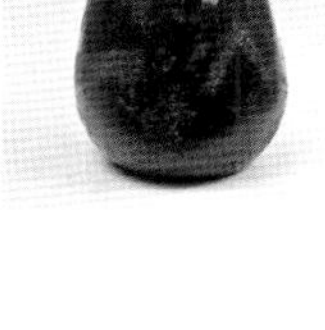

POT NUMBER **602**

Ukhamba, H: 246 mm

Provenance: eMbangweni. The owner, Khanyisele Ngubane,
who was 86 years old in 1996, came from eMkhuphula-
MaBomvini. She said she bought the pot in Mtubatuba a
very long time ago from a family who had moved there
– or who may have been expelled – from a farm called
Riverside at eMsamo near Muden. The text reads: 'WENA
PHUZA UthULE UMSINDO' (You, drink, stop the noise).
The use of text would suggest a date in the late 1950s. At
the earliest, the style and the history imply 1940s.

<1996> The tapered shoulder form with its small base is
characteristic of the Msinga region, whilst the design is
somewhat reminiscent of the Nongoma-Hlabisa region
(however cf. 6.04). The local people assured me that it was
an old Msinga design.

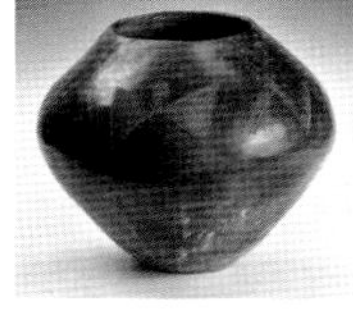

POT NUMBER **603**

Ukhamba, H: 228 mm

Provenance: Msinga [1980s].

<1995> Three incised motifs: butterfly, zigzag, and Greek cross
– the latter suggests the uMzinyathi area, but it could also
be Tugela Ferry as there was a fair amount of coming and
going between the two. The shoulder tapering to a narrow
base is characteristic of Msinga vessels.

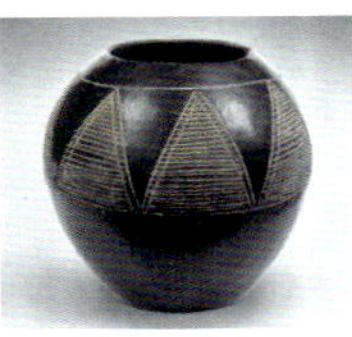

POT NUMBER **604**
M: 06 Jol 240
Umancishana, H: 180 mm
Provenance: KwaMajozi near Tugela Ferry. Mkhize
household, probably bought in Pomeroy [1980s].
<1998> This linear incised design (upright triangles on a base
line) was still fashionable in the Pomeroy area in the 1990s.

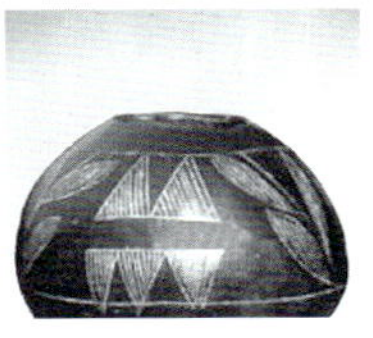

POT NUMBER **605**
Ukhamba, H: 265 mm
Provenance: Tugela Ferry area, Msinga [c.1980].
<1998> Leaf pattern with interspersed triangle motif using
broadly spaced incisions.

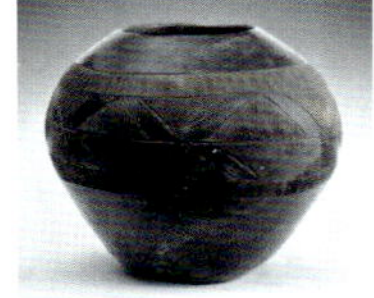

POT NUMBER **606.**
Ukhamba, H: 370 mm
Provenance: uMngeni valley, uMzinyathi region [1970s ?].
<1998> Incised band with geometrical motifs.

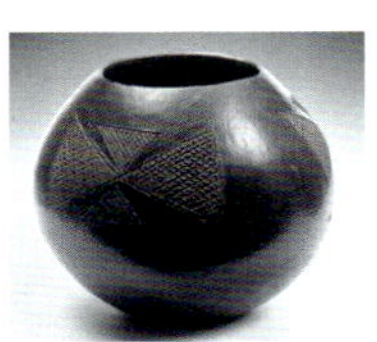

POT NUMBER **607**
Ukhamba, H: 289 mm
Provenance: KwaHlalele, opposite Mahlaba on eastern side
of uMzinyathi [1970s ?].
<2001> Though on the eastern side on the uMzinyathi, this
area belongs to the Msinga stylistic region where beadwork
is concerned, so I have included it here. It is an area in
which very few pots have survived. The broad band of
incised geometrical motifs bears some relationship to the
pots from the uMngeni valley a few miles downstream
on the western side of the uMzinyathi.

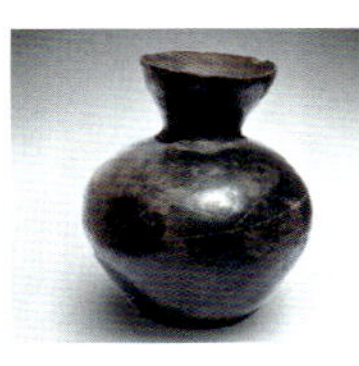

POT NUMBER **608**
Uphiso, also termed *ingcazi*: 'narrow-necked water pot'.
Provenance: bought from owner Gabusile Ndawonde (b.
07.06.1930) of *isigodi* Ekuvukeni, Muden Machunwini,
collected by Innocent Mkhize. <15.02.2012>. The pot
probably dates from the late 1940s.
Note the two small chips in the rim. One was taken before
the wedding and was given to the family of the boy she
was going to marry. The other was broken out when the
got married and was placed in the *insamo* at the girl's
home for the *amadlozi* to know that the girl was going to
another house, i.e. her husband's home.

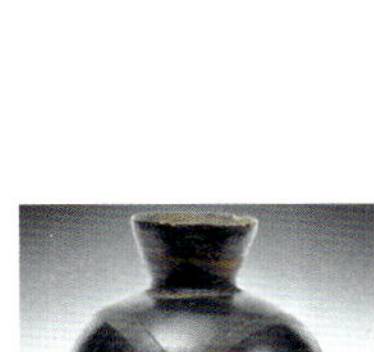

POT NUMBER **609**
Provenance: Embangweni, Msinga. OWNER: MaMkhize, born
1925 'When she came to be married the pot was already
here'. [1930s].

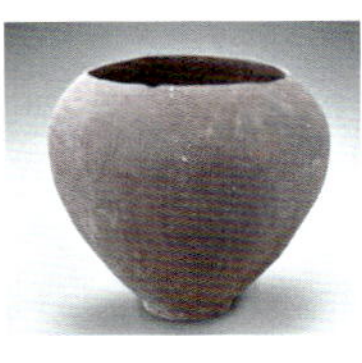

POT NUMBER **701**
Imbiza, H: 446 mm
Provenance: KwaMagwaza, Msinga. The owner, Mrs
MaMbatha Nogwazi, said it was bought more than 50
years ago (i.e. before 1946) at Phalafini, Msinga [1940s].
<1996> Characteristic broad-shouldered form (max. D: 515)
tapering to a very narrow base.

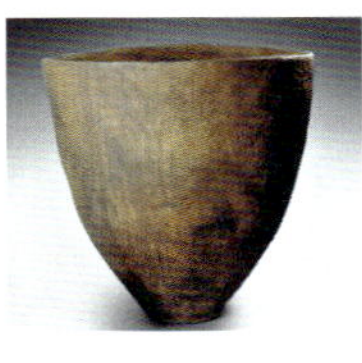

POT NUMBER **702**
Imbiza, H: 707 mm
Provenance: Embangweni, Msinga. The owner, Mrs
MaMkhize, said it was already in the household
when she married in 1964. Said to have been made at
eManzimhlophe, Opathe, Msinga, (Muden area), i.e. the
place at which the above celebration for the ancestors took
place (26 June 2011), p. 104.
<1999> The largest *imbiza* I have found – capacity over 450
litres – tapering from an elliptical opening (D at opening:
705 × 620 mm) to a narrow base.

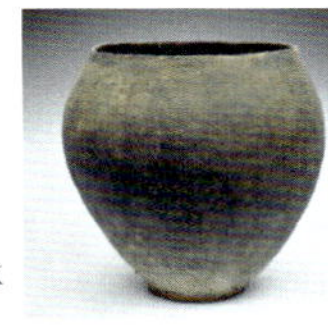

POT NUMBER **703**
Imbiza H: 412 mm
Provenance: Ngongolo, Tugela Ferry. Owner: Melika
MaDlamini. 'She bought it very long ago, can't remember
where, when she got married. At the great flu epidemic
(1918–24) she was already a lady but not married.' i.e born
around 1905. Her third child born 1944. [early 1930's?]

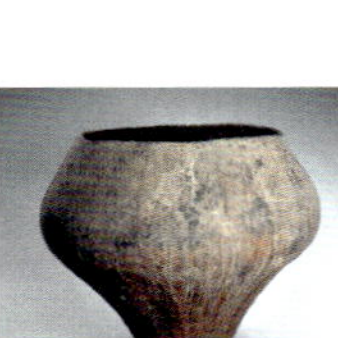

POT NUMBER **704**
Imbiza H: 452 mm, W: 510 mm, O: 365 mm
provenance: KwaMabaso, Msinga, (between Tugela Ferry
and Pomeroy). <1996> . The owner Mrs MaMbatha
Nogwazi, said it was bought more than 50 years ago (i.e.
before 1946) at Phalafini, Msinga [1940s]. Characteristic
broad-shouldered form tapering to a very narrow base.
PHOTO: Ian Carbutt.

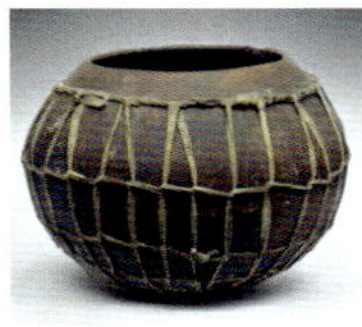

POT NUMBER **705**
H: 389 mm, W: 535 mm, O: 325 mm
Provenance: Buxedeni, but bought in Mgangatho, Nongome.
Owner: Mrs Judith Mtshali. She said it came from Richards
Bay originally but was purchased from the previous owner
in Msinga. [1990s] <16.05.2000>. PHOTO: Patrick Royal.
NOTE: Woven nylon tape used to support the sides of the
vessel. Largish chip in the rim may have been taken to leave
with the original owners when the vessel moved to another
home. (cf. p. 174) Some mends with cement

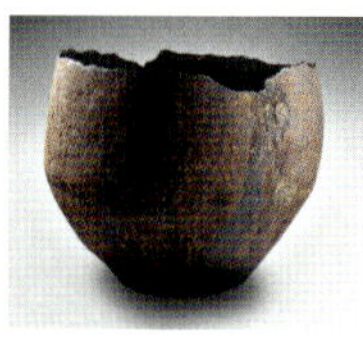

POT NUMBER **706**
Imbiza H: 515 mm G: 2100 mm O: 580 mm
Provenance: Magwanyana family, Muden/
    KwaManzimhlophe. [1900–1920] Phansi Museum
Photo: Patrick Royal

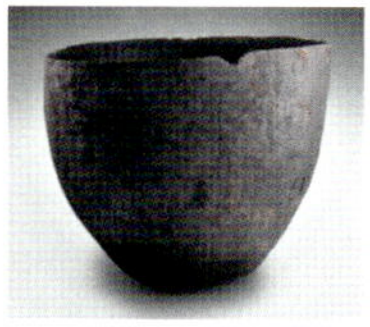

POT NUMBER **707**
Imbiza H: 595 mm, G: 2170 mm, O: 660 mm
Provenance: Not known. Chip taken from rim for the
    ancestors. Phansi Museum.
Photo: Patrick Royal

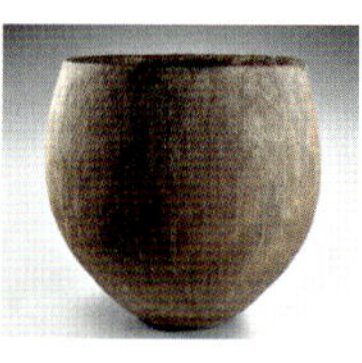

POT NUMBER **708**
Imbiza H: 610 mm, G: 2170 mm, O: 500 mm
    Provenance: Owner Sizwe Sithole (b. 1942).
    Ophathe Mission, Weenen. Phansi Museum.
Photo: Patrick Royal

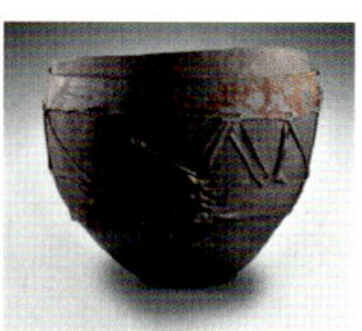

POT NUMBER **709**
Imbiza H: 595 mm, G: 1710 mm, O: 670 mm
Provenance: Owners: Langa Family, Makers: Magwanyana
    family, Muden, KwaManzimhlophe. Strapped with leather.
    Phansi Museum.
Photo: Patrick Royal

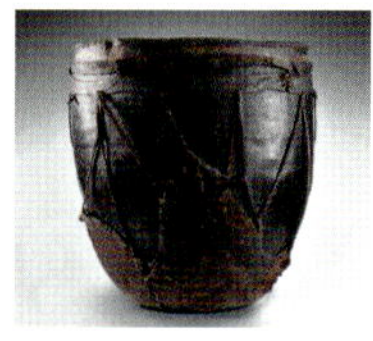

POT NUMBER **710**
Imbiza H: 635 mm, G: 1880 mm, O: 550 mm
Provenance: Owner Funani Langa (b. 1940). 'She came
    to this homestead in 1955. The *imbiza* belonged to her
    mother-in-law who has a dream [?]. She passed away. Her
    name was Nkone Langa. The *imbiza* was made here at
    Evukeni in Ophathe.' Weened/Munden. [1930s?]. Phansi
    Museum.
Photo: Patrick Royal

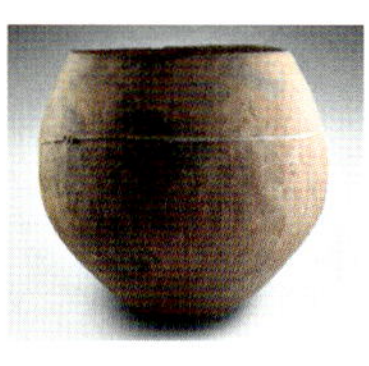

POT NUMBER **711**
Imbiza H: 690 mm, G: 2290 mm, O: 550 mm
Provenance: Nomhlangana Mkkize (1926–21010). Muden/
    Ekuvukeni. Phansi Museum.
Photo: Patrick Royal

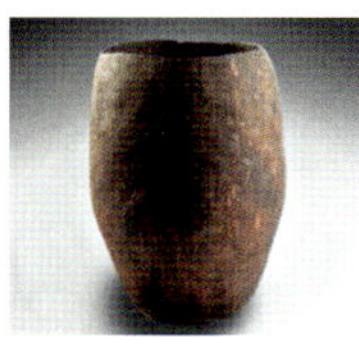

POT NUMBER **712**
Imbiza H: 845 mm, G: 1060 mm, O: 280 mm
PROVENANCE: Owner Sithile Ndawonde, Maker: Ntanazini
    Khumalo [1960s], Muden/Machunwini, Ophathe Kwa
    Mauzimhlophe. For storing water. Known locally as a
    'vase'. Phansi Museum.
Photo: Patrick Royal

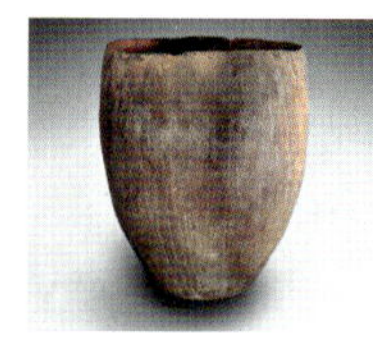

POT NUMBER **713**
Imbiza H: 545 mm
Provenance: From Ophathe mission near
    KwaManzimhlophe. [c.1960]. This one has been used for
    brewing beer. Two chips taken from rim for the ancestors.
Photo: Ian Carbutt

ACKNOWLEDGEMENTS

In the first place I wish to thank Kevin Conru for introducing me to the aesthetics of Zulu beer vessels (and the *utshwala* they contained) by inviting me to accompany him on one of his collecting trips back in 1991. My particular thanks are due to Ian Calder for his help in setting up a database, and for the many hours during which he shared his expertise in reviewing and discussing public and private collections of Zulu ceramics and to Paul Mikula for making available the collections of the Phansi Museum in Durban and for conducting forays into the remoter regions of the Drakensberg, also to Bill Simmons for allowing me to reproduce images of vessels from his outstanding collection. My special thanks go to Innocence Mkhize for guiding me safely more times than I can remember through the unmapped pathways of rural KwaZulu. Finally, I wish to thank the makers and original owners of the vessels illustrated here for their hospitality and patience in responding to my many questions: they are all named in the text or the database.

REFERENCES

ANGAS, G F. 1974 (1849). *The Kaffirs Illustrated*. Facsimile reprint, Cape Town & Rotterdam: AA Balkema.

ARMSTRONG, J. 1998. 'The Magwaza Family'. In: Bell, B & Calder, I., eds, *Ubumba. Aspects of indigenous ceramics in KwaZulu-Natal*. Pietermaritzburg: Tatham Art Gallery, pp 41–45.

BALLARD, C. 1989. 'Traders, trekkers and colonists'. In: Duminy, A & Guest, B, eds, *Natal and Zululand from earliest times to 1910: a new history*. Pietermaritzburg: University of Natal Press and Shuter & Shooter, pp 116–145.

BARLEY, N. 1994. *Smashing pots. Feats of clay from Africa*. London: British Museum Press.

BELL, B & CALDER, I, eds. 1998. *Ubumba. Aspects of indigenous ceramics in KwaZulu-Natal*. Pietermaritzburg: Tatham Art Gallery.

BERGLUND, A-I. 1976. *Zulu thought-patterns and symbolism*. London: C Hurst & Co., Cape Town: David Philip.

BROOKES, EH & WEBB, C DE B. 1987 (1965). *A history of Natal*. Pietermaritzburg: University of Natal Press.

COLENBRANDER, P. 1989. 'The Zulu kingdom, 1828–79'. In: Duminy, A & Guest, B, eds, *Natal and Zululand from earliest times to 1910: a new history*. Pietermaritzburg: University of Natal Press and Shuter & Shooter, pp 83–115.

CORY, GE, ed. 1926. *The diary of the Rev. Francis Owen, M.A., Missionary with Dingaan in 1837–38*. Cape Town: The Van Riebeeck Society

DAVIES, O. 1971. 'Excavations at Blackburn'. *South African Archaeological Bulletin* 37: 34–43.

DAVISON, P. 1985. 'Southern African beer pots'. *African Arts* 18 (3): 74–77.

DELEGORGUE, A. 1997 (1847). *Travels in Southern Africa*. Vol. 2. Webb, F trans., Alexander, SJ. & Guest, B, eds. Durban: Killie Campbell Africana Library, and Pietermaritzburg: University of Natal Press.

DOKE, E, MALCOLM, DM, SIKAKANA, JMA & VILAKAZI, BW. 1990. *English-Zulu; Zulu-English Dictionary*. Johannesburg: University of the Witwatersrand Press.

DUMINY, A & GUEST, B. 1989. Conclusion. In: Duminy, A & Guest, B, eds, *Natal and Zululand from earliest times to 1910: a new history*. Pietermaritzburg: University of

Natal Press and Shuter & Shooter, pp 428–37.

ETHERINGTON, N. 1989. 'The 'Shepstone system' in the Colony of Natal and beyond the borders'. In: Duminy, A & Guest, B, eds, *Natal and Zululand from earliest times to 1910: a new history*. Pietermaritzburg: University of Natal Press and Shuter & Shooter, pp 170–92.

—2001. *The great treks: the transformation of southern Africa, 1815–1854*. Cape Town: Longman.

FOWLER, HW & FOWLER, FG. 1966. *The concise Oxford dictionary of current English*. Oxford: Clarendon Press.

GARRETT, I. 1998. 'Nesta Nala: an overview'. In: Bell, B & Calder, I, eds. *Ubumba: Aspects of indigenous ceramics in KwaZulu-Natal*. Pietermaritzburg: Tatham Art Gallery.

GRAY, S, ed. 1992. *'The Natal papers of 'John Ross''*. Durban: Killie Campbell Africana Library, and Pietermaritzburg: University of Natal Press.

GUEST, B. 1989. 'Colonists, confederation and constitutional change'. In: Duminy, A & Guest, B, eds, *Natal and Zululand from earliest times to 1910: a new history*. Pietermaritzburg: University of Natal Press and Shuter & Shooter, pp 146–69.

HALL, M & MACK, K. 1983. 'The outline of an eighteenth century economic system in south-east Africa'. *Annals of the South African Museum* 91: 163–94.

HALL, M & MAGGS, TM O'C. 1979. 'Nqabeni: a Later Iron Age Site in Zululand'. South African Archaeological Society, *Goodwin series* 3: 159–76.

HAMILTON, C & WRIGHT, J. 1993. 'The beginnings of Zulu identity'. *Indicator SA* 10 (3): 43–46.

JOLLES, FEF. 1994. 'Messages in fixed colour sequences: another look at Msinga beadwork'. In: Sienaert, E, Bell, N & Cowper-Lewis, M, eds, *Oral tradition and its transmission: the many forms of message*. Durban: Natal University Press, pp 47–62.

—1997. 'Zulu earplugs. A study in transformation'. *African Arts* 30 (2): 46–59.

—2001. 'Tradition and innovation: woodcarvers at the confluence of the Umzinyathi and Umngeni rivers, KwaZulu-Natal, South Africa'. *Southern African Humanities* 13: 97–124.

—2004. 'Continuity and change in Zulu beadwork conventions: the interaction of color and pattern'. In: Washburn, DK & Crowe, DW, eds, *Symmetry comes of age*. Seattle and London: University of Washington

Press, pp 100–134.

JOLLES, FEF. 2012. 'Zulu ceramics in transition: Siphiwe MaS'Khhakhane Nala and her daughter Nesta Laudeleni Nala. *Southern African Humanities* 25:1–24

KRIGE, JE. 1950 (1936). *The social system of the Zulus*. Pietermaritzburg: Shuter & Shooter.

LABAND, J. 1995. *Rope of sand: the rise and fall of the Zulu Kingdom in the nineteenth century*. Johannesburg: Jonathan Ball.

LABAND, J & THOMPSON, P. 1989. 'The reduction of Zululand, 1878–1904'. In: Duminy, A & Guest, B, eds, *Natal and Zululand from earliest times to 1910: a new history*. Pietermaritzburg: University of Natal Press and Shuter & Shooter, pp 193–232.

LAMBERT, J. 1989. 'From independence to rebellion: African society in crisis, c.1880–1910'. In: Duminy, A & Guest, B, eds, *Natal and Zululand from earliest times to 1910*. Pietermaritzburg: University of Natal Press and Shuter & Shooter, pp 373–401.

LAWTON, AC. 1967. 'Bantu Pottery of Southern Africa'. *Annals of the South African Museum* 49: 1–440.

LEVY, D. 1990. 'Continuities and changes in Ndebele beadwork: c.1883 to the present'. MA dissertation, University of the Witwatersrand, Johannesburg.

MAGGS, TM O'C. 1976. 'Iron Age communities of the southern highveld'. Pietermaritzburg: Natal Museum.

—1982. 'Mgoduyanuka: terminal Iron Age settlement in the Natal grasslands'. *Annals of the Natal Museum* 25 (1): 83–113.

—1986. 'Spatial parameters of Late Iron Age settlements in the upper Thukela Valley'. *Annals of the Natal Museum* 27 (2): 455–79.

MEYER, 1909. 'Meyers Großes Konversations = Lexikon'. Leipzig and Vienna: *Bibliographisches Institut*, vol. 16.

REUSCH, D. 1996. 'Reflections concerning the pottery from KwaMabaso, Msinga. In: Wood, M, ed. *Zulu treasures: of kings and commoners*. Ulundi: KwaZulu Cultural Museum, and Durban: Local History Museums, pp 115–30.

PHILLIPS, T, ed. 1995. Africa. *The art of a continent*. London: Royal Academy of Arts, and New York: Prestel.

STUART, J & MALCOLM, D McK, eds. 1969 (1950). *The diary of Henry Francis Fynn*. Pietermaritzburg: Shuter & Shooter.

WASHBURN, DK. & CROWE, DW. 1988. *Symmetries of culture. Theory and practice of plane pattern analysis*.

Seattle and London: University of Washington Press.

WEBB, C DE B & WRIGHT, J, eds. 2001. *The James Stuart Archive of recorded oral evidence relating to the history of the Zulu and neighbouring peoples.* Vol. 5. Pietermaritzburg: University of Natal Press, and Durban: Killie Campbell Africana Library.

WOOD, M. 1996. Zulu Beadwork. In: Wood, M, ed., *Zulu treasures: of kings and commoners.* Ulundi: KwaZulu Cultural Museum, and Durban: Local History Museums, pp. 143–70.

Authors
Frank Jolles †
Karel Nel (Foreword)

Graphic designer
Kevin Shenton/Triple M Design, Johannesburg

Offset reproductions
Schwabenrepro Frischauf, Stuttgart

Photo credits
Patrick Royal
Ian Carbutt
Bruce M White

Printed by
Gorenjski tisk storitve, Kranj

Paper
Galaxi Keramik, 150 g/m^2

Printed on PEFC certified paper. This certificate stands throughout Europe for long-term sustainable forest management in a multi-stakeholder process.

Bibliographic information published by the Deutsche Nationalbibliothek
The Deutsche Nationalbibliothek lists this publication in the Deutsche Nationalbibliografie; detailed bibliographic data are available on the Internet at www.dnb.d-nb.de.

ISBN 978-3-89790-423-1

Printed in Europe, 2015

Cover illustrations
FRONT:
POT NUMBER 228 (see p. 68)
BACK (POTS FROM LEFT):
106 (see p. 39), 412 (see p. 1338), 414 (see p. 146)

ARNOLDSCHE art books are available internationally at selected bookstores and from the following distribution partners:

USA
ACC USA, New York, NY, sales@antiquecc.com

CANADA
NBN Canada, Toronto, ON, lpetriw@nbnbooks.com

UK | FRANCE | SOUTH AMERICA | SOUTH AFRICA
ACC GB, Woodbridge, Suffolk, sales@accdistribution.com

THE NETHERLANDS
Jan Smit, jan@jansmitboeken.info

SWITZERLAND
OLF S.A., Fribourg, information@olf.ch

SCANDINAVIA
Elisabeth Harder-Kreimann, Hamburg, elisabeth@harder-kreimann.de

SOUTHERN EUROPE
Joe Portelli, Bookport Associates, Corsico, bookport@bookport.it

EASTERN EUROPE and RUSSIA
Adriana Juncu, adriana@j4.ro

ASIA
Ralph & Sheila Summers, formtone@dircon.co.uk

CHINA
Benjamin Pan, benjamin.pan@cpmarketing.com.cn

JAPAN
Yasy Murayama, yasy@yasmy.com

INDIA, SRI LANKA, PAKISTAN, NEPAL
Surit Mitra, suritmaya@gmail.com

THAILAND
Paragon Asia Co., Bangkok, paragonasiabkk@gmail.com

AUSTRALIA | NEW ZEALAND
New South Books, Sydney, orders@tldistribution.com.au

For general questions, please contact ARNOLDSCHE Art Publishers directly at art@arnoldsche.com, or visit our homepage at www.arnoldsche.com for further information.